50 hikes in
Connecticut

From the Berkshires to the Coast

Fourth Edition

DAVID, GERRY, AND SUE HARDY

Photographs by the Authors

Backcountry Publications
Woodstock, Vermont

An Invitation to the Reader
Over time trails can be rerouted and signs and landmarks altered. If you find that changes have occurred on the routes described in this book, please let us know so that corrections may be made in future editions. The author and publisher also welcome other comments and suggestions. Address all correspondence to:

Editor, *50 Hikes*™ Series
Backcountry Publications
PO Box 748
Woodstock, VT 05091

Library of Congress Cataloging-in-Publication Data
Hardy, David, 1959-
    50 hikes in Connecticut: from the Berkshires to the coast/David, Gerry, and Sue Hardy; photographs by the authors. — 4th ed.
    p. cm.
    Rev. ed. of: Fifty hikes in Connecticut/Gerry and Sue Hardy. 3rd ed. ©1991.
    ISBN 0-88150-355-X (alk. paper)
    1. Hiking—Connecticut—Guidebooks. 2. Connecticut—Guidebooks.
I. Hardy, David. II. Hardy, Sue. III. Hardy, Gerry. Fifty hikes in Connecticut.
IV. Title.
GV199.42.C8H37 1996   95-50967
917.46'0443—dc20   CIP

Published by Backcountry Publications
a division of The Countryman Press
PO Box 748, Woodstock, Vermont 05091

Distributed by W.W. Norton & Company, Inc.
500 Fifth Avenue
New York, NY 10110

Printed in Canada

Text and cover design by Glenn Suokko
Maps by Dick Widhu © 1996 The Countryman Press
Photographs by the authors

DEDICATION

To the next generation, Nicholas and Anna

ACKNOWLEDGMENTS

Many of our thoughts were honed on our numerous hiking companions, to whom we are very grateful. The Appalachian Mountain Club groups we hike with provide an endless supply of wit and good fellowship. Above all, we would like to thank the dedicated chairmen of the Connecticut Forest and Park Association for the existence and maintenance of Connecticut's Blue Trails, members of the Connecticut Chapter of the AMC for maintaining the Appalachian Trail in Connecticut, and all those who laid out and maintain the many other fine trails in our state. For their help in the preparation of the fourth edition, we want to thank Jean Thompson, Marianne Pfeiffer, and Bob Buyak of Hartman Park and Walter Landgraf of Peoples State Forest for sharing their extensive knowledge of their woodlands. We would also like to thank Laura Jorstad and Chris Lloyd at The Countryman Press for their patience and perseverance in preparing this fourth edition.

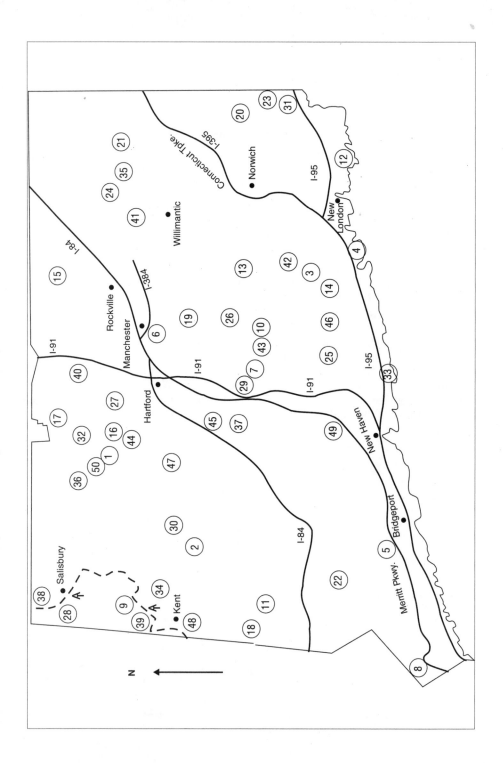

CONTENTS

Map Symbols

—— main trail

• • • side trail

Ⓟ parking

↑ view

⅄ Appalachian Trail

INTRODUCTION

Contrary to popular opinion, Connecticut is not all cities and suburbs. A gratifyingly high proportion of our state's woodlands are preserved as state parks and state forests. In fact, the only state in New England with more miles of hiking trails is New Hampshire.

These 50 hikes represent all areas of the state and traverse almost all the existing natural habitats. Naturally, this selection is only a sampler and, of necessity, somewhat reflects our own preferences and prejudices. We chose the hikes with an eye to the hiking family; most are suitable for families with young children (who are usually far more capable physically than psychologically). But remember, a hike adults and teenagers can cover in 4 hours may take all day with youngsters along, especially if they take time to examine their surroundings closely.

Revising a hiking guide is a never-ending task. A new edition becomes necessary due to the changes in trails, whether done by humans or by natural events. Outdated hiking guides can be particularly frustrating for new hikers.

This edition reflects trail changes in some of the hikes of the third edition (Wadsworth Falls, Sunny Valley, Northern Metacomet, Housatonic Range, Gay City, McLean, Talcott Mountain), new hikes in old haunts (Larsen, Greenwich, Hurd, Northwest Park, White Foundation, Westwoods), brand new hikes (Hartman Park, Lions Head), returns to old friends that have undergone significant change (Cathedral Pines, Mohawk Mountain, Mount Algo), and many minor adjustments. The hikes of this edition represent their trail status as of 1995; all the hikes were walked during that hiking season. Written comments by interested hikers like you were considered and field checked. Such notes are important in keeping this volume up-to-date, and any suggestions are appreciated. Connecticut was lucky in 1995 that nature didn't wreak any real havoc on the woods. Both Massachusetts and Vermont were hit with severe windstorms similar to the tornado that struck Mohawk Mountain and Cathedral Pines in 1989. Those storms altered hiking trails in both states, just as the '89 storm did in Connecticut.

This book is intended to please both the armchair and the trail hiker by fleshing out directions with photographs and snippets of natural history. We have also tried to answer some of the questions that you might ask while walking these trails. The phenomena we describe we actually saw on these 50 hikes (some hiked many times over the years); by being fairly observant you can see the same things. For this reason our descriptions are short on wildlife, which is seen only occasionally, and long on vegetation and terrain. Effective observation of animal life requires very slow movement (if any), blinds, and binoculars or scopes. In contrast, vegetation and terrain features require only an alert eye and an inquiring mind.

These hikes, which we feel represent some of the most attractive in the state, break longer trails into manageable sections. In addition to some of the best pieces of the Blue Trail System, the finest stretches of Connecticut's section of the Appalachian Trail (AT), and more interesting state park trail networks, we have included a few hikes in wildlife sanctuaries and in city- and town-owned, open-space areas.

CHOOSING A HIKE

The hikes are presented in order of their estimated hiking time; the first hike, Great Pond, is the shortest, and the last one, Ratlum Mountain, the longest. However, since difficulty is more subjective, owing to ruggedness of terrain as well as length and vertical rise (as well as vertical drop), the order does not necessarily reflect difficulty.

Total distance is the mileage walked if you complete the entire hike as described. Many of these hikes lend themselves readily to shortening if you desire an easier day. Some, with the help of local maps or the *Connecticut Walk Book,* can be lengthened. Trail distances are given in fractions of a mile for some hikes and in decimals for others. Fractional distances are estimates, while decimal distances have usually been measured with a wheel and are fairly accurate.

Hiking time is computed from a simple formula used all over the country: 2 miles an hour plus ½ hour for every 1000 feet of vertical rise. Thus, a 6-mile hike on flat terrain would have a 3-hour hiking time, but a 6-mile hike with 2000 feet of climbing would take 4 hours. If you are a middle-aged, beginning hiker you may not match "book time" for a while. A young, experienced hiker will consistently better these times. One word of caution—hiking time means just that and does not allow for lunch stops, rest stops, sightseeing, or picture taking.

The *rating* for each hike refers to the average difficulty of the terrain you traverse on the route we have described. The difficulty of a hike is relative. A tough section in Connecticut is far easier than a tough section in New Hampshire or Vermont. However, some of our rock scrambles, while shorter, can be just as difficult. The big difference between Connecticut and northern New England is our dearth of sustained climbs. Only Bear Mountain (see Hike 38) offers such an ascent.

Our rating system is the one used by the Connecticut Chapter of the Appalachian Mountain Club and is designed for Connecticut trails. It combines such factors as elevation gain, rock scrambling, footpath condition, and steepness. Hikes rated D are the easiest and A the most difficult. The seven categories used in our rating system are:

D   Flat terrain; little or no elevation change, easy footing
CD   Intermediate between C and D
C   Average terrain; moderate ups and downs with some need to watch footing
CB   Intermediate between C and B
B   Difficult terrain; steep climbs, considerable elevation gain or some poor footing or both
AB   Intermediate between A and B
A   Very tough terrain; maximum elevation gain, poor footing or hand-assisted scrambling up steep pitches or both

In an effort to limit grade inflation, an A rating is rarely given and *will* require the use of your hands on a steep pitch at some point in the hike. Where such a situation exists, it will be noted in the text.

When selecting a day's ramble, don't overdo it. If you haven't hiked before, try the shorter, easier hikes first and build up to the longer ones. Don't bite off more than you can chew—that takes all the pleasure out of hiking. As the saying goes, "Walk till you're half tired out, then turn around and walk back."

The *maps* listed are the United States Geological Survey (USGS) maps replicated as part of the route map provided in each hike description. You may wish to obtain some of these maps in their entirety to get a better sense of the region you're hiking in. They're available at some bookstores and outdoor equipment shops, from the Connecticut Department of Environmental Protection, and directly from the USGS.

ABOUT CONNECTICUT SEASONS

Hiking in Connecticut is a four-season avocation. Our winters are relatively mild—we rarely have temperatures below zero Fahrenheit or snow accumulations over a foot. In general, the snow deepens and the temperature drops as you travel north and west. Often the southeastern part of the state is snow-free much of the winter and is the first area in the state to experience spring.

Spring is usually wet and muddy, although there is frequently a dry period of high fire danger before the trees leaf out. Spring flowers start in April and peak in May. Days of extreme heat in the 90s can come anytime after the beginning of April.

The humid heat of summer demands short, easy, early-morning strolls and usually requires insect repellent. Beginners sometimes think summer is the best time to hike; veterans consider it the worst time! However, in summer the foliage is lush and botanizing is at its best.

Fall is the ideal hiking season. Cool, crisp days let us forget the enervating heat of summer; the colorful foliage and clear air make New England's fall unsurpassed. A better combination of season and place may exist elsewhere, but we doubt it.

Trailwork in Connecticut, on the Appalachian Trail's crossing of Guinea Brook

The color starts with a few shrubs and the bright reds of swamp maples. When other trees start to turn, the swamp maples are bare. Then tree follows tree—sugar maple, ash, birch, beech, and finally oak—turning, blending, fading, falling. There is no better way to enjoy a New England fall than to explore the woods on foot.

HOW TO HIKE
We do not mean to tell you how to walk. Most of us have been walking from an early age. Rather, we offer a few hints to help you gain as much pleasure and satisfaction as possible from a hike.

First and most important, wear decent, comfortable footgear that is well broken in. Children can often hike comfortably in good sneakers; adults usually shouldn't. We're heavier and our feet need more support than canvas offers. On the other hand, you don't need heavyweight mountain boots in Connecticut. A lightweight hiking boot or a good work boot with a Vibram or lug sole is ideal. While these soles may be hard on the woods trails, we do recommend them as most Connecticut hiking alternates between woods and rocky ledges, where the lug soles are very helpful. Your boots should be worn over two pairs of socks, one lightweight and one heavyweight. Wool or a wool-polypropylene blend is preferable for both pairs as it provides warmth even when wet.

Second, wear comfortable, loose clothes that don't bind, bunch, or chafe. Cotton T-shirts over a polypropylene mesh shirt are good; synthetics are comfortable. For our day hikes, except in winter, we favor cut-off jeans or hiking shorts; they're loose and have many pockets for storing a neckerchief, a handkerchief, insect repellent, film, tissues, and a pocketknife.

Establish a comfortable pace you can maintain for long periods of time. The hiker who charges down the trail not only misses the subtleties of the surroundings, but also frequently starts gasping for breath after 15 minutes or so of hiking. That's no fun! A steady pace lets you both see and cover more ground comfortably than the start-and-stop, huff-and-puff hiker. When you climb a slope, slow your pace so you can continue to the top without having to stop. Having to stop is different from choosing to stop at places of interest, although the clever hiker learns to combine the two! With practice you'll develop an uphill rhythm and find you actually cover ground faster by going slowly.

WHAT TO CARRY
You may have read articles on the portable household the backpacker carries. While the day-hiker needn't shoulder this burden, there are some things you should carry to assure a comfortable and safe hike. Ideally you will always carry your emergency gear and never use it.

Items 2–10 below live in our day packs:

1. Small, comfortable, lightweight pack.
2. First-aid kit containing at least adhesive bandages, moleskin (for incipient blisters), adhesive tape, gauze pads, aspirin, salt tablets, Ace bandage, and bacitracin. We always carry both elastic knee and ankle braces and Ace bandages—we have used them more than any of our other first-aid equipment.
3. Wool or polypro shirt or sweater and a nylon windbreaker. A fast-moving cold front can turn a balmy spring day into a blustery, snow-spitting disaster, and sun-warmed, sheltered valleys may contrast sharply with elevated open ledges.
4. Lightweight rain gear. In warm, rainy weather, hikers are of two minds

about rainwear—some don it immediately and get wet from perspiration; others don't and get wet from the rain. In colder weather, wear it for warmth. In any case, if the day is threatening it's wise to have dry clothes in the car. On a warm day, an umbrella may be preferable to rain gear. It may seem strange at first, but it's effective!

5. Water. Water in southern New England is rarely safe to drink. Always carry at least 1 to 3 quarts (more on hot summer days) per hiker. On cool days, a thermos of hot tea, cocoa, or broth is a good thing to carry along. Also, carry some water purifier or a filter in case you need to take water from a source in the woods.

6. Food. In addition to your lunch, carry high-energy food for emergencies. Sometimes you may feel nauseated when you need a bite to eat for energy, so carry stuff you like to eat. Hiking is no time to diet aggressively or to experiment in the food department. Gorp (Good Old Raisins and Peanuts)—a hand-mixed combination of chocolate chips, nuts, and dried fruit, is a good choice.

7. Flashlight with extra batteries and bulb. You should plan to return to your car before dark, but be prepared in case you're delayed. Be aware of the shorter daylight hours of autumn.

8. A well-sharpened pocketknife. This tool has a thousand uses.

9. Map and compass (optional). These items are not necessary for day-hikers in Connecticut who stay on well-defined trails and use a guidebook. However, if you want to do any off-trail exploring, you should learn to use a map and compass and carry them with you.

10. Others: toilet paper (always); insect repellent (in season); a hat or sunscreen lotion (always, especially on bright days); a wool hat and mittens (in spring and fall).

Winter hiking requires much additional equipment and does not fall within the scope of this book. Nonetheless, it is a lovely time to hike and we would encourage you to hone your skills in mild weather, consult experienced winter hikers, and consider hiking on winter's clear, crisp, often snow-white days. For additional information on winter hiking, we recommend John Dunn's *Winterwise,* published by the Adirondack Mountain Club.

HIKING CONCERNS

Footing is the major difference between road walking and hiking. Roads present a minimum of obstacles to trip you; at times hiking trails seem to have a maximum. The angular traprock cobbles on many of Connecticut's ridges tend to roll beneath your feet, endangering ankles and balance. An exposed wet root acts as a super banana peel and lichen on wet rock as a lubricant. Stubs of improperly cut bushes are nearly invisible obstacles that can trip or puncture. All these potential hazards dictate that you walk carefully on the trail.

It is far safer to hike with a companion than to venture out alone. Should an accident occur while you're alone, you're in trouble. If you must hike alone, be sure someone knows where you are, your exact route, and when you plan to return. *Don't* leave this information in a note on your windshield—it's only an invitation to a thief.

Every Eden has its serpent. Connecticut's, in warm weather, is its tiny biting pests. We've all seen horror pictures of hikers in the far north, their shirts blackened with blood-sucking mosquitoes. Explorers of the tropics fear not lions or tigers but biting insects most of all. In

Connecticut, you can avoid this problem by hiking in winter or on chilly fall and spring days, which are often ideal for hiking. For your summer excursions, understanding the problem and knowing its appropriate remedies will greatly enhance your enjoyment.

Most bugs can be kept at bay with insect repellent. Herbal repellents are quite effective for mosquitoes, while stronger concoctions, often containing DEET, are necessary for blackflies and are recommended for deer ticks. We recommend bug "juice" that contains a moderate amount of DEET, primarily for deer ticks, which can carry Lyme disease (see below). Studies, while not fully conclusive, seem to indicate that DEET isn't safe to use frequently or in high concentrations. For deer ticks it is best applied to clothes from the knees down, where they're most likely to land.

Lyme disease was named for a Connecticut town near Long Island Sound, where it was first identified in 1975. Carried by the very small deer tick (only ¼ inch in diameter even when fully engorged with blood), Lyme disease does not affect most nonhuman animals except for dogs, which may develop joint disorders. It is now the most prevalent tick-borne illness in the United States, and the number of cases increases yearly. Originally reported only in southern New England, Lyme disease has been found (using different tick carriers in different regions of the world) in 43 states and on all continents except Antarctica. European literature almost a century ago reported a similar group of symptoms. The airliner and similar forces that are "shrinking" the globe may have helped its dissemination, much as they have spread much more highly publicized "plagues." Fortunately, only a small percentage of deer ticks are infected, so the chances of contracting the disease are not high for hikers and other outdoorspeople; suburbanites seem much more susceptible. Also, proper treatment within a few weeks of infection is also very effective. While rarely fatal, untreated Lyme disease produces debilitating symptoms that can persist for a lifetime. Usually within a month of infection, a circular rash a few inches in diameter surrounds the tick bite location. Even at this stage, the illness is treatable with antibiotics.

The *Audubon* article referred to in Further Reading states: "For now, experts say the best way to protect yourself against Lyme disease is to wear long sleeves, tuck in your trousers, use tick repellent on clothing, and check yourself for ticks. If you have been bitten, contact a physician. No matter where you live, keep an eye out for [deer] ticks. Lyme disease isn't going to go away, nor are the ticks." This remains good advice. To put things in a reasonable perspective, we know literally hundreds of hikers, most of whom live in the Northeast. We know of only four who have ever had Lyme disease, and one of them has had it three times—all before he started hiking! He's sure he got it working in his garden.

Other hiking dangers are more minor. You should learn to identify poison ivy; it's a very common shrub or vine that can cause quite a bit of discomfort. If you stay on the trail, it shouldn't be a problem. It's most often a vine with little rootlets clinging to the bark of a tree or a shrub along old stone walls or a patch of plants on the ground. Its shiny, three-leafed arrangement is fairly unmistakable.

Snakes will not bite you unless you pick them up or step on them. Some nonvenomous snakes can deliver a nasty bite, but it will only require a good cleaning and maybe a tetanus shot. Connecticut has two native poisonous snakes and only rarely racks up a snakebite state-wide, almost never among hikers. The northern copperhead and timber rattlesnake are very rare creatures and very effective "mousers," which we need more of to keep the rodent population down. Rodents are not only destroyers of crops (and stealers of carelessly placed hikers' candy bars), but are also hosts for deer ticks, which are potentially infected with Lyme disease. Although rattlesnakes are considered much more venomous than copperheads, there have been *no* confirmed deaths from a New England timber rattlesnake bite. Ever.

Bees are more of a problem. If you are allergic, you should carry the kit to deal with anaphylactic shock. Twice as many people succumb to allergic reactions to bees as die from snakebite nationwide. Some people react more than others. Many people have little more than the local swelling usually associated with mosquito bites.

WATER WORRIES

Most of New England's open water sources probably contain the trophozoite Giardia. Warm-blooded creatures (like us) ingest tiny Giardia cysts (about 16,500 can fit on the head of a pin) from contaminated drinking water. In the gut, they will hatch, multiply, attach to the upper small intestine, and then do their damage, which can include diarrhea, cramps, and visible bloating. The cysts infest many warm-blooded animals, including the now numerous beavers; some people call these symptoms Beaver Fever. However, much of the problem has been caused by improper disposal of human waste and that other commonly seen trail beast, the family dog. Both carry Giardia, often without exhibiting any symptoms, and travel far more widely than any beaver we're aware of. Human and dog wastes should be buried in a shallow hole 6 to 8 inches deep (a "cat hole") at least 200 feet from water

and 50 feet from the trail to reduce the spread of disease organisms. Don't bother to burn the toilet paper; it breaks down quickly in our damp New England climate. Carrying a small trowel can make this chore easier. Giardia lurks in even the clearest, coldest running water. Therefore, never drink untreated water! This means carrying your own water while day-hiking and properly treating your drinking water while backpacking, with either a filter or iodine. Giardiasis, once correctly diagnosed, is easily treated.

POTPOURRI

While hiking, don't litter. The AMC motto, "Carry In—Carry Out," is a good one. Carry a small plastic bag in your pack for garbage, and pick up any trash you find along the trail.

On any hike, the minerals, plants, and animals you see have been left untouched by previous trekkers. You, in turn, should leave all things for the next hiker to admire. Remember to "take only pictures, leave only footprints, kill only time."

Connecticut has a limited-liability law to protect landowners who grant access to the general public free of charge. This saves property owners from capricious lawsuits and opens up more private lands for trails.

Hiking should be much more than a walk in the woods. Knowledge of natural and local history adds another dimension to your rambles. We dip lightly into these areas to give you a sampling to whet an inquiring mind. To aid further investigation, we offer a short, descriptive Further Reading section at the end of this Introduction. Using good field guides will add immeasurably to a hike.

Another fascinating aspect of hiking involves observing and considering your environment. Think about why some plants are found in southern but not in northern Connecticut. Why are our woods filled with old roads and stone walls and dotted with cellar holes? Why do some trees grow straight and tall, while others have outflung, low branches? Someone once said that "ecology is more complicated than you think; in fact, it is more complicated than you *can* think!" You will never run out of things to learn on your hikes! In these trail descriptions we have thrown in a smattering of natural history. We've only touched on a few things, and we've tried not to repeat ourselves from hike to hike. Much of what is described in one hike also applies to many of the others.

THE CONNECTICUT 400 CLUB

Many hikers collect attractive patches to signify completion of a goal. The AMC sponsors, among other things, the New Hampshire 4000-Footer Club and the New England 4000-Footer Club for those who have climbed the 48 mountains in New Hampshire or the 65 in northern New England that are over 4000 feet high. Special patches are awarded to applicants for a small fee.

Connecticut's peaks are less lofty. However, the Connecticut Chapter of the AMC has since 1976 sponsored the Connecticut 400 Club, whose members have hiked all the through trails (approximately 450 miles) described in the *Connecticut Walk Book*. Patches are awarded to applicants for a small fee. The Connecticut 400 Club was established not only to recognize those who have hiked the through trails but also, perhaps more importantly, to encourage hikers to explore all the trails in the state, thus reducing traffic on the famous but overused Appalachian Trail.

For the name and address of the current Connecticut 400 Club Patch chairman or for information on the Connecti-

cut Chapter of the AMC, write to the Appalachian Mountain Club, 5 Joy Street, Boston, MA 02108.

ABOUT TRAILS

Hiking trails do not just happen for our healthy enjoyment, and as we in Connecticut are well aware, they are impermanent at best. When the first *Connecticut Walk Book* was published in 1937, all the major trails in Connecticut were interconnected. The pressures of change have long since isolated most of these trails from each other. The major reason we still have good hiking trails is that hikers like rough, hard-to-reach land for their hikes, while builders prefer easily developed land. However, as time passes and populations grow, the hiker's land becomes more and more endangered. Let's examine the history of the Appalachian Trail (AT), which mirrors the problems that beset many hiking trails.

The bane of the hiker in our uncertain world is the continual loss of hiking trails to development, land-use change, or just plain unhappy landowners. The AT had been at the mercy of changes such as these since its inception in the 1930s. By the late 1960s, some 200 miles of this trail, once on private land, had been displaced onto paved roads. The volunteer Appalachian Trail Conference, located in Harpers Ferry, West Virginia, which coordinated the building and maintenance of the AT, was paying more and more attention to the loss of this "wild" land. Largely because of a major push by volunteers and pressure from the public, the US Congress passed the National Trails System Act, which President Johnson signed into law on October 2, 1968. While this potentially made the AT a permanent entity, no money was appropriated at that time to make the dream a reality.

In 1978 the act was amended, authorizing the National Park Service to acquire a 1000-foot-wide Appalachian Trail corridor on the private land where about half of the original trail was located. Fortunately, Congress also appropriated $90 million to effect the needed acquisitions. As of 1995, a number of parcels are still to be purchased, and hopes are that it can be completed by the end of the decade. Much has been done, but the toughest acquisitions remain. With the escalating cost of land and the uncertain attitude of recent administrations, it may take more time to complete this vital public acquisition.

What can we, the hiking public, do about this persistent problem? The hikes in this book are a direct result of the efforts of thousands of volunteers like you. Most of us do not have the time, ability, or money to make major contributions. However, we can all vote, support conservation-oriented politicians, and do some sort of volunteer trail maintenance. We must work to create an atmosphere of trust and understanding with private landowners. The hiker's cause is damaged by vandalism, rowdiness, and lack of respect for landowners' rights. But we all benefit from courteous hikers, diligent volunteer trail workers, and an understanding of landowners' concerns.

For more information about helping out, contact the following:

Connecticut Forest and Park
  Association
16 Meriden Road
Rock Fall, CT 06481

Appalachian Mountain Club
5 Joy Street
Boston, MA 02108

Appalachian Trail Conference
PO Box 807
Harpers Ferry, WV 25425

FURTHER READING

Connecticut is a small state with pleasing outdoor diversity. The hikes in this book touch lightly on many aspects of its ever-fascinating scene: flora, fauna, geology, and history. Since this is basically a hiking book, we have had neither the space nor the time to go into great detail, but we hope we have piqued your interest so you will want to become more knowledgeable about the outdoors and the history of Connecticut. The following books and articles should enhance your understanding of Connecticut's outdoors and add to your experience with this book. The following hiking guides are invaluable.

Among recently published books, the *Connecticut Walk Book,* published by the Connecticut Forest and Park Association, covers all the Blue Trails and many others in the state. The *Appalachian Trail Guide to Massachusetts–Connecticut* covers the AT through the northwestern corner of Connecticut. Susan Cooley's *Country Walks in Connecticut,* published by the Appalachian Mountain Club and The Nature Conservancy, presents details of many of The Nature Conservancy's holdings from a hiking naturalist's perspective.

A precursor to the *Connecticut Walk Book* is *Walks and Rides in Central Connecticut and Massachusetts* by C.R. Longwell and E.S. Dana, published by the Tuttle, Morehouse, & Taylor Company, New Haven, Connecticut. Because these Yale professors specialized in geology, this book is built around the forces that created and shaped the state's terrain.

Since this corner of the nation is composed of six diverse states, we often think of ourselves as New Englanders. A grounding in all of New England's changes certainly increases our understanding of Connecticut itself. We recommend *Changing Face of New England* by B.F. Thompson, Houghton Mifflin, 1958; *Changes in the Land* by W. Cronin, Hill & Wang, 1983; and *A Guide to New England's Landscape* by Neil Jorgensen, Pequot Press, 1977. Jorgensen's *A Sierra Club Naturalist Guide to Southern New England,* Sierra Club Books, 1978, examines a narrower section of the Northeast in greater detail, thus limiting the scope while broadening the understanding of our natural wonders.

Many of the Peterson *Field Guides* are invaluable aids in identifying the world met along the trail. Those of special value to us include: *A Field Guide to Wildflowers* by M. McKenney and R.T. Peterson; *A Field Guide to the Mammals* by W.H. Burl and R.P. Grossenheider; *A Field Guide to the Ferns and Their Related Families of Northeastern and Central North America* by B. Cobb; *A Field Guide to the Reptiles and Amphibians of the United States and Canada East of the l00th Meridian* by R. Conant; and *A Field Guide to Trees and Shrubs* by G.A. Petrides.

A special little softcover book, *Connecticut's Notable Trees* by G.D. Dreyer (Memoir of the Connecticut Botanical Society #2—1989), lists not only the dimensions and locations of all the known largest trees of each species in Connecticut, but also several large historic oaks and the largest known specimens of ash, eastern cottonwood, and elm.

Other good guides include *Stokes' Amphibians and Reptiles* by Tom Tyning, *Newcomb's Wildflower Guide,* National Geographic's *Birds of North America,* and *Tracking and the Art of Seeing* by Paul Rezendes. Audubon Society field guides are particularly helpful because of their extensive use of photographs.

If you want to go beyond the nuts and bolts of identification, the following books contain much of the lore that is so dear to the hearts of natural history buffs: *How to Know the Ferns* by F.T. Parsons, Dover, 1961; *A Natural History of Trees* by D.C. Peattie, Houghton Mifflin, 1950; *Trees of Eastern and Central United States and Canada* by W.M. Halow, Dover, 1957; and *How to Know the Wildflowers* by W.S. Dana, Dover, 1963.

The forces that shaped our land can also be found in *Underfoot: A Geological Guide to the Appalachian Trail* by V.C. Chew, Appalachian Trail Conference, 1988, which covers the trail's entire 2000 miles, including the trail section that passes through northwestern Connecticut. Excellent geological coverage of all of Connecticut for the layperson is provided by M. Bell's *The Face of Connecticut: The People, Geology, and the Land,* State Geological and Natural History Survey of Connecticut, 1985.

For more on Lyme disease, see "Something Scary Lurks Out There" by Edward R. Ricciutti, *Audubon* magazine, May 1981, pp. 89–93. Giardiasis is ably presented in the same issue of *Audubon,* pp. 95–97.

Finally, there are several books published on other outdoor aspects of our state. These include *Connecticut Railroads: An Illustrated History,* Connecticut Historical Society, 1986, and *Fishery Survey of the Lakes and Ponds of Connecticut* by the State Board of Fisheries and Game.

1

Great Pond

Distance: 1½ miles

Vertical rise: negligible

Time: ¾ hour

Rating: D

Map: USGS 7.5-minute Tariffville

This hike circles a delightful little body of water paradoxically called Great Pond. You will appreciate short hikes such as this one best when you take them slowly. Adopt a silent, hesitative step to enhance your chances of surprising wildlife. Try being first out on a Sunday morning to increase your chances even more.

From the junction of CT 167 and CT 10/US 202 in Simsbury, follow CT 167 south 0.2 mile to Firetown Road and turn right. Proceed down this road for 0.7 mile and then fork left onto Great Pond Road. The dirt entrance road to Great Pond State Forest is on your right in 1.6 miles. After passing an outdoor chapel, frequently used for weddings, the road soon ends at a parking lot with a wooden trail map in a dense grove of white pines.

We owe the preservation of this 280-acre state forest to James L. Goodwin, the forester and conservationist who established a tree nursery here in 1932. Twenty-four years later the nursery was designated Connecticut Tree Farm Number One by the American Tree Farm Program. The land was subsequently bequeathed to Connecticut by

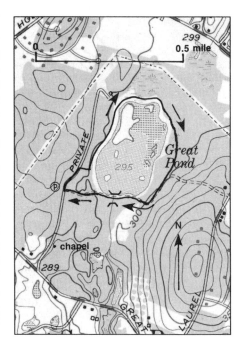

Mr. Goodwin and dedicated as a state forest in 1967.

Many unmarked trails crisscross near the parking lot. This hike starts at the far right corner of the lot and continues in the same direction as the entrance road. The wide (it was an old tote road), well-worn, horseshoe-pocked trail at first goes along the edge of the thick white pine grove and then passes through it. This pine plantation is so dense that no new pines have sprouted despite the millions of seeds shed by opening cones. Instead, the main understory tree is the shade-tolerant hemlock. In early summer, pink lady's slippers add color to the soft carpet of pine needles.

Turn right at the first four-way junction onto a woods road. The pond is visible through the trees. Turn left to follow the trail around the pond; keep the pond to your right. Following this rule of thumb, you may take an occasional dead end to the water's edge without getting lost—these inadvertent side trips permit you to admire the pond from many viewpoints. Cross a bridge over an arm of the pond and then follow a boardwalk through a marsh. You will pass a bull white pine 4 feet in diameter with enormous branches. The size of the branches indicates that the pine matured in a clearing, without any competition for sunlight.

Shallow Great Pond is strewn with lily pads and bordered with emergent vegetation and tree stumps gnawed by beavers. The moisture-loving royal fern stands on water-girt hummocks and even grows in shallow water. Dragonflies dance around and alight with their four wings outspread. Iridescent damselflies flap awkwardly and then perch with wings clasped together above a long, thin abdomen. From numerous spots around the pond you can see pine-dotted islands rising from the pond's north-

ern end—we noted that many pines have died in the last few years, probably from drowned roots.

In fall especially, the fallen pine needles on these tote roads create an interesting pattern. If it has been dry of late, a nice fluffy carpet of freshly fallen needles covers the road. If there have been heavy rains, the fallen needles outline the flow of the runoff water. Where the water has pooled, an even layer of flattened needles tells the story.

Needles falling? But aren't pines evergreens? Yes, to both questions. A needle grows in the spring, stays on the tree the first winter—creating the evergreen effect—and is joined the next spring by a crop of fresh new needles. Finally, about 1½ years after emerging, the needles die and fall. If you walk through a pine grove in early October, every little puff of air causes the needles to drift downward.

As your path enters more swampy areas, watch for the tupelo (or black gum) tree. Found from Maine to northern Florida, it has an exceptionally wide range but is only found growing naturally in swampy areas. The tupelo has glossy, leathery leaves, slightly teardrop in shape, and deeply furrowed, cross-checked bark that somewhat resembles alligator skin. As the leaves change color in the fall, this tree presents a deep burgundy red. A good-sized tree (1 or 2 feet in diameter with a record of 5 feet), the tupelo is unfit for most uses. It rots easily and its fibers are so intertwined that it is impossible to split. This tree is fairly common on the borders of the pond.

Just past a stand of great rhododendron—a native relative of our mountain laurel—and red pine, go straight through a woods road junction and bear to your right around the pond. In July the rhododendrons boast impressive white flowers.

In this area we froze at the sight of a large doe feeding in a clearing. By mov-

Great Pond through the trees

ing only when she lowered her head to feed and freezing during her periodic surveillances, we came within 30 yards of her before our suspicious forms elicited a steady stare. Mosquitoes feeding happily on our unmoving forms finally forced us to push on. Her instant flight was punctuated by the highly visible flag of her upraised tail.

At the next junction, turn right to cross a causeway offering views across the pond to the giant white pine and the red pine/rhododendron stand to its right. Soon cross a bridge at the small cement dam on the south end of the pond. Notice the beaver lodge and evidence of activity just past the dam. Shortly you come to another woods road to your left leaving the pond. Turn left and follow it uphill through the dense hemlock and pine grove to the parking lot.

2

Mount Tom Tower

Distance: 1.5 miles

Vertical rise: 360 feet

Time: 1 hour

Rating: C

Map: USGS 7.5-minute New Preston

Though short, this is a rewarding half-day hike. By using the swimming and picnicking facilities, you can profitably spend the whole day here. The tree-topping tower on the crest of the mountain offers a full 360-degree view of the surrounding countryside.

Mount Tom State Park is located just off US 202 southwest of Litchfield, 0.6 mile east of its junction with CT 341. Watch for the state park sign by the access road (Old Town Road). Once inside the 233-acre park (a fee is charged on most summer days), follow the one-way signs to a junction with a sign that directs you to the Tower Trail. Turn right and park in the picnic area.

Take the yellow-blazed trail through a wooden gate steadily up a gravel road (no vehicles allowed). Yellow birch and red oak predominate on this slope. In

early spring you will see the white blossoms of the shadbush, or Juneberry, so named because it flowers about the time the shad run up the rivers. This shrub, with its light gray bark, is much less noticeable at other times of the year. The juicy berries that ripen in July are edible

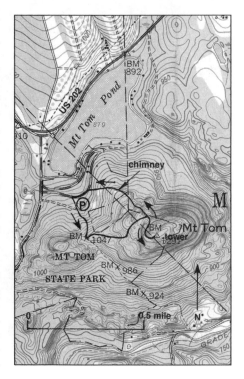

Stone chimney on Mount Tom

and taste not unlike huckleberries. The Native Americans used to dry and compress them into great loaves, chunks of which were broken off over the winter for use as a sweetener.

Turn left at the top of the rise and follow the ridge toward the top of the mountain. In about ¾ mile the trail ends at the base of a circular stone tower over 30 feet high. Wooden stairs inside lead you to a cement roof—watch your head as you emerge. This tower was built in 1921 to replace the original wooden structure. You may see turkey buzzards soaring on Mount Tom's thermals.

Below is spring-fed Mount Tom Pond, with its bathhouses and trucked-in sand beaches. Beyond Mount Tom Pond to the northwest you see the Riga Plateau with, from left to right, Mounts Bear (see Hike 38), Race, and Everett; the latter pair of mountains are in Massachusetts. To the right of the plateau and beyond Bantam Lake, a popular boating and fishing spot, white church spires mark the historic town of Litchfield. Toward the southwest the rugged hills contain New York's Harriman Park. On clear days, you can see Long Island Sound to the south with the outskirts of New York City at right.

To return by a different route, follow the yellow blazes back down, but at the first level spot turn right at the grassy area down a steep, rocky, yellow-blazed trail. You should have no problem following the well-worn treadway.

Near the bottom, as you approach a gravel road, you pass a handsome stone chimney and fireplace with nearby cement foundations. This is all that remains of Camp Sepunkum's assembly hall. The camp housed the Waterbury Boy Scouts, who helped with the development of the park between 1916 and 1934. Follow the gravel road to the left until it turns left, then take the path that branches to your right downhill. Log steps embedded in the slope reduce the erosion caused by the straight downhill route. Go left at the tar road and in about ¹⁄₁₀ mile you will see the marked Tower Trail that you started on.

In mid-April we encountered our first blackflies of the season here. Three biting insects are dominant in Connecticut: blackflies, mosquitoes, and deerflies. Blackflies need well-oxygenated, flowing water to breed in, so their season is mercifully short here. Farther north, they are a longer-term, merciless scourge. Only repellents that contain high percentages of DEET work against them. If the weather isn't too hot, long-sleeved shirts and trousers are often preferable to chemical defenses. Mosquitoes breed in stagnant water through most of the summer, but good herbal repellents work on them. In later spring, deerflies arrive, hovering around your head and waiting for a chance to land and dig in. Fortunately they rarely occur in great numbers, so by paying attention you can usually kill them as they alight and physically reduce your personal cloud of these pests, with great satisfaction.

As we stood by the car discussing the hike, a pileated woodpecker with red crest and white underwings flew overhead. This distinctive bird, as large as a crow, is the drummer that excavates great rectangular holes in unsound trees to reach infestations of carpenter ants.

3

Gillette Castle

Distance: 2 miles

Time: 1 hour

Vertical rise: 100 feet

Rating: CD

Map: USGS 7.5-minute Deep River

Most hikes in this book take you into areas where the pedestrian attractions far exceed those that you can see from your car. Gillette Castle can be considered an exception. A visit to this distinctive structure provides a grand excuse to explore by road the picturesque Haddam-Lyme countryside and to indulge in a short ferry ride. The two state-operated ferries across the Connecticut River hark back to the days of a more leisurely pace and are a fitting transition to this area with its turn-of-the-century aura. To get the most out of this trip, binoculars and a flashlight are recommended.

If you are starting somewhere west of the Connecticut River, come over on the Chester–Hadlyme ferry (CT 148), which off-loads a few miles from the castle, and return on the South Glastonbury–Rocky

Hill run about 25 miles north on CT 160. Both ferries cross at regular intervals during the warmer months and charge a nominal fee. From the Chester–Hadlyme ferry, continue east on CT 148 to River Road and turn left.

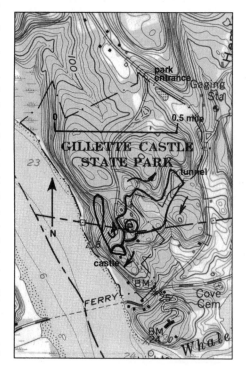

If you are starting east of the river, take CT 148 west 1.5 miles from its junction with CT 82 in Hadlyme and turn right onto River Road. Follow the signs on River Road ¾ mile to Gillette Castle State Park's entrance on your left; the main parking area near the castle is about 0.6 mile west from the entrance. On your way in, check out Castle Oak on the left side of the road, a giant white oak with a girth of 17 feet. Bear in mind that Connecticut's famous Charter Oak had a circumference of 33 feet!

Visit the castle first to put this hike into historical perspective. This eccentric edifice was built between 1914 and 1919 by William Gillette, one of the most popular figures of the American stage. Acclaimed for his portrayal of Sherlock Holmes, Gillette was born and bred in Connecticut; he lived in the castle until his death in 1937. Unbelievable though it seems, the interior of this building nearly outdoes the exterior. Granite walls, hand-hewn oak trim, built-in furniture, intricate wooden locks, and unique lighting fixtures are only some of its attractions. The castle is open daily from Memorial Day through Columbus Day, and on weekends well into the fall. Admission is charged.

After exploring the castle and perhaps lunching at a picnic table, walk the few yards north of the castle to the stone Grand Central Station, the main terminal for the now dismantled Seventh Sister Shortline. This 3-mile miniature railroad was Gillette's pride and joy. He often treated his guests to a ride while he manned the throttle. The park's trail system crosses, parallels, and follows this old miniature railroad bed. As you walk along this old railbed, imagine William Gillette delightedly piloting the train around the curves and by the rock walls while his passengers look on with amaze-

Gillette Castle above the Connecticut River

ment—or possibly some other emotion.

Pass through the station and follow the flagstone ramp to your right downhill along a fence. Turn to your left downhill before reaching a covered footbridge. You wind down through thick young hemlock interspersed with black birch. Please stay on the trail; hikers have caused too much unnecessary erosion by taking shortcuts down the fragile slope. The switchbacks in the area are designed to allow the maximum amount of use with the minimum amount of damage.

Look through the gaps in the trees for views of the Connecticut River. Where you first start on this trail, along the fence, there is an excellent cameo view of the ferry. The path boasts elaborate stonework for holding the hillside off the trail and passing over streams. Bear to your left at a junction to venture down to a wooden kingpost bridge. This truss design can support a significant amount of weight, far more than a simple stringer bridge. Return to the loop trail and bear left to follow the route to a hairpin turn, amid more impressive stonework and a trestle that hugs a cliff wall and takes you back up to the covered bridge. The covering over wooden bridges wasn't for romantic purposes, but for shielding the wooden roadbed from the elements.

Return to the main walkway, passing Grand Central Station. Continue past an ornate stone-and-cement gate that leads to an equally ornate stone outhouse. A short section of the original track has been put on display on the stone wall here. Follow the park entrance road over a small rise and turn right onto the road leading to a picnic area by a small pond. Follow this road past the pond, through a gate, and along the railroad grade to a wooden walkway offering a view of the pond below the castle. If you have brought binoculars, check the logs along the near shoreline of the pond. A mid-May visit rewarded us with the sight of painted turtles sunning themselves. While they're quick to take to water if you get close to the edge of the pond, with binoculars you can observe them from a distance without disturbing them.

Continue along the railroad grade and pass through Gillette's railroad tunnel. Here a flashlight makes the going a little easier. Just beyond the tunnel, follow a path downhill to your right to a woods road below. Turn right and follow the road to the pond. Bear left to walk along its southern edge before ascending to the parking lot and your car.

4

Rocky Neck

Distance: 3 miles

Vertical rise: 150 feet

Time: 1½ hours

Rating: D

Map: USGS 7.5-minute Old Lyme, Niantic

Families sometimes have difficulty finding a place everyone will enjoy. The outdoor activities at Rocky Neck State Park are varied enough to provide something for everybody. Youngsters can fish off the jetty, teenagers can loll on the beach, and hikers can explore the practically deserted woodland paths.

The park entrance is located off CT 156, 2.7 miles west of CT 161 in Niantic. If you are traveling on the Connecticut Turnpike (I-95), take exit 72 (Rocky Neck) to CT 156 and follow the signs east (left) to the park. In addition to complete day-use facilities—beach, bathhouses, rest rooms, and picnic areas—the park has a separate camping area. The attractive sites scattered amid trees may be reserved in advance. In

summer there is a weekend and holiday park entry fee. If you are going only to hike, you may choose to avoid this fee by parking on CT 156 about 0.5 mile west of the park entrance and starting this loop hike at the log gate there.

Within the park, drive into the first parking area on your right, 1.6 miles from the entrance (where park maps are available), just beyond the bridge over Bride Brook. Head for the far left corner of the lot and the picnic tables; the trail starts at a red blaze on a post to the right of the outhouses. The trail passes quickly through a fringe of oaks and maples to a short causeway leading across a marsh. While crossing the causeway and a small bridge, you are threatened by poison ivy, treated to the sight of large pink swamp roses, startled by ducks you have inadvertently flushed, and delighted by gracefully circling terns.

As you enter the woods beyond the marsh, mountain laurel, sweet pepperbush, blueberry, huckleberry, green-briar, and sassafras make up the bulk of the undergrowth. The shade of birch and oak provides relief from the summer sun. Occasional glacial erratics and rounded ledges complete this scene.

Cross a white-blazed trail that circles around the marsh behind you and leads to your right along Bride Brook. Gently

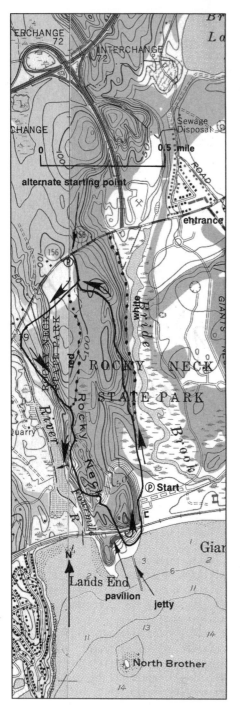

climb the ridge above the brook and reach another junction about a mile from the start. Take a short detour straight ahead here. The path leads to a field where Japanese honeysuckle, with its highly perfumed yellow or white blossoms, lines the edge. Just beyond is the wooden gate at the parking lot on CT 156 and this hike's alternative starting point.

Return from the highway and turn right (this is a left if you chose not to take the detour) to follow red and blue blazes west. Bear to your right to continue on the blue-blazed trail where the red-blazed trail turns left, and then take a sharp left on an old road to parallel the brackish Four Mile River. Cross Shipyard Field. A boatyard lying across the way reminds you of this hike's oceanside location. Follow the woods road over easy terrain, passing a junction with the red-blazed trail to your left.

Continue to the junction with the yellow-blazed trail near the top of the hill. Follow the yellow-blazed trail to your right and ascend a rocky ridge. Follow the ridge toward the ocean. Views of Four Mile River and the open bay await you from a vista called Tony's Nose, partially obscured at first by oak foliage. Clamshells litter the open ledges. Gulls drop clams from on high and then pick out the meat from the shattered shells.

At the end of the open ridge the trail drops down to your left to meet a path. A right turn soon takes you to a tar road. Proceed to your right through a small parking lot to the paved uphill walkway. Cross the arched bridge over railroad tracks to an imposing pavilion. A public works project of President Franklin Roosevelt's Works Progress Administration (WPA), the pavilion, completed in 1936, has given us more than full value! The walls of this massive building are made of fieldstone, and large fireplaces cheer the inside. The internal wood-

Four Mile River and the fogbound bay

work includes pillars made of great tree trunks; at least one trunk was taken from each then existing state park.

From the front porch of the pavilion, bear to your left toward a picnic area. A rocky fishing jetty thrusts into the water before you, and beyond it spreads the graceful curve of the beach. The rocky arms at either side of the bay provide shelter from all but the roughest storms. Turn left through the railroad underpass at the near corner of the beach. Swamp roses adorn the embankment here.

If you follow the road straight past the concession stands, you will find your car in the second parking lot on your right.

5

Larsen Sanctuary

Distance: 3 miles

Vertical rise: 100 feet

Time: 1½ hour

Rating: D

Map: USGS 7.5-minute Westport

Save this walk for a lazy summer day. An oasis in the urban sprawl of Fairfield County, the Connecticut Audubon Society's Roy and Margot Larsen Sanctuary is small, and its 6.5-mile trail network traverses flat, undemanding terrain. While it lacks the rolling hills and sweeping vistas of many Connecticut trails, intriguing names like Cottontail Cutoff, Dirty Swamp Trail, and Old Farm Trail hint at the diverse habitats to be discovered. Because of the predominance of low, marshy land so attractive to birds, the sanctuary makes a particularly fine birding area.

To reach the sanctuary from the eastbound lanes of the Merritt Parkway (CT 15), take exit 44 in Fairfield and immediately turn right (west). From the westbound lanes, take exit 45, and at the end of the ramp go left, then left again to pass under the parkway, and immediately turn right. Either way, you are on Congress Street, which you follow for 1.2 miles to Burr Street. Turn right and drive 1.1 miles to the sanctuary entrance on your left. A small fee is charged to enter the sanctuary. There is no charge, however, for Fairfield residents or members of the Connecticut Audubon Society. Pets are not allowed in the sanctuary.

A large, gray, contemporary building houses the nature center, which, in addition to the bookstore and exhibit areas, has a large auditorium and library. Both the studious nature lover and the casual browser can spend many a worthwhile hour here. The nature center is closed on Mondays, but you may still hike the trails.

You approach the trail system through a small, sheltered gateway to the right of the nature center. Pick up a trail map on the way through. From the multitude of loop opportunities, you'll follow a route that hits several points of interest. Although it was early March when we first explored this sanctuary, it was alive with birds. A trio of ducks flew overhead, and several other species sang from the trees and underbrush. We heard the distinctive flutter and owl-like coo of the mourning dove and the cheerful

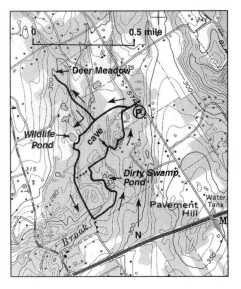

(though far from melodious) cry of that faithful harbinger of spring, the red-winged blackbird.

Follow the trail, strewn with wood chips, to your left through scattered overgrown apple trees past the Trail for the Disabled (on your right). Mountain laurel and rhododendron flank that trail, while a pair of open fences guide the way.

Shortly, go to your right on Garden Marsh Trail, cross a bridge, and bear right at the fork onto Old Farm Trail. As you pass Garden Marsh Pond, almost hidden on your left, note the wood duck nesting boxes set on poles above the water. Sweet-scented honeysuckle vines festoon many trees along the marshy pond's edge, and the heavy growth of sharp, spiny greenbriar vines guards both sides of the trail.

At the next fork, bear right; a left turn takes you on the circuit around Garden Marsh. Shortly you pass through a little clearing. Here a trailing vine of the blackberry family, the dewberry, winds around the tall grasses. Its rather sour,

edible, black berries can be refreshing on a hot, humid day.

Continue on the Old Farm Trail past the Azalea Trail (left), and bear right on the Wildlife Pond Trail (right). Bear right again on the Deer Meadow Trail to continue toward Deer Meadow. On a recent February hike in the sanctuary, a white-tailed deer burst out from a thicket alongside the trail. After crossing a bridge, gently ascend to an open meadow with occasional interpretive signs. At the top of the meadow is a raised observation deck. Turn around and retrace your steps to the Wildlife Pond Trail.

Turn right on the Wildlife Pond Trail and proceed to Wildlife Pond. Again, interpretive signs inform you about the pond's teeming plant and animal life. You'll turn left onto the Trillium Trail to follow a boardwalk along the western edge of Pin Oak Swamp. This not only keeps your feet dry, but also, more importantly, protects the trail. If it were not so elevated, the thousands of tramping feet would make a quagmire of the trail. Future users would edge to one side or the other to avoid the swampy mess and would only widen it.

Bear left onto Country Lane, an old woods road. Continue past Chipmunk Run and through a gas pipeline clearing along the old road, flanked on both sides by stone walls. In earlier days, the stone walls on either side separated farmers' fields from passersby. A route flanked on both sides by stone walls is almost surely a town road. Originally, the farmers erected wooden fences. However, wood eventually became scarce, and was more useful for buildings and fires for heating and cooking, so the farmers piled the ever-plentiful stones from their fields along the fences. Eventually the wooden fences rotted away, leaving the stone walls in their place.

Pass the southern loop of the West

Woods Trail to your right, cross over a brook on a bridge, and turn left onto the Dirty Swamp Trail. The trail can be somewhat difficult to follow, but it parallels the southern edge of the brook on its way from Dirty Swamp Pond. At the shore of the pond, you may choose to spend a little time at a park bench before proceeding to the left over the earthen dam. From the dam, follow the Dirty Swamp Trail north to Chipmunk Run, another significant woods road.

Turn right. A short distance past the end of Old Farm Trail (left), the trail forks at the top of a small rise. Azalea Trail goes to your left; stay to your right on Chipmunk Run. Follow a path down to the stream.

Just before crossing the brook below Wood Pond on a substantial wooden bridge, take a brief detour to your left and explore the cavelike rock ledge above. Little children love this sort of place. Cross the bridge and immediately go to your right onto Rock Ledge Trail (Streamside Trail goes left). Bear left at the top of the rise and follow the twists and turns of Rock Ledge Trail. Shortly after the two paths rejoin, you reach Farm Pond, which has large numbers of tame mallard ducks and Canada geese—a good place to dispose of leftover bread. If you have none, there are two food dispensers where for a quarter you may purchase seeds to feed the ducks. The pond has a wire fence around it to keep its inhabitants from wandering. All have malformed wings or other problems that keep them from flying.

At the junction, go right and con-

At the entrance to Larsen Sanctuary trails

tinue past Garden Marsh Trail (left) to the entrance. Before leaving the sanctuary, visit the compound for injured animals behind the center. Here, with a special permit from the state, the Connecticut Audubon Society treats more than 500 injured animals each year. Most are eventually returned to the wild.

6

Highland Springs and Lookout Mountain

Distance: *2.5 miles*

Vertical rise: *350 feet*

Time: *1½ hours*

Rating: *C*

Map: *USGS 7.5-minute Rockville*

Billed as the "Purest and Best Table Water in the World," bottled mineral water from the springs at Highland Park was once distributed throughout southern New England and as far away as New Jersey. However, while the water-bottling business is now flourishing as it did in the 19th century, this particular spring has been sealed off. The pollution that closed the spring may have come from the numerous housing developments that have cropped up in the area in recent years.

The loop trail begins at the Highland Springs parking lot. From eastbound I-384 in Manchester, take exit 4, Highland Street. From the end of the exit ramp, go right on Spring Street about 0.2 mile to the small parking lot at the bottom of the hill on your left. From westbound I-384, take exit 4 and go right at the end of the exit ramp to the traffic light. Turn right onto Spring Street, cross over the highway, and proceed as above. The town bought this area under the now defunct Open Space Program.

Before starting out, look for the large, piebald sycamore standing near the trailhead. The mottled effect results from the tree's normal growth; while the bark of most growing trees splits into vertical furrows as new wood forms just inside, the sycamore's thin bark periodically breaks off in plates, leaving a clean white surface that contrasts markedly with the older, darker bark.

From the parking lot, follow the gated paved road to Lookout Mountain uphill into a thick stand of hemlocks, keeping the chain-link fence on your left. Occasional white blazes mark your way. Soon the road becomes a wide gravel path. Turn right into the woods on a sparsely red-blazed trail in sight of new homes and a paved cul-de-sac (a key landmark for this turn) to your right. Shortly you reach the old, well-worn, but deeply eroded trail; turn left uphill.

In about ¾ mile you cross an old gravel road that goes directly to the lookout. If you had continued on the gravel

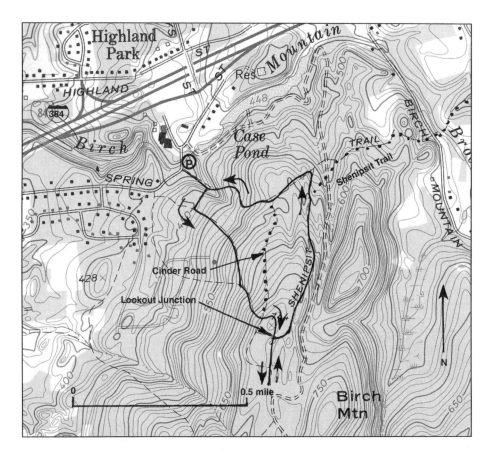

path, you would have run into this road. The hemlock begins to thin out until it is almost wholly replaced with oak and a scattering of maple, hickory, and black birch. The soil here may look the same to us, but the thirsty roots of the hemlock know the difference.

After another ¼ mile you come to a trail crossing known as Lookout Junction. A yellow-blazed trail goes right and a red-blue-and-yellow-blazed trail goes to your left, but you should continue straight ahead onto the blue-blazed Shenipsit Trail, which eventually leads to Gay City State Park (see Hike 19) some 6 miles to the south. Today you will follow the blue blazes only a short

distance past a screen of laurel to a 30-foot hemlock on your right. Look to your right—there is a mysterious clearing where only sedges and mosses grow. Surrounding the opening are numerous highbush blueberry plants that are heavily laden in season. Unfortunately, these berries, though beautiful, are extremely sour—perhaps because of very acidic soil. No woody plants grow within the opening; it is possible that the annual spring snowmelt flooding kills them. Such vernal pools provide spring breeding habitat for a host of amphibians and insects.

Retrace your steps to the junction and follow the yellow blazes to your left up a small rise to a gravel clearing, the summit of Lookout Mountain (744 feet). Note carefully where you enter the lookout clearing to ease your way back to the trail junction.

The view from the lookout depends upon the visibility; too often, especially in summer, Connecticut Valley smog reduces your horizon. Manchester lies in the foreground, but because of its well-treed streets, this city of 65,000 is hard to see. Only the broad, flat-roofed box of the high school and the white spire of Center Congregational Church are readily identifiable. In the middle distance the towers and high-rise office buildings of Hartford stand out, and on a very clear day you can see the white finger of the Heublein Tower rising from Talcott Mountain (see Hike 44) northwest of Hartford.

Return yet again to the junction and proceed straight across onto the joint Shenipsit Trail/Highland Park loop, marked here with red, blue, and yellow blazes. After the yellow-blazed trail peels off to your right, the trail curves gently left along the top of a ridge above an old stone quarry. To your right the land drops off quickly in stepped ledges to a flat forest floor. On your left lies a long, narrow depression, which snowmelt floods each spring. This is another vernal pool, a spring breeding ground for the wood frog.

These black-masked, tan-colored frogs are the earliest spring breeders of our native amphibians. Although probably more numerous than the familiar spring peepers, they lack the high-pitched carrying cry of the latter and

therefore are not as well known. You often hear their low croaks in this area as early as the fourth week of March. The tadpoles, though safe from most predators, must go through their metamorphosis and become small frogs quickly, since the depression is dry by early summer.

The thin, poor soil along the exposed ledges of the ridge dries out quickly and is largely treed with chestnut oaks, which are more tolerant of these conditions than the moisture-dependent hemlocks. With their deeply furrowed, dark gray bark, these oaks are distinctive at any season. The trail now slopes down toward the flat forest floor. After bearing right downhill, go to your left near the end of the ridge.

Hemlocks are thick about the trail again—a legacy of the moisture from Highland Springs on the other side of the hill. Watch for the turn where the blue-blazed trail bears right downhill. At this point continue straight ahead on the red-blazed woods road. Watch carefully for a large, double-blazed chestnut oak tree to the left of the trail near the end of the ridge. Turn left uphill.

The blazes lead to a rusted, open-mesh fence near the top of the rise. To your right you'll pass a lightning-riven hemlock. Notice the strip of removed wood and bark slashing down one side of the tree. The extreme temperature induced by the lightning vaporized the tree's sap, causing the wood to explode.

Although there are few blazes here, continue along and bear right on the old trail that leads to an old tote road. Follow it to rejoin the road you started up on. Go right, downhill, to your car.

7

Wadsworth Falls

Distance: 3 miles

Vertical rise: 200 feet

Time: 1¾ hours

Rating: CD

Map: USGS 7.5-minute Middletown

Moving water holds a special fascination for humanity that is rivaled only by the flickering of fire. The ebb and flow of ocean waves mesmerizes us, boiling rapids and cascades captivate our attention, and waterfalls enchant us wherever they occur. This hike features not one but two of these liquid attractions. Best viewed during spring's heavy runoff, the larger of this pair is worth a visit at any season.

From the junction of CT 66 and CT 157 in Middletown, take CT 157 southwest, following signs to Wadsworth State Park. You will reach the park entrance on your left in 1.6 miles. Since this park has swimming, there is a fee to park here on summer days. In addition to swimming, the park features bathhouses, picnic tables, fireplaces, and hiking trails.

Wadsworth Falls State Park was given to the state in 1942 by the Rockfall Corporation. This nonprofit group was established by the will of Colonel Clarence Wadsworth, a noted linguist and scholar.

A nice routed map of the park's trails has been set up just beyond the entrance. From this spot, pass through the picnic grove to the Main Trail, which begins by a culverted stream; this trail is blazed with orange paint.

Immediately after crossing a bridge over a small stream that splashes down a series of ledges, the trail forks. Bear right. Cedar, maple, birch, and poplar form the woods backdrop, while sweetfern, yarrow, blackberry, and a large patch of poison ivy line the path. On your left, the trail passes one of the largest mountain laurels in the state.

A short distance farther on you come to a second small stream. The stone bridge here is supported by sidewalls of masonry cloaked in mosses and lichens. It is said that Colonel Wadsworth himself used the bridge, and two dates are etched in the rock, 1910 and 1945. Here the woods are composed of tall straight hickory, oak, black birch, and hemlock. Red squirrels chatter loudly from safe perches far above the trail. Every so of-

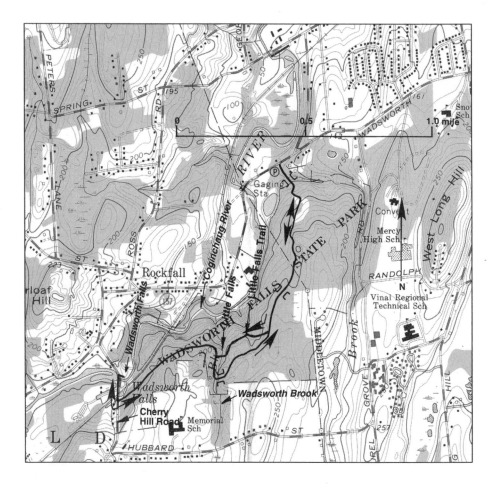

ten, unmarked side trails leave the well-worn main path, inviting exploration.

In ½ mile, when the trail splits, turn right on the blue-blazed fork toward Little Falls (you will return by the left path). Follow the blue blazes downhill as you wind through beautiful treed ravines and eventually parallel the small stream that glides over the mossy ledges. About ¾ mile from the start you reach Little Falls. Cross Wadsworth Brook below the falls and climb the steep hill on your right. Be careful, as this compacted soil can be slippery when wet. On the hilltop there is a falls overlook to your left.

When you have finished admiring the falls, return to the side trail, which continues to the nearby wide, worn main trail. Turn right. Less than ¼ mile from the falls and about 1 mile from the start, railroad tracks and power lines appear below on your right. In another ½ mile you'll reach the paved Cherry Hill Road.

Turn right to cross the railroad tracks. A short walk along the tracks in summer will reveal the blue bells of the creeping bellflower, and in season black raspberries tickle the palate. Great banks of multiflora roses and a few striking Deptford pinks will attract your attention.

Anglers at Wadsworth Falls

Continuing on Cherry Hill Road, cross a bridge over the Coginchaug River and an old sluiceway. The river provided water power to drive a textile mill by the falls. Nearby industries included a 19th-century pistol factory and a gunpowder factory that operated for nearly 100 years before blowing up in 1892.

On the far side of the bridge, cross a field beyond an established parking lot to your right, and descend a path to your left, which takes you to the river at the base of Wadsworth Falls. You may have to share this spot with anglers trying to entice the elusive brown trout. A fenced-in overlook provides yet another view.

To finish this hike, retrace your steps on Cherry Hill Road and the orange-blazed main trail, passing the blue-blazed trail to your left to Little Falls before and after crossing a plank bridge over Wadsworth Brook. Continue along the orange-blazed trail over the stone bridge back to the parking lot.

8

Audubon Center in Greenwich

Distance: 3 miles

Vertical rise: 300 feet

Time: 1¾ hours

Rating: CD

Map: USGS 7.5-minute Glenville

Mention Greenwich, and you may invoke visions of high-walled estates surrounded by dense urban areas and ribbons of concrete. Long ago, urban New York City engulfed this southwest corner of Connecticut. A visit to this 280-acre sanctuary, established in 1941, is a pleasant surprise; its woodland beauty compares favorably with that of many wilder, less accessible areas of the state. Rolling hills, large hardwoods on rich bottomland soil, swamps, a small river, and a pond attract many kinds of birds, as well as hikers.

To reach the sanctuary, take exit 28 from the Merritt Parkway (CT 15) and turn north (right) onto Round Hill Road. After 1.5 miles, turn left onto John Street. Drive for 1.4 miles to Riversville Road; the Audubon Center entrance and parking

lot are on your right. In addition to maintaining a network of hiking trails, the center, which is open Tuesday through Sunday 9 AM–5 PM, operates an excellent bookstore, an interpretive center with seasonal exhibits, and a variety of natural history programs and demonstrations on weekends. All are worth the nominal entrance fee. There is no charge for National Audubon Society members.

Before you begin walking, pick up a map of the trail system at the center. There are no painted blazes here to help you, but there are signs at all the trail junctions. As you can see from the map, there are many trails to explore here—we describe one loop—and you may want to try some or all of the others.

Starting by a large routed wooden sign showing the trail system in contrasting colors on the outside wall of the interpretive building, follow the paved trail to your left downhill, through an orchard dotted with birdhouses. A bit beyond where you turn left there is an apple tree with several rows of evenly spaced holes in the bark. These holes are the work of a provident woodpecker with the unglamorous name of yellow-bellied sapsucker. It drills the neat rows one day and returns on succeeding days to drink the sap that has welled up in the

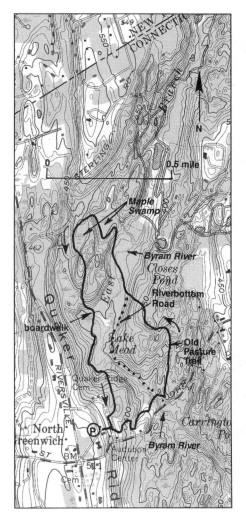

their formidable thorns. The trail tends downhill. Level log steps partially embedded in and perpendicular to the trail retard the erosion that running water causes as it courses down a trail. Without the steps, this well-traveled path would rapidly erode. The wood chips that you find elsewhere on the trail are not meant to ease your way but to protect the trail.

Most of this sanctuary, with its large, mature trees, is made up of rich bottomland hardwoods—beech, ash, tulip tree, oak, and maple. The woods are left to their own natural growth and eventual decay. Dying trees and fallen branches are left to rot where they fall, recycling their nutrients into the surrounding soil and contributing to the diversity of life in the sanctuary.

Turn right onto the Clovis Trail. Follow this trail to the small stream draining Indian Spring Pond and cross it before going downhill to cross the Byram River. Just beyond the river, reach an old woods road, the Riverbottom Road, and turn right. Soon bear left onto the Old Pasture Trail and follow this path through the woods past ponds and rock outcroppings. A holly tree, with its evergreen leaves, was very conspicuous on a gray day in February in the leafless hardwood forest. You'll pass through old pastures where evergreen eastern red cedars and various briars thrive in the sunlight. The red cedars' bark appeared gnawed by some hungry animal.

While traversing these trails in well-heeled suburbia, you may ponder the value of the land in this 280-acre oasis. Perhaps think in terms of the Crown Jewels of England. The value of their individual gems and precious metals is far less than their worth as a whole. So it is with this rare oasis—its value, if broken up and sold as lots, would be far less than its value to the present and future generations who will explore these woods.

holes and to feast on insects that have been attracted by the free lunch. After examining this tree, go back a few yards and head down the grass-bordered Discovery Trail, now a left turn.

Cross a bridge and walk along the left side of Indian Spring Pond, following signs to the Old Pasture Trail. You'll soon pass an old stone-and-mortar springhouse. In a short distance, the trail becomes surrounded by thick undergrowth, especially blackberry canes with

Skunk cabbage leaves and spathe in spring

Descend the hillside to the River-bottom Road. Its overgrown condition, a surprising development in recent years, is another example of nature absorbing our impact on the landscape. One of the conspicuous plants is greenbriar. The stem of this thorny vine is green year-round; its tangled masses are particularly distinctive during the leafless months. Turn right and follow the old road to cross Byram River upstream of Lake Mead on a bridge.

The muddy floodplain on the far side of the river is liberally dotted with skunk cabbage, a rather unattractive and mal-odorous plant that blossoms very early in spring. Its shape and smell are specially adapted to attract the only insects avail-able for pollination this early—carrion flies that search out the carcasses of ani-mals that died the previous winter. At-tracted by the dark reddish color of the hoodlike spathe and its fetid odor, the flies mistake the skunk cabbage flower for a dead animal. In the process of in-vestigating, the flies pollinate the tiny flowers inside the spathe.

After crossing the river, follow the trail up the slope through a large grove of beech trees. Riverbottom Road termi-nates at the top of this rise. Proceed left on Hemlock Trail. This route is neither blazed nor well worn, so be careful fol-lowing it. Be particularly alert because the trail zigzags sharply to your left near the top of the ridge. The Hemlock Trail skirts a swamp on your right, then rises sharply to its junction with Maple Swamp Trail. Turn right to circle another swamp to your left.

The Maple Swamp Trail climbs stead-ily to the Beech Hill Trail—again bear left. This trail ascends to the ridge and then drops gradually and merges with Dogwood Lane, which you also follow to your left toward Lake Mead. You pass more large beeches here. Unfortu-nately, defacing initials carved on the smooth, tender bark can still be easily deciphered after the passage of many years.

At a fork go left. You are now on the Lake Trail. Soon a right turn takes you out onto a boardwalk built in 1977. The numbers and variety of species growing in this swampy area are truly amazing. Soon you reach the west side of Lake Mead. Elaborate bird blinds hug the far shore. Turn left beyond the boardwalk and continue on the Lake Trail to its junction, just before the dam, with the Discovery Trail leading to the Center. Turn right.

Climb out of the hollow, passing an old root cellar in the apple orchard on your right. You may have noticed a strag-gly vine clinging to many trees and shrubs along the path. This vine, the Asi-atic or oriental bittersweet, depends on its coiling ability to work skyward, unlike poison ivy and Virginia creeper, which hold themselves up with the aid of aerial roots. Because its coils do not yield to tree growth, the host tree tries to grow around the vine, which cuts deep spiral ridges in its trunk, often girdling—and killing—the tree. This alien is consid-ered a pest in the sanctuary. Bear right beyond Indian Spring Pond and ascend the paved walk back to your car.

9

Pine Knob Loop

Distance: 2.5 miles

Vertical rise: 850 feet

Time: 1¾ hours

Rating: AB

Map: USGS 7.5-minute Ellsworth

Located on the edge of the Housatonic River Valley in western Connecticut, the double peaks of Pine Knob command excellent views of this beautiful river. In contrast to the large and rather dirty Connecticut River, the Housatonic here is a cozy little river winding down a scenic valley—its upper reaches are still relatively clean.

To reach this hike's start, drive north 1 mile on US 7 from its junction with CT 4 in Cornwall Bridge. A blue oval sign proclaims, "Pine Knob Loop." Although there is a parking area off the road, you may have to compete with trout anglers for a space—the Housatonic here is perhaps the premier trout river in the state.

The blue-blazed trail starts at a tote road on the north end of the parking area. Old house foundations and a pleas-ant crossing of Hatch Brook meet your eye immediately. This section of trail cuts through mixed woods of oak, ash, maple, and hickory, with a few crinkly-barked black cherry trees scattered throughout. Shortly the trail enters a planted white pine grove. The five-leafed vine climbing many of these pines is Virginia creeper; the leaves of this harmless vine turn flaming crimson in the fall. In 0.2 mile, you reach a trail junction. You will return on the blue-blazed trail to your left. Continue straight on the North Loop, which par-allels US 7 on your right. At a second junction in another 0.2 mile, follow the fork to your left. (The right fork leads to the campground at Housatonic Mead-ows State Park.) As you ascend the steep hill by switchbacks, stubby oaks pre-dominate on the thin, well-drained soil between ledge outcroppings.

Just beyond where the trail levels a bit, several chestnut saplings grow. Once considered one of North America's most important hardwoods—valued both for its extremely durable wood and for its tasty nuts—the chestnut has fallen prey to a deadly fungal blight. First no-ticed in New York's Botanical Gardens in 1904, the bark-girdling fungus spread quickly, almost eliminating the tree.

Housatonic Meadows Campground from the North Loop

The loss of the chestnut was one of our greatest natural calamities. Despite major efforts at Yale University and elsewhere, no sure solution to the disease has yet been discovered. Since the tree dies only from the girdled spot up and sprouts readily from its roots, the chestnut remains a common small tree.

In another 0.3 mile, a viewpoint reveals the campground almost directly below you, nestled among the trees across US 7. Circling left, the trail starts its final ascent of the first knob over displaced, tumbled ledges. After another 0.3 mile, the trail continues left along a rock terrace. As you face the river, the other peak of Pine Knob is visible to your extreme right. At left center on one of the rounded peaks well beyond the river, you can see Mohawk Mountain's distinctive towers against the horizon. The seemingly endless rounded hills

swimming across your vision help explain why northwestern Connecticut is the most popular hiking area in the state.

Your route turns right, off the overlook, and passes over the top of the wooded first knob (1120 feet), before dropping down steeply to the col between the two peaks. Here you join the Appalachian Trail on its way to Georgia. Pine Knob Loop and the AT run together for nearly ¾ mile. In another 0.5 mile, on the far side of the second knob (1160 feet), you come to another lookout. Stop and relax—perhaps you will see a pair of red-tailed hawks gracefully circling the valley, as we did! Continuing off this second knob, descend steeply while the sound of unseen flowing water gradually invades your subconscious.

In a small hemlock grove about 0.3 mile from the last lookout, watch for a blue arrow directing you sharply left.

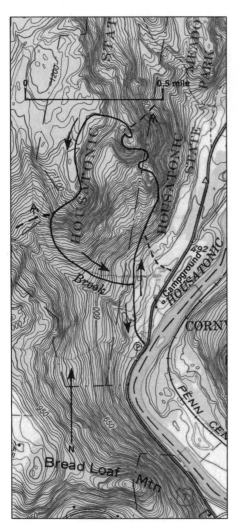

The depression containing Hatch Brook is visible on your right between two glacial erratics. Here you leave the AT as its white blazes continue south to CT 4 west of Cornwall Bridge. In another 0.5 mile, you reach the loop junction that you encountered on your way in. Your car is parked 0.2 mile on your right.

10

Hurd State Park

Distance: 3.5 miles

Vertical rise: 600 feet

Time: 2 hours

Rating: C

Map: USGS 7.5-minute Middle Haddam

Serendipity. It's a lovely-sounding word with a beautiful meaning: "the faculty of making fortunate and unexpected discoveries by accident." Perhaps the most important example of serendipity was Sir Alexander Fleming's discovery of penicillin while investigating the noxious green mold that was killing his bacteria cultures. For a hiker, serendipity should be a familiar byword. In this book we point out what we have seen, but you should always be prepared for serendipitous happenings. Remember that "adventure is not in the guidebook and beauty is not on the map."

With this thought in mind, pay a visit to Hurd State Park, perched atop the east bank of the Connecticut River. From the junction of CT 151 and CT 66

in Cobalt, drive south on CT 151 for 2.4 miles to a traffic light at a four-way junction. The road to your right leads to the park entrance. Park in the lot to the right of this road at the junction. This cross-country skiers' lot, with a large routed wooden sign showing the trails of the park, will be your starting point.

As we entered the park on a recent visit, we saw a bluebird, the first we'd spotted in a few years. Bluebirds are the same shade as the most breathtaking patch of sky you've ever seen. Unfortunately, their numbers have dropped because of competition from a pair of drab aliens—the English sparrow and the starling. A few people are trying to redress the balance by constructing bluebird trails with a series of specially built birdhouses along forest margins. With luck and the effort of these dedicated people, this rare bird might once again become common.

Pass the yellow metal gate and follow the right-hand road through the woods. The macadam surface is slowly breaking up after years of disuse. You'll soon pass a trail to your left; stay on the road and gently descend, following occasional green paint blazes. The hemlocks along this road look very unhealthy, and many have died, victims of the hemlock looper

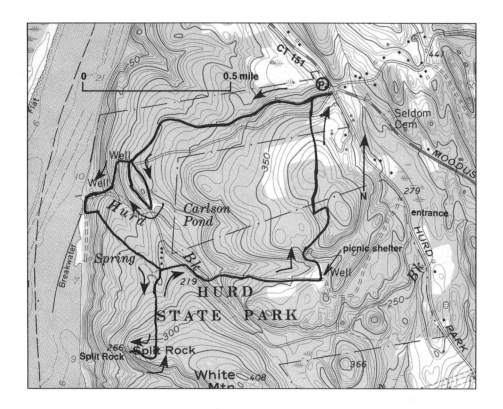

and the hemlock woolly adelgid. These pests feed on hemlock needles and twigs, respectively, and southern Connecticut hemlock stands, particularly along the Connecticut River, are the most noticeably affected. Salvage logging may be done in the park to remove some of the trees; we hope new trees will be planted to reduce the erosion that could result from the loss of these stands.

Follow the road to the paved circular loop road and another routed trail map. Take a side trip to your left, following the road to the dam by picturesque Carlson Pond, and inspect the 60-year-old stonework left behind by the Civilian Conservation Corps. A small quarrying operation left a cleft in a ledge along the road. Circle back to the trail sign and descend

on a gated road labeled River Trail. Follow the road down the steep hillside treed with black birches, tulip trees, and more unhealthy hemlocks.

Emerge at the bottom of the descent into the clearing along the Connecticut River. Follow the river downstream to your left. This grassy area is used mostly by boaters plying the river. Across the river to the right is the United Technologies jet engine facility. In addition to private craft, tugs pushing rusty barges occasionally chug by. Spend a while exploring the riverside. Wandering off to the right, we saw two young black ducks in a quiet spot. The trees here are different from those on the surrounding hillsides: sycamores, dying elms, tall sassafras, cottonwoods, silver maples, and

Tugboat and barge on the Connecticut River

willows form this canopy. Podded milk-weeds fringe the open areas, which are covered with coarse grass that glistens with dew on clear summer mornings. Across the river to your left is Bear Hill (see Hike 43). Only power lines (progress) mar this view of the hills along the river. Retrace your steps and continue left along the riverbank and cross the small stream over a stone slab.

After enjoying the riverside, climb the red-blazed trail to your left away from the river. Just before reaching the paved park road, you'll turn right at a four-way trail junction. Gently climb along the hillside, following the yellow blazes. At a junction with a woods road, marked with signs, turn right to Split Rock. Head downhill past a great white glacial boul-

der. Follow the trail down Split Rock, a ledge bearing a narrow crevasse 25 feet deep. This is a fine, sunny spot for lunch, with a good view of the Connecticut River 200 feet below.

After the respite, retrace your steps and climb back uphill, parallel to the ledge. Rejoin the trail and retrace your steps to the junction near the paved park road. Walking along this trail early one morning, we froze at a movement farther down the trail. A spotted fawn tottered to an uncertain stop, eyed us a bit, snorted to absorb our smell better, and—deciding that we were dubious characters—bounded away down the trail. Serendipity!

At the junction, turn right and follow the woods road to the paved road. Bear right and follow this road toward the park entrance. Shortly you'll see a gated road to your left. Take this road down to a stream crossing and then ascend on deteriorating macadam, following sporadic yellow blazes to the picnic area. Pass to the left of a large picnic shelter and follow the stone wall beyond it. At another routed wooden trail map, turn left toward an impressive white oak with great, gnarled, extended branches. This is a perfect example of white oak growth in an open field, complete with said field! Many hikes in Connecticut pass similar trees growing in the forest. These trees matured in open fields, and the forest has grown around them. Foresters know these trees as "wolf" trees. A white oak growing with other trees around it will grow straight and tall. To compete for sunlight, it will channel all its energy into growing tall, rather than broad.

Passing the white oak, take the left-most trail (to the right of the trail you arrived on) and follow a woods road past some intriguing stone ravines. A close inspection reveals a series of these ravines that must have been carved from the hillside. What these quarries yielded is open to speculation. The rock walls seem to have a fair amount of mica in them, so mica, used for early lanterns, might have been the miners' goal.

Bear right beyond the quarries to climb uphill, following red and orange blazes. You cross many stone walls while ascending the hill, which is covered with young hardwood trees sprinkled with occasional evergreen eastern red cedars. Pass just west of the hilltop and descend gently to cross through more old fields with abundant briars. Cross a woods road and soon reach a T-junction with another woods road. This is the road you started your hike on. Turn right to return to your car.

11

Sunny Valley

Distance: 3 miles	
Vertical rise: 700 feet	
Time: 2 hours	
Rating: C	
Map: USGS 7.5-minute New Milford	

A hike can be far more than just a bit of exercise in the woods or a chance to chin with a variety of like-minded folks. The woods are a wonderland where your depth of understanding can have no limit. The trees, the low-slung plants, the animals of chance encounter, the geologic clues, and our impact on the landscape are all there for us to see. The nicest thing about reading from nature is that, for the ever-curious amateur naturalist, there are no tests, no one to satisfy—except yourself! Some things are seasonal, some are around for decades, some date to colonial times, and still others go back to the Ice Age and beyond. An encyclopedia would be needed to detail each hike you take, especially if you take the time to look closely and return each season. We will touch briefly in this hike on three of these categories

of wonder—the Ice Age, trees, and traces left by the original colonists.

The Nature Conservancy's Sunny Valley Preserve provides trails as one facet of its multiple-use land management plan. The preserve's properties encompass nearly 1500 acres; trails are maintained on about 480 acres, with over 1000 acres managed as natural areas, woodlands, and farmlands.

From the junction of CT 67 and 133 in Bridgewater, go south on CT 133 about 0.7 mile, then turn right on Hat Shop Hill Road. After 0.6 mile, jog left on Christian Street, then right on Hemlock Road, which you follow for 1.7 miles to the gated Stony Brook Farm entrance. Park on your left just before the gate, where there is room for three cars.

Follow the Silica Mine Trail, which proceeds south, uphill, from the parking area. Climb the gently graded woods road, following blue blazes. Shortly your path levels and proceeds along an old tote road before climbing again. Gradually the grade steepens before reaching a white-blazed trail on your left. This is the trail to the Lookout, which will be part of your return route. Continue along the blue-blazed trail, passing numerous chips of quartz from the nearby silica mines along the path. You'll soon pass

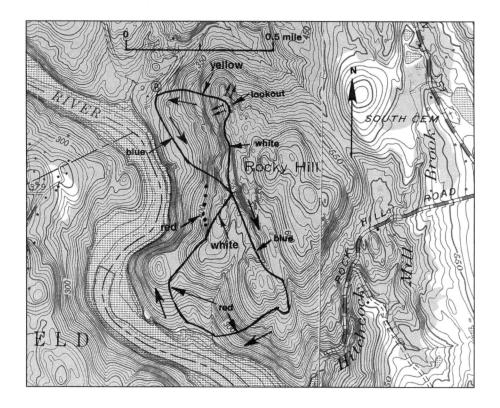

an old stone foundation to your left and descend through hemlocks. Cross a small swamp over puncheon, bridging made of local logs, and pass over a small ridge. Pass another swamp to your left and then follow a ridge with a deep ravine to your left.

The glaciers that covered our area over 10,000 years ago left many traces. There are thousands of these geological reminders in Connecticut—glacial erratics, old kettle holes, and dying ponds. The swamp, once a long narrow pond here on the side of the mountain, is such a remnant. The ice sheet gouged this depression in the ledge, the bottom of which is relatively impervious to water. The natural demise of all ponds comes sooner or later, depending on their original depth. Aquatic vegetative growth

and wind- and waterborne debris have all contributed to the filling in of the pond. The scum on its surface and the trail wending through its former outlet are signs of its return to dry land.

The blue-blazed trail comes to an abrupt end due to trail relocations. Take the red-blazed trail to your right through a clearing. Follow this trail up through a little ravine and then down an old tote road to Lake Lillinonah below. Turn right at the river and cross a small brook. We spotted a mink at the edge of the brook on a recent hike here! Climb away from the water's edge over a stone wall and parallel the shoreline northward. You'll turn right and ascend a series of ridges through thick hemlock woods.

Hemlock forests tell an interesting story. Look beneath this dense stand of hemlocks. The thick, acid bed of fallen needles and twigs and the tightly interwoven, light-intercepting foliage have banished all other plants from the forest floor, until only young hemlocks can grow. Connecticut's climax forest will then be maintained until fire, ax, or disease (see Hike 10) allows another cycle to start.

Just as the ascent eases, turn right onto a white-blazed trail to climb again to the crest of a ridge, where you'll descend briefly to a woods road, which is the blue-blazed trail you started on. Across from you are the old silica (quartz) mines that the colonists carved in the hillside. These abandoned silica mines are indicative of the lack of mineral wealth in New England. When our state was first settled, dreams of mineral wealth led to much part-time prospecting in Connecticut. Limited amounts of cobalt, iron ore, garnets, silica, and even traces of gold lured these early prospectors.

Most of the holes they dug have since filled in. In a few places some small successes caused larger diggings, where activity faded after the discovery of richer lodes elsewhere. This silica mine is a case in point. Like other local mines, it's just a relic from the past to stimulate our curiosity.

Bear left and soon arrive at the junction with the white-blazed trail now leaving to your right to the Lookout. Follow it and climb steadily but gradually past large stone slabs to the Lookout just to the left of the trail, with good views to the west.

As you leave the Lookout, go to your left downhill steeply on the yellow-blazed trail through mountain laurel and oak. Soon come to an old woods road, which you follow left, continuing on the yellow-blazed trail through another hemlock forest. When you reach the paved road, bear left to return to your car.

Looking west from the Lookout

12

Bluff Point

Distance: 4.5 miles

Vertical rise: 100 feet

Time: 2¼ hours

Rating: D

Map: USGS 7.5-minute New London

A combination of historical circumstances and heavy demand for shoreline property has kept most of Connecticut's short coastline inaccessible to the public. One of the very few state parks on this shore, Bluff Point State Park's undeveloped 800-plus-acre peninsula is a special place for the walker. The only such sizable acreage on the Connecticut coast, Bluff Point is free from concessions, cottages, and campsites.

There are signs to direct you to Bluff Point. From the intersection of CT 117 and US 1 in Groton, drive west for 0.3 mile on US 1 to Depot Road. Turn left, following this street past Industrial Road and under the railroad tracks (where the paved surface ends) until you reach a large parking lot and closed gate about 0.7 mile from US 1. You know that you have arrived when you spy a sign listing park regulations. There is an ample picnic area to the right of the gate.

Proceed on foot down the gated dirt road. Owing to the park's proximity to civilization, you'll share the roads with joggers and bicyclists. Fishing boats ply the bay to your right, and windrows of dead eelgrass, one of the few flowering plants that grow in salt water, line the rocky shore. The brant, a smaller relative of the Canada goose, feeds almost exclusively on this plant. When a mysterious blight in the 1930s all but exterminated the eelgrass, the brant nearly went, too. The emaciated flocks subsisted on a diet of sea lettuce until the grass came back. If you walk this way in the colder months, you may see a few of the hundreds of brant that winter along the shore of Long Island Sound.

Numerous side paths cut off from the main road. Due to the pervasive influence of the sea, the woods of Bluff Point are more varied than most inland forests. The tangle of vines and brambles— grape, red-fruited barberry, rose, blackberry, black raspberry, honeysuckle, oriental bittersweet, and greenbriar—is thick enough to make Br'er Rabbit feel at home. Various oaks, cherries, longthorned hawthorns, tight-barked hickories, shagbark hickories, sumacs, and

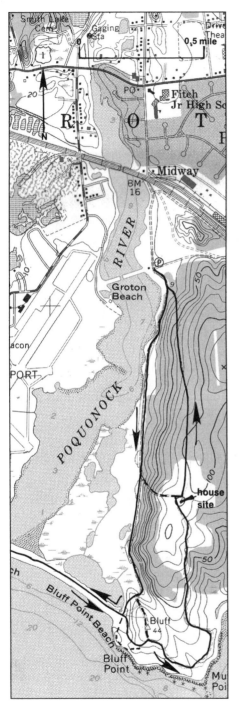

blueberries represent the deciduous trees, and an occasional cedar represents the evergreen trees.

You will probably see one or more swans gracing the bay on this hike. They will almost certainly be European mute swans. These birds are descended from captives escaped from various estates, mostly on Long Island. These descendants are now spreading rapidly throughout the waterways of the Northeast.

During an April visit you may hear the mating chorus of the male peepers and toads. These dry-land dwellers congregate, upon breaking hibernation, in various temporary waters to breed. The peeper has a high-pitched, two-note call, hence its name. The toad produces a long trill. If these amphibians mistakenly choose a permanent body of water in which to lay their eggs, various water-dwelling enemies will devour the tadpoles; if the pools they select dry up too soon, the tadpoles will die before completing metamorphosis. As with many things in nature, a very delicate balance exists.

The most common tree in this narrow strip of woodland is probably sassafras, usually recognized by its mitten-shaped leaves and greenish-barked twigs. Sassafras leaves usually come in three shapes—like a mitten with no thumb, one thumb, or two thumbs—often on the same branch. As a rule, those leaves nearest the end of a twig have the fewest thumbs. Henry David Thoreau found the fragrant leaves to be reminiscent of the Orient.

About 1.5 miles from your start, you reach the low bluffs on a point of land. Over the water to your right lies Groton Heights, and to your left, Groton Long Point. Fishers Island, part of New York State, lies to the right of center, while Watch Hill in Rhode Island is at left of center.

Bluff Point

A bit before the bluff, a boardwalk on your right detours you onto Bluff Point Beach. Wander down this beach a bit before continuing your exploration of Bluff Point itself. Castoff treasures from the sea await your curious gaze: rope, great blocks of wood, blue mussel shells, great whorled whelk shells, marble-sized periwinkle shells, scallop shells, rectangular shells from razor clams, flat wide strands of kelp, bladder-floated algae (seaweed), crab husks, and the everlasting, ever-present plastics—the bane of all the world's oceans.

When you have satisfied your yen for beach walking or have reached the end of this beach, retrace your steps, following sprawling masses of delicate beach peas back to the bluff. Before you start around this point, pause for a moment among the wild primrose and beach plum. You are standing on a terminal moraine. This hasty-pudding mix of rocks and sand was dumped here some 10,000 years ago, when the glacier that completely covered present-day New England retreated.

Follow the road around to the east. Soon after leaving the shore, take the better-worn path (inland) to your left; at the fork 50 yards farther on, bear right. (The trail to your left soon connects with the outward-bound leg of your hike.) Rounding the point, you look over a cattail swamp. These are being taken over throughout the state by the giant reed phragmites (pronounced frag-MI-tez). Here, their waving plumes stand sentinel by the sound. Across the bay, a seemingly solid wall of cottages stands in stark contrast to this wild oasis.

The trail moves inland to follow the center ridge of the peninsula. Stone walls stand in mute evidence of colonial cultivation. The trail forks after about 0.5 mile. Near this fork is the foundation at the site of the Winthrop house. Built around 1700 by Governor Fitz-John Winthrop, grandson of the famous Massachusetts Bay governor, it had a 300-foot tunnel to the barn and a room-sized brick chimney in the basement for protection from Native American raids.

Leaving this area, take the right fork (the left joins the bayside road you followed earlier). The path tends left until it joins the outbound trail near the parking lot. Go to your right to reach your car.

13

Day Pond Loop

Distance: 4 miles

Vertical rise: 500 feet

Time: 2½ hours

Rating: C

Map: USGS 7.5-minute Moodus

New England's forests, rock formations, and hills make a very nice setting for our hikes. We even have one feature that is world famous and almost unique—our glorious fall colors! Westerners may rave about their yellow aspen—we have not only yellows (including aspen), but also a riot of other colors that are beautiful in themselves and glorious together. What a grand and pleasant surprise it must have been for the Pilgrims to be greeted their first New England fall in 1621 by our magnificent colors!

Around Labor Day, the sumac and the red maple turn red and scarlet. Then the yellow of popple (Yankee for aspen) and birch appears, followed by seemingly translucent ash (perhaps our favorite), with deep purple on top of the leaf and yellow beneath; the wind ripples this two-toned effect beautifully. Our crown

jewels, the sugar maples, with their fantastic range of hues from yellow through orange to brilliant reds, burst into brilliance, and finally the various oaks, with their deep, long-lasting rusts, complete the tapestry.

The only area in the world with colors to rival ours is eastern China, but our far greater number of trees makes New En-

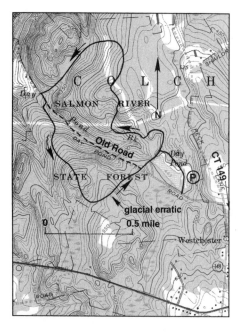

gland's show unsurpassed. You may wonder why only these two areas, half a world apart, are so blessed. One reasonable theory is that many millions of years ago, between ice ages, at a time when our present trees were developing, Greenland was a warm, forested island that served as a bridge over the pole between northern Asia and North America. The return of the ice pushed the forest south into both areas. The color genes were thus derived from a single source and spread into both eastern China and eastern North America.

To get to Day Pond, take exit 16 off CT 2 in North Westchester and go south on CT 149. In 3 miles, turn right at the sign for Day Pond State Park. After 0.4 mile, bear left on Peck Lane, then left again on Day Pond Road. The gate for Day Pond State Park is 1.1 miles north of CT 149. There is ample angle parking along the road around the pond. Several water-loving swamp maples surround the entrance. Various oaks and the yellow-leafed tulip trees are also found here. Follow the dirt entrance road around the pond on your left past a large picnic shelter, also on your left.

There are a few outhouses scattered about, but the next building (again on your left) is an elaborate bathhouse complete with water fountain. Such development is both good and bad. It can mean that the state is acquiring very few new parks and can thus put most of its money into developing existing parks. Sometimes such development is necessary to protect parks' resources. The multiyear, multimillion-dollar Heritage Program, started in the mid-1980s, aspires to double Connecticut's recreational land base before the century is out, ensuring the protection of more woodland for public use and enjoyment.

After curving around the beach and adjacent dressing rooms, turn right by a pair of outhouses just before the dam. The blue-blazed trail heads downhill on an old tote road. If you choose the latter part of October for this hike, you will find that the shorter hours of daylight, rather than frost, as is commonly believed, have painted the foliage lavishly with a spectrum of reds and orange.

In a few yards the trail turns sharply left off the tote road; you are still following the blue blazes. Jog slightly to your left and cross the gas pipeline easement; continue downhill toward the stream.

The outlet stream from Day Pond lends a cheery background to the first part of this hike. The stream moves quickly downhill, matching the trail and forming a series of small falls and rapids on its way to the Salmon River. Less than ½ mile from the pond, turn sharply right uphill away from the stream on the blue-blazed trail. Here, a blue-blazed trail also goes left to cross the brook and continues to the road that bisects the Day Pond Loop.

It is interesting to note the young beech at this turn in your path. Depending upon how late in the autumn you are walking, many of the trees may have lost their foliage. The red maple leaves are often off before the other colors have fully developed. The various oaks will usually hold their leaves until well into the winter. However, young (but not the old) beeches will often hold their leaves into early spring. By then the leaves are bleached almost white, but are still holding on.

Cross under the power lines and climb until you reach a rocky knoll nearly a mile from the start. The rock-strewn area (these are glacial erratics) culminates in a small, circular, almost flat top. The path starts down the other side, where a few cedars still reach the sun.

After several minor ups and downs, the trail changes its mostly northerly direction and heads west downhill, crossing a stone wall. Upon reaching a woodland valley, you go along the left side, following the blue blazes. You'll pass a number of stone walls and foundations in this valley. As the valley cuts deeper into the local water table, a stream becomes visible, growing as you proceed downhill, deeper into the valley. Soon you cross the stream.

The valley and its stream end at a deeper valley, with the larger stream coming directly from Day Pond. At the bottom of a hill the rough tote road you have been following hits a well-defined old road, where you turn left. After again crossing the smaller stream that you followed down the valley and starting up a gentle grade, turn right onto another woods road to continue along the blue-blazed trail.

Follow the blue-blazed trail into the woods, then turn right again and finally left across the larger stream from Day Pond; this can be challenging during the high-water period of early spring snowmelt. You are now better than halfway around the circuit. Go left along the bank of this stream beside a stone wall. Soon go right uphill away from the brook. Cross under the power line and wind slowly upward through what, at first glance, appears to be an almost featureless woodland. However, our woodlands are never featureless! Along here we saw a large expanse of white pine and eastern hemlock, a young deciduous woodland, and acres of club mosses, many carrying their spore stalks like banners.

After almost a mile of gentle upgrade, you crest the hilltop and then cross a linear clearing carrying a buried transcontinental cable. After crossing a small, mostly dry-bottomed valley, the blue-blazed trail resumes its gentle upward slope.

Day Pond

Pass on your right a 400-ton glacial erratic. Besides a patina of algae and lichen, this great rock supports a young black birch on its top and a clump of polypody fern clinging to a foothold on its side. You can estimate such things as the weight of this boulder, the grains of sand on a beach, or the number of leaves on a large tree quite handily by taking a small section and multiplying by the whole—you will definitely not be exact, but you will have a good idea of the actual number. For this boulder we estimated its weight at about 200 pounds per cubic foot (water weighs about 64 pounds per cubic foot) and its size as 20 feet square by 10 feet high. A simple calculation produces a volume of 4000 cubic feet and a weight of 800,000 pounds, or 400 tons.

As you reach the end of the loop, the path meets, parallels, and then crosses a stone wall. You soon cross an old tote road whose dirt surface is below much of the surrounding land—erosion from past heavy use! Shortly you reach the park road just south of the dam.

You then cross the pond's outlet stream and dam on two bridges, pass the two outhouses (to your left) where you started the loop hike, and retrace your steps to your car.

The two consecutive bridges over the pond's outlets are particularly interesting and show that the dam's designer knew what he was doing. The smaller stream's outlet in the dam is lower so that it will always carry some of the pond's overflow with its cheery burble. The second outlet is higher, but much wider than the first. In case of heavy floods, this can drain off a large amount of water, while the smaller dam is more limited. The two outlets prevent an unacceptable water buildup against the dam, which could result in overflow and increased erosion if the smaller outlet were unable to drain off the accumulating water. This pond then has the best of both worlds—it has the advantage of a small, compact outlet, with a safety valve that comes into play in case of heavy floods.

14

Hartman Park

Distance: 4 miles

Vertical rise: 600 feet

Time: 2½ hours

Rating: C

Map: USGS 7.5-minute Hamburg

This delightful woods ramble takes the hiker through three centuries of our history and is a result of the generous donation of 300 acres to the town of Lyme by John and Kelly Hartman. The nearly 10 miles of trails are the work of local volunteer hikers. Come and enjoy the fruits of their labors; maybe this example will inspire others!

Find Hartman Park from Hadlyme by taking CT 156 south from its junction with CT 82. Turn left on Beaverbrook Road, just past Lyme School. After 2.7 miles, turn left again on Gungy Road. The park entrance is 1 mile down this road on your right. There is ample parking near the gated road into the park. Take care not to block the road, which may be needed for emergency access.

The trails are marked with painted aluminum disks. You'll follow the orange-blazed Heritage Trail into the woods just before the metal gate. Soon you'll reach a junction with the Nature Trail, marked with green disks. Follow it to your right. This trail follows along the base of a hill and features painted stones, wooden mobiles, and hidden curios intended to surprise children. The open hardwood forest includes some prominent American hornbeam, once called blue beech. The gnarled trunks and thin gray bark give the tree its common name, musclewood. However, this tree's wood does not hold up well to the

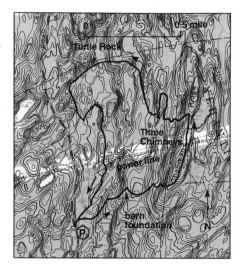

elements and rots quickly in contact with the ground.

Pass a junction with the yellow-blazed Lee Farm Road and continue on the Nature Trail to return to the Heritage Trail. Turn right to follow the orange disks up the hill to the impressive stone foundation of a barn to your right. On the way up the hill, check out the variably lobed leaves of sassafras. Its leaves resemble both right- and left-hand mittens, as well as double-thumbed mitts. A tea made from the roots of this plant was credited with keeping the Native Americans healthy. Hence, sassafras was the colonists' first export home from New England and matched tobacco as the largest export crop. The active ingredient in sassafras, safrole, has been found to be carcinogenic, so we do not use it in today's beverages.

The red oak in front of the barn foundation was struck by lightning a couple of years ago. Although only one branch showed signs of the strike, the next year the tree was dead and had no new leaves.

Follow the park road briefly past the foundation, and turn right up an old tote road opposite the foundation of the farmhouse. The 100-year-old white ash growing out of its cellar supports a large poison ivy vine. This house was probably built in the early 17th century and burned after the Civil War.

Climb over the hill and descend into a wetland. Cross it and ascend Chapman Ridge via switchbacks through mountain laurel. Following the ridge line north, you'll pass the remains of the Chapman Farm of two centuries past. Continue past the blue-blazed Chapman Path and cross a power line. The trail is marked with wooden stakes painted orange. After following the ridge a bit farther, drop to the valley to the west past a stone fireplace and turn right onto the worn park road. Follow the road until

the orange-blazed trail turns left to climb to the top of Three Chimneys Ridge.

On this ridge the small, pointed evergreen leaves of the striped wintergreen stood out among the brown leaves of late March. These leaves have prominent white veins, making the plant striking regardless of the season.

The orange-blazed Heritage Trail links up with the red-blazed Nubble and Ridges Trails, and all three stay together to the Three Chimneys to your left. Perhaps the most intriguing feature of the park, the chimneys may, it is speculated, be the remains of one of a series of forts Lyonel Gardiner was contracted to build for the original Puritan settlers of Saybrook Colony. In 1634, Gardiner was sent to build the forts in case the political and religious problems in England worsened. Oliver Cromwell's success made the forts unnecessary, and this fort possibly reverted to a farmstead. The arrangement of the chimneys resembles medieval forts of that period, and is similar to structures found at Plimoth Plantation. The Three Chimneys may be one of Gardiner's lost forts.

Follow the orange-blazed trail to your right soon after leaving the fort, and descend to a woods road at the base of the hill, where you'll turn right to follow the yellow-blazed road through a wetland. Bear left onto the red-blazed trail at a fork and eventually climb up to Jumble Ridge. The trail passes a number of rock formations, including Laughing Rock, Turtle Rock, and the aptly named Snout.

After passing below Coyote and Cave Cliffs, the red-blazed trail turns south toward Hartman Field. Turn left onto a yellow-blazed connector trail that follows a woods road. Cross over a bridge and turn right onto the orange-blazed Heritage Trail and pass a charcoal kiln to your right, marked with a white disk. The kiln is nothing more than a large,

"The Snout" in Hartman Park

circular, level spot in the forest with no large trees growing in it. The local farmers would pile up wood and cover it with soil to permit a slow-burning fire, thereby creating hot-burning charcoal for future use in blast furnaces.

Cross the power line clearing, passing the Flume, a cascade over moss-covered rock. Soon a yellow-blazed connector comes in from your left and then leaves the trail to the right. Follow it to your right and turn right again to a small cemetery on a rise. The unmarked stones probably indicate the graves of the less wealthy and those of lower social standing, such as slaves and itinerant workers. The only pertinent documentation in Lyme records is of a penniless man of partial Native American descent buried by a white landowner, who sought reimbursement from the town.

Turn left onto the red-blazed trail and follow it to the School Room, an open-air gathering site on the park road with an informative bulletin board and visitor register. Please sign in and let the park manager and volunteers know about your visit. From the School Room, take the orange-and-green-blazed trail south to the mill site just below an earth and stone dam. It was probably an old sawmill; however, there is no positive identification in the records. It is only known that 50 years after the settling of Saybrook Colony, there were complaints from Lyme of overcutting of timber in the uplands. Much of this was exported as wood products to lumber-starved England.

Below the mill, come out onto the gravel park road and turn right to pass through the gate and return to your car.

15

Soapstone Mountain

Distance: 4 miles

Vertical rise: 700 feet

Time: 2½ hours

Rating: C

Map: USGS 7.5-minute Ellington

Observation tower on Soapstone Mountain

Soapstone—an intriguing name for a mountain—sits in the midst of the 6000-acre Shenipsit State Forest. A quarry on the east slope used by Native Americans and early settlers once yielded the soft, talclike, greasy, lustered stone from which the mountain derives its name. In colonial times, this stone was valued for its high heat retention; flannel-wrapped hot soapstones lessened the shock of icy bedclothes.

Soapstone Mountain is located east of the Connecticut River in Somers. From the junction of CT 140 and CT 83, drive north on CT 83 for 4 miles to Parker Road and turn right. After 1.3 miles (the last 0.4 mile is a rough, three-season dirt road), at a four-way junction with Soapstone Mountain Road and Sykes Road, park across the way to your left.

Follow the gravel Soapstone Mountain Road east toward the mountain.

Pass some logging yards to your left and reach an old woods road flanked by boulders blazed with yellow and blue paint to your left. (If you miss this turn, follow the road to the summit of the mountain and then pick up these directions again from the tower.) Turn left onto the woods road and descend to where the blue-blazed Shenipsit Trail bears right uphill, away from the descending yellow-blazed trail.

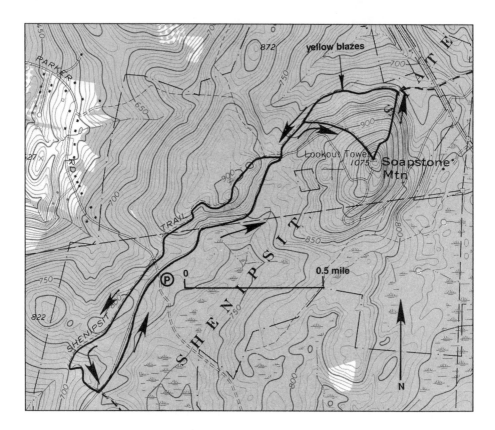

The Shenipsit Trail heads to the right up the main peak of Soapstone Mountain—a good steady climb. Climbing, you reach the top (1075 feet) ½ mile after leaving the road.

This summit is a good example of the sometimes rapid effects rendered by the hand of humanity. When we first wrote about this summit in 1977, the old fire tower that we had used so many times had been removed as unsafe, but the following year an observation tower was erected in its place. Now covered with graffiti, the structure nonetheless offers wonderful views.

An easy climb of the observation tower presents a bird's-eye view of the surrounding country. Off to the west is the flat valley land. To the north and south is the well-wooded mountain ridge of which Soapstone is a prominent part.

The trail down from the summit is a bit obscure due to removal of trees, a handy marking medium. You enter the woods just to the left of the telephone line. Your route threads down a rocky path through an attractive field of glacial erratics. After 0.3 mile, turn left on the yellow-blazed tote road. (The blue-blazed Shenipsit Trail continues to your right to the Massachusetts border about 6 miles farther on.)

Gently ascend on the yellow-blazed tote road around the north side of Soapstone Mountain. Continue climbing toward Soapstone Mountain Road and bear right onto the blue-blazed trail to climb the steep hill to the west. Eventually you'll stand on the rocky summit of West Soapstone Mountain (930 feet). Near the top in spring you may find an atypical species of violet, the northern downy violet. The leaves are long, oval, and fuzzy rather than the more familiar heart-shaped and smooth, but the familiar violet-blue flowers are unmistakable. There are dozens of species of violets, and with hybridization even the experts have trouble with some identifications. So we have a ready-made excuse if we cannot identify a violet—it must be a hybrid!

On a leafless day, the microwave tower on the summit of the main peak of Soapstone Mountain appears across the valley. The trail works downhill and passes another rocky outcropping over upward-tipped ledges. This is gneiss, the basic bedrock of much of Connecticut, which was laid down in flat layers hundreds of millions of years ago. These protruding ledges were tilted by subsequent crystal deformations.

Near a road crossing, you'll pass a swamp to your right. In spring, the swamp resonates with the high-pitched chorus of peepers. We have all heard countless thousands of these diminutive tree frogs with the big voices, but have you ever seen one in song? Cautious creeping in the evening with the subtle use of a flashlight may reward you with the sight of one of these small, tan frogs, whose throat swells into a great, white, bubble-like sound box from a body less than an inch long. Summer sightings are more a matter of quick eyes, quicker hands, and luck. Most of the woodland hoppers you find are the black-masked wood frogs, but occasionally you will find a tiny frog without the mask and a faint contrasting X on its back—this is the spring peeper.

In spring, fern fiddleheads pop up everywhere. Instead of growing gradually like most annuals, the fern uncoils like a New Year's Eve party favor from a tightly curled mass into a fully grown plant. In northern New England, the fiddleheads of the ostrich fern are considered a delicacy. We are told that our common cinnamon fern fiddlehead is also good to eat, but you have to remove all the light brown fuzz before you can eat it—seeing what a job that is, we have never tried it, nor have we found anyone who has!

Cross gravel Parker Road and continue east, following the blue-blazed trail. Carefully follow the blazes through here. There are many paths and old tote roads in this forest. If you are daydreaming or taking the path of least resistance, it is very easy to miss a turn or two and find that the worn path you are traveling is devoid of blue blazes. In that event, retrace your steps to the last blaze and try again.

In late spring, there are at least two aspects of the vegetation that you may have noticed and wondered about. One is the many groups of star flowers. Spreading mostly by means of underground rhizomes, they are usually found in large stands or not at all. There seem to be more multiblossom plants here than usual. Secondly, you may think the compact masses of moss have grown hair. Actually, in late spring, moss sends up flowering stalks that allow the resulting spores to spread further after they ripen.

The forest you're hiking through has a lovely, soothing sameness. An understory of maple and black birch struggles for sunlight in the gaps among large red oak. The leaf-littered floor is carpeted with masses of ground pine and wild lily of the valley. Many of Connecticut's forests are, like this one, all of a size. The last great timber harvests were in the early years of this century, and since then cutting has been sporadic—far less than the annual growth—resulting in many trees across the state being about the same age. The logging that does occur, some of which you pass by on this hike, appears to leave the trails virtually untouched.

Soon you bear left to cross Sykes Road. Turn left here to follow the road less than ½ mile back to your car.

16

Penwood

Distance: 4¾ miles

Vertical rise: 600 feet

Time: 2½ hours

Rating: C

Map: USGS 7.5-minute Avon

Lady's slippers

The traprock ridges flanking the Connecticut River Valley offer secluded hiking on the outskirts of the central cities. Penwood State Park sits atop one such ridge. Only a few minutes' drive from Hartford, the trails of Penwood carry you beyond the sights and sounds of our workaday world to a place where the most blatant intrusions are the blue blazes marking your route on the Metacomet Trail and the broken macadam of the closed access road.

The park entrance is on the north side of CT 185, one mile west of the CT 185 and CT 178 junction in Bloomfield. There is a large paved parking lot just to the right of the entrance. This park's proximity to Hartford, along with its paved circular loop road, makes it very popular with joggers, fitness walkers, and dog owners year-round.

Pass a plaque honoring Curtis H. Veeder, an industrialist, inventor, and outdoorsman who, in 1944, gave the state the nearly 800 acres that is now a state park. Pick up the blue blazes of the Metacomet Trail and follow them a short distance down the right-hand road (east). Just past a blocked tote road, bear left into the woods, climbing quickly onto the hemlock-shrouded traprock ridge. Once on the top, the trail undu-

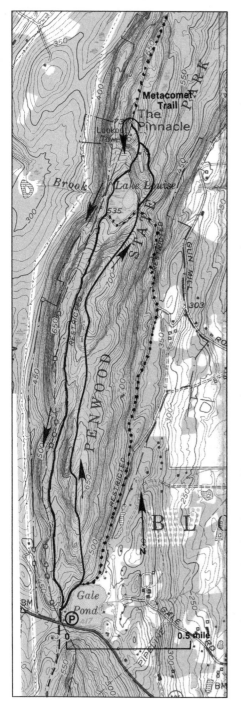

lates gently within the forest, passing a number of little-used side trails that lead north and south to the park's loop road. The forest dampens the sights and sounds of our harried world. Even the park road is invisible. Here the thick woods limit the undergrowth to a few striped maples, wild sarsaparillas, and mapleleaf viburnums.

In 1.8 miles, the trail crosses the tar end of the loop road. Take a break from the hike to explore the little ridgetop pond. Head across the pavement onto a short boardwalk leading through the thicket and onto the edge of the pond, grandiosely named Lake Louise, for Mr. Veeder's wife. The teeming fecundity of life here makes the dry, forested ridge look like a desert.

Discounting the usual forest birds that are drawn to this cornucopia, we saw or heard more varieties of living things in just a few minutes of standing by the pond than in our total time spent on the ridge—dragonflies with out-stretched wings, damselflies with folded wings, water striders miraculously skimming the pond's surface, circling whirligig beetles setting a dizzying circular pace when disturbed, and water boatmen riding just under the water's surface. Gaily colored butterflies displayed marked contrast with the mud perches on which they sat, absorbing moisture from their surroundings. Tadpoles were flitting into sight along the pond's edges when they came up for an occasional gulp of air. Through the water flicked aquatic green newts, the adult form of the red efts found on the springtime forest floor after a night of gentle rain. Here and there small frogs sat propped up, half in and half out of the water, still exhibiting the rounded softness of their recent tadpole stage, and we saw two small water snakes sunbathing near the boardwalk.

Even the vegetation here is varied and lush. Lily pads dot the surface. Marsh fern, swamp loosestrife, and buttonbush edge the pond, and a sour gum tree grows on your right. The white blossoms of swamp azaleas perfume the air. Look for the few clumps of swamp Juneberry amid the numerous smooth alders. Their lustrous black berries, which resemble huge huckleberries, make a nice snack. If such a place fascinates you as it does us, read the book *Watchers at the Pond* by Francis Russell.

When ready, return to the loop road and follow the tarred road east through a gate to climb a fine scenic lookout called the Pinnacle. The road leads to a clearing where Mr. Veeder's cabin of chestnut logs once stood, and you pick up the blue-blazed Metacomet Trail again to the right for the final ascent. Follow the trail to the Pinnacle. The ridge traversed by the blue-blazed Tunxis Trail lies to the west across the valley. To the south rises Heublein Tower on Talcott Mountain (see Hike 44) and farther left the great tilted volcanic slabs of Mount Higby (see Hike 29).

Return to the cabin clearing and stay to its right to follow a stone staircase down the steep slope back to Lake Louise. Bear left to continue your descent to the tote road around the lake, and then turn right to follow the old woods road around its north side. Cross the lake's outlet on a plank bridge, and follow a boardwalk through the swamp to the broken pavement of the loop road. Bear right on this road and follow it back to your car.

17

Northern Metacomet

Distance: 4 miles

Vertical rise: 500 feet

Time: 2½ hours

Rating: C

Map: USGS 7.5-minute Windsor Locks

Choose a cool, clear day for this hike. It begins with a pleasant walk along a traprock ridge of north central Connecticut, offering sunny vistas, and then a visit to the forbidding environs of the infamous Newgate Prison. The blue-blazed Metacomet Trail will take you along Peak Mountain's volcanic cliffs. After the hike, Newgate Road will lead to the prison site, which was also America's first copper smelter.

To reach the hike's start, follow CT 20 west 0.7 mile from its junction with CT 187 in Granby to Newgate Road on your right. Go north on Newgate Road a little way until you see the blue-blazed Metacomet Trail enter the woods on your right. The trail ascends from the second prominent pulloff to your right. There is room to park on the road. The path climbs steeply onto the traprock ridge

and then bears left along the top.

In leafless season the views here are particularly nice, but even in summer you catch glimpses of the countryside below through occasional breaks in the trees. The utility line you soon pass beneath services a string of beacons for planes approaching Bradley International Airport, which is just east of the ridge. The airplane buff will appreciate the procession of jet airliners and the myriad of smaller, private aircraft that come and go overhead. The exhilarating cliff edges and views offset the aircraft noise for the rest of us.

In a little under a mile you'll scramble up to a lookout about 300 feet above the valley floor. The USGS benchmark reads Copper Mountain. The Tunxis Trail follows the traprock ridge across the road directly west opposite you; to the south stretches the sinuous ridge curve that the Metacomet Trail follows. Penwood State Park (see Hike 16) straddles the nearest hump; Heublein Tower on Talcott Mountain (see Hike 44) stands out prominently behind it; and beyond the tower the tilted slabs of Mount Higby (see Hike 29) rise on the horizon.

Staying on the ridge, you'll reenter the woods and descend slowly but steadily and then climb again. Nearly 2

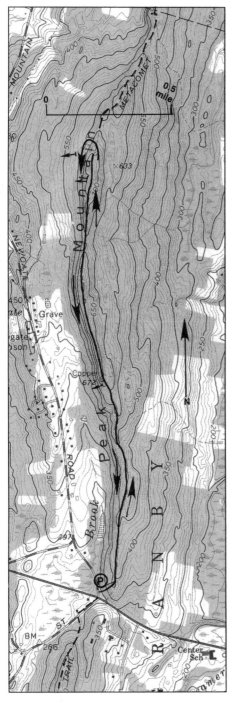

miles from the start, just beyond the third beacon tower, you reach an excellent lookout ledge with fine views to the west. Below you and to the south, there is a small paved road circle. To the left of that circle, on the main road below, you can spot the walls and front gate of Newgate Prison. Continue on the trail, soon coming to a grassy spot that overlooks the scree slope.

Retrace your steps to your car, and then drive north on Newgate Road for 1.1 miles. Before long you come to the impressive ruins of Newgate Prison on your right. Originally a copper mine (circa 1705), it was pressed into service as a prison just before the Revolutionary War. It became most famous as a prison for Tories during the war. The prison is open daily from Memorial Day through October. There is a small entry fee.

For a short excursion into the seamier side of our nation's past, join the line of waiting visitors. After descending 50 feet in a narrow shaft, you enter the mine proper. Water seeps down the walls. A motley crew of Tories, thieves, and debtors were forced to live and labor in this cavernous prison while fettered with leg irons, handcuffs, and iron collars. Marks worn on the floor by pacing prisoners are still visible two centuries later, and tales of barbarity seem to echo in the hollow chambers.

After exploring the prison, return to Newgate Road. The fresh air will be especially welcome after the dank dungeon. Above, the traprock ridges beckon to you for a return trip, perhaps a good idea after a visit to the prison.

18

Candlewood Mountain

Distance: 3.5 miles

Vertical rise: 1100 feet

Time: 2½ hours

Rating: A

Map: USGS 7.5-minute New Milford

Candlewood was a common name for pitch pine, a familiar tree to hikers of Connecticut's ridge lines and hilltops. This weather-beaten tree, often twisted by the prevailing winds, is easy to identify, as it is our only three-needled pine. Its wood contains so much resin, or pitch, that it is easily lit and was often used as a torch (before our modern flashlights) for lighting one's way, like a candle.

If scrambling over rocks and ledges interests you, here is your hike. This section of the Housatonic Range Trail does not require special rock-climbing skills and equipment, but it does have a challenging rock jumble and an interesting step ledge that demand careful use of both hands.

Remember that the Housatonic Range Trail depends on the deportment of the general public for its continued existence, because no state forests or parks protect this path. Built and maintained by volunteers, the entire trail lies on private land, and irate property owners could close the trail at any time. Do your bit to prevent this from happening by discouraging vandalism, picking up litter, staying on the trail, and greeting landowners pleasantly when passing through.

Candlewood Lake lies to the south of Candlewood Mountain. This 5420-acre body of water, the largest in the state, has a depth of 85 feet and supports both trout and warm-water fish. Almost all lakes in the state were either created or enlarged by artificial impoundments (dams). Candlewood Lake encompasses several lakes that were joined by an impoundment.

Watch for clumps of Dutchman's breeches in early spring. The yellow and white flowers look like old-fashioned pantaloons hanging upside down to dry.

From the junction of US 202 and US 7 in New Milford, drive north on US 7 for 2.6 miles to CT 37, a left turn. Watch for the blue-blazed trail just before you reach the junction with Candlewood Mountain Road—there is parking for a few cars at the trailhead. This hike con-

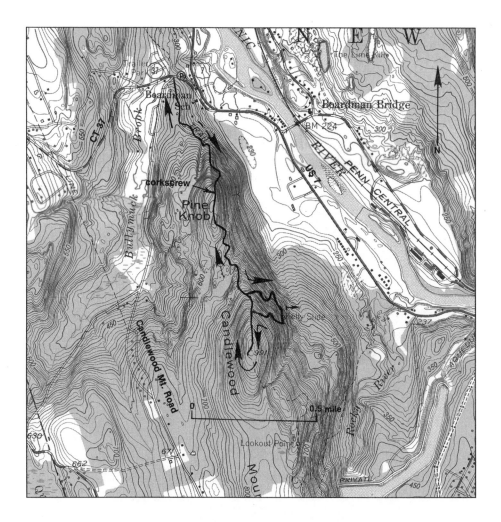

tinues to change with each edition of this book, due to quarrying operations and landowner concerns. The Housatonic Range Trail north of CT 37 is currently undergoing some changes from recent developments. We're hopeful a passable route through the development can be retained so that Suicide Ledges and Boardman Mountain to the north can continue to be linked by footpath to Candlewood Mountain.

Enter the woods just south of CT 37, following the blue blazes. There is a sign for the Housatonic Range Trail at the woods edge. Your route is shaded by a dense hemlock grove. After ¼ mile, cross a gas pipeline clearing. Gently climb through ledges and boulders amid hemlocks and white pines. The route can be tricky in here; follow the blue blazes carefully.

Climb a steep slab of rock and arrive at the base of the corkscrew, a rock jumble that will require careful placement of hands and feet. It is not recommended when wet or icy. At the top of

The Housatonic River from Kelly Slide

the corkscrew, bear left and gently ascend on the ridge to the top of Pine Knob, ¾ mile from your start. A grouse abruptly flew out of some shrubs on a recent hike here.

Descend to your left into Paradise Valley, the col between Pine Knob and Candlewood Mountain. The oak forest on the dry, rocky top of the knob gives way to hemlocks as you descend into the moister col. The trail soon climbs again toward the top of Candlewood Mountain. Turn left onto a side trail at a sign for Kelly Slide. This path seems to descend alarmingly to the bottom of the mountain as you drop steeply to the ledge known as Kelly Slide. After the trail finally bottoms out, you ascend on slabs to an opening in the forest above a precipitous ledge. The view from here is of the Housatonic River and the highlands south of the Housatonic Range. Your route crosses the ledge above the drop-off; this route is not recommended in wet or icy weather. You can always turn around if you're not sure. After crossing the ledge, climb over several step ledges, which can be difficult to negotiate. Then climb steeply in the woods to return to the Housatonic Range Trail.

Turn left and ascend to the top of Candlewood Mountain. Its top is quite ledgy, but the oak foliage blocks the view. Late fall might be the best time to visit. The trail to the south has been closed due to quarrying operations. Turn around and follow the Housatonic Range Trail 1½ miles back to CT 37 and your car.

19

Gay City

Distance: 5 miles

Vertical rise: 250 feet

Time: 2¾ hours

Rating: CD

Map: USGS 7.5-minute Marlborough

Gay City was founded in 1796 by a religious group led by Elijah Andrus. Andrus left town for reasons unknown and in 1800 John Gay, for whom the park is named, was appointed president of the remaining 25 families. They were known as an unsociable group; an itinerant peddlar was robbed, murdered, and thrown into a town charcoal pit, and a blacksmith's assistant was slain by his employer for failing to show up for work.

The two most prominent families were the Gays and the Sumners, whose rivalry outlasted the town. The Gays called the settlement Gay City, and the Sumners called it Sumner, although it seems the settlement was known locally as Factory Hollow. Ironically, when the Foster sisters, descendants of the Sumners, deeded the 1500-acre area to the state in the 1940s, they stipulated that it be called Gay City!

The town's decline, well under way before the Civil War, followed the usual pattern of hardscrabble areas: The old died and the young left. A paper mill outlasted all the houses; when it burned in 1879 the town was gone. Come hike along the now-empty dirt roads of this New England ghost town.

Gay City State Park is located off CT 85 just south of the Bolton-Hebron town line. In addition to the hiking trails, the park offers swimming and picnicking; facilities include outhouses, bathhouses, picnic tables, outdoor fireplaces, and, in summer, an open refreshment stand. There is a fee for parking inside the gates on summer weekends.

Emulating the thrifty Yankees, your hike avoids the toll by parking in a hiker's lot just north of the park entrance on CT 85. Pick up a park trail map at a bulletin board just above the parking lot. Walking in on the paved road, you pick up a few features that you might otherwise miss. Fields separated by stone walls grace both sides of the entrance road, and picnic tables are scattered throughout the area.

You will soon pass an old graveyard on your right—save it for your return.

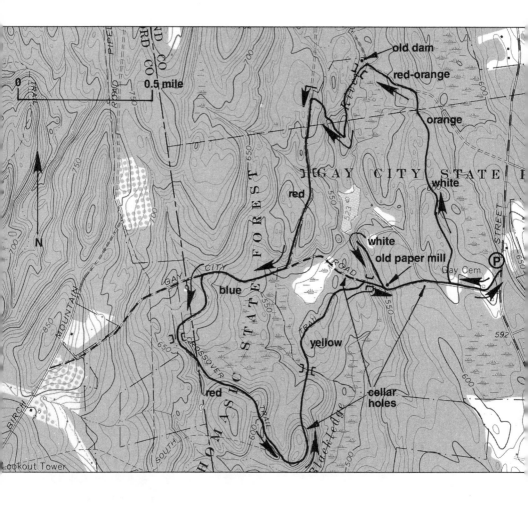

Leave the paved park road not far from the cemetery and enter the woods on an old tote road to your right, the white-blazed Pond Loop Trail.

After ¾ mile the Pond Loop Trail veers left. Stay straight on the woods road, now blazed with orange paint. Bear left at a fork and continue to a T-junction with the red-blazed Outer Loop Trail. Turn left to follow the red and orange blazes.

After about another 0.25 mile you will reach a place where the old road continues past a signpost with no signs; your route goes downhill (the old road continues out of the park) and crosses the Blackledge River on a small footbridge at the site of an old dam. Less than 100 feet beyond the bridge, you turn left, branching away from the river and proceeding uphill. From the top of the rise, take the well-used, red-blazed Outer Loop Trail that goes off to your right. Going downhill, you shortly cross a small brook and begin to climb. At the top of the rise, you reach a T-junction. Turn left here along an old woods road to continue following the red blazes. After a short distance, cross a brook on a small footbridge. Pass two white-blazed trails leading left to the pond, and then bear left, following the red blazes over a rise and then down to the blue-blazed Gay City Trail. Go to your right, uphill. This was the old Gay City Road, which was the main route to Glastonbury and the Connecticut River.

The old road climbs gradually. Alert ears may hear noises in the brush: the dash and chirp of the chipmunk, the heavy-bodied bouncing of the gray squirrel, the *drink-your-tea* call of the towhee, a common woodland bird with a black back, rufous sides, and a white belly.

Just after crossing a small brook with no bridge, turn left on the red-blazed Outer Loop Trail. Along this section in the spring, you may hear the low-pitched drumming of the male ruffed grouse. It perches on a good log to give its wings freedom to move and then beats them faster and faster until they become a blur. The resulting thumping attracts females and warns away other males. The first time you hear this sound you may think it is a distant motor running, or even wonder if you are really hearing anything at all. We like to think of this soft buffeting as the heartbeat of the New England woods.

In just under a mile, you reach the junction with the yellow-blazed South Connector Trail. Bear left and begin the final leg of your circuit. Continue following the yellow blazes to where a board-

Crossing a bridge at Gay City

walk crosses a swampy area and a brook. The trail then climbs gently to overlook a beaver pond below and to your left. The familiar stick-and-mud lodge is on the near bank of the pond.

Proceed downhill until you reach the blue-blazed Gay City Trail. Just before this junction note the old cellar hole to your left; it is one of many in the park. Turn right and cross the bridge over the Blackledge River; detour left briefly to view the remnants of the old paper mill. A bit past the old cut-stone foundation on your right is a ditch separated from the river by an artificial ridge. The small, now dry canal diverted water from the pond to power the mill downstream. The pond and the canal assured an even flow; the system dumped out the high water and accumulated water for controlled periods of operation during droughts. Just under 0.25 mile from the dam, the trail drops to your right off the canal and crosses a bridge over the mill's sluiceway. The squared blocks of the building's foundation and the square hole that diverted flow from the canal over the waterwheel to the sluiceway are very prominent. The canal was reputed to be 10 feet deep in its heyday. A bit farther on along the canal is the pond.

Retrace your steps and proceed to your left uphill, following the blue blazes, passing another old cellar hole on your right fronted by four decaying sugar maples. Pass the red-blazed Outer Loop Trail coming in to your right, and then bear right onto the paved park road.

Stop now at the graveyard to your left before returning to CT 85 and your car. It tells a poignant story of the dour little settlement. It is a small plot—a mere dumping ground for the dead. The rival Gays and Sumners are buried at opposite ends of the cemetery. The outlook and character of this vanished town may be reflected in the harsh epitaph on a 7-year-old girl's grave:

Com pritty youth behold and see
The place where you must shortly be.

20

Mount Misery

Distance: 5.25 miles

Vertical rise: 380 feet

Time: 2¾ hours

Rating: CD

Maps: USGS 7.5-minute Voluntown, Jewett City

The delightful little summit of Mount Misery belies its name. Set amid the flat pinelands of Connecticut's largest state forest, this prominent rocky mass adds a nice, short climb to an otherwise level hike. Your route to the top, where there are nice views across wooded terrain, follows the Nehantic Trail. This hike picks up the blue-blazed Nehantic Trail on CT 49 in Voluntown. From the intersection of CT 49, CT 165, and CT 138, head east on CT 165 to CT 49 north and turn left. The blue blazes of the trail run along the road. Continue 0.6 mile to the Beachdale Pond boat-launching area parking lot on the right opposite the forest access road to the west. There is a ramped wharf supplying fishing access for the handicapped here on the Pachaug River. The Nehantic Trail crosses CT 49 and goes off the Pachaug State Forest access road into the woods at the double blazes, about 100 yards beyond the parking lot.

As you enter the woods, even rows of white pines stretch away on either side. These conifers begin to thin out and are replaced by short, scrubby, head-high bushes of bear oak. These trees flourish (if that word may be used for these scraggly specimens) in dry, barren soil. Less tolerant but more vigorous trees prevent them from gaining a foothold in richer, deeper soil.

Almost immediately you reach a paved road; bear left and follow it. Very shortly the trail bears right on an old forest road softened by a carpet of pine needles. Next you walk under and then along utility lines before bearing right off this forest road into the woods. The blue-blazed trail here is well worn and not difficult to follow.

About ½ mile from the start, the Pachaug Trail enters from the right, and bearing to the left, the two trails continue as one over Mount Misery. From the trail junction, proceed downhill, bearing left; go under the utility line and continue through the open campground field to the stone-gated campground road. Cross the road and go

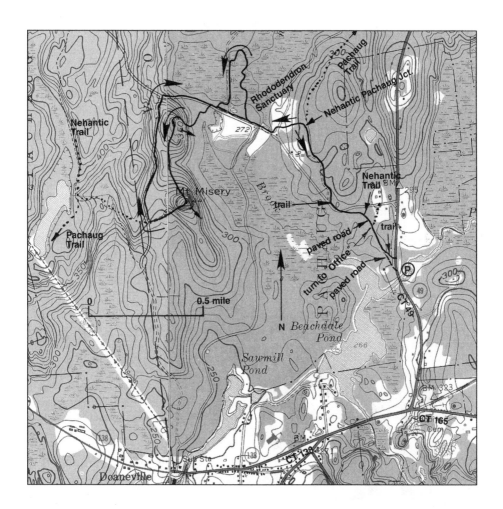

through the woods, shortly crossing Mount Misery Brook on Cut-Off Road. Follow the blue-blazed road to the Rhododendron Sanctuary, first passing a playing field that has a pump and excellent drinking water. The trail soon breaks to the right off the road and passes through a grove of young white oaks.

Presently you drop down into a cedar and rhododendron swamp; you will appreciate the dry, raised trailbed here. Along this stretch of the swamp, jungle-like rhododendrons flank the trail. This native evergreen can grow surprisingly tall—to 40 feet—and its leathery leaf can reach 8 inches in length. The combined effect of all that green is most impressive. In July these huge shrubs are dotted with white or pink bell-shaped flowers, creating a spectacular display. Here and there the straight, even boles of tall white cedars thrust through the mass. Their bark is soft and flaky; the greenish tint you see is algae growing on the tree's damp surfaces. The durability of its wood was so highly valued that cedars were once "mined" from beneath swamps and put to use.

Take care to stay on the blue-blazed trail, as other trails loop off it. Soon after the raised trail makes a sharp left and then another, your blue-blazed trail goes left into the swamp. Walk lightly; the ground is exceedingly wet and spongy. Follow the blazes carefully and in no time you emerge on a tote road (probably with wet feet). Note carefully where you reached the road, as you may return this way and this turn into the swamp is somewhat obscure. Turn left on the road and in less than ¼ mile, just before a gate and a small pond on the left, the trail bears right off the tote road.

Before you turn, stop and listen. On one mid-March hike here the sun beating down on the swamp to your right had aroused the resident wood frogs, despite the light coating of snow from a recent flurry. Their full, guttural chorus was broken only by the plaintive peep of

Pitch pine on Mount Misery

a solitary spring peeper too groggy to give the second half of his familiar call.

Soon you reach a dirt forest road, which you follow right for about 50 feet before turning left into the woods again. The level trail passes through oaks, hemlocks, and large white pines. A dead white cedar with a split down the center large enough to see through stands just to the left of the trail. What caused this hole? Did two trees once grow together? One of the pleasures of hiking is trying to figure out the reason for such strange phenomena.

Climb to the top of the ridge. A switchback makes the slope easier to surmount. Such trail design features not only make hiking uphill easier, but they also reduce the trail's susceptibility to erosion by avoiding the fall line of the slope. Turn left and soon emerge on open rock. Here, go to your right. A singularly misshapen, wind-twisted pitch pine grows on the ledge lookout. This distinctive old friend is one of our favorite trees in Connecticut, as well as a common sight on the dry, rocky ridgetops we frequent. Below are open fields popular with most of the forest's visitors.

The trail soon drops a bit and crosses a small brook before making its final assault on Mount Misery. The bolts you see in the ledges at the top used to support an abandoned fire tower. The picturesque fire towers dotting the woods of old have been replaced by the more efficient but far less romantic small spotter planes. Although Mount Misery, at 441 feet, is not very high, the summit provides a fine view of Voluntown, which lies to your far right, while Beachdale Pond is dead center.

On a calm day the open summit ledges also make a fine picnic spot. Be sure to carry out your garbage with you; even fruit scraps such as peels and cores should be carried out. The forest's animals should not be exposed to such popular throwaway items lest they become dependent on them.

Continue following the blue blazes down the backside of Mount Misery, soon joining a woods road. Bear right to proceed on the gravel road north opposite a gate; the blue blazes continue into the woods here. Follow this road to a T-junction with Cut-Off Road and turn right again, rejoining the Nehantic and Pachaug Trails where they enter the woods to your left toward the Rhododendron Sanctuary.

On this part of your return journey, as the day grows warm and your legs grow weary, you may shorten your hike and avoid the swamp by staying on Cut-Off Road. Continue past the playing field and water pump at your right. After crossing the brook, bear left onto the gravel road to the campground field. Turn right into the field and reenter the woods at the near corner across the field. At the junction of the Nehantic and Pachaug Trails, be careful to follow the Nehantic Trail to your right back to your car.

21

Wolf Den

Distance: 5 miles

Vertical rise: 600 feet

Time: 2¾ hours

Rating: CD

Map: USGS 7.5-minute Danielson

Some words roll off the tongue with melodious grace. Although Mashamoquet (mash-muk-it; "stream of good fishing") is definitely not one of those, this state park has a special beauty and grace due to its botanical and zoological diversity. Among the almost infinite attractions of this hike, you will find nestled within the park's 781 acres the legendary wolf den where Israel Putnam, of Revolutionary War fame, reputedly shot the last wolf in Connecticut.

From CT 101 just east of its junction with US 44 in Pomfret, head south on Wolf Den Drive (shown on the topographical map as Botham Road) for 0.7 mile. Turn left into the Wolf Den camping area, where there is ample parking.

The "No Pets" sign applies to the campground; pets are allowed on the trail if under control. Taking the family dog on a hike seems only natural to many owners. However, dogs do reduce your chances of seeing wildlife, can spread disease by tracking animal feces into streams and ponds, can dig up fragile vegetation, and can frighten other hikers, especially children. Pet owners can ensure hiking trails remain open to their dogs by controlling their pets, especially by burying or packing out their pets' feces and by leashing their dogs around open water and around people. It's also a good idea to carry food and water for Fido, especially on a hot day.

Start your hike by walking back up the gravel road and crossing Wolf Den Drive. The trail begins by going though an opening in a stone wall where "Mashamoquet" has been painted in yellow on a rock. The blue blazes lead you across an old field before the path turns left into a large stand of smooth alder. Here skunk cabbage spreads its large, aromatic leaves across the swampy, shaded ground. Within this thicket the hulk of a great black willow matches its vigor against the dissolution of age.

When you reach the edge of a field, turn left by a large shagbark hickory, go through a stone wall, and enter the woods. These first few hundred yards provide a wonderful illustration of the

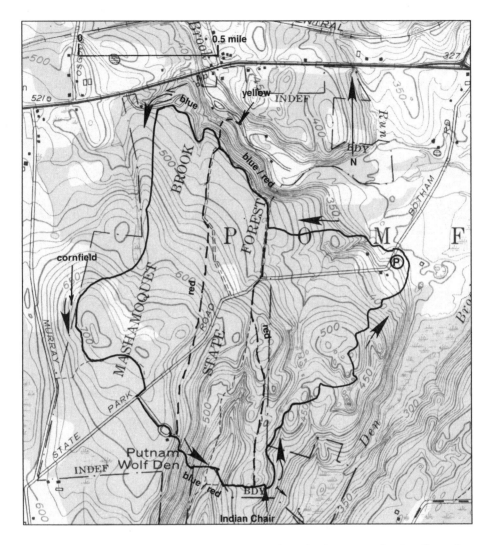

successive stages in the development of a mature forest. You first pass the open field, next the swamp-nurtured invading alder grove, and then cleared wasteland with juniper and red cedar. These trees are among the first to colonize open spaces. The forest is further advanced in the woods just entered; here large red cedars are losing the battle for sunlight to the taller, faster-growing birches. In time the birches too will be crowded out,

by the oaks that comprise the climax forest here. Then fire or lumbering will remove the oaks and succession will start all over again.

Beyond a stream, several large, plate-barked black birches guard the trail, which soon runs parallel to a stone wall. Where the stone wall turns a corner the trail joins a tote road. A red-blazed path goes left, cutting across the blue-blazed loop trail, but you bear right with the level, blue-and-red-blazed tote road through maturing oak and maple woods. Stay on the blue-and-red-blazed trail until the red blazes fork left. Follow the blue blazes—shortly a yellow-blazed trail veers right to both the campground and the picnic and swimming area.

Continue on the blue-blazed trail. Your route curves left through the woods, crosses a stream over a bridge, moves up a gentle slope through large hardwoods, and continues left along an open cornfield. It is easy to let your mind wander as your feet take you down worn old roads such as this one; we still miss marked turns off such an obvious path after thousands of miles of hiking experience.

The trail levels and then meets a gravel road. Turn right and then left almost immediately onto another gravel road, passing between a pair of well-built stone cairns. Each cairn contains a large stone with "Wolf Den Entrance" chiseled and highlighted with yellow paint.

Follow the dirt road back past thick clumps of laurel to a parking area with a few picnic tables nearby. Continue through the lot to the back of a small, circular drive and proceed downhill on a wide, eroded path. Soon the red-blazed trail comes in from the left. Directional arrows to Table Rock (left) and Wolf Den (right) are chiseled into a nearby rock. The red-and-blue-blazed trails now drop together steeply into the valley below on stone stairs. Less than halfway down you reach the fabled Wolf Den.

According to legend, it was here in 1742 that Israel Putnam slew the last wolf in Connecticut. In fact, the last wolf in the state was probably killed near Bridgeport about 1840. Putnam's wolf had preyed on local sheep for some years. Finally, after tracking it for several days from the Connecticut River some 35 miles to the west, the intrepid Putnam crawled into the den with a lantern,

saw the burning eyes of the trapped beast, backed out, grabbed his musket, crawled in again, and fired. Temporarily deafened, he backed out of the smoke-filled hole, paused, went in a third time, and hauled out the carcass.

As you peek inside, note the weathered initials on the sides of the den entrance. In the last century such graffiti were etched on rocks. Today's vandals are lazier—they use paint cans.

When you finish examining the den, continue down the slope on the red-and-blue-blazed trail. Cross the brook and climb the sloping ledges on the other side. Just over the crest of the next rounded hill, the red-blazed trail breaks off to your left. A short distance beyond, the trail bears left on the slope; here you go right a few feet to a ledge overlook and the Indian Chair. An appropriately shaped boulder, the chair commands a fine late-fall-to-early-spring view of the countryside.

Return to the trail and bear left, gently downhill, keeping the stone wall on your right. Shining clubmosses perch on some of the fern-framed boulders; wood, polypody, and Christmas ferns thrive in these shady woods.

Now climb the boulder-strewn hill ahead. The slope is softened near the top by a carpet of white pine needles. After dipping and hesitating slightly, the trail curves to your right up a rocky draw, turns right again, and descends, passing a black birch and a hemlock embraced in slow-motion mortal combat for the same piece of sunlight. To your right the sterile evergreen fronds of the maidenhair spleenwort are lodged in the cracks of a large, seamed boulder. The fertile fronds unfold in spring and die with the first frost.

The trail bends right and then zigzags down the hillside, crossing a stone wall before reaching the field that borders

The Indian Chair

the camping area where you started. Pause to admire the vegetation around the borders of the forest. Nature, with all her diversity, loves edges. Edges provide habitat for plants that can stand neither full sun nor full shade. Wild animals use the woods for cover and feed on the nearby field plants and border shrubs.

In the nearby woods is a backed-up pond where we flushed a great blue heron. This long-necked bird with a 6-foot wingspan uses its long legs to keep its plumage dry while wading in the shallow water. The sharp, pointed beak unerringly spears small fish, frogs, and other aquatic creatures that make up the heron's diet. Finally, cross the field to your waiting car.

22

Collis P. Huntington State Park

Distance: 5.5 miles

Vertical rise: 350 feet

Time: 3 hours

Rating: CD

Map: USGS 7.5-minute Botsford

Many of Connecticut's trails are easily found by the casual searcher. Collis P. Huntington State Park in Redding is off the beaten path and frequented primarily by local people. The trails within this park of over 800 acres, opened to the public in 1973, are on old woods roads that meander through this secluded area. The land was a gift from Archer M. Huntington, the stepson of the railroad magnate and philanthropist for whom the area was named. Archer was a noted poet and Spanish scholar in his own right. Two striking sculptures by the world-renowned Anna Hyatt Huntington (Archer's second wife) adorn this park. She is best known for her equestrian statues, including one of General Israel Putnam in nearby Putnam Memo-

rial State Park. It is appropriate that representatives of her wild animal tableaux decorate this park.

To get to this delightful out-of-the-way spot from the junction of CT 302 and CT 58 in Bethel, go south on CT 58 (Putnam Park Road) for 1.3 miles and bear left and then right on Sunset Hill Road. After 2.2 miles on Sunset Hill Road, turn left into Collis P. Huntington State Park. The entrance road is flanked by the wildlife sculptures by Anna Hyatt Huntington: wolves baying at the moon at left and a mother bear with cubs at right. There is a parking lot just inside the gate.

There are no trail blazes to lean on in this park, but the well-trodden paths or woods roads make it relatively easy to follow your route. Go downhill on a woods road on the right side of an open field; then the path narrows and goes down wooden stairs to your first junction. (You will return to these steps at the end of the hike.) Turn right on the well-defined trail through an open area plagued with a too-common choking alien—Oriental bittersweet. The animal and bird sounds you often hear in this area are reminiscent of the background noises of an old jungle movie! Surrounded by vines, the

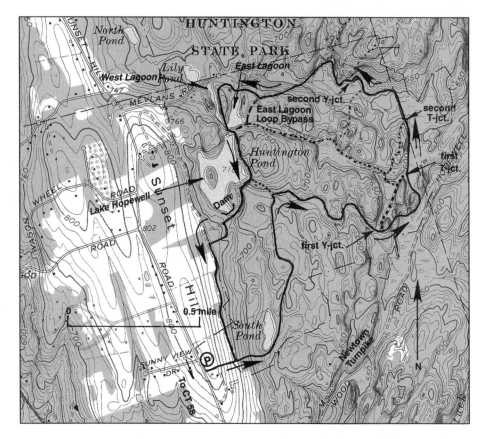

trail continues downhill, bearing left around South Pond. The left trail at the fork allows you to briefly skirt the edge of this pond before rejoining the main trail in a few yards. Shortly a trail heads to your right, out of the park. Continue straight past a low dam on your left and cross the bridge over the pond's outlet stream. Stay on the well-trodden trail as it curves left around the pond.

After passing a trail on your right, walk through a well-managed woodlot. Selective removal has been used to eliminate junk species such as black oak and wolf trees (oddly shaped trees that have grown in ungainly configurations, do not produce good timber, and shade out potentially valuable trees) and to create optimum conditions for the growth of usable trees.

Proceed past a trail at right by a huge split rock. Stay straight on a wide trail, soon passing another trail at your right. Pass several scarred beech trees. The beech's smooth, gray bark grows with the tree—it doesn't flake off with time, so marks or initials decades old still retain their shape. Daniel Boone carved his name into a beech tree when he once "cilled a bar" in Tennessee. The carving lasted for over 150 years before the tree finally toppled.

Bear right over a small rise and then cross the bridge that spans Lake Hopewell's outlet and immediately go right at the junction about 1¼ miles from the

Wolves baying at the moon

start. A stream comes in and soon parallels the trail on your right.

Shortly you reach your first Y-junction (see map) below a large rock face—go right. A short side trail here leads left to the top of the rock. Your route goes downhill and then bears left, reaching a small stream below still more rocks. Cross the stream on a bridge and soon you will cross still another stream running under a wooden plank bridge. Pass through an area of old blowdowns within a narrow stream valley. You can see Newtown Turnpike to your right through the trees in the distance.

Parallel the turnpike, climb uphill, bear left, and cross a stream on a small footbridge with a large boulder on your right. The boulder's source, a ledge, is on your left. At your first T-junction (see map), go right—there is now a swamp to your right.

Follow the trail to your left and reach the second T-junction (see map) with a generic park trail sign—go right. After crossing a stream, curve left and then right before reaching another junction with a trail leading to your left about 3 miles from the start—stay straight on the worn woods road. This route will quickly crest a rise and bear to the right. In about ¼ mile, go left on the lower woods road at your second Y-junction (see map). Your way curves right and then left uphill to a junction in another 250 yards—go left here along the base of an outcropping on your right, which the right-hand road ascends. Cross the stream. This area has a large number of tulip trees, a more southern species that is dominant in the Great Smoky Mountains National Park.

You climb, then level, passing a stone wall on your right about halfway up the hill. Continue through a rusted gate. Immediately go right on a less-used path, away from the wide old woods road. (If you wish, you may eliminate the loop around East Lagoon by staying on the main trail, which shortly crosses the lagoon's outlet on a wooden bridge and then rejoins your path at the bridge between East Lagoon and Lake Hopewell.)

Parallel a rusted fence, then bear right and uphill around East Lagoon. A parking area soon appears to your right. Turn left onto a narrow path through the laurel before descending toward the lot. Descend steeply over ledges to the shore of West Lagoon and follow the trail to the bridge over its outlet. Cross between East and West Lagoons on the footbridge. Immediately at the junction, go left over still another bridge with East Lagoon at left and Lake Hopewell at right.

At the junction just past this bridge, go to your right uphill on a gravel road that goes along and above Lake Hopewell. At the junction at the lake's end, cross the outlet stream on an earthen dam. At the end of the dam the road curves left to follow above the outlet's valley. You will shortly see a lightning-struck tulip tree. The tree was struck very high up and the ribbon of blasted bark can be traced all the way to its base. Such bark removal is caused by the instantaneous conversion of the sap to steam, which in its violent escape blasts off the bark. An extra-tall tree such as this one gets the lion's share of life-giving sunlight, but because it is the highest point around it is also a magnet for lightning bolts.

You parallel a fence, then reach a T-junction—go left. Shortly you will pass through a gateless, pole-flanked opening in the wire fence. Continue on the old road through seemingly impenetrable vine and brush thickets. In about ½ mile you reach the wooden steps (now at right) that you went down a few hours ago. Go back up the steps and follow the edge of the field uphill to your car.

23

Green Fall Pond

Distance: 5.7 miles

Time: 3 hours

Vertical rise: 540 feet

Rating: CD

Map: USGS 7.5-minute Voluntown

Far eastern Connecticut seems to have been forgotten by the 20th century. Roads change from tar to dirt, and stone walls are strikingly square and straight, evidence that they are not the trappings of gentlemen farmers but carefully maintained, functional components of working farms. Except for occasional fields and farmhouses, this untenanted, overgrown area is much as the westward-bound pioneers left it. Your hike on the Narragansett Trail to Green Fall Pond in Pachaug State Forest takes you through this secluded region.

From the junction of CT 49, CT 138, and CT 165 in Voluntown, drive south on CT 49 for 4 miles, then turn left on Sand Hill Road. In about a mile, turn right onto Wheeler Road—go 0.5 mile, where you will see the blue blazes of the Narragansett Trail. Park beyond the blazes, pulling off the road as far as possible; the traffic is minimal. In May, the flowering dogwoods punctuate the springtime greens with their white bracts. Their flowers are actually green clusters in the center of the white-colored, specialized leaves.

Enter the woods on the east side of the road (to your left as you drove down Wheeler Road from Sand Hill Road). The Blue Trail System marks trail changes with double blazes, usually offsetting the upper blaze in the direction of the turn. Follow the trail gently downward, with several seasonal streams interrupting the path and soothing the soul with their melodious chatter. This thin-soiled, rock-ribbed land is largely clothed in oak.

After 0.4 mile you'll descend a steep, rocky slope toward the valley. Parallel and then cross a stream. On your left you soon pass a 25-foot rock face graced with lichens, mosses, ferns, and even a few struggling trees. Just beyond is an even more impressive rock face, with larger trees growing from its sides. At its base lies a jumble of large rock slabs that were once part of the cliff but have split off since the glaciers bulldozed their way through here. Perhaps these slabs were forced off in years past by trees, since vanished, whose incessant

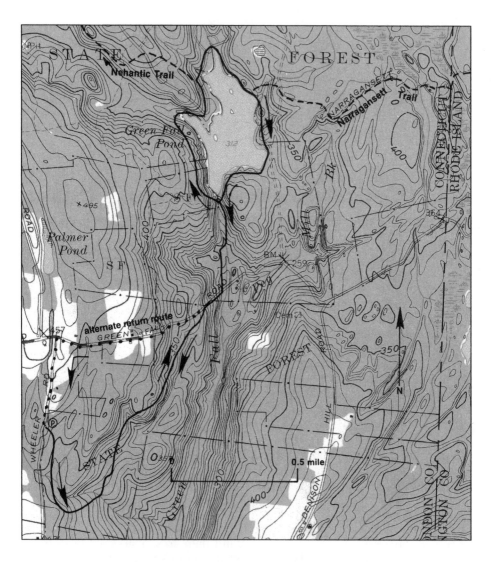

growth slowly but surely split the rock.

After crossing another stream, you soon find yourself on the edge of Green Fall River valley by a large, crumbling boulder. Look closely at this rock mass; its shade, moisture retention, and slant toward the sun create miniature ecosystems. While the stark, drier sides are gray with lichens, the shaded areas with pockets of soil hold a soft cushion of mosses. In wet times the surface of a moist, crumbly hollow is colored with light green algae. The thin soil of its horizontal surfaces supports clumps of polypody fern. Large birches buttress the sides of the boulder, which is crowned with an unexpected juniper; the rock's sunny, well-drained top provides the conditions that the juniper needs. An early settler of untended, tired fields, this prickly evergreen is ordinarily shaded out by taller successional trees.

Bear left, crossing two rocky seasonal streams. Step carefully; the smooth rocks become very slippery when their covering of mosses and lichens swells with moisture. After the second stream, proceed gradually uphill and along the valley rim to Green Fall Road, a dirt road 1.4 miles from your start. This road is an eastern extension of Sand Hill Road.

Turn right and follow the road downhill for 0.1 mile. Turn left off the road and follow the blue-blazed trail along the river, which is now on your right. The path climbs a rocky ridge before slipping down into a narrow ravine that speeds the river over boulders and ledges. About midway to the pond you cross the river at a shallow, rocky spot.

The trail clambers over boulders where root-hung hemlocks cling to a steep, eroding slope. The inward-pressing rock walls are thickly covered with mosses and lichens. Soon the trail climbs steadily up the side of the ravine to avoid a sharp drop into the river. Be careful not to trip on the exposed roots along the top.

You reach the base of Green Fall Pond Dam 1.9 miles from the start. Climb up the embankment to the right of the dam, and turn left to cross over the top of the dam on a wooden footbridge with handrails. Follow the route, now marked with blue blazes with orange spots (called orange blazes for simplicity), around the west side of Green Fall Pond. The Narragansett Trail goes around the east side of the pond—you will return that way.

Follow the orange blazes, first on a gravel road, then onto a footpath, keeping Green Fall Pond always on your

Green Fall Pond

right. This trout-stocked pond is one of Connecticut's nicest—it has lovely ledges dropping into the water, small islands, fully wooded shores, and no cottages.

The trail hugs a shore thickly grown with laurel, oak, birch, and hemlock. About 0.2 mile from the dam, the path crosses a feeder stream and continues rounding the pond. If you lose the trail here, head toward the pond—in most places the trail edges the shore. A ledge-tipped point across the bay to your right comes into view.

Soon you will reach the gravel road that services the campground; turn right. Continue following the orange blazes along the road. You'll pass the blue blazes of the Nehantic Trail to your left. Shortly after crossing the major inlet to the pond, the trail turns right at a sign for the Green Fall Trail. Many of the large outcroppings on your left bear patches of a large, thick-fleshed, curling lichen called rock tripe, which is considered nourishing in case of a dire emergency. Canadian voyageurs reputedly used it to thicken their soups.

The trail is now in sight of the pond. The orange-blazed trail ends at the blue-blazed Narragansett Trail 1.2 miles from the dam; turn right to continue along the edge of the pond. Cross a small brook on stepping-stones; at times of high water, an upstream detour will let you cross dry-shod.

The trail climbs a rocky ridge for the view of nearby rolling hills, drops down, and visits a rocky point. Enjoy these meanderings—a well-laid-out trail lets you explore all points of interest. Go right on an earth-filled auxiliary dam. The underwater face of the dam to your right is covered with rock riprap to minimize erosion.

The trail enters the woods just beyond the auxiliary dam. Follow the ridge overlooking the pond before descending diagonally down to the shore. Pass the dam to your right and descend the embankment. Retrace your steps down the ravine and back to your starting point. For variety, instead of reentering the woods on the other side of Green Fall Road, you may choose to continue along the gravel road, passing a farm, to the junction with Wheeler Road. Turn left onto Wheeler Road; your car will be ½ mile down the quiet road.

24

Northern Nipmuck

Distance: 5¼ miles

Vertical rise: 550 feet

Time: 3 hours

Rating: C

Map: USGS 7.5-minute Westford

The entire 14-mile section of the northern Nipmuck Trail, opened in 1976, offers delightful woods walking. This particular hike loops through the private Yale Forest and returns to your point of origin along two little-used gravel roads with the unusual names of Boston Hollow Road and Axe Factory Road.

The start of this hike is located in northern Connecticut, where the crisscross roads are as independent as the area's people. Follow CT 89 north for 4 miles from the junction of US 44 and CT 89 in Warrenville. Bear right at the Westford blinking traffic light. In 0.3 mile, where the tar road bends right, stay straight on gravel Boston Hollow Road. The blue-blazed trail crosses the road in another 1.3 miles. There is enough room for three cars to park on the left.

Follow the blazes north (left) into the woods. In late summer, the flat forest floor is liberally decorated with Virginia creeper, wild sarsaparilla, and fruiting blue cohosh, as well as interrupted and rattlesnake ferns. The latter is the largest and most common of the succulent grape ferns; the simple, large, triangular leaf and its early-season spore stalk are unmistakable.

Shortly the trail climbs steeply onto a hemlock- and oak-covered ridge and bears left. Boston Hollow Road, parallel to the trail, is visible below through the trees. Then, winding to the right through thickets of mountain laurel, the path gently climbs the side of a hemlock-covered hillside. Although the hiker finds mountain laurel lovely—in winter the evergreen leaves add color to the woods, and in late spring there is no more beautiful blossom—its tangled growth is the bane of the trail maintainer; it is a tough, stubborn bush whose stubs must be cut off lest they impale the stumbling hiker!

Jouncing up and down several small, rocky ridges, you will pass scattered patches of striped maple. Lovely views of the woodlands to the north, west, and south greet you as you reach the top of the ridge before bearing right (west) down-

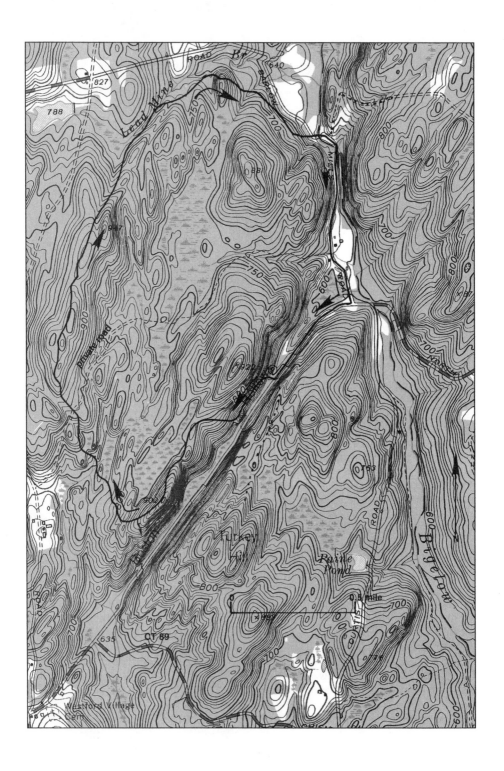

Black-eyed Susans at a field's edge

hill, away from Boston Hollow Road.

If you walk this way in mid-August, you can catch the first signs of the tipping of the year's seasonal hourglass. The lush vegetation looks slightly shopworn. Evergreen plants, previously overshadowed, sparkle with the fresh sheen of their new leaves, which will carry them through fall, winter, and into the start of yet another spring. Goldenrods and asters—fall's premier flowers—are prominent. The autumn spate of mushrooms has started: white and yellow puffballs, white *Amanita* that only the real experts dare to sort and eat (the deadliest is appropriately called the destroying angel—it tastes good going down, but with the passage of a few hours the fully absorbed nerve poison is 100 percent fatal), and the red-capped emetic *Rusala* (also poisonous, but fortunately it can't be kept in the stomach). Moss-bedded, dry, rocky rills recall spring's long-gone moisture. The ghostly Indian-pipes have become blackened skeletons, although they are just erupting through the forest litter in the mountains to your north. An admirer of a particular flower can often prolong the viewing season by moving north with the blooms.

In about 2 miles, you cross a private dirt road. After a little way the trail follows the remnants of an old tote road north, soon joining another tote road coming in from the southeast. There has been some recent logging on this ridge, but the trail remains easy to follow and well blazed. Connecticut's forests have been spared the ax (or the chain saw) compared to other New England woods, but its highly valued oaks appear to have reached a size suitable for harvesting. We hope that trails and logging can coexist; remember that a productive forest is one worth keeping and that interesting hiking trails need forests.

The trail then swings right (northwest) off this road to descend from the ridge and enter a small ravine. Finally, you ascend a hemlock-covered escarpment; below is one of Bigelow Brook's small, noisy tributaries.

In another ½ mile or so, after bearing left downhill, you emerge on gravel Axe Factory Road by a stream-threaded meadow. Although the woods vegetation has faded, late summer brings a riotous flowering in open fields and meadows. Great purple-crowned stalks of joe-pye weed, white flowering boneset (an herbal fever remedy), goldenrod, St. Johnswort, the three-leafed hog-peanut vine, and pealike clusters of groundnuts are everywhere. Blackberries invite you to snack, bumblebees engage in a final orgy of nectar gathering, and the sweet smell of pepperbush pervades the air. Here the marshy stream trickles through metal culverts; minnows and pickerel play a deadly game of hide-and-seek amid the waterweeds.

You are just under 1.25 miles from your car as you come out onto the road. Leaving the trail behind, return to your car by following Axe Factory Road to your right and then Boston Hollow Road, also to your right. Both these gravel roads are little used and a delight to walk. Cement and stone remnants of a mill wall are visible from the next bridge. Pasturing cows and a farm pond farther on compose a peaceful scene—a fitting conclusion to this relaxing hike through the countryside.

25

Chatfield Hollow

Distance: 5.5 miles

Vertical rise: 500 feet

Time: 3 hours

Rating: C

Maps: USGS 7.5-minute Clinton, Haddam

Hikers may complain about the overuse of a few select areas, yet Connecticut's trails are for the most part underutilized. As throughout the East, Connecticut's portion of the Appalachian Trail is heavily traveled, while most other trails are often practically deserted. If you feel that one of the joys of hiking is temporarily leaving behind the clamor of fellow human beings, consider Chatfield Hollow State Park. Despite several hundred carloads of people in the park on a summer weekend, on our visits we've met very few folks on this park's well-maintained trails.

Chatfield Hollow lies within that wide band of woodland separating the overdeveloped shore from the inland tier of cities. From the junction of CT 80 and CT 81 in Killingworth, drive west 1 mile

on CT 80. The park entrance is on your right. Park at the hikers' lot just to the right of the park gate.

Follow the tar road, keeping to your left to pass over the dam for Schreeder Pond. The pond, which offers fishing, swimming, and picnicking, is the focus of park activity. Turn left down the park exit road. A short detour to the right here leads to Oak Lodge, built, along with the dam, by the Civilian Conservation Corps in the 1930s. A marker honors CCC Camp Roosevelt, Company No. 171. Backtrack to follow the park exit road south. Beyond the maintenance buildings (the winter home of the Old Mill Pond waterwheel), turn right into the woods opposite a small grove of white pine trees on the orange-blazed Deep Woods Trail.

Climb up a rocky slope, atop which are open rock ledges decorated with mountain laurel. Whenever we mention mountain laurel to people, they often exclaim that they will have to go there in June to catch the display of gorgeous flowers. However, any one twig of mountain laurel blooms at best every other year, so you could conceivably have half the flowers in bloom each year. Most areas have a great year followed by a so-so year, when most twigs are busily putting

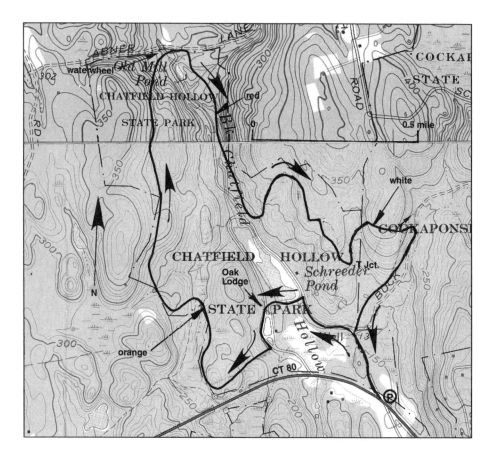

their energy into new growth instead of flowers. Once an area's pattern is known to you, you can usually depend upon hitting the great flowering every other year; mid- to late June is the best time.

One-half mile from the start, you'll curve left off the ledges, then pass beneath them. The ledges' rock faces are stained with mosses and lichens, and trees sprout from great cracks. You can use lichens as an indicator of air quality; an abundance of lichens signifies clean air, whereas pollution inhibits their growth and can even kill them.

Near a small brook crossing, a park naturalist once attached signs to many trees—among them yellow birch, black birch, chestnut oak, white oak, American beech, sugar maple, pignut hickory, and tulip tree. Most of the signs are in this area, but we saw a few signs scattered throughout the park.

Not very far from here Gerry once caught and released a hognose snake. This snake is so safe to handle that it makes the common garter snake look dangerous. When accosted, this slow-moving species will stop, flatten its head and throat, hiss, and otherwise threaten you. Unfortunately, this fearsome display has gotten the hognose snake killed on occasion.

If this ploy doesn't work, then it will writhe, turn over and play dead, and loll its tongue. To all appearances it is dead, but if you turn it onto its stomach, it will promptly roll over onto its back—a "dead" snake must be belly up! It will only play dead for a while before it will once again try to flee. The most annoying thing about these snakes, which we've never known to bite, is the foul-smelling fluid they leave on your skin when handled—it can take some time before this smell wears off or washes away. All things considered, snakes should be observed, but not picked up—it's safer for both the human and the snake.

After passing a blue-blazed trail twice, the orange-blazed trail ends at a tar park road well beyond Schreeder Pond. Proceed to your left along the road, across the bridge, and around the east side of dammed Old Mill Pond to pick up the red-blazed Ridge Trail. Initially this foot-path parallels the stream and passes abreast a waterwheel (an undershot wheel, wherein the water strikes the middle of the wheel and its falling weight turns the wheel). Bear left uphill just before reaching a covered bridge.

Follow the Ridge Trail generally uphill, passing beside and over several ledges. Finally turn left steadily uphill. After a few yards the trail curves back on itself. The park's trail system does a marvelous job of twisting and winding through and along the most interesting areas. You'll level off a bit, climb steeply again, and emerge on top of a ledge after passing around the left end of a large, almost perpendicular rock wall.

At a T-junction turn left, leaving the red blazes. Follow this trail to the white-blazed Look Out Trail. Bear left (north) on this trail. If you go right, you'll soon hit Buck Road and then the paved en-

Waterwheel at Chatfield Hollow

trance road, having completed about 4.5 miles.

In another ¼ mile along the Look Out Trail you'll reach an open ledge with a cameo view down the valley. Eventually you come out onto a ledge with a nice view south that encompasses Foster Ponds south of CT 80. Then curve around to your right and zigzag steeply down the slope. At a junction with the blue-blazed East Woods Trail, bear right to remain on the white-blazed Look Out Trail.

Several times, on your left, you will glimpse a gravel road (Buck Road) below you as you tend downhill. Descend through pines and sugar maples to the paved park road, and turn left. Follow that road to CT 80 and your car.

26

Great Hill

Distance: 5.5 miles

Vertical rise: 800 feet

Time: 3 hours

Rating: C

Map: USGS 7.5-minute Middle Haddam

This hike begins on the Shenipsit Trail near a long-abandoned cobalt mine in the obscure town of Cobalt. From there you climb a rocky ridge to Great Hill, which rewards you with a panoramic view over the Connecticut River. A short hike along the ridge brings you to a beautiful secluded cascade at the foot of Bald Hill.

From the junction of CT 66 and CT 151 in Cobalt, drive north on Depot Hill Road. At the first fork, keep right up a steep hill. After almost 0.8 mile, turn right onto Gadpouch Road, the first right after Stage Coach Run. The blue-blazed trail starts on the left in 0.5 mile, soon after the road becomes dirt. Park on the right nearly opposite the trailhead.

Before you start the hike, walk over to the large hemlock grove near your car. The entrance to the cobalt mine (sealed up at the time we visited) was down the hill in the shaded ravine. Deep pits on top of the hill, farther up the road to the right, tell of the cave-in of the mine roof. Originally opened by Connecticut Governor John Winthrop (son of colonial Massachusetts's John Winthrop) in 1661, the mine was active until the mid-1800s. The cobalt extracted was shipped as far away as England and China for use in the manufacture of a deep blue paint and porcelain glaze.

Return to the trailhead across the road and follow the blazes through ash-dominated hardwoods. These trees range from mature specimens 2 feet in diameter to fast-growing, strong, light-weight sprouts the size of baseball bats—in fact, ash sprouts are used to make all wooden baseball bats! This section of the trail, always wet and muddy, is at its worst during the spring thaw.

The trail starts climbing gradually. Look to your left for the round-leafed shoots of the wild onion. The leaves and bulb can provide a sharp-tasting treat. In spring, the skunk cabbage raises its hooded head above the soggy ground. Soon the trail climbs steeply before leveling off briefly. When you resume climb-

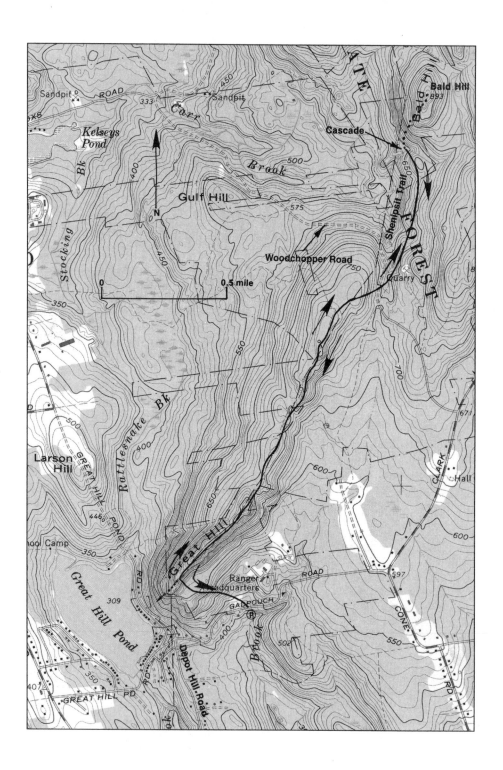

ing, look to your right for a patch of a creeping evergreen: partridgeberry. The tiny, heart-shaped leaves set off any of the bright red berries that may have been overlooked by ruffed grouse and white-footed wood mice. Oddly enough, this relative of the dainty bluet thrives in Mexico and Japan, as well as in most of eastern North America.

The trail zigzags steeply up the rocky side of Great Hill. At the crest, take the white-blazed trail left a short distance to a rocky lookout treed with oak and pitch pine. Follow the Connecticut River with your eyes. Directly below you is cottage-rimmed Great Hill Pond. In the middle distance are the smokestacks of the Middletown power plant. To your left, next to a girder-framed dock, the Pratt and Whitney Middletown jet engine facility sprawls over the countryside. At the dock, barges and small tankers off-load their cargoes of jet fuel. Continuing southward, the river's wanderings become lost to your eye amid the horizon's low rolling hills. The Mattabesett Trail follows the western horizon ridge. Northwest of the power plant, the bare slopes of the Powder Ridge Ski Area punctuate the hillside. The old colonial seaport of Middletown lies on the west side of the river.

Retrace your steps to the blue blazes. The trail continues north-northeast along the straight, narrow ridge for almost 2 miles before descending.

About a mile into the hike you'll see several deep holes in a live black oak just to the right of the trail. The pileated woodpecker cut these in its eternal quest for black carpenter ants. If you look closely, you will see the remains of the ant galleries at the bottom of some of the holes. By sound and/or smell the birds

Small cave in Great Hill

detect the insects in the rotten heartwood through several inches of living wood and use their great chisel beaks to reach them.

About 1½ miles into the hike, look for an attractive rock jumble on your right. Several of the larger, flatter rocks have masses of the evergreen polypody fern on them. The deep green leaves of this shade-loving fern arise from creeping rootstocks. It grows on rocks, cliff edges, and even downed trees where acidic humus has accumulated. In midsummer the undersides of the upper leaflets are decorated with double rows of red-brown spore bodies—the next generation.

The trail descends the ridge gradually and joins a tote road 1¾ miles from the start. Used mostly before World War I, tote roads were cut to "tote" logs from the woods. The soil became so compacted from this use that many of these old lanes are still virtually free of vegetation.

After another 0.2 mile of branching onto several tote roads, the trail crosses a gravel forest road (Woodchopper Road). As you cross to the west-facing slope along this gravel road, notice the scattered, straight, tall tulip trees that were absent from the east-facing slope. Here, near the northern limit of the tulip trees, minor differences of soil or exposure can create distinct demarcation lines. The large, tuliplike orange and green flowers and distinctive, four-pointed leaves with notched tips are unmistakable in summer. The numerous flower husks clinging to the upper branches make for certain winter identification.

Continue on the blue-blazed trail and you'll soon pass the remains of a small quarry and join a relatively recent lumbering road. Continue to follow the blue blazes along this road for about ¼ mile. Leave the road and follow the trail to your left downhill, soon crossing a small brook. After crossing a second, larger brook, you'll reach a cascade, which is at its best during the early-spring runoff. However, crossing the brook can also be problematic during runoff.

This is a favorite place. In spring, the sheet of water flowing evenly down the steep face of the moss-covered rock ledge creates a soothing sound. Bubbles formed in the turbulence glide merrily across the pool at the base of the cascade, accumulating in windrows of pollution-free foam. This is a fine place for a quiet picnic, a good book, or simply a restful interlude.

When you are ready, retrace your steps, taking care to follow the blazes through the maze of tote roads back to Woodchopper Road. Pause for a final view from the Great Hill lookout before returning to your car.

27

Northwest Park

Distance: 6 miles	
Vertical rise: 200 feet	
Time: 3¼ hours	
Rating: CD	
Map: USGS 7.5-minute Windsor Locks	

A major feature of the Connecticut River Valley is fading fast. Our world-famous crop of shade-grown tobacco, once the most valuable agricultural crop in the country, is about gone. In the late 1930s, Windsor alone had 3000 acres of shade-grown tobacco. Over 1600 square miles of tobacco, under its head-high cover of shade-cloth, were found in the Connecticut River Valley and dominated the landscape long after World War II. Cheaper tobacco from other countries, a reduction in the number of smokers, and the astronomical increase in the value of the land for housing have all contributed to the near extinction of our shade-grown tobacco.

Most of the state's thousands of imposing tobacco barns, where the crop was dried for use as top-quality cigar wrappers, were torn down for their weathered lumber, which, ironically, was extensively used in the same houses that contributed to the decline of this valuable crop. One of the special features of this hike is the still-looming presence of tobacco barns. A generation ago these barns were everywhere. Now they are about gone, but here you'll pass several of these reminders of bygone days on this 465-acre property now owned by the town of Windsor.

This park includes 8.2 miles of trail, and the hike we have chosen is about 6 miles long. Pick up a trail map on your visit to the park and invent your own loops to create shorter or longer hikes if you wish. To get to Northwest Park, take exit 38 from I-91 (about 7 miles north of Hartford). Go north on CT 75 (Poquonock Avenue) for 1.6 miles, then turn left onto Prospect Hill Road. After 1.2 miles, go right on Lang Road. Continue 0.4 mile to the parking lot at the entrance to Northwest Park.

Walk past the small pond to the interpretive nature center (call for hours; 860-285-1886). You may want to wait until after your hike to visit the center, but do go in before you leave. Trail maps are available near the door to the center. Go down the dirt road to the left of the nature center (playground at left) past the old tobacco barns. Follow the signs straight ahead to the Bog, Hemlock, and

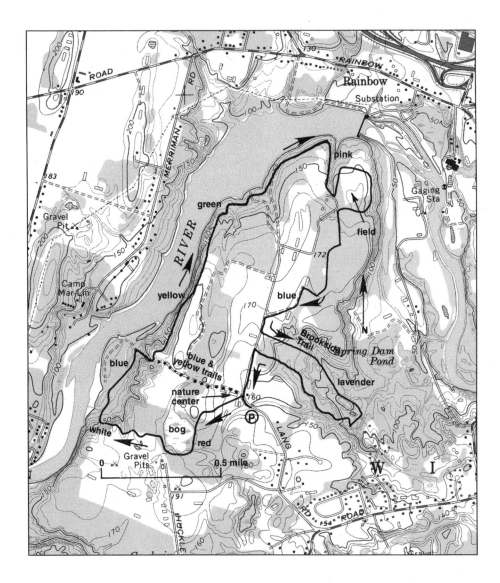

Pond Trails—there is a picnic area on your right. Shortly the Pond (and Wetland Forest) Trail goes straight, but you go left toward the Bog Trail on a red-blazed old road. At another junction, stay straight to follow the red blazes.

The Bog Trail is a 0.6-mile Braille trail, dedicated to the memory of Merlin W. Sargent in appreciation of his many years of service to the American Youth Hostels Yankee Council. The guide rope will conduct you around the bog and return you to the starting point. Once we had scouted this hike on a day that was warm and humid (ideal mosquito weather), we decided to continue straight ahead to the Hemlock Trail. Our decision was reinforced when a solitary hiker came by, telling us, "I just tripped over a mosquito in the bog!" However, in cooler weather, this is a delightful trail. A few interpretive signs provide some good forest and bog information.

Pass through a chain-link fence associated with the landfill to your left, and about halfway around the bog, bear left on the white-blazed Hemlock Trail. The trail is delightfully soft underfoot, thanks to the ground covering of needles, courtesy of the hemlocks. Switchback downhill toward the Farmington River. Notice the mole tunnels crossing the trail along the way. Stay on the white-blazed trail and go through another chain-link fence before reaching the Pond Trail junction.

At the junction, go straight ahead on the blue-blazed Pond Trail and soon loop to your right uphill and then down again. Stop and rest a moment at the large sitting log on your left, then cross an old log bridge, which may be slippery. Look out at the pond ahead, then bear right on another wooden bridge before bearing right uphill, following a gravel road.

At the top of the hill, go left on the yellow-blazed Wetland Forest Trail. If you go straight, the blue- and yellow-blazed trails run together until you reach a dirt road that leads back to the nature center in less than ½ mile. Continue downhill on the yellow-blazed trail, soon crossing an old road as the trail levels out. Soon after passing a large boulder on your right, you catch glimpses of the Farmington River below at left. You soon parallel the edge of a field to your right.

When you reach the next junction, leave the Wetland Forest Trail and continue straight on the green-blazed Connector Trail A. To your left there are intermittent views of the river as you drop down to the river bank. Soon the trail goes right and you cross a wooden footbridge before meeting the pink-blazed Rainbow Reservoir Trail. Continue straight, following the pink blazes. Pass a bench with a good view over the reservoir and bear right away from the river. Parallel the shoreline for a way before reaching a feeder stream. Here you'll turn right and follow it upstream to cross. On a recent March visit we observed a small flock of turkeys in this hollow. Near the U-turn in the trail, pass the green-blazed Connector Trail B to your right.

Stay on the Rainbow Reservoir Trail and head back toward the reservoir. After passing through a wet section of trail, you'll enter a field and bear right away from the reservoir again. Follow the road clockwise around the edge of the field. The route is sporadically blazed with posts, but the tobacco road is easy enough to follow. After traveling south along the eastern edge of the field, turn right to follow its southern edge.

You'll leave the field as the road enters the woods, passing the remains of an old gate. Soon you'll turn left at a woods road junction to follow the blue blazes of the Open Forest Trail. Turn right off the road and follow a path through the woods just west of a housing development that was visible through March's leafless forest.

Reenter the clearing that once boasted tobacco fields. Turn left on another farm road, passing the barns that were once full of curing tobacco leaves. Bear right onto a gravel road that leads back to the nature center. Within sight of the center, turn left to follow the lavender-blazed Brookside Trail. This path takes you down and back through a hollow filled with impressive trees: hemlock, white pine, American beech, and red oak. It is well worth the 1.1-mile walk. Upon returning to the gravel road, turn left back to the center and your car.

28

Lions Head

Distance: 5.4 miles

Vertical rise: 1000 feet

Time: 3¼ hours

Rating: B

Maps: USGS 7.5-minute Bash Bish Falls (MA-CT-NY), Sharon (CT-NY)

The federal land protection of the Appalachian National Scenic Trail (AT), begun in 1978, has greatly changed this hike in northwestern Connecticut's Taconic Mountains, in many ways for the better. Miles of Connecticut's AT once followed paved roads, and now many of those road walks have been eliminated. The old trail up Lions Head had been conspicuous for traversing an active open pasture, populated with cows and views of the surrounding countryside. Regrettably, economic forces shifted the area's land use away from farming to development, and the trail had to be rerouted away from the open fields. The new trail corridor passes below the abandoned pasture to follow a well-designed sidehill route.

To reach the start of this hike, follow CT 41 0.7 mile north from its junction with US 44 in Salisbury. There is a small parking lot nestled under pine trees just off the highway to your left. The lot contains a large bulletin board that carries the latest trail information, as well as Connecticut AT brochures providing handy parking, camping, and hiking information.

Follow the white-blazed Appalachian Trail uphill past the bulletin board. Utilizing switchbacks and old woods roads, you soon pass a campsite to your left. After a brief level stretch of trail, resume a gentle climb through a forest of beech, striped maple, chestnut sprouts, mountain laurel, and birch.

Staying just below the abandoned pasture to the west, follow an old barbed-wire fence and drop down a small ledge, which will require care. After passing a small (8-foot) glacial erratic boulder, continue traversing a sidehill route and drop into a dry wash, climbing on rock stairs on its opposite side. Soon the hardwood forest along the trail darkens as hemlock trees begin to dominate first the understory, then the whole forest. Hemlocks require shade to start as seedlings, and when given the chance by natural disturbance or die-off of pioneer species like aspen or birch, will shade

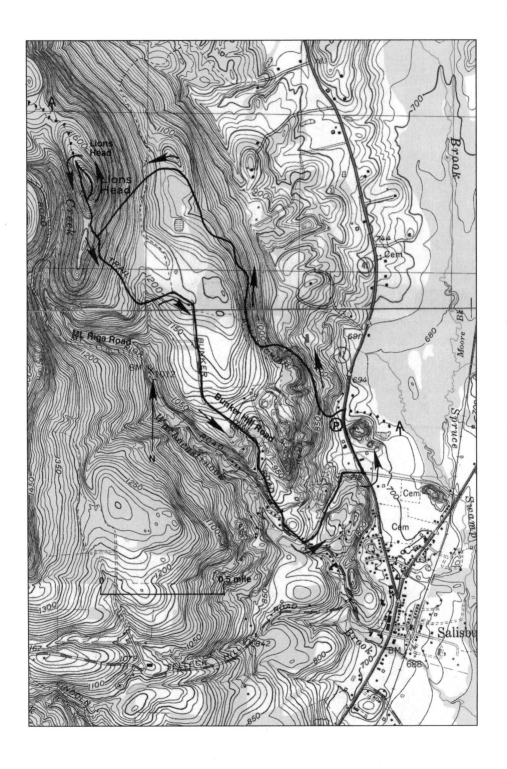

David Hardy on Lions Head (Bear Mountain in background)

out other trees to produce a dense, dark, climax forest.

Cross a stone wall, mute evidence of still older, long-forgotten pastures on the slopes of Lions Head. At 2.2 miles, cross two old charcoal roads. These roads delivered local timber and charcoal to Salisbury's renowned blast furnaces, producers of high-quality iron for nearly two centuries. Climb steeply to a T-junction with a well-worn trail. Turn right to continue following the white-blazed AT.

Ascend the rough and rocky trail to a small clearing, where the blue-blazed bypass trail goes to your left. From here, scramble up the final summit ledges to reach the crest of Lions Head at 2.7 miles. To your right, a short descent leads to an outcrop with fine views east and south toward Twin Lakes, Canaan Mountain, and the old farm below.

Continuing north on the AT, you reach the northern view just beyond the second junction with the bypass trail. From here you have a commanding view of the Riga Plateau, particularly Bear Mountain (see Hike 38) and Massachusetts's Mounts Race and Everett.

From here it is 3.2 miles farther north to Bear Mountain. However, your hike will turn around and head south, first following the blue-blazed bypass trail around the west side of Lions Head to the clearing below the summit ledges. Turn right and follow the AT to the T-junction where the AT turns left. Stay straight and follow the blue-blazed Lions Head Trail, formerly the AT.

Descend through an open hardwood forest of white ash, black cherry, shagbark hickory, and sugar maple. Near the base of the hill the trail becomes a more pronounced woods road and follows the edge of a field shielded with large white ash trees to your right. These trees are a special fall treat, with leaves turning a purplish red to contrast with the yellows, reds, and oranges of New England's birches and maples.

The trail ends at the gravel Bunker Hill Road at 3.5 miles. Just to your left is a fine view of Lions Head's ledges from the corner of a field. Turn right and walk along a field to your left that is slowly being reclaimed by nature. The road soon turns to pavement, and gradually descends to Salisbury past abandoned fields, although one pasture to your left still supports cattle. After passing Mount Riga Road to your right at 4.6 miles, turn left on Cobble Road at 5.1 miles. Descend to CT 41 and turn left again, taking care with the heavier traffic load. Soon you'll reach the AT parking lot and your car.

29

Mount Higby

Distance: 5 miles

Vertical rise: 1100 feet

Time: 3¼ hours

Rating: B

Map: USGS 7.5-minute Middletown

This is a hike that ancient vulcanism built; Mount Higby is a traprock ridge. The rough footing is counterbalanced by sweeping views of the woods and pastoral settings, or superhighways and development, depending upon where you look.

You start this hike at the junction of CT 66 and CT 147, west of Middletown. Park in the gravel lot well behind Guida's Drive-In. The access trail (blazed blue with a purple dot) starts from the west side of Guida's lot nearly opposite the side of the drive-in. It's always a good idea, when using a commercial lot, to ask permission to park. Reach the blue-blazed Mattabesett Trail after 0.35 mile and turn right. You may want to take a botany detour left to the ditch next to the paved road, where you can see some small, pinelike plants. These are horsetails, diminutive descendants of ancient

forests. Eons ago they dominated the land, along with clubmosses and ferns, towering over 100 feet high. The silica content of their cells not only betrays their origin at a time when carbon compounds in the soil were far less common than they are now, but also suggests their colonial use and name—scouring rush.

Heading back toward Mount Higby, the trail threads through hemlocks and chestnut oaks parallel to a tote road off to your right, but you soon cross the tote road and begin to climb the cobbly traprock slopes. After several switchbacks, you finally come out of the stony woods at the open rock Pinnacle, a great viewpoint about a mile from your start. Across CT 66 to the south is Mount Beseck, with Black Pond at its base. Continuing, you hike close to the cliffs, with excellent views to the west in a panorama that unfolds as you advance. West Peak and Castle Crag (see Hike 37) are visible in the middle distance; on your right is a traprock quarry. The fields below provide excellent examples of the stages of forest succession: In one field, immature evergreen cedars are just rearing up above the field's pioneer weeds; in another, mature cedars completely obscure the former pastures; and in still others, the succeeding hardwoods are

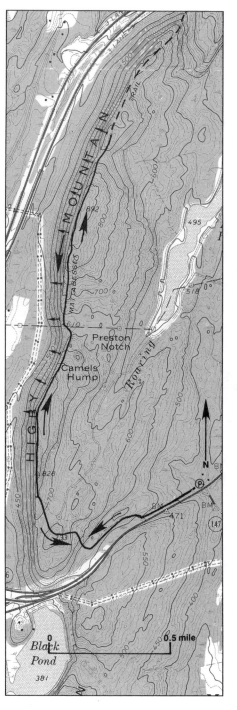

shading out the cedars. Forest succession silently continues.

At your feet along the ridge are large mats of a creeping evergreen shrub: bearberry. The white or pink bell-shaped flowers and tasteless, seedy berries are borne in terminal clusters. Native Americans smoked the foliage in a mixture with tobacco called by the Algonquin word *kinnikinnik* (reputed to be the longest single-word palindrome in the English language).

At 1.7 miles the trail drops down into Preston Notch. After crossing a brook and passing a tote road descending to your left, climb alongside a cliff with additional superb views. Near the top of the ascent look for a natural bridge formation with "NB" painted on it. Soon you'll reach the summit of Mount Higby. Scanning the horizon on a clear day, you will see to your left Long Island Sound and the New Haven skyline. To their left is the long traprock ridge traversed by the vandal-plagued Regicides Trail and the lumpy mass of the Sleeping Giant (see Hike 49). In front of you is an I-91 interchange; the large building on the right is the University of Connecticut Medical Center in Farmington.

This is also an excellent spot from which to review visually the northern Mattabesett and southern Metacomet Trails. Ahead, at the end of the ridge you are hiking, the Mattabesett follows Country Club Road (tar) over I-91, enters the woods, and climbs Chauncey Peak just beyond the traprock quarry. It continues back along that ridge over Mount Lamentation (partially hidden from view), ending on the Berlin Turnpike (CT 15/US 5).

The Metacomet picks up where the Mattabesett ends, heading west from the Berlin Turnpike over Castle Crag and West Peak. It then proceeds north over Talcott Mountain (see Hike 44) past the

Looking north along the cliffs of Mount Higby

Heublein Tower, and eventually reaches its terminus on the Massachusetts border at Rising Corners.

Leaving this cliff edge, the trail drops and then climbs to another viewpoint.

On a clear day you can see the Hartford skyline on your right, with Mount Tom, north of Springfield, Massachusetts, to the east. To the right of Mount Tom, the Holyoke Range stretches like a roller coaster. The gap between the two is threaded by the Connecticut River. The Massachusetts extension of the Metacomet Trail, the Metacomet-Monadnock Trail, traverses these two ridges. At this point, take the time to review what you have seen and implant it firmly in your mind; with time these mountains and ridges will become old friends.

30

White Memorial Foundation

Distance: 6.7 miles

Vertical rise: 100 feet

Time: 3½ hours

Rating: D

Map: USGS 7.5-minute Litchfield

The 4000-acre White Memorial Foundation wildlife sanctuary in Litchfield was established in the true spirit of multiple use. Within its boundaries lie more than 35 miles of crisscrossing trails, two family campgrounds, a marina, and the Nature Museum. To balance the more unusual sanctuary uses, over 200 acres have been set aside in four untouched natural preserves. These areas provide bases against which environmental changes on adjacent tracts can be judged. The hike described here explores only a small part of this special sanctuary.

Follow US 202 west 2.2 miles past its junction with CT 118 in Litchfield and turn left by the signs for White Memorial Foundation. The gravel entrance road leads 0.5 mile to a parking area just beyond the carriage house to your

right, which is used for staff housing.

The hike begins by following the gravel road east from the parking area past the Nature Museum. While there is a small fee, a rewarding half hour can be spent looking over the museum's attractive wildlife, geology, and Native American artifact exhibits. Especially interesting are old photos of the once open expanses of grassy fields, now completely forested.

A bookstore specializing in natural history sells pamphlets and maps relevant to the area. Since the numerous trails through the foundation's land twist, turn, and cross each other with bewildering abandon, a map is a good investment. We have seen even expert hikers have trouble following a particular route. However, if you visit this area several times and familiarize yourself with its lovely intricacies, it becomes relatively easy, and very rewarding, to follow the route we have outlined here.

Continue past the museum on the road. Large sugar maple and white ash grace the road to your left. Turn left onto a gravel road when your route straight ahead reaches a gated entrance blocked by a boulder and flanked by two large cement-and-stone posts. Follow this road north to the edge of the Bantam River and turn left into the woods.

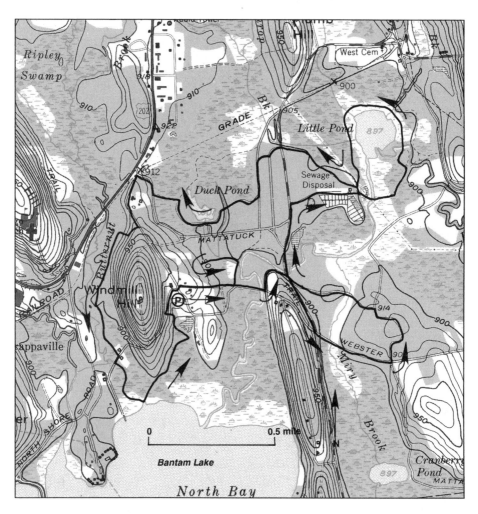

Follow this nature trail until you enter a stand of old-growth pines—trees more than 200 years old—at a junction with a closed trail. These majestic giants tower 100 feet above the forest floor and are well worth the visit. Return to the gated entrance by retracing your steps to the gravel road and turning right along the river to the paved junction.

Turn left through the gate on another gravel woods road. This route is marked with the blue blazes of the Mattatuck Trail, one of Connecticut's Blue Trails; 6.2 miles of this nearly 35-mile-long trail

are within the White Memorial Foundation. Soon the road crosses the slow-moving Bantam River on a substantial bridge. You may see a passing canoeist or two here. At the end of the bridge, go left, following the blue blazes along the woods road. Through the trees, you can see the Bantam River on your left. Hawking dragonflies skim over the water picking up and eating small flying insects such as mosquitoes—never hurt a dragonfly!

At your right there is a meadow where a few horses are often seen grazing happily. You may see late-summer flowers like joe-pye weed, boneset, various asters, hawkweed, and purple loosestrife, and hear the strident songs of grasshoppers and crickets. The volume from these singers will build up until the first frost: Light frost will slow them, a heavy frost will stop them. The round-leafed cornea species of dogwood with light blue berries is common here.

Shortly, you reach paved Whites Woods Road and turn right to follow it south to Webster Road. Turn left on the gravel Webster Road and follow it to the Mattatuck Trail crossing. Turn left on the blue-blazed woods road and enter the pine and hemlock grove that is Catlin Woods. Here, 200-year-old hemlocks and pines stand on land that was never cultivated, as indicated by the ancient pillows and cradles, or mounds and depressions, formed by the uprooting and decomposition of trees. Follow the trail left at a fork and leave the woods to cross a brook and pass through the marshy clearing. Near the road, pass through a stand of great bull pines. (These are white pines that gained their early growth in the open, with little or no competition for the sunlight; the numerous large branches create the wood known as knotty pine.) Reach the paved Whites Woods Road and bear right to follow it north past Bissell Road.

Turn right to follow the black-on-white-blazed Little Pond Trail along a tote road. Hike along the edge of a clearing to the swampy edge of the pond and bear right onto the loop trail, which soon passes through phragmites and crosses the arched Frances Howe Sutton Bridge. Follow the boardwalk around the pond. A late-August trip featured the bright red berries of honeysuckles along the way, as well as an occasional tasty blackberry.

A boardwalk gives you a fascinating look at one of nature's most interesting but least accessible areas—too wet to walk, too dry to canoe! Jumping frogs, innumerable buttonbushes, purple loosestrife, royal fern, meadowsweet, lily pads, pickerelweed—in terms of annual vegetation per acre, a swamp is one of the most productive areas of all.

After passing around the pond, the trail follows a woods road and reaches a junction with the red-triangle-blazed Pine Island Trail. Turn sharply right to follow it through hemlock woods to Whites Woods Road. Cross the road and continue on a woods road, staying to the right at the first junction, then turning left down another woods road at the next junction. Where the red triangles bear to your right off the road, continue straight to where the blue-blazed Mattatuck Trail bears right. Follow the Mattatuck Trail west, and follow the blazes to Duck Pond. Continue on the blue-blazed trail around the pond to Bissell Road, which you take nearly to US 202. Bear left down the foundation entrance road to the Pine Grove 1 camping area, and turn right on the green-blazed Windmill Hill Trail.

Descend on an old woods road past the campsites and walk around the thickly wooded base of Windmill Hill. The trail reaches a tote road T-junction with the yellow-blazed Lake Trail; turn right and then left to follow the Lake Trail down to the observation deck on the shore of Bantam Lake. White Memorial Foundation owns nearly 60 percent of the property bordering the lake, including nearly all of the visible shoreline.

Return north on the Lake Trail and bear right onto the Windmill Hill Trail past several large oaks. Bear left onto the orange-blazed Ongley Pond Trail, which skirts the western shore of the algae-choked pond, before returning to the Lake Trail near a stone wall. Follow the trail's yellow blazes back to the carriage house and your car.

Marsh in White Memorial Foundation

31

Bullet and High Ledges

Distance: 6 miles

Vertical rise: 600 feet

Time: 3½ hours

Rating: C

Maps: USGS 7.5-minute Voluntown, Ashaway

People talk of the megalopolis extending from north of Boston to south of Washington, D.C., but there is a gap in this urban sprawl. This hike is in the middle of this precious undeveloped area. Even as we write, pressure groups, in the name of economics and progress, are trying to run an interstate highway through this land. Hike here and judge the true value of this area for yourself!

The Narragansett Trail to Bullet and High Ledges leads west from CT 49, 4.8 miles south of its junction with CT 138 in Voluntown. Coming from Voluntown, pass Sand Hill Road on your left and then take a sharp right onto the second paved road. Park beyond the stop sign near a formidably spined honey locust tree.

Here, follow the Narragansett Trail along the road away from CT 49 and shortly leave the pavement on a dirt road, flanked by stone walls, to your left.

On your right stands a large sycamore with a massive poison ivy vine climbing on one side. A thick mat of fibrous aerial roots holds it in place. The "shiny leaves three" makes this vine easy to recognize in the summer, but you should become familiar with it in all seasons. The dormant winter vine is equally poisonous, especially when the sap courses up the stalks in preparation for spring growth.

Follow the woods road generally downhill and then along level ground. In 0.3 mile, turn right off the road, just before a gravel pit, and cross a stone wall. Here the forest floor is carpeted with clubmosses: first ground cedar alone (many capped with candelabrum-shaped spore stalks), then mixed with ground pine, until finally the ground pine predominates. Beyond the clubmosses, you may find rounded masses of gray-green reindeer moss. The winter mainstay of the caribou herds of the north, this "moss" is in fact a lichen.

Roll with the terrain, crossing and paralleling several stone walls before heading to your right along a seasonal stream and over another stone wall to Myron Kinney Brook—a river in microcosm. Nature's immutable laws are more

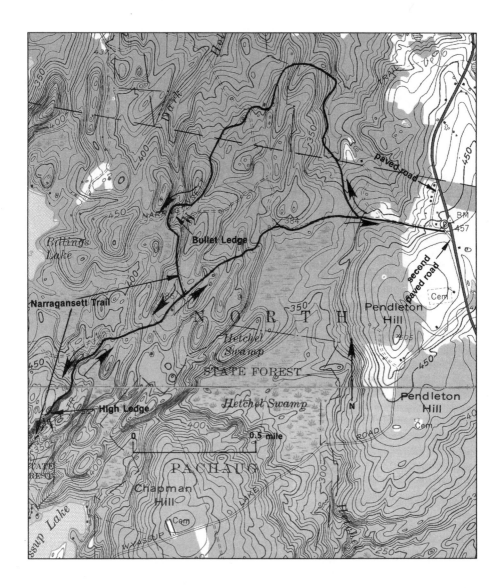

easily observed when the familiar is seen on a different scale. Spring runoff forms the seasonal headwaters of this small brook. Within a few tenths of a mile, small tributaries entering from both sides swell the brook many times. The water volume increases further from hidden springs where the stream cuts into the permanent water table.

Walk slowly along the stream with an alert eye—the forms darting across gravel riffles and through deep pools are native brook trout. Since these char need an unending supply of ice-cold water, you will see them in abundance only when you have passed the point where the brook has cut into the permanent water table.

Stone wall flanking the Narragansett Trail

While you are looking for trout, notice how the current rushes around the outer curves of the stream, undermining its banks. Sediment carved from these areas is carried downstream and deposited as sandbars on inside curves, where the current is slower.

You leave the brook in about ¼ mile and turn left uphill. The trail then dips to cross a small stream. Fleshy green ribbons cling with numerous short, hairlike roots to the sphagnum moss along the banks. This is liverwort; an evergreen closely related to the mosses, it is one of the most primitive living plants.

Across the stream, the trail hugs a stone wall going up the hillside. With posted land on the right and Pachaug State Forest land on the left, follow the blue blazes carefully through a network of interlocking stone walls and tote roads.

In an area of prominent ledges, bear left at a fork. After ¼ mile, merge with an old, eroded road. Follow the blue blazes as the undulating footpath passes through cozy-cornered stone walls and a partially cutover area with mountain laurel stems as thick as a man's arm.

At one point stay straight through a woods road junction. If you do detour right a bit on this second road, you will see at least two alien flowers—daylily and gill-over-the-ground—a sure sign that an old homestead existed here. Bear right at another woods road junction and continue generally upward with a rocky ridge to your right. Pass through a compacted dirt clearing in the woods. Just beyond this clearing, when the trail takes a steep right turn downward, continue instead straight ahead to the Bullet Ledge Lookout.

Return to the trail and descend steeply to the rocky valley floor. When you reach the tote road set between a rock ridge and a swamp, turn left. Following the blue blazes at succeeding junctions, you finally emerge on a deeply rutted old town road flanked by stone walls. To the left, this road leads back to CT 49. Generally when you find an abandoned road with stone walls on either side, it means that this was an old main town road leading from one place to another, rather than a wood-gathering tote road that goes nowhere.

Turn right on this old road, now the Narragansett Trail, for the climb to High Ledge. Fork left off the road, following the blue blazes up onto an oak- and hemlock-covered ridge. After about 0.5 mile it dips slightly into the valley before quickly rising to the edge of a steep hill. You wind through ledges before dropping into a narrow, rocky valley. Cross the stream and climb steeply, bearing left toward High Ledge.

A rocky point perched above the valley, High Ledge affords a bird's-eye view of nearby treetops. Island-dotted Wyassup Lake sparkles in the middle distance. On a clear day the faint line of Long Island Sound can be seen beyond the lake against the horizon. On the right you can pick out the fire tower on Wyassup Lake Road.

If you wish to hike an extra mile, just retrace your steps to your car. The 6-mile route described here leaves the Narragansett Trail to follow the rutted old town road, mentioned earlier, and continues directly to CT 49.

32

McLean Game Refuge

Distance: 6 miles

Vertical rise: 600 feet

Time: 3½ hours

Rating: C

Map: USGS 7.5-minute Tariffville

Tucked away in north central Connecticut, the privately endowed McLean Game Refuge was established in 1932 by George P. McLean, a former governor of Connecticut and US senator who wanted "the game refuge to be a place where trees can grow . . . and animal life can exist unmolested . . . a place where some of the things God made may be seen by those who love them as I loved them." Comprising nearly 3500 acres, the refuge is open to the public daily from 8 AM to dusk.

Today, be you hiker or cross-country skier, the refuge's excellent trail network provides access to acres of woodlands teeming with wildlife, as McLean had hoped. Although it is hard to predict what you will see on any given hike, on a mid-February day we watched a fairly common, but rarely seen, brown creep-

er moving in fits and starts up a shagbark hickory; a flock of bustling chickadees; and a chipmunk breaking its hibernation in the above-freezing temperatures. A small quick noise proved to be a ruffed grouse taking a few short steps before launching into flight with a thunderous roar.

The main entrance to this refuge is located on US 202/CT 10 in Granby, 1 mile south of its junction with CT 20. Year-round parking is available by a gate at the end of a short gravel road. Unauthorized vehicles are not permitted beyond this point. To the left of the gate is a beautiful trail map giving a sense of the trail system ahead of you.

At the right side of the entrance gate, nearly overwhelmed by faster-growing native trees, stands an old apple tree. Such trees are living mementos of the abandoned farms scattered through Connecticut's woodlands. The unnatural stretching of its upper branches bears witness to its losing battle for life-giving sunlight. Spring may bring a few delicate blossoms to this aging specimen; in the fall it yields tart, misshapen apples for the deer and the hiker.

Walk along the road a short distance to an old shelter on your left. Cross the bridge over Bissell Brook, which flows

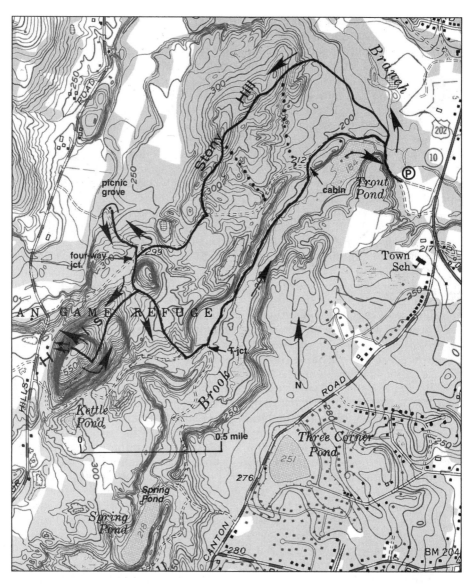

from the trout pond just beyond the shelter. The loop trails start here on the right. Follow blue, orange, and red blazes to ascend a small knoll. Look carefully down the slope to your right for two decaying butternut trees. A short-lived member of the walnut family, the butternut tree was used by the early settlers as a source of yellow, water-soluble dye. Bitternut dye was famous for coloring Confederate uniforms during the Civil War. The nuts have an excellent flavor, but their iron-hard shells beneath the sticky green covering are difficult to crack.

The trail, which has been paralleling Salmon Brook just out of sight to your right, bends away from the brook to the left. About ½ mile from the start, at the top of a small rise, the red-marked loop trail leaves to the left to return to the woods road west of the trout pond. Continue following the blue and orange blazes. However, first look back to the left of the trail and note what remains of the large, dead red pine with several narrow, 6-inch-long, vertical holes in its trunk. Only the jackhammer bill of the pileated woodpecker can make such an opening. Although this tree is now dead, newer growth around the hole indicates that the cavities were made while the pine was still living. The decayed, honeycombed interior indicates that the tree's center was infested with the fungus-eating, large, black carpenter ants that are the pileated woodpecker's favorite food.

After a level stretch, the blue-and-orange-blazed trail tends gently upward. In another ½ mile or so you will reach an overgrown clearing atop Stony Hill with the Barndoor Hills visible to the south through leafless trees. Shortly, the orange-blazed trail diverges left toward the valley below. Keep following the blue-blazed trail over a rise to a worn woods road. Here you would turn left to complete the loop. Another blue-blazed path goes straight into the woods. Turn right to follow the unblazed woods road over a rise to a woods road junction.

Turn right at this junction, following a sign to the picnic grove. Other choices, also with signs, were straight to Barndoor Hills Road and left to the summit. You'll return to this four-way junction (see map). The woods road goes downhill steadily to an open hardwood grove alongside Salmon Brook, where you'll find picnic tables, stone fireplaces, and a rustic log cabin that shelters still more picnic tables for the rainy-day tramper. This picnic area may be reached by car from Barndoor Hills Road, a left turn off CT 20, one mile west of Granby Center.

Retrace your steps to the four-way junction at the top of the rise and turn right onto the woods road following the sign to the summit. After a short ascent, pass a woods road to your left and resume climbing. As you ascend, the forest changes from the moisture-loving hemlocks to the oaks of well-drained hillsides. The woods road is more appropriately called a rock road as it hugs the steep western slope of Barndoor Hill. Near the top of the rise, turn right and follow a blue-blazed trail on a short, steep climb to the summit. This is an ideal lunch spot, with grand views to the north and west. The viewpoints along the cliff have fairly well trodden paths between them. Try not to wander off the path; the vegetation here is already stressed by the lack of moisture on this hilltop. Stepping on the plants can easily kill many years of slow growth. If you miss the trail to the summit, you'll continue on the woods road downhill to Barndoor Hills Road on your right; either retrace your steps or follow Barndoor Hills Road north (right) to the refuge entrance by the picnic grove.

When ready, retrace your steps to the woods road junction you passed just above the four-way junction. It will be your first right after descending Barndoor Hill. If you miss this unsigned junction, just follow the woods road straight through the four-way junction and return to the trout pond and the start of the loop trails. However, turning right on this woods road (it was a left on your way to the summit) is worth the effort. Pass through an impressive stand of white pines and bear left at a fork where the right turn is blazed with blue paint. Continue along the unblazed woods road to a T-junction (see map). Signs here tell you the road you were on leads back to the summit; to your right is

Canada goose on McLean's Trout Pond

Spring Pond and to your left is Route 10 Cabin. Turn left and follow this un-blazed woods road north, keeping a ridge to your left and Bissell Brook to your right.

Near the trout pond you'll reach another signed woods road junction. This time the road you were on leads back to Spring Pond; to your left is Picnic Grove and to your right is Route 10 Cabin. Bear right and soon you will pass a locked cabin to your right and then also the trout pond. Spend a few minutes at the pond's edge. This is an ideal place to identify fish swimming in the water. Tossing some small pieces of bread into the pond may attract some fish. Since fishing in the refuge is prohibited, they are quite tame. Watch for the flat ovals of the sunfish and bluegills, the former distinguished by sharper coloration and a sunburst of yellow on their breasts. The vertical-barred yellow perch, constantly cruising black bass with horizontal side stripes, and swarming shiners complete the list of the pond's bread-eating fish. Lurking in the weeds you may see a long, thin pickerel sliding in for a quick meal of one of the bread-eaters.

This fecund pond is also the annual breeding ground for Canada geese. If you look sharply to the right toward the pond's shallow end, you may notice a large brush pile—a beaver lodge. The beavers occasionally create trouble by damming up the pond's outlet. Leave the pond and follow the woods road to your right, passing the start of the loop trails you began on, and hike back to your car.

33

Westwoods

Distance: 6 miles
Vertical rise: 700 feet
Time: 3½ hours
Rating: B
Map: USGS 7.5-minute Guilford

This 1000-acre open space in Guilford, consisting of state forest, Guilford Land Conservation Trust, private tree farm, and town land, is an attractive woodland with a touch of salt. The lake at the south end is brackish, and as you hike the labyrinth of trails, gulls wheel overhead. Because it is so near to Connecticut's overdeveloped coast, Westwoods is especially prized.

From the junction of CT 77 and CT 146 in Guilford, follow CT 146 west 1.3 miles to Sam Hill Road to your right. Parking for the Westwoods trail entrance #3 is at this corner. The white-circle trail starts here.

Westwoods, like Sleeping Giant (see Hike 49), has an extensive trail system of over 40 miles. The hike described here tries to cover many points of interest. You'll follow the white-circle, yellow-circle, green-rectangle, green-circle, and orange-circle trails in a big loop. In the interest of clarity and brevity, we won't mention most of the numerous other trails you cross; directions to other routes in Westwoods are available in the *Connecticut Walk Book*. We will try to provide the numbers of trail junctions, which should match the map provided in the *Walk Book* and is also available at the Guilford Town Hall and the local bookstore. In general, however, the trails blazed with painted circles run north-south, and those with painted squares run east-west.

Mosquito repellent is a must on this hike in the summer, and we recommend this trip for early-spring and late-fall days to avoid these pests. Along the shore, because of extensive marshy breeding grounds, these bloodsuckers always seem bigger, bolder, and more numerous than elsewhere.

Follow the white-circle trail west from the parking lot along an old woods road paralleling the railroad tracks. Pass trail junction 29 (see map) and continue to follow the white circles past an old quarry bearing the drill marks where feather wedges split the rocks. You'll soon head north away from the tracks and rise into a dry, thin-soiled area cov-

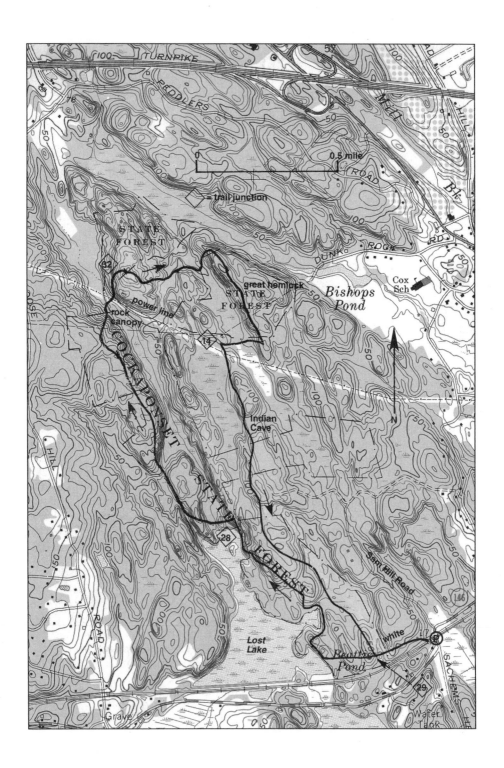

ered with laurel and hemlock. In general, the trails flirt with a multitude of rocks, ledges, and glacially rounded outcroppings; they were laid out with much thought and care. The terrain that made Westwoods a farmer's wasteland has given birth to a hiker's wonderland.

After crossing a stream, you'll climb an open ledge affording a good view south over Lost Lake. Near the top of the ledge, turn left at trail junction 28 (see map) to follow the yellow-circle trail. Descend by another quarry site passing a junction with an orange-square-blazed trail. Follow the yellow circles north over a hill, along a stream, and under a broken-up ledge before climbing through boulders and descending to a junction with the violet-circle trail. The yellow-circle trail joins it briefly as you hike uphill through an unhealthy hemlock stand (see Hike 10) to trail junction 36. Here you'll follow the yellow-circle trail straight to the top of the ledge that forms a great fallen cliff. Huge blocks from the cliff lie on the valley floor below you to your right.

Your route leads you along the top of the ledges. Often you climb in and out of nooks and crannies that keep the hike interesting. At one point you'll even use a short ladder to scale a wall of rock! After regaining the top of the ledge, follow a path down the hillside and cross a brook above a small waterfall. Climb more rock slabs whose wide expanse makes following the worn pathway difficult. Follow the yellow circles carefully through here. You'll pass over a cable leading down the cliff to your right and reenter the woods. Soon you'll see a huge slab of rock that has broken off the ledge to your right. This is the rock canopy. From this point on, you'll descend through the woods, enjoying a lowlander's view of the ledge and canopy above.

At trail junction 34, continue to your right on the yellow-circle trail along an old woods road. Cross a bridge and bear left to enter a power-line clearing. Pink lady's slippers grace the trailside and are scattered throughout the undergrowth. We have even heard that the elusive yellow lady's slipper grows in Westwoods. If you listen carefully you may pick out the *szweet-szweet-chur-chur-chur* of the cardinal. In wintertime the brilliant red of this bird against the snow is especially striking. The cardinal has become common in Connecticut only in the last few decades. Possible explanations for this northward expansion of its range include climatic change, extensive artificial winter feeding, and agricultural change.

Cross the clearing and climb yet another ledge along the long root system of a white pine. One enormous root is nearly as long as the tree is tall. You'll pass through the narrow openings in the ledges and boulders on top of this rise before reaching trail junction 32 (see map). Bear right on a green-rectangle-blazed woods road and enjoy its easy tread past junctions with the white-circle and orange-circle trails. Turn right off this woods road onto the green-circle trail and follow it over a hill to a sheltered stand of once majestic hemlock trees. The great hemlock is now dead, but its 6-foot-diameter trunk still stands, and a half dozen of the big trees are visible from the trail in a stand of smaller, unhealthy hemlocks. Before their recent demise, the hemlocks' combination of dense shade and tannin-rich needles nearly excluded understory shrubs. Now we'll watch for the beginnings of forest succession with the newly available sunlight.

Turn right on a well-worn, blue-rectangle-blazed woods road and descend the hillside. Continue on this road to trail junction 14 (see map) and the orange-circle trail. Turn left and soon cross the power line. You'll follow along a series of ledges, one of which contains an overhang called Indian Cave—one of at least a thousand so named in the state!

Cross a yellow-triangle-blazed horse trail. Stay on the orange-circle trail over and around ledges, and catch another glimpse of Lost Lake near a white-marked crossover trail. You'll join a woods road leading to trail junction 29, where you'll turn left on the white-circle trail to return to the parking lot.

34

Cathedral Pines and Mohawk Mountain

Distance: 6 miles

Vertical rise: 1200 feet

Time: 3¾ hours

Rating: BC

Map: USGS 7.5-minute Cornwall

Cathedral Pines, once the premier stand of white pines in New England, is still an impressive array of pines and hemlocks, even though a tornado knocked down much of the stand in July 1989. A recent relocation of the Mohawk Trail makes for an awe-inspiring beginning to a hike to one of western Connecticut's most familiar landmarks.

Mohawk Mountain rises 1683 feet above its surroundings, offering a 360-degree view from its summit tower. Mohawk State Forest boasts sections of the Blue Trail System's Mohawk (formerly Appalachian) and Mattatuck Trails within its boundaries. These trails, coming from divergent directions, meet near the summit and provide delightful alternatives to the summit road.

The hike begins at the base of the hillside that is home to the great pines. Take CT 4 west 0.5 mile from its junction with CT 125 in Cornwall. Turn left sharply on Bolton Hill Road and bear right immediately onto Jewell Street. After 0.5 mile, go left at the fork up Essex Hill Road 0.2 mile to a pullout on your left. A great scarred pine stands alone across the street. The blue-blazed Mohawk Trail enters the woods at the south end of the pullout by a Nature Conservancy sign. The drive to the trail prepares you for the damaged pines, as the sad condition of many nearby trees bears witness to the devastation of the 1989 storm.

Start the hike by climbing steeply up the hillside, aided by wooden stairs that keep the soil from washing away. The giant pines and hemlocks that survived the blow surround you immediately, and you'll pass over and around some that did not. Views through the trees to your left reveal the main path of the wind; few remain standing. Those trees that are still upright lost most of their tops to the windstorm.

Tornadoes are not thought of as a common New England phenomenon and occur much more frequently in the Midwest. However, we do get a few catastrophic storms (two such storms oc-

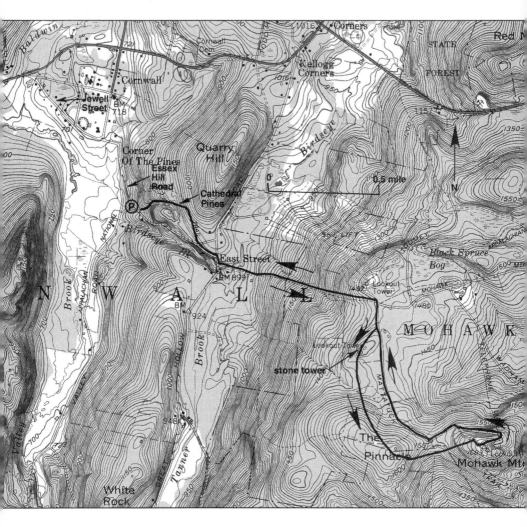

curred in different locations in New England in 1995) that, together with fire (another fairly rare occurrence), create natural clearings that nature soon fills in with a variety of early successional plant species. The 1938 hurricane spared Cathedral Pines, but knocked down comparable stands in New Hampshire's Harvard tract, now in Pisgah State Park.

The white pine is not a climax forest species, although its long life span and great height allow it to thrive above a climax forest. A pioneer species that grows quickly in fields, white pines filled untended fields when many of New England's farms and pastures were abandoned for the allure of the midwestern prairies. The white pine is now a common tree in Connecticut, and its abundance and great size make it one of the wonders of the hikes in this book.

Turn right onto an old tote road and descend gently out of the pines. Turn left on paved Essex Hill Road. Take care to hug the shoulder of the road; while this is not a busy street, drivers have little warning of pedestrians due to the many curves in the road. Bear right again, following the blue blazes, to take Great Hollow Road downhill to a driveway on your left at the base of the hill. In front of you, the effects of the storm on the west side of Mohawk Mountain are visible to the right of the ski area. On a warm July day we flushed out a group of wild turkeys in the woods on the east side of the road; such sights make a summer hike memorable when the haze reduces the bracing effects of the summit views.

Follow the driveway east toward the mountain. Bear left around a garage and through a metal gate and ascend steadily on an old tote road. The midsummer undergrowth can be thick here, owing to a lack of shade. Take care to follow the blazes, many of which are painted on rocks underfoot. Your route turns left to cross the top of the field you've been paralleling, then enters an open stand of hardwoods dominated by sugar maples. Pass to the right of a small red pine plantation and meet a well-worn path at the top of a rise. A sign identifies this as the Mattatuck Trail. You'll turn right here, toward Mohawk Mountain.

But before you do, the top of the ski area is visible to your left. A quick walk offers good views west over the terrain you've traveled. The hill below you again shows the effects of the 1989 storm; the green slopes are dotted gray with damaged trees. In early April there may be remnants of human-made snow here. Snowmaking is necessary in Connecticut to supplement our unreliable snowfall. Just north of the lift is a small stone lookout tower that predates both the ski area and, judging by its low height, the forest that surrounds it.

Return to the Mohawk/Mattatuck Trail junction and continue straight on

the blue-blazed Mattatuck, and soon you reach Toumey Road. Follow it straight (south) and soon bear right on the blazed path opposite a small picnic area. The trail curves up onto the extensive flat ledges. The ruins of a great stone tower dominate this rocky stretch. While the Civilian Conservation Corps built much of Connecticut's forest stonework in the late 1930s, this steel-braced tower with its magnificent fireplace was erected by Seymour Cunningham in 1915, before the state began to acquire land. Mohawk State Forest began with a 250-acre gift to the state from Alain C. White (who also founded White Memorial Foundation with his sister, May W. White—see Hike 30), in 1921.

You'll soon cross a field being reclaimed by the forest, enter some pine woods, and pass an abandoned well and hand pump. Pass through a swampy area where you will find several large bull pines and scattered spruce and black cherry trees.

On the far side of the swamp you cross a stone wall and follow left beside it. Pass a piped spring; a small cement cistern protects the source, and an adjacent pipe runs with cold, clear water. A friend of ours claims that a hiker should never pass a spring without drinking, even if only a sip—a symbolic thanks for the water, the trail, the day, and the good fortune to be there. But nowadays untreated water, even from a spring, may be contaminated with microscopic Giardia cysts. Even a symbolic drink may cause illness (see Introduction).

Soon you'll pass a clearing to your left where once stood an Appalachian Trail shelter. Climb up to and across a gravel tote road and continue to ascend the north side of the Pinnacle. Near the top you clamber over boulders. Across the valley, Mohawk's summit towers are visible when the trees are leafless. Descend

Cathedral Pines

along a stone wall, a remnant of open hillside pastures. Level out and cross a beautiful glade with ferns and a view south to Mohawk Pond. Cross a tote road and then climb a laurel-covered slope to the gravel summit road.

Head to your right up the blue-blazed road to the nearby top of Mohawk Mountain. There, dwarfed by radio towers, a lookout tower rises just high enough to top the trees. There are picnic facilities and a paved parking area for motorists who arrive on the gravel road. A March trip will reward you with a clump of pussy willows adjacent to the paved area.

Climb the steep wooden tower steps and enjoy the 360-degree view. Mounts Everett, Race, and Bear punctuate the Riga Plateau to the north. The Catskills rise on the western horizon. Farther to your left, in the distance, is the mountainous Hudson Highland in New York. The large, flat-topped mass in the middle distance to the right of the Riga Pla-teau is Canaan Mountain. If your eyesight and the visibility are good, you should be able to see Mount Tom in Massachusetts some 40 miles away. It lies about 30 degrees to the right of Riga, a distinctive blue outline protruding above the horizon with a gentle rise at left and a steep cliff on the other side.

When your eyes have drunk their fill, descend the gravel road to the east, which loops back west down the north slope of the mountain. Chestnut sprouts are common along the edge of the road. A little way down the road, you'll pass a clearing to your right opposite two imposing stone gateposts flanking a tote road to your left. Look over your right shoulder back to Mohawk. Rejoin the blue blazes of the Mattatuck Trail at the small picnic area on your right and follow them north, taking care to turn left down the Mohawk Trail just before reaching the ski area. Follow the Mohawk Trail back through the Cathedral Pines to your car in Cornwall.

35

Natchaug

Distance: 6.6 miles

Vertical rise: 300 feet

Time: 4 hours

Rating: CD

Map: USGS 7.5-minute Hampton

The woods of Connecticut contain many ghosts. Our human and natural histories bear the memories of Native American nations, early settlers and farmers, great forests come and gone many times since the *Mayflower*, and one of our greatest natural calamities, the chestnut blight.

The American chestnut, once comprising nearly one-quarter of all our hardwood forest trees, and particularly favored by farmers due to its tasty nuts, was allowed to grow to great size in their otherwise open fields. The blight was introduced to North America in a shipment of Asian chestnuts (which are immune to the blight) brought to New York City around the turn of the century. By the end of the First World War most of America's chestnuts had succumbed. Although no cure has been found for the blight, our chestnut is a vigorous sprout-

er, so the once mighty chestnut is now, ironically, a common small tree in Connecticut's hardwood forest. This hike takes you past two ghosts of chestnuts past in the Natchaug State Forest.

From the junction of CT 198 and US 44 in Phoenixville, drive south on CT 198 for 0.5 mile. Turn sharply left on General Lyon Road; in 0.1 mile turn right on Pilfershire Road (shown on the map as Pilshire Road), and then turn right again in 1.7 miles on Kingsbury Road where there is a sign for the state forest unit headquarters. In about a mile this road becomes dirt. Where the blue-blazed Natchaug Trail crosses, take a gravel road left to Beaver Dam Wildlife Management Area. There is a sizable parking lot at the end of this road.

Facing the pond, bear left out of the parking lot to follow the Natchaug Trail. But first explore the earthen dam backing up the pond to your right. A stone-and-concrete apron accommodates the pond's spring overflow, but the summer stream is usually handled by a vertical corrugated pipe, which also acts as a debris screen. The croak-jump-splash of thousands of frogs here heralds your approach to the water's edge. In the pond near the far shore is a brush, stick, and mud beaver lodge. You may see beaver

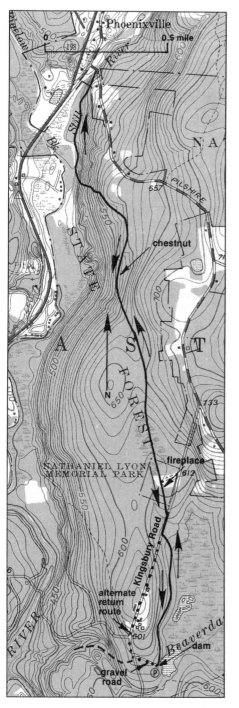

cuttings along the start of the trail. The pond's surface is almost completely covered in summer with floating and emergent vegetation, especially the rather dull, yellow-blossomed bullhead lily and the exotic white-flowered water lily. Tall, emergent purple spires of pickerelweed line the shallow shoreline.

Return to the trail that parallels the pond. Several highbush blueberry bushes tempt you to dally, and the summer perfume of the pepperbush lightens your way. In late summer the woodland birds are quiet; they anticipate the coming of fall sooner than we do. Swallows line the telephone wires (they are usually gone by Labor Day), and families of flickers and towhees rummage through the woods together.

After passing through a grove of red spruce and unhealthy red pine, you reach Kingsbury Road in about 0.6 mile. Follow the road to your right. There are two kinds of safe three-leafed vines along here: the hog-peanut, whose attractive lilac blossoms belie its name, and the virgin's bower.

About 0.8 mile from the start, the trail enters the woods to your left and soon passes through Nathaniel Lyon Memorial Park, named for the first Union general to die in the Civil War, at the Battle of Wilson's Creek in Missouri. Nathaniel Lyon was born in nearby Eastford, Connecticut. The park features picnic tables, outhouses, a water pump, and a great stone fireplace. Midway across this open area, bear left down an old tote road. On this stretch of the trail you wander through mixed hardwood forest, pass occasional stone walls, and finally invade the stillness of a hemlock grove.

In 1.9 miles the erect hulk of a giant chestnut tree, 15½ feet in circumference, commands your attention. It has been dead for generations, and its seemingly indestructible wood is finally break-

Hulk of a Great Chestnut

ing down. In the last few years the main branches have fallen and a portion of the trunk has split away—year by year you will notice more and more of the great tree's dissolution. Clearly it was once an open-field giant. Its great side limbs and their weight are hastening its decomposition by pulling the trunk apart. The photograph was taken in 1977—compare it to the way the chestnut looks now. Except for a few black birches, the space around the dead patriarch is respectfully empty. The chestnut sprouts nearby probably sprang from the still-living roots of the dead hulk.

While we were admiring this relic of our once most valuable hardwood, a small, chunky, brownish gray form circled a stub and disappeared into a knothole. This was only the second flying squirrel we have seen in broad daylight. This normally nocturnal animal is actually quite common in our woods. Its chunky look derives from the folds of skin joining the front and rear legs, which allow this little creature to glide (not fly!) from high points to lower branches.

A little farther along on the left stands a much smaller, but still huge, dead chestnut (everything is relative). Its lack of massive side limbs has kept much of the trunk intact. It's likely this tree grew in a woodlot, where side limb development was stifled by the competition for sunlight. Identification of dead chestnuts depends upon an unusual dissolution sequence: Most dead trees rot from the outside in—the chestnut rots from the inside out! The hard, intact surface hides a rotting interior. The chestnut's durability made it highly sought after for beams and lumber.

At 2.3 miles you come to a group of circular piles of stones, many perched on large rocks embedded in the ground. In the days of small hand-tool harvesters like scythes, this was an efficient method of clearing fields, quicker than building a wall; with today's straight-line mowing machines it would be unacceptable. Of course, running a mowing machine on these rocky hillsides would be a feat in itself.

The checkered leaves of the evergreen rattlesnake plantain are common along this section of the trail. Its faded spires of last year's orchids thrust upward here and there. This has to be one of the few plants whose foliage is more familiar than their flowers.

In about 2.6 miles, turn left down a rutted road. Soon turn right into the woods and bear right again at a wooded, grassy remnant of field dotted with eastern red cedars. Carefully follow the blue blazes through these reforested fields.

Dropping down a bank, you reach the Still River and follow it upstream. (This trout stream is a tributary of the Natchaug River.) In the next ½ mile, you alternately pass through typical woodland and grassy woods featuring the short-lived American hornbeam or musclewood, so called because its smooth, corded branches resemble muscular arms contorted with strain. For some reason, it does not shade out grass, unlike most trees.

After 3.3 miles you will reach Pilfershire Road at a bridge. On the upstream corner of the bridge is a large white walnut, or butternut—a not-too-common, short-lived tree. Retrace your steps over the trail.

You may choose to follow the gravel Kingsbury Road from Nathaniel Lyon Memorial Park past the Natchaug State Forest headquarters to your car at Beaver Dam Wildlife Management Area, and take in a CCC plaque, another familiar sight in Connecticut's woodlands. FDR's Civilian Conservation Corps did much work in the state's forests and parks during the Great Depression. Dams, trails, shelters, roads, walls, and other similar projects were completed by the corps, a unique mix of the Departments of War (now Defense) and Interior. The army ran the camps, and foresters, engineers, and land managers used the workforce to improve the country's abundant natural and recreational resources. You'll pass a marker honoring the workers of Civilian Conservation Corps Camp Fernow, Company No. 183. The marker notes the corps's origin: "Created by President Franklin Roosevelt, 1933–1942, Renewing the country's natural resources and challenging the human spirit of a nation in depression."

36

Peoples State Forest

Distance: 7 miles

Vertical rise: 1000 feet

Time: 4 hours

Rating: BC

Maps: USGS 7.5-minute Winsted, New Hartford

Good hiking trails do not just happen, nor are they maintained effortlessly. Three groups maintain most of Connecticut's trails. The Connecticut Chapter of the Appalachian Mountain Club does an excellent job of covering the Appalachian Trail. The unpaid volunteers of the Connecticut Forest and Park Association maintain the extensive Blue Trail System. Because each trail section in this system is the domain of a single individual who is subject to the vagaries of time and temperament, occasionally a section of blue-blazed trail is slightly unkempt. But overall, these volunteers do a superb job.

Conditions on state-maintained trails are the most variable, due to the demands of funding and priorities. Peoples State Forest is an example of an excellent trail system that benefits from a combination of volunteers and state funding. Not only are the trails in good shape, but also the Stone Museum described at the beginning of this hike has been restored and provides displays and programs for summer visitors.

From the junction of CT 318 and US 44 east of Winsted, proceed east on CT 318 across the Farmington River and take the first left onto East River Road. In 0.8 mile, by the Peoples Forest sign, fork right on Greenwoods Road, the paved state forest road. You have missed your turn if you come to a picnic area on your left. Then, in 0.2 mile, turn left up a short gravel road to a parking lot by a well-constructed trailside museum, a legacy of the Civilian Conservation Corps of the 1930s. Try to park efficiently so others visiting the museum can park here, too. In summer, it is recommended that hikers park on East River Road at the picnic area (nominal entrance fee) and take the blue-blazed trail uphill to the museum.

The Agnes Bowen Trail, named for a leader in the establishment of Peoples Forest, and marked with blue blazes with orange dots, starts into the woods here, across the parking lot from the museum. Follow this path through a stand of huge

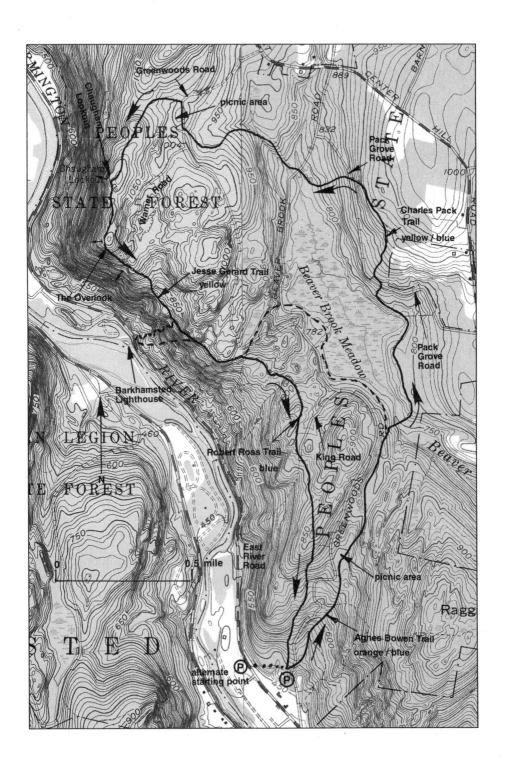

white pines. Shortly the blue-blazed Robert Ross Trail breaks off to the left; stay on the orange-on-blue-blazed trail as it curves downhill to the tar forest road. Turn right and follow the road for a few yards, then go left into the woods. Almost immediately you cross a small stream, which the now rocky trail follows uphill to the left. In ½ mile the trail passes through a roadside picnic area, turns right at a fireplace, and in another ⅔ mile intersects the Charles L. Pack Trail (yellow dots on blue).

Turn right to follow these blazes. In a few yards you reach Beaver Brook, which you cross on a footbridge (use caution: slick when wet) built by the Youth Conservation Corps in 1976. On the right you can see the old high-water double cable crossing; the cable crossing was used by walking on the lower cable and holding onto the upper one for balance. Here you'll find the red cardinal flower, a really striking midsummer bloom.

After crossing the footbridge, bear left across the hillside, keeping the Beaver Swamp on your left, and then curve to your right uphill. Beaver Swamp was once a meadow, and some of the Pack Trail follows the wagon path used to haul hay from these fields at the turn of the century. You'll pass a large foundation to your right, all that remains of a dwelling built before 1806 and torn down in 1880. In 0.7 mile from the junction with the orange-on-blue-blazed trail, you cross gravel Pack Grove Road. Climb among the beech trees (Pack Grove) and then descend to join the trail again in another ½ mile. Turn right onto the gravel road and then bear left to leave the road and continue to drop downhill to Beaver Brook Road. Turn left and recross the brook on a bridge. Watch for trout swimming under the bridge. Turn right off the road and reenter the woods on the stream's far side on

a woods road, and eventually ford a small feeder brook. Another ½ mile of woods walking brings you to Greenwoods Road, where this trail ends.

Turn right to follow the pavement through Big Spring Recreation Area and then turn left into the woods. Here you pick up the yellow-blazed Jesse Gerard Trail, which leads you to the escarpment along the Farmington River. Note the delicate spring blooms of Canada mayflower along the path here.

This trail traces an old tote road for a short distance before taking an obscure path uphill. After passing between two huge glacial boulders ⅓ mile from Greenwoods Road, the trail turns right, toward Chaugham Lookout. These open ledges, ½ mile from Greenwoods Road, provide an excellent view northwest across a wide, wild, wooded valley. The canoe-dotted Farmington River winds sinuously below. The village of Riverton in the valley to the north looks very New England–like with its white church steeple. Chaugham was a Native American whose cabin in the valley below, lit up at night, was a familiar landmark for stage drivers heading for New Hartford. His cabin, in an old Native American settlement, was called the Barkhamsted Lighthouse.

The well-worn trail continues through hemlocks along the ledge escarpment, reaching another overlook in ⅓ mile. Proceeding steeply down, you find sweet lowbush blueberries flanking the trail over erosion-bared basalt. The yellow-blazed Jesse Gerard and blue-blazed Robert Ross Trails run together here. They split about ¾ mile from Chaugham Lookout. A yellow-blazed trail turns right and descends 299 steps to the river at Barkhamsted Lighthouse. Continue on a yellow-and-blue-blazed trail until the yellow-blazed trail descends also to Barkhamsted Lighthouse, where you fol-

The Stone Museum at Peoples State Forest

low the blue-blazed trail up a steep hill beneath a ledge before resuming the descent. Pass over a rise and reach a wide road coming from your left. Bear right downhill and then turn left into the woods, following blue blazes.

Continue downhill on the blue-blazed trail to the orange-on-blue-blazed trail near the Stone Museum. Follow the blazes to the right back to your car. Take the time to check out the museum if it's open. The chestnut beams (see Hike 35) alone are worth the visit; however, there is plenty of natural and human historical information there to add to your day's enjoyment.

37

West Peak and Castle Crag

Distance: 6.4 miles

Vertical rise: 1200 feet

Time: 4 hours

Rating: B

Map: USGS 7.5-minute Meriden

Save this hike until your legs are in good shape (it's difficult), your mind is receptive to scenic beauty (the views are very special), and the day is clear and cool (visibility is very important).

Eastbound, take exit 5 from I-691; at the end of the exit go north (left) on CT 71 about 0.9 mile to a pulloff on the left side of the road, 0.1 mile south of the blue oval Metacomet Trail sign at Cathole Pass. Westbound, take exit 6 from I-691 and follow signs to CT 71, then go north (right) 0.5 mile to the pulloff below Cathole Pass. Your route starts up a blue-blazed steep slope on the west (left) side of CT 71 that has eroded to its volcanic traprock base.

The leafy green bower over the well-worn path opens a bit as you approach Elmere Reservoir. Swallows gracefully skim its surface in pursuit of tiny flying insectsor to sip water on the wing. After 0.2 mile, follow the trail across the dam, cross the rocky overflow channel, and continue straight ahead into the woods. If you are lucky and it is the right time of year, you may find a few double-blossomed rue anemones on the dam. In March, the spring peepers provide a high-pitched soundtrack to your hike over the dam.

In spring the pink wild geraniums along the trail divert your attention from the solid restful greens that fill the woods. An alcoholic decoction of wild geranium was once used to mitigate the effects of dysentery. Continue along a rocky, shaded hillside before dropping to your right to a dike with a swampy, unnamed pond on its left.

One mile from the start, emerge on paved Park Drive, which you follow across the dam at the north end of Merimere Reservoir. Here you can enjoy the fine view of the lake and the notch it sits in.

At the dam's end, turn left into the woods. After crossing an attractive rock-bound rill, you edge up the long west side of the reservoir. Then follow near the twisting shore of the lake—the

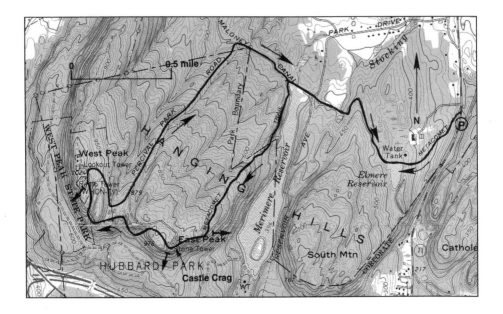

route is peppered with volcanic rocks. After leaving the shore, the way at first is very steep and rocky, but gradually the slope eases.

After 2 miles, you emerge on cliffs that rise 400 feet above Merimere Reservoir. Evergreen-covered Mine Island below you seems lifted from the Maine coast. Gerry first saw this island in the early 1960s on an autumn morning as the ground fog was lifting. Some sights plant themselves so firmly in your mind's eye that they are always there to delight you.

South Mountain rises from the far shore of the reservoir and Mount Higby's northern cliffs poke up at left (see Hike 29). On the far left you can make out the jagged Hartford skyline.

As you continue uphill along the cliff, several unmarked paths on the left lead to similar viewpoints with slightly different perspectives; all are spectacular on a clear day. One last lookout provides a glimpse of Castle Crag's tower. You follow the blue-blazed trail across a final dip before arriving at the base of Castle Crag's tower, 2.2 miles from your car. Climb the tower on metal stairs for a panoramic view.

The vista west is blocked by West Peak. Sleeping Giant (see Hike 49) and West Rock lie to the south and the Metacomet ridges to the north. Talcott Mountain (see Hike 44) is readily identifiable with its Heublein Tower. In the far distance you can see the east-facing cliffs of Mount Tom in Massachusetts, the Connecticut River gap, and the humps of the Holyoke Range.

Leaving the tower, continue on the Metacomet Trail across the parking lot. Be careful here; your route can be hard to locate. The trail goes across the near corner of the lot and continues up the slope near the cliffs. The route crosses more open cliffs and then drops down almost to the tower's access road.

Just before the road, a descending blue-blazed trail that avoids road walking by way of a series of ups and downs bears left away from the road. Take this trail and at the bottom turn right on a tote road. Soon turn right again, climbing diagonally left up an overgrown scree slope. A recent mid-March trip revealed a garter snake enjoying the early-season warmth of the hillside's southern exposure. Bear right and ascend a very attractive draw. Great traprock boulders are "flowing" down the intersection of the scree slopes. Look back—the sides of the draw frame the Sleeping Giant with his head to the right.

Near the top of this draw are a large elderberry bush and a stand of American yew. This is the largest, most southerly stand that we have encountered. A northern shrub, the yew ranges as far south as New England, so this may be one of its more southerly appearances.

The trail levels out before bearing left up the steep side a short way to the plateau top of West Peak. Here, the Connecticut Chapter of the Appalachian Mountain Club was formed in June 1921.

The club has held at least two reunions here since then, including one marking its 60th anniversary in June 1981. At this point you are 3.4 miles from Cathole Pass. You emerge onto an old road, which you follow left to a formerly fenced, rocky point. You can see the Tunxis ridge to the west. Several cliffs and headlands invite your careful exploration.

After a leisurely lunch—the surrounding thickets make nice spots for a nap—follow the park road down the north side of West Peak. As with most of Connecticut's traprock ridges, the side opposite the cliffs tends to slope gently as a result of the tipping of the layer of traprock. The break in the traprock is then exposed as a cliff. Be sure to turn left at the road junction that leads right to Castle Crag. When you reach Merimere Reservoir, cross the dam and follow the blue-blazed Metacomet Trail east, retracing your steps to your car.

From Castle Crag

38

Bear Mountain

Distance: 6.5 miles

Time: 4 hours

Vertical rise: 1600 feet

Rating: AB

Map: USGS 7.5-minute Bash Bish Falls (MA-CT-NY)

A rugged, windswept mountain with views into three states awaits you at the high point of this hike. On the way, you hike a portion of the justly famous Appalachian Trail (AT). At the top of Bear Mountain is a once magnificent stone monument that has partially crumbled but is still an imposing landmark. In late 1983 the rubble was stabilized, creating a lower monument. It was erected to proclaim (incorrectly) the highest point in Connecticut. In fact, as has been discovered since World War II, the state's high point is on a shoulder of Mount Frissell, another peak on the Riga Plateau just west of Bear Mountain, whose summit is in Massachusetts.

To reach the start of this hike, drive on CT 41 3.2 miles north from its junc-

tion with US 44 in Salisbury. There is a small hikers' parking lot on the left.

The blue-blazed Undermountain Trail, a feeder trail to the AT, starts at the back of the parking lot and soon passes a large bulletin board, which carries the latest trail information. There is also a box with a frequently replenished supply of AT information folders. These provide handy parking, camping, and route information.

Proceed across a field that is rapidly becoming overgrown. We have watched this area change from an open field to a young forest over the past 20 years. Enter the woods and soon begin to climb, gently at first, and then more steeply. This trail will present an almost unrelieved climb to its junction with the AT in 1.9 miles. It is a good test of wind and muscle and an excellent place to practice the mile-eating trick used by seasoned hikers: Set a pace you can maintain all the way to the top without stopping.

After 0.25 mile, you pass an eroded gully on your right and the hulks of several large fallen chestnut trees on your left. Although these trees have been dead for at least 70 years, their disintegrating trunks still litter the forest floor. The barkless remains, slowly decompos-

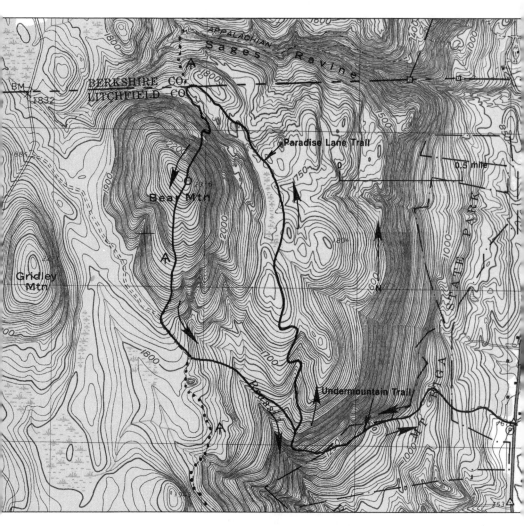

ing, have a weatherbeaten look unlike that of any other dead tree. Chestnut trees rot from the inside out, thereby maintaining their size and apparent integrity longer than most other deadfalls.

As you climb, it becomes more obvious that this trail is an old tote road whose surface has eroded several feet into the hill. This erosion was probably caused by countless horse and wagon trips scoring the surface, with rain and snowmelt doing the rest. Soon you encounter a bad washout. Hikers caused this unsightly scar, at least in part! The constant tramping of feet killed the stabilizing vegetation, and the deeply eroded road prevented the diversion of running water off the trail. Then a real gullywasher of a storm, probably in the spring when the soil was already saturated and unstable, caused the muddy earth to slide into the ravine at left, leav-

North from Bear Mountain to Massachusetts' Mounts Everett and Race

ing the gouge on the trail you see before you. Since the water now flows into the ravine instead of down the trail, and the Appalachian Mountain Club has rerouted the trail off the worst areas, the rest of the road should be fairly secure.

Two-tenths of a mile above the washout, go right off the Undermountain Trail onto blue-blazed Paradise Lane. Blazed trails may exhibit many different colors, but the white blazes are reserved for the AT, while AT side trails are blazed with blue. This blue-blazed trail joins the AT north of the summit of Bear Mountain in 2.1 miles. If you continue straight on the Undermountain Trail, you will meet the AT south of the peak of Bear Mountain. You will come back this way on the circuit described here.

Paradise Lane starts roughly parallel to the AT. In a short distance, the trail goes left off the old tote road and zigzags steeply up the hill. This trail has the densest population of chestnut sprouts we've seen in Connecticut, and a couple have grown to nearly 4 inches across. At

a relatively flat area on Bear Mountain, the trail levels a bit and even eases gently downhill until it reaches a swampy area on this side of the mountain.

Along this section of the trail Gerry once had a special experience. A ruffed grouse took off with the usual thunder of wings, without having run a bit, as they usually do. Why did it hold in one spot so long before flying? Having noted where it took off, Gerry went over and found a well-camouflaged, roughly circular nest with nine buff eggs in it.

After going along the level a short way, you will see the very steep south side of Bear Mountain at left. Cross a small seasonal stream and continue curving gently left. Soon you reach a small pond; the water is mostly filled with bushes. After crossing the pond's outlet stream on a log bridge, note the northeast corner of Bear Mountain as you go across an open ledge decorated with laurel and huckleberry. The line between Connecticut and Massachusetts is marked with yellow paint.

You reach the AT in a hemlock area, then turn left (south). A right turn will take you to Katahdin in Maine in about 800 miles. For years, members of the Appalachian Mountain Club used a group of five short-lived white birches to tell them where to turn off onto this end of Paradise Lane from the AT. Now that the National Park Service has bought this land, and this side trail can be officially signed, the trees' role as a landmark has ended; seeming to sense this, they have all died in the past 10 years.

Go diagonally left up the white-blazed, rocky AT on Bear Mountain. Some fine trail work has been done here to stabilize this steep route with large, erosion-proof rocks. After a long, steady uphill stretch, turn directly up the steep, ledge-dominated slope. Scramble over several steep pitches where you have to use both hands and feet, then enter some stunted pitch pines that perch precariously on rather bare open ledges. Almost immediately you will spot the monument on top of Bear Mountain.

While strolling around the open top, watch for large, dark, soaring birds—turkey vultures. These birds, with a 6-foot wingspan, are the largest of North America's vultures. They are common in the adjacent Hudson River Valley and are spreading throughout the Northeast. They use rising columns of air along the edge of the Riga Plateau to soar for hours without flapping their wings.

From the summit, the views are superb. To the east lie the Twin Lakes and Canaan Mountain. For the best view to the north, follow the AT north to a ledge on the edge of the stand of scrub pines. From there the mountain with a tower is Mount Everett (2602 feet), the apex of the second highest mountain mass in Massachusetts. The hulk in front of

Everett is Race Mountain (2365 feet).

When you are ready, follow the AT south off the top. Just as the trail starts seriously downward, there is a grand view to the south and west. Ahead is the relatively level Riga Plateau. To the right the mountains you see are, from left to right, Gridley (Connecticut), North and South Brace (New York), Round Mountain (Connecticut) with Mount Frissell (Massachusetts) behind it, and north of Frissell (you will have to go down the path a bit to see past obstructing trees) is Ashley (Massachusetts). The body of water left of Gridley is South Pond (1715 feet), and the Catskills can be seen off in the distance on a clear day. It usually takes several visits before these mountains become old friends, but the journeys are definitely worth the effort!

Continue, passing several pitch pines whose wind-distorted shapes would do credit to a bonsai artist. All lean east, away from the prevailing west winds. The cold, desiccating winds have sheared off any upward shoots that braved the elements so that the tops are flattened and bent eastward—the path of least resistance.

As you progress downward, the various hardy oaks rise slowly to obscure your view. Then you rise into the open again to a partial view of the mountains. However, each dip carries you into higher and higher trees until the trees win this game of hide-and-seek.

About 0.6 mile from the summit, a tote road comes in on your right from gravel Mount Washington Road; bear left on the AT. In another 0.2 mile, the blue-blazed Undermountain Trail leaves left steeply downhill at a well-signed junction. Take this trail; it leads you downhill past the Paradise Lane junction to your car in 1.9 miles.

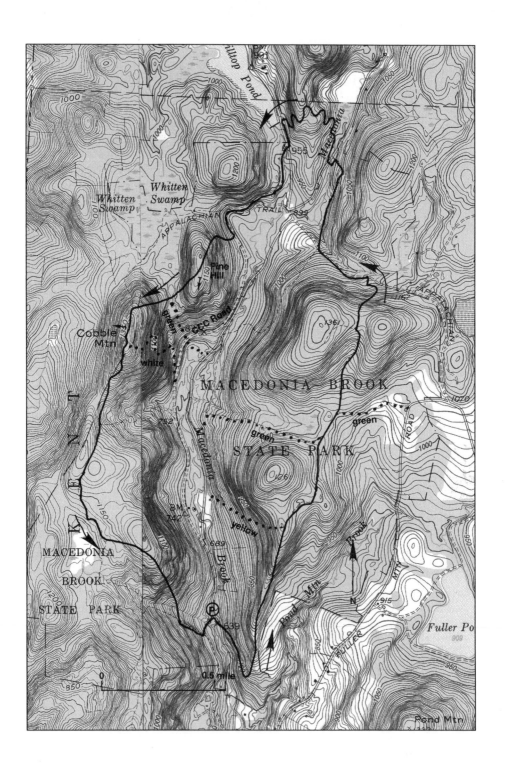

39

Macedonia Brook

Distance: 6.7 miles

Vertical rise: 1550 feet

Time: 4 hours

Rating: A

Maps: USGS 7.5-minute Ellsworth, Amenia (NY-CT)

A cluster of hills 1000 to 1400 feet high, separated by pure clear Macedonia Brook, make up Macedonia Brook State Park. This 2300-acre park boasts 13 miles of trails. The famed Appalachian Trail (AT) used to run through Macedonia Brook, but it was relocated in the late 1980s. Now what was the AT is part of the Connecticut Blue Trail System.

The park began as a 1500-acre gift from the White Memorial Foundation in 1918 (see Hike 30). Once the domain of the Schaghticokes (see Hike 48), Macedonia became a thriving community that supported the iron industry in nearby Kent. Because of charcoal production to feed the blast furnaces, all the local timber had been consumed by the 1840s. Competition with the larger Pennsylvania mines closed down the local iron opera-

tion in 1865. Macedonia Brook State Park, like many of Connecticut's state forests and parks, was home to a Civilian Conservation Corps company in the 1930s.

Macedonia Brook lies just inside Connecticut's western boundary. From the junction of CT 341 and US 7 in Kent, take CT 341 west for 1.7 miles to Macedonia Brook Road, where a sign directs you to the park down a paved road on the right. Bear left where Fuller Brook Road turns right 0.8 mile from CT 341, and reach the blue-blazed Macedonia Ridge Trail at a bridge over the brook after another 0.6 mile. There is parking on both sides of the bridge.

Enter the woods on the east side of the valley (to your right as you drive in from CT 341). Ascend the hillside, turn sharply left, and climb the ridge through open oak forest. On an early-morning hike in July a large hawk flew out of a tree ahead on the ridge. The remnants of an old apple orchard bisect the trail; many of the gnarled, unkempt specimens still bloom each spring.

After 0.9 mile, the yellow-blazed trail branches to the left as your trail bends right. Drop down the east side of a hill and join a green-blazed trail that comes in at your left from the park road. The blue- and green-blazed trails run together briefly. At the beginning of the next rise, bear left on the blue-blazed ridge trail where the green-blazed trail continues down the road and out to Fuller Mountain Road.

A short distance beyond the junction, you walk past several clumps of gray birches on the left. These dowdy cousins of the sparkling white birch have a grayer bark that does not peel with age. A short-lived tree with triangular leaves and black triangular patches beneath the base of each limb, the gray birch is an early colonizer of uncultivated open fields.

Your trail climbs easily and steadily up and over a col between two unnamed peaks. In spring the greenish yellow flowers of the many striped maples here lend a faint but delightful fragrance to the woods. The flower clusters dangle from the branches like exotic earrings.

From the col, the ridge trail drops steeply down to a deeply worn old town road (the former AT) where you turn left to follow it downhill. At a barricade, turn right off the woods road and cross a stream before climbing over a rise. Turn left to cross over a bridge on dirt Keeler Road. Bear right and follow Macedonia Brook before ascending a hill near the northern boundary of the park. We found a box turtle here on one of our recent hikes. The little 6-inch-long specimen was probably over 60 years old! Adult turtles have relatively few enemies except cars and can live to ripe old ages of more than 100 years. Pass over the crest of the ridge and drop steeply through a hemlock stand using switchbacks. Turn left on gravel Weber Road, then turn right on the old CCC Road at a park sign. Follow the road through gates at its crossing of the partially paved Chippewalla Road. Continue on CCC Road following blue blazes, and then turn right off the road to follow a footpath steeply up Pine Hill. Beneath an ash tree on the right we found two morels. Acclaimed as our best-tasting local wild mushroom, this hollow, light brown fungus with its exterior raised latticework is the elusive treasure of the dedicated mycologist. Always make a positive identification with a mushroom expert before nibbling!

At the top of the grade, the trail turns left into the woods, climbing steadily and fairly steeply. In June a few pink azalea or June pinks spot the trail with color and fragrance. Threading through the laurel undergrowth, the grade eases as you near the top of Pine Hill. As on most Connecticut hills, the steepest slope on Pine Hill is in the middle of the grade.

From the ledges on Pine Hill's far side, you have an excellent view down the valley. Close by from right to left are Cobble Mountain, South Cobble Mountain (both of which you climb on this hike), and Chase Mountain. In the center distance are Mounts Algo and Schaghticoke.

Follow the trail down over steep ledges, passing the green-blazed Pine Hill Trail to your left just before reaching the col. Continue uphill, passing through boulders before reaching the ledges above. Scramble over a boulder and up an 8-foot ledge with minimal handholds. This route is not recommended when it is wet or icy. Just above that ledge, follow the blue-blazed trail up a 30-foot sloping ledge. You have to either find a way around or use a crack for traction. This is definitely not recommended in adverse conditions. If you're uneasy with these ledges, you can return to the Pine Hill Trail and follow it ½ mile down to the park road, 1¼ miles north of your car. Your ascent soon moderates as you pass by several large beds of wild oats with their drooping, bell-shaped flowers.

Be prepared for superb views when you reach the top of Cobble Mountain, for the trail traverses its exposed western escarpment. The ridge across the valley is in New York, and beyond it are the Catskills. By dropping down the ledges a bit you can get a good view of Connecticut's northwest corner, the Riga Plateau. The tallest peak (topped by a fire tower) on the right is Mount Everett in Massachusetts. To its left is Bear Mountain (see Hike 38) in Connecticut.

Continue on these exposed ledges to their far end where the white-blazed Cobble Mountain Trail comes in from your left. Stay on the blue-blazed ridge trail, and drop steeply down the ledges into the col before rising up South Cobble Mountain. The trail passes to the left of the summit. Then follow the steep, rocky route down into the col. Head downhill to the park road and your car.

40

Windsor Locks Canal

Distance: 9 miles

Vertical rise: negligible

Time: 4½ hours

Rating: D

Maps: USGS 7.5-minute Windsor Locks, Broad Brook

By the middle of the 19th century, stiff competition from railroads brought about the collapse of New England's expanding canal system. The Windsor Locks Canal, built in 1829 to bypass the Enfield Rapids on the Connecticut River, was an exception. Here, the canal survived because water diverted from New England's biggest river not only served barge traffic but also provided power to mills, the last of which continued to operate until the 1930s. Today the Windsor Locks Canal still routes an occasional pleasure craft around the rapids, and its old towpath, now paved, offers a pleasant level trail for walking or bicycling.

To reach the towpath, follow CT 159 south from its southern junction with CT 190 for 0.1 mile to Canal Road on the left. The road ends in about 0.4 mile, with a large parking lot on your left. The size of the lot is not indicative of trail use; it is heavily used by anglers who congregate here from April to June. The famous Enfield Rapids provide the best ocean-run shad fishing in New England.

Head south down the river; pass through the gates and over the canal to the start of the towpath. These gates are locked from mid-November to the beginning of April to preclude towpath use, which could disturb wintering birds of prey. The impressive Enfield Rapids dominate the scene to your left. Your route simply follows the paved way 4.5 miles to its end; there are no side trails to mislead you. The towpath is a designated bicycle trail, so please give cyclists the right-of-way.

While the plants and wildlife along the way are the chief attractions of this hike, human-made constructions along the canal are not without interest. About 2 miles from the start, the blunt prow of heavily wooded, mile-long King's Island comes into view. Notice here that the banks of the canal are made of the soft Connecticut Valley red sandstone, best known as the rock used to build New York City's brownstone apartments. About ⅓ mile along King's Island, you cross a small overflow dam built to

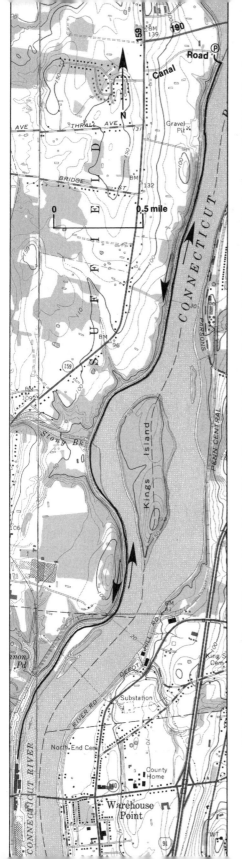

handle the floodwaters of Strong Brook; smaller streams run directly into the canal. A quarter mile below King's Island, you will pass alongside venerable stone abutments supporting a trestle over the Connecticut River; several trains whistled by as we hiked the towpath.

As you walk, maintain an alert eye. This entire trip is a veritable oasis in an urban desert. While humans create monotonous conformity, nature in all her diversity moves in wherever possible.

We came upon a young woodchuck caught between the devil (us) and the deep blue sea (the canal). Butterflies were constant companions. Besides the cabbage white (the only butterfly that is a common agricultural pest), we saw various swallowtails, skippers, wood satyrs, and a beloved ally, the red admiral, whose caterpillar ravages nettles.

From a botanical point of view, this walk is one of the best in the state. We identified ox-eye daisy, fleabane, yarrow, vetch, two varieties of milkweed, campion, St.-Johns'-wort, black-eyed Susan, several goldenrods, mullein, deadly nightshade, thimbleweed, Deptford pink, plantain (American and English), both bull and Canada thistle, roses, gill-over-the-ground, jewelweed, daylily, and lovely sundrop-like giant buttercups with cross-shaped stigmas. The clovers, legumes with built-in nitrogen factories on their roots, are well represented. In addition to white and alsike clover, we found at least two varieties of yellow-blossomed hop clovers.

Vines and bushes abound: poison ivy, several varieties of grapes, Virginia creeper, oriental bittersweet, sweet-smelling Japanese honeysuckle, scrub willow, various types of the smaller dogwoods, elderberry, alder (both smooth and speckled), sassafras, juniper, slippery elm, and smooth and staghorn sumacs with their great masses of red-

Windsor Locks Canal

ripening acid fruit. On a recent May visit, the white bracts of flowering dogwood punctuated the various shades of green along the canal's edge.

Here also, treetops that you usually see only from below stand open for your scrutiny. These trees growing along the riverbed, or on the canal's steep sides to your left, present their seldom-seen tops for your curiosity. The round buttons that give the sycamore one of its common names (buttonwood) are here at eye level, and the stickiness of the butternut tree's immature nuts can be tested in place. In mid- to late May the fluffs of cotton from the aptly named eastern cottonwood fill the air—in places we have seen a gossamer layer of this cotton two inches deep on the ground. In early summer you can pick with ease the tasty fruit of the red mulberry—if you can get there before the birds!

We talk of waste areas, but probably the only true wastelands are those areas sealed with concrete and asphalt—and even these are transitory. A constant rain of seeds awaits the smallest moistened crack, ready to sprout and grow. Near the end of the towpath, we found that a clump of field bindweed had wrestled a foothold in the junction between an old brick building and the asphalt drive. In the wild the small, white morning glory–like flowers of this "weed" have little appeal for most of us, but here they lighten a dingy corner.

A second set of gates 4.5 miles from the first marks the end of the towpath near CT 140. Turn around and retrace your steps to your car.

41

Mansfield Hollow

Distance: 8 miles

Vertical rise: 600 feet

Time: 4½ hours

Rating: CD

Map: USGS 7.5-minute Spring Hill

Because of its proximity to the University of Connecticut at Storrs, the Mansfield Hollow Recreation Area is sprinkled with temporary refugees from academia: jogging professors, strolling students, and young families with toddlers. In addition in picnic tables, fireplaces, ball fields, bridle paths, rest rooms, and boat-launching facilities, Mansfield Hollow also encompasses one of the two southern termini of the Nipmuck Trail, which stretches 34 miles north to Bigelow Hollow State Park near the Massachusetts border. This hike follows the blue-blazed Nipmuck Trail through a flood-control area and rolling countryside as far as 50 Foot Cliff, a nice little lookout.

From the junction of CT 89 and CT 195 in Mansfield Center, drive south on CT 195 for 0.5 mile to Bassett Bridge Road and turn left. After 0.8 mile, park in the lot to your left, on the right side of the entrance road to Mansfield Hollow State Park. To reach the start of the Nipmuck Trail, follow the gravel entrance road to a gated woods road through the open field fringed with white pine woods, keeping the flood-control causeway to your left. Turn right and follow the Nipmuck Trail's blue blazes into the young pine stand to your left. The flood-control reservoir is visible to the east.

The trail starts on sandy soil, where white pines grow very well. You reach a woods road in 0.1 mile; the blazes lead to the right before turning left into the woods. The reservoir is visible beyond the end of the road. Follow the blue blazes carefully through this maze of trails and woods roads. You may encounter recent relocations designed to prevent abrupt meetings between hikers and mountain bikers. On your right are patches of shinleaf, which you can distinguish by their almost round evergreen leaves. Although you will not see their spikes of nodding white flowers until June or July, the flower buds may be found nestled beneath forest litter, here mostly pine needles, in early May. This plant derives its name from the early custom of applying its leaves to sores and bruises—any plaster, no mat-

ter where applied, was called a shin plaster.

As you wend your way up onto a flat, the trail touches and then heads left off a bridle path. You will flirt with numer-

ous bridle paths strewn with strawberry plants and cinquefoils through the first part of the hike. The mixture gives you a chance to distinguish between these two plants with similar leaves: The strawberry has three-leafed bunches, and the local cinquefoils, five.

Beneath a blue-blazed white pine you will find the first of many hawthorns along the trail. This shrub is characterized by formidable 2-inch thorns, attractive white flowers with a rather disagreeable odor, and fall pomes suitable for making jelly. You encounter and cross a second bridle path, pass through another wooded section, and emerge once again on a bridle path.

At this junction, head right. After curving left through a small patch of woods, the trail continues along the right side of a ball field, Southeast Park, on a gravel road to CT 89, 1.5 miles from the start. Follow paved CT 89 to your left briefly and then cross to a grassy area. Bear right into the woods, then continue downhill by an old well and cellar hole. Cross the abandoned tar road. Soon the trail goes left on a dirt road to the bottom of a dry dike. In flood times the cen-tral gates of the flood-control dam can be closed to limit downstream flow. Several such dikes are found in this area. Bear left to cross the stream above the flood-control gate and turn right to return to the Nipmuck Trail.

Reenter the woods. White oaks (the bark is actually light gray) stand sentinel on the trail. Soon cross a gravel road, then turn right on a second road. This road to the left is the alternate white-blazed route. A utility pole footbridge carries the trail across the Fenton River. If the bridge is not usable, return to the white-blazed trail and follow it north to the Nipmuck Trail. After crossing the bridge, bear left over some wet ground before reaching a woods road that follows along the east side of the Fenton River valley. Blue blazes and painted wooden arrows guide you through this stretch. Robins fly ahead of you in the grass, and the soulful cry of the mourning dove echoes around you.

On the Nipmuck Trail

The path now angles up onto a small gravel ridge deposited by the glacier, with the river below you at left. To your left a small stream widens into swamp pools populated with frogs and painted turtles. Dropping off the ridge, you continue through a meadow brilliant with the yellows of the goldfinch and the swallowtail butterfly. Turn left into the woods just before you reach a second gravel ridge.

Shortly you come to the Fenton River again, which is spanned by another utility pole footbridge. After crossing, follow this 30-foot-wide trout river upstream (right), keeping a cornfield on your left. The white-blazed alternate route rejoins the Nipmuck Trail on the west side of the bridge. The blue-blazed trail winds among numerous anglers' paths along the river bank—watch the blazes carefully to avoid straying. A variety of ferns grace the low spots, while the aptly named interrupted fern stands tall throughout.

Two miles from CT 89, the trail cuts to the left away from the river and uphill to Chaffeeville Road. The trail crosses the road and ascends through hard-woods and hemlocks. About 25 yards beyond the second stream crossing, you reach the junction with the southern section of the Nipmuck Trail, which starts at Pudding Lane in Mansfield. Go right (north) and hike along the base of a large outcropping. Columbine hangs from the dripping-wet rock cliffs on your left.

Beyond the drier cliffs higher up, just before the blue-blazed trail bears right steeply downhill, leave the Nipmuck Trail and follow an unmarked trail to your left up along the base of the cliff. Known locally as 50 Foot Cliff, this lookout offers fine views of eastern Connecticut woodlands. Enjoy your lunch with a view and then retrace your steps south. To add variety to your return trip, stay straight at the trail junction before crossing the bridge over the Fenton River. Follow the white-blazed alternate route through a field and then up onto higher ground, eventually joining the blue-blazed Nipmuck Trail again above the flood-control plain on a gravel road. Bear right downhill and follow the blue blazes back to your car.

42

Devil's Hopyard

Distance: 7.5 miles

Vertical rise: 800 feet

Time: 4½ hours

Rating: C

Map: USGS 7.5-minute Hamburg

Water dominates the 860 acres of Devil's Hopyard State Park: water in the form of the rushing, turbulent Eight Mile River and its tributaries; water as the agent that shaped this rugged scenic area.

Throughout this state park, you pass beneath groves of great trees, primarily hemlocks, with wide boles, straight trunks, and first limbs often 20 feet or more above the ground. They create a brush-free setting for your explorations. The main attraction is the spectacular falls and giant trees that most come to see, but we have added a loop on the other side of the road that, while less spectacular, lets you stretch your legs quite a bit more.

Devil's Hopyard became a state park in 1919 and is fully developed, with picnic tables, fireplaces, rainy-weather shelters, a campground, and several miles of hiking trails. The origin of its colorful name is lost in a welter of fanciful stories, ranging from the simple corruption of "Mr. Dibble's hopyard" to tales of mist-shrouded forms seen dancing on the ledges amid spray from the falls.

From the junction of CT 82 and CT 156 in East Haddam, drive east 0.1 mile on CT 82 to Hopyard Road, following signs to the state park. Turn left (north); follow this road 3.4 miles past the picnic area entrance and turn right to the campground (signed) on Foxtown Road. Park in the small paved lot on your left just off Hopyard Road. The campground is just beyond the pond on the left.

Cross the road and go down the trail past the covered bulletin board. Follow the gravel trail past an unmarked trail to your right that passes under a bridge. Shortly you'll pass the Millington Trail going uphill to your right, sporadically blazed red (you'll follow this trail later in this hike). Bear left and descend gently past Chapman Falls to your left. Be sure to save some time to explore the falls area after your hike.

For over a century prior to its inclusion in the state park, this 60-foot waterfall powered a mill; remains of mills and mill dams abound in New England. The sheets of water now fall freely in a series

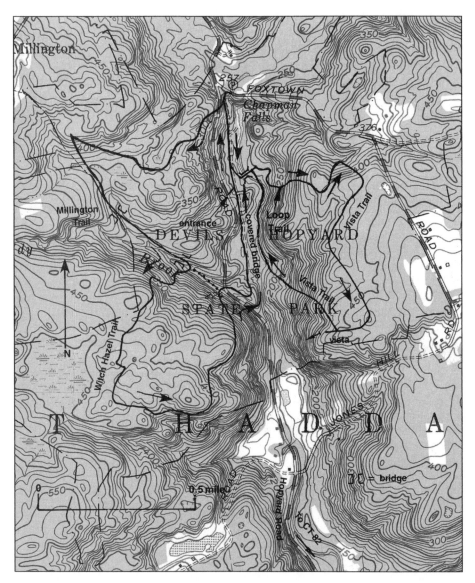

of cascades. To get the full impact of these falls you should view them from both above and below. The rocks beside the trail reveal many circular holes and a smooth, dry chute where the water used to go. The holes were formed when a hard, loose rock got caught in a small indentation in the ledge. The force of the flowing water caused this rock to gy-rate in the cavity, eventually wearing a circular hole. After the first rock has worn away, often another one falls in to continue the erosion.

Stop a moment to consider the "why" of a waterfall. It requires a special condition of hard rock overlying a softer rock, so the underlayer will erode at least as fast as the more greatly stressed upper layer. If these conditions do not exist, a waterfall will become a series of rapids or cascades that effectively move the water from a higher to a lower area, although not quite as dramatically.

You soon join the park road and continue below the picnic shelter to the covered footbridge. Cross the river (liberally stocked with trout) through the covered bridge and ascend the woods road, following blue and orange blazes on the other side. Turn left at a fork onto the blue-blazed Loop Trail. When the trail forks again, bear right and continue climbing, soon passing a large white oak with outstretched side limbs, which indicate the tree matured in a clearing or pasture. After topping the rise, come to a T-junction where you follow the sign leading to the vista, turning right on an orange-blazed trail.

Cross a brook and ascend to another fork, where you stay to the right. Pass over a rise featuring young, shade-tolerant hemlocks growing under tall pines and oak trees, biding their time for the larger trees to pass away. Descending, you'll pass another tableau of forest succession: large, dead hemlocks interspersed with oaks. The shade once cast by the tall evergreens no longer blocks out the sunlight. The tall, straight oaks in this stand will spread out their branches some more, and new trees will come in now that sunlight is again plentiful.

Cross another stream and pass over a rise, leveling out until you come to a large, dead hemlock blazed with an orange arrow directing you to the right. Proceed downhill, following the orange blazes toward the vista. Soon follow a footpath that breaks to your left off the main trail. Follow this path downhill for about 150 yards to a rocky outcropping on the edge of a steep drop.

The Eight Mile River valley lies below you. Hemlocks cloak the steep hillsides. The remains of a dammed pond form the centerpiece of your view; directly beyond, a single farm and a field break the undulating blanket of treetops. A closer look shows that the field is an alluvial fan. Eroding water tore this material from the hills behind it and, when the current slowed, dropped this debris in a fan-shaped area, flattening the valley floor and creating an optimal area for farming.

After enjoying the vista, retrace your steps to the main trail, watching carefully for the junction, and head left downhill. Your orange-blazed trail bears right toward the river and follows it upstream. After a bit, the trail passes over a stepped ledge to a hemlock-covered flat. It then runs gently down to the covered bridge, passing the blue-blazed Loop Trail to your right.

Cross the bridge and go right up the road toward the parking lot where you left your car. Turn left on the sporadically red-blazed Millington Trail. Follow the trail just below and then across the road. The well-used foot trail continues diagonally left, slabbing gently up the hill. Pass straight through two four-way trail junctions, following occasional ski markers. Follow a ridgetop to a sunken woods road. Turn left to take this road downhill. This junction is marked with an arrow on a large tulip tree, and the red blazes become more frequent.

Follow the woods road, and after passing some angular boulders you will cross a sturdy wooden bridge built by a Youth Conservation Corps team in 1978. Pass a woods road to your left. Stay straight here on the red-blazed woods road. Descend into a hemlock stand and cross a plank bridge over Muddy Brook just below Baby Falls. Immediately on the other side, a yellow-blazed trail cuts in; turn right to climb uphill away from the well-worn woods road. You soon pass the falls, which are on the right and down a steep hill.

View to Eight Mile River valley

When ready, continue following the yellow blazes uphill. You are now on the Witch Hazel Trail. Proceed up the steep grade and move away from the stream. Your climb will level out and cross the top of a rise, passing through an area lush with ferns: Christmas, cinnamon, beech, and New York. The woods here are a mixture of oak, black birch, and hickory.

Turn downward; at one point you pass under a canopy of ancient mountain laurel bushes. The tops are 10 to 15 feet above you, supported by boles almost as thick as your leg.

Finally, make a steep descent through a thick grove of hemlocks. Note the almost total lack of undergrowth where these trees grew thickest. Besides the shade, the strong tannin from years of accumulation of fallen needles and other debris prevents most plants from gaining a foothold, creating a practically monocultural grove. Now that these trees are dying out, we'll see how fast new trees and shrubs can move in.

Just as you emerge from the woods you join the red-blazed woods road that you left a mile or so back. Turn right and soon reach the paved road. Cross Hopyard Road and proceed down the now dark-red-blazed trail; the yellow blazes ended at the tar road. Pass through another grove of hemlocks. Bear left and join an old tote road. You will soon see the Eight Mile River on your right.

You come again to the stream that you crossed on the other side of the road. Now it is large enough that you may be glad to see the small footbridge a few yards downstream. Follow the red-blazed woods road to a gate at the tar park road that services the park picnic area. Follow this right past several small parking lots and up the hill to your car.

43

Seven Falls

Distance: 8 miles

Vertical rise: 900 feet

Time: 4½ hours

Rating: C

Map: USGS 7.5-minute Middle Haddam

Laying out a hiking trail is more an art than a science; the shortest distance between two points does not necessarily provide the most interesting hiking. A trail that is properly laid out directs you to the best of an area's natural features, thus offering you the finest hike possible. This stretch of the Mattabesett Trail, which starts at Seven Falls south of Middletown, does just that. Its corkscrew route approaches, circles, and often climbs the boulders and rock ridges that are so characteristic of the local terrain.

Another attraction of this hike is the number of loop trails. The main trail is blazed with blue rectangles and the loop trails, generally shorter, are marked with blue circles. We suggest that you go out on the main trail and return on the blue-circle loops to maximize hike variety.

While our route follows the Mattabesett Trail as far as Bear Hill and returns on several loops for a distance of just over 7 miles, you can shorten the hike by taking only the first or the first two loops for a total distance of 2.5 or 5.5 miles, respectively. This hike is far more difficult to describe than to follow, as the junctions are well signed to assist you in finding your way.

The hike begins by the Seven Falls Roadside Park on CT 154 south of Middletown. Leave CT 9 on exit 10 (Aircraft Road) and follow CT 154 south (right) for 0.8 mile. The park is on your left, and roadside parking is available just west of the park, where the Mattabesett Trail enters the woods.

Follow the rectangular blue blazes of the Mattabesett Trail down along the brook to the falls area. To your right, before reaching the brook, you pass the blue-circle trail to your left. Across the brook is the picnic area. About 100 yards from the road, turn left at the double blaze (the upper blaze is displaced in the direction of the turn) by a smaller brook. As we followed this brook upstream in early spring, we watched a water snake wind its way along the brook bottom. Not once did we see him come up for air.

Picnickers have worn an aimless laby-

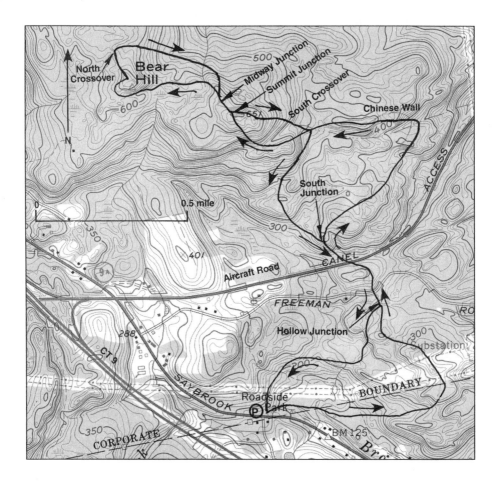

rinth of trails through this section; most go nowhere, so be careful to stick with the blue blazes. Shortly you cross this smaller brook near the power line clearing and wind up on a wooded hill. You soon reach and cross an old tote road; at a second tote road, go left, paralleling the power line. Along this stretch the trail skirts, surmounts, and circles numerous ledges and boulders. In 0.6 mile you pass a Middletown/Haddam boundary marker—a crosspiece with M/H on it on a rod set into a rock. From the marker ascend the ledge to your left and follow the blue blazes carefully. Several vantage points offer views of the numerous

forested, rolling hills with only a few houses nestled here and there.

Two high-voltage power lines cut through the woods 0.2 mile farther on. Be careful of this and all such crossings. The route rarely goes straight across the clearing, and except for a possible blaze on the poles there are frequently no markers between the parallel, but widely separated, forest walls. In partial compensation, the blazes on the forest edges are often deliberately made larger.

When you reach Hollow Junction, 1.4 miles from your car, the blue-circle trail bears uphill to your left, while the blue rectangular blazes continue straight

Nature's tic-tac-toe

downhill. Go straight here to descend to paved Freeman Road in about 0.1 mile, and then in another 0.1 mile, the busier, paved Aircraft Road (labeled Canal Access on the map). Climb the hill to South Junction (1.7 miles from the start), where a second loop trail bears left. Keep to the main trail, which forks to your right. The path tends generally uphill at first and then heads down, crossing a brook several times before climbing another ridge about 1 mile from South Junction. You cross another brook and scramble over ledges and across the top of the Chinese Wall, a long, uniform escarpment that ends just before reaching South Crossover, 1.2 miles from South Junction. This blue-circle trail crosses the main route here.

Continuing on the main trail, you reach Summit Junction (good view west across to Bear Hill) about 0.4 mile from South Crossover. In another 0.1 mile, you bear left on the main trail at Midway Junction. Climb to the top of Bear Hill (640 feet) on the main trail (rectangles) in another 0.5 mile, about 3.9 miles from the start. Look for the two US Geological Survey bench markers—one to your right, one to your left. The profusion of huckleberries here would have been a major attraction for bears, hence the probable origin for its name. Continue on the blue-blazed trail, turning left to descend on an old woods road, and then bearing left off that to stay on the ridge. Drop abruptly to another junction ¼ mile from the summit, the North Crossover. Bear right on this woods road blazed with blue circles. You are now on the Bear Hill Loop Trail.

Pass through the recovering burned-over north slope of Bear Hill. Many of the oaks and pitch pines bear the scorch marks of a small forest fire. After ½ mile, rejoin the main trail at Midway Junction and ascend to the rocky hilltop and Summit Junction. Bear left to follow the blue-circle trail down to South Crossover. Cross the main trail and descend ½ mile through open hardwood forest to the ledges of South Junction. Retrace your steps across Aircraft and Freeman Roads and soon bear right onto the blue-circle-blazed Seven Falls Loop, which passes over and around ledges, then skirts a pond just above a small cascade. Cross the power line clearing just before descending to the main trail, which you follow briefly to CT 154 and your car.

44

Talcott Mountain

Distance: 8½ miles

Vertical rise: 700 feet

Time: 4¾ hours

Rating: C

Map: USGS 7.5-minute Avon

Close by the city of Hartford is a large, attractive area of open reservoir land. Preserved to maintain water purity, areas such as this one in West Hartford are often open to nonpolluting activities. A nice day brings out an endless procession of walkers, joggers, bicyclists, hikers, and—in winter—ski tourers. The value of this land is incalculable. This hike will also take you over another of Connecticut's traprock ridges. We'll follow the Metacomet Trail over Talcott Mountain, passing by Heublein Tower, one of the state's most prominent landmarks. Metacomet, or King Philip, Wampanoag sachem, gave his name to one of our Indian Wars, the 17th-century King Philip's War.

From the junction of US 44 and CT 10 South in Avon, proceed east for 2.3 miles on US 44. On your left (north), a sign indicates Reservoir 6, Metropolitan District. Turn in here to park.

Walk to the far end of the parking lot, pass a mounted reservoir map, and bear left on the dirt road that is barred to motor vehicles. Pass the gate and proceed north. This soon becomes the blue-blazed Metacomet Trail. Along your route are the great rhubarblike leaves of the burdock; its nondescript flowers yield the round, multihook burrs that dogs and hikers pick up in the fall. These plants usually grow alongside trails and at hikers' campsites, because when hikers stop and remove them from their socks or pants they throw the burrs or seeds down where they are. The fresh green growth of grapevines edges out into the dirt road, where they are soon beaten back by the pounding feet of joggers. Shaded by hemlock, spruce, and pine, this west shore of the reservoir is lovely any time of the year.

The wind-stirred wavelets on the reservoir reflect the sun in a sparkling glitter that adds life to this shifting scene. Along the shallow edges of the water swim numerous species of the sunfish family, including the black bass; this border area provides protection from predators and is handy for snaring land-based insect life.

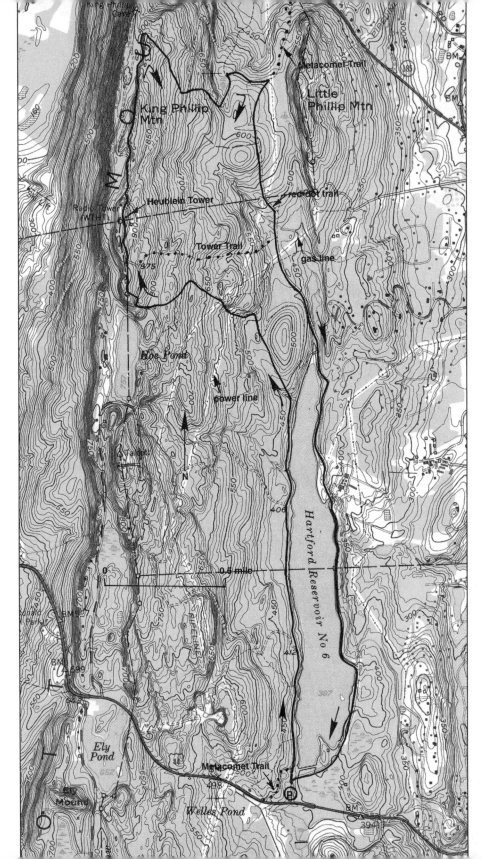

King Phillip Cave

Metacomet Trail

Little
Phillip Mtn

King Phillip
Mtn

Radio Tower
(WTIC)

Heublein Tower

reservoir trail

Tower Trail

gas line

Hoe Pond

power line

tangent

N

Hartford Reservoir No 6

0   0.5 mile

Donald
Park

BM 327

BM 539

Ely Pond

Ely
Mound

Metacomet Trail

Welles Pond

BM

394

The shiny-leafed vine on the reservoir side of a cement bridge is the harmless five-leafed Virginia creeper, but the small cement-and-stone bridge abutment used to be covered with great masses of poison ivy. There is still much poison ivy along the way; nestled within its foliage you may find its lovely, greenish yellow blossoms. Along here we saw a pair of 4-foot black rat snakes. Effective rodent eaters, they are now considered a threatened species by the Connecticut Herpetological Society. Like many of our larger creatures, its major enemy is man!

Farther along, the great torrent of water pouring into Reservoir 6 is ducted from another reservoir in an extensive system. Hartford gets most of its water from the Shepaug and Barkhamsted reservoirs in northern Connecticut; the West Hartford reservoirs serve largely for holding and storage, rather than as prime sources of water.

Continue along the west shore of the reservoir. Before reaching the north end and a bridge crossing, turn left to follow a woods road uphill away from the reservoir. The turn is marked with blue blazes and a small cairn. Continue uphill on woods roads and pass under a power line and, not long after, through a gas pipeline clearing. After passing through a stand of white birch trees, you'll reach the paved ridge road and bear right briefly before reentering the woods to the west to ascend to the traprock ridgeline.

Pass under a relay tower and continue to the summit development featuring stone garages, picnic pavilions, and a barbecue pit installed to entertain then General Eisenhower.

Soon you'll pass to the left of Heublein Tower. This 165-foot structure is the most ornate of the four towers situated on this ridgetop. Built in 1914, it was home to the family of Gilbert Heublein, the liquor magnate, for over 30 years.

The tower and almost 600 acres of land were protected by the state of Connecticut in 1965 through a coalition of government agencies and private conservationists and presently form Talcott Mountain State Park. The tower has visiting hours from mid-April to November; contact the Connecticut State Parks Division (860-424-3200) for details. The view encompasses nearly 1200 square miles; on the northern horizon you can pick out New Hampshire's Mount Monadnock (the second most climbed mountain in the world; the first is Mount Fuji in Japan) some 80 miles to the north; the Berkshires in western Massachusetts; the hills of eastern Rhode Island; and Long Island Sound to the south.

Follow the woods road north and bear right to remain on the ridgeline. After following the crest with intermittent views to the west, turn right on the blue-blazed Metacomet Trail and follow a winding woods road down the east side of King Philip Mountain. After a stream crossing, climb briefly over a small rise and descend to a power-line clearing. Turn right onto a woods road just before the clearing and soon find blue blazes with red dots marking your route south. Ascend gently past a solitary stone chimney and continue to the power-line clearing, where you briefly follow the service road to the right before entering the woods on the far side.

Cross a stream and then a pipeline clearing. You'll go straight through a woods road crossing; this is the old tower trail. Soon your woods road will reach the reservoir and you'll pass the bridge at the northern end to your right. Bear left to follow the reservoir's eastern shore. As you top a hill, the Metropolitan District Commission's filtration plant for Bloomfield comes into view. Beyond is the ever-growing Hartford skyline. From this point on, your route is in the open,

Talcott Mountain from Penwood's Pinnacle

fully exposed to cold winds in season. An extra sweater and windbreaker may be necessary. The dirt road joins and briefly follows the plant's tar road along the wooded shore.

Keep along the reservoir, following the lesser-used tar road. This road turns to dirt in a few yards and follows the length of the reservoir bank. As you look back, the Heublein Tower thrusts up above the ridge. The rock riprap lining the banks below you retards erosion.

When you come to a tar road again, stay on the path between it and the water. At the fork, bear left uphill away from the reservoir. (A right turn will take you out to the end of a point of land, which is worth the detour.) After crossing a causeway, you soon emerge on the road within sight of the parking lot.

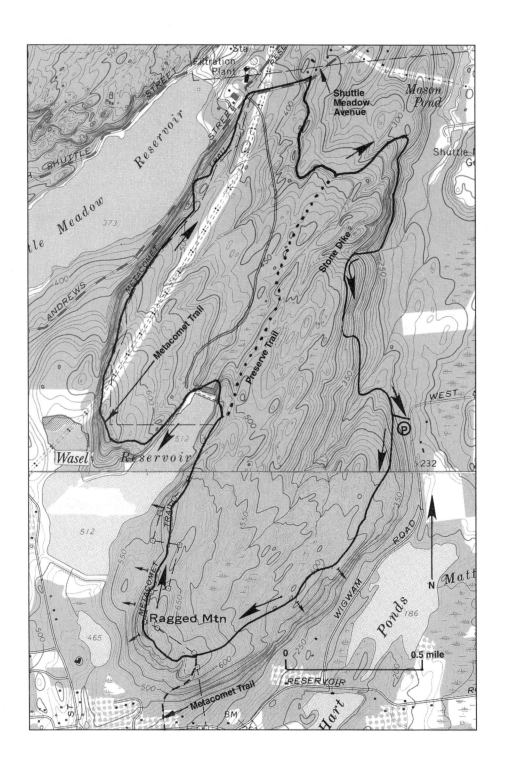

45

Ragged Mountain

Distance: 9.1 miles

Time: 5 hours

Vertical rise: 1000 feet

Rating: A

Maps: USGS 7.5-minute New Britain, Meriden

Rock climbing is a sport for people who want to mix physical and mental challenge with some risk. Perhaps the urge to rock-climb is innate, but the skills must be learned and learned well! Every year several neophytes take the rock-climbing course offered by the Connecticut Chapter of the Appalachian Mountain Club. Only a few graduate, but they are usually hooked for life.

This hike passes Ragged Mountain, the premier rock-climbing area in Connecticut (consult *Traprock* by Ken Nichols, published by the American Alpine Club), and the place where the course for beginners is given. You may see them in action (and marvel at their daring) on these cliffs.

To get to this area of volcanic cliffs, start from the junction of CT 372 and CT 71A in New Britain. From CT 372 (Corbin Avenue), take CT 71A (Chamberlain Highway) south for 1.1 miles. Turn onto West Lane. Proceed on West Lane for 0.6 mile to Ragged Mountain Memorial Preserve (563 acres) to your right. There is room for parking alongside the road.

Follow the blue blazes with red dots of the Ragged Mountain Preserve Trail about 100 yards to the beginning of the trail loop. You will start out on the left arm of the loop and return on the right.

Immediately bear left off the woods road. Be careful not to continue blithely along a well-defined woods road and miss the trail turn, which is easy to do. Bear left yet again away from the well-worn path, which continues straight. Climb gently on the trail, which is well marked with blue/red blazes. Soon you'll level out and go due south, then continue climbing past an old woods road on your right, and then level out yet again.

The Connecticut woodlands are crisscrossed with innumerable woods roads; some are easily followed, some have become choked with brush, and some are so faint as to defy certain identification. These roads were cut and used (usually for just a short time) to harvest the wood and charcoal that were major products

The top of Ragged Mountain's cliffs

of our woodlands in the last couple of centuries. The abandoned roads are slowly but surely being obliterated by the healing hand of nature. Pass over a rise and then turn sharply right to cross another old woods road. After another brief stint on a woods road, bear left and climb to a rocky ridge where Hart Ponds are visible through the trees. Continue on the ridge, soon climbing to an excellent lookout above the ponds. Drop down briefly and return to the ridgetop, reaching another fine viewpoint above Reservoir Road. Continue on open ledges with fine views to the south where West Peak (see Hike 37), with its towers (one of the highest traprock ridges in Connecticut), can be seen in the distance.

The trail drops into and then climbs out of another small ravine. Permanent water is rare in traprock—snowmelt and rain soon run off this impervious rock, leaving most ravines stark and dry. Continue south along a small, rocky ridge, and then turn down and left off the end of the ridge before climbing again to more views and a free-standing wall—difficult to describe but unmistakable when you see it—1.2 miles from the start. The tops of central Connecticut's traprock ridges provide exhilarating hiking with excellent views.

Join the blue-blazed Metacomet Trail on top of Small Cliff, south of Ragged Mountain's summit. Follow the blue blazes down into a ravine and then scramble up the traprock to the top of the cliffs, which are largely wooded here. In about another ¼ mile of gentle ups and downs you will come out into the open on the summit of Ragged Mountain. Here, of necessity, many of the blue blazes are painted on rocks instead of trees.

We've sat atop the cliffs and watched three sea gulls play follow-the-leader above the reservoir. Large birds often use the thermals associated with cliffs to soar for hours with nary a wingbeat. Far below you can see strollers sauntering along the reservoir dike.

Bear right away from the cliffs, drop down, and climb again as the trail undulates along the ridge. A final lookout offers views of the northern end of Wasel Reservoir.

Volcanic ridgetops are usually not good places to find large varieties of flowers, but we have found one especially favorite flower in Connecticut's traprock (but rarely elsewhere): pale corydalis, a member of the poppy family, closely related to bleeding heart and Dutchman's breeches. Whenever you traverse these ridges, be on the lookout for this striking rose-and-yellow flower.

Wind along the ridge down toward the reservoir's shore. The rugged trail surface requires proper hiking footgear—not street shoes. Near the end of the reservoir on an open rocky ledge, pass the blue-and-red-blazed preserve loop to your right. (You can shorten this hike by 3 miles by following this trail back around to the preserve.) Continue on the Metacomet Trail along the ridge and pass over a rocky promontory directly across from the dam below. Follow the trail east beyond the dam and then steeply descend some step ledges. This part of the trail requires some use of your hands to get down the rock wall. If this kind of hiking is more hair-raising than adventurous for you, we recommend returning to the preserve loop trail.

After reaching the floodplain below the dam, double back toward the dam and then cross the field to your right. Climb to the top of the dam's western end through a cleft in the ledge. Ragged Mountain's cliffs stand in profile across the reservoir. Cross the dam access road and bear left to follow a gravel road on the north side of the reservoir. This road is sparsely blazed, but the subsequent right turn off it in nearly ½ mile is well marked.

Ascend to the top of the ridge and cross a power-line clearing at its highest point. Bear right and soon reenter the woods to follow the northern escarpment over Shuttle Meadow Reservoir. The trail along the ridge is well shaded by pitch pine, red cedar, and hemlock. The thick woods can provide a much-needed windbreak on windy days and can be especially welcome after you've crossed the exposed top of Ragged Mountain. Follow this ridge for a mile, passing vistas over the reservoir, before coming out onto a grassy woods road. Proceed on the road until you reach Shuttle Meadow Avenue. Turn right and follow the pavement, taking care to stay on the edge of this fairly busy road.

Cross a canal and turn right to follow the feeder trail (blue blazes with red dots) south along it. After ½ mile, turn left at a well-signed junction. To the right, the preserve trail leads back to Ragged Mountain. Follow woods roads east and descend toward a meadow before curving to the right to stay in the woods.

After about ¾ mile, your trail turns sharply to your right and climbs alongside a small stream (crossing it once) to a lovely waterfall. Here you will find the remnants of a stone dike. Climb carefully up the loose traprock slope to the ridgetop and turn left as the trail continues south. Here, though not well worn, the trail is well blazed. Descend along the hillside, and descend again. Soon you cross a deeply eroded old road, then a brook, and then descend gradually to an old woods road.

Go right about 0.1 mile to reach the beginning of the loop you started a few hours ago. At the junction, go left to your car.

46

Cockaponset

Distance: 10.1 miles

Vertical rise: 900 feet

Time: 5½ hours

Rating: CD

Map: USGS 7.5-minute Haddam

Cockaponset State Forest is a 15,000-acre monument to the Civilian Conservation Corps (CCC). In its heyday (1933–1942), Cockaponset forest was home to three camps with a workforce three times as large as is presently employed in the entire state forest system. The passage of decades has not obliterated the roadside fireholes, stonework ditches, stepped trails, and tasteful plantings.

This hike starts by Pattaconk Reservoir in Chester. From CT 9 take exit 6 to CT 148. Follow this road west 1.5 miles to Cedar Lake Road and turn right. Go 1.5 miles to the entrance to the Lake Pattaconk State Recreation Area and turn left. In 0.4 mile (past the beach), there are parking lots on both sides of the road.

You are at the Filley Road crossing of the Cockaponset Trail. This 10.1-mile hike makes three loops and may easily be shortened to 2.3 or 5.8 miles by taking just the first or the first two loops. The entire trail has been wheeled (distances have been measured accurately using a calibrated wheel), and at all junctions away from the road crossings there are signs posting distances to various spots on the trail. However, signs at junctions are notoriously hard to maintain, as they are too tempting a target for vandals and souvenir hunters. Your hike follows the Cockaponset Trail (blue blazes) north to the Beaver Brook junction and returns using the loop trails (red dot on a blue blaze) wherever possible.

Proceed through the parking lot on the west (right as you're coming from Cedar Lake Road) side of the road, following the blue blazes as the trail leaves the far left end of the parking lot. Your trail soon goes right on a gravel road to Pattaconk Crossing (junction #4). Bear left to stay on the blue-blazed Cockaponset Trail, heading north to Old County Road. Cross a series of three woodland brooks, each one more lovely than the one before; all three flow into Pattaconk Reservoir.

When we first scouted this trail, thousands of chipmunks enlivened these

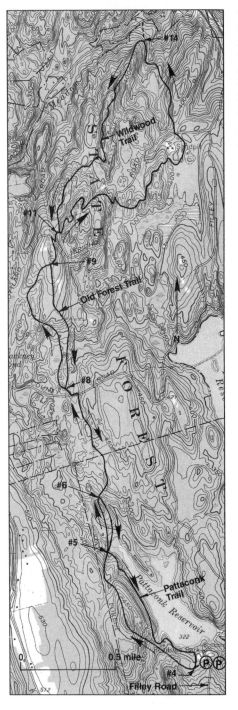

woods. Six years later we didn't see any. Chipmunks, like many of the small mammals whose numbers are not effectively limited by predators, go through population cycles. From a very low point, their numbers increase steadily year by year until they seem to be everywhere; then disease and/or starvation decimates their population and the cycle starts over again.

After crossing several more streams, the trail climbs and then descends gently to Pattaconk Brook at junction #5 (see map), 1.2 miles from your car. Cross the brook over stones arranged to keep your boots dry. Beware of slippery rocks! This is where you return on the Pattaconk Trail to your right if you wish to do only the 2.3-mile option.

Remain on the blue-blazed trail, reaching another brook crossing in 0.3 mile at North Pattaconk, junction #6 (see map). Just before the junction, look for the patch of bright red cardinal flowers. Here you rejoin the original Cockaponset Trail (now the Pattaconk Trail from junction #4 to #6), which is well worn and easy to follow. The Pattaconk Trail to your right ends here.

Follow the blue-blazed Cockaponset Trail north from junction #6 for 0.8 mile to Old County Road. In spring the ledges in this section are decorated with dwarf ginseng, white violet, wood anemone, Solomon's seal, and a profusion of mountain laurel.

Turn left on Old County Road and proceed for 0.1 mile before turning right at the bottom of a hill on a tote road. Pass Old County Road junction #8 (see map) where the Old Forest Trail bears to your right up a woods road. On your left is a laurel-covered hillside, on your right a brushy swamp. Follow the blue blazes north and uphill off the tote road, soon passing a small rock outcropping to overlook a dammed-up cattail swamp. Proceed with the swamp pond on your left, soon crossing the old dam. Originally built by the CCC in 1936, the dam's height was increased 3 feet in 1979.

Your blue-blazed trail bears left along the pond through azaleas and laurels. Passing a rock jumble to your right, proceed through a lovely laurel tunnel to another large rock jumble on your right. Follow the blue blazes through a recently logged area and cross a skid road. Timber harvesting appears to be increasing in Connecticut's woodlands. So far the hiking trails are still easy to follow. Such a collaboration between recreation and resource management can make a difference in favor of land for trails, when legislative appropriations for land protection are discussed.

Soon the trail joins a woods road and reaches Jericho junction #9 (see map), 3.1 miles from the start. Here is where you can head back to your right—following the red-dot-on-blue-blaze trail (Old Forest Trail)—if you wish to hike only 5.8 miles.

Just before you reach gravel Jericho Road, you pass a small stand of red spruce; this is the only native spruce found in any numbers in Connecticut. Its needle-covered twigs, when boiled with molasses or a similar sweetener and fermented, yield spruce beer, a good scurvy remedy. The colonists also used spruce to flavor homemade ales before hops were common in America.

Bear right a short distance on Jericho Road past an old CCC water hole on your left, then turn left back into the woods. Almost immediately you reach Wildwood junction #11 (see map), where the Wildwood Trail goes to your left. Stay straight along the blue-blazed Cockaponset Trail and ascend some stone stairs.

The next mile of trail to the second crossing of Jericho Road is a work of art: trail layout and construction at their best. It is stepped, curbed, graded, and routed by all points of interest. It was constructed only incidentally for the ease and comfort of the hiker; after 40 years of use, erosion here is practically nonexistent. Around Memorial Day weekend, lady's slippers are in bloom everywhere along this woodland path.

The trail in the midst of this scenic mile climbs and follows a brush-crowned, rocky ridge. At one point along this ridge are four spaced concrete blocks to your right, the underpinnings of an old fire tower. These remnants tell two stories: the prominence of this ridge as a lookout and the substitution of modern, efficient fire-spotting planes. To reach a fire tower with its warden standing his lonely vigil was once a favorite goal for hikers, for both good views and good stories.

After crossing Jericho Road again, the laurel-lined trail passes several low, protruding ledges patched with large clumps of rock tripe. Shortly, the trail skirts a swamp on your left, which is sprinkled with tiny yellow spicebush blossoms in early spring.

About 0.5 mile from the road crossing, watch the blue blazes carefully, as there are several unmarked trails leading left to a campground. Soon pass a small pond on your right and go through a field to cross Jericho Road again, 5.1 miles from your car. Continue gently downhill, then uphill through the laurel. You will first hear, then see, the brook rushing along to your left. Cross the brook and continue through a small stand of hemlock to a huge downed hemlock on your right—this giant broke off about 15 feet above the ground! Immediately cross another brook before coming to Beaver Brook junction #14 (see map), 5.6 miles from the start.

Here you start your return. You will take the loop trail whenever possible, marked with a red dot on blue blazes.

Small dam—Cockaponset State Forest

Leave the familiar blue blazes and bear left on Wildwood Trail. You'll meet and then cross a dirt road, turning south and climbing to a wooded hilltop. Dropping down, you'll soon level out and continue through a laurel tunnel and then through pines.

Cross Jericho Road for the fourth and last time just south of Wildwood junction #11, about 1.5 miles from junction #14. Follow the Cockaponset Trail to Jericho junction #9 and bear left on the Old Forest Trail, a deeply rutted tote road. Rejoin the blue-blazed Cockaponset Trail, proceed south past Old County Road, and bear left on the Pattaconk Trail at North Pattaconk junction #6. Follow this well-worn path, part of the old Cockaponset Trail, past junction #5 to the edge of Pattaconk Reservoir.

The rattling cry of the kingfisher frequently shatters the woodland silence here. From a well-chosen perch these brilliant blue-and-white birds spot a small fish and then plunge headfirst into the water to snare it.

After nearly a mile, pass a beach to your left and bear right uphill away from the reservoir. Soon you'll reach Pattaconk Crossover junction #4. Here take the blue-blazed trail to your left to the parking lot.

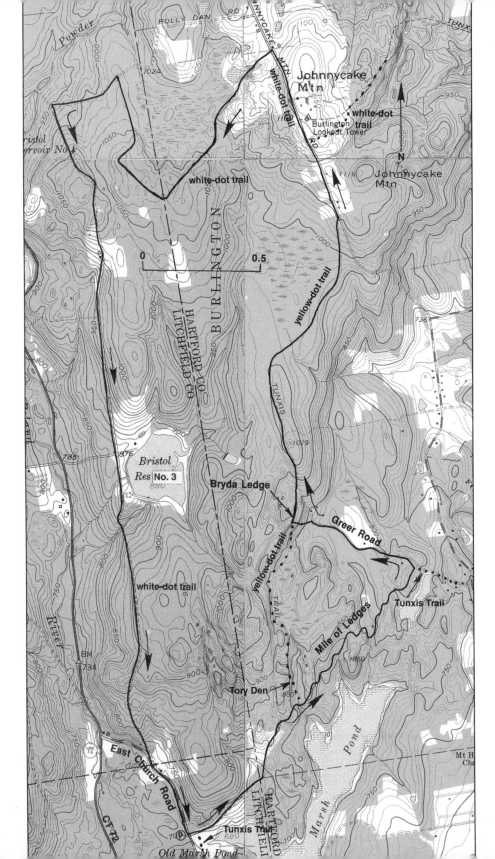

47

Tunxis Ramble

Distance: 9.5 miles

Vertical rise: 970 feet

Time: 5½ hours

Rating: BC

Maps: USGS 7.5-minute Thomaston, Bristol, Torrington, Collinsville

After a hiker gets his "sea legs," short, flat, often comparatively monotonous trails no longer hold the appeal they once did. Aesthetic sense demands a more varied terrain; toughened muscles, more of a challenge. The lengthy Tunxis Ramble with its Mile of Ledges should satisfy both these needs nicely. The loop route described here makes a delightful hike through the forest north of Bristol, particularly in June when the laurel is in flower.

From the junction of CT 4 and CT 72 west in Harwinton, proceed south on CT 72 for 4.4 miles. Turn left on East Church Road, and after 0.7 mile park on the left just past a gate. Walk around the gate to follow the well-worn tote road. Soon the Tunxis Trail, here marked with solid blue blazes, enters from your right. Continue on the tote road, now the blue-blazed "main line" of the northbound Tunxis Trail. Side trails, marked with blue blazes with a yellow dot in the center and blue blazes with a white dot in the center, will also be used to complete this circuit.

Proceed along the well-beaten tote road. Gill-over-the-ground, a little flower whose fanciful name rivals its delicate purple beauty, is plentiful here. On your left, at the edge of a large planting of red pines, a huge, gnarled maple exudes character. The maple's twisting, wide-spreading limbs overgrown with green plants and fungi are only part of the attraction. Here is the commonplace, blown up to heroic proportions!

Follow the tote road as it passes a swamp filled with skunk cabbage. About 0.6 mile from the start, reach a junction with the yellow-dot trail. Follow the yellow-dot trail briefly north to Tory Den, a small set of ledges with nooks and crannies to crawl through. This was a hiding place for Tories when the local Patriots rampaged. Return to the junction and turn left (east) to follow the blue-blazed Tunxis Trail to the Mile of Ledges. This part of the trail is a long series of boulders, ledges, and cleft rocks. In June, the faint perfume and showy flowers of

Along the Mile of Ledges

mountain laurel growing from dark recesses in moss-cushioned rocks heighten the beauty of each twist and turn. Pass a pond (to your right) sporting a prominent beaver lodge. As you leave the ledges, the twangs and jug-a-rums of the green frogs and bullfrogs echo through the humid air.

When you reach paved Greer Road, 2.2 miles from the start, turn left. After about 0.5 mile, just before the pavement ends, turn left to follow the blue-blazed trail into the woods and up the wooded slope to reach a junction at the top of the rise along Bryda Ledge. This route passes near a house to your left. Please respect the rights of property owners; much of our hiking is done on private land and is not a right, but a too easily lost privilege.

Here you take the trail marked with a yellow dot on a blue blaze to your right up the hill. To your left this trail leads back to Tory Den. Stout-stemmed bracken fern, a lover of dry ground, and yellow-blossomed whorled loosestrife are prevalent here.

The yellow-dot trail climbs over Bryda Ledge and soon reaches an old road. About 1 mile from the junction, bear left along the south slope of Johnnycake Mountain. After another 0.5 mile you reach gravel Johnnycake Mountain Road; bear left and soon continue straight on the now paved road. The next mile of road walking takes you by a private game farm at the top of the hill. Strutting peacocks utter unearthly cries from their pens. (The peacocks' showy beauty is balanced by their loud—and anything but melodious—cry.) The sides of the road are rife with vegetation: meadow rue, angelica, wild geranium,

yarrow, and horsemint are common, and orange daylily, an attractive alien escaped from colonial gardens, abounds.

Old Field Road, the white-dot route, turns to your right. Continue north on Johnnycake Mountain Road following the white dots for another ½ mile. Just before reaching a brick house on your right, turn left off the road and cross a field to a low point where a white pine and a maple are standing together. There has been a sign noting this trail relocation at this turn on the road. If you missed the turn, Polly Dan Road is 0.2 mile beyond it; turn around to look for the turn, now to your right.

Stay to the left of a field along a ledge in hemlock woods. Soon you'll stay on the high ground to the left of swamps. Occasionally you'll catch a glimpse of some trees killed when water from a beaver dam flooded them out.

Bear left on a woods road and gently descend. Turn left onto another tote road and pass over a rise through some recent logging. The trail on the worn road is easy to follow through the work area. Soon you'll pass a house on your right, and the road you've been walking becomes paved. Farther on, you cross Blueberry Hill Road and pass through a gate. Reservoir #3 is to your left. Continue straight on the gravel road on Bristol Water Department property. When the road bends left, proceed straight into the woods on an overgrown tote road with white-dot blazes. On this trail, continue downhill, cross a brook with steep banks, climb once again, level out, then descend gradually, reaching a gravel driveway that leads to East Church Road. Your car is parked 0.4 mile down the road to your left.

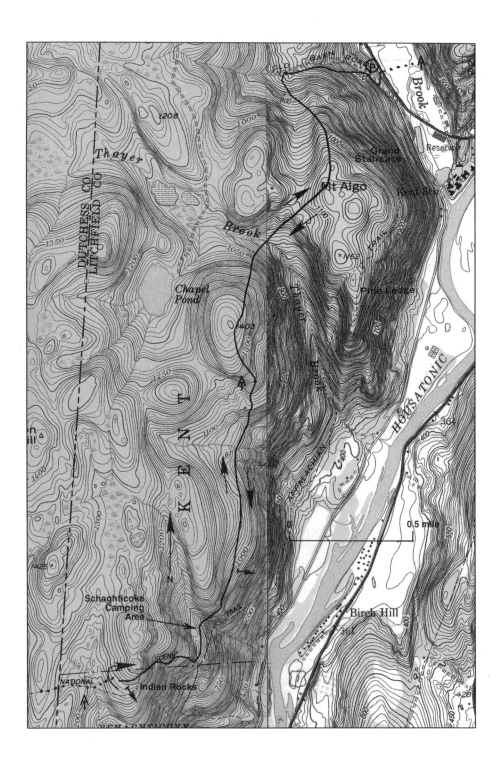

48

Algo and Schaghticoke

Distance: 7.6 miles

Vertical rise: 2600 feet

Time: 5½ hours

Rating: AB

Maps: USGS 7.5-minute Kent, Dover Plains (NY-CT)

The Appalachian Trail (AT) offers some of Connecticut's finest, and most difficult, hiking. Some folks opt to hike the entire trail, over 2000 miles from Georgia to Maine, in one season. This section of the AT is a fitting introduction to rugged New England for the northbound "through-hiker." The southern end of this hike goes through the Schaghticoke Indian Reservation.

The Schaghticokes are descended from Sassacus's Pequots, who were dispersed by the 1637 Pequot War, the first of America's Indian Wars. The surviving Pequots were scattered and enslaved by the victorious colonists. During the Revolutionary War over 100 Schaghticoke warriors joined the American cause; serving as a signal corps, they used drums and signal fires to relay messages from Stockbridge, Massachusetts, to Long Island Sound.

Timber rattlesnakes are seen occasionally on the Appalachian Trail, but are very rare and endangered in Connecticut. Snakes by nature want no part of humans and will quickly get away whenever possible. Unless you pick them up or step on them, no snakes found in Connecticut's woods will bite you. In all our years of hiking in the state, we've never seen a rattlesnake. If you should be lucky enough to see one, enjoy the sight from a safe distance, and let one of nature's most efficient rodent controls continue to grace its highland home.

Follow CT 341 0.8 mile west from its junction with US 7 in Kent to the Appalachian Trail crossing. Park on the left side of the highway. Opposite a field to the east, take the white-blazed AT west up the heavily shaded hillside. Turn right onto an old tote road through hemlocks, and then bear left, continuing steadily uphill. You'll cross several rock water bars installed to divert water from the trail before it can erode the path. Pass a blue-blazed trail to your right; it leads to the Mount Algo lean-to.

Continue the long, rocky ascent through oak and laurel to reach the height-of-land to the west of Mount

Algo from the Housatonic River

Algo. Descend to Thayer Brook and climb steeply to the high point of the hike on Schaghticoke Mountain. Here the woods are primarily the familiar oak and hickory of the dry, south-facing hillsides, with an occasional maple tree. The understory is composed of laurel and blueberry. From the height-of-land 2.1 miles into the hike, descend briefly to a ledge offering views of the Housatonic Valley. You will continue to follow ledges downhill, passing occasional vistas. In winter, the views are plentiful through the leafless trees.

Hike along the escarpment and take a sharp right turn uphill in a jumble of boulders next to a glacial erratic boulder to your right. Descend to a small brook crossing 3.2 miles from your car and pass a blue-blazed side trail to Schaghticoke Camping Area, a tenting site for backpackers.

Climb up from the brook through hemlocks, drop down briefly into Dry Gulch, and climb steeply out of this ravine on rock stairs installed by volunteers in the mid-1980s. Volunteers maintain the Appalachian Trail in Connecticut for the Appalachian Trail Conference and the Appalachian Mountain Club (two different nonprofit cooperative groups). The conference works with the National Park Service to manage and maintain the AT from Georgia to Maine. Individual trail clubs, like the Appalachian Mountain Club (AMC), maintain sections of the trail. The Connecticut Chapter of the AMC maintains the AT in Connecticut and mobilizes volunteer work parties for construction projects like staircases or basic maintenance like brushing and blazing. Volunteers also build shelters and bridges along the trail! Trail maintainers often start out simply as day-hikers and eventually show their appreciation of the trails by volunteering and "giving something back" to the trail.

After the steep climb and a brief up-and-down, you'll pass a rocky outcrop and view to your left. This is Indian Rocks, a fine eastern view of the Housatonic River just above Bulls Bridge. You are 3.8 miles from the start of the hike and just a short distance from the New York line. A brief descent on ledges takes you to a hiker's register, a popular way for AT through-hikers to communicate with each other up and down the trail and an important way to help locate lost hikers. You should at least sign in at trail registers with your name and the date. There is no obligation to write long messages, although you are welcome to do so.

From Indian Rocks, you retrace your steps to CT 341 and your car.

49

Sleeping Giant

Distance: Option A—4.8 miles; Option B—9 miles

Vertical rise: Option A—1600 feet; Option B—1900 feet

Time: Option A—3½ hours; Option B—5½ hours

Rating: A

Maps: USGS 7.5-minute Wallingford, Mount Carmel

Some hikers belittle the size of the Sleeping Giant, for he rises only 739 feet above sea level. They forget that he is lying down; were he to awaken and get to his feet, he would stand some 2 miles tall!

A series of folded, angular volcanic hills just north of New Haven defines the shape of the reclining titan. Legend has it that the giant was first recognized and named from sailing ships in New Haven Harbor many years ago. From the various parts of his anatomy you can see numerous peaks and ridges that other hikes in this book traverse. The giant is now contained in a 1500-acre state park. Only a short distance from downtown New Haven, it is a popular spot with campers, picnickers, and hikers. In 1977 the Sleeping Giant Trail System was dedicated as a National Scenic Trail.

From I-91, take exit 10 (Hamden/Mount Carmel) onto CT 40 north. After 2.6 miles on CT 40, follow CT 10 north 1.3 miles to its junction with Mount Carmel Avenue. Turn right and follow it 0.3 mile to the park entrance on your left. There is a large parking lot with a fee.

The 32-mile park trail system, designed by Norman Greist and Richard Elliot, key members of the Sleeping Giant Park Association, is ingeniously laid out in a series of loops. No matter how long or short a hike you wish, you need never retrace your steps. Six east-west trails, marked with blue, white, violet, green, orange, and yellow blazes, join the opposite ends of the park. Five north-south trails marked with red diamonds, squares, hexagons, circles, and triangles cut across the park. The loop combinations you may devise seem endless.

We have selected two pairs of trails in Sleeping Giant. Since they start at about the same location, you can combine them for a real leg-stretcher. The Connecticut Chapter of the Appalachian Mountain Club has offered all the trails in this state park on a single day to those who want to test their hiking ability!

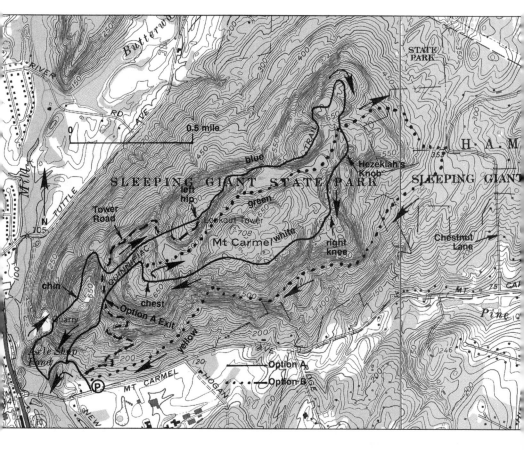

We favor the blue-white trail combination. It is the most strenuous, covers most of the giant's anatomy, and affords the best views. Alone, the blue-white circuit is Option A. Its combination with the easier green-yellow circuit is Option B.

Start up the right side of the paved picnic loop through the pine-shaded grove. To your right is a cluster of great red oaks. These tall oaks did not "from little acorns grow"; they are stump sprouts from a tree cut long ago. Tree clusters like this one are common in Connecticut's much cutover woodlands.

Follow the blue-blazed feeder trail to the right toward a gully before cutting left across the hillside. You will soon join the main blue-blazed Quinnipiac Trail, the oldest of Connecticut's Blue Trails. Bear right.

Shortly the first ascent takes you onto the giant's elbow. The trail follows the cedar-spotted basalt ridge of his crooked arm to the right, drops down, and then ascends his head. An old quarry drops off steeply to your left. The Sleeping Giant Park Association was formed in 1924 to protect the mountain from being torn down by a quarrying operation. This stretch is a long, difficult scramble—a good test of your hiking condition. Avoid this area in winter; the slope is usually icy and treacherous. An alternate

Mountain-laurel time in the Giant

route around the steepest ledges is available to your right; this route is not recommended in bad weather, either.

Back to the right you will see two ridges. The Quinnipiac Trail runs along the closer mass of shapeless hills; the Regicides Trail follows the long ridge of West Rock farther right. The neat lawns and tastefully spaced buildings of Quinnipiac College lie below.

Continue to the jutting cliff of the giant's chin. The wide path in the valley below is the Tower Trail; beyond it rises the giant's massive chest. Looking north you can see the traprock ridges known as the Hanging Hills of Meriden, where the Metacomet and Mattabesett Trails join. West Peak, a large rock mass with a crown of towers, lies at the left just beyond the rock tower of Castle Crag (see Hike 37). The flat-topped peak to the right is South Mountain. The city of Meriden fills the break in the ridge; the two hills farthest to the right are Mount Lamentation and Chauncey Peak. Lava flows formed all these traprock peaks and plateaus some 200 million years ago.

The trail zigzags steeply down the north end of the giant's head, crosses the tower road twice, and then climbs his left hip, also known as Mount Carmel, 1.5 miles from the picnic ground. Perhaps the best view in the park is from the top of the summit tower, a ramped rock structure built by the Works Progress Administration in the 1930s. The hilly panorama continues east and south; starting with Mount Lamentation, you see the impressive cliff faces of Mount Higby (see Hike 29), the gap through which US 6 passes, and the long ridge of Beseck Mountain. Like the hills to the north, these ridges are traversed by trails. The barrenness of the land makes landowners more willing to give hiking clubs permission to cut trails on hills than on their more fertile property. For-

tunately, hikers much prefer these barren hills to the low-lying fertile fields.

Follow the blue blazes past the tower and continue to the cliff edge, where you can look south to the giant's right hip, right leg, and right knee before dropping down to the right. After a level spell through white pines, dip down and then ascend his left leg. Drop again and go up the left knee. Note the pitting that centuries of exposure have produced on the weathered rocks; they contrast sharply with the smooth faces of a few recently uncovered rock surfaces nearby.

Working down the far end of the giant's knee, you encounter the first section of smooth, rolling, rock-free trail. Footing makes a tremendous difference in hiking difficulty, and the angular volcanic-rock ridges of central Connecticut are particularly treacherous. The size of the dogwoods here attests to the depth of the rich soil beneath them.

Begin your ascent of Hezekiah's Knob. As you near the top (3.2 miles from the start), look to the right for early-spring-blooming purple and white hepaticas with their characteristic three-lobed leaves left over from the previous summer's growth. The leaf's shape, supposedly like a liver, was the basis for its medicinal use for various liver problems.

The blue- and white-blazed trails meet on the knob. Proceed to your right down the hill on the white-blazed trail. When you reach the top of his right knee, look north across the valley to the giant's rocky left side, where you hiked earlier. Descend the stone-strewn slope and then climb up and down his right leg and right hip. The red-triangle trail cuts across the park by the base of the sleeping titan's chest—this path forms the last climb of this circuit. The trail winds up around the great boulders. In spring you may hear a stream echoing somewhere in the hollows beneath you.

White and green blazes mark the route here. With a last look at tiny Quinnipiac College below the giant's head across the way, you twist down off his chest on the white-blazed trail and join the Tower Trail for a short distance. The path leaves the road at right to follow a course tucked under the giant's chin to the picnic area. At the paved road, head left for the shortest route back to your car.

If you choose to hike Option B, turn right onto the green-blazed trail at its junction with the white-blazed trail on the giant's chest. The green-blazed trail crosses the park to the north side of the central spine. During the peregrinations of the trail, your path crosses many red-blazed north-south trails.

If you choose the proper season and year, the mountain laurel display will be magnificent. Almost your entire route is graced with these crag-loving bushes.

It becomes more and more obvious as you proceed that you are on an old tote road. Cross the blue-blazed trail between the left foot and Hezekiah's Knob and descend toward Chestnut Lane. Toward the east end of the park (you may have heard cars and glimpsed electric wires through the trees), the green blazes turn right into the woods. In just a few yards you come to a great meeting point where all the east-west trails converge at a gate and a bulletin board.

Go back on the yellow-blazed trail. Proceed to your right into the woods before the yellow-blazed trail straightens out and parallels the rest of the east-west trails. Even though this route is easier than most in the park, the numerous ups and downs and rough, rocky footing make it fairly tough. A few red "symbol" trails cross your path, but otherwise it is refreshingly uneventful and very quiet until you come within earshot of Mount Carmel Avenue. Near the end, our route was once blocked by the upper part of a fallen hemlock, blasted by lightning. The force of this electrical charge was so powerful it not only vaporized the sap, which lifted the bark along its path, but also snapped the tree completely off.

Soon the yellow-blazed trail joins a dirt road that goes left and continues to the beginning of the picnic circle, where you go left to reach your car.

50

Ratlum Mountain and Indian Council Cave

Distance: 13 miles

Vertical rise: 2250 feet

Time: 8 hours

Rating: B

Map: USGS 7.5-minute New Hartford

Although Connecticut does not have great bodies of water like those in New Hampshire's Lakes Region or the Great Lakes, we once had many lakes, compliments of the ice ages. Most of these have had their levels raised by dams, and many new lakes have been created by damming streams and rivers. Still, bodies of water are transitory. Natural succession proceeds from a lake or pond to a marsh or swamp, to a meadow, and ultimately to a forest. Connecticut is dotted with large, swampy areas that were once lakes and ponds. These continuing processes have occurred over the last 10,000 years since the glaciers retreated.

By building dams, we have temporarily increased our water acreage greatly, but we have only pushed nature back a few hundred, or at most a few thousand, years. Even as we push, nature continues to drop tons of alluvium and rotting vegetation into our lakes and ponds each year. The life of any body of water is dependent on many factors, including the size of inlet streams; the volume of silt and nutrients in the incoming water, which governs the growth rate of water vegetation; and the volume of the water body to be filled.

Some human actions greatly accelerate the filling of the bodies of water that we go to so much trouble and expense to create. Road cuts, developments, and poor farming practices continually supply lake-filling silt. Often the fertilizers put on farm fields and lawns ultimately enhance the growth of choking vegetation in our bodies of water. This hike passes many bodies of water at various stages of succession; no doubt some are now unrecognizable to the layman's eyes.

Drive to the junction of CT 219 and CT 179 in Barkhamsted. Go north on CT 179 one mile to an old gated town road on your left (west) just opposite Legeyt Road. There is room to park on both sides of CT 179. Do not block the gated road.

Go through the gate and follow the old road as it passes through Metropolitan District Commission land. At the start, you pass several white birch trees

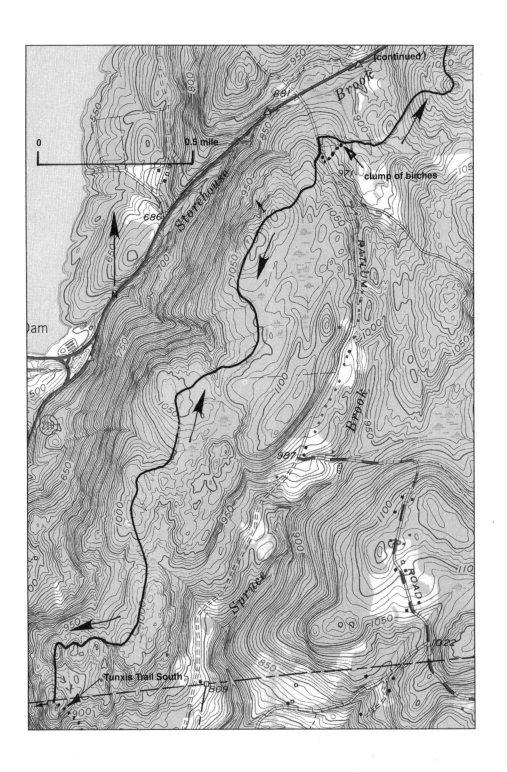

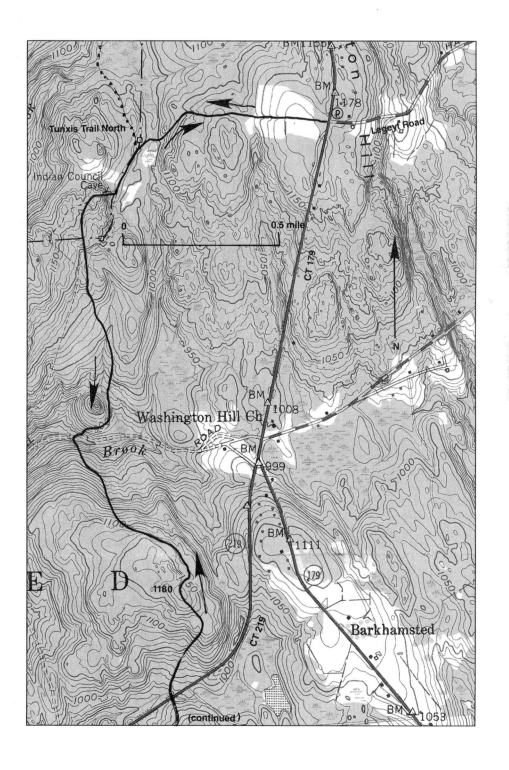

with their peeling bark and oval leaves; however, a single tall gray birch arches over the right side of the road. With its tight bark, large black triangles under its branches, and triangular leaves, this is a very different tree. A good way to learn to distinguish between similar trees is to find two species growing near one another. The white birch is considered a tree of the north, although more than a few are found in northern Connecticut. On the other hand, the gray birch, while not common in northern New England, grows naturally as far south as Virginia's Shenandoah National Park.

Just before a shallow pond at left we found a clump of pearly everlasting—clusters of round white flowers with a dull yellow center, which are popular with dried-flower enthusiasts. This is another northern species; sweet everlasting is more common in Connecticut.

At the bottom of a small hill, there is another small pond at left in the later stages of returning to the land. Try to visualize its original clear beauty. Now it is much smaller; trees are growing in its once open water, especially on the shallower inlet side. Submerged and emergent vegetation is adding to decay—as the pond becomes more shallow, its rate of filling increases. In a few hundred years someone may cross this area cussing the swampy wetness underfoot!

Opposite this pond, the blue-blazed Tunxis Trail goes off to the right on its way north to the Massachusetts border. Continue on the old road, now blazed blue, until still another pond appears at left; follow the Tunxis Trail south as it goes off to your right and climbs up through the Indian Council Cave. These are huge boulders reputedly used by Native Americans as a gathering place. Circle left up and around this rock jumble to a lookout on top with views of the surrounding forests. You will take the Tunxis Trail south to Ratlum Mountain.

Follow the blue blazes through this typical northern Connecticut forest over ledges and through laurel, crossing two small streams before reaching the wider Kettle Brook about 1 mile from the caves (2 miles from your car). Cross Kettle Brook on a dirt road, turn left into the woods with the blue blazes, and climb gradually through hemlocks. Enjoy the soft forest floor underfoot here. Cross a dirt road and pass through a small field thick with goldenrod. Soon the trail (now an old road) crosses a small brook and climbs steadily through mixed laurel and gray birch. Bear right off the old road, climb to a rock ledge, join another old road, turn right, and soon zigzag up yet another rock ledge. Although it has no views, this is the highest place around at 1180 feet. Follow the blue blazes downhill and then cross a stone wall by an immense spreading oak tree. Continue descending on the blue-blazed trail, crossing a woods road before reaching CT 219 about 3 miles from the start.

Cross CT 219, enter the woods, and climb gradually through laurel. Both forks join uphill. People have been cutting firewood in this area. Be careful to follow the blue blazes, as there are many woods roads traversing this section. Pass over a rise before crossing a brook and passing a clump of four white birches while climbing up to paved Ratlum Road, just under a mile from CT 219. The blue blazes are sparse on this hill. The well-trodden route bears left of the birches; however, there are no blazes. Bear right briefly on Ratlum Road to rejoin the Tunxis Trail on the road's west side. The blue-blazed route veers right at the clump of birches and bears left uphill to Ratlum Road. Turn left to follow the paved road to the Tunxis Trail on the other side.

On the west side of Ratlum Road,

Turkeys on the trail near Ratlum Mountain

climb uphill through the woods, soon reaching a lookout with fine views of Barkhamsted Reservoir to the west and northwest. Continue along the edge of the cliff and then roll along the ravines and rises of the ridge's west side. Cross old woods roads at about 1½ and 2 miles from Ratlum Road, then climb an overgrown rocky top, zigzag down and then up, again passing a third woods road. Stay on the blue-blazed Tunxis Trail

south and shortly you reach Lookout Point (1000 feet), about 6.5 miles from your car. Sign in at the trail register. This is an ideal lunch spot, with fine views of Lake McDonough below from ledges that are just downhill to your right.

After enjoying the view, retrace your steps to your car. Pause to admire the evergreen trailing arbutus, or mayflower, between the second and third woods roads on your return.

Trail Notes

Chapter 14
The 30-Minute Investor 285

Part V
Appendixes

Appendix A
Using MSN MoneyCentral's Investment Finder 293

Appendix B
Quarterly Flare-Out Growth Portfolios, 1998–1999   **309**

Appendix C
Stop Limits for Model Portfolios   **317**

Acknowledgments

This book was researched and written during the rainiest winter and spring on record in Seattle. Any hint of light a reader might detect in its pages must be a reflection of my three personal rays of sunshine—my children, Joseph and Janie, and my wife, Ellen. I could not have finished without their support, and I appreciate their good humor during the many blustery weekend afternoons when they ventured off to the museum, the movies, or the park alone to give me time to work.

I also owe a big debt to my colleagues at Microsoft who assisted with research—and who developed the software that made my work possible. First up is my editor at MSN MoneyCentral, Dan Fisher, who helped me articulate and execute on the SuperModels concept in late 1997. He's been a steadfast source of good judgment and helped with Chapter 8. Thanks too to Jim Jubak, a fellow columnist at MSN MoneyCentral, who provided research for Chapters 8, 9, and 10. And thanks to David Risher, Lewis Levin, Ken Moss, Neil Black, Dan Morrow, Walt Kennamer, Troy Zerr, Keith Birney, Malti Raghavan, Curt Fuhlman, Jim Simkins, and Eric Zinda—sponsors, designers, and developers of Investment Finder, Advisor FYI, Research Wizard, and other cool software at MSN MoneyCentral.

Thanks immeasurably to Terry Bedford, who has educated me almost daily on technical analysis and trading over the past two years. Thanks to Tim Allward and his team at Ford Investor Services for their price-momentum research and model backtesting. Thanks to Rick Hartley and Anthony Kolton at Logical Information Machines for their backtesting help. Thanks also to the following MoneyCentral editors and correspondents, who provided research or support: producers Justin Carder and Clay Martin; senior editor Eddie Yandle; copy editors Wendy White, Marian Prokop and Mike Wilenzick; correspondents Risa E. Kaplan (Chapter 12), Dr. George S. Mack (Chapter 10), Mike Robbins (Chapters 4 and 13), Randy Myers (Chapter 11), Tom Taulli (Chapter 9), and Eric Dubin (Chapters 8 and 9). My excellent editors and marketers at Microsoft Press were Amy Roberts, Anne Taussig, Barbara Ellsworth, Dail Magee Jr., Julie Xiao, Kimberly Dodge, Kristen Weatherby, and Susanne Forderer.

Finally, I'd like to express appreciation for some great editors and friends at the *Los Angeles Times,* who helped to form and inspire me as a journalist: John Arthur, Carol Stogsdill, Topy Fiske, Terry Schwadron, Marty Baron, Don Hunt, Bill Sing, and Terry McGarry.

This book is dedicated to my mother and the memory of my father, who always did the right things at the right time.

Introduction

Let's say Aunt Midge left you a million dollars five years ago and you wanted to invest it with care. Easy: You called up some big-city money manager who handles fat accounts for a 1% fee and handed over a check. With any luck, you watched the account grow simply by walking to the mailbox once every three months.

Now let's say you haven't got an Aunt Midge, you have only $20,000 to invest right now, and you swear you've heard your twins, Kelly and Courtney, trading differential equations in their cribs. Those girls are going to need million-dollar educations in 18 years. And it's your job to make it happen.

A few years ago, the effort to put the girls through Duke, Stanford, or even Eastern Alaska State would have sent you scrambling to the bookstore for thick, boring investment tomes or to some high-pressure salesman at a brokerage. Today, you can learn—slowly, steadily—to build your stake from the comfort of your home by harnessing a rich set of software tools and financial resources on the Internet.

The job isn't as easy as doing nothing—what worthwhile task ever is? But the digital age has improved and simplified few spins of the life cycle more than the task of investing. I'd argue that human relationships aren't better on the Net, and neither are sports, art, or religion. Yet finding and rapidly assimilating financial acumen is the kind of computational endeavor that is actually better accomplished on the Internet than on paper, on the telephone, or in person.

Indeed, today a dedicated mom, dad, or college student hooked up to the World Wide Web by modem from the Yukon can sneak through a strange crease of time and electrons to gather just about as much timely, relevant information about public companies as any money manager in Manhattan.

Fast, Tested Techniques

In this book, you'll discover easy, fast, tested, *new* ways to find, research, and track great stocks online. I have shared my methods to find the right stocks at the right time with millions of investors in the past two years via the MSN MoneyCentral personal-finance

site on the Web and the cable financial-news channel CNBC. Amid the market turmoil experienced in 1998 and 1999, these methods were a relatively steady beam of light, which resulted in stock portfolios that gained steam almost every month and beat the broad market by up to eightfold. MSN MoneyCentral's main momentum portfolio, in fact, gained 139% in 1998. That included a drop of 10% in the third quarter of 1998, when the Dow Jones Industrial Average plunged 13%, and a jump of 62% in the fourth quarter, when the Dow gained only 20%. For all of 1998, the Dow was up 16%—eight times less than our strategy.

It's not hard to learn how to build great portfolios like this online. Here's how you'll do it:

- In Part I, you'll learn how to use online stock-screening tools to build successful portfolios, whether you fancy yourself a momentum, growth, or value investor.

- In Part II, you'll learn how to find and exploit more new stock ideas by being disciplined and focused about frequently visiting and understanding a select number of online news publications.

- In Part III, you'll learn how to thoroughly research all of those ideas online with a plethora of fundamental and technical-analysis information and software.

- In Part IV, you'll learn how to use online brokers and portfolio managers to buy and track the stocks you've chosen. You'll also learn how to fit all these ideas into your lifestyle at your own pace.

Whether you're a beginner or an expert, the emphasis in this book will be on showing you how to use mechanical, unemotional, thoughtful investment strategies to get better and more consistent results over time than speculative or intuitive stock-picking. You really can leverage the power of the Web to build powerful, lucrative portfolios in whatever amount of time you desire to spend—whether it's five minutes a month or five hours a day.

Here's what you need to bring to use this book: an interest in meeting your financial goals by using the Web to find great stocks and mutual funds, a personal computer, a connection to the Internet, a Web browser such as Microsoft Internet Explorer 5 or Netscape Navigator 4, and a basic understanding of stocks and the stock market. To take advantage of some of my more advanced suggestions, you'll also need a spreadsheet program such as Microsoft Excel or Lotus 1-2-3.

Now let's get going.

Part I
Building Model Portfolios

Chapter 1
Introduction to Model Portfolios

How do you find the right stocks at the right time by using software and online information? Let's start by considering the objectives:

- You want to find stocks that go up.

- You want to know when to sell them before they go down (much).

- And you want to do this without spending more than, say, a few hours a year because financial stuff makes your eyeballs spin backwards.

I know it's not just me that hates squinting at numbers all day and trying to guess whether nanoseconds come in six-packs or how the El Niño weather pattern will affect copper prices in Peru. I just want to use the Internet to find some good investments and spend the rest of the day concentrating on work, my family, and my community.

That's where model building comes in. I'm not talking about those gray plastic kits that you stick together with brain-buzzing glue but investment-portfolio models that you assemble in minutes via stock-screening engines on the World Wide Web.

What's cool about model portfolios is that they can make you money in almost any economic environment, they remove emotion from decision-making, and they don't require you to own more than 3, 5, 10, or 15 stocks. Moreover, you don't need a finance Ph.D. to use them to your advantage. You just fire up a Web site, run the stock-screening software just the way I'm going to describe, print out a list of stocks, and then click over to your Web-based stock brokerage to make a purchase.

Then, with any luck, you click out, kick back, and relax. Or if you have the interest, you can monitor the progress of your stocks by reading news stories about the companies, monitoring quarterly securities filings, studying their technical trends in charts, or joining

online discussions about their prospects. All from the comfort of your den at home (or office, if the boss isn't watching). But fundamentally, all the watching, reading, and fretting in the world isn't going to help you be a more successful investor—though it *might* help you be a better conversationalist.

In the next three chapters, you'll learn exactly how to build great portfolios using stock-screening software. But first some background on how and why screening works.

Improve Your Odds

The core of the model-building approach focuses on ways to use software and online resources to improve your odds when launching into investments. That's not to say that investing is like betting. But when embarking upon any endeavor whose outcome is essentially unknown—whether it's a vacation overseas, a game of blackjack in Las Vegas, or an investment in stocks—your potential for fulfilling results will improve with careful study of success factors.

The beauty of investing in major U.S. stocks is that, due to the advance of securities law and technology, so much is known about them today. Ten years ago, you had to order annual reports and wait for them to arrive in the mail. Quarterly financial data came in the mail weeks late. If you wanted charts of stock prices, you had to create them day after day by hand or pay an outrageous sum of money to specialist firms to send them. And if you wanted statistics revealing how a stock had performed in the past, forget it. Even if you could find data providers that held such statistics, you probably couldn't afford them. And the information was typically far from timely.

Today, almost any current data point you could crave about a public company is available somewhere online. If you're willing to pay a few bucks, you can get tons of historical data as well. The key, then, is to determine which data points, or factors, are important and then go one step further and settle on the ones that have characterized the best stocks of the past 10 to 25 years.

Determine Success Factors

The good news is that a handful of bright finance professors, stock researchers, and money managers in recent years have already done much of the hard work. Analysts have crunched decades of statistics on the shares of tens of thousands of companies, many of which have long-since disappeared as a result of merger or bankruptcy. This work has identified a few key conclusions that help us use online tools to find the best short-term

and long-term investments. Some of the evidence is contradictory, to be sure. But there is little disagreement on the facts that should help to shape solid model portfolios:

- Stocks in motion tend to stay in motion.

- The strongest stocks often do violent head fakes, consolidating their gains by going flat or declining for a short period before advancing further.

- The stocks of companies with strong earnings and revenue gains tend to outperform those with weaker growth.

- Cheap stocks ultimately outperform expensive stocks but only once they clearly attract buying momentum.

- Portfolios balanced between "growth" and "value" investment styles tend to outperform portfolios that are biased in favor of either growth or value alone.

These findings sound simple, and they are. But mind you, none of these concepts would work at all if the markets worked as purists believe they should. In the world that many market idealists inhabit, stock prices should move up or down in lockstep with earnings gains. Every quarter, stock prices should move at the precise pace of earnings, and they should stay there for three months until the next earnings announcement.

That does not happen because markets are forecasting mechanisms—always attempting to price the future rather than the present. Because the future is inherently unknowable, it is in that cove of prediction that stock prices get wacky, whether a company sells Internet content or toothpaste.

That nuttiness makes day-to-day trading much more like a short-term wager—sort of a vote on who's most likely to be elected Wall Street prom queen. The stocks that go up the most each day are the ones that were the most popular *that day or week*. There were more buyers than sellers. End of story. Maybe a company released knockout earnings or announced a new gizmo that dissolves fat via the Internet. Or maybe people just thought something like that *might* happen. The reason matters little. It's all about investors casting votes on the winners with their dollars, every minute of the trading day.

But do you really have to trade every day to be successful? Of course not.

The Yeartrader

I developed many of the models described in Part I because I and many of the readers of my columns at the *Los Angeles Times* and later at MSN MoneyCentral Investor (*http://moneycentral.msn.com/investor*) were seeking a way to take advantage of the day-to-day liveliness of the market's most volatile stocks while not actually trading day to day. Yes, we

wanted the best of both worlds. We were searching for a rationale and methodology that would help us buy zoomy tech stocks while still holding down our day jobs. We wanted to become a different kind of daytrader. Call it a 365-daytrader, or better yet, a yeartrader.

To become successful yeartraders,

1. We had to learn to handicap how the Wall Street popularity contest would turn out over any 12-month period. The effort required consideration of what the country's biggest investors—pension and mutual-fund managers—were likely to consider attractive a year from now regardless of the prospective economic and market cycle.

2. We had to test those factors against historical data, as well as in the real world with real money.

3. We had to determine the right length of time to hold the stocks that matched those factors.

4. We had to figure out how to keep our hands off the stocks that the model—or handicapping system, if you will—picked. In other words, we had to learn that a yeartrader must settle on a model and leave it untouched.

Why would we trust models over our own intuition and intelligence? That's simple. Good models, it turns out, are more reliable and far less emotional than humans. They're more reliable than I am, certainly; and I'll bet they're more reliable and less emotional than you are too.

Money manager and market researcher James P. O'Shaughnessy noted in his seminal book *What Works on Wall Street* that models beat humans at investing "because they reliably and consistently apply the same criteria time after time. In almost every instance, it is the total reliability of the model that accounts for its superior performance." O'Shaughnessy added, "Models never vary. They never fight with their spouse, are hung over or get bored. They don't favor vivid, interesting stories over reams of statistical data. They never take anything personally. They don't have egos. They're not out to prove anything. If they were people, they'd be the death of any party."

Passive-Aggressive Investing

To be sure, the yeartrading of computer-built models is not exactly new. It's really just a rather lively form of passive investing. Let's call it *passive-aggressive* investing. To grasp this concept, consider for a moment that investors generally can be classified as either "active" or "passive."

- Active investors are those smart-looking men and women you see on financial news channels who tell call-in viewers whether they should buy, sell, or hold a stock. They believe they can pick equities one by one that are superior to all other stocks at that

time on the basis of certain fundamental or technical characteristics, such as a strong business model or low price compared to earning power.

- Passive investors are those who believe that stock-picking cannot beat the market over extended periods. Therefore, they simply buy a mutual fund that holds a group of stocks that are characterized by one or two common features, such as membership in the Standard & Poor's 500 Index.

O'Shaughnessy pointed out in his book that the majority of active investors have not beaten a broad-market benchmark like the S&P 500 Index over either short or long periods in the last 50 years for which there are good statistics. In fact, he noted, the best 10 years for active managers, ending December 31, 1996, saw only 26% of actively managed mutual funds beating the index. As a result, ownership of index funds has multiplied virally in the United States, with more than $800 billion managed in this way at last count.

In the case of the enormously popular S&P 500 Index mutual funds, such as the $78-billion Vanguard Index 500 Trust, the success factor that the managers target is companies with very large market capitalizations (stock price multiplied by shares outstanding). The median market capitalization of companies in the index is about $8.5 billion.

But is large capitalization the only great success factor? No, not by a long shot. It's just the easiest to identify if you don't have a computer or much data to work with. Fast new microprocessors and software have allowed investors to identify many more success factors that beat the pants off size alone.

And that computing power allows investors to *aggressively* magnify the best attributes of passive investing with the benefit of advanced knowledge of the success factors that boost stock prices.

The Four Key Factors

For prom-queen voters in high school, the list of success factors was usually limited to some mélange of smile, shape, and personality. For equity investors, research has shown that the success factors at work for stocks today are:

- consistency of sales and profit growth
- large capitalization
- high volume of shares traded each day
- strong stock-price momentum

And to cut to the quick, you can move straight to stock-price momentum, trading volume, and capitalization because the biggest companies in each sector today are generally being voted as the most *consistent* growers, even if they're not the *fastest* growers.

The pointy-headed fundamentalists in their ivory towers can spout all day for the financial-news shows and magazines about how they determine future winners via the study of esoteric statistics. These include "days sales outstanding" (don't ask) or nominal GDP rate (I have no idea how to calculate it either). But don't let their big intellects scare you. In the end, investors' knowledge about all that stuff should be wrapped up in a single, pristine, undisputed data point: the stock price. If it's up smartly ahead of the pack over the past year but conforms to certain norms of recent regression to the mean (which I'll discuss at length in Chapter 2), the stock has what the technicians call good "relative strength" and should be considered a top candidate to continue outperforming.

Harindra de Silva, manager of one of the nation's top large-cap mutual funds for the past five years, is a leading adherent of the passive-aggressive style. In 1998, he told me, "If you're looking for the ideal stock just look for really strong price momentum over the past 11 months and high amounts of cash for the price. You're going to see more and more of these stocks purchased."

Big, Reliable Quality Wins

Traditional yardsticks of value, such as a high dividend yield or low price-to-earnings ratio, are still valuable gauges for investors with a three-year to five-year time horizon for their investments to pan out. But over the past couple of decades—and probably over the next few years at least—large companies that have succeeded most in the past will probably continue to win even with relatively high price-to-earnings ratios. (Also known as the P/E ratio, the price-to-earnings ratio is the latest closing price of the stock divided by the latest 12 months' earning per share. The P/E ratio is perhaps the most widely used factor in assessing whether a stock is pricey or cheap.) In other words, the high-priced stocks of big, reliable companies will probably beat the low-priced stocks of small, unproven companies.

Richard Bernstein, chief quantitative strategist at Merrill Lynch, explained the view well to Dow Jones Newswires. He noted that institutional investors responsible for managing large sums of money are highly focused on buying shares in companies that are not likely to disappoint them. These investors will pay a premium for peace of mind. Call it the "sleep-easy" premium. "What the market is valuing in stocks is not the fundamentals but the *certainty* of those fundamentals," Bernstein said. If you include

an intangible variable for certainty when you value stocks, he added, it makes the large companies look especially attractive in comparison with smaller companies.

If you still think the best big stocks are too expensive today or any other day, here's another way to think about them: only a handful of today's publicly traded companies will be around 30 years from now. And their prices will probably be much, much higher.

Building Yeartrading Models

How can you find those stocks with the right factors that will be much higher in the context of an aggressively passive investment strategy? You could paw through thousands and thousands of pages of financial documents, scratch your head, and do a lot of math on paper.

Or you could use an online "stock-screening engine" like Investment Finder, shown in Figure 1-1, at MSN MoneyCentral. It lets you identify the right stocks in seconds, which you can then buy without further decision-making or analysis as a model portfolio to hold for a year.

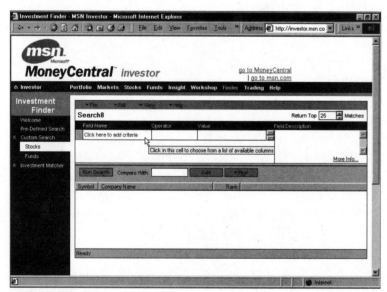

Figure 1-1.   April 28, 1999

Investment Finder, the stock-screening engine of MSN MoneyCentral Investor.

Before going on, let's consider the difference between stock "screens" and stock "models."

- Screens are lists of stocks that meet certain criteria for price, volume, and value. You can generate these lists using software such as Investment Finder, which searches its database of 8,900 stocks for ones that meet the criteria you specify. For many investors, screens are just a starting point; they're used to find stocks that merit further research. An active investor might buy only one or two of the stocks netted in the screen, if any.

- Models are mechanical, programmatic, tested ways to use screens to choose stocks. They direct an investor to purchase the top 3, 5, 10, or more stocks netted by a screen and hold them for a set period. Models are used by investors who believe that it's easier to find groups of stocks likely to turn in great performance than to pinpoint individual stocks that will outperform.

Models are marvelous because they provide an extremely valuable framework of discipline to investors who have a hard time deciding exactly when to move into and out of stocks, and that includes just about everyone. They're also a little like a religion, in that they precisely rank every stock in their hierarchies. If you "believe" in a stock-investing model and are curious about how a particular stock fits it, you can run the

Stock-Screening Engines

A screening engine is essentially just a big electronic filing cabinet packed with ever-changing stock-market data. New data flows in every day to fill that cabinet from multiple sources. Current price data comes from one vendor, and fundamental data, analyst estimates, historical prices, and insider-trading data come from others. To allow you to highlight the information that matters to you most, screening engines let you apply software "filters" against that data stream. Filters allow you to tell the filing cabinet, for instance, that you want to see only stocks whose market capitalization is greater than $1 billion—and no others. In more sophisticated screening engines, you can apply multiple filters, or "criteria," against the data stream. For example, you can look for stocks with market caps greater than $1 billion and P/E ratios lower than 20. In the most sophisticated screening engines, you can filter the data stream in more than 500 ways and create screens that include mathematical formulas. This chapter and Appendix A provide more detailed information about the Investment Finder screening engine.

screen at any time and find out. The model then becomes your Talmud, or law book, against which all future situations—in their infinite variety—are measured.

Although models can be rewarding in the right market climate, they can also be highly volatile. That's a fancy way of saying their results can vary a lot from day to day and from month to month. Sticking with models that work even when they don't *appear* to be working is where discipline comes in. Once you're committed to a model for some portion of your portfolio, it's best to generally leave it alone and let it work.

Preparing to Invest in Models

To execute a yeartrading strategy, you must first decide on the type of investment model that's most appropriate for your investment goals. Then you determine the amount of money you wish to invest and the number of stocks you wish to buy. You might be 40 years old, have just switched jobs, and have a $100,000 IRA rollover account to invest, for instance. If so, you might allocate 70% to the stocks of large growth companies, as described in Chapters 2 and 3, and 30% to the stocks of small or value stocks, as described in Chapter 4. Some passive-aggressive investors prefer to use momentum-stock models like the ones described in Chapter 2 simply to spice up their reliance on an S&P 500 Index fund. They will apportion 80% to 90% of their retirement money to index funds and apportion the rest to momentum stocks.

A model portfolio, by definition, equally distributes the amount invested among the stocks it contains. To create a $25,000 momentum portfolio consisting of five stocks, for instance, you would subtract the cost of commissions from your kitty and divide the resulting sum by five. That's the amount you will invest in each stock. Finally, divide that sum by the current price of the stocks you plan to buy, and you'll have the number of shares to buy.

Table 1-1 on the next page shows an example. Suppose you were to settle on a model portfolio of the five U.S. stocks with the highest market capitalizations, and you were going to buy them using an online discount brokerage like E*Trade. You would divide the amount you want to invest ($25,000) by the number of stocks in which you want to invest (5) to get $5,000. Then subtract the cost of commission ($15) to get $4,985, which is the amount to invest in each stock. Divide $4,985 by the price of each stock, and you have the number of shares to buy. You can buy odd lots of each stock— that is, 21 of one, 47 of another—or round up or down to buy even amounts of shares within your budget. (If you round off, you will end up putting *slightly* more money into some stocks and slightly less into others, which is fine.)

Table 1-1. **Model Portfolio for Five MegaCap Companies**

Total funds to invest	$25,000
Stocks to buy	5
Commission per trade	$15
Funds after commissions	$24,925
Funds per trade	$4,985

Stock	Price	Shares to buy
Microsoft	$82.00	61
General Electric	$113.00	44
Intel	$58.00	86
Exxon	$78.00	64
Merck	$75.00	66

Learning to Use a Stock-Screening Engine

One of the great things about becoming a yeartrader investing in models is that only one skill is really required. You must take an hour to learn to build stock screens with the criteria you've identified. After they're built and saved to your computer, you need only click a button with your mouse once a year to update the list.

You can find the best online screening software for this purpose at MSN MoneyCentral, a Web site published by Microsoft, in a section called Investment Finder. The Finder, as it's known, is not difficult to use once you understand the rules. It works only on Windows-based PCs, so if you've got a Macintosh, you'll have to get hold of a Windows-based machine either at the library or a friend's house. Appendix A gives detailed instructions on using the Finder and a few exercises, but here are the basics:

1. Visit MSN MoneyCentral's investment area by typing *http://moneycentral.msn.com /investor* into your browser address bar.

2. On the MSN MoneyCentral / Investor home page, click the word Finder on the top navigation bar (which will take you to the page shown in Figure 1-2). Then click *Custom Search* on the left navigation bar.

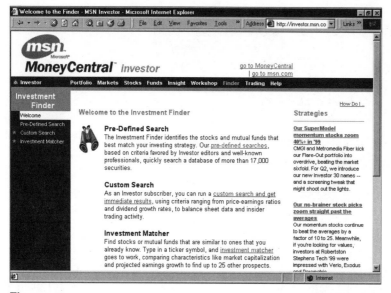

Figure 1-2.   April 28, 1999

The Investment Finder Welcome page.

3. If you are visiting the site for the first time, you are asked to register and then download the software. You have to do this only once, and it is free. Accept the software download when a dialog box appears on your screen, and then follow the instructions that appear. After about five minutes (if you're connected to the Internet via a 28.8-Kbps modem), a chart appears on your screen. Click the words *I see the chart*, and the software download will complete.

4. You now face software that looks vaguely like a spreadsheet program. The software has four key areas: a menu bar across the top (File, Edit, View, and Help), a criteria-entry section, a comparison section, and a results section.

5. To build a screen in the criteria-entry section, click the words *Click here to add criteria* in the Field Name list box. A menu then appears that allows you to choose criteria from 13 categories. To add a criterion, point to a category, such as Stock Price History. A submenu slides out (as shown in Figure 1-3 on the next page), allowing you to choose a specific criterion, such as % Price Change Last Month, by clicking it. Your criterion is inserted into the Field Name box.

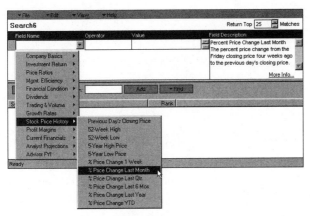

Figure 1-3.   April 28, 1999

Choosing a criterion in Investment Finder.

6. Click the words *Choose an operator* in the Operator column. Then choose a mathematical symbol or relationship, such as >= (for greater than or equal to) or High As Possible, by clicking in the menu that slides out.

7. If you choose an operator that requires a value, click the words *Click here to add a value* in the Value column. You can choose from among the categories you first saw in the Field Name column, or you can choose Custom Value or Ticker Symbol to enter either a number or a company's stock-ticker symbol.

8. After you finish entering criteria, click Run Search. The Finder searches the 8,900 or so major stocks listed on U.S. exchanges for the ones that match your criteria, as shown in Figure 1-4.

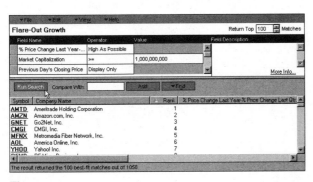

Figure 1-4.   April 28, 1999

Investment Finder results.

As you'll learn in Appendix A, the software gives you a break after you've created a screen. You can save the screen to a file, give it a name that's easy to remember, and run it in a flash the second time. You can even export the results to a spreadsheet, such as Microsoft Excel; send them to a friend via e-mail; send them to your online portfolio manager; or print them.

Using Models: The Investor 30, the CNBC Top 100, and Your 10

In the summer of 1998, the financial-news channel CNBC asked me to use my strictly mechanical online stock-screening techniques to come up with 100 momentum, growth, and value stocks that would outperform the major averages over the rest of the year. The list, shown in Figure 1-5, was turned into a Labor Day special and heralded as the CNBC Top 100. The gains of those 100 names crushed the broad market over the rest of the year, advancing 36.4%—10.2 percentage points better than the Standard & Poor's 500 Index.

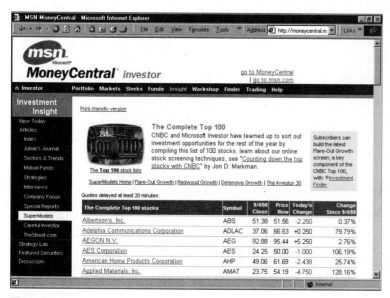

Figure 1-5.   April 28, 1999
The CNBC Top 100.

That success was no fluke. Lots of folks duplicated it simply by running the same screens that I created for the show and posted on the CNBC, MSNBC, and MSN MoneyCentral Web sites. Since then, I've built and published many more models under

the name Investor 30, shown in Figure 1-6. Regular private investors have utilized my models for their trading or retirement accounts and have beat the market by two to nine times. They found, as I hope you will, that it can really be very easy—even fun—to become a yeartrader because the technique requires so little time and usually works so well. It puts you in control of your portfolio, demands very little trading, and saves hundreds or even thousands of dollars in commissions and taxes.

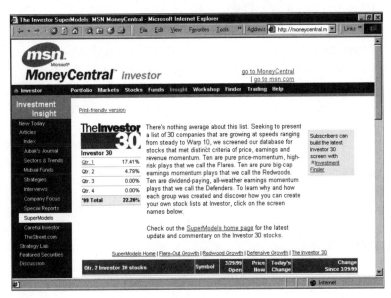

Figure 1-6.   April 28, 1999

The Investor 30 at MSN MoneyCentral Investor.

No individual should own 100 stocks or create models every three months. But the exercise of creating many big, diversified portfolios will serve us as a useful avenue for investigating portfolio-building techniques of which anyone can take advantage at any time.

In the rest of Part I, you'll learn how to use online stock-screening engines to narrow down the mind-bending list of choices you're confronted with each day to build three types of successful models yourself.

Chapter 2

Momentum Models

Let's start with the models that have succeeded best over the past decade: ones that capture momentum stocks.

First, it's important to understand that momentum stocks are hard to value by traditional means. To determine the right price to pay for shares of a company's equity, traditional analysis calls for investors to review the quality and value of a firm's current earnings and cash-flow streams and to estimate the growth of those streams in the future. (I'll talk about how to follow this method of analysis a lot more in Part III.)

One reason that many smart people who run mutual funds underperform the broad-market averages, however, is that they do not seem to have a good strategy for dealing with stocks that rise seemingly for no fundamental reason. Stocks that go up because, well, they're going up. Stocks that defy the textbook logic of market behavior. Stocks that the pundits like to deride as being in the thrall of *retail* investors or worse yet, *momentum* investors.

Yet these stocks are often responsible for the bulk of the gains of most stock indexes' advances in any individual year—and they're often precisely the stocks that growth-oriented private investors should want to own. The pundits would have you believe that there is something morally wrong with owning stocks that go up a lot if they can't understand exactly why they're going up. They can't abide stocks whose prices respond to demand-and-supply disequilibrium more than to fundamental value. I'll never forget the smug look on a traditional growth-fund manager's face, back in January 1998, when he told me that "only yahoos would buy Yahoo!."

I'm not going to debate whether Yahoo! was fundamentally worth a $3-billion market capitalization then or a $40-billion market cap a year later. But it's common sense that investors in the traditional manager's funds would have preferred the 615% gain of Yahoo!

that year over their manager's valuation ideology. The cost of his smugness? Millions of dollars of lost opportunity to own one of the great growth stories of the decade. In this case, and many others, price action preceded news. Our momentum model caught this Internet stock in January 1998 and held it for at least the next two years. In the face of fundamental analysts' skepticism, Yahoo! registered a 940% gain over 18 months. Only in mid-1999, *after* its largest gains under the sponsorship of early momentum buyers, did Yahoo! gain the status of Internet blue chip and a place in mainstream mutual funds.

In this chapter, I'll show *you* how to build great momentum-stock portfolios online that are likely to defy the conventional wisdom. Historical testing shows that my best model gained 70.1% per year on average since 1986, turning $10,000 into $11.3 million by the middle of 1999. The same amount in an S&P 500 Index fund would have netted only $66,378 over the same period. In real-life testing at MSN MoneyCentral, an early version of that model pulled in a return of 139% in 1998 and 53% in the first half of 1999—five and four times the broad market, respectively.

Understanding Momentum Stocks

So how should you value ordinary growth stocks that have caught momentum fever? First, take the exercise out of the Finance 101 classroom. Don't even try to use traditional, fundamental yardsticks. They'll only drive you crazy.

Instead, think of a restaurant. When you go into a fine dining establishment, do you try to determine the price-to-book ratio of the fresh scallops in white-wine sauce before determining whether to try them? Of course not: you accept the price on the menu. You don't care that the cost is substantially inflated over the dish's asset value. By convention, the restaurateur has the right to name his price based on the scarcity of the item (if you don't buy it now, someone else will) and your desire for the item (you came here for the fabulous scallops, didn't you?).

Now what if you and the person at the next table simultaneously want the same dish, and only one portion is left in the kitchen? It wouldn't be too cool, but theoretically the maitre d' could make you two bid for it—with the scallops going to the top offer. Now let's go one step further and say that just as you were about to dig into your winnings—knife and fork poised—another diner suddenly decides he must have the last portion of scallops and offers 10% more than what you paid. You might reluctantly agree that the money was worth more than the dish and hand the meal over.

Finally, one last metric: let's say that you walked into the restaurant with no knowledge of its specialty. By looking at the menu, you could easily guess that the high price associated with the scallops meant that the owner believed that item was his scarcest and

most precious. And if you watched the scene above unfold and fancied a fine dinner, you could reasonably conclude that if you paid the high price for any scrap of scallop left in the kitchen, you'd be satisfied with your choice. Surely three gourmands and the restaurateur couldn't all be out of their minds! Seven times out of ten, you'd be right.

The movement of stocks in the thrall of momentum buyers is similar. There are never enough shares to go around, they advance sharply on high and emotional demand, and their prices often bear little resemblance to their true value. Yet they continue to advance, often by leaps instead of steps. Outside observers who don't have the same appetite for these stocks will never understand their appeal. But the skeptics are missing one key concept. If enough people jump into the bidding with enough fervor over a long enough period of time, the correct prices for most stocks generally emerge.

That's a long way of saying the market is *usually* right. Yet it's not a contradiction to add that the market can also be wildly, amazingly wrong sometimes. It can be insanely overoptimistic on a stock when things seem to be going well and far too pessimistic when things seem to be going poorly. These extremes of greed and fear cause investors, operating as a herd, to overshoot the "right" price of stocks on both the high and the low side during any individual day, week, or month. Ultimately they determine their folly and bring prices back to beam. So if you wish to initiate a new position in a momentum stock, you need to look for those moments when utter excess has been wrung out of it and it's just *very* expensive rather than *incredibly, stupidly* expensive.

Finding the Best Momentum Stocks

Luckily for us, it is not too hard to find good momentum stocks—and determine the right moment to buy them during pullbacks amid their advances—in an Investment Finder screen.

First though, a couple of observations from the halls of academe.

- I won't bore you with the citations, but studies have shown that the long-term stock-price appreciation patterns shown by great momentum stocks tend to persist into the future, while short-term share-price appreciation patterns tend to reverse.

- These two stock-price tendencies—persistence for the long-term, reversal for the short-term—tend to occur without regard to the way you define long- and short-term. If you wish to trade on these tendencies during the day, for instance, the long term might be two hours; the intermediate term, 30 minutes; and the short term, 10 minutes. If you wish to trade on these tendencies from a broader perspective, the long-term should be seen as 12 months; the intermediate term, as 3 months; and the short-term, as 1 month.

My momentum-stock screen capitalizes on these observations by attempting to buy high-flying stocks during a period of short-term price reversal, or consolidation. To be sure, this is counterintuitive. Why would you want to buy hot stocks that appear to have suddenly turned cold, and how can you call them "momentum" stocks if they're actually falling or moving sideways at the time of the purchase?

The answer is that intuition is wrong. A stock-research team at Ford Investor Services in Del Mar, California, discovered that this pattern plays out again and again in the market's best stocks. Not only that, but you can capture the pattern in a mathematical formula to apply against any stock at any time.

I stumbled upon Ford's technique in 1997 when I was seeking a screen that would help me mechanically, unemotionally buy high-momentum stocks like Yahoo!. Like many investors with a fairly early understanding of the likely pace of growth of media on the Internet, I instinctively believed that Yahoo! and Amazon.com would be worth a lot to investors in the future, but I could not wrap my brain around their valuations. I decided I needed to find or create a valuation method that did not rely on the traditional stock-measurement gauges, which compare prices to revenue or earnings growth. A mathematical formula that pinpointed moments when the purchase of high-momentum stocks held the most promise appealed to my need for a rational—if radically different—solution.

At the time, Ford was using its momentum formula as the last of a three-part screen to purchase cheap stocks. I turned that concept on its head by applying the formula all by itself to determine the right time to purchase *expensive* stocks.

The Original Flare-Out Growth Model

After obtaining permission from Ford, I borrowed the formula for my first momentum-stocks model in January 1998. I named the model Flare-Out Growth because the stocks' chart pattern resembles the "flare-out" play in sandlot football. In this play, a wide receiver runs straight downfield, then suddenly swerves to the side, slows and turns around, catches the ball, and resumes his fast run to the goalposts.

The original Flare-Out screen on which the model is based begins by seeking stocks with $1 billion market values. Then it seeks stocks that have advanced the most in the last 12 months but which have swerved sideways in the most recent three-month and one-month periods. This lets us find the stocks that have gained the most in the past year (the momentum part of our search) but have then consolidated, or taken a breather, as investors step back, take profits, and assess their next moves.

Mean Regression—or "Bull Flag"

Mathematicians and technical analysts, who have a jargon all their own, call this a *mean-regression* methodology of seeking stocks. The trajectory along which the Flare-Out stocks have gone straight up is considered their *mean*. The path they take back to that trajectory after going sideways, or consolidating, is considered their *regression*. When viewed on a chart, this pattern is called either a *bull flag* (if the consolidation takes just a few days or weeks) or a *wedge* (if it takes longer). (See Figure 2-1.)

Figure 2-1.   April 29, 1999

The stock of Web auction house eBay made two bull flags from February to April of 1999. The first flagpole started in mid-February with the stock at $70. The stock subsequently ran up to $171 by March 8, and then it backed off and slid up and down in a narrow range until April 7. The stock then exploded upward again (back toward its mean) on April 8 and April 9 before backing off and making another flag until another explosion upward on April 23. The Flare-Out Growth screen attempts to find stocks that are in the middle of one of those "backing-off" periods because of the frequency with which such stocks ultimately bound much higher.

For years, investors who wished to find stocks that traced out these explosive patterns had to flip through hundreds and hundreds of charts that they either crafted by hand or received by mail from a subscription service. But now we can find the 3, 5, or 10 stocks that best fit this pattern in seconds, at any time, via online stock-screening engines such as Investment Finder.

1998 and 1999 Flare-Out Growth Portfolios

So how exactly do you find these names? If you can't wait to see the screen recipe, skip ahead to page 26. But if you're patient, here's a little more background.

My first Flare-Out Growth screen was strictly based on the formula handed down by Ford Investor Services. According to Ford analyst Tim Alward, a portfolio managed under the 10-stock strategy advanced at an annualized clip of 22.8%, including dividends, from 1976 to 1996. That compared with a 14.6% advance in the S&P 500 Index.

The portfolios I built from that screen did a whole lot better than Alward's estimate in 1998 and the first half of 1999, however. They posted the gains of 139% and 53% I mentioned above. Indeed, in the 18 months that I have run real-time model portfolios with the screen, their worst results were still two times better than those of the broad market over any stretch of time longer than six months. And they have regularly done as much as four to eight times better over longer stretches.

Take a look at the Flare-Out Growth portfolio built in January 1998, for instance. As shown in Table 2-1, the Flare-Out screen netted stocks in a mix of industrial sectors. Although you might have imagined that momentum was purely the province of technology stocks, you can see that the picks were actually scattered among businesses in technology (Dell Computer, ASM Lithography), media (Yahoo!), retail (Best Buy), medical devices (Arterial Vascular), biotechnology (Immunex), trucks (Navistar), oil drilling (Varco International), and air freight (Airborne Freight).

If you look at the sixth column of the chart, you'll see that almost all of the stocks ended the first quarter of 1998 with gains that resembled those of Internet stocks. This shows that momentum investing doesn't play by any rules except price and volume. It is *sector agnostic*. That means you don't have to wrack your brain to determine the right industries in which to invest at any given time. The market decides, and you just need to follow.

If you look at the columns showing the 12-month and 18-month changes, you can see that, for the most part, the stocks continued their upward bias. Yahoo! started 1998 with a modest 39% gain in the first quarter and went on to record a 615% gain for the year. Even electronics department store Best Buy, not exactly a sexy name, expanded its incredible first-quarter success of 81% by posting a 233% gain over 12 months. Investors who held the portfolio for one year—which I believe is the best duration—ended 1998 with a 138.6% gain. Not bad for a strategy that takes less than 30 minutes to execute and requires no extra news-following, TV-watching, broker-calling, or chart-reading. Buy once a year and you're done.

Table 2-1.   1998 Flare-Out Growth Portfolio

The 1998 Flare-Out Growth portfolio gained 39% from January 2 to March 31, 1998. Through December 31, 1998, the one-year portfolio rose 139%—five times better than the S&P 500 Index.

	1/2/98 Close	3/31/98 Close	12/31/98 Close	6/30/99 Close	3-Mo. Chg.	12-Mo. Chg.	18-Mo. Chg.
Yahoo!	$16.56	$23.11	$118.47	$172.25	39.5%	615.4%	940.2%
Dell Computer	$10.72	$16.94	$36.59	$37.00	58.0%	241.4%	245.1%
Best Buy	$9.23	$16.67	$30.69	$67.50	80.6%	232.5%	631.3%
Immunex	$27.19	$33.69	$62.91	$127.44	23.9%	131.4%	368.7%
Arterial Vascular*	$31.82	$38.56	$52.88	$58.38	21.2%	66.2%	83.5%
Airborne Freight	$30.78	$37.63	$36.06	$27.69	22.2%	17.2%	-10.0%
Navistar	$24.44	$35.00	$28.50	$50.00	43.2%	16.6%	104.6%
ASM Lithography	$34.00	$46.22	$30.50	$59.38	35.9%	-10.3%	74.6%
Varco International	$20.63	$25.75	$7.75	$10.81	24.8%	-62.4%	-47.6%
			Total		38.8%	138.6%	265.6%
			S&P 500		13.0%	28.0%	43.0%

Merged with Medtronic; last price was January 28, 1999.

Portfolios purchased on the first day of subsequent quarters in 1998 did equally well. A Flare-Out Growth portfolio bought on April 1 was up 86% over the next 12 months. A portfolio bought on July 1 was up 168% over the next 12 months, and a portfolio bought on October 1 was up 98.6% over the next 9 months. See Appendix B for details.

A Flare portfolio purchased on the first trading day of 1999 also started off strong, as shown in Table 2-2. The screen, in this case, picked five Internet companies (CMGI, Yahoo!, MindSpring, Amazon.com, and Earthlink); four technology companies (EMC, Dell Computer, Apple Computer, and New Era of Networks); and a telecommunications company (Metromedia Fiber Networks). These 10 stocks beat the market by a whopping margin over the first three and six months of the year, despite some extreme turbulence in the second quarter.

Table 2-2. 1999 First Quarter

The Q1 '99 Flare-Out Growth portfolio gained 48.5% from January 4 to March 31. Through June 30, 1999, the portfolio rose 53%—four times the broad market.

	1/4/99 Close	3/31/99 Close	6/30/99 Close	3-Mo. Chg.	6-Mo. Chg.
CMGI	$28.63	$91.53	$114.06	219.8%	298.5%
Metromedia Fiber Network	$17.25	$25.91	$35.94	50.2%	108.3%
Yahoo!	$124.00	$168.38	$172.25	35.8%	38.9%
MindSpring Enterprises	$33.00	$43.03	$44.31	30.4%	34.3%
EMC	$43.50	$63.88	$55.00	46.8%	26.4%
Apple Computer	$41.25	$35.94	$46.31	-12.9%	12.3%
New Era of Networks	$41.50	$67.75	$43.94	63.3%	5.9%
Amazon.com	$118.31	$172.19	$125.13	45.5%	5.8%
Dell Computer	$37.09	$40.88	$37.00	10.2%	-0.3%
EarthLink Network	$62.44	$60.00	$61.44	-3.9%	-1.6%
			Total	48.5%	52.8%
			S&P 500	5.0%	12.0%

These stocks absolutely flew into the middle of January as if drawn by a powerful magnet. They were collectively up 33% only two weeks into the year. But the magnet turned out to be merely the earnings-release date of Yahoo!. The day before it released its earnings, Yahoo! actually had an intraday move of $51 before settling with a gain of $35. The company disappointed investors by announcing merely a 2:1 split rather than a 3:1 split, though, and its stock subsequently fell from a split-adjusted high of $222.5 to a low of $124 over the next 28 trading days. Many of the rest of the stocks in the portfolio followed in sympathy, with Amazon.com sinking from a high of $199 on January 11 to an intraday low of $92 just 10 days later.

But guess what? They all came back—with a vengeance. Performing just the way we expect these momentum stocks to act, the stocks rose about half as fast as they plunged, but they did rise. By the end of the quarter on March 31, they had registered a 48.5% gain in three months, which was nine times better than the broad market. A week later, they had advanced briskly enough for a 71% year-to-date gain, though they all slumped sharply after that by the end of the second quarter. Despite the turbulence, the portfolio was still ahead 53% after the first six months of the year, which was four times better than the broad market.

New Flare-Out Growth Screen: Quality Momentum

Clearly, the Flare-Out Growth strategy had a terrific 18 months, starting at the beginning of 1998. But have the past year and a half been *unusually* kind to momentum investors, and will it work every year? The answer is yes—and no.

I built the 1998 and 1999 Flare-Out Growth portfolios using screening criteria that were the best I had at the time. Testing results for models built with those original criteria were great: a seven-stock version of the original models showed a 55% annual return with a 58% standard deviation in historical testing. This isn't bad at all, considering that $10,000 turns into $2.9 million in 13 years. A $10,000 investment in an S&P 500 Index fund would have turned into just $57,000 over the same period.

But portfolio experts believe that whenever a model's standard deviation is higher than its return, its risk is too great: You're not getting enough return for the volatility you're forced to endure. Standard deviation is a measure of a portfolio's volatility; the higher the number, the more it tends to skitter above and below its average return. By definition, the return of a portfolio in any single year is expected to differ from its average return by no more than plus or minus the standard-deviation figure about two-thirds of the time. Thus, models for which the standard deviation is lower than the return should rarely go into the red.

I hate volatility just as much as the next person, so I embarked upon a quest to improve the original, bare-bones Flare-Out Growth screen. I spoke to numerous technical and quantitative analysts around the country, and I was aided by the "backtesting" software of a company called Q·Analytics. (The company ceased operations in June 1999.) This research led me to add a few criteria to the classic Flare screen that promised even better—and steadier—returns. The improvements lean on these themes:

- **Quality.** I learned that portfolios tend to be hurt more by stocks that collapse than they are helped by stocks that soar. An important way to avoid disaster is to demand a minimum amount of quality from the companies you will potentially own. Every investor has a different definition of quality. For my purposes, it means looking for companies that have figured out how to generate at least $50 million in sales and any profit at all. (Is that so much to ask?)

- **Size.** The market decides who shall be big and who shall be small. And the market is usually right. I've discovered it's best to seek companies that are growing from small- to medium-size with at least $1 billion in market capitalization. These stocks tend to be less risky than smaller ones, but they have more room to grow than much larger ones.

- **Liquidity.** The market trades the stocks it loves most. Stocks with the highest trading volumes tend to be the most loved. Sometimes that's good; sometimes it isn't. By itself, volume means less than when paired with the two criteria above. Generally, I prefer stocks that are in the top 300 to 500 most actively traded issues over the past month. (In mid-1999, that meant about 800,000 shares daily.)

- **Relative strength.** Stocks that have performed the best in the past tend to continue to perform the best, all other things being equal. I use the Flare-Out Growth formula to rank all stocks netted with the criteria above. To ensure a stock has decent momentum at the moment of purchase, historical testing suggests it's best to require positive returns in the last month and quarter.

- **Selection.** Testing shows emphatically that the fewer high-ranked stocks you pick from a screen, the better. Every good screen will beat the market, no matter how many stocks you pick from the top, but fewer is definitely finer. Most mutual funds have to own at least 25 stocks, but you need only 3, 5, or 10. Most momentum screens that I have tested have the best risk/reward balance with three to five top-ranked stocks. That's also the number of momentum stocks that most of my readers have said they'd prefer to buy for this portion of their overall portfolios.

- **Time.** Most momentum portfolios do best when purchased in November, December, January, or February and held for one year. Most do poorly when purchased in August, September, or October. Rebalancing monthly or quarterly also works, but that is more labor-intensive and less tax-advantaged.

Creating the Screen in Investment Finder

Creating the Flare-Out Growth screen in Investment Finder, as shown in Figure 2-2, is easy. You can find detailed instructions on using the Finder in Appendix A and more concise instructions in the previous chapter. Now here's the recipe that would potentially have made you a multimillionaire if you'd started with $10,000 on January 1, 1986, and stuck with this plan. Enter these criteria into Investment Finder:

1. Market capitalization of at least $1 billion. (In Investment Finder, choose *Company Basics* / Market Capitalization >= $1 billion.) The market of the 1990s prefers larger cap, highly liquid stocks for reasons I'll discuss further in the next chapter.

2. Revenue of at least $50 million in the past 12 months. (In Investment Finder, choose *Current Financials* / 12-Month Revenue >= $50 million.) Companies that have figured out how to wrest $50 million from customers in a year probably have real businesses.

3. Return on equity greater than 0.1%. (In Investment Finder, choose *Investment Return* / Return on Equity > 0.1%.) Companies with any return on equity at all have earned money in the past 12 months, which is a sign of quality and potential stability. A 1999 survey of institutional investors by Merrill Lynch showed that a high return on equity was the primary criterion sought by the market's biggest buyers of stock.

4. Current price greater than the price three months ago. (In Investment Finder, choose *Stock Price History* / % Price Change Last Qtr. >= 0.) Momentum stocks should be bought above their prices of three months ago.

5. Current price greater than the price one month ago. (In Investment Finder, choose *Stock Price History* / % Price Change Last Month >= 0.) Momentum stocks should be bought above their prices of one month ago.

6. Average daily volume over past month greater than 800,000 shares. (In Investment Finder, choose *Trading & Volume* / Avg. Daily Vol. Last Mo. >= 800,000.) No market moves are valid without strong volume, because volume shows buyers are acting with conviction.

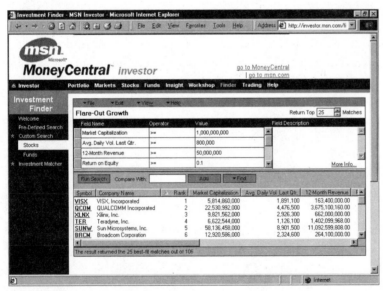

Figure 2-2.   July 15, 1999

You can create and run the Flare-Out Growth screen in MSN MoneyCentral's Investment Finder in less than 30 seconds. This list shows the top stocks on July 15, 1999.

7. Rank these stocks by the Flare-Out Growth Index. (In Investment Finder, choose *Stock Price History* / % Price Change Last Year - % Price Change Last Qtr. - 3 * % Price Change Last Month. Choose High As Possible as the operator.) The Flare-Out Growth Index, or FOG Index for short, is the momentum formula that mathematically replicates technicians' bull-flag chart pattern.

8. Run the search. The stocks will be ranked in descending order by the FOG Index.

9. Buy the top three, five, or seven stocks listed. You should buy the stocks in equal dollar amounts, and the number of stocks you buy should depend on your risk tolerance. Fewer stocks means higher potential reward (and risk).

10. That wasn't so hard, was it? Start a portfolio near the beginning of the year—any time from November 1 to January 15—and hold it for one year. Repeat the screen the following year. This will be your "core," or main, momentum-stocks portfolio. If you find it impossibly boring to buy stocks just once a year, you can create a separate portfolio the same way and trade the top-ranked stocks each month.

Historical testing suggests that portfolios bought using the improved Flare-Out Growth screen would have returned 70.1% on average annually from 1986 through mid-1999 with a standard deviation of 46%. A return that's higher than the standard deviation indicates that the model would be relatively easy to hold. Testing suggests the model would have suffered no losing years over that 13-year period, and it would never have underperformed the S&P 500 Index. Only three stocks turned in negative full-year performances.

The results show that $10,000 invested on January 1, 1986, in the stocks turned up by the model every year through 1998 would have turned into $5.4 million. The three stocks that were turned up on January 1, 1999, rose 110% collectively in the first six months of the year, so the portfolio would have been worth $11.3 million by the middle of 1999. Table 2-3 lists the stocks that would have been purchased over that period. (Only one stock met the criteria in January 1988, but two more would have been netted in February of that year.)

A note about the testing: All historical-testing calculations were performed in Q·Analytics' Q-Investor software. The results were confirmed by Camelback Research Alliance, a consulting firm directed by Carr Bettis, a finance professor at Arizona State University. The results were also confirmed by researchers at Ford Investor Services and Logical Information Machines of Austin, Texas. No historical database or back-testing software is perfect, however. Results from testing in other databases may vary, and there are no guarantees that past results will be repeated.

Table 2-3. Flare-Out Growth, 1986–1998

Historical testing suggests that the three-stock Flare-Out Growth model would have turned $10,000 into $11.3 million between January 1986 and July 1999. In this table, purchases are made on the last day of the first trading week of the year. The sales occur on the previous day (except for 1999, when the sell date is June 30).

	Buy	Sell	% Return
1999			
CMGI	$28.63	$114.06	298.50%
MindSpring Enterprises	$33.00	$44.31	34.30%
Dell Computer	$37.09	$37.00	-0.30%
1998			
Best Buy	$9.09	$30.69	237.50%
Schering-Plough	$31.22	$55.25	77.00%
Costco Companies	$44.00	$72.19	64.10%
1997			
PeopleSoft	$24.50	$37.88	54.60%
BMC Software	$22.19	$32.47	46.30%
Global Marine	$19.88	$24.19	21.70%
1996			
Global Marine	$8.50	$19.88	133.80%
Ascend Communications	$35.13	$59.69	69.90%
Maxim Integrated Products	$18.38	$22.19	20.70%
1995			
StrataCom	$17.13	$33.25	94.20%
Micron Technology	$21.69	$39.13	80.40%
Atmel	$16.63	$22.00	32.30%
1994			
Tellabs	$3.08	$6.72	118.30%
EMC	$9.38	$10.75	14.70%
DSC Communications	$33.13	$34.63	4.50%

(continued)

Table 2-3. *(continued)*

	Buy	Sell	% Return
1993			
Newbridge Networks	$10.31	$27.38	165.50%
Informix	$9.06	$10.63	17.20%
International Game Tech.	$25.44	$29.50	16.00%
1992			
International Game Tech.	$11.22	$25.44	126.70%
First Health Group	$19.13	$15.00	-21.60%
Ivax	$38.38	$29.25	-23.80%
1991			
Amgen	$5.00	$18.69	273.80%
Novell	$8.22	$30.44	270.30%
Chiquita Brands Int'l	$31.50	$39.25	24.60%
1990			
Home Depot	$2.79	$4.17	49.40%
Barrick Gold	$8.50	$10.38	22.10%
American Greetings	$17.88	$16.56	-7.30%
1989			
Fannie Mae	$4.34	$9.00	107.60%
MCI Communications	$11.50	$20.19	75.50%
Albertson's	$9.56	$14.25	49.00%
1988			
GPU	$14.19	$19.00	33.90%
1987			
Amdahl	$11.81	$17.63	49.20%
Walt Disney	$3.74	$4.94	31.90%
Digital Equipment	$105.75	$135.00	27.70%
1986			
Liz Claiborne	$12.13	$21.75	79.40%
Limited	$10.38	$16.50	59.00%
Kellogg	$8.66	$13.19	52.30%

The aggregate annual results, shown in Table 2-4, show that 1998 and 1999 stand out among the top years in the past 13 for this strategy. However, 1991 (coming out of the 1990 recession) was the very best.

Table 2-4. Flare-Out Growth 1986–1999 Annual Returns *

Steady application of the three-stock Flare-Out Growth strategy since 1986 would have turned $10,000 into $11.3 million by July 1999, according to historical testing. Compounding in final years ramps the final amount.

Year	% Return	Pct. Pts. Over S&P 500	Portfolio Value**
1986	63.6%	46.7	$16,360
1987	36.3%	36.0	$22,299
1988	33.9%	21.5	$29,858
1989	77.4%	51.9	$52,968
1990	21.4%	30.2	$64,303
1991	189.6%	158.9	$186,222
1992	27.1%	23.2	$236,688
1993	66.2%	59.2	$393,375
1994	45.8%	47.8	$573,541
1995	69.0%	35.1	$969,285
1996	74.8%	53.5	$1,694,310
1997	40.9%	10.5	$2,387,282
1998	126.2%	100.1	$5,400,033
1999**	110.0%	98.0	**$11,340,069**
Avg. Ret.		70.1%	
Std. Dev.		45.8%	

* Portfolio starts January 1, 1986, with $10,000.

** 1999 return through June 30.

Could you live with returns like this? These stocks can be yours any year you wish to try them by clicking a few buttons on the Web. No need for any newsletters, TV financial-talk shows, or even prowling the Internet looking for ideas. This is all because the Internet and a few smart software developers and program managers made it possible to bring the tools and data that the top pros have been using for years down to your desktop.

Now let's learn to find a much tamer brand of security in the next chapter: great growth stocks.

Chapter 3

Growth Investing Models

It's not too hard to figure out why you'd like to buy stock in companies that are growing earnings and revenues faster than their peers. At the end of the day, stock-price growth *always* follows reliable, high-quality earnings growth.

But exactly which growth stories should you buy into? The legend of classic growth companies often outlives reality. Individual investors often keep paying for great advances that have been made in the past without real regard to whether the company is making the same magnitude of advances in the present. The spring of 1999 provided a good lesson in that regard, as private investors were slow to respond to marketplace stumbles by Coca-Cola and Gillette. They continued to bid up their shares even as professionals were bailing out.

An online screening tool such as the Investment Finder at MSN MoneyCentral Investor is ideally suited for finding the right fast-growing companies at the right time. The Finder acts like a market X-ray machine, shining through the opaque outer layers of companies' press releases and promises—and investors' hopes and myths. It helps you find the firms with the correct combination of growth factors at the moment you are interested in purchasing shares.

In one successful method of using the Finder, for instance, you can screen for big companies that reported earnings and revenue gains greater than 15% in the past year and are expected to do so again in the coming one-year and five-year periods. Then you can rank those companies according to the ardor with which investors have rewarded them for growth over the past year—and buy shares in the top 4 to 10. I'll describe this technique in much more detail later in this chapter. As simplistic as it sounds, this technique has, over the past decade, netted great stocks to hold for at least one year, and it will probably continue to do so over the next few years. In early 1999, it would have kept you far away from old growth, like Coca-Cola and Gillette, and steered you instead to new growth, like low-cost printer maker Lexmark International and electronics retailer Best Buy.

Why emphasize big growth stocks over small ones? The universe of growth stocks is truly divided by size. In recent years, *large* companies with good growth have been sharply rewarded by investors, while many *small or mid-sized* companies with good growth have been treated as time bombs ready to go off. It's as if investors are just waiting for small companies' growth to be proven false—that is, with dishonest accounting or overly rosy promises.

For the most part, investors have been right. The nation's largest companies have reported consistent, reliable growth while an astonishing number of supposedly fast-growing small firms have blown up. Every time this scene plays out, another nail is set in the coffin of the small stocks. One stark example came on April 7, 1999, when Alcoa, the world's largest aluminum producer, reported a sharp earnings increase and Engineering Animation, a small but impressive software maker, announced an earnings shortfall. (See Figure 3-1.)

Alcoa was not exactly a true growth stock at the time. It had reported a 4% earnings increase in the past year, though it was expected to grow the following year by a respectable 34% and over the next five years by 12%. On April 7, however, the company reported that its first-quarter net income had risen sharply above year-ago levels—reflecting successful cost-cutting and tax-minimizing measures. Investors immediately bid the $16-billion company's shares up 7% to a 52-week high of $44 that day. They might have figured that, as an analyst at Scott & Stringfellow said, "If this kind of cost-cutting execution can continue, then everyone's estimates are too low for this year and next year."

Meanwhile, shareholders of one-time high-flying small-cap Engineering Animation suffered a shellacking that day. On paper, their design-software company looked a lot cooler than dowdy old Alcoa. Earnings were expected to grow 53% in 1999, another 35% in 2000, and 40% over the following five years. Moreover, the Iowa-based firm's client list ranged from Ford Motor to Lucent Technologies. Yet on April 7, the stock lost half its value when company executives announced that, because of failure to close several key contracts, they expected their first-quarter earnings and revenues to fall below analyst expectations. The stock fell $18, sinking to $21.50 from a 52-week high of $72. Matthew Rizai, president of the firm, said, "While we are confident that our business prospects remain strong, we simply did not execute as well as expected in the first quarter."

It's exactly that kind of uncertainty that investors have punished in small caps in recent years. The serious private investor is better off purchasing the shares of larger, steadily growing companies whose balance sheets are more transparent and whose prospects are more reliable, if not exactly failsafe. After all, big but boring Alcoa ended the month of April with a whopping 58% gain, while small, flashy Engineering Animation concluded the month with a 60% loss.

So now let's see how to hunt down those reliable large-cap stocks.

Figure 3-1.   April 30, 1999

The market's uneven treatment of small-cap and big-cap stocks in the late 1990s was well-illustrated by trading in aluminum producer Alcoa and software maker Engineering Animation after each reported earnings results in April. By the end of June, Alcoa shares had risen 50% while EA shares had fallen 50%—even though the software maker had been expected to grow twice as fast as the smelter.

How to Build Large-Cap Growth Models

Need more reasons to focus on the nation's largest companies with the best current combination of growth factors? Consider that they are the most widely recognized and arguably the most important companies in each sector of the economy. They are the companies that the smaller firms must figure out how to compete with, dance around, or ally with. They own the most popular brand names. They are the power brokers. And when they're hitting on all cylinders, they're really fun to own. Just ask anyone who snagged a 98% gain in the stock of discount brokerage Charles Schwab in the first six months of 1999.

Yet not all large companies are created equal, and not all are run well from the shareholder point of view. The lovely old cemetery at Broad and Wall streets in New York could be filled with executives of large companies that simply did not deliver the goods on their stock price and were fired by their boards after months or years of disappointing patient shareholders. Their firms might have been big, but they were also complacent and slow-moving. They might have had market share of 50% in their very

large niche but had not figured out how to grow that business by more than 5% a year. That kind of growth might be good enough for them, but it doesn't have to be good enough for *you.* As an investor armed with the online tools to readily determine and monitor who's doing best *right now,* you owe it to yourself to stay invested in the winners and let someone else own the rest.

Redwood Growth: Bigger Is Better

Betraying my California roots, I've nicknamed my best screen for big-cap stocks Redwood Growth because the market seems willing to bet that these companies will grow to the sky. In recent years, portfolios built from these stocks have rarely underperformed the market over any time period longer than three months. You just can't keep a good set of companies down. In January 1998, for instance, I launched a model portfolio built from an early version of the Redwood Growth screen. That portfolio scored a return of 68.6% by the end of the year, beating the S&P 500 Index by 41 percentage points, as shown in Table 3-1.

Table 3-1. **Redwood Growth in First Quarter 1998**

The Q1 1998 Redwood Growth portfolio rose 69% from January 2 to December 31. With just 9 stocks, it advanced 2.4 times faster than the broad market.

	1/2/98 Close	12/31/99 Close	1-Yr Chg.
Dell Computer	$10.72	$36.59	241.4%
The Gap	$15.53	$37.42	141.0%
Safeway	$31.44	$60.94	93.8%
Pfizer	$25.23	$41.67	65.2%
Compaq	$29.81	$42.00	40.9%
Fifth Third Bancorp	$54.33	$71.31	31.3%
Nordstrom	$29.25	$34.69	18.6%
Coca-Cola Enterprises	$35.00	$37.44	7.0%
Computer Associates	$54.56	$42.63	-21.9%
		Total	68.6%
		S&P 500	28.0%

Six months later, I created an improved 15-stock Redwood Growth portfolio that also soundly beat the market over 6 and 12 months, as shown in Table 3-2. I'd love to say I was smart enough to do this kind of individual stock-picking. The truth is that anyone can do this at any time by using the right screen and exercising enough discipline to hold on through any short-term calamities.

Table 3-2. **Redwood Growth in Third Quarter 1998**

The 15-stock Q3 1998 Redwood Growth portfolio rose 29% from July 1 to December 31— more than triple the market. Through June 30, 1999, the portfolio rose 47%—more than double the market.

	7/1/98 Close	12/31/98 Close	6/30/99 Close	6-Mo. Chg.	12-Mo. Chg.
EMC	$22.81	$42.50	$55.00	86.3%	141.1%
Airtouch Comm	$59.00	$72.44	$107.00	22.8%	81.4%
The Gap	$27.97	$37.42	$50.38	33.8%	80.1%
Microsoft	$54.69	$69.34	$91.19	26.8%	66.7%
Dell	$23.48	$36.59	$37.00	55.8%	57.6%
Home Depot	$42.50	$61.19	$64.44	44.0%	51.6%
Tyco Intl	$64.75	$75.44	$94.75	16.5%	46.3%
Walgreens	$21.22	$29.28	$29.38	38.0%	38.4%
MBNA	$22.33	$24.81	$30.63	11.1%	37.1%
Lowe's	$42.00	$51.19	$56.69	21.9%	35.0%
Costco	$61.56	$72.19	$80.06	17.3%	30.1%
Carnival	$40.00	$48.00	$48.50	20.0%	21.3%
Safeway	$41.69	$60.94	$49.50	46.2%	18.7%
Schering-Plough	$47.00	$55.25	$52.50	17.6%	11.7%
Household Finance	$51.56	$39.63	$47.38	-23.2%	-8.1%
			Total	29.0%	47.3%
			S&P 500	8.0%	21.0%

The screen is easy to create at any time, and the stocks are generally easy to hold. Purchase the top 4 to 10 stocks ranked this way, and then forget about investing for a year. Then it will be time to screen again and buy a new set. Despite what your stock broker or the television talking heads might say, buying big stocks doesn't have to be

much harder than this, now that you have the power of the Web at your disposal. Here's the Redwood Growth screen recipe:

1. **Market capitalization of at least $10 billion.** (In Investment Finder, choose *Company Basics* / Market Capitalization >= $10 billion.)

2. **15% growth in revenues and earnings per share in the past quarter and year and 15% growth in earnings per share expected over the next year and five years.** (In Investment Finder, choose *Growth Rates* / EPS Growth Qtr vs Qtr >= 15; *Growth Rates* / EPS Growth Year vs Year >= 15; *Growth Rates* / Rev Growth Qtr Vs Qtr >= 15; *Growth Rates* / Rev Growth Year Vs Year >= 15; *Analyst Projections* / EPS Growth Next Yr >= 15; *Analyst Projections* / EPS Growth Next 5 Yr >= 15.)

3. **Earnings surprise in the most recent quarter.** (In Investment Finder, choose *Analyst Projections* / Recent Qtr Surprise % >= 1.)

4. **Rank by 52-week stock-price percentage gain.** (In Investment Finder, choose *Stock Price History* / % Price Change Last Year "high as possible.")

This screen appears to work well because it encompasses the five principal characteristics that money managers seek in growth stocks today: size, fast earnings growth, fast sales growth, an earnings surprise, and great relative strength. Let's look at each of these more closely.

Targeting Hugeness

How big is big? Many money managers and market historians, such as Ken Fisher of Fisher Investments in California, believe that because the extremely large companies today have put so much distance between themselves and everyone else, true bigness doesn't start until around $80 billion. In early April of 1999, that would have netted an investor 41 stocks, starting with Microsoft at $475 billion and ending with Philip Morris at $84 billion. That's about 0.5% of all 8,900 stocks in the Investment Finder database. If you wish to follow Fisher's lead, as documented in his *Forbes* magazine columns over the past several years, just adjust the Market Capitalization figure in the Redwood Growth screen to read $80 billion rather than $10 billion.

North Carolina money manager Robert Sheard—author of *The Unemotional Investor: Simple Systems for Beating the Market*—prefers to start at $20 billion. That was about the top 2% of all stocks in the Finder database in mid-1999. At that time, 150 firms met that criterion, and they ranged from Microsoft at the top to Eastman Kodak at the bottom.

The finite definition of size doesn't really matter, however. The real *value* of size in a screen is that it is a measure of quality. Unless they're a brand-new Internet company with a great scheme to somehow make a profit by selling dollar bills for seventy-five cents,

companies don't generally grow to a market cap of $10 billion or more unless they've been measured by the market over time and judged worthy, or at least reliable. The bigger you go, the more reliability you're requiring. The more reliability you demand, however, the more reward you sometimes have to sacrifice. In my own research, the best compromise between risk and reward for stocks like these is around $7 billion to $10 billion.

Targeting Earnings Growth

Earnings growth is the best measure of a mature growth stock, and investors have prized it since trading began in the mists of time. It's not enough to have succeeded in the past, however; the company must be expected to succeed at similar or better rates in the future. Although everyone knows that analyst projections are often faulty and overly optimistic, they are the only statistical measure that we have for estimating future earnings in a screen.

Before online screening engines came along, it was difficult for a private investor to figure out which stocks, in aggregate, were growing fastest. About the best you could do was buy a copy of *Investor's Business Daily* at the newsstand (if you lived in one of the large cities where it was distributed) and painstakingly go through the EPS Growth column in its financial tables. A lot of private investors used to do this; presumably, many still do. The wider availability of this data online today is just another reason why it's so much easier to be your own money manager now and not have to rely on expensive experts or mutual funds.

In the Redwood Growth screen, I set the target for earnings growth at 15% because it is quite high without being ridiculous. If you wish to be more stringent, set the value at 20% or more. If you wish to be less stringent, set the value at 5% or 10%. In my research, 15% seems to be a good compromise between fast and flamboyant.

In mid-April of 1999, 328 stocks in the Investment Finder database had market caps greater than $10 billion. Of those, only 110 recorded revenue growth greater than 15% in the most recent quarter compared to the quarter one year ago. Of those, only 81 recorded revenue growth greater than 15% in the most recent 12-month period compared to the previous 12 months. Of those, just 55 recorded earnings per share growth greater than 15% in the most recent quarter compared to the year-ago quarter. And of those, just 45 recorded earnings growth greater than 15% in the most recent year versus the previous year.

Those 45 were pretty awesome. Microsoft had the largest market cap, and Qualcomm had the smallest. The list also included such great companies as Wal-Mart Stores, Citigroup, and BankAmerica. But I demand even more of the Redwoods. Of those

45, only 25 were expected by analysts to record 15% earnings growth in the following year as well. And of those, just 24 were expected to continue to record EPS growth of greater than 15% over the next five years. Wal-Mart and Citigroup fell off the list because analysts expected them to record growth of only 13% to 14% over the next one and five years. See ya later!

For the final 24, I then add one last test. Did they surprise analysts in the most recent quarter? Research has shown time and again that companies that do better than analysts expect in one quarter will do so again in the following quarter—and that investors fail to accurately adjust their expectations upward for the stock's future performance after just a single surprise. That is to say, a single surprise is often followed the next quarter by an even larger surprise.

When I applied that gauge, I was left with just 16 stocks. Common sense suggests that these companies are less likely to disappoint us because their track record is so solid. Of course, that doesn't mean that they won't disappoint us—only that they're *less likely* to. Statistically, you should be willing to take that as enough of a guarantee. At least it's better than guessing.

Targeting Relative Strength

After narrowing down the number of growth stocks to buy from 8,900 to just 16, there's still a little more work to do. You must rank them. As discussed in Chapter 2, stock-price performance over the previous 12-month and 6-month periods impressively predicts price performance over the next 12-month to 6-month period. Skeptics always complain that this method of determining a portfolio is wrong-headed because they don't believe the past holds any sway over the future and that stocks must be picked one at a time from a quality list like this.

But recent research—even by value-stock proponents such as Robert A. Haugen, recently retired from the University of California, Irvine, and the author of the seminal book *The New Finance*—shows emphatically that relative strength works well as a forecasting tool. To create our final Redwood Growth portfolios, I use the simple technique of ordering our list of stocks by 52-week price performance and choosing the 10 with the highest returns.

In Table 3-3, you'll see the stocks that made the cut for the Redwood Growth portfolio of our CNBC Top 100 and their market-beating returns from September 4, 1998, through June 30, 1999. That 10-stock group returned 47% by the end of the year and 69% by June 30, 1999. These results were 20 and 27 percentage points better than the broad market, respectively.

Table 3-3. Redwood Growth / CNBC Top 100

On September 4, 1998, the Redwood Growth screen sought the best big growth stocks. With just 11 stocks, the model performed 75% better than the market over four months and 65% better than the market over 10 months.

	9/4/98 Close	12/31/99 Close	6/30/99 Close	4-Mo. Chg.	10-Mo. Chg.
The Gap	$23.78	$37.42	$50.38	57.4%	111.9%
AirTouch Comm	$56.88	$72.44	$107.66	27.4%	89.3%
Microsoft	$48.31	$69.34	$90.19	43.5%	86.7%
Carnival	$26.13	$48.00	$47.88	83.7%	83.2%
Lowe's	$32.19	$51.19	$56.69	59.0%	76.1%
Tyco International Ltd.	$54.50	$75.44	$94.75	38.4%	73.9%
Home Depot	$38.31	$61.19	$64.44	59.7%	68.2%
Clear Channel Comm	$42.56	$54.50	$68.94	28.1%	62.0%
Costco	$49.75	$72.19	$80.06	45.1%	60.9%
Dell	$27.38	$36.59	$37.00	33.7%	35.1%
Safeway	$43.25	$60.94	$49.50	40.9%	14.5%
			Total	47%	69.2%
			S&P 500	27%	42.0%

Suspicions that those first three portfolios were a fluke might have been put to rest in the first quarter of 1999, when a new 10-stock Redwood Growth portfolio was launched for MoneyCentral readers. That portfolio, shown in Table 3-4 on the next page, was up 80% more than the broad market by June 30. Michigan-based software maker Compuware had fallen out of favor with investors, plunging by 53% at its springtime low. Yeartrading investors sticking with the model portfolio should not have flinched, however. By July, Compuware was down just 15% from its January 1 value and gaining steam again.

If you look closely at the tables, you'll see that I've put anywhere from 10 to 15 stocks in each Redwood portfolio. Research suggests that four to seven are really enough, but that it's important not to "cherry-pick" the list. Just take the top four, five, six, or seven, not a random sampling from the screen. Try this technique on your own—perhaps "paper-trading," or just watching, one portfolio for three to six months before actually committing real cash. You may be surprised at how quickly screening for stocks online will allow you to move *away* from relying on hot tips or bland mutual funds and *toward* your own good sense and the historical odds.

Table 3-4. Redwood Growth / First Quarter 1999

The 12-stock Q1 1999 Redwood Growth portfolio rose 13% from January 4 to March 31—more than double the market. Through June 30, 1999, the portfolio rose 22%—almost double the market.

	1/4/99 Close	3/31/99 Close	6/30/99 Close	3-Mo. Chg.	6-Mo. Chg.
Charles Schwab	$27.50	$48.06	$54.40	74.8%	97.8%
Solectron	$46.00	$48.56	$66.69	5.6%	45.0%
Cisco Systems	$47.66	$54.78	$64.44	15.0%	35.2%
The Gap	$37.75	$44.88	$50.00	18.9%	32.5%
Microsoft	$70.50	$89.64	$90.18	27.1%	27.9%
EMC	$43.50	$63.88	$55.00	46.8%	26.4%
Lucent Technologies	$57.09	$54.00	$67.44	-5.4%	18.1%
Home Depot	$58.81	$62.25	$64.44	5.8%	9.6%
Staples	$30.17	$32.87	$30.94	9.0%	2.6%
Dell	$37.09	$40.87	$37.00	10.2%	-0.3%
Compuware	$37.56	$23.88	$31.81	-36.4%	-15.3%
Safeway	$60.81	$51.31	$49.50	-15.6%	-18.6%
			Total	13.0%	21.7%
			S&P 500	5.0%	11.7%

Screening Tip

To play with a screen like Redwood Growth a little more, it can be interesting to apply a final filter that determines which of the stocks are the farthest from their 52-week highs. This allows you to put on your contrarian cap while still looking at some of the best big-cap growth stories in the market. Many investors believe that all good growth stocks ultimately return to and surpass their 52-week highs, so choosing the ones that are farthest from that goal often proves fruitful. To do so in Investment Finder, add this formula as a final criterion: Previous Day's Closing Price / 52-Week High "low as possible." The value will be less than 1.00, such as 0.89. That means the stock's current price is 89% of its 52-week high.

How to Build Defensive-Growth Models

When the going gets tough on Wall Street amid fears of war, recession, or overseas crisis, many growth-portfolio managers turn their attention to owning stocks they consider "defensive." The theory is that some sectors of the economy—drugs, soap, groceries, beverages—are considered less vulnerable to economic and market instability than others.

The concept is not universally admired, and it may simply not be valid. Some portfolio-management experts believe that there are no truly defensive stocks, and they suggest that investors seeking to dampen risk in their equity portfolios simply raise cash. "If you wanted to diversify your real-estate risk," asked Terry Bedford, a hedge-fund manager in Toronto, "would you buy more houses?"

RBI Growth—Bat 'Em In!

Still, it makes sense to consider ownership of mature, steady growth stocks with solid, well-defined sources of income *without regard to economic sector.* I've named this model RBI Growth (for Revenue/Beta/Income). Over the past 13 years, it has reliably turned up large retail, pharmaceutical, financial service, consumer product, and technology companies that made reasonably steady investments. If these stocks were baseball players, most would be considered MVPs.

You can use the following factors to identify stocks in this category:

- steady returns, as characterized by betas between 0.5 and 1.9

- strong business model, as characterized by revenues greater than $500 million over the past 12 months

- profitability and growth, as characterized by earnings growth greater than 1% over the past 12 months and net income greater than $30 million

- appreciation by investors for their good deeds, as characterized by market capitalizations among the top 350 stocks at the time and high 52-week returns

I have never run this model in real-time, but I have tested it against historical data stretching back to 1986. A four-stock RBI Growth portfolio has returned 42% on average over the past 13 years with a standard deviation of 30%. The portfolio recorded no years of negative returns, and it underperformed the S&P 500 Index only once in that period (by 3 percentage points in 1992).

Here's the recipe:

1. **12-month revenues greater than $500 million.** (In Investment Finder, choose *Current Financials* / 12-Month Revenue >= $500 million.)

2. **12-month income greater than $30 million.** (In Investment Finder, choose *Current Financials* / 12-Month Income: Cont. Ops. >= $30 million.)

3. **Earnings growth in the past 12 months greater than 1%.** (In Investment Finder, choose *Growth Rates* / EPS Growth >= 1%.)

4. **Beta greater than 0.5.** (In Investment Finder, choose *Trading & Volume* / Beta >= 0.5.)

5. **Beta less than 1.9.** (In Investment Finder, choose *Trading & Volume* / Beta <= 1.9.)

6. **Current price greater than the price three months and one month ago.** (In Investment Finder, choose *Stock Price History* / % Price Change Last Mo. >= 1 and *Stock Price History* / % Price Change Last Qtr. >= 1.)

7. **Market capitalization within the top 350.** (In 1999, the smallest capitalization in the top 350 is $7 billion. In Investment Finder, choose *Company Basics* / Market Capitalization >= $7 billion.)

8. **Rank by 52-week return, and take the top four.**

According to my testing in Q·Analytic Inc.'s software and confirmed by LIM Research, a single portfolio constructed in 1986 in this manner would have turned $10,000 into about $1.16 million by mid-1999. The same amount invested in an S&P 500 Index fund would have turned into $66,378. (See Tables 3-5 and 3-6.)

Table 3-5. **RBI Growth, 1986-1999**

Testing suggests that the four-stock RBI Growth model would have turned a $10,000 investment in 1986 into $1.2 million by mid-1999.

Year	% Return	Pct. Pts. Over S&P 500	Portfolio Value*
1986	50.90%	34.00	$15,090
1987	21.50%	21.00	$18,334
1988	33.90%	22.00	$24,550
1989	80.40%	55.00	$44,288
1990	28.10%	37.00	$56,732

Year	% Return	Pct. Pts. Over S&P 500	Portfolio Value*
1991	122.50%	92.00	$126,230
1992	1.20%	-3.00	$127,745
1993	32.20%	25.00	$168,878
1994	13.00%	15.00	$190,832
1995	46.50%	13.00	$279,570
1996	51.50%	30.00	$423,548
1997	42.80%	12.00	$604,826
1998	31.00%	5.00	$792,322
1999**	40.9%	28.90	$1,116,382
Average	42.60%		
StdDev	29.8%		

Portfolio starts with $10,000 invested on January 1, 1986.
*** 1999 results through June 30.*
Source: Q•Analytics Inc.

Table 3-6. RBI Growth, 1986-1999

Since 1986, testing suggests that the four-stock RBI Growth model would have chosen just six stocks that lost money over a calendar year. In all cases, the purchases are made at the end of the first trading week of the year. Sales occur at the end of the first trading week of the next year (except for 1999, when the purchase was made on January 4 and the sale occurred June 30).

	Buy Price	Sell Price	% Return
1999			
Best Buy	$31.75	$67.50	112.6%
Lexmark	$49.18	$65.50	33.2%
Lucent Technologies	$57.09	$67.44	18.1%
Dell	$37.09	$37.00	-0.3%
1998			
Schering-Plough	$31.22	$55.25	77.0%
Fifth Third Bancorp	$54.33	$71.31	31.3%
First of America Bank	$76.06	$86.50	13.7%
Coca-Cola Enterprises	$35.00	$35.75	2.1%

(continued)

Table 3-6. RBI Growth, 1986-1999 *continued*

	Buy Price	**Sell Price**	**% Return**
1997			
EMC	$16.69	$29.38	76.00%
Microsoft	$21.16	$32.78	54.90%
SunAmerica	$28.67	$42.13	46.90%
STMicroelectronics	$69.75	$65.00	-6.80%
1996			
Nike	$33.06	$60.50	83.00%
Monsanto	$24.75	$39.63	60.10%
Loral	$36.25	$51.88	43.10%
Thermo Electron	$33.08	$39.63	19.80%
1995			
Safeway	$7.78	$12.09	55.40%
Becton, Dickinson	$12.56	$18.66	48.50%
Capital Cities/ABC	$86.13	$125.38	45.60%
Electronic Data Systems	$39.00	$53.25	36.50%
1994			
Lowe's	$13.78	$16.69	21.10%
Computer Associates	$12.55	$14.41	14.70%
Wells Fargo	$130.75	$148.75	13.80%
Cisco Systems	$7.40	$7.58	2.40%
1993			
Computer Associates	$6.00	$11.85	97.50%
Intel	$5.44	$7.75	42.50%
Chase Manhattan	$14.25	$16.94	18.90%
Winn-Dixie Stores	$38.31	$26.81	-30.00%
1992			
Home Depot	$11.61	$16.88	45.40%
United HealthCare	$19.78	$28.44	43.80%
United States Surgical	$115.75	$68.75	-40.60%
The Gap	$13.05	$7.33	-43.80%
1991			
The Gap	$3.79	$13.05	244.20%
Microsoft	$2.11	$4.71	123.30%
Nike	$9.34	$18.25	95.30%
PG&E	$25.13	$32.00	27.40%

	Buy Price	**Sell Price**	**% Return**
1990			
Microsoft	$1.24	$2.11	69.80%
Home Depot	$2.79	$4.17	49.40%
LM Ericsson Telephone	$3.77	$3.86	2.30%
UNUM	$12.47	$11.31	-9.30%
1989			
LM Ericsson Telephone	$1.49	$3.77	152.90%
Fannie Mae	$4.34	$9.00	107.60%
UST	$9.97	$15.25	53.00%
Sonoco Products	$14.94	$16.13	8.00%
1988			
GPU	$14.19	$19.00	33.90%
1987			
Walt Disney	$3.74	$4.94	31.90%
Digital Equipment	$105.75	$135.00	27.70%
Merck	$7.00	$8.80	25.80%
Becton, Dickinson	$6.33	$6.38	0.70%
1986			
Becton, Dickinson	$3.98	$6.33	59.10%
Walt Disney	$2.37	$3.74	58.10%
Browning-Ferris	$15.69	$23.25	48.20%
Sara Lee	$3.13	$4.33	38.20%

Considering that you would have invested in some of the biggest brand-name companies—including Monsanto, Nike, Microsoft, Cisco, Safeway, and The Gap—this is a nice "sleep easy" model to consider.

Now, on to the bargain bin!

Chapter 4

Value Investing Models

So far I've focused on growth and momentum stocks—those darlings of the market that seem to have done nothing but swell in price over the past 10 years. The sole purpose of momentum and growth investing, indeed, appears to skeptics of the style to be nothing more than to buy high and sell higher. A fool's errand.

So now let's take a look at using online screening tools to identify stocks on the other side of the equation. First, I'll focus on former growth stocks that have just recently fallen on relatively hard times, and then I'll turn to absolute crash-and-burn cases. Finally, I'll look at possibly the best values of all, which are growth stocks that just happen to be relatively cheap.

Growth and Value: What's the Difference?

Before hitting the screens, it's important to understand that the growth and value styles of investing have alternated in irregular frequency throughout history.

Growth stocks dominated the market in 1998, for instance. The Russell 1000 Growth Index rose 38.7% while the Russell 1000 Value Index advanced 15.6%. That difference of 23 percentage points was the largest in the 20-year history of those indexes. (The Russell 1000 Growth Index measures the performance of the largest 1,000 public companies sporting the highest forecasted growth rates. The Russell 1000 Value Index conversely starts with the same 1,000 stocks and measures the performance of the ones sporting the lowest price-to-book ratios and forecasted growth rates. For more information, see Frank Russell Co.'s Web site at http://www.russell.com.)

Investors who thought a contrarian value strategy was the way to go in 1999 were proven wrong in the first three months of the year. A look at history could have prevented their pain. A study by Charles Schwab broke down the 19-year history of the Russell indexes through the end of 1997 into the extended periods in which growth stocks dominated and the extended periods in which value stocks dominated. It found that the perceived periods of style dominance have been as short as three years or as long as seven. The current growth cycle just started in 1998.

On the other hand, many observers believe the market through mid-1999 had not been in a growth phase so much as it had been in a *large-company* growth phase. "People are focused on the growth/value cycle," said Ken Fisher of Fisher Investments in an interview in early 1999. "But at the moment, the big/small trade-off is much more primary than the growth/value trade-off. The biggest stocks simply tend to be growth stocks."

It's always hard for value investors to maintain their focus in the face of the growth-stock onslaught. Heck, even the nation's No. 1 value mutual fund, run by investment bank Legg Mason, scored its 1998 victory by twisting logic sharply enough to justify owning such traditional growth names as Dell Computer, America Online, and Microsoft. (The manager said he bought each when they were down and simply never sold.)

So how do smart value investors remain dedicated to their style using online tools? It's most important to invest in a value *strategy*, not just what you perceive as a value *stock*. Value investors do get to invest in trendy growth stocks. They just do so when the stocks are temporarily out of favor. "We don't think you can make a distinction and say, 'This is a growth stock, and this is a value stock,'" said Robert Sanborn, longtime manager of the Oakmark Fund, one of the most successful value portfolios in the nation. "We just like to ask the question, 'Is this business selling for significantly less than it's worth?'"

Indeed, it's essential to realize that the scary stretches of time when a stock, sector, or market trips up are precisely the moments that value investors get their shot at companies that might traditionally be considered growth companies. "These can be terrific buys," said David Dreman of Dreman Value Management and author of the book *Contrarian Investment Strategies*. In an interview in early 1999, he noted, "Citicorp and Merrill Lynch had great runs after falling into value territory in 1998. And tobacco stocks like Philip Morris (MO)—selling well off its five-year highs—are really classic growth stocks that are out of favor."

According to Dreman, specific measures of value might mean less than you think. "We've looked at all the measures: price/book, price/earnings and price/cash flow measures, and so forth, and they all perform very close to each other," he said. It's more important that you stick to whatever style you select for an extended period—at least a year.

Value stocks do not generally turn on a dime. You might have to wait 18 months to three years or more, and then you might see your stock double in a single week or month. Witness Alcoa, mentioned in the previous chapter, which traded between $20 and $40 for five years before rocketing to $65 in a single month, April 1999. Dreman favors stocks in the lowest 20% of any time period's rankings in terms of P/E ratio. Sanborn looks for stocks trading at below 60% of their enterprise value, a figure he determines through proprietary analysis.

The Value-Growth Transition

So how long does a value stock remain one after its turnaround from hitting a price bottom? That is, when do value investors hand off their ownership stakes to growth investors? The subject is shrouded in mystery.

Warren Buffett is widely considered to be a value investor. However, he's owned and profited most from former value stocks Coca-Cola, McDonald's, and American Express long after they moved into the growth camp.

Still, many value investors stress the need for a disciplined sell strategy. "Most of the successful value investors I've spoken with know the price they'll sell the stock at the day they buy it," said Jan Squires, professor of finance at Southwest Missouri State University. Occasionally, that means leaving money on the table.

Sanborn said he sells stocks when they reach 90% of the company's enterprise value, and he often watches stocks he's sold continue to rise. "If you're going to be a successful value investor over the long haul, it's what you have to do." Sanborn noted, with just a touch of regret, what happened to the cable stocks after he bought them in 1996 and 1997 when you couldn't give them away. "We bought TeleCommunications Inc. for less than $12 and sold when it was in the high $30s," he said in early 1999. It rose to $71 before disappearing into the maw of AT&T. "Value investors can't always get every last dollar out of a stock. In other words, don't be a pig," Sanborn said.

How to Build Value Stock Models

That brings us to the question of how precisely to find value stocks in any market environment.

When I created four value portfolios for the CNBC Top 100, I leaned on the published screening recommendations of money managers James O'Shaughnessy, David Dreman, and Ralph Wanger. Then I added a few elements of my own. Some worked very well, and others, well, let's just say we were *early*.

Good news first: Value investing, done well, can be incredibly rewarding, both intellectually and monetarily. Psychologically, it's a rush to find a diamond where everyone else just saw rocks. And for the sake of your portfolio value, it can be a huge win to hit within 10–20% of the exact bottom of a stock.

Just ask anyone who managed to buy Ascend Communications in January 1998. Almost from the day of its initial public offering in May 1994, Ascend was one of the killer growth stocks of all time. A maker of networking equipment, it rose 3,731% from its IPO date to the middle of 1996, paused for a few months in a sickening slide, and then stormed up again to top out in early 1997 with a fantastic three-year gain of 4,171%. An investor who bought $10,000 worth of the stock at its IPO was holding stock worth $427,000 in January 1997. For comparison, consider that growth favorite Dell Computer advanced just 981% in that period, and America Online grew just 274%. Microsoft was up just 301% in that span. It was an amazing ascent.

And then something happened. There was an earnings disappointment, and investors grew worried about the company's product pipeline. Then executives failed to provide adequate explanations and skipped an important investment conference. Suddenly, all the confidence rushed out of the stock, and it deflated like a pricked balloon. From January 23, 1997, to November of the same year, Ascend stock plunged 70%! A stock that once traded hands for $80 was now going for $23. *Nobody would touch it.*

Well, not quite nobody. After seeing Ascend stock skim along its trough for a couple of months, suddenly investors decided the news wasn't that bad after all. The value investors who specialize in technology stocks (yes, there are a few) started kicking the tires. Hey, wasn't the product pipeline looking a lot better? And this cheap, wasn't the company a buyout candidate? Sure enough, slowly and steadily, the stock began to rise. The psychology shifted. A couple of earnings reports came in above expectations. And by the time communications-equipment maker Lucent Technologies bought and assimilated Ascend, the stock had risen 371% from its 1997 low to an all-time high of $108.

Great GARP!: Growth at a Reasonable Price

Online screening tools could have helped *you* find Ascend in the low $20s just as it helped us find Tellabs at its low in September 1998.

Tellabs, another great communications-equipment story, had risen 10,850% from its IPO in early 1990 to the day in July 1998 when it announced it would buy competitor CIENA Corp. Wall Street didn't like the terms of the deal, and investors shot the stock in the heart—taking it down from a high of $93 that month to an eventual low of $33.50 by September.

The screen I created to find stocks like Ascend and Tellabs was based on a concept called "Growth at a Reasonable Price," or GARP. The theory suggests that if you can buy growth stocks when their price-earnings ratios are lower than their estimated long-term growth rates, you might have a bargain on your hands. It seems to have worked in our case, as you can see in Table 4-1 on the next page. We placed Tellabs in our Great GARP! portfolio for the CNBC Top 100 at a split-adjusted $20.44 on September 4 only to see it fall another 20% before bottoming out in the great 1998 sell-off of October 8. From there, it rose in just about a straight line and closed June 30 at $67.56—a 231% gain.

Here's the screen:

1. **Market capitalization greater than $1 billion.** (In Investment Finder, choose *Company Basics* / Market Capitalization >= $1 billion.)

2. **Earnings growth next year greater than 15%.** (In Investment Finder, choose *Analyst Projections* / EPS Growth Next Yr >= 15.)

3. **Earnings growth in the next five years greater than 15%.** (In Investment Finder, choose *Analyst Projections* / EPS Growth Next 5 Yr >= 15.)

4. **Past five years' earnings growth better than 15%.** (In Investment Finder, choose *Growth Rates* / 5-Year Earnings Growth >= 15.)

5. **Past year's earnings growth better than 15%.** (In Investment Finder, choose *Growth Rates* / EPS Growth Year vs Year >= 15.)

6. **Price-earnings ratio based on next year's estimated earnings lower than next five years' estimated growth rate.** (In Investment Finder, choose *Analyst Projections* / Forward Year P/E <= *Analyst Projections* / EPS Growth Next 5 Yr.)

7. **Current stock price no more than 20% above the stock's 52-week low.** (In Investment Finder, choose *Stock Price History* / Previous Day's Closing Price <= 52-Week Low * 1.2.)

Examining the screen closely, you can see that all it does is pinpoint stocks that are big, fast growers historically and are expected to keep on going. It's just that they've hit potholes in the road—the screen, of course, doesn't know why—and are now trading within 20% of their 52-week lows. Other great pick-ups in this screen were Citigroup (then trading as Citicorp) and global electric-power plant operator AES Corp. Less fortunate were generic-vitamin maker Rexall Sundown, nursing-home operator HCR Manor Care, oil driller Transocean Offshore, and enterprise-software maker PeopleSoft.

Table 4-1. Great GARP! Stocks / CNBC Top 100

On September 4, 1998, this screen netted seven companies in different sectors that had fallen from grace as growth stocks. By the end of the year, three were recovering nicely. After 10 months, each of those three posted returns double those of the market.

	9/4/98 Close	12/31/99 Close	6/30/99 Close	4-Mo. Chg.	10-Mo. Chg.
Tellabs	$20.44	$34.28	$67.56	68%	231%
AES	$24.25	$47.38	$58.18	95%	140%
Citigroup	$26.04	$33.18	$47.50	27%	82%
HCR Manor Care	$24.63	$29.38	$24.19	19%	-2%
Transocean Offshore	$28.50	$26.81	$26.25	-6%	-8%
Rexall Sundown	$17.40	$14.00	$12.19	-20%	-30%
PeopleSoft	$30.94	$18.94	$17.25	-39%	-44%
			Total Ret.	21%	53%
			S&P 500	27%	42%

By the spring of 1999, PeopleSoft was still coming up on the Great GARP! screen even though it had fallen another 56%. New to the list in April 1999 were formerly high-flying enterprise-software makers BMC Software, Compuware, and Keane. Were they all hurt by an overreaction to gloom in their sectors or were there specific problems at these firms? Value stocks always look worst before they turn back up, so the answer won't be forthcoming until at least the end of 1999. But BMC Software, Compuware, and Keane were up 64%, 42%, and 32% from April 1 to July 15.

One caveat: It's hard to test the Great GARP! screen against historical data because it contains criteria not collected in most commercial databases until recently. It can pin-point good ideas, but you'll benefit from learning about the stocks' recent news, funda-mental and technical health, and regulatory filings before buying. For more information on how to do this kind of research, see Chapters 8 through 11.

Cornerstone Growth: Cheap Value on the Move

Connecticut-based money manager Jim O'Shaughnessy wrote two books in the mid-1990s that made him a new star both in the community of quantitative stock analysts and among private investors. *Invest Like the Best* and *What Works on Wall Street* showed laymen for the first time how portfolios built mechanically from screens could soundly beat port-folios in which stocks were picked one by one. To measure how quickly times have changed, consider that when *What Works* was published in late 1996, stock-database firm

S&P CompuStat was able to charge investors $200 a pop to run the book's most popular screens just once. Two years later, you can run the screen online as many times as you like all day long—and you can tweak it any way you see fit—for free.

O'Shaughnessy's signature finding in *What Works* was the power of the price/sales ratio, also known as the PSR, as a measure of value. His conclusion: Companies with good 12-month relative strength trading at price/sales ratios lower than 1.5 were bargains that the market had already noticed—and thus potentially due for explosive lift-offs. He particularly likes stocks with PSRs of less than 1. After all, wouldn't it be cool to buy $1 of sales for less than $1?

Well, yes and no. The screen worked well historically for him in backtesting against the CompuStat database, and a mutual fund that he runs based on it has beaten the average small-cap mutual fund and the Russell 1000 since inception. But it hasn't proven yet to be a world-beater. It underperformed against the S&P 500 Index, 69% to 34%, over that period. The jury is still out, however, because two years is too short a time to judge whether the strategy's long-term success in practice will match its success in testing. I am fond of the screen because it makes a lot of sense. Part of the reason Cornerstone Growth has had relatively modest success in the real world for O'Shaughnessy is that the value style of investing has been out of favor since its inception. Another reason, however, might be the fact that he puts 50 stocks into the portfolio due to his beliefs about diversification and risk. (The higher the number of stocks, he says, the lower the risk.) My own research suggests that portfolios with fewer stocks actually work a lot better and *don't* carry outrageous risks. But the individual investor has an advantage over a pro like O'Shaughnessy. *You* need only three to five stocks of this type, not the much greater number required of a mutual-fund manager. I ran the screen in the CNBC Top 100 in two flavors: one to capture large stocks and one to capture small stocks. Tables 4-2 and 4-3 on the next page show the results. Here's the screen:

1. **Market capitalization greater than $150 million** (for Little Cornerstone) **or greater than $5 billion** (for Big Cornerstone). (In Investment Finder, choose *Company Basics* / Market Capitalization >= $150 million or $5 billion.)

2. **Price/sales ratio less than 1.5.** (In Investment Finder, choose *Price Ratios* / Price/Sales Ratio <= 1.5.)

3. **Earnings in the current year greater than in the past year.** (In Investment Finder, choose *Growth Rates* / EPS Growth Year vs Year >= 0.1.)

4. **Rank by 12-month relative strength.** (In Investment Finder, choose *Stock Price History* / % Change Last Year "high as possible.")

5. **Choose the top three, five, or seven, and hold one year.**

Table 4-2. Large Cornerstone / CNBC Top 100

On September 4, 1998, four of the top seven stocks netted in this screen were big retailers that posted market-beating returns. Only a disastrous merger by McKesson brought the model down over the 10-month period.

	9/4/98 Close	12/31/99 Close	6/30/99 Close	4-Mo. Chg.	10-Mo. Chg.
Lowe's	$32.19	$51.19	$56.69	59.0%	76.1%
Staples	$17.63	$29.13	$30.94	65.2%	75.5%
Wal-Mart Stores	$29.25	$40.72	$48.25	39.2%	65.0%
Fred Meyer*	$38.44	$60.25	$54.88	56.7%	42.8%
Ford Motor	$41.88	$58.69	$56.44	40.1%	34.8%
US Airways Group	$48.88	$52.00	$43.56	6.4%	-10.9%
McKesson HBOC	$76.38	$79.06	$32.19	3.5%	-57.9%
			Total Ret.	38.6%	32.2%
			S&P 500	27.0%	42.0%

* Fred Meyer merged with Kroger; last price May 27, 1999.

Table 4-3. Little Cornerstone / CNBC Top 100

On September 4, 1998, this screen netted an eclectic group, ranging from retailing to construction equipment. The model doubled the market's return by year end, and it was still beating the market after 10 months.

	9/4/98 Close	12/31/99 Close	6/30/99 Close	4-Mo. Chg.	10-Mo. Chg.
Best Buy	$23.11	$30.69	$67.50	32.8%	192.1%
Labor Ready	$13.75	$19.69	$32.50	43.2%	136.4%
Astec Industries	$16.22	$27.81	$40.75	71.5%	71.5%
Tarrant Apparel	$19.13	$39.75	$22.75	107.8%	18.9%
First American Fin.	$27.44	$32.13	$17.88	17.1%	-34.9%
			Total Ret.	54.5%	76.8%
			S&P 500	27.0%	42.0%

Both models beat the market by the end of the year, gaining 39% and 54%, respectively. The Little Cornerstone model went on to almost double the market over 10 months with a 77% return. But Large Cornerstone was dragged down to slight underperformance after one stock (McKesson HBOC) blew up as a result of a disastrous merger. It's important to note that Little Cornerstone also doubled the performance of the Russell 1000 small-stocks index over both the short and long periods.

Sleepers!: The Best Stocks in Slumbering Sectors

Another way to hunt for dirt-cheap value online: Screen for the best stocks in the worst-performing industrial sectors. For the CNBC Top 100, I determined the doggiest sectors of the market in September by running an Investment Finder screen for the 100 stocks trading the farthest from their 52-week highs. I then tallied the industrial groups most represented. Oil drillers won this pathetic contest by a mile: 11 stocks. They were followed by the oil and gas equipment/services companies and the semiconductor manufacturing-equipment makers.

You can do this at any time. (In April 1999, for instance, the business-software group that includes BMC Software, Keane, and Compuware would have been seen as the worst sector of the month.) After identifying the worst sectors, seek the stocks in those groups that have current price-earnings ratios lower than they had a year ago. (This criterion proves that the stock has truly been bombed with its group.) To find the best stocks left standing, seek the ones with the largest market capitalization (size matters in a recovery), price no worse than 60% of its 200-day moving average (a pretty low bar), a relatively strong balance sheet, and high past and estimated future growth. Then rank the stocks by one-year price change.

In September 1998, I advised readers and viewers of the list not to expect any changes in the oil patch until global prices improved and that semiconductor manufacturers would be constrained for some time by worldwide over-capacity. But I noted that the world depends desperately on the products that these two groups make to fuel mobility and the digital revolution; when they recovered, share prices and earnings ratios should expand rapidly.

Sectors fall out of favor because of excessive pessimism. But that sentiment will almost always change during the next 12 to 36 months. It certainly did for the semiconductor-equipment group. Table 4-4 shows that the screen caught these stocks very

close to their bottoms in the summer and hung with them all the way through a spectacular recovery. In many cases, brokerage analysts didn't start recommending these securities until they had already bounced 50% to 100% from their summer-low values. Meanwhile, by April 1999, a recovery also seemed to be underway in the oil group, as shown in Tables 4-5 and 4-6.

Table 4-4. Chip Equipment Sleepers / CNBC Top 100

On September 4, 1998, this screen sought the best stocks of the beaten-up semiconductor-equipment industry. The model performed three times better than the market over four months and four times better over 10 months.

	9/4/98 Close	12/31/99 Close	6/30/99 Close	4-Mo. Chg.	10-Mo. Chg.
Teradyne	$18.56	$42.38	$71.75	128.3%	286.6%
Applied Materials	$23.75	$42.69	$73.88	79.7%	211.1%
KLA-Tencor	$22.25	$43.38	$64.88	94.9%	191.6%
ATMI	$13.00	$24.63	$29.75	89.4%	128.8%
Etec Systems	$29.25	$40.00	$33.25	36.8%	13.7%
			Total Ret.	85.8%	166.3%
			S&P 500	27.0%	42.0%

Table 4-5. Oil Drilling Sleepers / CNBC Top 100

On September 4, 1998, this screen sought the best stocks of the beaten-up oil-drilling industry. The model underperformed the market over 4 and 10 months by a wide margin. Were we early or wrong? Give it another year before you decide.

	9/4/98 Close	12/31/99 Close	6/30/99 Close	4-Mo. Chg.	10-Mo. Chg.
Nabors Industries	$14.94	$13.50	$24.34	-9.6%	63.2%
Noble Drilling	$14.38	$12.94	$19.69	-10.0%	36.9%
Global Marine	$11.75	$9.00	$15.50	-23.4%	31.9%
Diamond Offshore	$23.63	$23.69	$28.38	0.2%	20.1%
Transocean Offshore	$28.50	$26.81	$26.25	-5.9%	-7.9%
			Total Ret.	-9.8%	28.8%
			S&P 500	27.0%	42.0%

Table 4-6. Energy Services Sleepers / CNBC Top 100

On September 4, 1998, this screen sought the best stocks of the beaten-up energy services industry. The model sharply underperformed the market over 4 and 10 months. But note how the biggest stocks (Baker Hughes and Schlumberger) powered past the smaller fry.

	9/4/98 Close	12/31/99 Close	6/30/99 Close	4-Mo. Chg.	10-Mo. Chg.
Baker Hughes	$21.75	$17.63	$33.50	-19.0%	54.0%
Schlumberger Ltd	$50.00	$46.34	$63.67	-7.3%	27.4%
Veritas DGC	$16.00	$13.00	$18.31	-18.8%	14.5%
Willbros Group	$9.56	$5.56	$8.50	-41.8%	-11.1%
Lufkin Industries	$26.00	$18.50	$20.00	-28.8%	-23.1%
			Total Ret.	-23.1%	12.3%
			S&P 500	27.0%	42.0%

Here's the screen we used for the semiconductor-equipment makers. Alternatively, in step 1, fill in the name of any industrial sector that you believe is unjustly beaten up.

1. **Industry name is Semiconductor Equipment & Materials.** (In Investment Finder, choose *Company Basics* / Industry Name = *Electronics* / Semiconductor Equipment & Materials.)

2. **Price-earnings ratio less than a year ago.** (In Investment Finder, choose *Price Ratios* / P/E Ratio: Current <= P/E Ratio: 1 Year Ago.)

3. **Revenue and earnings growth last year, next year, and next five years as high as possible.** (In Investment Finder, choose *Growth Rates* / Rev Growth Year vs Year "high as possible"; *Growth Rates* / EPS Growth Year vs Year "high as possible"; *Analyst Projections* / EPS Growth Next Yr "high as possible"; *Analyst Projections* / EPS Growth Next 5 Yr "high as possible.")

4. **Current price no worse than 60% below long-term support.** (In Investment Finder, choose *Stock Price History* / Previous Day's Closing Price >= *Trading & Volume* / 200-Day Moving Average * 0.6.)

5. **Low debt.** (In Investment Finder, choose *Financial Condition* / Debt to Equity Ratio <= 1.0.)

6. **Strong balance sheet.** (In Investment Finder, choose *Financial Condition* / Current Ratio >= 2.0.)

7. **Market capitalization high as possible.** (In Investment Finder, choose *Company Basics* / Market Capitalization "high as possible.")

8. **Long-term price momentum high as possible.** (In Investment Finder, choose *Stock Price History* / % Price Change Last Yr "high as possible.")

RBI Value

Remember RBI Growth from Chapter 3? Well, a value-oriented version of the model does very well in historical testing. The only change from the growth version of the model: require that the stocks have a price-sales ratio of less than 4.

While 4 is almost triple the 1.5 price-sales ratio O'Shaughnessy requires—and might make true value investors blanch—it still cuts out the outrageously overvalued companies. Of all stocks with market capitalizations greater than $7 billion in June 1999, only 50% would have made the cut.

Table 4-7. RBI Value, 1986-1999 Annual Returns

Steady application of the RBI Value strategy since 1986 would have turned $10,000 into $2 million by July 1999, according to historical testing. Compounding in final years ramps the final amount.

Year	% Return	Pct. Pts. Over S&P 500	Portfolio Value*
1986	48.1%	31.3	$14,810
1987	20.1%	19.9	$17,787
1988	33.9%	21.5	$23,817
1989	89.5%	64.0	$45,132
1990	14.1%	23.0	$51,496
1991	122.3%	91.7	$114,476
1992	35.0%	31.1	$154,542
1993	36.7%	29.6	$211,259
1994	16.5%	18.5	$246,117
1995	49.8%	16.0	$368,683
1996	62.1%	40.8	$597,635
1997	48.2%	17.9	$885,695
1998	29.4%	3.3	$1,146,089
1999**	75.0%	63.0	$2,005,656
Avg. Ret.	48.6%		
Std. Dev.	30.3%		

* Portfolio starts January 1, 1986 with $10,000.

** 1999 results through June 30.

Source: Q•Analytics Inc.

Table 4-8. RBI Value, 1986-1999

Since 1986, testing suggests that the three-stock RBI Value model would have chosen just three stocks that lost money over a calendar year. The purchases are recorded at the end of the first trading week of the year; sales are recorded in the first week of the following year (except for 1999, when the sale is recorded June 30).

	Buy	Sell	% Return
1999			
Best Buy	$31.75	$67.50	113.00%
Lexmark	$31.75	$65.94	108.00%
Staples	$30.17	$31.63	5.00%
1998			
Banco Bilbao Vizcaya, SA	$10.88	$16.00	47.10%
Coca-Cola Enterprises	$35.00	$35.75	2.10%
Omnicom Group	$41.75	$58.00	38.90%
1997			
Coca-Cola Enterprises	$16.00	$35.00	118.80%
IBM	$39.78	$52.81	32.80%
STMicroelectronics N.V.	$69.75	$65.00	-6.80%
1996			
Loral	$36.25	$51.88	43.10%
Monsanto	$24.75	$39.63	60.10%
Nike	$33.06	$60.50	83.00%
1995			
Becton, Dickinson	$12.56	$18.66	48.50%
Capital Cities/ABC	$86.13	$125.38	45.60%
Safeway	$7.78	$12.09	55.40%
1994			
Computer Associates Int'l	$12.55	$14.41	14.70%
Lowe's	$13.78	$16.69	21.10%
Wells Fargo & Co.	$130.75	$148.75	13.80%
1993			
Computer Associates Int'l	$6.00	$11.85	97.50%
Intel	$5.44	$7.75	42.50%
Winn-Dixie Stores	$38.31	$26.81	-30.00%

(continued)

Table 4-8. RBI Value, 1986-1999 *(continued)*

	Buy	Sell	% Return
1992			
Conrail	$41.06	$47.50	15.70%
Home Depot	$11.61	$16.88	45.40%
United HealthCare	$19.78	$28.44	43.80%
1991			
The Gap	$3.79	$13.05	244.20%
Nike	$9.34	$18.25	95.30%
PG&E	$25.13	$32.00	27.40%
1990			
Home Depot	$2.79	$4.17	49.40%
LM Ericsson Telephone	$3.77	$3.86	2.30%
UNUM	$12.47	$11.31	-9.30%
1989			
Fannie Mae	$4.34	$9.00	107.60%
LM Ericsson Telephone	$1.49	$3.77	152.90%
Sonoco Products	$14.94	$16.13	8.00%
1988			
GPU	$14.19	$19.00	33.90%
1987			
Becton, Dickinson	$6.33	$6.38	0.70%
Digital Equipment	$105.75	$135.00	27.70%
Walt Disney	$3.74	$4.94	31.90%
1986			
Browning-Ferris Inds.	$15.69	$23.25	48.20%
Sara Lee	$3.13	$4.33	38.20%
Walt Disney	$2.37	$3.74	58.10%

According to testing in Q·Analytics' software, a three-stock model run (as shown in Tables 4-7 and 4-8) since 1986 in this way never has a losing year. Moreover, it never underperforms the S&P 500 Index. It gains 49% a year through June 1999 with a reasonable standard deviation of 30%, and it turns $10,000 into $2 million. (If you prefer to take more stocks, a four-stock version gains 40% annually with a 26% standard deviation, turning $10,000 into $792,000 through December 1998. A five-stock version gains 35% annually in historical testing with a 21% standard deviation, turning $10,000 into $527,000 through December 1998.)

Here's the recipe:

1. **12-month revenues greater than $500 million.** (In Investment Finder, choose *Current Financials* / 12-Month Revenue >= $500 million.)

2. **12-month income greater than $30 million.** (In Investment Finder, choose *Current Financials* / 12-Month Income: Cont. Ops. >= $30 million.)

3. **Earnings growth in the past 12 months greater than 1%.** (In Investment Finder, choose *Growth Rates* / EPS Growth >= 1%.)

4. **Beta greater than 0.5.** (In Investment Finder, choose *Trading & Volume* / Beta >= 0.5.)

5. **Beta less than 1.9.** (In Investment Finder, choose *Trading & Volume* / Beta <= 1.9.)

6. **Current price greater than the price three months and one month ago.** (In Investment Finder, choose *Stock Price History* / % Price Change Last Mo. >= 1 and *Stock Price History* / % Price Change Last Qtr. >= 1.)

7. **Market capitalization within the top 350.** (In 1999, the smallest capitalization in the top 350 is $7 billion. In Investment Finder, choose *Company Basics* / Market Capitalization >= $7 billion.)

8. **Price/sales ratio less than 4.** (In Investment Finder, choose *Price Ratios* / Price/Sales Ratio <= 4.)

9. **Rank by 52-week return, and take the top three, four, or seven.**

Performed with discipline and thoughtfulness—rather than just contrariness—value investing can be both rewarding and satisfying. Even for a year-trader.

Now let's put away the Investment Finder and our spreadsheets for awhile and learn some more conventional—and unfortunately less steadfast—ways to uncover interesting stocks by using the Web. First, we'll look at online news and newsletter sites, and then we'll move on to fundamental and technical analysis, regulatory filings, and community discussion groups.

Part II
Using News and Commentary

Chapter 5
Web News Organizations

Imagine the tension felt by investors in past centuries who sought news about their stakes in risky enterprises far from home. In the 1600s, shareholders in British or Dutch cargo ships often waited years for word of their captains' bounty. In the 1800s, investors in the eastern United States waited months for the Pony Express and later the telegraph to deliver word from the American frontier of the success of gold mines, cattle drives, or logging claims. As recently as the early 1990s, serious investors were obligated to subscribe to tens of newspapers and magazines and paw through mountains of paper to find news items that could mean success or failure in new ventures.

Today we have quite the opposite problem. So much news barrels toward us through dozens of outlets on the Internet that our real problem is deciding what *not* to read. Every major Web site provides business news from wire services as a staple, and dozens of sites focus on the aggregation and dissemination of specialized business news.

Sheer quantity doesn't help the investor, however, and the measure of greatness in news organizations has been their ability to reliably winnow down the day's umpteen million data points to just a few important ones. In the physical world, we depend upon the editors of the *Los Angeles Times* or *Wall Street Journal* to front-page just the dozen or so most important stories of the day. And likewise in the virtual world, investors have come to rely on the editors of a few key news Web sites to funnel all the news of the hour or day into a single home page for digestion.

If you follow the yeartrading style of investing that I have described so far, news has more value as education and entertainment than as a source of trading ideas. It *might* help you make more intelligent dinner-party conversation about the market or your stocks, but it won't necessarily help your returns. If you like to pick stocks one at a time, however, news events are extremely important.

In Part II, I'll show you some of the best sites for the fire-hose style of news and those whose editors do the best job of saving you time by narrowing your choices. In this chapter, I'll examine Web-based news organizations. In Chapter 6, I'll investigate mainstream news organizations that have set up online delivery. In Chapter 7, I'll examine a few good investment-newsletter sites.

First, let's take a swing through news on the Net in a hunt to separate fresh facts, ideas, and insightful perspective from rumors, gossip, and hallucinations.

The Nightly Round

For the serious private investor, the process of news gathering should start each week on Sunday night and continue most nights thereafter. Create bookmarks for the sites in this chapter that suit your style, and then visit them one after the other in the same sequence every night. It's useful to create a regular pattern as a financial news hound so that you don't make mistakes and miss something important. It's also important to have an agenda for your nightly rounds so that you don't get distracted and wander off into non-financial matters. Your purpose is to find tradable information, not merely to be amused.

Almost anyone can benefit from the general-news sites, and investors who specialize in particular industries will want to focus later in the evening on niche news sites. I'll cover the general sites first and then look at the others.

Touring Yahoo! Finance

The granddaddy of Web sites for news still rocks. I first encountered business news at Yahoo! in 1995 well before the company had made the transition to fame and fortune as a public company. I was working at the *Los Angeles Times* as an executive news editor, and a colleague told me about a cool location on the Internet where you could read news for free without belonging to an online service like Prodigy, CompuServe, or America Online. In the newsroom, we had access to all the news we could eat through dedicated workstations on our desks, but at home or on the road we were out of luck.

When I first visited Yahoo! via a cranky old MCI Internet access service at home, I was amazed. It was a crude, text-only aggregation of bookmarks that required rudimentary knowledge of UNIX programming to navigate. But I was instantly hooked, and I've used Yahoo! virtually every day since for gathering financial news. There are hundreds of ways to use Yahoo! to find relevant business news, so poke around for an hour after you try this straightforward approach.

The Yahoo! Finance Home Page

On the Yahoo! home page (*http://www.yahoo.com*), click Stock Quotes, and you'll arrive at the area of the site devoted to financial and other business news, called Yahoo! Finance (*http://quote.yahoo.com*), shown in Figure 5-1. This is an outstanding control center for business-news seekers.

Figure 5-1.   May 4, 1999

The Yahoo! Finance home page is a command center for news gathering at the popular Web portal. In a compact space, you can view price and volume levels of the major indices, as well as the time left in the day to make a trade.

Starting at the top of the page, you'll see a table that lists the status of the Dow Jones Industrial Average, the Nasdaq Composite, the Standard & Poor's 500 Index, and the 30-Year U.S. Treasury Bond. Check these figures every day after the markets close at 4 p.m. Eastern—or even during the day. This will give you a good feel for the stock and bond markets' movement over time.

Study the volume of the New York Stock Exchange (NYSE) and Nasdaq frequently as well, so that you become familiar with whether a strong move up or down has been accomplished on high volume or low volume. Low-volume moves—for instance, NYSE daily volume of less than 600 million shares—are much less important or trustworthy as indicators of investor sentiment than high-volume moves. If you see a 2% move upward in the Dow on NYSE volume of 1 billion shares or more, the move is legitimate. The same move on volume of 600 million shares is less meaningful if you're trying to determine

the market trend. In this table, you'll also see a counter that shows the number of hours and minutes until the close of trading, which is deceptively useful.

The heart of Yahoo! Finance's news control station is in the middle of the page under the title banner. You'll want to pay attention to at least 6 of the 11 sections: U.S. Markets, World Markets, Research, Editorial, Financial News, and Latest Market News.

U.S. Markets

In the U.S. Markets area, start with Major U.S. Indices, shown in Figure 5-2. This page lists the levels and changes in all the major domestic stock and commodity indices.

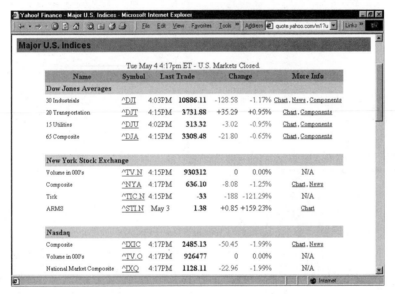

Figure 5-2.   May 4, 1999

Yahoo! Finance puts all the major U.S. indices on one page. You can click links to see their charts and news. In some cases, you can also get easy access to quotes for an index's components.

Major U.S. indices shown include:

- The Dow Jones Averages (Industrial, Transportation, Utility, and Composite)
- The Nasdaq Composite and Nasdaq 100
- The S&P 500 and its cousins the S&P 100 (the largest of the S&P 500 stocks); the S&P MidCap 400 (largely stocks with market caps from $1 billion to $10 billion); and the S&P SmallCap 600 (largely stocks with market caps less than $1 billion)

- Specialized indices of the American Stock Exchange, such as ones focused on Internet stocks (IIX and DOT) and major big-cap stocks (XMI)

- The Philadelphia Stock Exchange's semiconductor index (SOXX)

- The Pacific Stock Exchange's Technology Index (PSE)

It's productive to scan the list at least once a day to learn which parts of the market are moving. If you fancy yourself a momentum trader, you want to look for the sectors and sizes of stocks that are moving up; if you're a contrarian trader, you want to focus on the ones that are moving down.

All in all, you'll see that even when the market moves extremely well, as it did on March 5, 1999, not all parts of the market move equally: While the Dow Jones Industrial Average had a spectacular 2.8% move that day (up 268 points to a record 9,736), the Dow Transports moved just 1.7%, the Nasdaq Composite Index moved 0.9%, the S&P MidCap 400 moved just 0.8%, and the S&P SmallCap 600 advanced a paltry 0.7%. The best movers of the day were the Philadelphia Semiconductor index, up 6.2%, and the Major Market Index, up 2.9%. This suggests that investors were not treating all stocks equally. Trend followers were well-advised to focus on large stocks, particularly the biggest companies in the semiconductor sector, such as Intel, Texas Instruments, STMicro-electronics, Applied Materials, Broadcom, Xilinx, and Linear Technology. (Those stocks

How to Use the News

I learned in my weekend prowl through Yahoo! Finance's indexes on Sunday, March 7, that large stocks and semiconductor stocks had performed best the previous trading day—Friday, March 5. If that trend continued, a reasonable strategy might have been to find the largest semiconductor stocks that were the farthest from their 52-week highs. A strong market would at least carry them back to those highs.

To find these stocks, open a new browser window, and visit the Investment Finder stock-screening engine at MSN MoneyCentral (*http://moneycentral.msn.com/investor/finder/customstocks.asp*). Then follow these steps to get a list similar to the one shown in Figure 5-3:

1. Create a screen with the following criteria:

   - Market Capitalization >= $5 billion

   - Industry Name = Electronics—Semiconductor - Broad Line

   - Previous Day's Closing Price / 52-Week High (Display Only)

   - Previous Day's Closing Price (Display Only)

(continued)

went on to post gains over the next two months of 12%, 54%, 17%, 41%, 155%, 52%, and 50%. Over the same period, the S&P 500 was up just 10%.)

Most Actives

Check the Most Actives section to learn which stocks are seeing the most trading action. Volume is the fuel of the market, so it behooves a trend-following investor to know which stocks on which exchanges are moving the most. Big volume increases generally precede and precipitate big price moves, both up and down.

To discover why a stock on the list is moving, click its News link. Yahoo! Finance keeps two weeks of news items about each stock, so it's likely that you'll find a reason, or at least a rationale, behind every moving stock.

How to Use the News *(continued)*

2. Export that list to a spreadsheet by using the options on the Finder's File menu as described in Appendix A.

3. Repeat the screen with the Finder's four other semiconductor groups:

   - Semiconductor - Specialized
   - Semiconductor - Memory Chips
   - Semiconductor - Integrated Circuits
   - Semiconductor Equipment & Materials

4. After you've run each of these four screens, open the Finder's Edit menu, and then choose Copy Results To Clipboard. That puts the result set in your computer's short-term memory.

5. Then return to your spreadsheet, and use its pasting function (Ctrl-V in Microsoft Excel) to insert the screen's result set into your spreadsheet, below the rows that are already there.

6. When your list is complete, use your spreadsheet program's sorting function to arrange the list according to the parameter that the market seems to favor most at the time. Figure 5-3 shows a screen I created on March 7, 1999. In that case, market capitalization won out because the large-cap stocks of the Dow and the Major Market Index had performed best the previous trading day. This would be a good list of stocks to research further, with the largest ones theoretically more favored by the market than the smaller ones. I exported the list in Figure 5-3 to Excel, as shown in Table 5-1.

Market Digest

In the Market Digest section, shown in Figure 5-4, you'll learn how many issues on each major exchange advanced compared to the number that declined and the number of new highs compared to the number of new lows. Technical traders hate to see big market advances in which the number of declining issues is larger than the number of advancing issues or in which the number of new lows is larger than the number of new highs.

If the market moves up sharply but the advance/decline and new high/new low ratio is even or weighted heavily toward decliners and new lows, you should visualize a big red warning flag over the page. On the other hand, bearish contrarians look for moments when the number of new highs sharply swamps the number of new lows. They believe it signals an overabundance of optimism and potentially a market top.

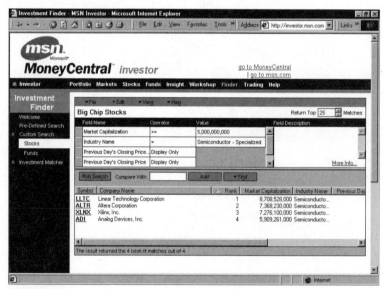

Figure 5-3.   March 7, 1999

You can create screens in MSN MoneyCentral's Investment Finder to take advantage of news insights. In this case, I created a screen to seek large-cap semiconductor stocks that were farthest from their 52-week highs.

(continued)

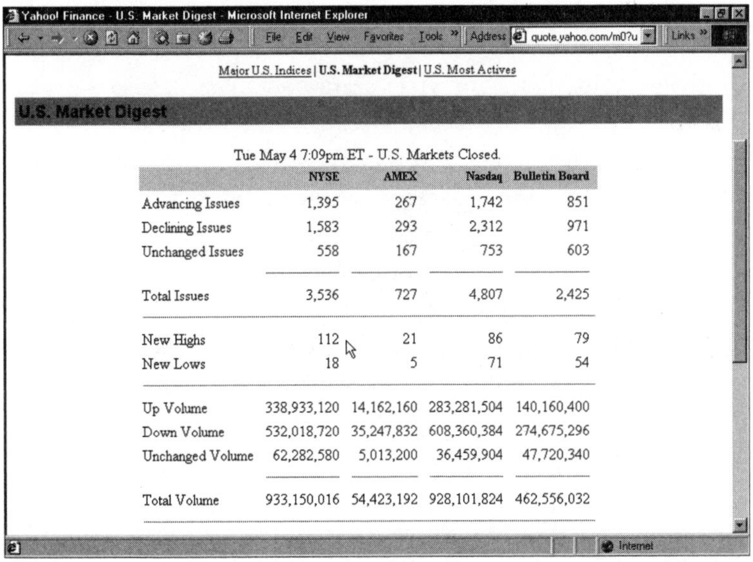

	NYSE	AMEX	Nasdaq	Bulletin Board
Advancing Issues	1,395	267	1,742	851
Declining Issues	1,583	293	2,312	971
Unchanged Issues	558	167	753	603
Total Issues	3,536	727	4,807	2,425
New Highs	112	21	86	79
New Lows	18	5	71	54
Up Volume	338,933,120	14,162,160	283,281,504	140,160,400
Down Volume	532,018,720	35,247,832	608,360,384	274,675,296
Unchanged Volume	62,282,580	5,013,200	36,459,904	47,720,340
Total Volume	933,150,016	54,423,192	928,101,824	462,556,032

Figure 5-4. May 4, 1999

The Market Digest page gives a concise view of the day's trading. On this day, the Dow fell 125 points, but many more stocks hit new highs than hit new lows on the New York Stock Exchange and the Nasdaq. That suggests the market, which looked sickly on the surface, was fundamentally healthy.

How to Use the News *(continued)*

Company Name	Market Cap	Price / 52-Wk High	3/5/99 Close
Intel	191,194,500,000	79%	$113.40
Texas Instruments	39,312,175,000	88%	$92.50
Applied Materials	22,692,611,000	80%	$57.60
Micron Technology	14,843,941,000	66%	$53.00
STMicroelectronics	12,447,934,000	80%	$85.70
Linear Technology	7,023,310,000	83%	$44.50
Maxim Integrated Circuits	6,199,752,000	80%	$45.50
Xilinx	5,929,925,000	79%	$69.10
Altera	5,600,486,000	75%	$53.90

Table 5-1. Investment Finder Data in Microsoft Excel

You can export data from Investment Finder to Microsoft Excel for further analysis. This table would help an investor determine how to potentially take advantage of the market's March 1999 interest in large-cap semiconductor stocks. The third column shows, on a percentage basis, how far each stock was from its 52-week high. Two months later, this group was up 31% on average while the S&P 500 was up 10%.

Initial Public Offerings

The IPOs section at Yahoo! Finance contains a richly detailed, comprehensive list of companies that either plan to launch an "initial public offering" of stock to the public soon or have done so in the recent past. Visit a couple of times each week to discover the latest companies to join the public equity markets and the performance of companies that have preceded them recently. The section, shown in Figure 5-5, is divided into six parts:

- **Pricings** The price at which a company will begin trading, which is set by its underwriter. This section includes links to registration documents filed at the U.S. Securities & Exchange Commission, or SEC.

- **Filings** The date on which private companies have filed financial documents with the SEC that indicate their intention to go public

- **Withdrawals** Companies that filed but decided against the move

- **Latest IPO News** News about recent public offerings or filings

- **Post-IPO Performance** Best and worst three-month, six-month, and one-year stock-price performance by IPOs

- **Resources and Web Sites** A glossary, a list of relevant Web sites, and Yahoo! message boards devoted to IPOs

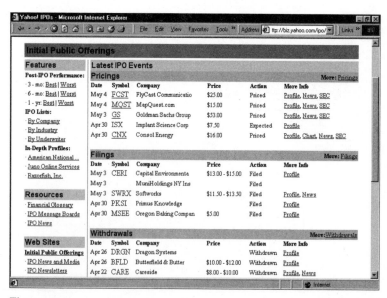

Figure 5-5.   May 4, 1999

The IPO section of Yahoo! Finance's U.S. Markets section offers a succinct view of the action for initial public offerings. Although not the most complete Web site for IPO news, it's among the most compact and useful.

Using IPO Information

First the bad news: recent academic research shows that most initial public offerings make bad investments. In 1998 and 1999, investors' perspectives on the value of IPOs was skewed by the spectacular success of a few that soared the first day and kept on running. For the most part, only company insiders, venture-capital investors, and major customers of the full-service brokerage taking a company public can buy stocks of potentially hot IPOs at their opening prices, although an increasing number of online discount brokerages now offer shares as well. However, your chances of receiving a significant number of pre-open IPO shares of top companies from online brokers are similar to your chances of winning the lottery.

E*Trade and Wit Capital assign shares of IPOs to investors expressing interest in the order in which they send e-mail. Fidelity and Charles Schwab allocate IPO shares on the basis of fuzzier criteria that include the size of one's account. But reports from users suggest that very few online investors actually get these IPO shares. Until that changes, you're better off keeping a full-service account for this purpose. See Chapter 13 for more information on brokerages.

World Markets

Check the Major World Indices page in the World Markets section at least once a week to learn how stock markets around the world are faring in comparison with U.S. markets. (See Figure 5-6.) On March 5, for instance, the S&P 500's strong performance was actually dwarfed by a 3.3% gain in Hong Kong's Hang Seng Index, a 5% gain in Japan's Nikkei Index, a 6.9% gain in Thailand's SET Index, and a 3.4% gain in Germany's DAX Index.

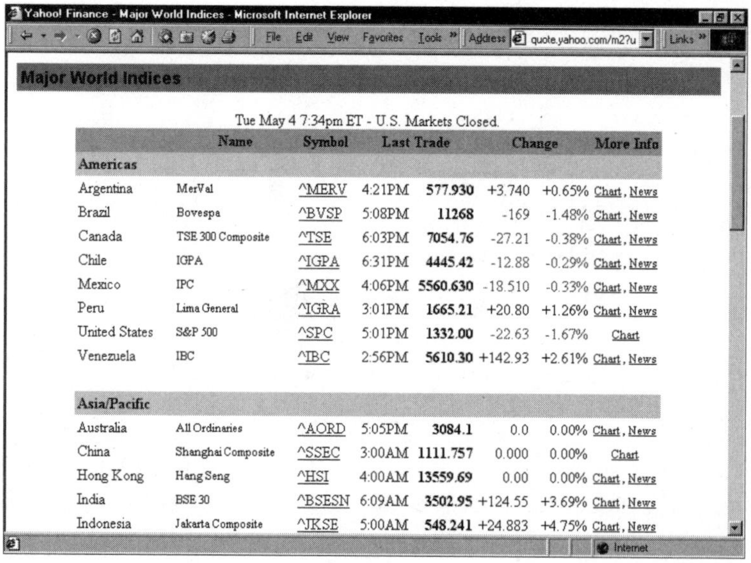

	Name	Symbol	Last Trade		Change		More Info
Americas							
Argentina	MerVal	^MERV	4:21PM	**577.930**	+3.740	+0.65%	Chart, News
Brazil	Bovespa	^BVSP	5:08PM	**11268**	-169	-1.48%	Chart, News
Canada	TSE 300 Composite	^TSE	6:03PM	**7054.76**	-27.21	-0.38%	Chart, News
Chile	IGPA	^IGPA	6:31PM	**4445.42**	-12.88	-0.29%	Chart, News
Mexico	IPC	^MXX	4:06PM	**5560.630**	-18.510	-0.33%	Chart, News
Peru	Lima General	^IGRA	3:01PM	**1665.21**	+20.80	+1.26%	Chart, News
United States	S&P 500	^SPC	5:01PM	**1332.00**	-22.63	-1.67%	Chart
Venezuela	IBC	^IBC	2:56PM	**5610.30**	+142.93	+2.61%	Chart, News
Asia/Pacific							
Australia	All Ordinaries	^AORD	5:05PM	**3084.1**	0.0	0.00%	Chart, News
China	Shanghai Composite	^SSEC	3:00AM	**1111.757**	0.000	0.00%	Chart
Hong Kong	Hang Seng	^HSI	4:00AM	**13559.69**	0.00	0.00%	Chart, News
India	BSE 30	^BSESN	6:09AM	**3502.95**	+124.55	+3.69%	Chart, News
Indonesia	Jakarta Composite	^JKSE	5:00AM	**548.241**	+24.883	+4.75%	Chart, News

Figure 5-6. May 4, 1999

The Major World Indices page of Yahoo! Finance provides a compact view of the trading in all major markets around the globe, as well as easy access to charts and news.

To learn more about one of these indexes, click its Chart link, and then click Moving Avg in the lower-right corner to display the 50- and 200-day moving average, as shown in Figure 5-7. To see the data on which the chart is based, click the Table link at the bottom of the chart for the interval that interests you (daily, weekly, or monthly). If you want to archive the data behind the chart, click the Get Historical Data button, and click the Download Spreadsheet Format link at the bottom of the page to store the data in a spreadsheet program such as Microsoft Excel.

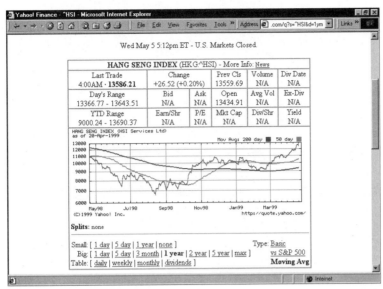

Figure 5-7.   May 5, 1999

Yahoo! Finance provides one-day to five-year charts for the market indexes of most major countries. In this one-year chart, it's easy to see that Hong Kong's Hang Seng Index broke above resistance in March and kept on chugging.

If a recent gain has pushed a depressed index back above the "resistance" of its long-term moving averages, it can be productive to discover the major stocks in the index that are responsible for much of the advance. Many countries' economies are so heavily consolidated that just a handful of large industrial and financial firms are responsible for a bulk of their markets' movements.

To learn more about which companies might be behind the gain, click the News link, if any, and read newswire articles about the previous days' advance. In the case of the jump in Japan's beleaguered stock market on March 5, wire stories pointed out that industrial giants Sony and Toshiba were expected to create an unprecedented joint venture focused on creating parts for Sony's popular Playstation gaming console. The Nikkei that day edged up above its 200-day moving average for the first time in eight months, and Sony's price also had just edged up above its own 200-day moving average to $82.25. The stock's three-year high at the time was $101, which it hit back in July 1997.

If the Japanese market were to stay strong, an investor could have easily concluded that Sony might make a decent play. *The New York Times* had just that day published a business-section cover story describing Sony's potential to become the leading maker of operating systems for the next generation of computer-powered consumer electronics devices. While investors highly attuned to Sony and Japanese stocks might have already

known that for weeks, if not months, this combination of price action and media buzz constituted potentially tradable news for an online investor. Sure enough, two months later, Sony had eclipsed its old high. It closed on July 6 at $111.18.

It's quite sensible for private investors to own shares in overseas firms that trade in U.S. markets in the form of American Depositary Receipts, or ADRs. These represent shares of foreign companies traded in U.S. dollars on U.S. exchanges. For all intents and purposes, they are just like shares; you buy and sell through a broker, pay a commission, and so forth. Technically, though, ADRs are tradable receipts for actual shares on deposit at a bank. Foreign companies use ADRs to make it easier for Americans to buy their shares.

Research

The Upgrades/Downgrades and Earnings Surprises sections of the Research area at Yahoo! Finance are worth a visit more than once a week. Upgrades/Downgrades shows the stocks about which brokerage research analysts have become either more or less optimistic. When analysts become more sanguine on a stock, they describe their reasoning to their firm's retail and institutional stock brokers. (See Chapter 10 for more information on this.) The brokers are then, of course, supposed to recommend the stock more heartily to their clients. The often-complicated string of reasoning is condensed into a rating at most brokerages that ranges from "sell" or "hold" on the low end to "strong buy" on the high end.

Every brokerage has its own rating system, and Yahoo! Finance provides a very handy secondary page, called Equity Ratings, that shows the precise range of ratings for individual brokerages. On March 5, 1999, the Upgrades area showed that Morgan Stanley Dean Witter had upgraded large semiconductor makers Altera and Microchip Technologies from "outperform" to "strong buy." The Equity Ratings area shows that Morgan Stanley's ratings are "underperform," "neutral," "outperform," and "strong buy," so the two chipmakers were now getting the firm's highest ratings. The news coincided with the information discovered earlier that the Philadelphia Semiconductor Index had jumped that day.

To learn about *previous* upgrades or downgrades on a stock that catches your eye, click the History link in the final column. That leads to a page that lists all previous times in the past year or two in which the stock's rating had changed.

Checking Altera's history (Figure 5-8), I learned that the stock had been downgraded by four brokerages—including Morgan Stanley—in January. It had since been upgraded by five brokerages in February and March, with Donaldson Lufkin Jenrette making it a "top pick" on February 4, 1999. The prior round of upgrades for the stock had occurred almost exactly a year before, with Morgan Stanley upgrading it from the same "outperform" to "strong buy" on March 20, 1998.

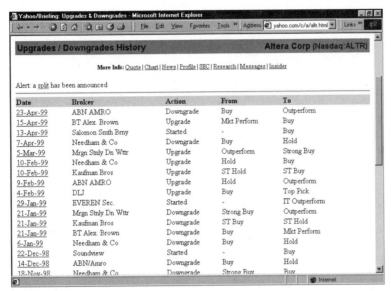

Figure 5-8.   May 5, 1999

Between March 5 and April 23, 1999, Altera had been upgraded, downgraded, and upgraded again. At least a year of ratings changes on most large stocks is available on Yahoo! Finance's Upgrades & Downgrades history page.

Using Upgrade Information

To investigate how well Morgan Stanley had called Altera's price moves in the past, you can follow these steps:

1. Open a new browser window, and load MSN MoneyCentral Investor (*http://moneycentral.msn.com/investor*).

2. Type the symbol for Altera (ALTR) in the text box in the upper-left corner of the front page, choose Chart from the drop-down menu, and click Go. The default chart shows one-year price performance.

3. Open the Chart menu, and choose Investment Growth. Open the Period menu, and choose Custom.

4. In the date-range dialog box, enter the date ranges that coincide with Morgan Stanley's rating changes.

Earnings Surprises

Check the Extreme Surprises page of the Earnings Surprises section regularly to find stocks that really creamed analysts' expectations. Several academic studies have found that stocks that surprise once generally surprise again and again. The notion has become colorfully known on Wall Street as the "cockroach theory." If you find one, there will probably be a lot more.

On March 5, 1999, the only interesting "extreme surprise" was from ABR Information Services (ABRX). The stock of the small-cap company, which provides benefits and payroll administration on an outsourcing basis, surged 8.5% following its earnings announcement. It popped through its 50-day moving average for the first time in a month. The last time it jumped above its 50-day moving average, back on December 9, 1998, the stock went on to climb from $15 to $23—a 58% jump. If that had happened again, the stock would have risen from its current $20.62 to $32.50. To discover more about the fundamentals of ABR's business, I clicked the News link. There I found a press release that declared the firm's net income had jumped 35.7% in the past quarter compared to the year-ago period on an 80% jump in revenue. The company's chief executive remarked in the release that it was the firm's 20th consecutive quarter of better than 30% revenue

You will discover that after the "strong buy" upgrade on March 20, 1998, Altera fell by 6% over the next month but ended up rising 14% by May 5. Looking out farther, the stock fell by a total of 25% to its lowest point during the 1998 summer correction, but it turned around to ultimately climb 79% by mid-January 1999. Morgan Stanley then lowered its rating to "outperform" on January 21, and the stock plunged 19%. Apparently figuring the security had been punished enough, the brokerage then decided to start over again with the "strong buy" upgrade on March 5. On that date, the stock jumped 6.7%, about the same as other semiconductor stocks and three times better than the overall market. What goes around comes around. By May 5, the stock was up another 37%. More importantly, however, you can see that if you had simply bought on the upgrade on March 20, 1998, and never sold, you'd be up 101% in Altera by May 5, turning $10,000 into $20,100.

growth. Certainly one to keep an eye on. (The stock ultimately traded down during the next two months to a low of $13.50 before leaping to $25 on the strength of a May 3 takeover offer from Ceridian.)

Editorial

The editorial premise of Yahoo! generally is to provide a thin sheen of branding on top of partners' content, leveraging other firms' efforts for its own purposes. Nowhere is this more evident than in its business-editorial area, where you can obtain a quick overview of at least three major online news providers without ever leaving the friendly confines of Yahoo!.

The Motley Fool

Yahoo!'s offerings are liable to change at any time, but let's start with The Motley Fool. The most useful links are to the Fool's Lunchtime and Evening reports on market movers, plus its Daily Double and Daily Trouble reports. The Motley Fool, one of the first financial Web sites, has a staff of journalists who provide news analysis that's occasionally keener and more quickly produced than what you'll find at the *Wall Street Journal* or *New York Times*. On March 9, 1999, for instance, its noon report on the split-up of RJR Nabisco was finely tuned to the valuation metrics that investors use but that aren't typically articulated by the financial press. The report went on with 22 more meaty paragraphs on the day's winning and losing stocks. This is a lot more than a standard Reuters report. The "Double" column examines a stock that has doubled in the past year and how investors could have caught onto the story before the run-up. The "Trouble" column examines a stock that has dropped by more than 50% over the past year and how investors could have avoided it. The focus is on useful trading ideas, which is a key advantage.

TheStreet.com

TheStreet.com has an outstanding mix of free articles and columns about investing and a good mix of premium columns. I'll give you more information on this leading financial journalism site later in this chapter. For now, note that much of its best free content is posted on Yahoo!, including excellent mutual-fund coverage (FundWatch), a regular report on tech stocks (Silicon Valley), and a regular report on online brokers. You'll also find a new piece, titled Wrong! by fast-trading columnist James J. Cramer every day. The columns are published on Yahoo! a day after they appear on TheStreet.com's own site, but it doesn't matter. Cramer rarely puts any truly tradable information in his column. He's more like a sports columnist in that way. You might not find out the score of yesterday's game, but you'll discover how Cramer felt about it and maybe pick up a tactical tip.

Individual Investor

In early 1999, Yahoo! added Individual Investor to its editorial lineup. This is a solid research outfit headed by Jonathan Steinberg that has published a good list of stock picks known as the Magic 25 the past few years. It has not beaten the market every year, but the methodology behind its stock-picking and articles are strong. It relies on screening to find good revenue growth, insider buying, and cash flow.

Individual Investor's columns in Yahoo! Finance are argued well and packed with strong investment ideas. On March 9, for instance, its Industry Analysis column presented a fresh, persuasive take on why Hewlett-Packard might acquire Novell. The latter had been rumored as a takeover candidate by *Barron's* magazine the week before, but this was the first piece to detail reasons why Hewlett-Packard could and should do the deed.

Financial News

Finally, cruise through the Financial News area of Yahoo! Finance. What was the rest of this stuff, if not financial news? You'll find out in this area, where you can mainline raw feeds from Reuters' general business, securities, and international wires; the Associated Press; and Standard & Poor's, as well as press releases from Business Wire and PR Newswire. On a weekday in March, the U.S. Markets news area alone had seven pages of Reuters Securities wire news from 3:30 p.m. to 7:30 p.m. To get full value out of Yahoo!'s offerings for investors, subscribe to the MyYahoo! feature on the home page. This allows you to set up your own command center for financial information—including views of several portfolios, top news stories on each of the stocks in those portfolios, and a daily list of analyst-ratings changes, earnings announcements, and split dates.

Touring CBS MarketWatch

The CBS MarketWatch site (*www.cbs.Marketwatch.com*) was launched as a joint venture between Data Broadcasting Corp. and CBS in 1998. Since then, it has steadily gained momentum to become one of the top five places on the Web to find high-quality financial news and analysis at no charge. In 1999, it capitalized on its first-mover advantage and excellent branding to become the first financial site to go public.

Far from just a pretty face with good parentage, MarketWatch's strengths run deep. Its predecessor site, DBC.com, was one of the first places that investors could get delayed price quotes and a smattering of specialized news. Today, MarketWatch carries

that innovation forward. Start with its home page, shown in Figure 5-9. It's designed like a newspaper's front page, with a big headline directing readers to the most important story. That shows its editors understand their job is to guide readers to the most important stuff. This is a rarity among news sites, which are largely more egalitarian, showing a list of equally weighted headlines.

Figure 5-9.   May 6, 1999

CBS MarketWatch presents a newspaper-like front page that displays the top three or four stories of the hour plus dozens of columns. Visit this site for IPO coverage, breaking news, and the StockWatch and Internet Daily columns.

MarketWatch's daily news reporting is unparalleled in its breadth, though depth is often a problem. Many articles are just a few paragraphs long and therefore barely worth the effort to click. It has bright concepts such as the Clueless Investor column, which beats up on brokerage analysts who make bad calls on stocks. Daily news columns are devoted to everything from IPOs to mergers to Internet stocks to Hollywood stocks. In May 1999, the site had at least 20 distinct investment-news columns, 25 commentary columns, 7 columns just about IPOs, and 9 columns about personal finance. If you can't find a good idea here, you aren't looking hard enough.

One more word about breadth: this is one of the few places to find regular news updates about the futures market, which is far bigger than the equities market. You'll find out when crude-oil, cotton, and pork-belly futures are soaring or falling overnight and why. Such information is critical for forecasting the fate of companies in the oil-drilling, apparel-making, and food-processing industries.

Touring MSN MoneyCentral Investor

I'll spare you any superlatives about MSN MoneyCentral Investor (*moneycentral.msn.com /investor*), shown in Figure 5-10, because they'd be self-serving. Rated by *Barron's* as the top all-around financial Web site in 1998 and 1999, MSN MoneyCentral Investor has a wide variety of news resources. Each day of the week, the site runs at least two financial articles or columns, each with a strong point of view in one of these categories: Sectors & Trends, Mutual Funds, Strategies, Interviews, and Company Focus. In addition, Money-Central offers commentary from up to 12 columnists, money managers, or investment researchers each day.

Figure 5-10.   May 6, 1999

The home page of MSN MoneyCentral's investing section is a command center for the site's rich array of columns, news, and stock-portfolio descriptions. News, commentary, and stock-pick headlines appear in the middle of the page, as well as behind the Insight link on the top navigation bar.

Start with the Insight section by scanning the New Today page. You'll find articles and columns for the past seven days on subjects ranging from prospects for Internet stock brokerages to accounting problems at enterprise-software firms. To see past stories in a particular department—such as Strategies—click Articles in the left navigation bar, choose the Departments option from the choices across the top of the page, and then click Strategies. You'll see all the stories in that category published in the past year. Likewise, you can search for articles by author (for example, Jon Markman or Jim Jubak), company (for example, Microsoft or IBM), or topic (for example, Retirement or Banking).

For expert commentary, click Jubak's Journal, SuperModels, Strategy Lab, and Careful Investor in the left navigation bar. More on the first three below; the latter is authored by Mary Rowland, a veteran journalist who addresses the needs of conservative investors with columns about such topics as asset allocation, municipal bonds, and value stocks. I write the SuperModels column, which is published at least once a month to follow the results of the model portfolios I described in Part I. In addition, MSN MoneyCentral regularly creates special reports on topical issues of interest to investors, such as Internet stocks, taxes, and year-end reviews.

SuperModels

The SuperModels column, shown in Figure 5-11, monitors the performance of my year-trading style of investing. It also offers a convenient place to discover the latest stocks that investors following the SuperModels style should consider for purchase.

Figure 5-11.   May 6, 1999
The monthly SuperModels column monitors the progress of a 30-stock portfolio of price- and earnings-momentum stocks chosen in a strictly mechanical fashion from Investment Finder screens.

To view a Flare-Out Growth or Redwood Growth model portfolio, click the Portfolio link under the model that interests you on the left side of the page. The portfolios are updated at the beginning of each quarter with the current set of picks. In the lower-right corner, you'll find the quarterly return of the model and the return of the S&P 500

Index for comparison. In the upper-left corner of the portfolio page is a list of returns by quarter and for the year to date. To see the returns by quarter of each model from inception to the present, click the Qtr. link.

To view the current picks of each SuperModel, click Today's Picks. That displays the Investment Finder with the model's screen. (See Chapters 2 and 3 to learn about the Flare-Out and Redwood Growth models.) Readers interested in following the strategies are instructed to buy the first 3, 5, 7, or 10 stocks listed—in order.

Jubak's Journal

Jim Jubak, the senior markets editor at MSN MoneyCentral, writes twice a week on topics that range from stock-valuation principles to global trends. Jubak's professorial tone is refreshing and reassuring on the Web. He's one of the most readable financial journalists around, and he's certainly one of the most knowledgeable.

For Jubak, the process of finding profitable stocks is almost as rewarding as the results. So he tends first to write about the strategies, trends, and emotions of Wall Street. Then, to separate what actually works from what only seems like a great idea, he tries to find individual stocks that embody a particular approach. Finally, he tracks those stocks to see how the ideas play out in Jubak's Picks. He also maintains, prunes, and comments upon a list of the 50 greatest stocks in the world. You can reach Jubak's Picks and his list of the 50 best stocks from links in the sidebar of his regular column.

Quotable Jubak: On the Value of News

Here's a passage from March 16, 1999, concerning news that sent one of his favorite stocks, Saville Systems, plunging:

> *Sometimes the internal working of the market itself is news. I think it's important to remember that the market for any stock is composed of investors who not only have different amounts of access to the news—usually because they expend the time and money to dig for it—but that also have different interpretations of the news. On any trade, after all, both buyer and seller are convinced that they are getting the best end of the deal. Over time, one or the other of them will turn out to be wrong. In Saville's case, the market is divided between those who see recent news from the company about rising expenses and new product introductions as negative events for the stock and those who see the same items as positive.*

(continued)

Strategy Lab

On most financial-news sites, there is plenty of opinion without accountability. Writers and pundits comment on stocks and strategies in great gales of glibness, but they seldom follow up to let you know whether they were right or wrong.

Frustration over the lack of accountability gave rise to the Strategy Lab feature at MSN MoneyCentral, shown in Figure 5-12. It gives readers an inside view as six professionals practice the art and science of investing in real time. At six-month intervals, the site starts a new round of the Lab by giving each pro a hypothetical $100,000 with one rule: pick a strategy and stick to it. The pros must run their portfolios as if they belonged to clients and comment on transactions at least once or twice a week in "journal" entries. This makes the Lab function much like a newsletter advocating six investment approaches.

The first page of the lab is accessible from the home page of MSN MoneyCentral. That page provides a weekly summary of the managers' successes and failures, a running total of the amount of money in their portfolios, and navigation to their individual journals and portfolios. Next, I'll show you how to explore the feature more deeply.

Click a manager's photo to read his or her latest journal entry. It's refreshing to hear pros admit defeats and fun to see them revel in victories. Even if you never make a trade alongside them, there's typically plenty of practical advice to improve your own investment skills.

Quotable Jubak: On the Value of News *(continued)*

Look at a list of pros and cons for Saville's stock right now; they are virtual mirror images of each other. Profit margins are likely to be under pressure for the next quarter or two, but that's because the company is spending money on marketing to new customers. Product introductions are risky times for companies and the possibility of error is high—but the company is introducing six new products that should lead to big earnings gains in the not-too-distant future. It's this battle over how to interpret the news that currently is driving the stock's price....

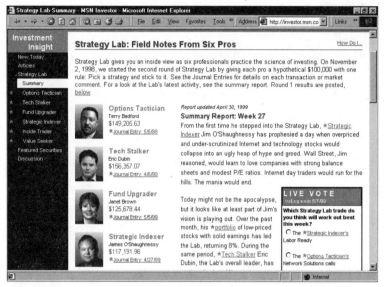

Figure 5-12.   May 6, 1999

In Strategy Lab, six professional investors buy and sell stocks in hypothetical portfolios in full view online, and they describe each transaction in a running journal. Click the dates beneath their totals to display journal entries, current picks, and a how-to manual on their strategic styles.

The journal entry provides navigation to the four additional components of Strategy Lab: Strategy, which is a manifesto from each manager describing how and why they have chosen their strategy; Portfolio, an account of the stocks or funds they currently own and the values of those securities; Transactions, a list of all previous journal entries; and Biography, an essay describing how and why the manager decided to devote their lives to creating wealth. The Biography page provides all relevant contact information, including Web sites, phone numbers, and addresses.

Touring Briefing.com

Briefing.com was one of the first Web sites to take financial news seriously. Right from the start, it offered a smart real-time market-news feed. Founded in 1996 by refugees from Standard & Poor's, it is still one of the few places an investor can visit to take the pulse of the market at any time of day. It is updated many times each hour, including

before the market's open and after its close, and it is one of the few sites well worth its monthly subscription.

Let's start with the free offerings. Without charge, Briefing.com offers investors a peek at its hourly Story Stocks news section. The commentary is sharp and to the point—no messing around with detours into the kind of bright but diverting writing styles of other sites. You will seldom find so much good, relevant information packed into a single paragraph, online or anywhere else. The site excels at providing solid thinking about stock-price movement before and after earnings releases, economic reports, and merger deals. It's as good as any stockbroker or analyst you're likely to find—and a lot more accountable. In one memorable post-close report on March 19, 1999, Briefing.com picked through Adobe Software's first-quarter earnings announcement and declared that the stock would benefit short term. It ramped from $54 to $87 over the next three months.

Quotable Briefing.com

Here's a Briefing.com "Story Stocks" report from May 7 about a monthly employment report from the federal government. What's cool is that Briefing.com published this report only 30 minutes after the government issued its report. With the perspective and trading advice it offers, Briefing.com's commentary represents a tremendous advance in speed-news quality for private investors.

> *EMPLOYMENT DATA. The April employment figures released at 8:30 ET this morning have the bond and stock markets up strongly. This is a bit surprising, because the numbers aren't really that surprising. What is really happening is that **the markets are relieved that the data do not show signs of any inflation pickup.** After Greenspan's comments yesterday which implied that the Fed might be willing to allow interest rates to rise, due to tightening labor market conditions and improved global economic conditions, the bond market was worried that maybe today's employment report would show signs of inflation. Well, it didn't. Average hourly earnings, a reflection of wage pressures, rose a mere 0.2%, leaving the year-over-year gain at just 3.2%. That is down from the year-over-year gain of 3.6% last month. No problem there.... The employment report thus once again shows strong economic growth and very little inflation pressure. The interest rate fears that had built up have been relieved, at least for now. **Cyclical stocks, which have been pushing the Dow up in recent weeks, could benefit from this report.** They are the ones most vulnerable to interest rate fears.*

Stock Analysis

If you pony up for a subscription, your first stop each day should be at the site's Stock Analysis area. Coverage here is divided into five sections: Live (fast-breaking headlines), Daily (analysis), The Market (statistics), Calendars (upcoming events), and Research (proprietary ratings). Here's a look at a few key pages in those sections.

Live

Visit here for four pages that offer a successively more detailed view of the day's action. Start with In Play and Stock Ticker, shown in Figure 5-13. These provide running commentary on market events with no more than a few sentences for each hour of the day. Both read like the stream-of-consciousness transcript of an announcer describing the action of horses rounding a track over the course of a day. Along with descriptions of action

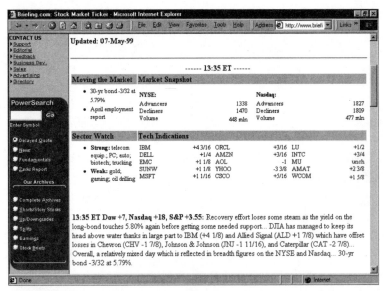

Figure 5-13.   May 7, 1999

In its Stock Ticker section, Briefing.com covers the action in the stock and bond markets as if it were a sporting event, succinctly offering up-to-the-minute statistics, play-by-play coverage, and analysis. It's indispensable for the serious private investor trading during the day.

in individual stocks, the announcer blends in a personalized view of the market conditions and a forecast for where the market might end the day. Here's a typical comment, from 3 p.m. on March 19: "Market got broadsided by the cautious comments from Morgan Stanley Dean Witter with respect to IBM's prospects, but is now attempting to repair the damage... Nervousness surrounding IBM coupled with the options expiration should make for an interesting finish...."

Next, Short Stories offers brief descriptions of interesting action in individual stocks throughout the day. Story Stocks augments that coverage with longer descriptions of action in individual securities—capturing broader themes. Often these are acerbic, skeptical accounts of strange occurrences in trading. They are not to be missed both for entertainment as well as tradable ideas. If you miss it during the day, it's still worth a few minutes' look at night.

Daily

This area offers deeper analysis of broader themes. In Stock Brief, the editors succinctly review and comment on market issues, such as investors' changing valuation of Internet portal companies or ways to play the craze over the Linux operating system. The Tech Stocks section, updated nightly, provides concise, insightful analysis of online investors' favorite sector. Visit to catch up with the day's price action and get a forecast for the next day. Comments here are more useful to private investors than almost anything on the Net, including any brokerage analysis or bulletin-board chatter. Trader's Edge provides in-depth analysis of a single stock—pro and con. Market View offers the editors' idiosyncratic look at the broad indexes' prospects. The trading-oriented nature of the report is noted in the fact that long-term is described as the span of one year, while intermediate-term is two months. Over the course of early 1999, the editors grew increasingly skeptical of the indexes' advance, as noted in this report from March 17: "**Bottom Line:** Valuations are at all-time highs while profit growth has been declining. True believers will say that profit growth is just around the corner, and that low inflation and interest rates mean that stocks can go higher. Briefing.com does not doubt that they can indeed go higher, but that will be due to the speculative nature of the market rather than the fundamentals. The bubble may very well keep expanding until something drastic occurs to change long-term

expectations about profit growth or interest rates. When it does change, though, the risks will be very high."

Research

In this area, the editors offer their own long-term stock and sector picks. The Core Update page lists Briefing.com's top recommendations for one-year holds. In early 1999, choices included mostly big-cap blue-chips, such as Charles Schwab, General Electric, MCI WorldCom, Dell, and BankAmerica. Considering how closely these editors watch the market, their views carry considerable weight with the site's growing roster of subscribers.

Likewise, the Sector Ratings page offers Briefing.com's prognosis for various industrial groups. The site regularly upgrades and downgrades sectors according to its own proprietary system. This section is less useful than the rest of the site, because it requires more conjecture and crystal-ball gazing. It is also updated less often. Still, it can contain real gems, such as this comment from March 16 that describes an upgrade of oilfield-equipment suppliers: "It seems like every two or three months the Oil Equipment & Services group stages a recovery try. We are in one of those periods right now. The big question for analysts and investors is whether the current rally is just another temporary blip in an otherwise extended bear market, or if it is the beginning of a legitimate rebound. Recent talk out of OPEC concerning additional production cuts, combined with the much stronger than expected domestic economy and an improved economic outlook in the Asian/Pacific region, has driven the price of crude sharply higher over the past few weeks. But is the advance in crude prices sustainable? Briefing.com says no."

Calendars

Briefing.com's straightforward tables for Earnings Calendar, Earnings Surprises and Warnings, Splits, Events, and Economic Reports are so strong that many other sites license them. All of these might look simple on the surface, but they are actually difficult to maintain, freshen, and keep accurate. Some contain analysis. Each is worth a quick scan a few times a week.

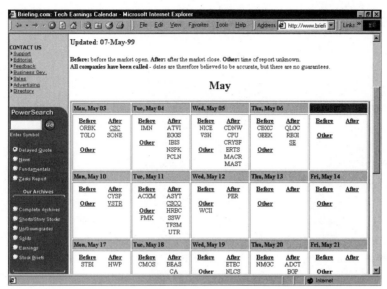

Figure 5-14.   May 7, 1999

Briefing.com's Tech Calendar is the Web's most complete list of days and times at which high-tech stocks are expected to release earnings reports. Many tech stocks tend to run up in price in advance of their earnings reports and sell off after the report. At the bottom of the page is a list of companies that will hold public conference calls after their earnings announcements, and the phone numbers to call.

All in all, Briefing.com is a tremendous resource that fulfills the Web's promise to put professionals' tools in the hands of private investors.

Touring TheStreet.Com

TheStreet.com is one of the Web's most promising news sites for investors because it is staffed by a growing number of solid journalists and columnists with a good feel for the market and a buoyant attitude. Hard-core traders might shun the site, shown in Figure 5-15 because style tends to take precedence over substance. But seldom a day goes by without its editors providing at least a few good nuggets of tradable news or analysis—making the subscription for premium columns worthwhile for private investors.

James J. Cramer's column, Wrong!, is the 800-pound gorilla of this site: hard not to notice, but not the best companion. Cramer is a hedge-fund manager in addition to being co-founder of TheStreet.com and a columnist. He attempts to be the Martha Stewart of financial media, creating a television, online, and print brand all at once. But his column is essentially a trader's journal, which makes it alternate between being manic, ecstatic, senseless, and depressing. While it can be occasionally brilliant, it's seldom truly useful. Primarily the column's value is in its insights into a trader's lifestyle. But it won't necessarily

Figure 5-15.   May 7, 1999

TheStreet.com's home page gives mostly equal weight to about 15 news stories and 10 columnists a day.
Top columnists to consider reading regularly are Jim Seymour, Gary Smith, Helene Meisler, and Adam
Lashinsky. Also occasionally instructive or amusing is columnist and site co-founder James J. Cramer.

help you make money because Cramer's own ethics rules prohibit him from mentioning
stocks that he favors in a timely manner. So while Martha Stewart genuinely gives home-
makers the recipes for success in the kitchen, Cramer essentially just describes a dish and
expects the reader to figure out the ingredients and cooking times on their own. Good luck.
His cowboy style of buying stocks one a time for largely short-term plays relies on analyst
recommendations, store visits, or raw hunches. This is the antithesis of the yeartrading
strategy I described in Part I. It seems like a hard way to make a buck or build a retirement account.

Market Updates

The thrice-daily Market Updates at TheStreet.com are generally excellent, with bright
writing and useful insights. They are not as savvy as Briefing.com's summaries, and you
have to fight through a lot more style to find the meat. But they occasionally feature outstanding reporting on issues of the day. Also, the weekend report, called The Coming
Week, is a worthwhile stop on Sunday nights because it is one of the few places on the
Web to get caught up on all the overseas trading and Sunday newspaper stories that might
affect Monday's tone of trading.

Commentary

Columns by technical trader Gary B. Smith are often the most useful on TheStreet.com, offering specific recommendations and answering a ton of reader mail in short, helpful bursts. Smith uses the effective technique of pasting his own one-liners to technical charts that illustrate his point—a universal language that traders understand. Unlike Cramer and most of the other columnists on the site, Smith also has a definable, defensible strategy. He buys or shorts stocks that are making upside or downside breakouts from congestion patterns. What's cool is his breezy way of describing the technique to new and experienced investors alike, and he mixes in personal news about his swim-champion daughter to humanize his content. He made dead-on accurate calls on Amazon.com's bullish charts in the fall of 1998, helping a lot of readers make a lot of money, including me. Among my favorite columns was one on the "Seven Deadly Sins of Technical Trading." Here's an excerpt: "Sin No. 3: Emotions. Dealing with your emotions is so important, I could have made it sins 3 through 7 … as it's one of the most, if not the most, critical aspects of trading. As an example, after many years of trading, I know I require a system that is almost totally mechanical with nondiscretionary stops and targets. Why? Because Gary B. Smith is weak! Gary B. Smith will crack under the pressure! Gary B. Smith needs a method that takes himself out of the trading equation! Take a look through the TSC archives, and you'll see I wrestle with my emotions constantly. You will, too, and if you don't find a way to deal with them, you'll quickly wind up back in a mutual fund. Which, for many of you, is probably the correct place to be."

"The Chartist" column by Helene Meisler is unique on the Web. It offers the kind of reliable daily technical analysis of market trends that previously only brokerage professionals had. From Singapore, Meisler advises whether technical indicators suggest that the overall market is overbought or oversold and what you should do about it.

Other strong columnists include:

- **Jeff Bronchick,** who gives a view of the perilous lives led by those heroes of the bull market—fund managers.

- **Herb Greenberg,** late of the *San Francisco Chronicle,* who gives a daily view of companies that are doing something wrong (usually in their accounting) and are potentially good candidates to sell short.

- **Adam Lashinsky,** late of the *San Jose Mercury News,* who brings years of experience covering high-tech companies and venture-capital firms to the task of analyzing and forecasting stock trends.

- **James Padinha,** an economist, offers his reflections on the growth or decline of goods and services produced in the United States and the rest of the world.

- **Jim Seymour**, a long-time technology columnist and consultant. He may not always be right about stocks, as proven by his advice to purchase Yahoo! and Amazon.com at their highs in mid-January of 1999. But he's always provocative about the direction of technology.

Conference Coverage

TheStreet.com's editors have taken on the Herculean task of attending most of the major brokerage investment conferences around the country. The site will send as many as four or five reporters to take notes at the presentations of the top companies, and their dispatches are posted throughout the day. In addition, the reporters schmooze with buyside and sellside analysts and managers and pick up tradable gossip.

This kind of information was previously available only to institutions, so it's an example of the democratization of news. At the Robertson Stephens Tech '99 Conference in San Francisco, for instance, TheStreet.com posted a report about investors' warm acceptance of Internet venture-capital firm CMGI's presentation. In a period of consolidation, CMGI's stock had been trading at about $130 for two months. After the TheStreet.com published its report, the stock immediately began to move, reaching a high of $226 a month later. That's the kind of information that can pay for many, many subscriptions.

Mutual funds

This is an area where TheStreet.com shines because it has a band of reporters that really dig out news on America's favorite investment vehicles. Most mutual-fund columnists just report on the best funds, but TheStreet.com often goes behind the numbers to determine if fund managers are playing by the rules. A column from March 1999 explained that most Fidelity funds underperform the market because their managers are strait-jacketed into a single style of investing, such as big-cap, small-cap, value, or sector stocks. But the column pointed out that three Fidelity funds aren't bound by those restrictions, and those funds have posted the best returns as a result. That's truly useful information.

Touring Bloomberg.com

To its credit, Bloomberg (*http://www.bloomberg.com*) has refrained from adding dot-com to its official corporate name, as the Web has overrun its business of offering proprietary real-time financial news and data to the professional investment community. In 1999, the company took a radical turn for the better in its Web operation (shown in Figure 5-16), creating an outstanding site that offers one-stop shopping for data, editorial, commentary, and perspective. (Yes, the Web site is called Bloomberg.com.)

Figure 5-16.   May 7, 1999

Previously available only to institutional clients, Bloomberg's breaking-news coverage is now available at its deep, well-organized Web site.

Financial News

Start with the news coverage on the front page of the site. Keep in mind that the quality of any news organization starts with the experience level of its editors and writers and the quality of their information sources. Bloomberg has one of the largest and most respected financial-news organizations. This quality shows up virtually every day, as the stories are written with conviction and perspective, and content is rooted in fact rather than opinion. On March 23, 1999, for instance, Bloomberg had the best and fastest coverage when

emerging biotech darling PathoGenesis plunged in the morning after reducing estimates for sales of its inhalable antibiotic. One reason is that the smartest analysts and money managers are fastest to return the calls of the reporters whom they know have the biggest audience and the most clout.

Continue on to each of the successive news links on Bloomberg in order: Top World News, Technology, and U.S. Economy. Just note the headlines before opening the excellent pages of data: Stocks on the Move, Movers by Exchange, Industry Movers, Most Active Options, and IPO Center. The options page, shown in Figure 5-17, is just about unique on the Web. It's one of the few really crystal-clear keyholes through which you can see what the big money is doing in the market. On March 23, 1999, for instance, the page showed heavy option buying in calls for regional Bell operating company SBC Communications, America Online, and retailer T.J. Maxx. Because they were all going down at the time, this suggests that smart money was buying into the decline. America Online proceeded to advance 38% over the next two weeks, while T.J. Maxx and SBC Communications were each up about 12%.

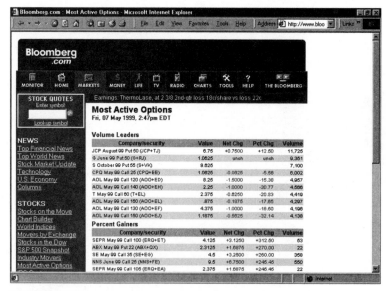

Figure 5-17.   May 7, 1999

The Most Active Options page at Bloomberg.com is a good place to see where the market's biggest players place their bets each day. On May 7, 1999, America Online stock was under a lot of pressure, but there was heavy buying of call options on the stock that would expire two weeks later.

Moreover you can't beat Bloomberg for coverage of commodities and currencies. Check out the Most Active Futures and Commodity Movers pages to get a read on the direction of basic elements of the world economy, such as the U.S. dollar, U.S. Treasury bonds and bills, oil, sugar, and cotton. Those pages will tell you more than reams of punditry about the direction that stock prices and the economy are headed. Besides, haven't you always wanted to enliven your lunchtime conversation with the latest word on the movement of copper futures?

Columns

Although they are hidden a couple of layers deep and seldom highlighted on any front page, several fine columnists write for Bloomberg. Whenever you have some free time, take a spin and read author Michael Lewis, economist Caroline Baum, and Kathryn Harris. Under the Finance heading, check out Susan Antilla and John Dorfman. Under Companies, check out IPO Focus and Insider Focus, and, in the Markets area, check out the Flow of Funds column on mutual funds. If you're going on a business trip, print some of these and carry them with you instead of a magazine.

Touring Other Sites

Dozens of additional news sites are worth visiting every so often. Here are five of the more notable ones:

- **CNET's News.com** (*http://www.news.com*) came out of nowhere in 1998 to become one of the leading Web sources for news about technology companies. Although it gets most of its investment information from wire sources like Bloomberg and Reuters, it also has tons of proprietary content as well. And if you invest more than half of your funds in technology stocks, you should spend at least 30 minutes a week buzzing through the site's news headlines, special packages, and commentary—particularly the CNET Investor and Perspectives sections.

- **Worldlyinvestor.com** (*http://www.worldlyinvestor.com*) has quickly become a standout source of news and commentary about international investing opportunities. The site includes proprietary reports on countries and regions as well as columns on subjects ranging from foreign value stocks to currency trading.

- **Bridge** (*http://www.bridge.com*) is one of the largest providers of financial information in the world. Though not as well known to consumers as top rivals Bloomberg and Reuters, it is considered by professionals to be one of the most dependable

sources of tradable hard news. Its Web site in mid-1999 was subpar, but any improvements in its navigation would make it well worth a visit for economic, political, and international news oriented toward investment.

- **CNBC.com** (*http://www.cnbc.com*) is a useful companion to the popular cable television financial channel. It offers distinctive, well-researched articles and columns each day, transcripts from television appearances by anchors and guests, a calendar of television appearances, and terrific stock-screening and charting technology.

- **CNNfn.com** (*http://www.cnnfn.com*) is a useful companion to another popular financial channel on cable television. It offers excellent news and analysis columns, easy navigation, and a neat feature called "Executive Summary" that provides a quick summary of top stories.

Figure 5-18.   July 14, 1999

CNET News.com has established itself as the Web site of record for technology news on the Internet. Its home page provides links deep into the site, including special packages on breaking stories. Many technology investors consider a quick run through its news-section links at left (Enterprise Computing, E-Commerce, Communications, and so on) as essential at mid-day and the end of the day.

Chapter 6

Newspapers and Magazines Online

Newspapers and magazines should have carved out the best Web sites for investors early on. After all, at the start of the online revolution they owned most of the best minds in finance journalism, a lot of the data, and consumers' trust. They just needed to roll their products out electronically with a little software finesse to become instant winners in this space. But most were too concerned about protecting their investments in printing plants and delivery trucks to expend much time and money on cyberspace. While they dawdled, their online-only cousins quickly blew past them in delivering large quantities of news, data, and commentary at top speed to the fast-growing, brand-conscious Web community.

With notable exceptions, by the middle of 1998, the financial-news content of the nation's great newspapers and magazines had become largely just a commodity to be displayed and distributed by the new media kingpins—portals such as Yahoo!, Excite, and MSN. Soon after print publishers lost the race to be *first* in online investors' hearts, they began falling behind in the race to be *best* too, as competitors such as TheStreet.com, Briefing.com, and CBS MarketWatch provided a finer focus on market-moving stock news. By March 1999, figures from Web ratings service Media Metrix showed that TheStreet.com had edged out the *Wall Street Journal's* Web site in the number of visitors per month. (Traffic at broader sites Yahoo! Finance and MSN MoneyCentral eclipses them both.)

Nevertheless, many big newspapers and magazines began to rally online by mid-1999; some may yet succeed in winning back their natural audience. Several individual columnists are well worth regular visits in your quest to find the right stocks at the right time on the Web.

Los Angeles Times

The *Los Angeles Times*' well-regarded business section has made a half-hearted effort to extend its content online. If you can ignore the clumsy navigation, you'll find two of the best financial columnists online or off: Tom Petruno and Jim Flanigan.

Petruno's copy is consistently spare and smart. His "Market Beat" column (*http://www.latimes.com/HOME/BUSINESS/COLUMNS/PETRUNO/*) contains top-notch analysis of the equity and bond markets at least twice a week. In a column from March 1998, for example, he wrote with insight about the surprising rebound in emerging overseas markets. Other columnists and economists had dismissed the revival as just an irrelevant phenomenon of gamblers, but Petruno took a contrarian approach. He wrote, "It's worth remembering that short-term speculators usually precede long-term investors into dicey markets. Somebody has to go first, and that generally means those willing to take high risks. Some Wall Street pros believe there is, in fact, an economic message in markets' recent moves: a growing belief that the global economy is finally turning away from the specter of deflation/depression that has haunted it since the Asian economic crisis began in mid-1997."

Anyone following Petruno's advice could have stocked up on mutual funds specializing in emerging markets. These invesments were the spring quarter's best performers. Jim Flanigan (*http://www.latimes.com/HOME/BUSINESS/COLUMNS/FLANIGAN/*), Petruno's colleague at the Times, writes a couple of times each week with grace and intelligence on a wide range of macroeconomic, corporate, and market issues. It's rare to find analysis of this caliber at the new financial portals, so for now you'll have to go to the source.

New York Times

The *New York Times,* so gray and sober for decades, has surged to become a force on the Web (*http://www.nytimes.com*). The site's Business section, shown in Figure 6-1, is lively, fresh, colorful, and easy for investors to navigate as they hunt for tradable ideas. Because the *New York Times* continues to hire many of the smartest financial editors in the business, its story ideas are among the most topical, sharply argued, and useful.

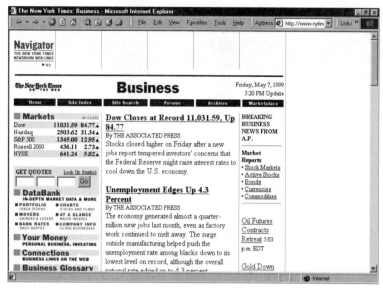

Figure 6-1.   May 7, 1999

The home page of the New York Times' *online Business section displays live market stories from wire services during the trading day, but it features exclusive stories and columns in the evening and the morning.*

Pay special attention to stories labeled "News Analysis" and "Market Place." If you're a technology investor, also scan for anything written by Silicon Valley reporter John Markoff. In mid-March of 1998, for instance, Markoff wrote persuasively about the rising fortunes of Sony and its new gaming console, Playstation II. Investors who followed up by studying Sony more closely or seeking out the makers of key, high-value components for the Playstation II were well-rewarded for their effort. Over the next few months, the stocks of the Japanese electronics maker and its semiconductor suppliers soared.

Washington Post

The political and overseas reporting staffs at the *Washington Post (http://www.washington-post.com)* have long eclipsed the newspaper's business-reporting team. But the paper has one exceptional columnist: James K. Glassman. Check out his column, shown in Figure 6-2, titled "Glassman on Wall Street." It's as useful for veterans as it is for beginners because he mixes plenty of education with keen insights.

The *Post* combines all of his columns, tips, and tutorials on a single page for easy access—an outstanding feature unmatched by other Web sites. So what will you learn? In mid-March of 1999, Glassman told readers not to get so caught up in Dow 10,000 mania

Figure 6-2.   May 7, 1999

James Glassman's column at the Washington Post *site is one of the most useful on the Web for novice and intermediate investors. He explains well-worn concepts in fresh ways; check out his archive of past columns and chat transcripts.*

that they ignored "signs of life abroad" in Asia, Latin America, and Europe. He noted that the stock markets in Italy, Spain, and France had all topped the 29% return of the S&P 500 Index in the prior year, and he specified individual companies in those countries that would benefit from deregulation, the unification of the currency, and consolidation.

Glassman closed the column on an important point: international diversification dampens the volatility of an all-U.S. portfolio. From 1976 to 1998, he pointed out, a stock account with 80% U.S. shares and 20% foreign shares would have produced returns almost exactly the same as an all-domestic portfolio—but at lower risk. He concluded, "Have your gateau and eat it, too."

For a real test, I looked at Glassman's columns during the time of the scary downturn in the stock market in the late summer of 1998. I found a gem from August 13 in which he gave the following advice to investors who might be worried about further skidding in the market: "How to change your frame of mind? Make a wish list. Write down the stocks you would truly love to own if only prices were more reasonable. Then, next to each, write down a reasonable—or more than reasonable—price. Put the list in your pocket and check out the stocks every once in a while. One purpose of the wish-list approach is to change the way you view market declines: They're good, not bad. They give you the chance to own great companies at good prices."

This was exactly the kind of thing you needed to know. Unfortunately, however, Glassman went on to recommend three marginal stocks to put on that list: funeral-home operator Stewart Enterprises (STEI), home-security specialist Pittson Brink's Group (PZB), and gum maker Wm. Wrigley (WWY). An investor who bought them a couple of weeks later during the August 31 plunge would have, six months later, been underwater on the first two by 25% and up just 18% on Wrigley. (A much better choice would have been to run the Redwood Growth screen I describe in Chapter 3. Those big-cap leaders turned out to be the best rebounders. In the same six months, America Online soared 482%, data-storage king EMC was up 191%, and Cisco Systems rose 91%.)

Dallas Morning News

Many regional newspapers have terrific columnists that aren't nationally known. One that fixed-income investors should read regularly is Scott Burns, shown in Figure 6-3, at the *Dallas Morning News* (*http://www.dallasnews.com*).

Burns is one of the few news columnists who pays any attention to municipal bonds, Treasuries, and the like. He invented the Couch Potato Portfolios for conservative investors who want a mix of low-risk growth and income. He answers questions about both portfolios in his column and at his own Web site (*http://www.scottburns.com*). In March 1999, an investor asked him how to diversify a portfolio of corporate bonds. Most columnists today wouldn't have a clue how to answer. But Burns offered this: "With yield in short supply, investors need to take every possible avenue to increase their interest income. That means supplementing a portfolio of Treasury obligations or bank CDs with holdings in high-yield bond funds and Ginnie Mae funds."

Here is Burns' recipe for his two basic approaches:

The Basic Couch Potato Portfolio is simple and cheap. Take your money, divide it in two equal piles, invest one pile in the Vanguard Index 500 Fund (VFINX) and invest the other in Vanguard Intermediate Term U.S. Treasury Fund (VFITX). Then watch TV for a year, preferably evening sitcoms or other shows likely to render you intellectually inert. This strategy produced a return of 18.04 percent in 1998.... The Sophisticated Couch Potato Portfolio is just as cheap but involves fractions. In spite of this, the SCP can still be done in the privacy of your own home, without supervision from a Designated Financial Professional. Take your money, divide it into four equal piles, invest one pile in Vanguard Intermediate Term U.S. Treasury Fund, and invest three piles in Vanguard Index 500 fund. This method produced a return of 22.96 percent in 1998.

Though it's meant to be amusing, this approach is probably right for many conservative private investors.

Figure 6-3.   May 7, 1999

Scott Burns' column in the Dallas Morning News *is one of the few on the Web or in print that consistently and eloquently explains the advantages of fixed-income investments to private investors.*

The Wall Street Journal (and Family)

The *Wall Street Journal* (*http://interactive.wsj.com*) has defined high-quality financial journalism around the world. In the mid-1990s, its Web site was one of the first to include briefing books on all major companies—something that became ubiquitous later on. But its Interactive Journal site, at $59 per year, was essentially just an online version of the newspaper. As the decade wore on, the site's value was eclipsed by its younger, more nimble cousins in the Dow Jones family: Barron's Online, SmartMoney.com, and DowJones.com. The quantity of good information in these publications is staggering. Investors who are just getting started in the late 1990s have no idea how hard it was previously to find ideas of this quality before the Net.

Barron's Online

The contrarian columnists of Barron's Online (*http://www.barrons.com*) may not always be right, but they are erudite, entertaining, and carry clout. Become a subscriber, and read it every weekend if you want to know what traders are going to be talking about—and potentially buying or selling—on Monday. Barron's Online, shown in Figure 6-4, also offers new trading ideas Monday through Thursday under the Weekday Trader heading.

During the first week of March 1999, several stories were posted on a resurgence in beat-up airline and technology stocks, as well as medical-device maker Medtronic. Each was a solid piece of journalism packed with good reasoning, facts, and interviews. In addition, the columns carry addenda that look back on the last time the author wrote about a stock and how it has fared since. That's responsible journalism and well worth a look a couple of times a week.

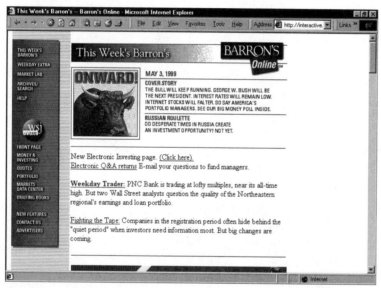

Figure 6-4.   May 7, 1999

Barron's *is the leading weekly journal of financial opinion in print, and its Web site offers the same acerbic, eccentric, and erudite point of view daily. Click the Market Lab link in the upper left to see interesting SEC filings and other useful data.*

SmartMoney.com

SmartMoney.com has staked out a well-deserved reputation as the most technologically adroit news site on the Web. This is, in part, because it's loaded with nice, small Java-based software applications that help tell stories. Start at the site's Hourly Stock Update, an excellent place to catch up with the Dow Jones wire's news on overnight events in Europe and Japan as well as domestic markets during the day. Packed with good graphics and sharp writing, the Market Digest page is typically a strong, idiosyncratic take on the day's hot IPOs, winners, and losers.

Unlike most sites, SmartMoney.com also keeps a daily record of the stocks it has recommended over the past year. (Surely you've seen magazine cover stories like "19 Stocks Starting with the Letter C to Buy Today!") To its credit, SmartMoney.com is keen to come clean on its losers as much as it likes to brag about its winners. In 1998, it offered eight portfolios for different budgets and tastes in different copies of its magazine, and it still keeps track of each one.

My favorite section of the site is the Daily Screen, shown in Figure 6-5. This column starts with an anecdote or concept (for example, that cable stocks are on the move) and then uses a screening engine to find stocks that match the theme. On March 9, 1999, the column started with the premise that Microsoft co-founder Paul Allen and investor Warren Buffett had each made cable-TV franchise investments in the past six months. The writers then came up with a method for discovering values in that industry. Their picks were MediaOne Group, Cablevision, and TCA Cable. (The three were up 31%, 16%, and 11%, respectively, two months later.)

Finally, keep an eye on the Pundit Watch section. This feature tracked the recommendations of 12 Wall Street wise men and women through 1998 and 1999 and gave them batting averages as if they were baseball players. The section provides fairly deep information about each of its pundits, who range from bullish technical analyst Ralph Acampora, of Prudential Securities, to bearish economist Edward Yardeni, of Deutsche Bank Securities. It's worthwhile to check up on the players every week to find out what they're saying now and how it's being spun.

Figure 6-5.   May 7, 1999

Check the Daily Screen section at SmartMoney.com regularly. After reading the column, click the menu along the top to run the featured screen yourself, visit past screens, or hop over to one of SmartMoney.com's many other excellent features. These include Dueling Portfolios, Pundit Watch, and the Hourly Stock Update.

Forbes

Forbes magazine (*http://www.forbes.com*) has taken its lumps from readers over the years because of its elitist presentation, dowdy appearance, and persistent coverage of heavy industry at the expense of livelier parts of the economy. But around 1997, the magazine came under new management and began to turn up the volume—and it became a much more important resource for both online and offline investors. Its advantages include a great staff of reporters, superior columnists, and editors who know how to keep stories to the point.

Forbes' Web site, shown in Figure 6-6, is hard to navigate, but here's the best way to read its coverage online:

- **The cover story** is almost always a great read because it's packed with figures, perspective, and steady (if not bright) writing.

- **Special reports** are typically very well done. In late March of 1999, for instance, the magazine produced the best first-day piece on the Web about Comcast's surprise announcement that it would merge with MediaOne. The article untangled the many strings attached to the broadband-cable deal, which involved such heavyweights as AT&T, TimeWarner, and Microsoft. Anyone interested in investing in this deal was well served by a read (even though the deal did not ultimately work out).

- **The columnists** are great. Favorites include editor Rich Karlgaard and money managers Kenneth L. Fisher and Laszlo Birinyi. Here are a few typical paragraphs from Karlgaard, delightful in their bombast and liveliness: "A guy with a drink at a lawn party last summer says to me: 'Whoa! You'll never catch me typing out my credit card number onto a freaking Web page!' A few months zip by, and I bump into the guy again. It's as if we were having the same cocktail chat, and the mint julep had never left his hand. But now he boasts: 'Let me tell you about the Civil War bayonet I bought for a song on Ebay.' That's an attitude shift."

When you find someone like Karlgaard or Birinyi with something truly different to say, it's wise to bookmark their spots on the Web and revisit them at least a couple of times a month. They will either bring you new insights or reinforce old ones. And if there's anything in short supply these days, it's fresh ideas.

Quotable Fisher

Check out longtime Forbes columnist Kenneth L. Fisher every couple of weeks, particularly if you favor big-cap growth stocks and a perspective on market history. Here's an excerpt from a column published in May 1999 that was helpful as the market stutter-stepped near Dow 11,000 and many pundits mongered fears of a crash:

SOME READERS ARE ASKING when, if ever, I will turn bearish. I've done so twice during my tenure here. But I couldn't now if I had to. Longtime readers know I won't call a peak until at least three months after I think it has already happened....

I stole my three-month rule from Joe Goodman, a tremendous timer, super stock-picker—and a stunning simplifier. Goodman knew bull markets have long, rolling tops, and bear markets are painfully slow. If he got you out three months after a top, you missed most of the drop, and he would be a hero.

He knew it was vastly easier to see a peak afterward, more so if you don't clutter your brain with prior biased forecasts. Joe simply waited until he could look back

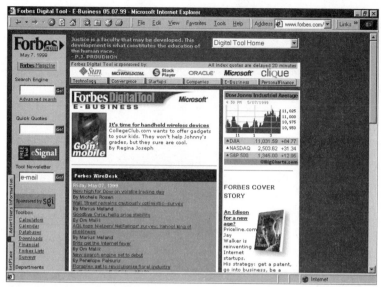

Figure 6-6.   May 7, 1999

Forbes *magazine is a great resource for investors, but its Web site tries to do too much at once, making navigation tough. Visit the columnists, listed in the sidebar, as well as the cover stories and feature packages.*

and see higher prices three months earlier. Then he looked for problems that weren't widely appreciated. If he found them, he turned bearish. Following this practice helps me avoid getting spooked by corrections. Here are some other classic Goodman pearls:

1. *Don't be a bull or bear all the time.*

2. *There is a time to buy, a time to sell and a long time to do nothing.*

3. *Never buy a stock that didn't rise in a bull market. Smart guys are out of it.*

4. *Don't buy the sympathy stock. Don't buy a weak railroad because a strong one has started to move. Everyone does this, and it is rarely profitable.*

5. *When a bull market peaks, sell the stock that rose most. It will fall fastest. Sell the stock that rose least. It didn't rise, therefore it must fall.*

6. *In a high market, confine yourself to high-quality stocks.*

Fortune

Fortune, the venerable TimeWarner publication, has its act together on the Web. Shown in Figure 6-7, *Fortune*'s site (*http://www.fortune.com*) packs a powerful 1-2-3 punch of useful editorial, decent presentation, and tons of software tools. The hallmark of Fortune's offering is the eccentric, fun Street Life column. Three writers trade off on the byline, but Andrew Serwer has been the signature author. It's a high-adrenaline look at the day's market action, with attitude, humor, and flavor. The best thing about it is that you can receive it by e-mail for free. It puts a nice exclamation point at the end of any day, if you like this sort of thing. Here's a typical paragraph from a report in late March:

> *TECH STORY....Dell was down $2 to $38, stock was downgraded by Mr. (don't call me Eugene! or Joe! or Charlie!) McCarthy of DLJ, who lowered his numbers from 17 cents to 15 cents. Dude is worried about top line and ASPs (that's average selling price, greenhorn!). He says it's fairly valued in the mid-thirties!!.... Much general worry about a slide in PC demand. So sick of this.... IBM is also a real concern. Morgan Stanley bopped 'em last week, and now the grim reaper himself, Dan Niles (a very serious young man—but he's been right!) bashed 'em. Also, he said Dell still has to cope with the sub-$1,000 market. Gee, Dan, don't you think Mikey D. is all over this? My money is with Dell....*

After Street Life, click over to the magazine's cover stories, where you can read some of the most colorful writing in business journalism. In late March, the offerings included a look at the high-stakes world of NASCAR racing, the unraveling of denim maker Levi Strauss, an interview with the creator of the new low-price Web site Buy.com, and a personal essay by Hewlett-Packard chief Lew Platt on why he broke up the company.

What's notable about Fortune is that its writers and editors give the sense of being self-aware. They often reflect on past stories and muse about potential ideas. This gives the reader the feeling that they are watching a work in progress—a publication constantly attempting to improve itself.

A reader gets the sense that really smart editors are having a good time riding the crest of investor interest in these companies. If journalists at Barron's write as if they've seen it all before and attack the news from the most cynical perspective, Fortune's team appears to always see the world fresh. In every publication, they uncover at least a couple of solid nuggets of tradable stuff. The site also has some excellent investment aids in its Tool section, including one of the Web's better stock-screening engines.

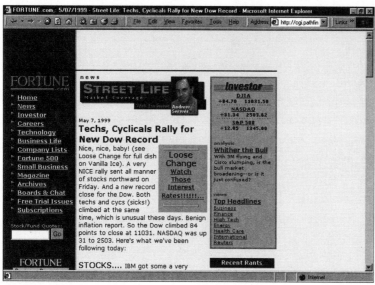

Figure 6-7.   May 7, 1999

The hyperactive Street Life column in Fortune's Investor section is the most entertaining piece of finance journalism on the Web every day. Sign up for free e-mail delivery for a fun, educational exclamation mark at the end of the day.

Other Notable Publications

There are dozens more financial publications with decent Web sites. Here are three more to consider in your daily or weekly spin through the Net for market news:

- **Money.** The personal-finance magazine in the TimeWarner family (*http://www.money.com*) does a great job of writing about stocks in an easygoing manner that's both educational and practical. Its site includes a few useful tools as well, including an I-Watch feature from Thomson Investment Network (*http://www.money.com/iwatch*). This tool combines software and commentary to explain where the big money is flowing in the market every day.

- **Financial Times.** Unless you live in a major city, it's pretty hard to find copies of the great financial newspaper *Financial Times* at the corner newsstand. That makes its online site (*http://www.ft.com*) a fantastic resource if you have any interest in overseas investments. It combines news, commentary, briefing papers, and foreign-stock

quotes in one easy-to-navigate site. Sign up to receive your favorite features in e-mail for free.

- **The Economist.** A lot of people think that this is the best-written financial publication in the world, and that's hard to argue against. Its Web site (*http:// www.economist.com*) is spare, elegant and easy to navigate—full of as many great insights on U.S. markets as on markets overseas. Stop here for perspective, crisp writing, and an outstanding archive of articles on big issues (the euro, the continuing Korean conflict, the economic history of the Balkans, and the impact of the Internet, to name just a few).

By the time you're done reading all this journalism, you may be overloaded with facts. Now let's look at some places online to find reliable interpretations of those facts.

Chapter 7
Newsletters

Trolling for new investment ideas in stock-screening engines, news Web sites, and online brokerage reports can take a lot of time. And all that information can be so contradictory—and confusing.

Perhaps you'd rather find just one advisor, a guru, who would do almost all the work for you. Someone who would tell you when to pile into hot stocks before they're barely warm and when to sell before they chill out.

That's where the investment-newsletter industry comes in. The ease and low cost of online publishing has encouraged dozens of bright, not-so-bright, dim, and outright crooked writer/traders to hang a digital shingle on the Internet with the promise of offering you independent advice via e-mail or their Web sites for a fee. Unlike stock brokers and brokerage analysts, these writers argue that they work only for you, not for the benefit of their firms' investment-banking arms or for a trading commission.

For many serious private investors, these letters are a great tool. Hardworking newsletter publishers succeed in their businesses by being right over long, long stretches of time and by following through with strong customer service. Don't think for a minute that their advice is just for amateurs. Plenty of pros working institutional money and large pools of private money scan the top newsletters religiously for trading ideas. Yet separating the terrific few from the terrible or even dangerous is a tough errand. Before learning about some of the best sites for finding and using newsletters, here are a few things to keep in mind:

- **Set reasonable expectations.** Subscribing to an investment newsletter is different from subscribing to a magazine. You *should* expect to find specific, tradable ideas, not just general news and commentary. But you should not expect every idea to be successful.

- **Determine your trading time horizon.** The most timely and useful advice will be the most expensive. Some newsletters publish once or twice a month, while others publish as often as five times a day. If you tend to hold onto stocks and funds for extended periods of time, it doesn't make sense to subscribe to an expensive letter for daytraders.

- **Determine the writer's track record.** The best online newsletters publish a running total of their past trading ideas and a record of their success or failure. If more than 70% of the recommendations are claimed as successful, exercise caution and ask questions. Even the best traders are rarely right much more than half of the time. (They make their money earning tons on their successes and cutting losses quickly on their failures.)

- **Determine the newsletter writer's reputation.** Just as you probably wouldn't hire someone to paint your house or baby-sit your kids without a recommendation from prior customers, you shouldn't subscribe to an investment newsletter without attempting to check the writer's integrity. Ask the author for referrals, or search for the writer's name at forums such as Silicon Investor (*http://www.techstocks.com*). A lack of positive comments on the boards shouldn't scare you away, but a plethora of complaints should obviously raise a red flag.

- **Demand a one-month free trial, and use it wisely.** Almost all of the good newsletters allow potential new subscribers to take a month free. During that month, keep track of the writer's advice carefully, either on paper or in an online portfolio tracker. (See Chapter 13 for more information about online portfolio trackers.) Watch for slippage in the prices of the investments that the writer recommends. For example, if the advisor recommends buying a stock at the next day's opening price and the stock opens higher than where it closed the previous day, make sure the record shows the higher price. Building a track record on prices unobtainable by subscribers is a trick unscrupulous traders use to enhance their published results.

- **Beware of à la carte pricing.** Some newsletter writers allow you to purchase their ideas à la carte, charging as little as $1 for one month's commentary or $5 for a list of current stock picks. Although this sounds attractive, you run a risk choosing investments from writers one at a time rather than as part of an overall strategy that suits your lifestyle, temperament, age, and risk tolerance. If you're hunting for a guru, you're better off choosing one and sticking with him or her for at least six months before changing your mind.

So where you should you hunt for the best newsletters? Many of the best today are aggregated at financial portals like INVESTools (*http://www.investools.com*) and The Financial Center (*http://www.tfc.com*), while many others float untethered in cyberspace.

INVESTools

INVESTools.com was launched in 1995 as one of the first Web sites to group dozens of newsletters in one location, and it continues to represent the best selection and presentation. The site, shown in Figure 7-1, integrates more than 30 subscription-only newsletters; in mid-1999, it claimed more than 190,000 registered users.

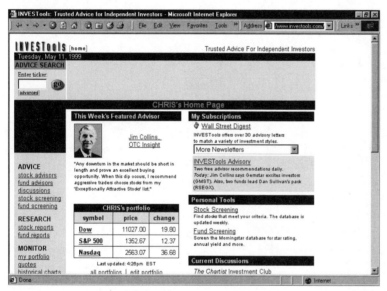

Figure 7-1.   May 11, 1999

INVESTools offers more than 30 investment newsletters at a single site. The aggregation allows users to easily compare publishers' prices, frequency, and philosophies.

The good news about starting your hunt for a stock-trading guru at INVESTools: You can compare a wide variety of newsletters' advice and prices side by side. In addition, if you decide to subscribe to more than one, INVESTools offers you a single place to take advantage of all your subscriptions at once. INVESTools provides a lot of "back-end" services to newsletter owners as well, such as e-mail to customers and a payment system. For subscribers, this alleviates a lot of the headache of multiple passwords and billing statements.

Getting Started

To determine the best newsletter for you, start by clicking the Stock Advisors or Fund Advisors link on the home page. INVESTools provides a short statement from each writer and groups the newsletters by investment style. When you view these descriptions, try to read between the lines. A little savvy can go a long way toward weeding out the worst. For example:

- **How long has the writer been publishing?** It's a bad sign when they're not proud enough to say. A minimum of five years is best.

- **How cogent is the writer's investment style?** The advisors who can state their missions clearly in the few sentences allowed in this forum are probably the ones who can state their trading ideas clearly in their newsletters as well. Look for buzzwords like "growth" and "capital appreciation" if you're seeking high-octane returns. Look for words like "capital preservation" and "dividend paying" if you want returns that'll just help you keep ahead of inflation. Avoid words like "options" and "margin" if you're looking for any sort of low-risk strategy.

- **How's their personality?** You'll be surprised to discover how much you can learn about an investment manager's public personality in just a few short sentences. If they're boastful, mocking, or ambiguous here, they probably will be the same in their newsletters. Annoying managers can still be effective. But because you're considering putting serious cash behind the advisor's picks, you'll probably feel better about following one whose temperament suits your own.

Get Philosophical—Study the Mission

After narrowing down the list of advisors that suit your style, click the links to their home pages on the INVESTools site. Then click the links for "Suggested Readings" or other background material on the publisher's philosophy. Some of these readings are highly educational, while others are merely promotional. Stick with the advisors that attempt to draw you in as an equal partner, explaining their styles in a way that's fresh, easy to comprehend, and sensible. If advisors seem vague here, they will tend to be vague in their newsletters as well, and you definitely do not want to take stock picks from an advisor who can't articulate a clear methodology.

Among the best in this regard is Al Frank, who runs The Prudent Speculator, a highly rated newsletter. In his statement, Frank declares, "Over the years we have developed the acronym PASADARM for speculating in the stock market. Patience And Selection And Diversification And Risk Management is the foundation of our investment philosophy." That's pretty straightforward. I particularly like the last line of his commentary: "Eternal vigilance coupled with benign neglect is the curious nature of speculating. By keeping daily track of things yet not fussing with portfolios and positions until well and truly indicated, the prudent speculator is likely to obtain optimum results."

Get Practical—Take a Sample

To learn more about an advisor, you should sign up for a one-month free trial. You must go through the hassle of giving the site your credit-card number to sign up, but it's easy to cancel before the month is over if you ultimately don't like the advisor's ideas or style.

The leading reason people bail on an advisor isn't the lack of trading ideas, however. It's too many. Many newsletter advisors at INVESTools and elsewhere offer 10 to 80 or more trades at a time, but they offer little advice on cutting down the list to a reasonable number. These laundry lists of stocks are a cop-out, giving the advisor a better shot at claiming success for the three or four ideas that pan out.

During your trial period, it is important to focus not on how many trades panned out for the advisor—but on how many would have worked out for *you*. When you keep a paper record of the trades the newsletter writer suggests, mark in advance the trades that you would have actually done. If you can't follow the advice adequately during the trial period, you probably won't be able to do it when you're paying for the newsletter.

One Favorite: The Chartist

Published by Dan Sullivan, The Chartist focuses on market timing and momentum stocks. The performance of its model portfolio has consistently ranked very well against its peers, according to the bible of newsletter performance, The Hulbert Financial Digest (*http://www.hulbertdigest.com*). The Chartist, shown in Figure 7-2, includes both a long-term model portfolio and a trader's portfolio. The latter is more aggressive and includes fewer stocks. Sullivan is considered one of the best practitioners of the dark art of market timing, so many investors read the letter not for his calls on individual stocks but for his calls on market direction.

Figure 7-2.   May 11, 1999

The home page for The Chartist at INVESTools allows potential subscribers to read excerpts from past hotlines and learn the newsletter's philosophy. After subscribing, readers can return here to see the current newsletter.

Sullivan's timing served readers well in 1998 when he suggested stepping aside from the market in July near that year's summer high. Just as importantly, near the lows of mid-October, he also told readers to jump back into the market with both guns blazing—100% invested in equities with their own money and 100% invested in equities with money borrowed from their brokerages on margin. Both were great calls. Sullivan's sense of timing was less acute in early 1999, when he told readers to bow out of the "vulnerable" market on February 17. The Dow Jones Industrial Average was coughing and sputtering at 9,195 after peaking around 9,650 in January. About three weeks later, the Dow kicked into overdrive, ultimately rising to 10,462. Sullivan issued a new buy signal on April 16 and recommended that readers return to 100% equity exposure in 27 stocks.

The fact that Sullivan missed 1,267 points in the Dow isn't as important as the fact that he swallowed his pride and recommended that readers return to the market at higher prices. If you must follow a guru, it's important to find one who publishes regularly, admits mistakes, and offers specific advice on buying, selling, and stop limits.

Quotable Dan Sullivan

A newsletter publisher should offer more than just stock picks. He or she should also offer perspective and education. I particularly liked the following passage in Sullivan's letter from April 17, 1999. He mentioned that the book that had made the greatest impact on him was *The Battle for Investment Survival* by Gerald Loeb. The book was published during the Great Depression in 1935, but the advice was timeless. Here's an excerpt from Sullivan's newsletter:

> *Loeb's basic investment philosophy of market timing, cutting losses and taking profits to avoid lengthy bear markets and possible financial disaster, has been all but pushed into the background in recent years. There is no question that his methodology is out of favor. Conventional wisdom now dictates that the surest way to Wall Street wealth is to buy and hold for the long-term. It was only a few years ago that conventional wisdom was the opposite of today. Investing in the stock market was viewed to be a highly speculative venture suited only for sophisticated investors. One of the safest predictions we can make at this time is that Loeb's philosophy will come back into vogue over the next several years [...] The current generation has a painful lesson to learn. They will come to realize that Loeb's principles are far from outmoded. The following are some of Loeb's ideas and principles:*

> 1. *To achieve success one must set their investment goals very high.*

> 2. *Investing actually is the most inexact sort of science. This is especially true because of the important part psychology plays in shaping stock prices.*

> 3. *One's effort should be concentrated first on deciding the trend and next in seeking out the most responsive stocks.*

> 4. *During a market correction in a bull market, nine times out of ten, the active stock which declines the least will be the one that advances the most in the next surge into new high ground.*

> 5. *Accepting losses promptly is the most important single investment device to insure safety of capital—it is also the action that most people know the least about and that they are least likely to execute.*

> 6. *Never average down.*

The Financial Center

The Financial Center (*http://www.tfc.com*), shown in Figure 7-3, has also done a good job of aggregating top investment-newsletter publishers in one place. Calling itself the "Home of Wall Street's Market Mavens," the site distinguishes itself by providing a lot of decent daily and weekly market and stock commentary for free.

These teasers can be a good entrée for private investors seeking a newsletter. Start with the daily comments in the middle of the page, under the Updates heading. Click any headline for the writer's view of the market, and then click links on the page that appears to dig further into the newsletter's philosophy, publication frequency, and pricing.

The site's home page also lists about a dozen categories of letters to choose from, including ones that follow U.S. Federal Reserve policy, Internet stocks, futures, and options. Its list of authors includes some heavyweights, including John Bollinger, the inventor of the Bollinger Bands technical indicator; Mark Leibovit, inventor of the "volume reversal" indicator; and Bert Dohmen, a good market timer and old-fashioned stock picker.

The Financial Center offers a reasonable deal on bundled newsletters—that is, you can subscribe to four Internet newsletters at once for one low introductory price. In addition, the site offers a good newsstand of books, as well as audio and video tapes, on trading.

Figure 7-3.   May 11, 1999

The Financial Center offers one-stop shopping for about a dozen high-quality newsletters. Read the free commentary for a few days or weeks to learn which newsletter might be right for you, and then take a free trial before subscribing.

One Favorite: Bert Dohmen's Smartfax

One of best newsletter publishers listed at TFC is Bert Dohmen. Based in Honolulu, Hawaii, he offers specific trading advice at regular intervals in a range of publications, as well as good macro-economic perspective. He publishes a variety of letters (*http://www.dohmencapital.com*), ranging from the monthly Wellington Letter to the almost-daily Smartfax. A single solid trading idea from a letter like Smartfax, shown in Figure 7-4, can pay for the high cost of the subscription very quickly. (Smartfax costs $3,000 a year for a guarantee of 52 letters. In practice, he often sends three to four per week.)

Here's a passage from the April 8 Smartfax, the day after the Dow had stormed strongly past the 10,100 mark in defiance of conventional wisdom.

> *Market strength has improved greatly over the past two days. Today once again the internet stocks had extraordinary gains, but other sectors did very well also. The financial stocks are booming. So are discount retailers. Communications, and even the casino industry are suddenly very strong. It appears that this market wants to prove wrong all those who had correctly detected the subsurface weakness of the market and had been giving warning signals of an imminent correction. As you know, when many investors get on one side of the fence, the market usually does the opposite. But sometimes it also means that the inevitable is only delayed.*

> *We will continue to go with the flow. This once again demonstrates that it's better to go with a strategy rather than fighting the trend. Many traders have been selling the market short because of the technical sell signals. They will now have to close-out their short positions in a hurry. That will produce further market strength. I really don't know how far this market upmove will go. If it stalls-out soon, it could get ugly. But the further it goes, the more the 10,000 DJI level will become strong support.*

Dohmen followed up this letter with individual picks that performed extremely well the next day. More importantly, he kept readers in the market just before the market advanced rapidly past strong negative sentiment to Dow 11,000.

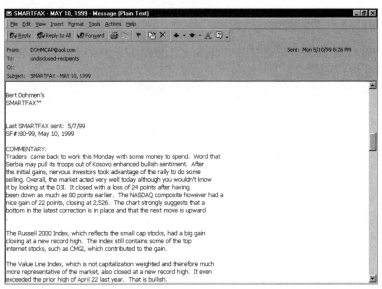

Figure 7-4.   May 11, 1999

A subscriber can choose to receive Bert Dohmen's newsletter Smartfax by e-mail or fax. If you choose e-mail, the letter arrives one to five times a week in the evening. It contains market commentary as well as up to a dozen stock and option picks.

Fination.com

Fination.com (*http://www.fination.com*) is the only newsletter aggregator that helps you determine the type of commentary that might be most appropriate for your investment style. It uses simple database software to help you find a match between your risk tolerance and time horizon and more than 60 newsletters.

Start by clicking the Newsletter Finder link on the home page. Then answer the questions, shown in Figure 7-5, that attempt to build your profile. Once you tell the software that you incline toward high-risk, daytrading technical approaches to the market, for instance, you are shown a page of newsletters that might suit you.

The attractive, well-organized site offers a page displaying each letter's philosophy, a link to free articles by the author, and a link for a free trial sign-up.

Figure 7-5.   May 11, 1999

The Newsletter Finder feature of Fination.com helps you quickly zero in on the newsletters that might be most appropriate to your investment style.

One Favorite: Bedford & Associates

Many good newsletter writers are independent souls. They don't hang around other newsletter writers at the aggregation stations; they just ply their trade and wait for customers to drop by as a result of good word of mouth. Their letters can be hard to find, even if you search for "investment newsletters" in a search engine.

Canada-based hedge-fund manager and market researcher Terry Bedford has his own excellent site (*http://www.baresearch.com*), shown in Figure 7-6. But he also makes himself available at Fination.com for investors who want to view all their newsletters in one place.

Bedford, a specialist in the technical art of money-flow analysis, publishes four newsletters: CycleWatch for investors, Bedford Option Review for options traders, OEX Advantage for index traders, and New DayTrader for daytraders. Although he is always happy to follow a trend, Bedford excels at helping institutional and private investors put money to work during market declines and sell into advances.

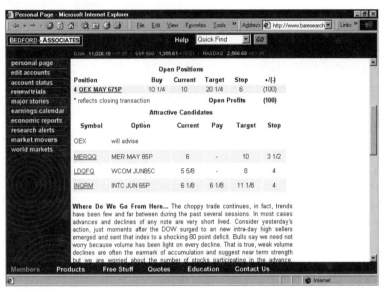

Figure 7-6.   May 11, 1999

Bedford & Associates' OEX Advantage arrives by e-mail four times a day—once in the evening to advise on trades for the next day and three times during trading hours. It provides specific entry and target prices, as well as commentary.

Here's an example of the OEX Advantage newsletter from the same day as the Smartfax excerpt above. Like Dohmen, Bedford was wary of the market advance in early April but was willing to participate as long as the trend continued up.

> ***Where Do We Go From Here...*** *It is almost laughable how the market continually fools the pundits. For weeks the market has exhibited extremely poor internal technical behavior. Breadth and upside volume have been abysmal. However, even as the broad market slipped further into the abyss, the biggest stocks have been very well behaved, in fact, key stocks in the Nasdaq and DOW have moved to one new high after another. If you look at leading stocks you might be inclined to conclude the market is healthy—but that is not at all the case. The big question, indeed the only question is how long can this type of behavior last? We are forced to conclude the market will be relatively firm into the April 15 time frame. We should see money inflows come to an end near that date as investors top-up retirement accounts.*

Readers of this letter (which costs $1,000 per year for four updates a day via e-mail) are interested in the shortest of trends. The above advice proved fruitful for them, as the market sank 5% by April 20. Bedford's commentary in his mid-day updates sounds like a football coach calling in plays to the line of scrimmage (*"Buy these OEX calls at this price—go!"*). Definitely not for everyone, but this kind of advice proves that there's no reason anymore to trade alone.

Other Notable Newsletters

There must be some connection between the crafts of trading and writing that makes so many traders want to write. If you use common sense and avoid newsletter publishers that make outlandish and unprovable claims, this type of commentary can prove a lot more trustworthy than advice from conventional journalists, stock brokers, or investment analysts. The key is to find an advisor who suits you and whom you can stick with. Just keep in mind that trading activity does not necessarily lead to trading success.

Two of the better newsletter sites not mentioned above are:

- **Tradehard.com.** This operation (*http://www.tradehard.com*) bills itself as the "ultimate supersite for traders," which would normally wave a big warning flag. Yet it really is filled with solid trading ideas, educational articles, and good commentary. Writers include pro traders Kevin Haggerty (formerly head of trading for Fidelity Capital Markets), Jeff Cooper (author of three good, short books on momentum trading strategies), and Bob Pisani (an options-trading pro and finance professor). Tradehard.com has come on strong for aggressive traders and daytrading wanna-bes, and it costs a lot less than most newsletters, at $10 per month.

- **Jagnotes.com.** This outfit (*http://www.jagnotes.com*) every morning somehow publishes a comprehensive, consolidated list of recommendations and research from dozens of top brokerages, newsletters, and independent buyside researchers before the market's opening bell. The service has been used by institutions for the past decade, but the cost was prohibitive for individuals at close to $2,000 per year. Now running at $10 a month, it's just another example of the way the Web has leveled the playing field for private investors.

Before considering a subscription to any newsletter, read the promotional materials from as many as possible, then take a free trial subscription to a few, and conscientiously trade the suggestions on paper. Keep in mind that no advisor is going to be right all the time. But if yours turns out to be wrong most of the time after three to six months, don't hesitate to bail and find a new one.

Still, it's not hard to become your very own guru if you master fundamental and technical analysis using online tools. In Part III, you'll learn how to study the fundamentals, regulatory documents, and charts of any stock, and I'll show you where to discuss your findings with fellow investors.

Part III

Researching Investment Ideas Online

Chapter 8
Fundamental Analysis

So far, we have used an online screening engine and news resources on the Web to turn up the right stocks at the right time. If I've persuaded you to become a dedicated yeartrader—to purchase 3 to 10 stocks based on model criteria once every 12 months and benignly ignore the market the rest of the time—you have to go no further in this book. But if you still want to buy the right stocks *one at a time,* you need to use the Web to understand companies thoroughly before you own their shares.

Imagine, then, that you're a frontline diagnostic physician at a big-city hospital. The companies that have piqued your interest so far as a result of screening or news events are similar to patients walking in off the street. Your staff has just completed the admissions process—asking a lot of mild questions and nodding at the answers—but now it's time to perform a series of tests to learn what really makes the companies tick.

To determine whether it's the right time to buy shares or short them "all the way to zero," as a cynical editor of mine used to say, you must find the answers to two very different questions:

- Is the company healthy?
- Is the company's stock healthy?

The answer to the first question requires something the investment community calls *fundamental analysis.* You need to determine exactly what goods or services the company makes or sells, whether consumers like them, and how much power the company has over setting their prices. You need to figure out whether the company is financially sound, whether it's growing faster than its peers, and whether the marketplace appreciates the company for its deeds. You need to use traditional techniques to measure whether the current stock price fairly reflects its fundamental value. Finally, you need to know

whether any catalysts on the horizon (such as management changes or product introductions) might *change* the market's perceptions of the company's value.

The answer to the second question requires something investors call *technical analysis*. This might sound scary, but it's really just an investigation of the balance between supply and demand for the company's stock. You need to determine how much investors have been willing to pay for shares of the company in the past and how much they're likely to pay for it in the future. You also need to know whether the stock price trend is essentially up or down, and whether that trend is likely to change soon.

In this chapter, you'll learn ways to use the Web to find the statistics that make up the lion's share of fundamental analysts' arsenal, and I'll show you how to wield that data effectively. In Chapter 9, you'll learn about the documents that companies file online with federal securities regulators. You'll also see how to mine those documents both to evaluate the health of particular companies and to identify new trading ideas. In Chapter 10, you'll learn all about the new mandarins of the market—brokerage stock analysts—and how to find and interpret their reports online. In Chapter 11, you'll learn to use online charts to study stock-price movement over time as investors react to news of companies' successes and failures. Finally, in Chapter 12, you'll learn to use Internet bulletin boards and chat rooms to bounce your ideas off other investors.

The process of evaluating a company's health comprises eight stages. The first of those is simple but deceptively important.

What does the company do?

Not too long ago, most private investors bought shares in companies with brand names that they used and liked—firms such as Coca-Cola, AT&T, Colgate-Palmolive, and Wal-Mart. Today, however, you're just as likely to have your interests piqued by a company in an industry you've barely heard of and which might not have even existed three years ago.

For this reason, Web sites that provide thorough descriptions of a wide range of companies' businesses and histories have become an important component in any private investor's toolkit. All of the major financial sites provide at least a sentence or two about thousands of companies, but only a few reach beyond the simplistic.

Hoover's Online

Hoover's Online (*http://www.hoovers.com*) offers, by far, the most informative descriptions of the greatest number of public and private companies. If Hoover's doesn't have at least a five-sentence blurb about a public firm, you can just about stop your investigation right away. In mid-1999, for instance, I searched MSN MoneyCentral's 8,900-stock database

for the public companies with the 10 smallest market capitalizations. Then I checked whether Hoover's, shown in Figure 8-1, had a description of each. The site had a capsule on every one, including two with market caps less than $1 million that were based in South Africa and the Grand Cayman Islands.

What makes Hoover's Online a gem is not only its completeness but also the liveliness of its writing. Whether its editorial staff is writing about mighty Alcoa or minuscule Grand Central Silver Mines, the capsules are thoughtful, careful, and fun. Here is Hoover's description of Grand Central, an Idaho firm with the extra-tiny market cap of $700,000:

> *The canary is gasping at Grand Central Silver Mines, formerly Centurion Mines. The company buys land (or the mineral rights to land) that is likely to have deposits of copper, silver, gold, or other minerals. Grand Central capitalizes on its holdings through property sales and joint ventures with larger companies. However, poor market conditions and recent additions to federal mining regulations have the company back-pedaling to cut losses. The company's operations have been slashed by staff reductions and the liquidation of many of its unpatented mining claims. Grand Central has never operated a working mine on any of its properties.*

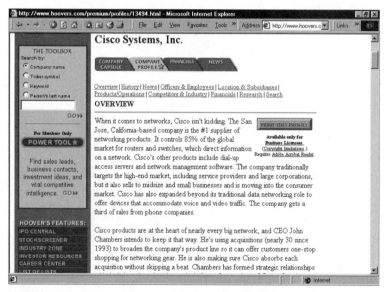

Figure 8-1.   May 18, 1999

Hoover's Online offers subscribers a vast collection of data about nearly all large companies, including corporate history, top officers and their pay, locations of headquarters, lists of products, and competitors.

Hoover's supplies its company capsules to many Web sites, including MSN MoneyCentral. If you want much more detailed descriptions of companies and their corporate histories, you can read those at Hoover's own site. If you want still more background, you can pay $14.95 a month for access to premium content, such as lists of products and competitors.

SEC Filings

If Hoover's can't satisfy your curiosity about a company's business, you can check a few other places.

Every U.S. company must file detailed financial reports annually with the U.S. Securities & Exchange Commission. I'll cover the details of key SEC documents in Chapter 9. For now, note that the Business section of Form 10-K, which is filed annually, contains excruciatingly detailed descriptions of corporate affairs.

For instance, Metromedia Fiber Network, a mid-sized telecommunications company, filed a Form 10-K in December 1998. This form contained a Business section that rattled on for 10,450 words. It included a description of Metromedia's complex plans for installing intracity fiber-optic networks, a treatise on its technology, a list of competitive risks, a long chapter on its licensing and franchise agreements, and an equally long review of its sales and marketing efforts.

MSN MoneyCentral Investor provides easy access to this kind of information in its SEC Filings section, as shown in Figure 8-2. On the site's home page, click Stocks on the top navigation bar, click SEC Filings on the left navigation bar, and then click Business on the submenu. Type a company's ticker symbol at the top of the page, and then click Go. The company's latest quarterly report loads quickly. Pay special attention to the section on Sales and Marketing and the section on Competition, which appear midway through most of these reports.

Another site that provides easy access to this material, as you'll learn in Chapter 9, is FreeEDGAR.com (*http://www.freeedgar.com*). You simply enter a company's ticker symbol on the home page, click Search, and then click View Filings on the page that follows. Next scan the list of the company's most recent filings for the latest Form 10-K. Click the form name, and the long document loads quickly. To move directly to the proper section, click Business or Management Discussion in the left frame, under the Table Of Contents heading.

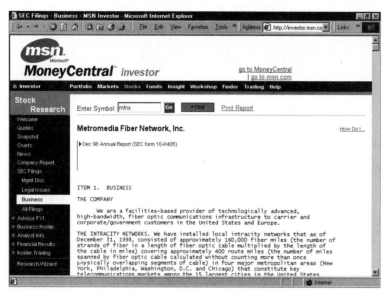

Figure 8-2.   May 19, 1999

The Business section of Form 10-K, which most publicly owned U.S. companies must file with the Securities & Exchange Commission, offers a wealth of information. MoneyCentral offers easy access to these forms, as do most other major finance portals.

How much does the company sell?

When long-term investors buy a company's stock, they buy a slice of the firm's future stream of earnings. Therefore, they need to know how much stuff or or how many services a company sells and how much revenue it keeps as income (or profit) to grow its business or return to shareholders. The more of each, the better. In general, you should look for companies that sell and earn more than their peers.

Of course, it's not that simple. It might not be fair, but investors judge public companies more on their sales and earnings *growth rates* than on the absolute value of their sales and earnings. So it's more important to look for companies that are growing *faster* than their peers than to look for ones that simply sell or earn more at the moment than their peers.

Every financial site on the Web displays figures that reflect earnings and sales growth. I'll use the Financial Highlights page of MSN MoneyCentral Investor for examples because it's as good as any and better than most.

Revenue

The term *revenue* sounds simple, and for the most part, it is. Also referred to as *sales,* it is most of the money (or other items of value) that comes into a company's coffers as a result of its business operations. The revenue figure typically includes product sales and license fees but not interest income or proceeds from the sale of subsidiaries. The more sales, the better.

Revenue figures are often the most reliable statistics with which to judge a company's success. Unlike *net income* figures, sales figures are not subject to various accounting and managerial judgments. To discover the amount that a company sells using MSN MoneyCentral Investor, click Stocks on the top navigation bar, click Financial Results and then Highlights on the left navigation bar, type a ticker symbol into the box, and click Go. As you can see in Figure 8-3, sales and income for a company's past 12 months are displayed in the upper-left corner of the page.

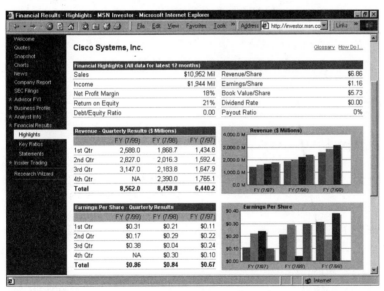

Figure 8-3.   May 20, 1999

The Financial Highlights page at MSN MoneyCentral Investor offers a quick overview of a company's revenue and income results over the past three fiscal years. Look at both the raw data in the table on the left and at the bar charts on the right. Companies that increase revenue and income every quarter generally make superior investments.

Understanding Revenue Growth Acceleration

Now look in the middle of the Financial Highlights page, and determine whether sales at the company you are investigating are rising or falling. On the left, you can compare the company's raw revenues and income results for the past three fiscal years as well as for each quarter within those years. On the right, you can view a bar chart that gives you quick visual impressions of the rates at which a company's revenue and income are growing. Ideally, the bars should rise as they move to the right. (Companies in seasonal businesses—such as apparel or PC sales—will always show lower revenues in certain quarters; in those cases, compare like quarters.)

Most of the time, it's good news when growth at a company accelerates. This means that customers are snapping up a new product, a competitor is losing market share, or the sales force is firing on all cylinders. The company could be on a roll that will produce quarter after quarter of accelerating growth.

If a company is growing faster than its industry, you have a powerful indication that it has found an advantage over competitors. The Growth Rates page of MSN Money-Central, shown in Figure 8-4, lets you quickly find out how a particular company's growth compares to its industry.

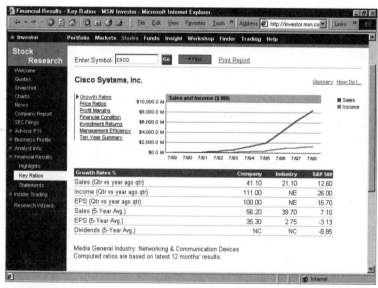

Figure 8-4.   May 21, 1999

The Growth Rates page of MoneyCentral Investor's Financial Highlights section offers a quick overview of a company's sales, income, and EPS growth rates as well as a comparison to its industry, its five-year average, and the average of the companies that make up the S&P 500 Index.

Revenue growth isn't *always* great news, however. If you learn in the SEC documents, a press release, or Hoover's Online that the company has added sales by acquiring other firms, for instance, revenue growth might not be so exciting. You'll need to look at earnings as well to see whether the purchases are paying off with profits.

Likewise, if the company is in a cyclical industry, you'll need to consider the economic cycle. For example, automobile manufacturers tend to do well only when the economy expands. Sales at companies in cyclical industries tend to accelerate most quickly just before consumers decide to start sitting on their wallets.

Once you've noticed that sales are accelerating, do some sleuthing to determine how the growth is affecting other parts of the firm's business. For example, check what the new growth rate has done to net profit margins. If growth has sped up but margins have fallen, management might be losing control over expenses. Perhaps the company is hiring too many salespeople.

Also check whether the company is getting paid on time for all these sales. Accounts receivable is the figure on the balance sheet (see Chapter 9) that measures how much money customers owe the company for goods they have received. If this number climbs from quarter to quarter, watch out. Management might be pumping up revenue figures by booking sales made to customers before actually shipping them merchandise. That tactic almost always blows up on the company and on investors because customers can later cancel their orders.

Finally, check the company's cash flow statement to determine whether financing all this growth is putting a strain on the company. Fast growth in sales often leads to big expenditures for new plants and new people. Is the company able to pay for expansion out of cash reserves or current earnings? Or is it going to have to issue new stock or float new bonds, which might dilute the value of your shares?

Understanding Revenue Growth Slowdowns

If a company's revenue-growth rate falls dramatically—for instance, if its annual revenue growth falls below its five-year average—it's seldom good news. To see how bad the situation is, you've got to dig out the reasons behind the slowdown.

- **Worst case:** A decrease in growth could be fundamental to the company's business if customers are rejecting a new product, a competitor is stealing market share, or the sales force quit, for example. It takes a long time to reverse conditions such as these.

- **Not quite so bad:** Customers could be waiting for the company's new product before buying. Sales could quickly accelerate after the product ships.

- **Neutral:** If the company has sold off a division or two, this would reduce sales, but it might raise profits. You'll have to read news reports or documents filed with the SEC more closely.

- **There is no problem:** A slowdown in a particular year might result from problems in a single quarter that have been fixed.

Companies will usually try to explain any slowdown in their growth in the press release that accompanies their quarterly earnings announcement. But you should do some sleuthing on your own, too.

Check what the new growth rate has done to profit margins. If growth has slowed but margins have held firm, management is doing a reasonably good job at handling the business and probably saw the problem coming. Cut them a little slack. If margins are falling, management was either blindsided or couldn't do anything to prevent the problem. Look for a convincing plan from the company for reversing the situation.

If growth slows, profit margins fall, and accounts receivable climb quarter to quarter, be careful. Management could be trying to stuff the distribution pipeline to make revenues look better than they really are. This underhanded tactic, sometimes used even by very large companies, always eventually becomes visible—and will ruin a stock.

How much does the company earn?

Earnings is just another word for profit or net income. In most cases, the relevant figure is the sum of the trailing four quarters' net income from continuing operations. However, most Web sites, including MSN MoneyCentral, principally display the figure for net income from total operations.

Types of Earnings

Understanding income figures on the Web is not a simple matter because many companies try to put a positive spin on their earnings reports. They might emphasize a flavor of the facts that shows their results in the best light. Investors need to understand the types of earnings presentations to get a clear picture of a company's financial situation. Here are the three types of earnings most often presented:

- **Actual earnings.** This amount is what a company earned, including all current revenue and expenses.

- **Operating earnings.** This amount includes only revenue and costs from ongoing operations. It excludes one-time non-operational charges, such as gains or losses on

sales of assets or one-time acquisition costs. For example, proceeds from the sale or purchase of a business unit are not tallied. Inventory write-downs and currency impacts, however, are included in operating earnings.

- **Pro-forma earnings.** This amount is based on some assumptions described in the company's press release. For example, it might refer to earnings that would have been generated if a newly acquired business unit had contributed to the company's business for an entire year.

When companies report how much they made or lost each quarter, seasoned investors look first at their *earnings per share* figure. This is the net income divided by the number of common shares outstanding. A company that earns $1 million for the year and has 1 million shares outstanding has an EPS of $1.00.

The EPS figure, which represents how much of the company's earnings each share is entitled to, is important as the basis for various calculations an investor might make in assessing a stock's value. The most widely used indicator of whether a stock is over- or undervalued, for example, is the price/earnings ratio, which relates the price per share to the earnings per share.

Companies report earnings in press releases that they distribute by wire services to all financial Web sites. Earnings are typically reported either before trading begins for the day or after it ends. Stock prices often rise or fall in anticipation of or reaction to these announcements. See Figure 8-5 for an example of a relationship between earnings releases and stock price.

Many Web sites offer calendars of expected earnings-release dates. None is 100% reliable, because each relies on users' or clerks' efforts to call the companies for the dates. Sometimes the dates are recorded incorrectly, and sometimes company leaders change their minds. If it's critical that you know the exact time and date, call the company's investor-relations department yourself.

The best calendar for technology stocks can be found at Briefing.com (*http://www.briefing.com*). It shows not only the dates but also whether the release is expected before the market opens or after it closes for the day. This is important because high-momentum technology stocks typically run up in price before earnings releases and sell off afterward, no matter what the news is. Timing is everything. The calendar also lists phone numbers for many analyst conference calls.

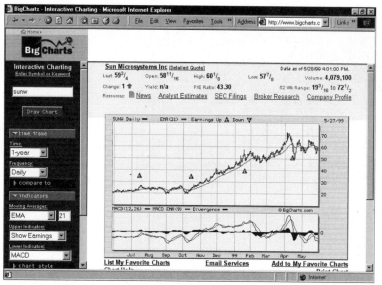

Figure 8-5. May 28, 1999

It can be very useful to see earnings-release dates matched up against a stock's price chart, as shown in this graph from BigCharts.com (http://www.bigcharts.com). It uses upward-pointing arrows for dates when the company reported an increase in its earnings and downward-pointing arrows for dates when a profit decline was reported.

The following list names other sites with good earnings calendars:

- **CBS MarketWatch** (*http://cbs.marketwatch.com/newsroom/EarnCal.htx*). This one is nicely organized by weeks, and it gets the data from a company called Net Earnings. The calendar offers reports from a wide range of companies and quick links to quotes and more data.

- **MSN MoneyCentral Investor** (*http://moneycentral.msn.com/investor/calendar/earnings/current.asp*). This comprehensive calendar also relies on Net Earnings for data, but it is laid out so investors can easily page forward and back by day or week to find a particular stock. Estimated earnings are listed too. To visit from the site's home page, click Markets on the top navigation bar, and then click Calendar on the left navigation bar.

- **Silicon Investor** (*http://www.techstocks.com/investor/earningscalendar*). This calendar, shown in Figure 8-6 on the next page, is less complete than the others because it is solely powered by the discussion community. But it also sometimes provides useful comments from members of that community.

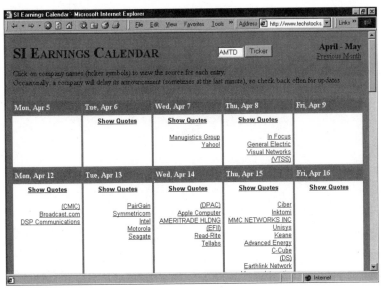

Figure 8-6.   May 28, 1999

The earnings calendar at Silicon Investor is maintained and monitored by the site's users, so it includes mainly technology stocks. You can search by ticker symbol and read comments from users who called the companies to confirm the dates.

Understanding Earnings Acceleration

Many well-managed companies chug along with profits rising at rates in what executives euphemistically call "the mid-single digits." But it's typically best to find companies that exceed that level by a wide margin. Companies that are well worth your time to own grow 15% annually, even exceeding their five-year averages by as much as 15%. (See Appendix A to learn how to find these stocks in a stock-screening engine such as MSN MoneyCentral's Investment Finder.)

Even in very prosperous times, only a few great firms can improve their earnings growth by more than 15% a year. If you find a company that reports extraordinary growth, dig into reasons behind the acceleration before starting your celebration.

- Determine how earnings growth relates to the company's revenue growth over the same time frame. Perhaps revenue accelerated even faster than earnings in the last year, and in reality, the company's profits shrank. On the other hand, if earnings accelerated at a faster clip than revenue, this could signal some fundamental improvements that bode well for the future. Perhaps management has installed some great new technology that has sharply reduced expenses.

- Read the company's earnings announcement carefully, and listen to its conference call with analysts to see how executives explain their latest results. Was there some extraordinary item that caused the jump, or are recent gains truly based on improved operations? An extraordinary item speaks less about the overall direction of the firm.

- Accelerating earnings growth typically leads to a higher stock price. But perhaps investors have already pushed share prices up in anticipation. Check the company's current price/earnings ratio, which is one of the more common measures of stock value. Where does the current P/E ratio stand compared to the range this company has seen over the last five years? You can find the high and low P/E ratios for the company in MSN MoneyCentral's Financial Results / Price Ratios section. Note also how the company's current P/E ratio compares to the average for its industry. A P/E ratio that is above both its own norm and that of its industry indicates that the market views the firm as an industry leader. You'll need to decide whether the accelerating earnings growth justifies the premium.

- Investigate what analysts are saying about the company. Do they think it can maintain its new, higher rate of earnings growth for the next year—or five years?

Earnings Conference Calls

Most companies follow up their earnings announcements by speaking to major shareholders and a select group of analysts on a telephone conference call. These calls are extremely important because they allow executives to give color to the report's dry list of figures, describe the firm's view of the future, and answer questions.

For years, individual investors were not privy to the calls, which deprived them of a critical source of information. But the Web has helped end the shut-out. Today, several financial sites list the phone numbers that investors can call to listen either by phone or by Web audio. Here are the best Web sites to check for this kind of information.

- **BestCalls.com** (*http://www.bestcalls.com*). Register for free at this site, shown in Figure 8-7 on the next page, to search for dates, phone numbers, and passwords for thousands of companies' conference calls. You can sign up to be alerted by e-mail seven days before a call.

(continued)

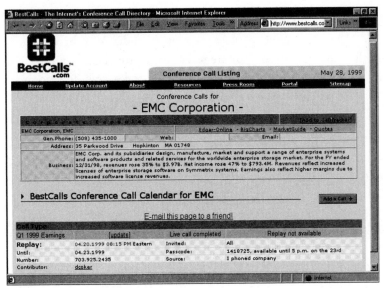

Figure 8-7.   May 28, 1999

At the BestCalls.com site, private investors can register for free to have e-mail sent seven days before conference calls or other corporate events. In the lower-left part of the page, the site lists a phone number for one of EMC Corporation's calls, as well as the password for listening to a replay of the call.

Earnings Conference Calls *(continued)*

- **Briefing.com** (*http://www.briefing.com/sub/stocks/techcal.htm*). Scroll to the bottom of the Tech Earnings Calendar to see a long list of technology companies' conference-call dates, phone numbers, and passwords.

- **Motley Fool** (*http://www.fool.com/Calls/Calls.htm*). The Motley Fool editors blazed the trail for individual investors who wanted in on conference calls. They provide a report on major calls each day and sometimes even transcripts of the proceedings.

- **Vcall** (*http://www.vcall.com*). Vcall calls itself "the bottom line online" and has the greatest number of links to Webcast conference calls. You'll need to load Windows Media Player (*http://www.microsoft.com/windows/mediaplayer*) or a RealAudio player (*http://www.real.com*) to listen.

Understanding Earnings Growth Slowdowns

Deceleration of earnings growth is always troubling, especially when the decline occurs over a period as long as a year. The reasons behind such declines and the prognoses they imply are the same as for slowdowns in sales growth, described earlier in this chapter.

Keep in mind when you're examining growth rates that earnings growth doesn't have to be explosive to make a good stock. A company that consistently makes more profit year after year might be a lot more attractive an opportunity for conservative investors than a firm that makes a ton of money one year only to see profits drop the next. In the best of all worlds, of course, a company not only improves its earnings every year but improves them substantially. If you find a company like that, you have a potential winner. (The Redwood Growth model portfolios, described in Chapter 3, are made up of stellar companies like these.)

How profitable is the company?

Profit margins tell an investor all about the rate of income generated by a company's operations, though they leave aside capital investments (the purchase of new machinery, for instance), depreciation, and other indirect expenses. Gross margins are calculated by subtracting the cost of goods sold from net sales and dividing the result by net sales. For instance, if an apple-cart owner pays an orchardist 25¢ apiece for apples and sells them for $1 each, his gross profit margin is 75%. You can research the history of a company's profit margins with MSN MoneyCental Investor, as shown in Figure 8-8 on the next page.

Companies with razor-thin profit margins generally are less attractive to investors than ones with fat profit margins. But like all such measures, this one varies greatly by industry. Profit margins for software firms and movie studios can be quite high, while profit margins for even successful retail stores tend to be low. So it's important to determine whether the profit margins of the company you're investigating are rising or falling compared to its own history and how the firm's margins compare to those of its industry.

You can measure profit at many levels of the income statement. (For more on these statements, see Chapter 9.) Each level tells you something different about the company. Here are the three main flavors of profit margin to examine:

- **Gross margin.** This is the broadest measure of a firm's profitability. Gross margin is a good way to assess the profitability of the company's core operations, aside from depreciation and other accounting stuff. Essentially, it tells you how much

more a customer pays the company for its products than the company pays to make those products. No company pockets all its gross margin. The costs of selling its product, keeping payroll, and the like are paid from this amount. But gross margin tells an investor how successful a company has been at the business of buying or manufacturing the raw materials and components it needs cheaply—and selling its finished products dearly.

- **Pre-Tax Margin.** This is the latest 12 months' pre-tax income divided by the latest 12 months' sales. Because different companies within an industry might have different tax rates, this is occasionally the best gauge for comparing profitability.

- **Net Margin.** This is the latest 12 months' net income from total operations divided by the latest 12 months' sales. Net margin includes all the factors—whether under management control or not—that influence profitability. Net profit margin varies widely by industry. In the supermarket business, for instance, enormous sales are generated to produce relatively modest profits. Software firms and drug companies show the opposite pattern. Because net margin sums up in one number how successful a company has been at the business of making a profit on each dollar of sales, it is the most common metric for comparing one company's profitability against another's.

Figure 8-8.   May 21, 1999

The Profit Margins page of MSN MoneyCentral Investor's Financial Results section offers a bar chart that quickly lets you see whether a firm's net profit margins are declining or rising. The page also shows data that allow you to compare current gross, pre-tax, and net margins with a company's industry, its own five-year average, and the average of the S&P 500.

Understanding Profit Margin Improvements

Increasing profit margins should not be enough to impress you unless you also understand the source of those higher margins. If the increase comes from lower costs, for instance, you should dig deeper to determine how much control the company has over those costs. A dip in the price of raw materials could vanish in a short time. On the other hand, a major change in the manufacturing process that cuts the amount of raw material needed to produce a product is a permanent savings.

Improving margins can provide a company with a sizable competitive edge. A company with higher gross margins has the ability to spend more on marketing its product than its competitors can. In an industry-wide downturn, it might still be able to make money when competitors slip into the red. An aggressive management team would use that edge to pick up market share during the tough times.

However, beware of companies that get a big boost to their margin from a lower tax rate, for example, because of a write-down of an asset to its current value. The extra points of margin are likely to be transitory, and investors who count on them could get a shock when the tax rate returns to normal levels.

Understanding Profit Margin Declines

If a company has suffered through a long string of consecutively lower profit margins, watch out. It's rarely anything but bad news for current shareholders and a red flag for prospective shareholders. Investors, after all, bid up the shares of a company anticipating an earnings stream. If the company is progressively earning less profit on each dollar of sales, the earnings stream might be threatened.

If revenues are growing very rapidly, of course, the decreasing profit margin might not be a big worry. Perhaps the company's margins started from an unsustainably high level. Or perhaps the company is reacting to increasing competition by reducing prices while investing in new products or technology that promises healthier profits in the long run. It's only really long margin declines that you must be wary of.

On the other hand, if you're studying the company as a new investment, it's possible that it is attractive as a potential turnaround play—a diamond in the rough, just on the verge of dramatically reversing course. Investing in distressed merchandise of any kind is more of a gamble than many might find comfortable, and that certainly holds true for companies. But if you uncover a budding turnaround, the profits can be great. You might want to look into this company more deeply if value investing is your style.

Some questions to consider include whether management has changed recently. If so, does the new team have a track record in guiding stale corporations back to vigorous health? Have they proved willing to take difficult actions, such as rapidly writing off, or selling, outdated assets?

A prospective value investor should also check how the firm compares to its industry average in terms of key measures of value, such as price-earnings, price-cash flow, price-book, and price-sales ratios. If the P/E ratio, for example, is far enough below both the norm for the company and the norm for its industry, the price might have been discounted enough to make for an attractive risk-reward tradeoff.

How is the company's financial health?

Many investors measure a company's financial health by weighing its debts and liabilities against its equity and physical assets. You can easily evaluate all of these considerations online at sites like MSN MoneyCentral Investor, as shown in Figure 8-9.

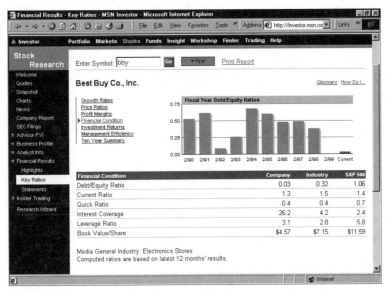

Figure 8-9.   May 21, 1999

The Financial Condition page of MSN MoneyCentral Investor's Financial Results section offers a bar chart that shows whether a firm's debt/equity ratio is declining or rising. (In this case, electronics retailer Best Buy's is falling dramatically.) Data here also let you compare a company's debt/equity ratio, current ratio, quick ratio, and leverage ratio against those of its peers and the S&P 500 average.

Debt/Equity Ratio

This is a measure of the extent to which a firm's capital is provided either by its shareholders or its lenders. The figure is calculated by dividing the dollar amount of a company's long-term debt by the dollar amount of shareholder equity.

Aggressive companies in capital-intensive industries, such as telecommunications, often rely more heavily on its lenders than conservative companies in more mature industries do. A greater reliance on loans can mean greater profitability for shareholders down the road but also greater risk in the event that things go sour.

As a rule of thumb, look for companies with a debt/equity ratio of 50% or lower. Companies in industries that aren't very competitive or are subject to tight regulation—such as telecommunications or cable companies—can afford to carry more debt.

Understanding a Declining Debt/Equity Ratio

If a company's debt/equity ratio declines, something good is happening. The company is borrowing less money. Companies borrow money because it is often a cheaper way to fund their businesses than selling stock if they don't have enough cash flow from operations. Companies also borrow when it makes sense to match the duration of the obligation to the duration of the need for cash or to the life expectancy of the asset being purchased.

A debt/equity ratio falls when a company pays off debt. A company contemplates this alternative only when it generates excess cash flow. Paying down debt is a good use of cash when the debt that's being retired carries a high interest rate. Money that goes out the door to pay banks and bondholders will become earnings that should drive the stock price higher or pay higher dividends. This kind of decline in a debt/equity ratio can be great news for investors.

An investor will get the most bang out of an improving debt/equity ratio when a company has been so highly leveraged that its debt level raised market concerns. A company's stock will get a boost if one of the rating agencies—such as Moody's or Standard & Poor's—upgrades its opinion of the company's debt. That upgrade by itself will lower a company's cost of borrowing and add dollars to the bottom line.

Understanding a Rising Debt/Equity Ratio

When a company's debt/equity ratio rises, the meaning is clear. The company is borrowing more money. It's up to you to figure out whether that's a danger sign.

Companies get into trouble when they borrow so much that their ability to pay interest on the debt decreases. (If nothing else, this doubt raises the interest rates that a company must pay on its debt.) There's no specific number at which the debt/equity ratio goes from safe to dangerous, although a ratio of 0.5, sometimes rendered as 50%, is obviously safer than a ratio of 1.5. (Compare the company you're studying with other companies in the same industry.)

Debt Ratings Changes

Changes in a company's debt ratings are extremely important and among the least understood phenomena affecting stock prices. Debt analysts generally get more respect from the market than equity analysts do. Much more money is at stake, and their audience is both more sophisticated and less tolerant of error. When a major debt-ratings firm, such as Moody's Investors Services or Standard & Poor's, announces it might downgrade a company's bonds because of the risk of default, seasoned investors pay attention. A lower debt rating can translate immediately into higher costs of borrowing and, therefore, lower profits.

Check regularly for ratings changes at Moody's (*http://www.moodys.com*), shown in Figure 8-10, or Standard & Poor's (*http://www.standardandpoors.com/ratings*). The reports are easy to read and full of great information. Here's an example in which Moody's warned investors about shoe retailer Just For Feet on May 28, 1999:

> *New York, May 28, 1999—Moody's Investors Service placed the B1 rating of Just for Feet's 11% senior subordinated notes due 2009, and the Ba2 rating of the company's guaranteed revolving credit facilities, on review for possible downgrade.*
>
> *The review action follows disclosure of excess inventories at the company's specialty store division. Although the division accounts for only 15% of the company's sales, inventory had ballooned to about 25% of the company total. Management has announced decisive plans to clear the inventory through the superstores' Combat Zone during the summer. However, this action will lower anticipated profitability in the near term because it will replace full-margin sales, therefore leading to likely delays in improving effective leverage and debt coverage in the near term.*
>
> *Moody's review will focus on revised expectations for performance and growth plans for the company's specialty and superstore businesses, and expectations for the company's financing needs and debt profile based on changes to its business plan. The review will also take into account the benefits of the company's strong market presence, the opportunities to improve operations of the store specialty group through improved controls and corporate oversight, and the opportunity to free up working capital by reducing inventory carried throughout the chain.*

Don't worry about the debt-industry mumbo-jumbo in the first paragraph. What's important to note is that Moody's is paying attention to the firm's inventory and profitability on behalf of institutional clients paying huge fees; only the Web puts some of that data and analysis in your hands for free.

Figure 8-10.   May 29, 1999

Moody's Investors Service provides sophisticated daily analysis of the prospects of numerous companies and industries for free at its Web site. On May 28, 1999, it analyzed the prospects of Just For Feet, Deutsche Telekom, Apple Computer, Ceridian, and Amerada Hess.

Current Ratio

The current ratio is a measure of a firm's current financial health and its ability to meet current obligations. It's calculated by dividing the most recent quarter's current assets by current liabilities of the same period. (See Chapter 9 for more on these terms.)

Generally, the current ratio should be 2:1 or higher, usually just rendered as 2.0. The higher the current ratio, the more conservative the firm, although a high current ratio can mean less profitability than that of a competing firm with a leaner current ratio. Also, like so many ratios, this one can vary by industry. Restaurant companies, for example, often have current ratios of less than 1.0. However, this low ratio raises few eyebrows because customers pay for services immediately, but vendors, who typically grant credit, aren't paid as quickly.

Understanding Current Ratio

When people start falling behind on their monthly bills, they're probably having trouble finding the cash to pay up. Other factors might come into play. Maybe they fell behind while on an extended vacation. But that's not the reason that first jumps to mind. The same is true for corporations.

If a company's business is growing, it's reasonable to expect its bills, or *accounts payable*, to grow proportionately. But if accounts payable rise significantly more than a measure of its overall business activity, such as sales, it's worth checking out. There are benign reasons for a disproportionate rise in accounts payable. Perhaps the company anticipates a supply shortage or a price increase for some critical component or raw material, and it has increased its inventory to protect itself. But an increase in accounts payable could also signal trouble. Failure to pay debts on time might damage the company's credit rating, which might mean the company will face higher interest rates when it needs to borrow. In extreme cases, bad debt management can bring a company to the brink of bankruptcy.

The company's current ratio offers a classic test of its short-term debt-paying ability. Check industry comparisons to see how a company matches up against its peers.

Quick Ratio

The quick ratio assesses a company's ability to meet short-term obligations. Also known as the *acid test*, it's calculated by adding cash and receivables from the most recent quarter and dividing that sum by the total current liabilities from the same quarter.

In general, the quick ratio should be 1.0 or better. A high quick ratio is usually a sign of a solid, conservatively run company in no danger of imminent demise even if, for some awful reason, sales immediately ceased. A firm's quick ratio might be of special interest to investors anticipating some kind of downturn in the firm's business or the economy at large.

Interest Coverage

Interest coverage measures a company's ability to handle debt service, and it tells investors whether the company is overburdened with debt. It is calculated by dividing the latest 12 months' earnings before interest and taxes (EBIT) by the latest 12 months' interest expense. EBIT should be several times the annual interest expenses, but the higher this ratio is, the better.

Leverage Ratio

This figure gives some indication of how highly leveraged a company is. It's calculated by dividing total assets by total stock equity. If the ratio is high—that is, if assets far exceed stock equity—the company is quite leveraged. This can be lucrative during good times, when assets bought with borrowed money earn more than they cost. But if things go bad, the company could have trouble servicing the debt implied by all this leverage. Look for a number that's lower than those listed for a company's peers.

Book Value

Book value per share is simply the company's net worth from the most recent quarter divided by the shares outstanding. Often of interest to value investors, the book-value-per-share ratio expresses how much actual value would be left for each share if the company went out of business. This figure can be especially noteworthy when considering a turnaround situation. Sometimes a firm's stock is so beaten down that shares are trading at or below book value, implying either a real bargain or a balance sheet that overstates the company's assets. In such circumstances, a look at cash and marketable securities per share can help.

Book value per share is not to be confused with "break-up value," which attempts to determine what the parts of a company might be worth if sold off. Break-up value is much harder to pinpoint, but it's considered more realistic by many analysts. It is usually higher than book value.

What's the company's return from investments?

Institutional investors often report that they consider companies' returns on investment, such as those shown in Figure 8-11, to be their most important valuation criteria. Let's look at these critical factors and see how you can find the data online.

Figure 8-11.   May 21, 1999

The Investment Returns page of MSN MoneyCentral Investor's Financial Results section showcases companies' investment-return ratios. It also lets you compare them to those of their industry and the averages of the stocks in the S&P 500 Index.

Return on Equity

Return on equity (or ROE) is the most widely used measure of how well a company is performing for its shareholders. It's a relatively straightforward benchmark that is easy to calculate, works for the great majority of industries, and sums up a lot of the more complicated criteria noted above in a single number. Return on equity is calculated by dividing the latest 12 months' net income by the common-stock equity recorded in the most recent quarter.

Return on equity for most large companies should be in the double digits, but value investors often look for 15%. A return of more than 20% is considered excellent, and 26% is often named as a gold standard for use in screens. But the importance of consistency makes the five-year average especially noteworthy.

Understanding Return on Equity

If a company's return on equity is high and rising, bravo. The company is using shareholders' money more and more efficiently. To get the most insight out of return on equity, you should look at the number in two ways:

- **Look at the company's ROE trend.** A rising return on equity could indicate that the company's customers are willing to pay more for new products than they are for products that are older or offered by a competitor. A new management team could have invigorated the sales force, instituted brilliant new marketing, or found a way to outflank the competition. New products with higher margins could make up an increasing part of sales. A climbing return on equity inevitably leads to a climbing stock price as investors realize that each dollar invested in the company is earning more and more with each quarter.

- **Compare the company's ROE with that of its industry.** Companies with a high return on equity relative to their peers are probably taking market share away from competitors. Such companies certainly have an easier time attracting investment capital for new factories and new products. When looking at return on equity, also check a company's debt/equity ratio. Because return on equity divides only earnings by shareholders' equity, a company that has funded itself using bonds and other debt instruments could show a higher return on equity than a competitor without actually managing capital more effectively. To be safe, check return on equity and the more comprehensive ratio called "return on investment," which considers total debt and equity invested in the company.

If a company's return on equity declines, either its customers aren't willing to pay as much for its products as they were in the past or the products are getting more expensive to produce. New competition could be forcing the company to spend more on marketing and sales support. Aging products that command only a commodity price could be making up a bigger and bigger part of sales.

Beware: a falling return on equity generally leads to a falling stock price as investors realize that each dollar invested in the company is earning less and less each quarter. Companies with lower returns on equity relative to those of their peers are probably losing ground to competitors, who have an easier time attracting investment capital for new factories and new products. A company with a low but steady return on equity is not necessarily going out of business. It might occupy a niche in its industry that none of its more profitable competitors find attractive. Moreover, a company with a low and falling return on equity could make an attractive turnaround investment for value-stock pickers who can see signs that the company has adopted a more viable strategy.

Return on Assets

This ratio measures a firm's effectiveness in using the assets at hand to generate earnings. It's calculated by dividing the latest 12 months' net income by the total assets recorded in the most recent quarter. (See Chapter 9 for more on this term.) Return on assets (ROA) should be of special interest to investors in banking and manufacturing stocks. Compare a company's current ROA to its five-year average for insight into the trend.

Understanding Return on Assets

Assets are listed on the company's balance sheet and include such items as inventory, plants, and equipment. ROA tells investors how productively a company and its management use the physical resources they own. The higher the ROA, the better. To get the most insight out of return on assets, you should look at the number in two ways:

- **Look at the company's ROA trend.** A rising return on assets is caused by events similar to those that cause a rising return on equity. It also generally leads to a rise in stock price as investors realize that management is skilled at getting profits out of the resources that the business owns.

- **Compare the company's ROA with that of its industry.** Companies with high returns on assets relative to their peers own a very powerful weapon. They are getting more profit out of each dollar of machinery or inventory, for example. That means they have more money to devote to marketing or research, and such companies certainly have an easier time attracting investment capital for new factories and new products. Be careful in this comparison, though. Companies in the same industry can actually specialize in niche businesses that require very different amounts of assets to produce each dollar of sales.

How efficient is the company's management?

Many investors look at management's efficiency measures, such as those shown in Figure 8-12, for insights into the extent to which executives get the most out of their employees.

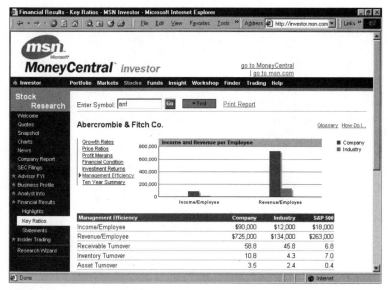

Figure 8-12.   May 29, 1999

Investigating the amounts of revenue and income a company wrings out of each employee can be very useful when comparing companies within an industry. Specialty youth-apparel retailer Abercrombie & Fitch, for instance, was on a roll in 1999—a phenomenon confirmed by its terrific management efficiency comparisons.

Income and Revenue Per Employee

Labor is a huge expense for most businesses. Studying how effectively a company can turn the wits and brawn of its workforce into earnings yields powerful clues for investors. These figures are calculated by dividing the net income by the number of workers recorded at the end of a company's fiscal year. Note that these figures can be deceptive in the middle of the year because they do not account for any new hiring.

Understanding Income and Revenue Per Employee

If income and revenue per employee rise—and especially if they're above the industry averages—good things might be happening at this company. It could mean that the company's products take fewer hours to sell than those of competitors, perhaps because they leap off the shelf. Or it could mean that management has found a way to trim the time it takes to make its goods. Executives might have reorganized the paper flow in a company to reduce overhead. If any of this is true, this is definitely a stock to watch.

But don't jump to any conclusions until you've watched the company for a few quarters. Some efficiencies turn out to be very short-lived. For example, companies that cut their workforces will often see a temporary jump in income per employee as the survivors work harder and pick up the tasks done by the recently departed. Research shows, however, that the effect can be temporary. Workers might burn out under the load and perform less efficiently, or the company might be forced to outsource the work formerly performed in-house. If this is the case, management has succeeded in reducing headcount, but it hasn't succeeded in increasing productivity per capita.

If income and revenue per employee at a company fall—especially relative to those of its industry—bad things might be happening at this company. Such a drop could indicate that the company's products take more hours to sell than those of competitors. Perhaps customers don't understand what makes the product so special. The product might take longer to make than is common elsewhere in the industry, or employees might be so disgruntled that they are quitting en masse. The company would then face big expenses for training and have an inexperienced staff running the show.

If any of this is true, this is definitely a stock to avoid. But, again, don't jump to any conclusions until you've watched the company for a few quarters. A company that is staffing up quickly to prepare for expected growth will show a declining ratio of income per employee. If the company's expectations prove accurate, that temporary dip was actually a sign of good things to come. If management has inaccurately forecast company growth, however, the firm will find itself saddled with expensive workers it doesn't need.

Inventory Turnover

A company's inventory-turnover rate indicates how well its products are succeeding in the marketplace. In general, the higher this number, the better. It's calculated by dividing the latest 12 months' cost of sales by the average inventory recorded in the most recent quarter and the same quarter from the previous year.

Understanding Inventory Turnover

It's critical to keep an eye on a company's inventory levels. If a company has too much inventory, it's wasting money by tying up capital that could be better used elsewhere. But if it doesn't have enough, it risks losing business because a potential customer would rather shop elsewhere in order to get immediate delivery. That makes inventory control an important issue for managers and investors alike.

Inventory turnover is thus considered a key measure of management efficiency. It measures how often, during the course of a year, a company sells its final products and replaces its inventory of component parts and materials. As a general rule, the higher the inventory turnover, the better, although the standard varies dramatically from industry to industry. A fast-food chain, such as McDonald's, has high inventory turnover because hamburger meat is not the kind of thing a company wants to keep in storage for very long. Boeing, on the other hand, tends to have considerably lower inventory turnover because airplanes don't spoil, are more complicated, and take longer to build than Big Macs.

A common way to assess a company's inventory-control procedures is to determine how long, on average, it holds its inventories. A significant increase in a company's inventory-turnover rate is probably a good sign, suggesting that management has fewer dollars tied up in inventory and that it is filling customer orders more efficiently. On the other hand, if the firm had been losing sales and profits because it did not have product in stock ready for sale, holding more inventory could be a good move.

Compare potential investments to others in the same industry by this ratio to see sharp contrasts. In May 1999, for instance, apparel-retailer Abercrombie & Fitch had an inventory-turnover rate of 10.8—more than double its industry average of 4.3. In contrast, struggling discount variety store Dollar General had an inventory turnover of 3.4—less than half its sector's average rate of 6.4.

How does a company's stock price compare to its earnings and sales?

Price ratios, such as those shown in Figure 8-13, are the most common means of comparing the valuations of companies. Let's look at the main ones and learn how to find and interpret them online.

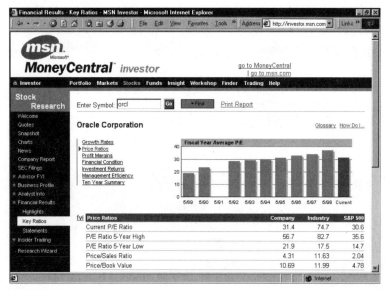

Figure 8-13.   May 29, 1999

The Price Ratios page at MSN MoneyCentral Investor concisely displays companies' price-to-sales, price-to-earnings, price-to-cash flow, and price-to-book values. It also shows comparisons of these ratios to those of the companies' industries and the S&P 500 average. In May 1999, Oracle's ratios were well below those of its industry, which suggested it might have been undervalued.

Price/Earnings Ratio

The price/earnings ratio, also known as the *P/E ratio* or the P/E *multiple,* describes how much an investor is willing to pay for a company's earnings power. It is calculated by dividing the latest closing stock price by the latest 12 months' earnings per share. The P/E ratio is perhaps the single most widely used factor in assessing whether a stock is expensive or cheap.

In some respects, the P/E ratio can be considered the true price of a stock. Investors assign high P/E multiples to companies and industries with the best growth prospects, and they assign low P/E multiples to companies and industries with the worst growth prospects. Indeed, when large numbers of investors decide that a stock or industry has higher or lower growth prospects than previously believed, they expand or contract the stock or industry's P/E multiple. This action changes the stock price without any specific news or earnings event.

A company's P/E ratio should be compared to those of similar companies and the stock market as a whole. High-tech companies often trade at P/E ratios above 60, which is double the P/E ratio of the overall market. Banks and auto makers, on the other hand, typically have below-market P/E ratios.

P/E ratios, therefore, are all about expectations, high or low. Value investors buy stocks with low P/E ratios because they believe the market is unreasonably pessimistic in its expectations. They later sell those stocks if the P/E ratios rise to reflect overly rosy expectations. Investors need to understand and track their investments' historic ranges.

Understanding a High or Rising P/E Ratio

A company sporting a P/E ratio substantially higher than the average for its industry is seen by investors as having greater earnings power than its peers. Perhaps it's the industry leader in key product lines, or it has exceptional management. But a higher-than-average P/E ratio also can mean greater risk. If something goes wrong with either the company or the industry, the stock price might fall very fast.

If a company's P/E ratio is 25% or more above its industry average, for instance, its stock is probably worth extra attention. Does the firm clearly stand in the forefront of its industry? Is its edge sustainable? The following factors are among those you might check:

- **How does the company stack up to its peers by other measures?** Compare its price-to-sales, price-to-book, and price-to-cash flow ratios with those of its industry. Do these ratios confirm that the company is a leader?

- **How about the company's sales-growth and earnings-growth rates?** If a company's earnings-growth rates match or exceed its P/E ratio, many investors would still consider its stock fairly valued, or even undervalued. But if its P/E ratio significantly exceeds its growth rates, the stock could be vulnerable.

- **What are analysts' expectations for the company?** Perhaps they see the company's earnings growth accelerating compared to its recent track record. But if the outlook is for slower growth, it might raise more questions about the company's P/E ratio.

Understanding a Low or Falling P/E Ratio

Investors who specialize in undervalued stocks take note when a company's P/E ratio falls significantly below the average for its industry and the overall market. That happens when the company's stock price falls disproportionately in relation to its profits, or its profits rise disproportionately to its stock price. Either way, the P/E ratio suggests that this is a firm whose stock has room to move up in price.

Whether it will, of course, depends on many other factors. A disproportionate drop in the price of the stock, for example, might mean that analysts have lost confidence in the company's ability to maintain its current level of profitability. But a P/E ratio below the industry average might also mean that the market hasn't yet caught up to a buying opportunity.

Using the P/E Ratio to Set a Price Target

Analysts fix near-term price targets for most stocks by estimating a company's fiscal-year earnings per share and then multiplying that figure by its current P/E ratio. (That's why the P/E ratio is often called a stock's multiple.) You can do the same without calculating your own earnings estimate simply by starting with the brokerage analysts' average estimate, which is also known as the *consensus estimate.*

For instance, the consensus estimate for earnings in fiscal year 1999 of consumer-products giant Johnson & Johnson was $2.99. The company's P/E ratio in late May 1999 was 39.9. Multiply $2.99 times 39.9, and you get a target price for the stock of $119.30 by December 1999. That would be a 28.8% gain from the May 1999 price of $92.63. Not bad!

If your research leads you to believe that a company's stock is undervalued or overvalued compared to other stocks in its industry, you can also calculate an alternate price target based on that assumption. Just multiply the average P/E ratio for a company's industry by the consensus fiscal-year earnings estimate for the company you're studying. In the case of Johnson & Johnson, the average P/E ratio for its industry was 38.1. Multiply 38.1 by $2.99, and you get $113.92—a bit less than the first estimate.

At MSN MoneyCentral Investor, a Research Wizard can perform all these calculations for you, as shown in Figure 8-14 on the next page. Click Stocks in the top navigation bar on the site's home page, and then click Research Wizard in the left navigation bar. Type a ticker symbol into the box at the top of the page, click Go, and then click Price Target in the left navigation bar. Price targets for the current and next fiscal years appear in the middle of the page.

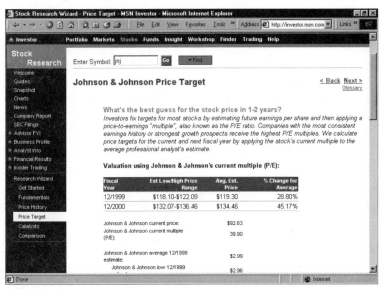

Figure 8-14.   May 29, 1999

MSN's Research Wizard calculates price targets for the next two years on all stocks with P/E ratios. In May 1999, the wizard multiplied Johnson & Johnson's current P/E ratio by analysts' consensus earnings estimate. This generated the prediction that the drug giant's price would rise from $92.63 in May 1999 to reach $119 by December of the same year and $134 by December 2000.

Charting a Stock's P/E Range

Just as stocks trade within a range of prices over the course of a year, they also trade within a range of P/E ratios. To understand more clearly whether a stock is overvalued or undervalued at any given time, you might be better served by examining a chart of its P/E range rather than its price range.

BigCharts.com (*http://www.bigcharts.com*) is the best place to chart P/E ranges for free on the Web. On the site's home page, type your stock's ticker symbol into the box, and then click the Interactive Chart button. Next click Time Frame, and choose a multi-year period, such as 3 Years. For frequency, choose Weekly. Then click Indicators, and under Lower Indicator, choose P/E Ranges. For Upper Indicators, choose Show Earnings. Finally, click Draw Chart.

You'll see a chart in the page's main frame that shows the weekly P/E range for a stock over the past three years. If your stock's P/E ratio is far above the average for the period, beware. It's likely to contract, bringing the stock price down with it. If the ratio is significantly below its P/E range, it's likely to ultimately expand back to normal, taking the stock back up.

In Figure 8-15, you can see clearly that Microsoft was trading at the low end of the middle of its P/E range in late May 1999; in fact, it was trading at the same P/E ratio as it had when the stock was 30 points lower. That suggested the stock price had ample room to move back up over the next couple of months, particularly if investors believed the next earnings report would be favorable.

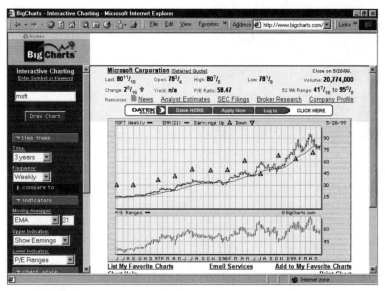

Figure 8-15.   May 30, 1999

BigCharts.com's Interactive Charting feature allows investors to study stocks' P/E ranges over time. In this case, Microsoft's P/E ratio in late May of 1999 appears to be at the low end of the middle of its three-year range. This suggested it had room to move up if earnings trends were favorable.

The "E triangles" on the chart show the dates of earnings-report releases. If you switch the Time Frame in the left navigation bar to Monthly, it becomes clear that the stock's P/E ratio tends to peak in the months prior to earnings releases. An investor might conclude, therefore, that Microsoft's P/E ratio would re-expand—and its stock price would increase—by July 1999. (In fact, the stock price rose from a low of $75 in May to $100 in July.)

The data-analysis company Baseline (*http://www.baseline.com*) also provides an excellent format for helping investors understand companies' P/E ranges. Baseline provides its charts, such as the one in Figure 8-16 on the next page, to several online discount brokerages, such as E*Trade and Suretrade.com. The most useful Baseline chart shows clearly that stocks trade in a limited P/E range each year. If you identify the past high and low P/E ratios of a stock, you can improve your chances of developing a solid entry and exit strategy.

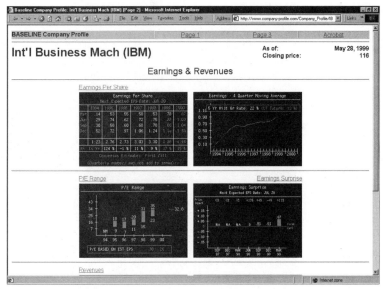

Figure 8-16.   May 30, 1999

Baseline provides a unique set of charts that show the precise P/E ranges of stocks over the past several years. Knowing the range should help you be more patient with entry and exit decisions because you might not want to buy a stock trading at a P/E ratio near the top of its historic annual range or sell when it's trading near the bottom of its range. In May 1999, IBM stock was clearly trading near the top of its range. Patience for new buys would have been prudent.

Understanding the P/E-to-Growth Rate Ratio

Investors intent on buying growth at a reasonable price, as explained in Chapter 4, like to compare a company's P/E ratio to its estimated rate of growth. This comparison is called the PEG ratio, which is short for "P/E ratio divided by Growth." The usefulness of this number is based on the notion that the ratio of a company's current stock price to its current earnings per share is less interesting than the ratio of a company's current price to its future earnings per share.

The PEG ratio is calculated by dividing the current P/E ratio by the company's projected growth rate of earnings per share over the next year. If the resulting value is less than 1, the stock might be undervalued; if the resulting value is more than 1, the stock might be overvalued. The farther from 1 the value is, the stronger the signal. Some dedicated value investors prefer to look for stocks with PEG ratios no higher than 0.5, which means the company's P/E ratio is 50% below its growth rate. Even many growth investors consider a ratio of greater than 2.0 to 3.0 as overly generous, and they might pare their holdings in a stock as soon as its P/E ratio exceeds its earnings growth rate by 100%.

Determining a company's PEG ratio online on the fly can be a great way to get a quick read on whether its shares are relatively cheap or expensive. Here's what to do:

1. **Determine the company's current stock price.** At MSN MoneyCentral Investor, type the stock's ticker symbol into the box on the home page, and click Go. Record the price in your memory or on paper. (Example: On May 29, 1999, the closing price of major credit-card issuer Providian Financial was $95.88.)

2. **Determine the company's consensus earnings estimate and growth rates for the current year and the next year.** At MoneyCentral, click the Analyst Info link on the left navigation bar to land on the Estimates page. For Providian Financial, the consensus estimate for earnings in fiscal year 1999 was $3.53. You can see this in Figure 8-17 if you look at the table in the lower half of the page. The average earnings estimate for fiscal year 2000 was $4.86. The company's estimated growth rates—shown in the table's bottom row—were 73.01% for fiscal year 1999 and 37.83% for fiscal year 2000.)

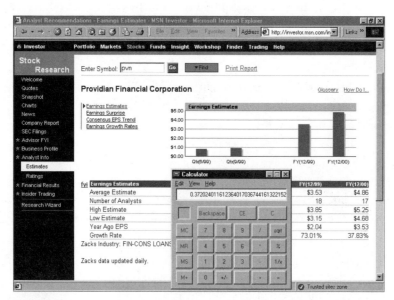

Figure 8-17.   May 31, 1999

To determine a company's PEG ratio on the fly, load the Windows calculator. Divide the stock's current price by its earnings-per-share estimates for the current and next fiscal years to get forward P/E ratios. Then divide those P/E ratios by the company's estimated growth rates. A PEG ratio less than 1.0 suggests a stock is undervalued compared to growth expectations.

3. **Get out a calculator.** If you're using Windows 95 or Windows 98, load the onboard calculator. To do this, click Start in the lower-left corner of your screen, point to Programs, point to Accessories, and then click Calculator. A calculator application appears on your screen. (Of course, you could use a handheld calculator—or even, gulp, do long division on paper!)

4. **Calculate the company's P/E ratios for the current year and the next year.** Enter the stock's current price into the calculator, and then divide it by the consensus estimates for earnings in the current and next fiscal years. (For Providian Financial, that meant dividing $95.88 by $3.53 and $4.86—yielding P/E ratios of 27.16 for fiscal year 1999 and 19.73 for fiscal year 2000. These differ from the P/E ratios reported elsewhere in the site or on the Web because they're calculated on forward-estimated earnings per share, rather than on the actual earnings per share of the most recent four quarters.)

5. **Calculate the company's PEG ratios for the current year and the next year.** Divide the two P/E ratios from the previous step by the company's estimated growth rates. (For Providian Financial, that meant dividing 27.16 by 73.0 and 19.73 by 37.8. By these calculations, Providian had a PEG ratio of 0.37 for fiscal year 1999 and 0.52 for fiscal year 2000.)

6. **Decide whether the stock is expensive or cheap.** If the PEG ratios are less than 1, the stock's price can be considered cheap relative to its estimated growth rate. If the PEG ratios are greater than 2, the stock is considered to be generously priced— or even overpriced. (By this measure, shares of Providian Financial appeared to be substantially undervalued compared to growth expectations. This might have been because the company's lending practices were under investigation by San Francisco authorities at the time. If you believed that fears over the investigation's impact on future earnings were unwarranted, it would have seemed to be a good buy.)

The Investment Finder stock-screening engine at MSN Investor makes it easy to determine a particular stock's PEG ratio or to find all stocks with high or low PEG ratios. See Appendix A for detailed instructions on finding and using the Investment Finder, and then try this screen, an example of which is shown in Figure 8-18:

1. **Market capitalization is greater than $3 billion.** From the drop-down list under Field Name, point to Company Basics, and then click Market Capitalization. Under Operator, choose >=. From the drop-down list under Value, choose Custom Value, and then type *3 billion* in the box.

2. **Stock price rose 75% or more over the past 12 months.** From the drop-down list under Field Name, point to Stock Price History, and then click % Price Change

Last Year. Under Operator, choose >=. From the drop-down list under Value, choose Custom Value, and then type *75* in the box.

3. **PEG ratio is as low as possible.** From the drop-down list under Field Name, point to Price Ratios, and then choose P/E Ratio: Current. Then type a slash mark (/), which is the divisor sign, directly after the *t* in *Current*. Without moving your cursor, click the drop-down list under Field Name again, point to Analyst Projections, and choose EPS Growth Next Year. Under Operator, choose Low As Possible.

4. **Click Run Search.**

The results pane lists all stocks with market caps of $3 billion or greater that have had stock-price gains greater than 75% in the past year. They are ranked by PEG ratio, with the lowest at the top. To see how a stock that you own compares with these, enter its ticker symbol in the Finder's Compare With field, and then click Add. The results for your selection appear in the comparison pane just above the results pane. If the stock appears in both places, it appears in red.

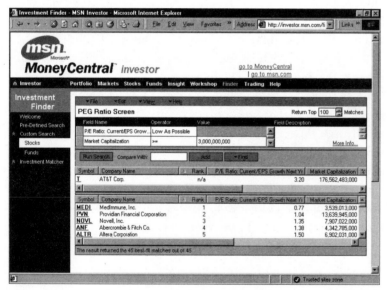

Figure 8-18.   May 30, 1999

Sometimes it's useful to uncover stocks that remain relatively cheap despite strong price run-ups. This screen in MSN Investor's Investment Finder looked for stocks with market caps greater than $3 billion and one-year stock-price gains greater than 75%. Then it ranked those stocks by PEG ratio, from lowest to highest. The screen found MedImmune, Providian Financial, Novell, and Abercrombie & Fitch to be relatively low-priced compared to their growth rates—with PEG ratios under 1.5. In contrast, AT&T had a PEG ratio of 3.20, which is quite high.

PEG ratios don't help you evaluate companies that are losing money. They are also considered less useful in assessing cyclical stocks, as well as those of companies in industries like banking, oil, or real estate, where assets are more important indicators of value. Regardless of industry, you shouldn't base a decision to buy on the PEG ratio alone. A company's growth rate might be exceptionally high for reasons other than the ongoing strength of its business, and the rate might, therefore, be unsustainable. Be aware also that a low PEG ratio might reflect high risk.

Price-to-Sales Ratio

In the past few years, investment strategists paid more attention to sales as an indicator of a company's prospects. The price-to-sales ratio (PSR) is calculated by dividing the latest closing price of the stock by the trailing 12 months' sales per share.

Investors who follow the "value" approach to assessing stocks, as described in Chapter 4, are always on the prowl for out-of-favor companies ripe for a turnaround. Because these firms often have minimal, if any, profits or cash flow, valuations based on such common benchmarks as price-earnings (P/E) or price-to-cash flow ratios are useless. Similarly, cyclical stocks—those that tend to rise and fall in lockstep with the overall economy—might look the best by these common benchmarks at the very time when they are about to hit the skids. In both cases, the PSR can be a useful proxy.

A low PSR suggests that a firm has turnaround potential. This view shows that the company already has significant revenues, so it just needs to squeeze more profit out of each dollar in sales. As profits rise, so will the stock price. That's the theory, anyway. In his book *What Works on Wall Street,* money manager James O'Shaughnessy made a persuasive case for using this ratio instead of the P/E ratio to determine a company's value. He sets the maximum PSR for stocks in his value funds at 1.50. You can find out more about O'Shaughnessy's strategies by reading monthly commentaries at his Web site (*http:// www.osfunds.com/comment/commentary.html*). In my own work, I've found that a maximum PSR of 4 is more effective.

Price/Book Ratio

This is the granddaddy of all value ratios, but it's frequently the hardest to use. It's calculated by dividing the latest closing price of a stock by the most recent quarter's book value per share. (Book value is simply a company's assets minus its liabilities.)

A favorite of strict fundamental investors, the price/book ratio gives some idea whether you're paying a little or a lot for what would be left of the company if it went out of business immediately. A price/book ratio of less than 1.0 causes value hunters to salivate. One reason is that basic accounting principles are geared to err on the side of conservatism. So they typically understate a company's book value because assets must be accounted for at cost less depreciation. Thus, a factory could have little or no value on the balance sheet even though, if it were for sale, it might bring millions. Given all this, a very low price/book ratio makes some fundamental investors feel that an ability to generate earnings as well is almost gravy.

As with most ratios, this one varies by industry. The price/book ratio can be especially useful in any field where asset values are fairly certain. The thrift industry is one example. Because a thrift's assets are largely financial and, therefore, much easier to value than those of an industrial concern, the price/book ratio for a thrift is not as subject to accounting vagaries. But beware: the stock price of a buggy-whip company would be low because of the lack of demand for buggy whips. Therefore, the book value of its factory would be largely irrelevant.

Price-to-Cash Flow Ratio

The price-to-cash flow ratio is often used to analyze companies in industries with huge depreciation expenses, such as cable TV, as well as cyclical industries, such as automobiles, steel, mining, and paper. This ratio is calculated by dividing the latest stock price by the company's cash flow per share from the last 12 months. (See Chapter 9 for more about cash flow.)

An alternative to the P/E ratio, the price-to-cash flow ratio removes depreciation and other non-cash charges from the valuation calculation. Like the P/E and P/S ratios, this ratio should not be considered in a vacuum but compared with similar companies.

Understanding Price-to-Cash Flow Ratios

Some analysts consider cash flow as perhaps a company's most important financial barometer. Many favor the ratio of stock price to operating cash flow over the P/E ratio as a measure of a company's value. Operating cash flow is composed of net earnings minus preferred dividends plus depreciation, and it's arguably the best measure of a business's profits. A company can show positive net earnings and still not be able to pay its debts. Cash flow pays the bills and underwrites dividend checks to stockholders.

Price-to-cash flow ratios vary widely from industry to industry. Capital-intensive industries, such as auto manufacturing or cable TV, tend to have very low ratios; less infrastructure-heavy industries, such as software, sport much higher ones. In 1999, for instance, the average price-to-cash flow ratio for companies in the Standard & Poor's 500 Index was about 14. For every $1 that flowed through those companies, their stock price was $14. But the average price-to-cash flow ratio in the auto industry was 5; in the software industry, it was 39.

Conclusion

Fundamental analysis of a company's business and growth rates gives an investor a lot of details to consider before buying or selling stocks at the right time. It should be clear by now that you can find almost every statistic online and that you need to consider each in the context of time and industry.

Now let's move on from the dry recitation of numbers and facts to the somewhat more lively view a company gives federal regulators in its disclosure forms. Investors have never had more information available to them than they do today, and many of the best gems are lying in wait for you online in SEC documents, if you only know where to look. Let's go find those hidden places.

Chapter 9

SEC Documents

America's financial markets are the most honest and admired in the world primarily because of the extraordinary level of disclosure required by U.S. securities laws. No other country in the world requires most corporations to blab their secrets in such detail at least four times a year, and no other country's regulators release most of that data to the public online within 48 hours.

The U.S. Securities & Exchange Commission (*http://www.sec.gov*), known commonly as the SEC, was founded in 1934 and chartered as America's top stock cop amid the devastation left by the Great Crash. In keeping with the free markets whose functioning it seeks to preserve, the agency's approach is heavily weighted toward laying corporate facts bare without passing judgment on those facts. A company might have John Dillinger as chief executive, Willie Sutton as chief financial officer, and a business plan focused on selling bikinis in the Yukon, and it's perfectly all right with the SEC, as long as these facts are clearly disclosed.

Indeed, all material information that could affect an individual's investment decision has to be revealed by law in at least one of many dozens of forms labeled in an alphabet-soup language that only a bureaucrat could love. The first disclosure comes in a document named S-1, which describes a company's initial public offering. The company later provides quarterly and annual reports, known as 10-Qs and 10-Ks, and such sundry documents as the DEF-14A proxy and the 13-G beneficial-ownership statements.

The assumption is that investors are big boys and girls who can make their own decisions as long as they have all the facts. The system seems to work. America's securities markets are models of efficiency and integrity, and the SEC plays an important role in keeping them that way. "We are the investor's advocate," said William O. Douglas, SEC chairman in 1937.

The SEC's public face to online investors is a project known by the acronym EDGAR. Short for the Electronic Data Gathering, Analysis, and Retrieval system, it receives and disseminates corporate filings electronically. EDGAR rules have required all domestic public companies that trade on exchanges to file almost all their data online since May 1996.

Prior to the establishment of the EDGAR system, investors had to wait patiently for all disclosure forms to be filed on paper in Washington. Then they had to know exactly which document to request, either from the SEC or a company, and wait for those forms to be mailed. All of that information had to then be sorted and catalogued by hand. It cannot be mere chance that the rise in the power and importance of the individual investor coincided neatly with the rise of the EDGAR system. For the first time in history, EDGAR put the power of information into the hands of private and institutional investors at the same time.

New investors should not underestimate the importance of the information treasure trove that was denied to their predecessors in decades past. I'll start with suggestions on where to find EDGAR data online, and then I'll explain what to look for in some of the key forms.

Retrieving the Forms Online

Examining a company's financial-disclosure forms can be fun if you're in the right frame of mind. To be sure, they are written mostly by junior attorneys fearful of liability laws and thus can be good cures for insomnia. But after you begin to read them regularly, you'll be surprised to find lively dissertations on businesses and industries in which you're interested, occasional corporate gossip, and even flashes of good humor. Rather than getting information on corporate performance and risks filtered through the media or analysts, you're hearing it straight from the source.

More importantly, you can use the documents to spy on the world's greatest investment minds as they disclose details on stock purchases and sales that they'd never tell a news-media interviewer. In many cases, you'll learn that you can invest right alongside them. In sum, you'll be rewarded well by acquiring the habit of dropping in on EDGAR at least once a week.

The Original EDGAR

The first site on the Internet to display EDGAR data was the federal agency's own site at *http://www.sec.gov/edgarhp.htm*. It was extremely cool for the short period of time when it was the only game in town. But it has been far surpassed by non-government sites that get

their data from the SEC and provide rich search features and document formatting. (Two pages at the EDGAR site that are still valuable compose a glossary of all SEC forms and schedules. You can view them at *http://www.sec.gov/edaux/forms.htm and http://www.sec.gov /edaux/forms/edgform.htm.*)

FreeEDGAR

FreeEDGAR.com (*http://www.freeedgar.com*) was one of the first sites to figure out how to pretty-up electronic filings, and it is still among the best. Even better, FreeEDGAR provides a ton of data for free, including unlimited access to its vast archive of fully indexed EDGAR filings and current data as soon as they become available.

View a Company's Filings

To see a company's most recent filings, type its ticker symbol into the box in the middle of FreeEDGAR's home page, and then click Search. On the page that follows, click View Filings to see a chronological list of all filings made by the company in the last three years. Figure 9-1 shows an example. The sizes of the documents are listed on the right, in case you're accessing the site over a slow modem connection and don't want to download a big file. (In July 1999, FreeEdgar was purchased by rival EdgarOnline.)

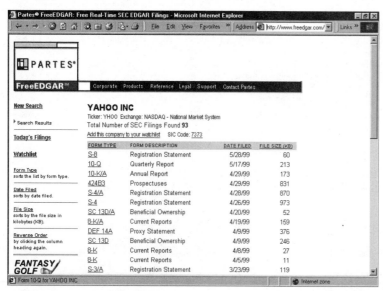

Figure 9-1.   May 31, 1999

FreeEDGAR houses up to three years of SEC documents on public companies. Create a watchlist containing all the stocks that you own to receive timely e-mails when they file new documents.

Click a link in the Form Type column to view a document. Then use the Table of Contents in the left frame of the document page to navigate. Unless you're looking for a particular section, it's usually best to click the link for Body: Entire Filing and then scroll through (or print) the document.

A few nice features of FreeEDGAR:

- To receive notice by e-mail of a company's filings as soon as they become available, click the link labeled Add This Company To Your Watchlist. You'll have to register, but the process is painless and unintrusive. It's a good idea to register to receive SEC filings on all the stocks you own or are considering owning. (It's easy to come back and turn off the function if you decide you're receiving too much mail.)

- To sort the filings by form type or file size instead of by date filed, click the appropriate column heading. (To reverse the order, click the heading a second time.)

- To save paper if you're printing a document, reduce the font size by choosing an option from the drop-down box at the top of the right frame of each document page. Conversely, if you're myopic and can't find your glasses, you can enlarge the font size.

View Today's Filings

Another way to use FreeEDGAR, if you've got the time and inclination: check the running stream of current filings. This is not everyone's idea of a good time, but it can be a useful way to hunt serendipitously for new ideas during the day. It's sort of the EDGAR equivalent of television channel surfing.

To get started, click the Today's Filings link. You'll see documents in the order they were received by FreeEDGAR. You can choose to view only a particular form type (for example, 13-G Beneficial Ownership statements) by selecting that option from the drop-down box at the top of the list. You can then click a column heading to sort those documents either by company name or filing time. You can also add any of the companies to your watchlist by clicking one of the Add buttons on the right. To see all filings by a company's peers, click the SIC Code number that appears next to the View Filings link.

View Money Managers' Filings—Forms 13-D and 13-G

It's not just public companies that have to file documents with the SEC. Money managers who buy 5% stakes in public companies do too, and that is an incredible boon to the individual investor.

Have you ever longed to get a real-time peek at hedge-fund manager George Soros' buy and sell decisions? How about a look at the latest big bets by TheStreet.com colum-

nist Jim Cramer or anyone over at the Boston-based mutual-fund giant Fidelity Investments? FreeEDGAR gives you the next best thing by allowing you to search SEC documents by the names of the filing hedge-fund, mutual-fund complex, or individual money manager. You have to know which names relate to your interests, but it's not too hard to compile a short list of folks whose filings you might want to scrutinize from time to time.

To look for Cramer's latest filings, for instance, visit the FreeEDGAR site's home page, type *Cramer* into the Company Name dialog box, and then click Search. In late May of 1999, five Cramers were listed but just one *Cramer J. J. & Co. Inc.* Regular readers of the money manager's columns would recognize this as one of his corporate entities. Click links to 13-D or 13-G filings to view documents disclosing his latest transactions in companies in which he owned at least a 5% stake. These forms must be filed within 10 days of the transaction, and they include a lot of specific information about sales and purchases. After a 5% stake has been purchased, all additional transactions affecting ownership by more than 1% must be reported too.

In May 1999, FreeEDGAR displayed six pages of J. J. Cramer & Co. transactions dating back to 1996. On April 23, 1999, a Form 13-D/A (the A stands for amendment) was filed that reflected the purchase of 69,600 shares of tiny UFP Technologies, a maker of specialty foam cushioning products. As shown in Figure 9-2 on the next page, the shares were bought between April 15 and April 20 at prices that ranged from $4.11 to $4.19. On the day the form was filed, 25,000 of those shares were sold at $3.18. (A DEF 14A proxy statement filed by UFP Technologies 10 days later showed that a Cramer partnership was the firm's second largest shareholder.)

You might be surprised to discover the number of minuscule companies in which managers of giant hedge funds buy stakes. One caveat: these names can serve as great investment ideas, but you should never buy a stock just because Mr. Big owns it. The hedge-fund manager's opinion can change at any time, and when these guys want out of a stock, they can knock the price down in a hurry as they rush out the door. In addition, their positions in small companies often amount to mere pocket change; it can be "gambling" money for a roll of the dice, not necessarily a long-term investment. Here are a few names of managers and fund companies to check on, just to get you started:

- **FMR.** This is short for Fidelity Management & Research, the arm of the Fidelity Investments empire that buys and sells securities for all of the company's mutual funds. Fidelity buys stakes of 5% or more in hundreds of companies. (*FMR* is not a ticker symbol; you must type it in the Company Name box on FreeEDGAR's home page.)

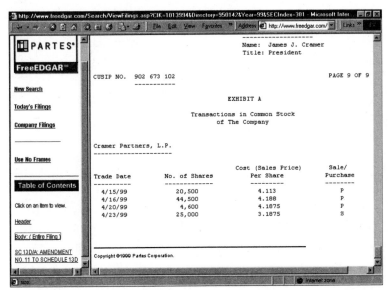

Figure 9-2.   May 31, 1999

Viewing the 13-D and 13-G forms of top fund managers might feel like espionage, but it's completely legal. Type the name of a manager or fund company into the Company Name box on FreeEDGAR's home page. Select the name from a list on the next page, and then click any form name to see what the manager or fund company has been up to. Scroll to the bottom of the form to see the actual prices and dates of the manager's purchases and sales. In this case, you can see when J. J. Cramer & Co. bought and sold shares of tiny UFP Technologies in April 1999.

- **Soros.** You can see information on most of hedge-fund manager George Soros' many funds, including the Quantum Fund and the Soros Fund. (On May 19, 1999, for example, a form disclosed the holding of a significant stake in small-cap Sensormatic Electronics, among many other investments.)

- **Tiger Management.** You can see information on the main fund run by investor Julian H. Robertson Jr. (On February 16, 1999, for example, forms disclosed the purchase of more than 10% ownership in companies as diverse as tiny sub-prime lender American Business Financial Services and mighty brokerage house Bear Stearns.)

- **Van Wagoner.** You can see information on the most recent filings of star small-cap fund manager Garrett Van Wagoner. (A July 12 filing disclosed that his firm, Van Wagoner Capital Management, owned a 9.2% stake in Midwest barbecue-restaurant chain Famous Dave's of America.)

You can also search on the name of any investment bank—for example, Bear Stearns or Goldman Sachs—to see their current holdings. Although many financial portals on the Web list the top 10 holdings of individual mutual funds, peeking at Forms 13-F or 13F-HR is the only way to view all holdings of an entire brokerage.

Peering into amendments

Companies often file amendments to their SEC documents. These newer documents, marked with the letter A, occasionally provide surprising insights if they reflect management's change of mind or a change in forecasts. If you have a recent version of Microsoft Word, you can use a technique recommended by TheStreet.com columnist and SEC hound Adam Lashinsky to determine the differences between an original document and an amendment:

- **Copy the original SEC document.** In FreeEdgar, display the "body" of any document—an S-3 registration, for instance. Then select all of the text in the document using your browser's menu system or, if you're using a Windows-based PC, pressing Ctrl-A. Then copy the selection into temporary memory. (Press Ctrl-C if you're using a Windows-based PC.)

- **Paste the original into a new Word file.** Start Word, and then paste the text of the original SEC document from temporary memory into a new Word file. To do this, you can either select Paste from the Edit menu or, if you're using a Windows-based PC, press Ctrl-V. Then save the Word file, and remember the name you give it.

- **Copy and save the amended SEC document.** Repeat the steps above with the amended document (an S-3/A, for instance). Select its text, copy and paste the text into a second Word file, and save the file.

- **Compare the two documents.** After saving the second document, click Word's Tools menu, and then choose Track Changes. From the submenu, choose Compare Documents. Browse to the first document you saved, and click Open. After Word does its magic, which can take up to a minute, you'll see all the differences between the two documents highlighted in red on the second document. Look for material differences in numbers, forecasts, executives' pay or titles, and even whole new passages. You might find a hidden gem.

Edgar Online

Edgar Online (*http://www.edgar-online.com*) was one of the first companies to fully exploit the commercial potential of organizing and nicely presenting EDGAR data. The company has done a fantastic job of making it easy for investors to *quickly* find relevant SEC data on individuals and public companies, and it lays out that data in common formats such as Microsoft Word, Corel WordPerfect, and Microsoft Excel.

Although almost everything at FreeEDGAR is free and requires no registration, much of the really good stuff at Edgar Online is cordoned off for paying subscribers only, and everyone must register.

View a Company's Filings

Edgar Online distinguishes itself from FreeEDGAR and other competitors by allowing very detailed searches. It can also take excerpts from key sections of forms and present them as tight, readable chunks. An example of this process, called *parsing*, is shown in Figure 9-3.

After you register for a free visitor's pass, click Full Search on the site's home page. Then type a date range and a company name, a ticker symbol, or a form type into the page that follows. Type the ticker symbol for Internet retailer Amazon.com (AMZN), for instance, to see a page similar to the one shown in Figure 9-4. You can request to see only

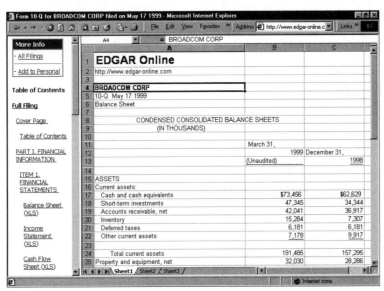

Figure 9-3.   May 31, 1999

Edgar Online accurately parses the 10-Q for data from the balance sheet, the income statement, and the cash-flow statement. It then allows you to view and download the data as a Microsoft Excel spreadsheet.

Form 10-Qs for the past six months, for example, and then choose from one of four options: view the whole document, view a glimpse of key information, view an FDS (financial data schedule), or view a list of people mentioned in the document.

If you choose to view the whole document electronically, Edgar Online lets you specify whether you want to view it in HTML (with your browser) or in Rich Text Format. The HTML option features a detailed table of contents in a frame on the left, which lets you narrow your scan of the document. You can, for instance, choose to view only the document's Income Statement, and you can choose to view that statement as a Microsoft Excel worksheet instead of as plain text. This option is terrific if you want to save and manipulate the information for your own financial modeling.

If you choose Glimpse, you see just the Management Discussion portion of the 10-Q, along with a few odds and ends such as the Legal Issues, Risk Factors, and Year 2000 Compliance sections. If you choose FDS, you see just a short, formatted list of the key financial data contained in the document. If you choose People, you see a list of the principal people named in the document, along with links to other documents in which they might be mentioned elsewhere on the site.

Figure 9-4.   May 31, 1999

A search for Amazon.com's SEC filings at Edgar Online yielded nearly a dozen public documents. The Glimpse view of the 10-Q (quarterly report) highlights that document's sections on Management Discussion and Risk Factors. You can easily jump off to more research, news, and quotes by clicking links on the page of the company you're researching.

Edgar Online has, furthermore, turned itself into an impressive portal for financial information that relates to companies in its database. A click or two away from each search are links to charts from BigCharts.com; news from CBS MarketWatch, CNNfn, and the wires; stock quotes from Island, a private electronic communications network; company capsules from Hoover's Online; and research reports from Multex.com. (See Chapter 13 for more information on electronic communications networks, or ECNs.)

EDGAR on the Financial Portals

You don't actually have to visit FreeEDGAR or Edgar Online to view SEC documents anymore because most of the financial portals have brought the basic forms into their offerings.

MSN MoneyCentral Investor

EDGAR data resides in three places at MSN MoneyCentral (*http://moneycentral .msn.com/investor*):

- For the principal text documents, click Stocks on the top navigation bar of the home page. Then click SEC Filings in the left navigation bar, type a stock's ticker symbol into the text box at the top of the page, and click Go. You'll find the Management Discussion, Business Issues, Risk Factors, and Legal Issues sections of the company's four most recent Forms 10-Q and 10-K arranged in chronological order. To view the rest of a company's documents, click All Filings on the left navigation bar. You can then search for any document type.

- For a compact view of just the financial statements from the latest Forms 10-Q and 10-K, click Financial Results in the left navigation bar, and then click the Statements link on the submenu that appears. Type a stock's ticker symbol into the text box at the top of the page, and then click Go. A consolidated view of the company's past five annual income statements appears. To see a different statement, choose it from the drop-down box on the upper-left side of the page. To see quarterly data, select Quarterly in the View drop-down box in the upper right. For the most consolidated view, choose "10-Year Summary" from the drop-down box in the upper left.

- For Forms 4 and 144, which contain data on corporate officials' stock trades, click Insider Trading on the left navigation bar. The default view is a list of Form 4 filings that indicate completed transactions by corporate insiders or major shareholders, including the number of shares purchased or sold, prices, and values. Click an individual's name to see his or her corporate title and learn whether he or she sold stocks or options. To see Form 144 transactions, which have been proposed but not yet acted upon, click Planned Sales on the left navigation bar. Click an individual's name to see his or her corporate title and learn whether he or she sold stocks or

options. To see Form 144 transactions, which have been proposed but not yet acted upon, click Planned Sales on the left navigation bar. Click an individual's name to see all of his or her planned sales over the past year and the name of the brokerage slated for the transaction.

Yahoo! Finance

EDGAR data resides in two places at Yahoo! Finance (*http://quote.yahoo.com*). For the main text documents, click SEC Filings in the Research section of the home page. The default is a streaming list of the latest Form 10-Qs and 10-Ks filed at Edgar Online. Click a name, and you'll get the same page as you'd get if you chose the Glimpse option at Edgar Online itself. Type another ticker symbol in the text box at the top of the column to see any other company's 10-Q. To see insider-trading data, type the ticker symbol for a stock at the top of any page, and then click the Insider link.

Quicken.Com

Quicken.com (*http://www.quicken.com*) offers a good mix of consolidated and expanded SEC data. Type a ticker symbol into the text box at the top of the site's home page, and click Go. On the subsequent page, click SEC Filings, Financial Statements, or Insider Trading in the left navigation bar. On the Financial Statements page, a link in the upper right lets you switch quickly from an annual to a quarterly view.

Two elements stand out on this page. Links at the bottom of the Financial Statements pages lead to excellent educational articles on using the data properly. Also, the Insider Trading tables contain a unique and hard-to-find piece of data: the amount of stock each insider retains after the sale. This helps you understand whether it's noteworthy if Mr. Big sells 300,000 shares of BigFat Co. If he still owns 30 million shares, it's not necessarily remarkable.

InsiderTrader.com

InsiderTrader.com (*http://www.insidertrader.com*) has emerged as a leading compiler and explainer of insider-trading data on the Web. Founded by a former research director at *Individual Investor* magazine, InsiderTrader.com has sophisticated database programs that slice and dice the confusing information contained on Forms 3, 4, 5, 13G, 13D, and 144 until it makes enough sense to be tradable. The site requires a subscription of $50 per year for its core content and newsletter, which seems fair.

Although most of the financial portals let you search for insider data only by company name and offer no analysis, InsiderTrader.com lets you search by the names of individual insiders, and it provides weekly commentary on the most interesting transactions.

The former could be helpful, for instance, if you find that a chief executive has done a great job of picking the low in his own stock and you wonder whether he's done just as well with the stocks of companies for which he serves as a board director. For example, Microsoft executives rarely buy stock on the open market, but Jeff Raikes, vice president of marketing, picked up 100,000 Microsoft shares in May 1998, when the stock was languishing. The stock was up 100% eight months later. A search of Raikes' name at InsiderTrader.com shows that he made an even better purchase of shares of Nextlink, where he served as board director, that same month; those shares were up 145% 12 months later. You can set up a watchlist to be notified the next time Raikes makes a purchase. Other features at the site include a newsletter and powerful insider-accumulation screens.

InsiderSCOREBOARD.com

InsiderSCOREBOARD.com (*http://www.insiderscoreboard.com*) takes the analysis of SEC documents for insider data to a whole new level. Editors of this site rank all the top corporate insiders in the United States by their success at purchasing or selling their own stock; the insiders are ranked both in relation to peers in their own industry as well as against all insiders. The insider data is highly searchable and stretches back as far as 10 years; the user interface is attractive and intuitive. Some of the brightest minds involved with insider-trading analysis are behind this site, including Craig Columbus, vice president of research at Primark, and Carr Bettis, professor at Arizona State University.

Now let's go on to learning the purposes of the various SEC forms.

Primer on the Forms

It's really important to know the alphabet if you want to read and understand SEC documents. Rather than just giving its forms names such as Quarterly and Annual Report, the U.S. government has forced investors and corporate treasurers to learn dozens of combinations of letters and numbers.

Although they might seem a little bit boring at times, it's important to keep in mind that almost all fundamental data that you see on public companies are originally reported in these forms before being extracted and manipulated. Here are brief descriptions of the most important forms found online and suggestions on how to use them.

Forms 10-Q and 10-K—Quarterly and Annual Reports

The SEC requires most public U.S. company to file a comprehensive accounting and explanation of its financial condition and business prospects each year. The statement, on

Form 10-K, is due 90 days after the close of a company's fiscal year. It isn't as pretty as the glossy annual report that the company sends out to shareholders, but it generally has a lot more useful information in it.

The government requires companies to report an abbreviated version of the same information on a quarterly basis as well in the Form 10-Q. When reading both 10-Ks and 10-Qs, remember that companies are good at putting a positive spin on everything. Take their comments with a grain of salt.

Business Description

Most Form 10-Ks start with either a letter to shareholders or a lay description of the company's business. This is the chief executive's chance to describe events of the past year and his vision of the future in plain English. Keep in mind that you are entrusting this person with your hard-earned dollars. Make it personal. Pay attention to whether the corporate chieftain is a good communicator and whether the vision statement is not only persuasive but also aligned with what you believe the company's mission should be.

Try to assess whether the company has faced up squarely to any past failures and whether it presents a reasonable plan to prevent them in the future. In particular, read the description of competitive risks and expansion carefully and try to determine whether they make your investment too risky.

Letter to Shareholders

Occasionally, companies do not put their "Letter to Shareholders" in their 10-Ks; they place it instead only in their glossy annual reports. Some post these letters in the Investor Relations sections of their own Web sites, however, after juicing them up with photographs, animations, and even video. Visit the Dell Computer Web site (*http://www.dell.com*), shown in Figure 9-5 on the next page, for an example. Click the About Dell link on the left of the site's home page, then click the Investor Relations link on the subsequent page, and then click the link for 1999 Year In Review, Annual Report On 10-K & Proxy Statement. Finally, click the link for 1999 Annual Report—HTML Format And PDF File. To go to this page directly, type this address into your browser address bar: *http://www.dell.com/corporate/investor/annualreports/report99/fromtheooc/fromtheooc.htm*

(continued)

If you're just starting to research a company, pull its 10-Ks from the past few years, and compare the opening comments. Has the chief executive changed direction often? Has he or she executed well?

Balance Sheet

The financial statements in the quarterly and annual reports are broken into three parts: the balance sheet, the income statement, and the cash-flow statement. I won't describe how to read them in great detail because there are dozens of books on that topic alone. But here are a few pointers.

Letter to Shareholders *(continued)*

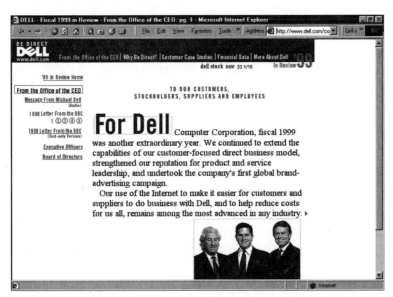

Figure 9-5.   June 1, 1999

Dell Computer and many other companies have started placing enhanced equivalents of their glossy annual reports in the Investor Relations sections of their Web sites. Some companies are going further, putting all of their SEC documents on their sites within easy reach of current and potential investors.

You can find another good example, from an industrial concern, at Alcoa's Web site, *http://www.alcoa.com*. To go directly to the chairman's letter, visit *http://www.alcoa.com /investor/chairmanletter.asp*.

A firm's balance sheet is a snapshot of its financial picture on a given day. One side of the balance sheet totes up assets, moving from the most current, or liquid (for example, cash), to the least liquid (for example, equipment and good will). The other side of the balance sheet lists liabilities in order of their immediacy (that is, how soon debts must be paid back) and shareholders equity. Assets must equal liabilities plus shareholder equity.

The balance sheet is an important tool for analyzing the financial health of a company. Using only this document, you can compare current assets against current liabilities to assess the degree to which a company can meet near-term payment obligations, compare debt-to-shareholder equity to see how leveraged the company is, and learn whether the assets might include hidden value. Let's look more closely at the key sections of the balance sheet, using Dell's 1999 10-K occasionally as a marker.

Assets   Current assets are expected to be converted to cash within one year. They include:

- **Cash.** More is usually better, but too much might mean that the company isn't investing enough in its business. After all, interest on short-term Treasury bills is around 3%; surely the company doesn't want too much lying around in what amounts to a passbook savings account. Then again, you want to make sure a company has enough cash to pay its bills and invest in new technology.

- **Accounts Receivable.** The buyer of a company's products usually has 30 days to pay up. The money expected from those unconsummated sales is called accounts receivable, or A/R for short. When accounts receivable grow faster than sales, it's a red flag that suggests a company's customers are not paying on time. That can cause serious cash-flow problems down the road. (A company must also disclose its "allowance for doubtful accounts," which is an estimate of uncollectable A/R. If this amount starts to increase faster than sales, you should be concerned.)

- **Inventory.** This is the value of products piled up in a company's warehouses. It is expensive to hold inventory because the company must pay for storage and might have paid for those items well in advance. Successful companies turn over their inventory quickly, getting their money back from their investment as quickly as possible. Dell is a master at this.

Non-Current Assets   Technically, these are assets not expected to be sold, converted into cash, or exchanged within a year. This category basically refers to plant and equipment. It can also include such miscellany as deferred income taxes, investments in other companies, and intellectual property acquired from other companies.

Pay special attention to good will, if it's listed separately. This typically results from buying out a company for a price greater than its book value. Suppose a company has a book value (assets minus liabilities) of $10 million, but it is purchased for $100 million. The $90 million difference between the two is considered good will. This amount must be charged against earnings annually for 5 to 40 years, and it can be a drag on future earnings.

Liabilities   Liabilities are the opposite of assets; they're obligations to pay. Current liabilities are debts that must be paid within one year, such as accounts payable. Non-current liabilities include such IOUs as long-term debt.

Accounts payable, or A/P, are among the most important liabilities because they measure the amount a company owes for such things as inventory. It is a bad sign if A/P increases faster than sales because it suggests a company is having cash-flow problems.

The current ratio, which I mentioned in Chapter 8, is the easiest way to assess the balance between a company's assets and its liabilities. As you might recall, the current ratio is calculated by dividing current assets by current liabilities. If the result is less than 1.0, a company might not be able to pay its bills. A ratio of 2:1 is considered healthy, although such guidelines depend on the industry. More important than the actual number is the trend. A declining current ratio is bad news.

Another way to assess the health of a balance sheet is to compute the quick ratio, which I also mentioned in Chapter 8. This is calculated by subtracting the value of inventory from current assets and dividing the result by current liabilities. Inventory is subtracted from the current assets because it isn't always liquid. So the quick ratio is a more conservative indicator of a company's liquidity. In general, a quick ratio of 1:1, often rendered as 1.0, is considered strong.

Non-Current Liabilities   These are debts due more than a year from the report date. Companies might have a diverse mix of non-current liabilities, including bonds and notes (typically debts payable more than 10 years from the issuance date), real-estate and equipment leases, and pension liabilities.

A common indicator of health here is the debt-equity ratio. In general, a ratio higher than 0.5—or 50%—might mean trouble. To calculate it, divide the amount of long-term debt by the total amount of stockholder equity. In Dell's case, divide $512 million by $2.32 billion. That yields a debt-equity ratio of .22, or 22%, which is great.

Shareholder Equity   This is the amount by which a company's assets exceed its liabilities. Most companies are worth far more than this because *worth* means what someone is actually willing to pay, and few good companies can be acquired for this baseline amount.

Income Statement

The income statement starts with the amount of a company's total sales and subtracts the costs of obtaining the products or services to make those sales. That equals gross income. The statement then subtracts operating expenses (including administrative, marketing, and research costs), depreciation, amortization, financing expenses, and taxes to reach a *net-income* figure. That figure is then divided by the number of common shares outstanding to reach an earnings per share figure on the statement's bottom line.

That bottom line is what a successful business is really all about: making money. Net income is probably the most closely watched item in a company's financial reports, yet it is subject to many judgments by both corporate managers and accountants, as well as various charges that exist largely on paper. Net income can also be swollen by earnings from discontinued operations (meaning net income will probably be much lower next year). Many investors prefer to focus on measures of profit that remove some of the smoke and confusion generated by such variables as taxes and depreciation. That leads them to the cash-flow statement or to just observe the amount of the earnings *before* interest, taxes, depreciation, and amortization, a figure known by the acronym EBITDA. Still, you can't get around examining the income statement. Here are a few key lines to watch:

- **Cost of Goods Sold.** The cost of producing whatever it is the company sells, including material, labor, and overhead. As a company increases its sales, it hopes to realize economies of scale. Look for a company at which the cost of goods sold (COGS) is declining as a percentage of revenue.

- **Research and Development.** If you're investigating high-tech stocks, look for ones that spend a healthy amount on R&D, especially in comparison with competitors. You can compare industry peers' commitment to innovation by dividing the amount each spends on R&D by its total sales. In addition to comparing those percentages, you should also check news reports and press releases to determine whether companies have spent R&D funds effectively by regularly rolling out new products.

- **Selling, General and Administrative.** Keep an eye out for corporate waste in this section, often called the SG&A line. This is the line swollen by expenses like posh offices, corporate jets, excessive executive salaries, and so on. Make sure the number is not growing as a percentage of sales.

Management Discussion and Analysis

This section, known as the MD&A, is a concise summary of the company's operations, and it typically focuses on acquisitions, strategic relationships, and major investments. For example, in Yahoo!'s 1998 10-K, you'll find a detailed discussion of its purchases of Four11, ViaWeb, GeoCities, WebCal, and Yoyodyne Entertainment. It also includes insights on the company's strategic partnerships with credit-card company Visa. For potential investors, this is a good place to learn about how management thinks through its business. For shareholders, it's a great place to determine whether management is still on track with comments it made in the same space in the previous year.

Risk Factors

In many cases, the Risk Factors section is dull, legal boilerplate. Still, a close look at this section can raise important red flags. Be wary of companies that rely heavily on a few customers, have negative gross margins, or have defaulted on debt. The disclosures in this section can be extremely instructive, so pay close attention.

Legal Proceedings

Do not be too quick to dismiss the troubles that protracted legal proceedings can cause a company, particularly if it's young. They are unpredictable, and surprises can sink a company's stock. Tobacco leads the league these days in litigation, and the legal-proceedings section in Philip Morris' 1998 10-K runs on for pages and pages. Here's just a snippet of that filing: "In recent years, there has been a substantial increase in the number of tobacco-related cases being filed. As of March 1, 1999, there were approximately 500 smoking and health cases filed and served on behalf of individual plaintiffs in the United States against PM Inc. compared with approximately 375 such cases on December 31, 1997, and approximately 185 such cases on December 31, 1996." The section contains juicy details of the lawsuits. It's up to you to decide whether the threat is already priced into the stock or whether further surprises lurk.

Statement of Cash Flows

It takes lots of cash to run a successful business. Smart investors examine the cash-flow statement carefully because the income statement alone does not reflect the liquidity of a company. In fact, a company can be profitable and yet run out of money. Conversely, a company can show no profit and yet rake in tons of cash. The cash-flow statement has three components:

- **Net cash from operations.** This shows the amount of cash a company hauls in from its regular operations. (It doesn't include one-time events, such as the sale of fixed assets.) Look for companies that grow this number steadily every quarter and year. *No other statistic so clearly separates the winners from the losers.* Look at the 10-Ks of Dell Computer and Microsoft for prime examples of strong operating cash flow, and then compare them to a company you are investigating.

- **Net cash from investments.** This one's a bit tougher. It's the sum of the sale of property, plant, and equipment; the sale of short-term investments; the purchase of property, plant, and equipment; the purchase of short-term debt; and other investing charges.

- **Net cash from financing.** This is often critical; it is the sum of the issuance of debt, the issuance of stock, the repayment of long-term debt, the payment of cash dividends, and other financing charges. For a lot of Internet companies, this is the only positive figure. For any company, that's a big red flag.

To see a troublesome cash-flow statement, look at the 1998 10-K of Internet music retailer CDnow, shown in Figure 9-6. The company had $49 million in cash at the end of 1998 (as shown in the line that reads "Cash and Equivalents, end of year"). But if the company had not received $88.5 million in cash from the issuance of stock during the year ("issuance of capital stock"), it would really be hurting. CDnow burned through $40.3 million in cash during the course of its operations for the year ("net cash from operating activities").

Despite what the company might say in press releases or what you might think of its Web site, the cash-flow statement shows when a company can stay above water only by issuing stock to the public. That might be all right as long as the public equity markets stay friendly. However, you might conclude that a company like CDnow would be unable

Figure 9-6.   June 3, 1999

Several financial portals post companies' annual and quarterly financial statements in their research areas so you don't have to go through the trouble of finding them at FreeEDGAR or Edgar Online. At MSN MoneyCentral, these statements can be displayed from a single location in the Financial Results/ Statements section. In the case of CDnow, you can see that cash flow from operations is negative, which is a bad sign.

to fund its operations in a downturn, and your investment in its shares would plunge in value. The company's shares fell as low as $7 from a peak of $39 as it struggled to keep the music going. On July 13, 1999, CDnow finally agreed to merge with music club Columbia House, owned jointly by Sony and Time Warner. This document clearly showed that it needed deep-pocket partners.

Notes and Footnotes

Companies love to hide the bad stuff here. Thus, make sure you read all the notes and footnotes. The following list contains things you should look for:

- **A change in accounting policies.** Beware of a firm that changes an accounting policy that is standard with its industrial peers. It might mean the company is in trouble and is trying to hide things with accounting gimmickry.

- **Lawsuits.** These can be wildcards for companies, and when they're embarrassed, they sometimes provide just footnotes about them.

- **Auditors' Opinions.** A third-party accounting firm will analyze a company's accounting statements to see if they are in accordance with Generally Accepted Accounting Principals, or GAAP. If no problems appear, the accounting firm will give an unqualified opinion. However, if the accounting firm has concerns, it will give a qualified opinion. Even though financial statements are audited by independent consultants and regulated by the SEC, this does not mean they are foolproof. An audited company can still defraud investors.

Proxies

You might think of proxy statements as those intimidating ballots you get in the mail. In fact, proxies are very revealing documents, typically sent once a year, that disclose and explain issues up for shareholder vote. They list the amounts that top executives and directors wish to be paid, as well as all the management perks, like corporate jets, home theaters, and mortgage allowances. If you already own the stock, executives hope that you'll ignore these proxies and let them vote for you.

When looking up proxy statements at FreeEdgar or Edgar Online, you'll find they are usually referred to as DEF-14, which stands for definitive proxy. Here are some items to look out for.

Option Repricing   When executives are hired, they are typically granted stock options that have an exercise price equal to the stock price at that time and that vest over four or five years. The options have value only if the stock price increases above the exercise price, so they are supposed to act as incentive for executives to get the stock price moving up.

If management has been terrible, however, and the stock price has collapsed, some executives will propose that their options be repriced lower. An outside shareholder's cost basis in the stock isn't repriced downward; this gimmick benefits only bad managers. It's a big red flag. Stay away, or if you own the stock, vote no. One example came in 1997 when telecom-equipment maker General Datacomm repriced options on 863,400 shares for management from $16 to $6.75. If you had seen that in the proxy and stayed away from purchasing shares, you'd have been wise. The stock was trading at around $3 by mid-1999.

Poison Pills   If a stock has been beaten down, executives commonly institute provisions that seek to preserve their tenure—and lucrative compensations plans—in the event of a takeover attempt. Beware. Many of these measures aren't necessary, and they are occasionally adopted by managers who do not have shareholders' interests at heart.

Executive Compensation   Proxies contain lots of juicy details about the compensation of officers and directors—usually going back three years. You will see salaries, bonuses, stock options, and even retirement plans. Many executives are worth all the money that their boards throw at them. Yahoo!'s 1998 proxy, for instance, revealed that its excellent chief executive, Tim Koogle, received 550,000 stock options in addition to his $290,000 salary. Here are a few other notable data points from the "Employment Contracts" section found at Edgar Online:

- America Online's 1999 proxy shows that the company must purchase president Robert Pittman's house if he's ever fired. What's more, the proxy reveals that AOL pays Pittman to fly his private jet for company business.
- Amazon.com's 1998 proxy shows that chief executive Jeff Bezos was paid $81,840 that year and that he opted not to take a bonus. He also decided not to take any new stock options. (Don't fret: he already owned 58.7 million shares.)

Authorization of New Stock   Many proxies contain proposals to authorize more shares. These usually indicate that the company plans to engage in a lot of acquisitions. That can be a good thing if the company has a high valuation and will pay for the purchases with stock rather than cash. This was the case with Amazon.com in 1998, when the company sought permission, in its proxy, to issue up to 1.2 billion shares. It then came as no surprise that, in the first half of 1999, the company followed through by issuing millions of shares of new stock to buy several companies.

Major Shareholders   The proxy statement usually lists individuals, institutions, and strategic investors that own more than 5% of the firm's common stock. If you're studying new firms, look for ones that have smart-money backers, such as Intel, Microsoft, or major venture-capital firms, such as Benchmark or Sequoia.

The Vote   Voting your proxy is becoming simpler. Some companies let you vote by phone or even over the Web. You can also go to the annual shareholders meeting and vote in person. If you have time and money, that can be a great idea. It gives you a chance to see the management team and meet other shareholders.

Form S-1—IPO Registration

When executives at a private company decide to go public, the first thing on their agenda is the filing of a Form S-1 with the SEC. This document, also known as the *prospectus,* is loaded with most of the information an investor needs to make an informed decision on whether to buy shares in the company's initial public offering, or *IPO.*

Because an IPO is so risky for investors, the SEC loads higher-than-normal disclosure rules on the S-1. That can make it the most revealing document a company will ever file—and very, very long. Here are the items to look for:

Underwriters

The underwriter is the firm that takes a company public. The strongest companies generally go with the strongest underwriters—ones that have the greatest resources to support the stock after it starts trading with favorable investment recommendations through their "research," or sales, departments. If a company you're investigating went public under the wing of a minor-league underwriter, beware. These companies are not as well supported with favorable research, and they can get lost in the shuffle. You will find the list of the underwriters on the first couple of pages of the prospectus. Top ones include Goldman Sachs, Morgan Stanley Dean Witter, Merrill Lynch, BancBoston Robertson Stephens, Bear Stearns, Gruntal & Co., J. P. Morgan, Lehman Brothers, Credit Suisse First Boston, Hambrecht & Quist, Banc of America Securities, and Thomas Weisel Partners.

An example of a poorly executed S-1 and IPO came in the spring of 1999 with COMPS.com, a provider of information on commercial real estate. This was the first Internet company IPO in 1999 to fall before its initial offering price on the first day of trading. Tiny underwriter Volpe Brown Whelan was unable to give the stock enough after-market support, and it quickly dived from an opening-day high of $15 to as low as $6.50 two months later.

Risk Factors

Many risk factors are exaggerated to cover the company against liability, but this section can make fascinating reading nonetheless. In Internet companies' S-1s, you will see a lot of paragraphs that start off like this: "Limited Operating History," "No Assurance of Profitability," "Risk of Systems Failure," and so on. Pay attention: they're not kidding. But these boilerplate risk factors pale next to some real humdingers that you'll find from time to time:

- **Litigation.** This can kill a small company. If the wording is strong, particularly in regard to patents, and you believe the lawsuit could prevent a company from selling its products, stay away. Distasteful legal matters pertaining to executives should come up as red flags as well. One case of note was Jenna Lane (JLNY), a maker of women's sportswear. Its S-1 disclosed that an executive had been convicted of theft and had signed a consent decree with the SEC over securities violations. Why anyone

would invest in such a company after reading that disclosure is hard to understand. The stock opened at $10 in March 1997 but fell to $1.50 after 15 months of trading.

- **Dependence on a Few Customers/Suppliers.** It is common for small companies to rely on a few customers. However, you might see an S-1 that shows a firm has just one customer. That's a danger sign.

- **Shifting Business Model.** Be concerned if a company jumps from one business to the next. This indicates that the company has no vision and likely never will. The company, in a sense, is experimenting with your investment dollars.

- **Debt Payment.** Some companies state that they will use the cash from an IPO to pay off debts. If most of the IPO proceeds are used for that purpose, it's a danger sign because there will be little money left for the growth of the firm. Also avoid companies that state they have defaulted on debts in the past.

- **Limited History of Profitable Operations.** If a company has been in existence for three to five years and has yet to make a profit, chances are good that it never will. Stay away. One example is interactive-TV hopeful Celerity Systems. When it filed its initial small-business registration, called Form SB2, in 1997, the company stated that it had lost money in all but one year. (In 1995, it made $9,900.) The stock opened at $7.50 but fell to 50¢ by May 1999.

Lock-Up Period   Most underwriters prohibit a company's officers from selling shares for six months after an IPO so that there is no undue selling pressure on the stock as it's born. However, after the lock-up period expires, you might see the officers sell a great deal of their holdings, which puts downward pressure on the stock price. This can be an opportunity to purchase the young company's shares at a lower price. You can find the terms of the lock-up period in the Shares Eligible for Resale section of the S-1.

Business/Industry/Management

Here you'll find a mother lode of details about the company's business and goals, as well as trends in its industry. Read it carefully. The S-1 of eBay serves as a great primer on this form, particularly because the company went on to have one of the most successful IPOs in history. In its Business section, the first sentence says: "eBay is the world's largest and most popular person-to-person trading community on the Internet." The company claimed to be the undisputed leader in its category. It wasn't bragging. It was the leader when it opened and still led at the time of this writing. The Industry section of eBay's S-1 claims that the online, person-to-person auction model addressed a market that had the

potential to be worth at least $50 billion in sales. The form also stated that eBay would serve a "global marketplace" that allowed for an incredibly broad selection of goods and sellers, as well as 24/7 convenience and continually updated information. It made a persuasive argument.

The eBay S-1 went on to describe the company's management team in great detail. If you'd read the document at Edgar Online in the summer of 1998, you would have learned that founder Pierre Omidyar had abdicated major management responsibilities. He hired Margaret Whitman, who had been the general manager of the preschool division at Hasbro as well as chief executive at FTD, the floral-products company. The management section also told investors about the hiring of several other experienced executives as well as the assembly of an impressive board of directors that included Scott Cook (founder of Intuit and director of Amazon.com) and Howard Schultz (founder and chief executive of Starbucks).

Finally, the S-1 lists the company's major shareholders and early backers. For most companies these days, this includes venture-capital firms. The big ones bring more than money to a company; they help to bring in a top executive and directors team and build strategic alliances. Top venture-capital firms include Kleiner Perkins (Amazon.com, Netscape, Intuit), Benchmark (eBay), and Sequoia Capital (Yahoo!). If the S-1 lists these names, you know instantly that you are in good company.

Forms 4 and 144—Insider Trading

Insider trading got a bad rap from the likes of Ivan Boesky in the late 1980s. But there is really nothing sinister lurking in these forms. They are filed by a company's officers, directors, and major shareholders whenever they sell or purchase any of the company's shares. Disclosure forms are intended to prevent these folks from taking unfair advantage of their knowledge of their company's affairs.

Craig Columbus, president of InsiderSCOREBOARD.com, believes that corporate insiders are in a unique position to evaluate the assets of a company. He therefore advises clients to own fundamentally undervalued stocks that are being bought by corporate insiders with the most intimate knowledge of their business. Because he thinks that the information asymmetry is greater in the shares of small companies than large, he advises focusing your insider-trading attention toward smaller firms.

Form 144

This document indicates the amount of stock an insider plans to sell within the next three months. There are so many reasons that corporate insiders might want to sell—for instance,

to diversify their holdings, buy a house, or handle a divorce—that they are not good indicators of panic.

On the other hand, a large amount of insider selling that represents a significant amount of insiders' stakes might be a danger sign. Also beware when insiders propose to sell a lot of stock when their stock is hitting new lows and the fundamentals of the business appear to deteriorate.

Form 4

Insiders file this document when they plan to buy or sell stock. Except for stock that many directors are ordered to buy as a result of joining a board, the only reason an insider purchases stock is that he or she believes it will go up. The form lists the insider's name and title, the number of shares bought, and the price. You'll also learn whether the trade was made on the open market or as part of a stock-option exercise. An open-market transaction is more unusual and meaningful, because option exercises almost always result in instant gains. Open-market transactions reflect risk-taking.

Errors abound in these filings because many executives file them without legal counsel. A form might list the wrong amount of stock sold, and many executives file forms as much as a month or even a year late. They are also not adjusted for splits, so you must make the calculations on your own when looking at forms filed before a company has split its stock. Finally, some insiders are just bad at timing. Look at Web sites such as InsiderSCOREBOARD.com and InsiderTrader.com to separate the savviest insiders from the rest. Some other items to watch when examining insider-trading data online:

Cluster Buying   Look for sudden bursts of insider buying from two or more insiders—a phenomenon known as *cluster buying*. The insiders should preferably be involved in the company on a day-to-day basis, such as the chief executive, the chief financial officer, or the vice president of sales. Insider buying from directors and major shareholders is less significant. For an example, visit MSN MoneyCentral Investor and look at the insider transactions at IT Group, a company that manages hazardous waste. During the last half of 1998, you'll see that a variety of insiders made 168 purchases at prices ranging from $5.44 to $10.30. By May 1999, the stock was trading at $17.50.

One caveat: Columbus advises investors to ignore cases in which the cluster buying occurs at exactly the same price or for exactly the same number of shares. Those conditions usually suggest that the purchases are part of a secondary offering or some type of orchestrated accumulation.

Silence Is Golden   One indication that a company is talking with a suitor about a takeover comes when frequent insider activity suddenly stops. This happened at grocery chain

Fred Meyer in 1998. The company showed a lot of insider activity until late July of 1998 when transactions suddenly ceased. Four months later, Kroger purchased Fred Meyer at a big premium to the July price.

Turnarounds   Often, heavy insider buying is a signal that executives believe they're successfully turning a money-losing operation around. One example is Callaway Golf, which hit hard times in mid-1998. Its stock fell from $38.50 to $9.37 amid intense competition, knock-offs of its signature Big Bertha club, and the development of a golf-ball division. In the second half of the year, however, insiders were big buyers of the stock. The chief executive, Ely Callaway, purchased 300,000 shares of stock at prices ranging from $9.93 to $11.14. Frederick Port, the senior vice president of international sales, purchased 27,100 shares at prices ranging from $9.63 to $13.75. Another vice president, Richard C. Helmstetter, purchased 100,000 shares at prices around $12.25. All of those purchases were visible for months online by the time the stock started to rise; by May 1999 the stock had moved up to $17.

Industrial and Seasonal Trends   If you follow a particular industry, watch the insider activity across several companies to get a feel for its seasonal trends and insider habits. For example, Columbus notes that utility-industry insiders rarely purchase more than a few thousand shares. If an insider purchases 5,000 shares, you have a very bullish indicator in a utility stock. Likewise, he says, the computer disk-drive business is very seasonal, and insiders are notorious for conducting transactions at certain times of the year. If they vary from that pattern, it could be bullish.

Furthermore, Columbus says his research suggests that insider buying is more predictive of stock-price movements in certain industries, such as biotechnology, real-estate investment trusts, and regional banks, to name a few. In the case of biotechnology stocks, for example, new products must wend their way through complicated clinical trials whose results are subject to a wide range of interpretation. As a result, insiders are uniquely positioned to provide valuable insights, particularly those with extensive industry experience and multiple board affiliations.

Impact of Filing Requirements   Corporate insiders must report their trades to the SEC by the 10th of the following month. So if an insider buys shares or exercises stock options at any time in September, she has until October 10 to notify the SEC. It then takes the SEC a couple of days to process the filings and release the information.

Nearly three-quarters of the filings come during a five-day span each month. Insiders can file their forms immediately after their transactions, but most wait until the deadline. The reporting lag can cause problems. By the time we outsiders learn of the insider buying, the price of a stock might have risen dramatically from the levels at which the

insiders were motivated to act. Columbus usually advises investors not to initiate a position in a stock based on insider trading unless it is still within 10% of the average price at which the insiders bought it. Still, insiders tend to be very early in their purchasing, so there's usually plenty of time to watch their moves and tag along.

If you want to lead rather than follow, however, you'll next need to learn how to put the billions of statistics discovered at SEC sites into context by focusing on the bottom line: which companies are expected to turn their hopes and dreams into the fastest earnings-per-share growth over the next few years? The investment-banking community puts a lot of time and attention into answering that question. Now you'll discover where to go online to find the pros who do the best job of bottling this blur of data and conjecture into buy, hold, or sell recommendations.

Chapter 10

Analyst Recommendations

More than 3,000 securities analysts working for many dozens of brokerage and independent stock-research firms study about two-thirds of the companies traded publicly in the United States. Celebrated lately as never before, these researchers issue judgments that are acted upon by investors at the speed of the Net—driving prices of favored stocks to the moon faster than you can say "upgrade."

The attention is largely unjustified; academic studies have revealed that analysts' estimates of corporate earnings are wrong about 80% of the time. Many critics of the investment-banking profession complain that brokerage analysts are little more than salespeople for the stocks that they cover. They routinely urge investors to buy shares in companies from which their firms have earned hefty underwriting fees or whose underwriting business they would like to snag in the future. Analysts are likewise accused of being loathe to speak plainly in their recommendations. To avoid riling a current or potential client, they use code words like "hold," "market performer," or "long-term accumulate" when they mean "sell."

Some analysts are indeed frequently off-base, but others are brilliant and will lead you to solid trades. Analysts on the "buy side" work for money-management firms that are net purchasers of stock. These researchers are the generally the most respected by institutional traders, but they are also the most reluctant to publicly announce their opinions. Analysts on the "sell side" work for brokerages that are net sellers of stock to the public, both through underwriting initial public offerings and trading on commission; they're the ones you hear from every day. Even though most smart investors recognize brokerage analysts' conflicts of interest, analyst pronouncements make news. And in the bull market of the late 1990s, news makes stocks groove. So regardless of your opinion of the profession,

you need to keep tabs on brokerage analysts' comments about stocks you are researching, even if you consider their opinions contrarian indicators.

Fortunately, the advent of the Web has made it a lot easier to learn analysts' declarations fast, receive their reports on the same day as publication, and figure out which ones are any good. In this chapter, you'll learn where on the Internet to hunt for analyst groupthink on stocks (called their *consensus*), where to find their individual reports, and what to do with the information you uncover.

What Analysts Do

Analyzing someone else's prospects for success has to rank as one of the world's oldest professions. Back in the mists of time, we can imagine the Cro-Magnon equivalent of a Harvard MBA earning piles of prehistoric wampum for his keen critiques of some rival's chisel-making production line.

Securities analysts in today's Wall Street caves all work in pretty much the same way. After conversations with corporate and industry insiders, they tote up the dollar value of all the contracts that a firm says that it has or will have with customers, and then they apply the profit margin that the firm says it expects to earn from those sales. They subtract a percentage for taxes, press a button to recalculate their spreadsheets, and, voilà, they have earnings estimates for the next quarter, year, and possibly five years.

For this they earn more than $1 million a year? Most brokerage analysts study only a handful of companies in a single industry, such as wireless communication or medical devices; that becomes their "universe," in analystspeak. Ingredients for their estimates come from guidance that the company offers in the form of press releases, conference calls, or one-on-one discussions with decision makers. But some analysts add other elements to the recipe. One might visit the company's customers and discover that sales of certain products are not as brisk as the company has publicly declared. Another might determine that the company is going to qualify for a lower tax rate than is generally expected or that a company is facing a price war that will grind down profit margins. An analyst with a medical degree might see something wrong with a drug company's research plans. Others appear to sniff incense and pull cards from a tarot deck.

At least once every three months, all of this number crunching, phone dialing, jawboning, and crystal rubbing results in a document that declares the analyst's judgment on the company and its shares. He or she first reports the findings to institutional clients by phone, e-mail, or fax, and then the data is uploaded to earnings-data aggregation firms such as First Call, Zacks Investment Research, and I/B/E/S. Next, a press release is often broadcast around the Internet, and sometime later, the upgrade, downgrade, or announcement of the start of coverage is sorted into the appropriate news or analyst-ratings sections

of major finance Web sites. If it seems as though stocks start moving well before you learn of a change in earnings estimates or ratings, it's because the private investor is usually the very last person to hear about those kinds of changes. (Another good reason to become a yeartrader, rather than a buyer of stocks one at a time.)

Each brokerage has its own ratings rules and lingo, but most insist that brokers grade companies in their universes on a curve. This would mean that the top 20% get "strong buy" recommendations, the middle 60% get "buy" recommendations, and the rest earn the label "hold" or "neutral" even if the firm's chief executive is being hauled off to prison and creditors are closing in. (In April 1999, chief U.S. securities regulator Arthur Levitt complained about this practice, citing a study that found only 1.4% of all analysts' opinions were a "sell," while "buy" ratings accounted for 68% of their advice.)

By the time a company's earnings are actually announced each quarter, it doesn't really matter which analysts are right and which are wrong, however. Numbers from all of the analysts are smushed together by the analyst-info aggregators to form a consensus expectation. It's incredibly important for companies to match or beat that consensus by at least a penny or face the wrath of investors.

All of the major finance portals list analysts' high, low, and consensus earnings figures for public companies and a list of the day's upgrades and downgrades. Many today provide access to the actual report as well. Almost all of the finance portals receive their analyst data funneled through Zacks Investment Research, I/B/E/S, or First Call. The numbers can vary slightly, so if you suspect that a figure is wrong, check a site that uses a different data provider. I'll use MSN MoneyCentral Investor (a Zacks customer) to explain the broad picture, and then I'll take a quick tour of additional value added by other sites. Finally, I'll show you where to find key analysts' comments at their own Web sites.

MSN MoneyCentral

To see most of the information on analysts' aggregate opinions, click Stocks on the site's home page. Click Analyst Info in the left navigation bar, enter a ticker symbol in the box at the top of the page, and click Go. The section is arranged in two parts: Analyst Estimates and Analyst Ratings.

Analyst Estimates

Investors should focus on four components of analysts' statistical work. You want to know the highest, lowest, and average earnings estimates for the coming quarters and fiscal year; whether a company has consistently beat consensus expectations in the past; whether analysts have raised or cut estimates in the most recent 90 days; and whether those earnings estimates add up to a belief that the company's earnings are growing or declining.

MoneyCentral starts with a page of quarterly and annual earnings estimates, shown in Figure 10-1. You can click links on each page to reach the other three sections of this area: Earnings Surprise, Consensus EPS Trend, and Earnings Growth Rates.

Earnings Estimates   Almost all Web sites and brokerage reports divide analysts' estimates into two groups by time frame: estimates for the current and next quarter and estimates for the current and next year. Most sites also show the company's earnings in the previous periods as well, and they provide the percentage change between the previous period and the estimate.

You certainly want to find companies that are expected to grow income by at least high single-digit rates both sequentially (quarter to quarter) and annually (year to year). A less obvious yet important element to focus on is the spread between the high and low earnings estimate for a stock.

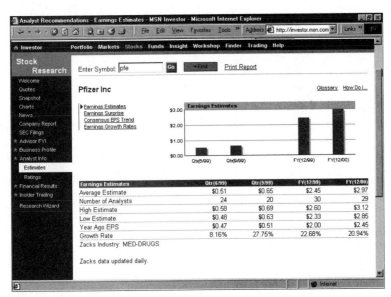

Figure 10-1.   June 10, 1999

At MSN MoneyCentral Investor, start investigating analyst estimates on the Earnings Estimates page. For example, drug giant Pfizer was expected to record earnings per share of $0.51 in the quarter ending in June 1999, $0.65 in the quarter ending in September 1999, $2.45 for all of 1999, and $2.97 in 2000. These figures are compared with figures from the previous year to yield the growth rate on the bottom row. To determine the spread between high and low estimates, subtract the low estimate from the high estimate, and divide by the low estimate. In the case of fiscal year 1999, ($2.60-$2.33)/$2.33 equals 11%. That suggests a reasonable amount of certainty among analysts about Pfizer's prospects.

For the country's oldest and most established industrial concerns, analysts' estimates are usually close—certainly within 5% to 10%. But estimates for the country's newest companies, particularly high-tech companies, can range all over the map. In June 1999, for instance, 37 analysts estimated America Online's earnings per share for fiscal year 2000. Those estimates ranged from $0.30 to $0.45, a difference of 43%. In contrast, the 20 estimates for General Electric's fiscal year 2000 ranged from $3.12 to $3.23, a difference of merely 4%. When some analysts are wildly bullish and others are wildly bearish, a stock price can fluctuate wildly between the two scenarios. To avoid that kind of volatility, look for stocks for which the spread is narrow or narrowing, which is a sign that the analyst community is now or is becoming more certain of a company's prospects. A big spread is one of many measures of a stock's riskiness. If you decide to ignore this particular risk factor, at least keep in mind that you should expect a high return. If risk is high and you are expecting only a *modest* return, you should probably forego purchasing the stock.

Earnings Surprise   Click the Earnings Surprise link on the Earnings Estimates page to learn whether the company you're researching has exceeded analysts' expectations in the past. Figure 10-2 on the next page shows part of America Online's earnings-surprise history.

Most companies work hard to manage analysts' expectations by providing lots of access to sales data. Executives know that beating the consensus earnings estimate for a quarter—even if only by a penny or two per share—is necessary to keep their stock price on track. In contrast, missing the consensus by even a penny is likely to mean a stock will get pummeled. The latter is known as a *negative earnings surprise,* or an *earnings disappointment,* and few words are more dreaded by shareholders.

Numerous studies have shown that companies that consistently beat analysts' consensus estimates tend to see their stocks rise faster than their peers. So be choosy, and consider investing only in companies with a strong track record of surprises. Analysts reward positive surprises by raising future earnings estimates and targets for share prices. Some investors build a buying strategy around this earnings-surprise cycle using the so-called cockroach theory, which holds that one surprise will be followed by two or three more.

Of course, companies that consistently fail to match or exceed analysts' consensus estimates tend to see their stocks sink faster than those of their peers. Analysts hate to be fooled, and they regularly lower estimates and price targets soon after a company announces disappointing earnings. Why? If a company said in analyst meetings that it expected to enjoy a 40% profit margin on a product line but got only a 30% margin because expenses got out of control, analysts figure something else will go wrong next time.

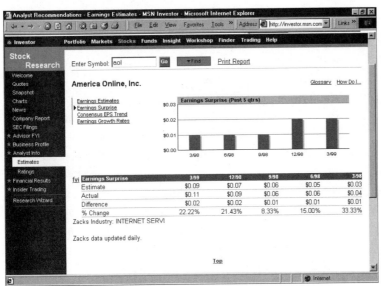

Figure 10-2.   June 10, 1999

*Companies that consistently beat analyst estimates generally see their shares rise in price. America
Online's shares jumped 703% over the five quarters shown here when the company beat estimates by
8% to 33%.*

By itself, however, a string of positive or negative surprises is not a reason to buy or
sell a stock. You should examine a company's earnings expectations for yourself to determine whether another positive quarter is likely and whether the price of obtaining a share
of those potential earnings is reasonable. Also, be aware that there has been a growing tendency to focus on the *whisper number* for a company's anticipated earnings. This is the
highest estimate of earnings that analysts relate to their private clients, and it tends to be
7% to 10% higher than the consensus estimate for top companies from which much is
expected. When a stock gets punished after a company announces seemingly strong results, it's usually because the company failed to beat its whisper or it made cautionary
comments to analysts in its conference call. (See Chapter 8 for more information on conference calls that accompany earnings announcements.)

To see MSN MoneyCentral's list of the top 10 positive and top 10 negative earnings
surprises of any week, click Markets on the top navigation bar. Then click Top 10 Lists on
the left navigation bar, and click Earnings Surprises in the list that appears.

Consensus EPS Trend   The consensus EPS Trend page, shown in Figure 10-3, charts
the *direction* of analyst groupthink about your stock. (If you visited the page with the top
10 earnings surprises and you want to return to the page with earnings surprises for your

stock, click Stocks on the top navigation bar, and click Analyst Info on the left navigation bar. Type a ticker symbol in the box, click Go, and click Earnings Surprise.)

These estimates are important because investors generally make judgments about the future price of a stock by multiplying the consensus figure by the stock's P/E ratio, also known as the P/E *multiple*. (For a complete description of P/E ratios, see Chapter 8.) These multiples vary by industry, with the highest multiples assigned to industries and stocks that grow fastest every year without interruption.

If you learn that a stock's mean fiscal-year estimate is sinking or has fallen since the last time you looked, you should apply the security's current P/E multiple to the new figure to determine a new target price. (See Chapter 8 for the formula to calculate estimates using a P/E multiple.) The reasons for the decrease in the mean number might include such bad news as the unexpected failure of a new product, shrinking profit margins, or the rise of a competitor. In these cases, it is reasonable to multiply the new mean estimate by a lower P/E multiple than the stock currently enjoys. This sort of *multiple contraction* is a key reason that stock prices sink dramatically after a negative change in analyst estimates.

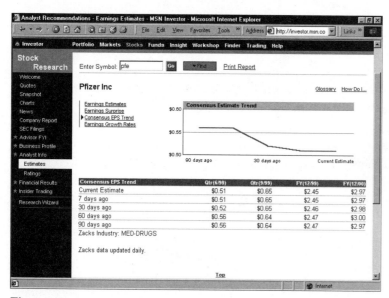

Figure 10-3. June 10, 1999

On MoneyCentral's Consensus EPS Trend page, you can learn whether analysts in aggregate have recently grown more or less bullish on a stock. In this case, you can see that Pfizer analysts cut estimates for the quarter ending in June 1999 from $0.56 to $0.51 over the 90 days that preceded when this list appeared. Estimates for later earnings remained steady, but those could also soon be cut, and the stock, which had already been hammered, could have much farther to fall.

By itself, however, a falling mean estimate is not a reason to sell or avoid a stock. Here are some things you can do to follow up:

- Determine whether the new, mean-changing figure is among the lowest, among the highest, or right in the middle of the pack of estimates for the stock. If the new estimate is the lowest on Wall Street, it might be considered an extreme view and therefore carry less weight.

- Determine which analyst downgraded the estimate. Look for an alert in the News section of Stock Research, and check the analyst's track record at Yahoo! Finance or Multex.com. (I'll discuss how to do this in more detail later in the chapter.) Almost every stock has bulls and bears in the analyst community, and some are considered more accurate than others.

Earnings Growth Rates   Click the Earnings Growth Rates link on the Consensus EPS Trend page to compare your stock's estimated earnings growth with those of its industry and the S&P 500. (See Figure 10-4 for an example.) The key figure to study on this page is the comparison between the current year's P/E multiple and the current year's estimated growth rate. If the estimated full-year P/E multiple is much more than twice the estimated growth rate, investors are showing a lot of exuberance for the stock. Any little misstep could sink it.

If you're a conservative or value-oriented investor, look for stocks with *forward-year* P/E multiples that are at least equal to, but preferably lower than, the growth rate. (Forward-year P/E ratios are based on the current full fiscal year, rather than just the trailing four quarters.) For these stocks, little is expected, and any unexpected positive news can boost the price dramatically.

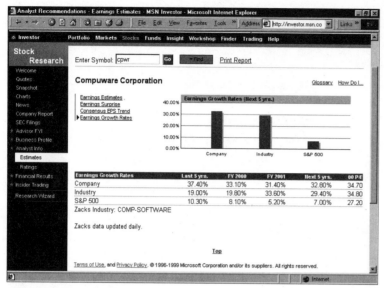

Figure 10-4.   June 10, 1999

On MoneyCentral's Earnings Growth Rates page, you can compare your stock's estimated earnings growth rate with those of its industry and the S&P 500. Compare the forward-year P/E ratio to the estimated growth rate to determine whether earnings expectations are high or low for a stock. In the case of Compuware in June 1999, the P/E ratio for fiscal year 2000 was just about even with the estimated growth rate. This indicates relatively low expectations—just right for value investors.

Analyst Ratings

Analysts sum up all their beliefs about the companies they cover with ratings similar to those in a report card, shown in Figure 10-5. Although each brokerage has its own rating system, each is a variation on a theme. At the top is "strong buy," which generally means the analyst expects the stock to rise by at least 50% over the next 6 to 12 months. Lower ratings include "hold" and "neutral," which mean the analyst believes the stock will either stand pat or sink. Very few brokerages issue "sell" ratings.

The most significant upgrades or downgrades typically come when an influential analyst changes his or her rating from "buy" to "strong buy," or vice versa. You should definitely take note when something so dramatic occurs that a stock is upgraded or downgraded two levels, for example, from "hold" to "strong buy." Very often, other lesser-known analysts will follow that top-ranked analyst—called an *ax* in Wall Street slang—like sheep.

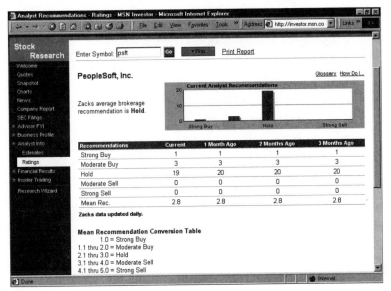

Figure 10-5.   June 10, 1999

On MoneyCentral's Analyst Ratings page, you can discover how many analysts have rated the stock a "strong buy," "buy," or "hold." Some investors use these ratings as contrarian indicators. In the case of PeopleSoft in June 1999, analysts were nearly unanimous in their "hold" ratings. As a result, a little bit of good news could cause a flurry of price-boosting upgrades.

Sadly, the ratings mean very little. America Online, for instance, was upgraded to "strong buy" by more than 10 Wall Street analysts in the early spring of 1999 after it shot up from around $70 in January to around $165 in April. All kept their "strong buy" ratings in force even as the stock slid back under $90 by mid-June. Indeed, a flurry of "strong-buy" upgrades can be used as contrarian indicators because it means no one is left to recommend the stock! One hedge-fund manager told me that he has a rule along these lines: if he sees more than five analysts upgrade a stock at the same time, he sells it. "They're just as emotional about stocks as retail investors—always bullish at tops and bearish at bottoms," said the fund manager. "They move in packs. You want to bet against them."

Yahoo! Finance

Few financial portals distinguish themselves with unique presentations of analyst estimates and ratings. Yahoo! breaks away from the pack by putting all of the information noted above on a single page, rather than forcing its customers to make multiple clicks. It also contains a few more nice features:

- Yahoo! provides a record of all rating changes in a stock. For example, you can go to *http://biz.yahoo.com/c/p//pfe.html* to see the dates of all ratings changes for Pfizer in the past couple of years and the names of the brokerages behind them. Also, as described in Chapter 5, you can print the list and then click over to MoneyCentral's Investment Growth charting tool to see which brokerages have a good record of calling each stock's price movement.

- Yahoo! provides a daily list of the top earnings surprises at *http://biz.yahoo.com/z /s_hs.html*.

- Yahoo! provides a unique list of analyst ratings from about 50 top brokerages at *http://biz.yahoo.com/f/bc.html#ratings*. You'll see that few have a "sell" rating. Gruntal & Co.'s lowest rating is "speculative," which is a nice euphemism, while most use "underperform" or, my favorite, "source of funds."

Zacks, First Call, and I/B/E/S

Zacks Investment Research, First Call, and I/B/E/S are the leading aggregators of earnings data and analyst ratings, both offline and online. They all focus primarily on their wholesale business to institutions and major Web sites, and that means they are loathe to compete with their clients for customers.

- **Zacks** (*http://www.zacks.com*) has done the most, among these three, for the individual investor. For a subscription of $150 a year, Zacks' own site provides tremendous detail on changes in analysts' ratings and revisions of their earnings estimates over the short-term and the long-term, as well as lots of daily or weekly commentary from its own analysts. Zacks also ranks stocks from 1 to 5 in timeliness, much like Value Line, and it ranks all top brokerage analysts against each other for accuracy in predicting individual companies' earnings results and stock-price targets. The latter sounds like a great feature, but its usefulness is modest. The rankings are based on data that can be as much as two years old, and the site provides no way to hunt for an analyst's current choices. Zacks does provide access to research reports from hundreds of analysts, but due to onerous rules imposed by brokerage firms, most are at least 45 days old. In mid-June, for instance, the most recent report on oil giant Chevron was originally published in mid-February; the most recent report available on Cisco Systems was published in early May.

- **I/B/E/S** (*http://www.ibes.com*) is an institutional favorite that did not have a retail strategy through mid-1999. Professionals subscribe to its trapeze.net or its Instant Access service, which delivers intraday earnings revisions and upgrade data almost as

soon as they're off the analysts' desks. Contributors run from A to Z around the world (that is, from A.B. Asesores Moneda of Spain to Zivnostenka Banka of the Czech Republic).

- **First Call** (*http://www.firstcall.com*) was originally a brokerage-industry cooperative. It became the first company to aggregate and transmit analyst data from brokerages and banks around the world, and it is still the gold standard. Through mid-1999, First Call lacked a retail presence, but it showed signs of starting one by the end of the year.

Where to Find Analysts' Reports

One of the most remarkable developments in the late 1990s has been the sudden willingness by many investment brokerages to move their written research online. Until about 1997, most firms considered stock-research analysis to be their crown jewels—the sparkle that differentiated their businesses in the eyes of institutional and retail customers. They kept it hidden and guarded, available only to clients.

In contrast, research is now being wielded as a marketing weapon, with many analysts getting the green light from their firms to disseminate their commentary as widely as possible. Indeed, I've heard individual analysts describe their aggressive new publishing efforts as attempts to build their own personal names into brands.

This has been a boon to private investors, as they face the opportunity, suddenly and for the first time, to hear from the men and women who advise institutions on investments. Putting aside the question of whether analysts' estimates are right or wrong in aggregate, some individual analysts' research reports can be terrific sources of information and perspective about companies and industries. I'll start with the best places to find reports online for free, and then I'll lead you to the growing number of places that aggregate this material for a fee.

BancBoston Robertson Stephens

The analysts at Bay Area boutique investment bank Robertson Stephens have had new bosses every few months over the past couple of years. The firm was independent until 1996, when Bank of America bought it. Then NationsBank merged with Bank of America and sold Robbie Stephens to BancBoston. That name lasted just about nine months until BancBoston was sold to Fleet Financial. Stay tuned for the next installment of the saga; by the time you read this, they might well be owned by someone else.

In the meantime, however, the high quality of research at this house has continued unabated. It is still among the best and the most widely available to private investors. Start with the work of Keith Benjamin, who publishes his work on the Web site Internetstocks.com (*http://www.internetstocks.com*). Every Friday morning before the market opens, Benjamin publishes The Weekly Web Report, shown in Figure 10-6. It clearly shows deals, personnel and valuation changes at Internet companies, and their effects on stock prices. I highly recommend that you sign up at the site for e-mail delivery of the newsletter if you're interested in this sector.

Benjamin was an early supporter of America Online, Amazon.com, CNET, Sportsline, Network Solutions, CMGI, and eBay. In many cases, he banged the drum for these stocks in an intelligent manner well before most of his colleagues did. By the end of 1998, the market began to catch up with his views and follow his advice. Whether Benjamin declared his appreciation for a stock or declared it undervalued, it began to move immediately. That quickly made him the ax on on many of the stocks in his universe.

Here's an example of the specificity and skepticism characteristic of Benjamin's commentary. The excerpt came from a report filed March 19, just before the reporting season

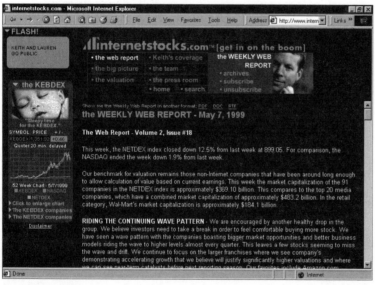

Figure 10-6.   May 7, 1999

InternetStocks.com is the product of Web analysts Keith Benjamin and Lauren Cooks Levitan of BancBoston Robertson Stephens. They post updates of their views on Internet stocks every Friday. Sign up for e-mail delivery, so you don't have to remember to visit the site.

for first-quarter earnings. Most of the stocks moved to new highs by early April but were cut in half again by mid-June.

> *EXPECT SOLID REPORTING SEASON - We expect AOL to show record sub-scriber growth and Network Solutions record registration growth, suggesting strong trends for growth in consumer and business audiences. Advertisers seem to be using direct marketing tools to make increased spending more effective as consumers buy more online. We remain focused on two stocks, Amazon and Lycos, where we be-lieve near-term confusion about sequential growth and price competition at Ama-zon and the deal terms at Lycos are distracting investors from superior fundamental positioning to grow into bigger valuations. We expect results at Amazon will now beat lowered expectations and that complaints about the Lycos deal will draw at-tention to the stock, which will rise one way or another.*

> *STOCKS MOVING ON STOCK SPLITS MORE THAN FUNDAMEN-TALS - We had little patience for school, particularly business school, finding expe-rience much more valuable. To twist Paul Simon, after all the stuff we were supposed to learn in school, it's a wonder we can think at all. The textbook chapters that rationalized market efficiency in reaction to stock splits should be updated for the irrational impact of day-traders after the stock splits of eBay, CNET, Double-Click, CMGI, and now NSOL. While the fundamentals of each company appear great, we find it difficult to chase each stock near term. We believe it might make sense to divide our universe into two groups, day-traded and non-day-traded, fo-cusing on smaller news items as catalysts for the former and strategic positioning for the latter.*

Benjamin's co-conspirator in the Weekly Web Report is analyst Lauren Cooks Levitan, a former Crate & Barrel sales clerk. She earned an MBA from Stanford and moved over to Robertson Stephens from Goldman Sachs in 1995. She and Benjamin claim to have invented the term *e-tailing* in a report in February, 1996, more than a year before online retailer Amazon.com went public. An early and ardent backer of eBay, Levitan's advice to Internet stock-pickers in an online report from March 1999 was useful:

> *My single biggest piece of advice is to try to understand the business model and un-derstand why over the long term any particular company has a chance of success. The critical success factors for an e-tailer are largely the same as critical success factors as a retailer. Are they good product pickers? Are they establishing a brand that has meaning? Are they going to be competitively differentiated from both the physical world players and the pure-play e-tailers? Is the company actually bringing*

something extra by using the distribution channel? Just simply offering products online and expecting people to shop there, I don't think that's a strong enough proposition. I think people really need to be looking for which of these companies have the ability to be enduring and that requires a combination of brand power and execution excellence.

Software investors should also visit sister site Softwarestocks.com (*http://www.softwarestocks.com*) once a week. That site showcases the analysis of Robertson Stephens software hawk Marshall Senk. His reporting is steadfast and pointed, with little embroidery around the edges. The posts always include information that the pros know and that private investors need to learn. Over the remainder of 1999, more Robertson Stephens analysts were expected to roll out newsletters about hardware and networking stocks.

Prudential Securities

Prudential (*http://www.prusec.com*) lists all of its analysts' "strong-buy" recommendations at its Web site, shown in Figure 10-7. In addition, Prudential offers daily commentary from celebrated technical analyst Ralph Acampora and investment strategist Larry Wachtel (*http://www.prusec.com/daily.htm*).

Figure 10-7.   May 7, 1999
Daily market commentary from technical analyst Ralph Acampora and investment strategist Larry Wachtel is available at the Prudential Securities site in both written and audio formats.

This tremendous resource is worth a look at least once a week. In late March of 1999, the Dow Jones Industrial Average slid back from its attempt to rally over 10,000. This was related to fears that NATO troops would begin to bomb Serbia and that large high-tech companies would preannounce a slowdown in earnings. Here were Acampora's prudent comments:

> *Since our secular trending bull market began in November 1994, we have seen six milestones: 4000, 5000, 6000, 7000, 8000, 9000 and now 10,000. The Dow closed above its 5,000 and 6,000 levels fairly quickly (8 and 4 weeks respectively). The other milestones took at least 6 months, if not about one full year to break, on a sustainable basis. History is telling us to be patient—it will take time for the Dow to close above 10,000 but, in the meantime, most of its 30 components still look attractive to us, which is by far the most important consideration. Expect more of the same choppy activity as the Dow meanders around the 10,000 level. Unfortunately, the leadership is expected to remain very narrow as the negative breadth problem continues. We can not defend the poor performance of so many individual stocks but we are saying that this negative divergence need not result in a major sell off for the DJIA. We feel comfortable in saying that the Dow's support in the 9000/ 9100 area is very strong as the support of 1200 is formidable for the S&P 500.*

Acampora gave the same advice to Prudential brokers at just about the same time, so a private investor was essentially getting a full-service brokerage's professional advice for free. This is not a bad deal, as long as it's also good advice. Acampora's comments proved their worth when the Dow proceeded to blow right through 10,000 and hit a high of 11,107 by mid-May. The site also provides support and resistance levels for each of the Dow 30 components.

Gruntal & Co.

Gruntal & Co. (*http://www.gruntal.com*) is one of the oldest specialty brokerage and research houses on the Street, claiming a heritage that stretches back to 1880. Almost every day, the company posts short extracts of a couple of its recent research reports on its Daily Research Summaries page (*http://www.gruntal.com/research/daily.html*). Although short, these snippets definitely qualify as responsible advice directly from professionals. More broadly, Gruntal's bullish chief investment strategist, Joe Battipaglia, posts a weekly summary of the firm's investment opinions as Market Commentary (*http://www.gruntal.com/ research/joeb.html*).

Bear Stearns

Bear Stearns (*http://www.bearstearns.com*) is well regarded for its economic research. I like to check in on its Web site, shown in Figure 10-8, from time to time to catch up with the views of Wayne Angell, a former Federal Reserve governor. Here's some commentary posted on the site's Economic Update page in March 1999, when many investors were concerned about the potential for the Fed to raise interest rates:

> *With little more than a week to go before the March 30 FOMC meeting, the infla-*
> *tion data for February should have removed any lingering uncertainty over the*
> *outcome of the meeting. Following a surprisingly good wholesale price report and*
> *further moderation in average hourly earnings in February, the latest consumer*
> *price report showed core inflation falling to 2.1%, which was the slowest 12-month*
> *rate of change in ten months. With absolutely no evidence of any smoking gun on*
> *the inflation front, we do not see how Fed Chairman Alan Greenspan could bow to*
> *any pressure to adopt a tightening bias at the upcoming FOMC meeting. In addi-*
> *tion, the February earnings and inflation data have provided another important*

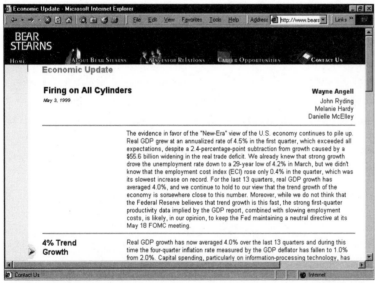

Figure 10-8.   May 7, 1999

Bear Stearns publishes the views of former Federal Reserve governor Wayne Angell and his economics staff regularly on its Web site. The firm does an admirable job of making economics understandable and (almost) interesting.

reminder to bond investors that real yields are attractive when the 30-year Treasury yield exceeds 5½%. Moreover, with gold at $282 an ounce, which is toward the lower end of the range that has prevailed since late 1997, our favorite leading indicator continues to present no pressures on the inflation front. Meanwhile, the latest readings on activity continue to point to strong economic growth in the first quarter.

Those were very calming words and, previous to the Web, the kind of thing reserved strictly for Bear Stearns brokers and clients. (Never mind that Angell turned out to be largely wrong this time, as the Fed ultimately did adopt a tightening bias in May 1999.)

S.G. Cowen

The French banking conglomerate Société Générale purchased the investment banking house Cowen & Co. but didn't change its style. The Cowen analysts are first class, and the free research they offer can be excellent. Their key contribution: the Internet Capitalist, a twice-a-month look at trends in Internet stocks. It's not easy to find, but visit the S.G. Cowen Web site (*http://www.sgcowen.com*), click Research, and then click the link for Internet Capitalist in the middle of the main frame. You'll see an archive of past editions as Adobe Acrobat files. (To read the reports, you'll need to download a free Acrobat reader from Adobe Systems at its Web site, *http://www.adobe.com*.)

S.G. Cowen states that it publishes the report in an attempt "to place both anecdotal and concrete data within a thematic context that will help institutional investors gauge where the greatest shareholder value will be created over time in the Internet universe." The report is often long-winded, but it offers detailed reports on analysts' interviews with company management, vendors, and customers. You sense that you are getting a really close-up view of an analyst at work. You can sign up to receive the report free by e-mail. Just send a message to infomail@sgcowen.com, and put the words "subscribe capitalist" in the body of the message.

Lehman Brothers

Lehman Brothers has been generous with its research reports for two years. It files dozens of them each day to its public Lehman Brothers Equity Research Web site (*http://www.lehman.com/Research/Equity/equity.shtml*) with a two-day delay from its institutional delivery. Although that's clearly not as fast as some of the younger brokerages, the timing is much better than almost any of the traditional brokerages such as Salomon Smith Barney, Merrill Lynch, and Bear Stearns. The coverage is very widespread, from electric utilities to software, and it is also quite good.

Salomon Smith Barney

This unit of financial-services giant Citigroup offers a lot less than Lehman Brothers does but more than many other brokerages of comparable size. The Salomon Smith Barney research Web site (*http://www.salomonsmithbarney.com/inv_up/*), shown in Figure 10-9, is attractive and well-organized, offering three or four investment ideas each week. The reports are cut up into sections such as Reason to Buy Now, Technical Analysis, and Investor Profile, which describes the type of investor for whom a stock is appropriate. If you're looking for a quick idea that won't make you think too hard, this is a good option once a week.

Figure 10-9.   May 7, 1999

Salomon Smith Barney provides weekly reports on stocks and sectors for free. Daily reports are available to customers only, although non-customers can sign up for a free trial.

Multex.com

The stranglehold professional investors had over Wall Street research was broken forever in 1997. Multex Systems provided only back-end technology support to brokerage research departments before it decided to turn its business model inside out. Taking baby steps that led to giant leaps, Multex managed to persuade Merrill Lynch, Salomon Smith Barney, Prudential, and more than 400 other firms to provide their research to the public, on a delayed basis, for a fee. By the middle of 1999, Multex Systems changed its name to

Multex.com and launched a slick consumer-oriented site that, for the first time, provided private investors a crack at analysis formerly available only to the pros.

Multex.com (*http://www.multex.com*) offers reports through partnerships with most of the major financial portals on the Web. It also offers a variety of free trials and free material at its own site, shown in Figure 10-10. You should prowl around it until you feel comfortable. At its core are tens of thousands of pay-per-view research reports available on thousands of domestic and foreign companies. (Most are available only in the Adobe Acrobat format, which is sometimes referred to by its file extension, .pdf.)

To start, type a ticker symbol into the box in the middle of the Multex.com home page. You'll first see a list of free, same-day research, which is sponsored by brokerages such as Merrill Lynch or Salomon Smith Barney as a teaser. Next you'll see a list of reports available from brokers, at prices ranging from $10 (for a two- to five-page report on a single company) to $150 or more for an industry report. Most are at least two weeks old. Before you click and buy, check the report's headline to make sure that the name of the stock you're researching is really a key part of the report. (If you're not satisfied, Multex will refund the purchase price.) Finally, you'll see a list of reports from third parties, which are usually independent, buy-side research firms.

Figure 10-10.   June 14, 1999

Multex.com offers tens of thousands of analysts reports at prices of up to $150. The site also offers a free compendium of analyst coverage in its Analyst Corner feature, which is available through a link on the left navigation bar of all its research pages.

Deconstructing the Reports

If you've been investing for any period of time, odds are 100% that you've owned a stock that's blown up despite your painstaking research. One of the great ways to learn skepticism about a company's plans—and analysts' enthusiasm—is to spend the money to read several interpretations of the same set of facts. Indeed, it's useful to begin your foray into the analyst *demimonde* at Multex.com not with a strongly positive or negative view, but rather with the posture of a scientist. You may have a bullish or bearish hypothesis about a company and its stock that you wish to prove. But you must be willing to incorporate countervailing evidence in your ultimate decision to buy or sell. When you visit Multex.com, keep in mind that you seek facts in a world of opinion. Be wary of comments that include the words *should, could, might, ought,* and *assume.*

Every analyst and brokerage has its own reporting style, but most follow a familiar format. Somewhere near the top is the name of the analyst. If you're studying companies in technical or scientific fields and you believe in pedigrees, look for analysts that show off their erudition with a Ph.D. or M.D. after their names. Next to their names will normally be their e-mail addresses and direct phone numbers. But don't hold your breath waiting for a return call or e-mail. Unless you're a money manager or a buy-side analyst, they are not likely to respond.

Whom to Believe

So which of these opinions are worth reading? That's hard to answer, because picking a good analyst is almost as hard as picking a good stock. A couple of companies have tried to make the job easier by ranking the rankers:

- **Institutional Investor.** Every October, industry trade magazine Institutional Investor (*http://www.iimagazine.com*) compiles a list of top research teams. Industry insiders admit that winning a place on that list is as much about politics as prediction strength because inclusion is based on a vote (like the Oscars). But you've got to start somewhere. In 1998, Merrill Lynch won the contest for the fourth year in a row. It was followed, in order, by Goldman Sachs, Morgan Stanley Dean Witter, Salomon Smith Barney, Donaldson Lufkin & Jenrette, Credit Suisse First Boston, PaineWebber, Lehman Brothers, Bear Stearns, and J. P. Morgan. To see the full list, visit Institutional Investor's site, register for free, and go to the rankings in its research section at *http://www.iimagazine.com/research/98/aart/index.html.*

(continued)

The analyst's rating is usually prominent at the top of the page, along with standard vital statistics for the company and the analyst's estimates for the next quarter and year. Some analysts also include a projected 12-month price target in this space. Next come bulleted points that summarize the report to follow. Following that, you'll see the meat of the report, which describes recent business and industry trends that will lead the stock to be worth more (or less) than it is today. And finally, you'll usually see an itemized income statement, or *model,* that gives projections for far into the future. You can trace the analyst's thinking from the top line to the bottom and determine whether it follows logically from descriptions of the business.

Discount Brokerages

In the past year, a few of the online discount brokerages have swooped into the business of providing real-time research from some of their full-service rivals. These odd-couple marriages started off a bit rocky, but they have gained traction as each party found something to like about the relationship. Top efforts include the following companies:

E*Trade

This pioneering online discount brokerage (*http://www.etrade.com*) offers recommendations and analysis from BancBoston Robertson Stephens before the bell each morning. It's a great service from one of the best boutique investment banks. You can find leading-edge analysis of the high-tech, medical-device, and consumer-product sectors, but you've got to subscribe to E*Trade's premium Professional Edge service.

Whom to Believe *(continued)*

Click each brokerage's name to see a list of its top-ranked analysts, as well as the analysts' photos, biographies, and detailed descriptions of their best calls over the previous year.

- **Zacks Investment Research.** Zacks (*http://www.zacks.com*) and the *Wall Street Journal* team up each year to publish a more objective list of the best analysts. The study ranks the top five analysts in each industry based on the historical performance of their recommended stocks and the accuracy of their EPS estimates. The list becomes available if you pay $150 to subscribe to Zacks' Web site. If you a subscribe to the *Wall Street Journal*'s Interactive Edition (*http://wsj.com*), you can hunt for the annual article on that site's Publications search page. Then you need to pay only $2.50 for the same information.

Charles Schwab

The San Francisco-based giant (*http://www.schwab.com*) offers its high-end clients free access to morning and afternoon research notes from high-tech/biotech investment bank Hambrecht & Quist (*http://hamquist.com*) and Credit Suisse First Boston (*http://www.csfb.com*). Reviewing this better-than-average material is a good way to start the day if you're an active investor with a Signature-class account at Schwab. (See Chapter 13 for more details.)

DLJdirect

The online offspring of major merchant bank Donaldson Lufkin Jenrette (*http://www.dljdirect.com*) offers daily reports from its parent's research department, as you would suspect. To get you hooked, all new DLJdirect customers get 60 days of research free; after that, you have to maintain a $100,000 account balance.

Discover Brokerage

Morgan Stanley Dean Witter's online offering (*http://www.discoverbrokerage.com*) is more complicated. Customers can pay for a subscription that includes a specific number of reports per month, but the subscription is free to holders of $100,000 accounts.

In conclusion, it's hard to overestimate the value that the Web has brought to investors interested in the work of fundamental analysts. But the Web brings even more value to investors interested in technical analysis. Let's go there next.

Chapter 11

Technical Analysis: Following and Forecasting Trends

Some successful stock-market strategists don't even pretend to be investors. They're just traders with a single goal: get the money. "Every day we think of ourselves as sending out a little squad of army men to capture capital and bring it back. Then we lock it up and go out for more," said Terry Bedford, a Toronto hedge-fund manager who is one of the best of this ilk.

To find the right stocks at the right time each day in the market, speculators like Bedford almost never pay attention to the fundamentals of a company's business or anything else I've discussed in Chapters 8 through 10. They don't look for great new products, earnings growth, low P/E ratios, or a smart chief executive. Instead, they monitor technical trends in stocks' recent price movement with online charting software, seeking patterns that tend to repeat.

Successful technical traders generally do not have long-term opinions on the direction of the broad market. Investors may be bullish or bearish, but many traders dedicated to technical analysis—called TA for short—try to be neither. They believe that stock prices tend to move, or *trend*, in one direction for a period of time and then change direction abruptly. Successful analysis, based on a blend of mathematics and psychology, helps traders forecast changes, and it tells them whether changes are likely to be permanent or temporary. Said Bedford, "The market tells you what you have to be because the market is always right. A lot of people say you can make money as a contrarian. But they're wrong. If a train is going 100 m.p.h. in one direction, and you stand in front of it with a picket sign and say, I'm Joe Smith and I say you're wrong, you're going to get run over 100 times out of 100."

Most successful technicians are not the risk-blind Wall Street cowboys of myth. Instead, they generally use TA to time the movement of their money into and out of positions when risk is lowest. By learning to thus manage risk with technical analysis, even private investors with time horizons that extend months or years instead of minutes can start and maintain stock positions with a higher probability of success.

There are at least four main disciplines for technical analysis:

- **Wave theory** examines long market or stock cycles over time.

- **Point-and-figure theory** examines stock-price movement without the backdrop of time.

- **Candlestick theory** examines the relationship between opening, high, low, and closing prices for each trading period (whether days, hours, or minutes).

- **Bar-chart theory** couples pattern recognition with mathematical formulas (called indicators) to forecast changes in stocks' demand and supply.

You can find dozens of books and Web sites that specialize in each of these methods. I'll focus here on the most widely used online tools, which help traders monitor bar charts. I'll start by examining a few of the best places on the Web to draw pictures of stock movements, and then I'll plunge into a description of the most useful tools. To learn more about chart and wave patterns online, visit the daily Chartroom column at Bedford & Associates (*http://www.baresearch.com/chartroom.htm*), the daily Technician's Take column by Gary B. Smith at TheStreet.com (*http://www.thestreet.com*), Today's Ideas at LIM Research (*http://limresearch.com*), or the Education section at ClearStation (*http://www.clearstation.com/education/patterns.shtml*). To learn more from books, order these classics from your favorite online store: *How to Make Money in Stocks* by William O'Neil, *Technical Analysis of Stock Trends* by Robert D. Edwards and John F. Magee, and *Technical Analysis of the Financial Markets* by John J. Murphy.

Charting Engines

First let me acknowledge that no Web-based product yet matches the sophisticated capabilities of shrink-wrapped software like TradeStation 2000 and SuperCharts 4 from Omega Research (*http://www.omegaresearch.com*) or MetaStock from Equis International (*http://www.metastock.com*). These software suites allow traders to build and test their own technical-analysis systems, study charts in real time, and set up alerts to buzz when favorite patterns emerge. A professional trader would sooner walk onto the floor of the New York Stock Exchange naked than work without TradeStation or MetaStock.

Most private investors, however, will do fine at any of the three best places on the Web for examining stock-price movements from a technical point of view: MSN MoneyCentral Investor, BigCharts, and ClearStation. The main differences between the trio: MSN MoneyCentral allows the most flexibility in examining custom time periods, focuses only on the most popular technical-analysis tools, and offers the best chance to compare historic returns. BigCharts offers the most complex technical-analysis tools and does a great job with short time periods. ClearStation does an unparalleled job of offering well-integrated instruction and community discussion.

MSN MoneyCentral

The charting features at MSN MoneyCentral Investor (*http://moneycentral.msn.com/investor*), shown in Figure 11-1, were created by some of the same developers that created the charting features of Microsoft Excel. The tools' flexibility stems from the fact that they are actually software rather than just a fancy Web page.

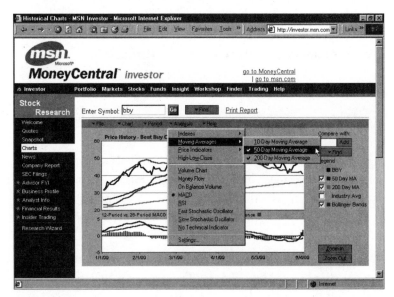

Figure 11-1.   June 6, 1999

Set analysis and time-period criteria at MSN MoneyCentral's charting engine by opening the Analysis and Period menus at the top of the chart and making successive choices from pop-up menus. In this year-to-date chart, the 50- and 200-day moving averages and MACD for Best Buy have been chosen from the Analysis menu. In addition, Bollinger Bands have already been selected, as you can see in the list of criteria on the right.

To start, click Stocks in the top navigation bar. Then click Charts in the left navigation bar, enter a ticker symbol, and click Go. The first time you visit, you will need to download the site's full suite of software; this takes about five minutes using a 28.8-Kbps modem. In the next few sections, I'll give a quick overview of the functions to investigate.

Time Period

When doing technical analysis on stocks, it's important to study price movements over a variety of time frames. The default time-period view here is the *one-year daily,* or a full year of prices in which each plot point equals one trading day. To change the length of time to display, click Period on the top of the chart. From the menu that appears, choose any option from Intraday to All Dates (which is the public lifetime of the company). To choose a specific period in the past, click Custom, and then type in a date range in the dialog box that appears. You can see the histories of some stocks as far back as 1970 and some indexes dating from 1928. Note that the level of detail shown changes as the period changes. If you choose to view a 3-year chart, for instance, each point on a price chart and each bar on a volume chart represents one week. If you choose a 5-year or 10-year chart, each point and each bar represents one month. You can change these settings in the Custom box as well—to view, for instance, weekly changes in a 10-year chart.

Chart Type

The site offers three types of charts from which you can choose by clicking Chart on the top of the chart.

- **Price History.** This is the default and the standard way to view the daily closing price and volume of a stock over time. This is the only view for which the technical-analysis tools apply. To compare up to 20 stocks or mutual funds against the stock or fund with which you started, type their ticker symbols into the Add box, and then click Add.

- **Price Performance.** This view shows the return on a stock over various time periods, for example, a 30% annualized return over the past five years or a 50% return in 1994. Use the Period menu for this chart to compare stocks' returns over a Recent period (a week, a month, six months, and year-to-date); a Long-Term period (an annualized value for 1 year, 3 years, 5 years, and 10 years); or an Annual period (a calendar year in the public life of the company). Use Add to compare multiple stocks.

- **Investment Growth.** This view shows how an initial investment in a stock would have grown over time (including dividends) both in total dollars and in total percentage return. The default investment is $10,000, but you can change it to any value by choosing Display Options from the Charts menu. To see the absolute value and percentage gain of the investment at any point in the chart, move your cursor over the line and a box appears with the numbers.

Analysis

This menu is where all the technical-analysis tools are found. Users can choose from the following:

- **Indexes.** Use these to compare your target stock or fund with a relevant benchmark. Choose from four major indexes: the Dow Jones Industrial Average, the S&P 500, the Nasdaq Composite, and the AMEX Composite. Or choose Relevant Industry to plot the average price of the stocks in your target's industry.

- **Moving Averages.** Use these to view the average price paid for your target stock or fund over the past 10, 50, or 200 days. Technical traders see bullish or bearish signals when a stock's price rises above or sinks below its moving averages or when short-term averages rise above or sink below long-term averages.

- **Price Indicators.** Choices here include a stock's Moving Average Envelope, Bollinger Bands, and Price Channel. Each shows a type of trading band around the current price. I'll discuss Bollinger Bands in more detail later in the chapter. To learn about the other trading bands, see the site's Help section.

- **Technical Indicators.** Choices here include Volume Chart, Money Flow, On-Balance Volume, MACD, Relative Strength Index, and Stochastics. (More detail will follow on each of these options later in the chapter.)

- **Settings.** Choices here allow you to change settings for the technical-analysis tools and display preferences for the price-history tools. For instance, most technical analysts prefer the site's default setting for the MACD of 12-26-9, meaning the first moving average is set over 12 days, the second is set over 26 days, and the signal line is set at 9 days. However, others like to set the averages at longer or shorter periods. As for display preferences, you can set the price charts to display dividend and split dates, as well as the dates on which your MSN MoneyCentral portfolio manager shows that you bought and sold individual stocks.

File

This menu contains two important options in addition to Print:

- **Save Chart Style.** Once you configure a chart with moving averages, time period, volume, indexes, and so on, you can click this menu option to save the configuration on your PC. The next time you want to use that configuration, return to this menu, and choose Apply Chart Style.

- **Export Data.** Click this option to quickly send all the high/low/close price and volume data from a chart to a spreadsheet. If you have Microsoft Excel on your computer, the program automatically starts and fills a spreadsheet with the data. If you display a one-year chart with daily prices, you export daily prices and volume. Likewise, if you're viewing a 10-year chart with monthly prices, you export monthly prices. Very cool.

Zoom In / Zoom Out

The chart's Zoom In button works like a magnifying glass that you can hold up to any part of the chart to see a shorter time period and greater detail. Drag the pointer from one place to another on the chart. Click the Zoom In button to get closer or Zoom Out to step back. Click Zoom In or Zoom Out repeatedly to see progressively finer or broader levels of detail.

In addition, you can point anywhere on a chart to display the date, close, change, and volume information on the top line of the chart.

BigCharts

BigCharts (*http://www.bigcharts.com*) was one of the first independent sites to focus solely on charting, and it has emerged as the best for intermediate-level technical analysis. Although it has a fine free-standing site of its own, BigCharts also sells its charting technology to dozens of major financial sites around the Web, such as TheStreet.com, Money.com, Charles Schwab, and the *Wall Street Journal* Interactive Edition. Many of these partners cripple the full functionality of BigCharts so that their clients don't get confused. It's therefore best to hit the unadulterated version of the technology at the BigCharts site itself, shown in Figure 11-2.

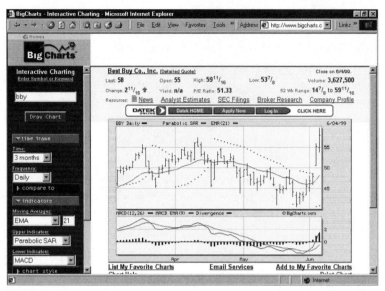

Figure 11-2.   June 6, 1999

Select a time frame and a set of technical indicators at BigCharts by making choices from drop-down lists in the left frame and clicking the Draw Charts button. This figure shows a three-month daily chart of Best Buy with a 21-day exponential moving average (EMA), Parabolic SAR as the Upper Indicator, and the MACD as the Lower Indicator. Note how the MACD exhibits an upside crossover on June 1 just as the stock breaks out above the 21-day moving average. Also the Parabolic SAR shows it's time to switch from short to long positions on the stock when the dot moves from above the price bar to below. Very bullish.

Two shortcomings of this site are that it is not easy to determine the exact prices on its charts. (Other sites use Java or ActiveX software to display precise prices when your mouse hovers over a line on a grid.) Also, the 10-day charts at BigCharts do not adjust properly for splits. Three nice surprises on the site include the fact that clicking the Email Services link under any chart sets up daily or weekly delivery of the chart via e-mail. The Add to My Favorite Charts link lets you set up a ready-made library of charts. Finally, the Store Settings link allows you to preserve chart styles between visits to the site.

To start at BigCharts, type a ticker symbol into the text box on the home page, and then click Interactive Charts. The page will be refreshed, and two frames will appear. In the right frame is your chart, which starts out quite plain; in the left frame are four categories of input, which help you dress your chart up.

Time Frame

Technical analysis is mostly about judging the movement of prices and volume against the backdrop of time. Changing your time perspective from one-minute intervals to one-hour, one-week, one-month, or one-year intervals might change your interpretation of price patterns. This is roughly analogous to saying that a century is a long span in human time but only a speck in geological time.

Short-term traders watch 1-minute, 5-minute, or 10-minute charts to catch buy and sell signals all day long. Traders with broader time horizons prefer daily one-year charts or weekly three-year charts. Of course, you can use more than one time frame. Some traders use daily charts to compile a list of stocks with the best long-term momentum. Then they zero in on the best stocks' hourly or 10-minute charts to determine exactly the right time to buy.

To set your initial period of examination, click the Time Frame button in the frame on the left. In the Time field, start with a long period of time, such as one year; in the Frequency field, choose Daily. Now click Draw Chart, and look at the chart on the right. Experiment with different times and frequencies. The periods between 1 day and 10 days allow you to look at frequencies that range from one minute to one hour. The periods between 1 month and 10 years allow you to look at frequencies that range from daily to annually.

When I study a chart at BigCharts, I almost always begin with the three-year weeklies, then move to the one-year dailies, and then move to the 10-day hourlies for a finer focus on the action. It's like climbing up to the balcony at a theater to survey the whole stage, pulling out a pair of binoculars to zero in on the actors' bodies, and finally adjusting the lenses to focus on their faces. I almost never look at the 5-minute or 15-minute charts; that's like staring at the actors' lips.

Compare To

Traders often like to compare stocks against either other stocks or a benchmark, which is typically a broad-market index. Click the Compare To button in the left frame, and then choose from about 15 benchmarks in the Index field or type a ticker symbol into the Symbol field.

Indicators

This is the main attraction at BigCharts. You can explore all the indicators on your own by clicking the Indicators button in the left frame, but here are explanations of the indicators that I find the most useful.

Moving Averages   Moving averages plot the average price of a stock over a period of time. They smooth out all the "noise" of a stock's day-to-day meandering to reveal overall trends. If a stock's daily price fluctuations are random waves on an ocean, moving averages are the tide. Like the tide, they tend to move slowly and purposefully in one direction before reversing.

Moving averages come in two main flavors: simple and exponential. To calculate a simple 50-day moving average for a stock, the software adds the stock's closing prices for the past 50 trading days, and then it divides that figure by 50. To calculate an exponential short-term moving average, the software gives greater weight to the most recent prices.

Traders observe a stock's current price in relation to different lengths of moving averages depending on whether they're trying to understand the short-, intermediate-, or long-term trend. The most popular short-term trend is 10 days; many traders like 21 or 50 days for the intermediate term and 200 days for the long term. Personally, I have had the best luck with a 21-day exponential moving average to best understand weekly and monthly trends.

So what's the purpose? It's all about forecasting *changes* in trends. When a stock's current price breaks above its 50-day moving average, for instance, it is considered to have broken its trend, or recorded an *upside breakout*. This is bullish because it means that every new buyer of the stock is willing to pay more than the average price paid for the past 50 days. Likewise, a breakout below a moving average is considered bearish.

Technical traders believe that the short-term and long-term moving averages of a stock form lines of resistance or support that are difficult for a stock to penetrate on its way up or down. Once the stock does penetrate these lines of resistance, however, technical traders believe that the smoke clears, and the stock has a clearer shot at moving higher or lower. Essentially these levels can act like intense battlefields for a stock's bears and bulls. Once the battle over a weakened stock is lost by bulls, technical analysts believe that the stock has a better chance of sinking toward new lows. Likewise, once the battle over a recharged stock is lost by bears, it is more likely to achieve higher highs and higher lows as it moves up.

By themselves, however, breakouts are not reasons to buy or sell a stock. They're just clues that the stock is in greater or less demand than it was on average over the past 10 to 200 days. Technical analysts believe that these kinds of trends tend to continue, all other things being equal.

It's much easier to understand moving averages if you see them represented on a chart. To put a 21-day exponential moving average on your chart, click the Indicators button, choose EMA from the first drop-down list, and then type *21* into the text box on the right. Click Draw Chart, and the moving average appears in the right frame. Experiment

with various types of moving averages (SMA or EMA) over different time frames (for example, 10-day hourly or 1-year weekly). Also try the 2-line and 3-line versions, which automatically augment your first moving-average choice with averages set at longer time intervals. Figure 11-3 shows an example.

You may find that different setups work better at helping you understand the support and resistance levels of different types of stocks. For instance, try the 50-day EMA 3-line with Cisco Systems (CSCO) for the year prior to June 1999. You'll see that the 50-day average provided support most of the time, while the 100-day average provided excellent support for all but the breakdown in October 1998.

Upper Indicators   There are 10 choices here, but I'll focus on volume by price, Parabolic SAR, and Bollinger Bands. To learn about the others, click Chart Help.

Volume By Price. The volume-by-price indicator shows you the amount of trading volume relative to the price of the stock. For example, if you apply the volume-by-price indicator to a chart for IBM, BigCharts creates a bar chart on top of the price

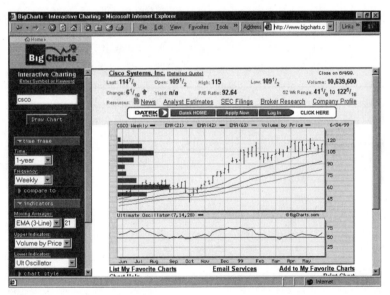

Figure 11-3.   June 6, 1999

Here's a three-way view of Cisco Systems in the year prior to June 1999. First, traders showed a strong willingness to keep buying Cisco at its 21-day exponential moving average (the highest of the three lines). Second, the Volume by Price indicator (the bars extending from the left) shows the stock was bought in high volume at $60 and $105, which suggests that the $105 level should hold amid any weakness. Third, the Ultimate Oscillator in the Lower Indicator suggests that five months of consolidation were about to conclude with a breakout to the upside.

chart showing the distribution of trading volume at different price levels. This is useful in determining where the majority of historical trading volume occurred, and it may help you find meaningful support and resistance lines. Support lines are used to determine the price at which buyers are likely to come into the market and support a stock. Resistance lines are used to determine the price at which "weak hands," or investors without conviction, may unload their stock, thereby driving the stock price lower.

America Online stock, for example, was under attack in June 1999 by bears who had driven it down from $165 to $105 over the previous two months. At that time, the volume-by-price indicator showed a ton of volume around the $120 level. That was an indication that whatever else the moving averages might show, the future of the stock during any rebound would be fought most fiercely at around $120.

Parabolic SAR. Parabolic SAR is one of my favorite indicators. This "stop and reversal" system (that's what SAR stands for) was developed by pioneering technician Welles Wilder to help answer the toughest question of all: exactly when should traders sell a successful long position or even immediately go short? Most systems of setting stops fail because the stops are set too tightly at the start of a trade and too loosely after the trade becomes profitable. The Parabolic SAR, in contrast, allows more leeway for price fluctuation early in a new trade and then progressively tightens a protective trailing stop as the trend matures. According to BigCharts, the indicator accomplishes this by using a series of progressively shorter, exponentially smoothed moving averages for each period that the price moves in the expected trend direction.

Just try it on a few stocks that you own, and experiment with different time frames. In the Upper Indicators drop-down list, choose Parabolic SAR, and then click Draw Chart. You'll see red dots below a stock in an uptrend and above a stock in a downtrend. (See Figure 11-2.) Traders following this indicator would close long positions when the price fell below the SAR dot and close short positions when the price rose above the SAR dot. If you are long (that is to say, the price is above the SAR), you will see the SAR move up every day, regardless of the direction in which the price is moving. The amount the SAR moves up depends on the amount that the price moves. Some traders like to use a short-term Parabolic SAR (for example, 10-day hourly or 1-month daily) when initiating or selling positions in very volatile stocks, but they turn to a longer-term SAR (for example, the 1-year weekly or 3-year weekly) when it comes to core positions in big, steady stocks such as Cisco or Merck.

Bollinger Bands. You can use Bollinger Bands to determine whether a stock price is high or low relative to its recent trading history. Bands are plotted two standard deviations above and below a stock's 20-day moving average. The usefulness of the bands is rooted in the elementary observation that stocks tend to trade within a range over a

period of time and that excursions above or below that range may signal changes in the stock's price trend. The bands widen during periods of volatility and narrow (or *squeeze*) during periods of calm. The behavior of a stock when it approaches these bands offers clues to its future direction, either by clarifying past trading patterns or by confirming buy and sell signals generated by other technical indicators.

Two concepts to watch: when bands squeeze, a price breakout becomes more likely. And once a stock starts moving away from one band and toward the other, it tends to complete the trip. A sell signal isn't automatically generated when a stock price finally arrives at the top band from the lower band, however, because the price can climb the upper band for weeks. In an interview, inventor John Bollinger said, "If prices run up to the upper band, and another indicator does not confirm that strength, you have a sell signal. Likewise, if prices fall to the lower band and whatever indicator you're using doesn't confirm that weakness, then you have a buy." In other words, it's only by coupling the action of another indicator with the action of the prices within the bands that you can have success with this indicator.

Lower Indicators   The site offers 26 more indicator options to place on your customized Interactive Chart page. I'll mention my favorites, but you should explore the rest on your own. Click Chart Help to learn their functions.

Volume +. This enhanced volume indicator simply uses different colors to signify when the period's trading volume contributed to a gain or loss in price: red for down days and black for up days. The indicator helps you quickly understand whether the investors behind a particular move (for example, above or below a moving average) had conviction.

RSI. The Relative Strength Index is a momentum indicator that measures an equity's price relative to its own past performance. The RSI therefore indicates a security's internal strength and quantifies momentum, or *velocity*. The RSI represents the average of the closing price on days (or hours, if using an hourly chart) on which the stock closed up divided by the average closing price of the days on which the stock closed down. The RSI ranges between 0 and 100, and it is said to indicate an *overbought* condition when it is above 80 and an *oversold* condition when it is below 20. In general, traders try to initiate long positions in stocks that have RSIs greater than 50 and rising.

MACD. As shown in Figure 11-2, the Moving Average Convergence/Divergence is composed of one line (called the "slow line") that represents the difference, or *divergence,* between 12- and 26-day simple moving averages. A second line (called the "signal" or "fast" line and usually colored red) represents a 9-day exponentially smoothed moving average. Although this explanation makes it sound complicated, the MACD is actually one of the easiest indicators to use. When a stock moves up powerfully from a trough, the slow line crosses decisively up and over the signal line. This indicates that the stock price

is not just advancing: it is *accelerating*. Math majors will note that the slow line rises because the difference between the 12-day and 26-day moving averages is growing. The MACD histogram—vertical bars plotted beneath these lines—is another, more graphic, picture of exactly the same divergence.

The key trading strategy for the MACD is the concept of *crossovers*. Generally, technical traders see a buy signal when the slow line crosses above the signal line, and see a sell signal when the slow line crosses beneath the signal line. Crossovers above the 0 line (x-axis) on the chart are considered especially strong. One of my favorite strategies—if trading, rather than investing—is to look the MACD on three-year weekly or one-year daily charts. I initiate long positions in stocks that are turning MACD positive (meaning the MACD indicator is rounding up) and exit long positions when stocks turn MACD negative (meaning the MACD indicator is turning down, or "rolling over," in the lingo). The three-year charts filter out a lot of day-to-day noise and throw into sharp relief those key moments when a stock that was once hot is turning cold even as it limps to new highs. It's usually smart to exit trading positions when a stock makes a new price high but its MACD high is lower than previous MACD highs on the same chart. (An *investor* should ignore this and all other indicators entirely, except as an odd source of entertainment.)

ROC. The Rate of Change (ROC) measures a security's percentage change in price over rolling 10-bar (hourly, daily, weekly, or monthly) time periods. For example, if you plot the daily price performance of Oracle and you apply the ROC indicator, you see a line that plots the percentage change in price of Oracle over rolling 10-day periods. The ROC helps you understand visually whether a stock's trend is intensifying or waning.

Ultimate Oscillator. Oscillators generally compare a security's smoothed price with its price some number of periods (hours, days, weeks) ago. The value of oscillators can vary greatly depending on the number of time periods used during calculation. The Ultimate Oscillator, developed by Larry Williams, uses weighted sums of three oscillators, each of which uses a different time period. The three oscillators are based on Williams' definitions of buying and selling pressure. Williams recommends that traders initiate positions following divergences and breakouts in the Ultimate Oscillator's trend. Try this indicator with various stocks and various time periods. You'll see what works pretty well at showing sharp breaks in trends over any time frame you pick.

Slow Stochastic. This oscillator compares a security's *closing* price with its price *range* for a given time period. The premise is that when a security rises, it tends to close near its high for that period. When it falls, it tends to close near its low. The slow stochastic indicator shows when a rising stock starts to close near the low end of its trading range or a falling stock starts to close near the high end. Such shifts in momentum often predict changes in the stock's price trend. Inventor George Lane likened the classic momentum

pattern of a security to the path of a rock that's launched into the air. As the rock approaches the highest point that it's going to reach, it starts to slow down. Only then does it turn and head back to Earth. Similarly, a rising stock begins to rise more slowly before it turns down and vice versa. In other words, its momentum changes before its price does. At both BigCharts and MSN MoneyCentral, the Stochastic Oscillator is displayed as two lines. The main line is called %K and calculated using the security's high, low, and closing data. The second line, called %D, is a moving average of %K. Both are typically calculated using daily price data, but some traders prefer to use weekly numbers. Readings below 20 strongly indicate that a stock is oversold, and readings over 80 strongly indicate that it is overbought. In general, traders try to buy a stock when the stochastic is turning up from an oversold condition, and they try to sell a stock when the stochastic is turning down from an overbought condition.

P/E Ranges. This is a great way to determine whether a stock is relatively cheap or expensive compared to its own history. The indicator is available only when you choose weekly, monthly, quarterly, or yearly time periods to chart. It displays the range of the stock's P/E ratio, over given periods of time, as solid bars. The top of the bar is the high end of the range for that period, and the bottom is the low. (See Figure 10-18.)

ClearStation

ClearStation (*http://www.clearstation.com*) emerged in May 1998 as the premier place on the Web to learn about, practice, and discuss technical analysis. A smart, congenial young trader named Doug Fairclough founded the company in the heart of San Francisco's financial district and called his creation the "intelligent" investment-analysis community. ClearStation largely lives up to that moniker. Although many sites featuring technical analysis and message boards focus solely on tools and hard-selling products, ClearStation focuses on education and camaraderie. Purchased by the online brokerage E*Trade in 1999, the site uses screening software in the background to push good new trading ideas at users, rather than forcing them to grope around on their own. More importantly, ClearStation's community discussions are much smarter and better focused than you'll find at competitors' sites. (See Chapter 12 for more on community discussion.) Here's a quick tour of the site's tools for budding technical traders.

Home Page

ClearStation's home page, shown in Figure 11-4, is one of the most useful on the Web, and it shows off the site's excellent navigation scheme. Editors use the A-List column to display their best trading ideas of the moment according to the dicta of technical analysis.

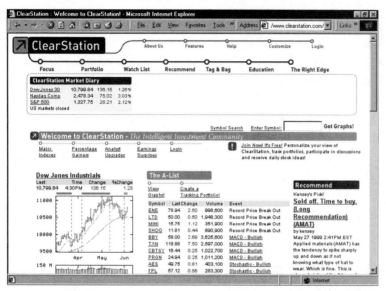

Figure 11-4.   June 6, 1999

The ClearStation home page is nirvana for intermediate-level technical traders because it lists stocks that are making bullish or bearish patterns in an easy-to-read format. With a quick glance at the A-List, you can get numerous fact-based trading ideas with which to start your day's research.

These stocks have either begun bullish or bearish MACD or stochastic patterns, have broken out to new highs or lows, or are being recommended by analysts or ClearStation community members.

After you complete the free registration and set up a real or watch portfolio, as I describe in Chapter 12, click Focus at the top of the home page to see a list of all the technical events that have occurred in your stocks during the past day. The organization of this page is very useful. For example, rather than just listing your stocks in alphabetical order, ClearStation arranges them by Price Performers, showing which of your stocks are "Doing Well" or "Doing Poorly." It also shows Portfolio Events, displaying which of your stocks are MACD bullish/bearish, are stochastics bullish/bearish, are crossing above or below moving averages or recording price breakouts, have stock splits pending, or were the subject of analyst upgrades or downgrades. Click the ticker symbol of a stock to see headlines from a variety of news organizations, charts, and community comments.

Tag & Bag

Click the Tag & Bag link at the top of ClearStation's home page, and you'll find yourself in the virtual TA drawing room. If you click links to New York Stock Exchange, Nasdaq, or Amex stocks, you will see a list of the stocks that ClearStation's software has identified

as making the most significant bullish or bearish moves either from a technical or fundamental point of view. These are terrific trading ideas from which to launch into research;
the best are collected in the A-List mentioned earlier. The section is separated into Today's
Trending Issues (MACD); Today's Timing Signals (Stochastics); Record Activity (highs or
lows); Most Actives and Price Movers; Price Action Events (crosses above or below moving averages); Continuing Trends: Bullish and Fundamental Events (for example, analyst
upgrades, earnings expected or announced, split pending, or dividend declaration).

Quote and Chart Detail

Type one or more ticker symbols into the text box on the site's home page, and then click
Get Graphs!. You are taken to a page that instantly graphs the security's price, volume,
MACD, and stochastics. Figure 11-5 shows an example.

Figure 11-5.   June 6, 1999

*Quote pages at ClearStation are the most informative on the Web. In one place, they show a stock's price
and volume chart, its MACD and stochastics charts, news, and community postings. On this page, note
the little green trending indicator at the far right of the MACD that shows the stock has entered an
uptrend in early June. All price and volume bars are color coded: red volume bars for down days, blue
for up days. Price bars that show new 52-week highs are also blue. Along the top of the price chart are
colored trending bars: red for strong downtrends and green for strong uptrends. Finally, look at the complete set of data along the top of the page. ClearStation lists price, volume, percent change in volume,
and the community's vote on a stock.*

The charts include trending bars along the top that turn green when a stock has started a definitive uptrend and red when a definitive downtrend begins. This is a great help to novice or intermediate investors who have a hard time telling the difference amid all the noise of a chart. A feature called "three-point view" provides automated interpretation of the current technical and fundamental state of the stock. This description explains in *almost* plain English how long a stock has been in its current trend, the date of the next expected earnings release, and a vote from users on the price action. Below the charts is a list of user comments on the price action. Click a headline to see the full message, and then click Say Something! to join the discussion. If you like a comment, click the writer's name to see all the messages that person has left on that and other stocks. The link also shows the writer's portfolio, if it was opened for public view. Here's a nice touch: attached to your message is a chart with a blue circle highlighting the spot at which you made your comment.

ClearStation pays a lot of attention to volume, using blue bars in its volume charts for days on which the stock finished up and red bars for days on which the stock finished down. This allows you to tell at a glance whether buyers or sellers are in charge of a stock. Fairclough notes in his educational material that if the blue volume bars predominate and stack much higher than the red bars, buyers rule. Essentially, it means that there is more conviction among bulls than bears. The volume chart also furnishes a moving-average line so that you can tell at a glance whether a stock exceeded its average volume on a particular day. To learn more about ClearStation's views on the importance of volume or any other indicator, click the link next to the appropriate chart.

Annotate

Technical traders like to draw *trend lines* on stock charts so that they can see the likely support and resistance points for stocks. ClearStation is the first company to bring that functionality to the Web. On the quote-detail page, click Annotate. Then click an option button for either Support, Resistance, or Trend Line, and follow the instructions for creating a custom view of your chart. The software makes it easy to start over if you make a mistake, and you can also add multiple trend lines for further analysis. These lines are visible only to the user, unless you choose to recommend a stock to others.

Recommend

ClearStation was the first Web site to allow users to create portfolios that could easily be shared among members of its community, either at the site or via e-mail. If you get excited about the technical characteristics of a chart, click Add to Recommend. I'll discuss this more in Chapter 12, but note that every recommendation includes a technical chart

that you can annotate to your heart's content with commentary and trend lines. Clear-Station lists the names of all public portfolios that are performing well at the moment; click a name to see all of the stocks within the portfolio and their annotated charts.

Education

ClearStation excels at teaching users about technical analysis. Click Education on the home page to see articles written by Fairclough under the *nom de guerre* Kensey in a lively style. His topics include Reading Graphs, Trending, Oscillating, Patterns, Portfolio Management, and Trading Basics. Follow the Next links from each topic's first page to get a lively, well-illustrated explanation of a TA concept. Return occasionally even after you've read through the content once to gain new insight.

Volume and Money Flow

Now that you know where to go to perform technical analysis on your stocks, let's take a much closer look at the mother of all indicators: volume.

Reading trends accurately involves more art than science, but most technicians believe you must always pay special attention to the average daily volume of trading in your stocks as well as that of the New York Stock Exchange and the Nasdaq Composite. No market move means anything without volume because the market is essentially a giant consensus engine. To see the consensus take hold, you need big, big volume—at least 10% higher than usual in a market and 50% higher than usual in an individual stock. Indeed, volume plays a starring role in the four phases of a stock trend's life cycle as seen by technicians:

Accumulation. This is the period of time, sometimes called *congestion,* when a stock is being bought a little at a time by institutional investors. On a chart, the stock might look like it's going sideways—up two days, down two days, up four days, down three days—for weeks or months. Large institutional investors are generally able to hold positions longer than the average private investor. They may ride out two quarters of poor earnings in anticipation of a major fundamental turn.

Markup. This is the period that gets everyone excited, because it's when a stock price breaks out of the accumulation phase and starts to rise exponentially every day on higher and higher volume. This phase is often characterized by hints of positive fundamental developments to come. The firm may announce new management, a new product, or the beginning of a pickup in earnings. Wall Street analysts normally are skeptical during this phase, preferring to wait for an actual manifestation of the positive fundamental development. You want to initiate a long position soon after the start of this phase.

Distribution. This is the period to be wary of. The stock moves sideways after the markup phase on flat volume. Everyone who wanted into the stock is in, and now some are stealthily taking their profits. During the distribution phase, earnings improve, and the positive fundamental picture is finally complete. Several "buy" recommendations from Wall Street analysts arrive, and an era of good feelings seems to begin. Initially, the stock may zoom higher, but the smart money is selling positions it accumulated during the first phase. Most stocks give good clues when the end is near. Failing to rise on good news is the most noteworthy clue that the jig is up. For example, America Online failed to rally substantially after five separate "buy" recommendations in early April of 1999. A technical clue: This is when the three-year weekly and one-year daily MACD turn down, even though the price hits a high.

Markdown. This is when the stock begins to collapse—a little at a time at first and then sometimes in a cascading waterfall of lower prices on higher volume until all sellers are done and a stock finds a new equilibrium between demand and supply. Typically, analysts will begin to talk about slowing profit growth, weaker margins, or increased competition. A clue that marks the end of this phase: the stock stops declining on negative fundamental news, and the long-term MACD turns up even though the price looks flat. At that point, the accumulation phase begins anew.

Most TA indicators described in this chapter are oriented toward the belief that the ideal time to buy comes right after the initial move of the markup phase. That move is often called a *flagpole* in TA lingo, and it's the hardest to predict. It is usually driven by an event, such as a great earnings, product, or restructuring announcement. Afterward, a stock will often drift down on lower volume, and that is the time to buy. Some technicians say the "spring" of the markup phase is getting "coiled up" during this time. Others describe it as a "bull flag," as noted in Chapter 2. Indeed, some believe technical analysis is all about missing the first move but catching the second move that follows a bull flag, in which the stock advances a ton on high volume.

The Source of Volume

What or who causes volume? It's the institutions—the pension funds, the mutual funds, the hedge funds, the endowments, the foundations, the trusts, the banks, the insurance companies, and the program trades launched by the big brokerages. Depending upon whose estimate you use, these big guns account for 75% to 90% of all stock trading. And they often move in herd-like fashion. Buy a stock when this mob is selling it, and you'll have about as much luck as a wrong-way driver on a one-way street. But buy when they're buying, and you could see your stock soar like a jet with a good tailwind.

Some traders believe that watching volume trends works because the so-called "smart money" is always first in and first out of huge moves in prices. These giant financial

institutions are like elephants: they leave big footprints. As a private investor, you want to follow those footprints because they mean good support for a stock. The reason stocks go up in general is that there are more big buyers than big sellers. If you can find the stocks where the imbalance is greatest before the rest of the crowd does, you will find the greatest winners.

Using Volume Charts

To be sure, spotting signs of institutional buying and selling isn't an automatic ticket to riches, but it can be an important tool. Volume charts at each of the Web sites noted above make it easy. To start, just load a Volume + stock chart at BigCharts or any volume chart at ClearStation. Focus on the changing colors of the volume bars, and try to become as comfortable reading the trend in quantity as you may already be reading the trend in prices. "If you see periods where the up days are accompanied by heavy volume and the down days by lighter volume, it suggests the stock is being accumulated," said Tony Dwyer, chief market strategist for the New York brokerage firm Ladenburg Thalmann & Co. Conversely, heavy volume associated with a declining price suggests that one or more big shareholders is selling.

To track the elephants' footsteps, many technical traders like to look at the money-flow indicator, which measures money flowing into and out of a security by multiplying the number of shares traded by the change in closing price. If prices close higher during the time frame you're examining, money flow is a positive number. If prices close lower, money flow is a negative number. A running total is kept by adding or subtracting the current result from the previous total. A stock's money-flow line varies depending on the time frame you are studying.

Using Money Flow Charts

Money flow is more art than science. You are mainly looking for divergences. If a stock hits a high, a trader wants to see the money flow hit a high. The money flow should therefore mirror the stock chart. When it doesn't, you've got trouble. Why? When a stock makes new highs but the money flow declines before the move, you have distribution—or selling. This is particularly true when a stock makes new highs on weaker and weaker volume.

How does that happen? Again, the market is nothing but monetized consensus. Take the case of trading in a stock like Cisco Systems. Investors might like Cisco Systems at $60 because the price/earnings ratio is relatively low and a new product cycle is starting. After a ton of buying, the stock is suddenly at $100. At that point, smart investors might not sell, but they won't buy either. They hold. As the stock rises higher and higher

above its historic valuation range, the bulls have to convert more and more people to their way of thinking to keep it going.

At some point, the bulls hit the law of diminishing returns. They just can't find any more people to convert at the higher valuation. Then ultimately you have a new high with fewer and fewer people trading the stock every day. Weak volume and declining money flow at a historic high is a sure indication of a top, and it's easy to see in charts.

For a classic example of a divergence between price and money flow, look at the one-year chart of Yahoo! at MSN MoneyCentral Investor for the period ending in April 1999 (shown in Figure 11-6). The stock hit an all-time high of $221 on April 5, but money flow was deteriorating rapidly. After hitting $28 million at its previous high of $207 in January, money flow on April 5 had fallen to just $19.3 million. The result was that 45 days later, the stock had sunk 100 points to $119. Amazon.com rose from $118 to $199 on low volume and waning money flow in January 1999. But it quickly plunged all the way to $92 before enjoying a high-volume recovery.

Figure 11-6.   June 8, 1999

The divergence between Yahoo!'s price and money flow in April 1999 is a classic example of what can happen when a new price high is not accompanied by a money-flow high. Money flow deteriorated in early April as the stock rocketed to $220. This suggested that small investors were bidding the price up even as large investors were bailing out. The divergence was followed by a 45% decline in the stock price over the next 45 days.

You always have to look at volume because it's more honest than any analyst report or wishful thinking. Whenever one of your stocks hits a new 52-week high, check its volume and money-flow charts for a confirmation. If they clearly look weak, you might sell into the rally. For confirmation, check the stock's MACD chart. If price momentum and volume momentum both look weak at the price high, consider bailing fast!

Why Volume Works

Why do volume and money-flow indicators seem to work? Institutions typically can't build a position in a stock in a single day. It could be weeks or months until they're done buying a single stock. Likewise, it takes the same amount of time to liquidate a position.

Said Steve Hayward, who managed the Marshall Mid-Cap Growth Fund: "Each of my stocks accounts for about 2% of my portfolio. That's $5 million, which means that even with a $50 stock, I need 100,000 shares. So I'm going to start with a respectable position of 25,000 shares or so and build from there. In some cases, I can do it in a few days; in other cases it may take a few weeks."

For larger institutions, the numbers can be much, much bigger. "A normal-size block trade these days is easily a quarter-million shares," said Mark Edwards, a trading consultant from Santa Monica, California. "Some of our clients can truly work million-share orders in a day; others may take two or three days to work 100,000 shares. And then some will trade a single position for two months."

Of course, not all stock accumulation is the result of institutional buying, because millions of individual investors are exerting new levels of influence on the market as well. But if you keep as close an eye on volume and other indicators as on price alone, you'll end up ahead of the crowd.

Now let's move on to discover the best places on the Web to talk about all these indicators and other stuff with fellow investors.

Chapter 12

Community

Just before heading to work every morning from my home in the Madrona section of Seattle, I hit MSN.com to eyeball the day's news and the market. Usually I glance and go, but on the morning of May 19, 1999, I just about spit out my Starbucks special blend. Providian Financial—one of the stars in my trading portfolio—was down $12 in the first hour of the NYSE session, and it was still gathering downside speed.

The issuer of credit cards to high-risk borrowers had advanced 80% so far in 1999 (from $70 to $130), but those gains were disappearing faster than a sunbreak in the Cascades. I gulped more coffee and searched my usual Web news sites. Did the company announce weak earnings? Did the chief executive resign? Was there an analyst downgrade? Had they announced a dilutive merger or secondary stock offering? I ticked through the possibilities in my mind as I surfed, but I could find no news items or press releases anywhere online.

That's when I turned to the digital communities of the Web for help. I first scanned primo bulletin-board site Silicon Investor (*http://www.techstocks.com*) and found nothing. Not surprising: Providian's not a tech stock, though it trades like one. Then I turned to the message boards at Yahoo! Finance, where I found my answer. Six investors from the Bay Area had already reported that a San Francisco television station disclosed that Providian was under investigation by the city attorney's office for suspected fraud. One investor had provided a link to a San Francisco newspaper's Web site, and I quickly confirmed the posts. The stock had sliced through support at its 50-day moving average without hesitation on heavy volume, so I sold my shares at Fidelity's Web site before the news was even more widely disseminated, managing to get out at $112. It bottomed out around $78 a few days later.

The moral of this story: Web communities are the one resource that can keep pace with the market's fearsome flood of information. The Providian problem wouldn't be worth a Bloomberg or Reuters wire story for another few hours; brokerage analysts wouldn't comment for another day. But investors today are always running on Internet time, using new-age discussion formats such as electronic message boards and chat rooms to keep pace. The best of these communities turn the ideas, discoveries, opinions, and questions of private investors into useful tools that can help solve the puzzles of investing as fast as a few odd pieces can be posted.

Now you never have to trade alone; thousands of fellow shareholders are just a click away. To be sure, you'll sometimes need to wade through dozens of useless messages, sidestep stock-hyping or shorting scams, and ward off a few morons. Moreover, you must still ultimately make buy and sell decisions on your own. But with your skepticism radar fully engaged, you can leverage the cunning of the Web collective for help in narrowing your focus, discarding bad ideas, and hanging tight when the market just makes no sense. Online communities are divided into bulletin boards and chat rooms. Let's look at each.

Bulletin Boards

Make no mistake: if you decide to become a dedicated yeartrader, bulletin boards and chat rooms can be a drain of time and energy unless you enjoy their camaraderie. The Motley Fool and ClearStation boards can serve a terrific social and educational purpose, and other boards excel at filling news voids, as Yahoo! Finance's did in the Providian example above. But many lesser boards will just cloud your brain with trivia, mutterings, lies, and well-meaning comments that are just plain wrong. I'll give you a quick tour of the best communities to visit, and I'll score each community as a time-saver or waster.

Silicon Investor

Silicon Investor (*http://www.techstocks.com*), shown in Figure 12-1, is the gold standard among financial-discussion sites on the Web. After it gained popularity in 1995, SI (as it's known to fans) started to attract many of the best bulletin-board posters away from the Motley Fool area of America Online. Soon it gained pre-eminence as the main place to swap ideas on high-tech stocks and strategies. Its founders, amiable Kansas-born brothers Brad and Jeff Dryer, sold the site in 1998 to Web conglomerate Go2Net. But it's never lost its earnest charm. By mid-1999, more than 300,000 messages were being posted per month, and the site had recorded its 10 millionth post since inception. Useful posts: 30%. Chance you'll find an answer: 70%.

Figure 12-1.   June 20, 1999

*Silicon Investor boards are the class of the Web, with archived messages stretching back to the mid-1990s
and serving as a verbal history of tech stocks. After subscribing, add Bookmarks to your favorite threads;
identify People of interest; check Hot for the liveliest boards of the day; create public Portfolios for others
to see via the New link; check the user-powered Earnings calendar via the Earnings link; or click headlines to start reading messages and posting replies. At the Applied Materials board, click Start to see the
first 100 posts from 1995.*

Roadmap

To start exploring, visit the home page, and type the ticker symbol or name of a company
in the box. Select Subject, and click Search. You'll then see a screen containing links to
one or more discussion "threads" dedicated to that stock. Each of those links has three
bits of information attached: the name of the thread's SI department (for example, Communications or Software), the number of posts in the thread, and the date and time of the
last message. Click the thread with the greatest number of recent posts. (Anyone can start
a discussion thread at SI, but many threads are quickly abandoned.) You'll then see the
first message posted in the thread. If it's a very popular board, you'll see number links
such as 18,100; 18,200; and 18,300 below the message. Behind each link are 100 messages, listed in chronological order. As a beginner, you should skip those links and look
down the list of headlines now facing you; they're also listed chronologically. Sometimes,
you'll see that messages arrive at a rate of more than two a minute! Find a headline that
looks interesting, and click its link. That takes you into the body of the message. You can

page forward or back, or you can just read the replies to that message. You'll also see links to standard stuff such as company profiles, earnings, news, and charts.

Anyone can *lurk,* or read posts without commenting. You'll need to pay up to $120 per year for a subscription to post a message, set up a public portfolio, bookmark a favorite thread, or check the profile and past messages of another poster. After you sign up, it's fun to join in a stock or strategy debate right away. But you may find that until you slowly establish a bond with natives of the boards, it can take awhile until anyone responds. The biggest boards (for example, Dell, Microsoft, and Intel) can be cliquish. The less-trafficked boards (covering small companies or value investing) can be great places to learn from 3 to 10 people having an intimate, public conversation. Click the Hot link at the top of any page to see the liveliest boards at the moment; click the New Subjects link to see discussion groups started in the past few days.

To navigate quickly around SI, use the excellent Search function found on every page. Search for words such as "communications semiconductor" or a technical-analysis technique, such as MACD. If you seek comments about a particular person—for example, futurist pundit George Gilder or CNBC pop icon Maria Bartiromo—just type the name, click Full Text, and then click Search. You'll soon be searching messages from the past 120 days. This function can be great for researching any subject. I typed in "nanotechnology" and found several dozen mentions in a variety of contexts. Another good use: type in the name of your online brokerage—or one you're considering—and see what others have to say about it. A mix of news hounds, amateur analysts, traders, and a handful of professionals keep SI on top of nearly every press release, new product, insider trade, brokerage recommendation, and rumor that comes down the pike. The subscription requirement keeps out much of the garbage messages that plague other Web discussion boards.

When should you visit? It's easy to get hooked into long-term discussions about obscure companies that might be changing the world. It's a little less interesting to drop in regularly on the big favorites such as Dell or Intel because there's so much information available already in the media and analyst community about them. Visit the boards when confusing news breaks and you need perspective, or visit when you feel euphoric or depressed about a stock and you need ballast or commiseration. Also visit when you're researching a small-cap or value stock and you want to research what people were saying about it two or three years ago. Unless you have the time to engage in endless debates or have made good friends, though, you might not need to visit every day.

ClearStation

Drop in on the boards at ClearStation (*http://www.clearstation.com*) and you'll feel like you've got a personal session with a team of technical analysts. Organized around the site's strong charting features, the messages here are highly focused on buy/sell recommendations generated by users' interpretations of four of the key technical indicators I mentioned in Chapter 11: moving averages, MACD, volume, and stochastics. Don't come here looking for discussions of fundamentals and P/E ratios. ClearStation generally begins and ends with charts, as veteran technicians and sloppy amateurs get together to throw around terms like *cup-and-handle, head-and-shoulders,* and *breakout* to describe short-term and long-term trends in stock-price movement. The analysis can be extremely inconsistent, but much is very good. Almost every post is, at least, earnest. Unlike most sites, records of past messages and trades are available with a single click. Useful posts: 80%. Chance you'll find an answer: 60%.

Roadmap

Start by becoming a registered member. It's free, and the registration process introduces you to the all of the site's features in an unusually friendly fashion. All sites have a tone, and the hip, buoyant sensibility encountered here right from the start is refreshing. Whereas Silicon Investor can seem gruff and cliquish, the Motley Fool can seem cloying, and Yahoo! Finance seems faceless, this site is all San Francisco cool.

The registration process leaves you at the site's Focus page, a good place to begin research on stocks believed to be turning bullish or bearish for technical or news-related reasons. To visit the message boards, type a ticker symbol into the box in the upper right, and click Get Graphs!. Just below the site's five standard charts is a list of the community's 10 most recent messages. Click a headline to read a particular message; then click Say Something! to respond, or click List All to see all messages on the subject. After you type a response, click Preview to make sure you didn't say something you didn't mean, and then click Submit. Voila, you are now a card-carrying member of the ClearStation community.

Next, click Recommend to visit the area of the site where users put their trading acumen to public test (as shown in Figure 12-2). Here you'll find a table of recommended portfolios by ClearStation's core staff of experts as well as the top 20 public portfolios

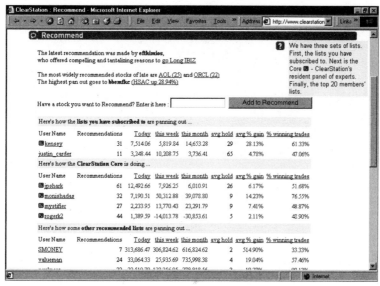

Figure 12-2.   June 20, 1999

The Recommend area of ClearStation offers a uniquely useful angle on community. Any registered user can "recommend" long or short stock positions to others; the top 20 recommenders' portfolios are listed here. Click a person's name to see his or her portfolio, and click Subscribe if you want to receive an e-mail message every time he or she makes a new pick. Your subscription list appears at the top of the page along with the portfolios of the ClearStation staff, which is led by Kensey (the nom de guerre of founder Doug Fairclough).

from ClearStation members. Click column headings such as This Week or % Winning Trades to sort from high to low. Then click the name of a high-ranked recommender to see his or her whole current portfolio and the gains and losses of each pick, along with the purchase dates. Click Graphs: In Bulk to see an annotated chart and detailed recommendation of each stock in the portfolio. If you find someone with a track record and a trading style you like, click Subscribe at the top of their portfolio page. Each time he or she makes a recommendation, his or her pick and commentary will be sent to you in e-mail. (Don't worry; it's easy to unsubscribe. See the instructions at the bottom of every e-mail message.) The most widely recommended stocks are listed at the top of the screen, as well as the recent community pick that worked out best.

When should you visit? When you're getting ready to buy or sell a stock, visiting the ClearStation boards might save you from a mistake. If you like to trade, visit the Focus page every few days for new long or short ideas. And if you've got a technical bent, check regularly for community commentary on stocks that you own. Few questions are posed from one user to another, but you can certainly see several interpretations of the technical action on your positions.

The Motley Fool

The multimedia extravaganza that investors now recognize as the Motley Fool (*http://www.fool.com*) actually started as a very modest group of text-only message boards in the ancient DOS version of America Online (AOL) in the early 1990s. In the middle of the decade, AOL switched to the colorful Windows 3.1 format, carpet-bombed the United States with start-up software CDs, and made a force of the Fool channel. Brothers Tom and Dave Gardner were truly online discussion pioneers. Their literate, high-spirited, and educational boards at AOL taught thousands of new investors how to shirk their mutual funds and ride the decade's mighty bull market in individual stocks.

The Motley Fool's popularity at America Online waned, however, with the advent of the Web and browsing software around 1996. And their boards on the Internet, while excellent, have never regained the influence that they held in the early days. Still, the discussion is well-directed and fun, and posters are relatively nice to newcomers. Useful posts: 50%. Chance you'll find an answer: 50%.

Roadmap

Visit the Motley Fool's home page, and click the Messages tab in the upper left. (See Figure 12-3.) On the boards' main page, click Stocks A To Z, and then click the first letter of the stock of your choice. Next, keep clicking until you find your stock, or search for it using the text box at the bottom of the page. After that, you can add a bookmark for faster access. To determine whether a stock is more widely discussed at Silicon Investor or the Fool, compare the number of messages next to its name here with the number at SI. For example, the Micron Technology thread at the Motley Fool in June 1999 held 350 messages; at Silicon Investor, there were 44,000. To determine which board you'd rather hang out at, read through a few dozen recent messages at each. You'll quickly learn the flavor and seriousness of each community.

The Motley Fool does have real advantages over its rivals because its zeitgeist puts learning first. The site has plenty of helpful advice boards, grouped under "The Information Desk" section of the Messages area, as well as boards devoted to such topics as investment clubs, financial books, and even model portfolios. These boards are well focused and generally friendly to strangers. Plus they're surrounded by a lot of solid Motley Fool editorial content to serve as fuel.

Although the Fools that gather here may not be as quick to react to the news of the day as the folks at SI are, they're more likely to provide serious, outside-the-mainstream analysis. Anyone can lurk, but you need to register (it's free) to post, put up your own profile, and send e-mail to fellow denizens of the boards. The boards are monitored by staffers who delete spam and off-topic messages. Throw in some nifty tools—such as the

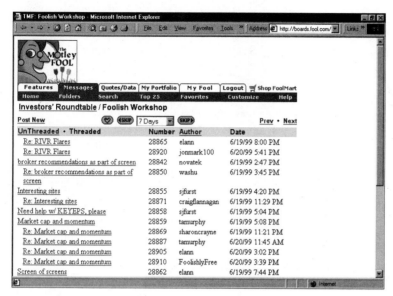

Figure 12-3. June 20, 1999

The Motley Fool has a committed community and well-polished boards. Its Favorites feature allows you to zip straight to the most recently posted messages on your favorite boards—and see them nicely organized by topic. In this Favorite, I could quickly view replies to my RIVR Flares message, as well as several other threads.

ability to organize messages by topic, create a list of favorite boards, or hide posts from users—and you have a powerful resource. If you're bored, check out the "Top 25" list to see the day's most popular boards.

When should you visit? Pick a few stock threads, and bookmark them as Favorites. Then pull up the Favorites tab every few days to check the number of new posts, and dive in.

Yahoo! Finance

About 60% of the stock-message boards on Yahoo! Finance (*http://messages.yahoo.com*) are worthless—loaded with spam, infantile gibberish, foul language, hostility, and stock-hyping mystery men. A few are great. This ratio, biased toward infamy, is a shame when you consider the splendid quality of the site's financial-research tools. But it's a reflection of what happens when message boards are unmonitored and do not require a subscription. Useful posts: 20%. Chance you'll find an answer: 30%.

Roadmap

It's a hassle to get to the stock boards via Yahoo! Message's front door. It's actually easier to visit Yahoo! Finance (*http://finance.yahoo.com*) first as shown in Figure 12-4. From there, type a ticker symbol in the box, and click Get Quotes. On the subsequent page, click Msgs in the More Info box. At that point, the format will be familiar—you face a list of messages. Click the headline of any to see the text, and then use links to page forward or back. Click List to see about 100 messages at a time. You must register to post.

The only reason to visit the boards of Yahoo! Finance is the sheer volume and breadth of messages. Look there if you strike out in finding news or a forum at Silicon Investor, the Motley Fool, or ClearStation about some obscure stock. Even the least sexy stocks, such as Eskimo Pie (EPIE), garner at least a post or two per week. Now where else are you going to pal around with EPIE shareholders?

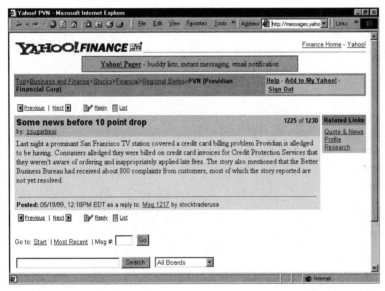

Figure 12-4.   May 19, 1999

Yahoo! Finance message boards are inconsistent but notable for breadth. This was one of several posts about Providian Financial that explained why the stock plunged May 19, 1999. The newswires didn't pick up on the story until hours later. Click List to see all messages, or click Start to display the beginning of the thread.

Bulletin Board Etiquette

The most efficient way to take advantage of the stock-discussion groups is to speed through, search for what you need, and move on. But eventually you'll feel the need to post a question or whack down a weak argument. When that happens, do it with class. Here are five tips to keep you from being lumped in with spammers, hypsters, and newbies:

- **Where's the URL, Pearl?** If you're going to post about something you've read elsewhere on the Web, don't forget to include its address in your message. Doing so lends credibility and is a big help to the board. If you're using a Windows-based PC, copy the Web page's URL by clicking in the address field of your browser and then pressing Ctrl-C (to copy). Then move back to your discussion-message form and press Ctrl-V (to paste). If you post text from an article, keep in mind that brevity is the soul of wit; judicious editing to post only the key passages will win you friends on the board.

- **Two sentences, good; one sentence, bad.** Nothing gums up a message board like endless strings of one-question, no-commentary messages. *"Should I buy this stock now?"* doesn't cut it. But it's OK if you tell why you're interested in it before asking for others' opinions. Simple rule: never post fewer than two sentences.

- **OT is not OK.** Some people seem to think that it's fine to post jokes or personal stuff to an investing thread as long as they mark the message "OT," shorthand for "off topic." But listen: the people on the thread are your stock buddies, not your work or basketball buddies. Talk stocks.

- **Learn the TLAs PDQ, OK?** Net discussion groups are filled with TLAs, or three-letter acronyms. A few of the key acronyms are IMHO (in my humble opinion), JK (just kidding), FWIW (for what it's worth), YMMV (your mileage may vary, meaning *your results/interpretation might differ from mine*), LOL (laughing out loud), and DD (due diligence). For more cyber-acronyms and emoticons, visit *http://www.mirc.co.uk/emote.html.*

- **Count to 5.** When you're done typing a message and you are about to post, sit back, count to five, and then read it again. If it doesn't seem as important as you imagined or you'd be embarrassed to say it to somebody's face, spike the message. If you still want to post, count to five again. Ten seconds is time well spent if it helps you avoid angry messages from irritated message-board users.

Chat Rooms

Chat rooms are like bulletin boards on amphetamine-spiked steroids. If you think it's hard to follow threads on the Silicon Investor boards, drop in on #daytraders (a chat channel I'll discuss in detail later), where snippets of coded conversation rush over your screen in a multicolored cascade of fact, foresight, fib, and outright fantasy.

MSN MoneyCentral Investor, America Online, and Yahoo! Finance have much tamer chat rooms. These are typically amiable discourses that can be fun and educational. The number of participants at any one time will vary from one person muttering to himself all the way up to 1,000 people or more. Some are hosted by investment celebrities; most are hosted by whoever shows up. But the daytrading chat rooms of Internet Relay Chat (IRC) are entirely different beasts, where widely followed speculators tell legions of fans which equities or options to hold onto for half a point and when to dump. Here's an overview of two leading investment-chat sites—the G-rated type—and then the Badlands. Chats on all other financial portals are similar; just click the Chat links on their home pages to start.

Yahoo! Chat

Yahoo! Finance's chat rooms are a lot more easygoing than its message boards are. Because of the portal's size and reach, a decent chat is almost always going on, day or night. Yahoo!'s chat technology is also superior and easier to use than most. You'll need to register at Yahoo! first and then visit *http://chat.yahoo.com/c/roomlist.html*. Click the News And Business link on the top navigation bar, and then choose Biz:StockWatch. That launches a Java chat application. After it loads, you'll find yourself in a virtual room with anywhere from a half dozen to several hundred people. On the right is a pane listing all the chatters. On the bottom is a box of Tools that will help you discover who's chatting, change rooms, or create a private room.

Unlike the bulletin boards noted above, the chat rooms are generally free-for-all conversations with many threads going on simultaneously. This is not a place to hang out if you need to feel focused and in control. Watch for awhile, and then throw out a comment or a question. Someone will usually respond after a few beats. If you strike up a nice conversation with someone, you can start a private conversation. Click his or her name in the Chatters pane, and then click the PM (private message) button at the bottom of the

pane. A window will open, and you can begin a conversation that's not much different from a phone conversation. Occasionally, Yahoo! holds chats hosted by gurus ranging from Individual Investor chief Jonathan Steinberg to TheStreet.com columnist James Cramer and *Fortune* magazine writer Andrew Serwer. Check the Events Calendar at *http://chat.yahoo.com/c/events/calendar.html* for a schedule. If you have a My Yahoo! account, you can click a link to add the event to your Interactive Calendar, and the site will send you a reminder in e-mail.

MSN MoneyCentral Chat

MSN MoneyCentral's open (unmoderated) chats are not as well attended as the ones at Yahoo! are. But its hosted chats are great places to get questions answered and meet fellow investors. From the site's investing home page (*http://moneycentral.msn.com/investor*), click Insight on the top navigation bar, and then click Discussion in the left navigation bar. On that page, you'll see a schedule of hosted events that occur at regular intervals, including a weekly one-hour chat with markets editor Jim Jubak and a weekly one-hour chat with me. The chats usually start with topics and then become open forums for questions. Almost every question is ultimately answered, if not by the host, then by fellow chatters. A group of chat-room regulars has become so friendly that they've actually gotten together in person a couple of times—once on the South Carolina coast and once in New Orleans.

To start, click the event link on the Discussion page at the listed time, or click the Open Chat link on the left navigation bar at any time. Type a handle (nickname) into the text box at the top of the page, and then click Join The Chat. During a hosted chat, you'll see a list of 50 to 150 guests in the right pane; the host's name is bold and has a gavel icon next to it. Type your question or comment in the pane at the bottom of the screen, and then click the blue cloud icon on the right to send your message. You'll see your comment on the screen, and fair questions rarely go unanswered. You have to read fast, though, because comments whiz past. Use the scroll bars on the right side of the pane to display missed comments. To preserve the whole chat, if you're using a Windows-based PC, click inside the chat pane, press Ctrl-A to select all the text, and then press Ctrl-C to copy. Open a word-processing application, and press Ctrl-V to paste the entire chat transcript into a document for later review.

Internet Relay Chat

If you have a taste for frontier life, you'll want to check out investment conversations in Internet Relay Chat, or IRC. This is the home of those infamous daytrading chat rooms that you may have heard the media finger as the birthplace of every ill that has befallen U.S. equity markets in the past half a decade. To get started, you'll need to download

some software and then configure it. Remember that this is the Badlands. It's not supposed to be easy.

Visit mIRC (*http://www.mirc.com*) to obtain the software required to run Internet Relay Chat. (See Figure 12-5.) On the home page, click the Download mIRC link, and then choose the download site closest to you. Follow the directions on the screen for installation.

Run mIRC from your computer as you would any program. On mIRC's first screen, click Introduction to learn more about the program, and then close the dialog boxes by clicking the Close buttons in the upper-right corners. You'll face an Options dialog box. In the middle of the box, type your full name, e-mail address, and nickname. Then choose a server from the drop-down list at the top of the dialog box. In the server drop-down box at the top, choose Othernet: US, MS, Vicksburg, and then click the Connect To IRC Server button.

A short scrolling notice from the server will then appear on your screen, followed by a dialog box titled mIRC Channels Folder. Type "#activetrader" in the narrow entry line, then click the Join button, and you're in. The #activetrader channel bills itself as the #1 Live Free Financial Chat service on the Internet, and it's hard to dispute the claim. It seems to be busy day and night with users from around the world. The denizens seem savvier as a rule than the Yahoo! crowd as well, possibly because it's harder to find. Type a message or comment in the entry box, and it will instantly be visible to everyone on the channel. The channel's organizers have talked about moving their discussion group to the Web as a Java-based chat room; check *http://www.activetrader.com* to check on their progress.

Another top channel to visit is #daytraders. Although these channels look raw compared to Yahoo! and MSN MoneyCentral, they are usually monitored by "Ops," or systems operators, who boot users that employ foul language or go off topic. The Ops' names and directions for contacting them are displayed every time you log on. Press the Status button atop any screen to see them again.

If you like #activetrader and #daytraders, you might consider taking a look at pay-only trading chat rooms. You can find these rooms on the conventional Web at Underground Trader (*http://www.undergroundtrader.com*), Daytrader (*http://www.daytraders.com*), or Mtrader (*http://www.mtrader.com*). At these sites, stocks are announced much like a football coach calls "plays" in what seems like real-time. For that reason, the day trading rooms can read like virtual casinos. But beware: just as in Las Vegas, the odds are stacked against you. Many of the self-appointed gurus making trading-room calls have uncertain motives, and they may not themselves be doing what they're telling you to do. Indeed, it is suspected that many of the gurus hang out in secret chat rooms (or, um, talk by phone) before announcing their picks to the dozen or so big chat rooms. The plays have been pre-determined based on certain criteria. The stock is usually inexpensive with low average

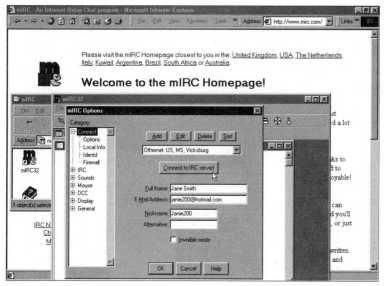

Figure 12-5.   June 20, 1999

To join the IRC community, you must first download and configure mIRC software. After loading, choose Othernet: US, MS, Vicksburg from the Options drop-down box, and then click Connect To IRC Server. After a few seconds, you'll be online. In the dialog box that follows, type "#activetrader" or "#daytraders," then click "join," and you're in business. Have fun, but beware.

daily volume, and it has decent-looking charts showing strong support at the present price. Gurus surreptitiously place rumors about deals in hand at bulletin boards at Silicon Investor or elsewhere to set the scene.

Let's say a stock whose symbol is HYPE is trading at $5 with an average daily volume of 50,000. The guru group starts the day by buying 200 to 5,000 shares each. The price immediately starts lifting because of the multiple orders. The group then begins posting its play in various chat rooms, hoping newbies will buy just on the basis of its recommendation. If 500 people pick up on the concept and each take 100 shares, the volume could easily reach its daily average in just a couple of hours. That will set off alerts on thousands of more legitimate traders' screens. The guru posts on the channel at every uptick to create even more excitement. The stock is now at $7.50. At that point, the guru announces a target of $8.50. Some observers buy at $8, believing there is still 50 cents to be made. Meanwhile the guru and his gang are selling HYPE. When the stock hits $8.38, it begins to drop like a rock. Within seconds, it is at $6.50.

The guru pats himself on the back, declaring to the room, "We hit the target." Few in the room realize that the guru and his gang have set sell limits well below that target. Some observers have scalped an eighth or quarter of a point, and the early buyers maybe made two or three points. But newbies are still holding at the high, rolling their eyes.

They realize they have just become long-term investors, having paid $8 for a stock that in a few days will be back to $5. Tomorrow the newbies looking for counsel will post, "Is anyone still in HYPE?" And they'll get no answer.

Here are some basic rules of the road for chat rooms: assume everyone in the chat room is lying, even though most are actually friendly and helpful. Be wary of rumors that are hard to check out. Beware of posters who repeat a stock idea over and over without any explanation. And don't ever think you're going to double your money in a week by hanging out in a chat room, even if other people tell you that they did. Finding the right stocks at the right time is much harder (and more rewarding) than that.

In sum, talk is cheap, but a misplaced bet on a low-priced, low-volume stock can cost you a small fortune. If you feel that you must trade on someone else's advice, you're much better off paying to subscribe to a legitimate online newsletter with a good public track record, as described in Chapter 7.

20 Seconds in a Daytrading Room

IRC trading chat rooms are not the sorts of places that long-term investors hang their mice. You probably won't get many bites on attempts to talk about the five-year prospects for Wal-Mart. It's almost all about digesting news, interpreting technical indicators, and gambling on hunches. The channel text moves quickly throughout the day as plays are called. With more than 1,000 players in a room, the screen scrolls at the speed of light. Instant news from various feeds and rumors about stock deals, buys, and sells are posted. After trading hours, the pace of the room slows, and subjects vary from opinions about tomorrow's market to politics. Here's a typical conversation:

TheTiger: i have a stock that looks good but it's not ready yet, i'll let you know
Cheetah: SPDE is going BOOM
TheTiger: buys 1,000 SPDE —5 1/4.
IPOshorter: shorts SPDE at 5 ¾
hottubsheik: SPDE UT FIREEEEEEEEEEEEEEEEE
Sheeple: What does UT mean
DaDog: SPDE just announced a deal with CSCO
BocaMan: uptick DUH!!!!!!!!
Treeman: SPDE 7 it is going to run
DaDog: SPDE is shaking
Scamman: JoeK is doing the CSCO deal on CNBC YES!!!!!!!!
Sheeple: What is SPDE target Tiger?
TheTiger: SPDE 8 we were early, we hooked one, we banked

Part IV

Managing Your Portfolio

Chapter 13

Buying and Tracking Stocks

My first experience with a stock broker came in 1982, soon after I was married. My wife, Ellen, and I had a short appointment at Dean Witter's sleek, black-on-black Universal City office. That meeting culminated in our purchase of a single Franklin mutual fund with a 5% load. It proceeded to go straight down, and we quickly realized that we had been over-charged and under-advised. (If we had put the same $10,000 into Wal-Mart stock, the investment would be worth $1.5 million today.)

Later we had successful stock and fund accounts at other full-service brokerages for our buy-and-hold strategies, but we never found a truly good value. Then the pioneering Lombard Institutional Brokerage burst upon the nascent online scene around 1994 with the stunning price point of $19.95 a trade. The glory of cheap transactions made through a browser instead of a broker soon faded, however. I proceeded to make a mistake common to many investors new to the online world then. I clicked way too many buttons, turning those supposedly cheap trades into expensive losses.

Five years later in the online revolution, investors have gotten a lot more sophisticated about taking advantage of low-cost trading—a factor that no doubt has provided plenty of fuel to the 1990s bull market. Indeed, the most reliable way to leverage the Net isn't by investing in Internet stocks; it's by investing through strong, experienced, Internet-powered brokers such as E*Trade, Charles Schwab, and Brown & Co. Today you can buy and sell with confidence for as little as $5 a trade, which is a fraction of the price even discount brokerages charged a few years ago.

I'm not saying that price is the only factor to consider when choosing a brokerage or that Internet trading is perfect. Virtually every online trader can tell grim tales of system failures, lost account documents, trades so slow to execute that thousands of dollars in potential profits were lost, and customer-service phone numbers that required interminable waits. Visit the online-brokerage bulletin boards at Silicon Investor, and you'll find horror stories fit for a Stephen King novel on just about any outfit you can name.

Still, thousands of investors open online accounts every month, and the brokerage business has changed forever. Gomez Advisors, an e-commerce research service, reports that investors will hold 10 million online accounts by the end of 1999—a jump of 47% from the previous year. More than 30,000 investors were hitting Charles Schwab's site each morning in mid-1999. Even mighty Merrill Lynch has reluctantly joined the revolution, promising to open up low-cost online trading by late 1999 for customers who wish to bypass its sales force. It has proposed to munge the best of the full-service, discount, and online brokerage models into a service that allows investors to make an unlimited number of trades for a flat fee online. This plan, coupled with the fact that users will still have access to the guiding hand of a human broker at moments of uncertainty, shows real promise.

If you become a dedicated yeartrader to buy and sell the right stocks at the right time, as described in Part I, you'll be happy with almost any first-tier online broker. If you're just starting out, set your expectations low. Trading online is definitely not as easy as working with a caring, intelligent human being at a good full-service brokerage. But it's not nearly as expensive either, and you'll never have a high-pressure salesperson calling you at all hours, pitching a firm's latest underwriting project masquerading as a research-department idea.

If you're an investor, you are unlikely ever to have the worries about system outages or execution problems that are the bane of daytraders' interactions with online brokers. Even if you ultimately decide to trade much more frequently, it's not hard to minimize the potential damage from online-trading problems and enjoy all the benefits. Some online investors open accounts with more than one firm so that they have a backup should their primary brokers experience problems. Others largely eschew market orders in favor of limit orders to avoid trading at unfavorable prices if execution is slow. Although no broker is problem-free, many investors have learned that it pays to stick with the biggest brokers with long histories of handling complex documentation.

The bottom line: your choice of brokerage isn't nearly as important as your choice of stocks and holding period. If you buy the right shares at the right time and elect to hold them for the right number of weeks or months, even Attila the Broker will probably do just fine. Most of the terror tales you hear about online brokerages stem from

investors' misunderstanding the role technology plays in making good trades. The most important trading tool is between your ears.

First I'll discuss what to seek in an online broker and look at a few of the leading firms. Then I'll comment on the trend toward trading directly in the market via new electronic communications networks, and I'll conclude by examining the best portfolio managers on the Web.

Choosing an Internet Broker

By mid-1999, the number of online brokers listed at the financial-services aggregation site Investorama (*http://www.investorama.com*) had grown to 72, while Yahoo! Finance's online-brokerage page listed 93. This explosion can only mean that it must be incredibly easy to set up an online brokerage—a fact that should give you pause about moving your account to the latest new company with a nice-looking Web site, low prices, and a promise of fast fills. They're practically the corner grocery store of the digital age.

Which one is right for you? The answer is surprisingly simple, whether you're an active or infrequent trader. Select the online brokerage that couples the lowest trading costs with the most reliable service. And don't buy anything you don't need, such as streaming real-time quotes.

Don't fret about making exactly the right choice either. Think about the top-tier online brokers as you would Ford, General Motors, Chrysler, and Toyota. The automakers all sell products—cars and trucks—that are more similar than they are different. Each of the products is configured slightly differently in its exterior color, interior trim, or engine size. But ultimately each is just a set of four wheels packaged with a different marketing campaign. Likewise, all the online brokers essentially sell one product: a trade. Except for a few standouts such as E*Trade and Schwab, the variations in cost, presentation, customer service, research, and data availability are really minor.

Rating Services

Because the number, variety, and quality of online brokerages changes so frequently, it's difficult to put a stake in the ground and declare one or two brokers right for everyone. Almost any of the top 10 firms will suit most purposes. To find the one that's best for your needs, visit one of several publications that review and rate brokerages regularly whenever you're ready to make your first choice or switch to another broker. Here are the top reviewers.

Gomez Advisors (*http://www.gomez.com/Finance/Brokers/Scorecard/*). Founded by a former Forrester Research e-commerce analyst, Gomez had the clever insight that consumers and companies might be confused about the plethora of brokerage choices on the Internet. In 1997, the firm launched its first Internet Brokerage Scorecard. The site, shown in Figure 13-1, rated 27 online firms, and it's been among the best sources of objective information about the industry since. (The site also rates banking, travel, shopping, and auction sites on the Web.) It names a top Web broker each quarter, but it also ranks all sites by ease of use, customer confidence, on-site resources, relationship services, and overall cost. In addition, Gomez divides the brokerages by customer profile, helping you decide on the best brokerage, depending on whether you consider yourself a Hyper-Active Trader, a Serious Investor, a Life-Goal Planner, or a One-Stop Shopper. Its top five choices in June 1999 were E*Trade (*http://www.etrade.com*), National Discount Brokers (*http://www.ndb.com*), Charles Schwab (*http://www.schwab.com*), DLJdirect (*http://www.dljdirect.com*), and Discover Brokerage (*http://www.discoverbrokerage.com*).

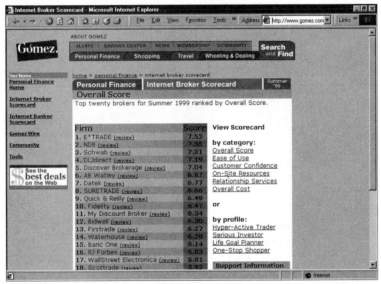

Figure 13-1.   June 23, 1999

Gomez Advisors has emerged as the leading ratings service on the Internet. Its Internet Broker Scorecard ranks Web-powered brokers by a variety of metrics, and it helps you determine the best service for your style of investing.

SmartMoney.com (*http://www.smartmoney.com/si/brokers/online/*). The online version of the personal-finance magazine has done a superb job of rating online brokers ever since anyone started caring about them. It rates brokerages by the following criteria:

- commission costs
- amount of real-time data
- abundance and availability of account information (for example, whether your balance updates in real time or once a day)
- fees (for example, the cost of wire transfers)
- number of products under one roof (for example, access to initial public offerings, mutual funds, and bonds)
- research (for example, institutional reports from full-service brokerages)
- services (for example, free check-writing and debit cards)

The site has a terrific interactive tool that allows you to specify the information you care about the most to come up with a personalized ranking. You can find the tool by clicking the Discount link at the top of the home page and then clicking Complete Rankings: A Sortable Table on the subsequent page. Its own top five in the mid-1999 survey were QuickWay Net (*http://www.quickwaynet.com*), SureTrade (*http://www.suretrade.com*), Web Street Securities (*http://www.webstreet.com*), Discover Brokerage, Waterhouse Securities (*http://www.waterhouse.com*), and Datek (*http://www.datek.com*). I ran the interactive test and ranked the brokers by their trading costs rather than services, research, or breadth of products. My top-ranked sites turned out to be Waterhouse, SureTrade, QuickWay Net, and Brown & Co. (*www.brownco.com*). The site also offers a fun application, called the BrokerMeter, that shows which sites are running fastest on any given day (*http://www.smartmoney.com/si/brokermeter/*).

Barron's Online (*http://www.barrons.com*). The estimable weekly magazine of Wall Street opinion runs a cover story once a year, typically in the spring, on the top online brokerages. It's a tour-de-force examination of the elements that serious, but not overachieving, investors look for in a Web brokerage. You can subscribe to the Web site to view its archives easily or find the relevant issues at a local library for free. In the survey from March 1999, the magazine rated these sites as the top 10: DLJdirect, Discover, National Discount Brokers, Web Street Securities, Datek, E*Trade, A.B. Watley Ultimate (*http://www.abwatley.com*), SureTrade, Charles Schwab, and Muriel Siebert (*http://www.msiebert.com*).

Narrowing Down

Many of these online brokerages offer a dazzling amount of high-level research, analytical tools, news feeds, and mutual funds. But if all you really want is a trade, do you really need to pay for all the infrastructure required to produce and maintain that other stuff, when so much is available at the top financial portals for free? It depends. First I'll list reasons to consider a top-tier brokerage, and then I'll make the case for going with a brokerage that just offers the least-expensive trades.

One-Stop Shops: E*Trade, Charles Schwab, Fidelity, DLJdirect

If you crave all the latest bells and whistles—and there's no reason why you shouldn't—consider E*Trade, Charles Schwab, DLJdirect, Fidelity (*http://www.fidelity.com*), or Discover. All were charging $15 to $29 for the lowest-priced market orders placed online in mid-1999. I use Fidelity for my individual retirement account and Schwab, shown in Figure 13-2, for two other accounts. Each of these five brokerages offers nearly every financial convenience imaginable, including credit or debit cards, research, and access to IPOs. They all also have hundreds of well-informed agents who answer the phone promptly at all hours of the day and on weekends. As long as your actual trades are made on the Web site, you get the low Internet-trade price even if you spent an hour on the phone asking a broker questions.

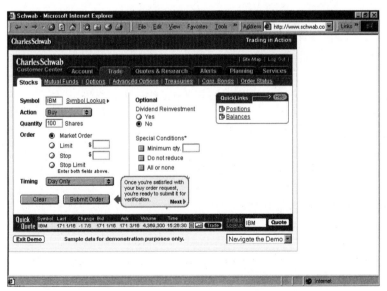

Figure 13-2.   June 23, 1999

Most online brokerage sites offer step-by-step demonstrations. The Charles Schwab demo explains how to enter a trade for 100 shares of IBM. The site offers real-time quotes and balances on the trading page, which is a big plus.

Schwab, Fidelity, and Waterhouse also have retail outlets across the country, and they encourage online customers to call or stop by with questions. Not confident with computers? Drop by a Schwab office and say you'd like to sign up for an online account, but you need some help first. A Schwab representative can walk you through the Web site and even help you make a trade right there in the office. "Our goal is fully integrated service in person, over the phone or online," said a Schwab spokesperson. "It's very difficult to have a relationship just through a computer monitor." To encourage that bond, Schwab has gone the extra step to create Schwab Signature Gold for online customers who make at least 24 to 47 trades a year or have at least $500,000 in Schwab accounts. Qualifying customers get toll-free numbers that link them to their own eight-person broker teams and free high-level research, among other benefits.

E*Trade, in turn, has done more than any other brokerage to push the envelope on creating a holistic financial experience online. The brokerage offers good educational content, a clean trading interface, and a staggering array of products (mutual funds, bonds, options, loans, IPOs, and banking). Moreover, the company has moved fast both to take the online trading revolution overseas and to bring IPOs to the private investor. E*Trade has suffered a few well-publicized site outages, to be sure. But such growing pains should be expected from a technology that's developing at the speed of light around the globe. The problems from the past have seriously irked active traders, but they would be of little consequence to an investor or yeartrader.

Brown & Co.: Cheap and Reliable

If you're the kind of person who buys fresh bread at a bakery, flowers at a florist, and meat at a butcher instead of buying everything at a supermarket, then as an investor all you will probably care about is finding a responsible brokerage that's good at making low-cost trades. One top choice is Brown & Co. (*http://www.brownco.com*), which is a unit of the nation's second-largest bank, Chase Manhattan Bank.

Brown requires a minimum opening balance of $15,000 and doesn't typically rate highly overall in the Gomez or SmartMoney surveys because of its lack of frills. But it has staked out a nice niche as low-cost leader, with $5 market orders for less than 5,000 shares of any equity and equally low prices for options. The site offers low margin rates, real-time quotes, and up-to-the-minute account balances—but no analytical tools or advice. Don't confuse a lack of products for a lack of service, however. I have used Brown for two years and been amazed at the high level of customer attention despite the low prices. Brown isn't just for the little guy either. A manager of a multimillion-dollar hedge fund who runs his block trades through Goldman Sachs told me that he uses Brown for his personal account due to its solid order handling and low cost.

Initial Public Offerings (IPOs)

In 1998, online brokerages finally broke the stranglehold traditional brokerages held on the shares of companies going public for the first time. So many initial public offerings of Internet stocks in 1998 and 1999 shot to the moon on their first day of trading that new investors got the mistaken impression that all IPOs were a ticket to instant riches. The truth is far different, because historically IPOs have dramatically underperformed the broad-market averages. One academic study published in 1998 showed that the better a stock performed in its first week as an IPO, the worse it performed in ensuing years. Nevertheless, the public's thirst has continued unabated. Here's a quick guide to finding and snaring the best IPOs online.

- **Find the best businesses.** Generally only the best private companies with unique products and business plans will have knockout IPOs. To find the coolest high-tech IPOs, read Red Herring magazine regularly at *http://www.redherring.com*. It's the voice of the venture-capital community in Silicon Valley.

- **Find the new IPOs.** Visit Renaissance Capital at *http://www.ipo-fund.com* regularly to track when a company first announces plans to go public, files a prospectus, and sets an offering date and price. (Figure 13-3 shows some examples.) The site has a lot of competitors (for example, IPO Monitor at *http://www.ipomonitor.com* and IPO Central at *http://www.ipocentral.com*), but Renaissance seems to stay a step ahead of them. On its home page, focus on the This Week, Next Week, and Coming Attractions links.

- **Stick with the best underwriters.** The list of new IPOs can be long. To narrow the field, investigate only the ones with the highest-quality underwriters—well-known names such as BancBoston Robertson Stephens, Hambrecht & Quist, CS First Boston, and B.T. Alex Brown. IPOs backed by these firms are the best supported with institutional purchasing and high-powered analyst recommendations after the first day of trading.

- **Read the prospectus.** Each entry at Renaissance and other sites includes a link to the company's Form S-1, or prospectus, at EDGAR Online (*http://www.edgar-online.com*). Read it carefully, as described in Chapter 9, paying particular attention to the risk factors.

- **Demand the best genes.** The best venture-capital companies get to invest in the best young firms, and they should be listed in the prospectus. Top names include Kleiner Perkins (Amazon.com), Sequoia Capital (3Com, Apple), Accell Partners (RealNetworks), Hummer Winblad, Mohr Davidow (Rambus), and Benchmark Capital (eBay).

- **Demand the best management.** Read the management biographies in the S-1 closely. Many young firms have experienced executives with long track records of success at other firms.

- **Bid for shares.** Each online brokerage hands out its allotment of IPO shares differently. Most get very few shares and distribute them upon request on a first-come, first-served basis following an e-mail message to all clients; others distribute them only to their biggest clients. Ask the customer service representative at your brokerage for the rules.

- **Wait awhile if you miss out.** If you don't get the low-cost IPO shares, wait a few days, weeks, or months before you buy shares on the open market. Very few IPOs don't come back to Earth after an initial moon shot. Amazon.com traded near its IPO price for weeks after going public, but it shot up 5,900% over the next two years; eBay traded at less than half its opening-day price a month after going public, but it rose 1,260% over the next eight months. But beware: more than half of all stocks trade below their IPO price after two years. Make sure you're investing in a *company* and not just an interesting product or concept.

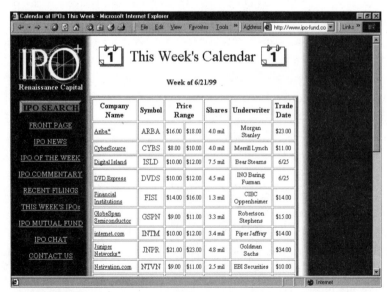

Figure 13-3.   June 25, 1999

*The IPO calendar at Renaissance Capital's site (*http://www.ipo-fund.com*) is among the most comprehensive on the Web. Check out the IPOs with the best underwriters and venture-capital backers. If you don't get an allotment of shares from your online brokerage, wait a few days or weeks before you buy to get the next best prices.*

Getting Started

To get started in choosing an online brokerage, visit Gomez Advisors and Smart-money.com, as noted above, and pick a couple of sites for your short list. Before you make your final choice, run through these checks:

- Visit each site and try its online demo, if one's available. (Schwab and National Discount Brokers have two of the best demos.) Does the site feel good to you? Is it working smoothly? Get quotes for stocks and options, and see how you like the presentation. Read the free educational materials, if any. Are they clear and friendly? Try all of these at different times of day. If the site is balky when you're a guest, it'll also be balky when you're a customer. .

- Call the brokerage, and talk to a sales agent. Tell him or her that you're considering signing up, and ask some questions. See if they can explain the commission schedule succinctly, for example, or describe their policy on stop limits and margin. Did the phone ring a long time, and were the brokers courteous? First impressions matter. You're entrusting these people with your money—it's not a game. Make sure you really like them from the start.

- Visit Silicon Investor, The Motley Fool, and Yahoo! Messages. Search for the name of a brokerage that interests you, and then read through the relevant posts. Almost everything you read will be a complaint, but you'll quickly get a feel for which appear legitimate and which are irrelevant. Post your own questions to the board, follow up on any questions you see, and leverage the community for your purposes.

When you've finally chosen a broker, click the button in the firm's Web site that is labelled Open An Account. Some brokerages will allow you to open the account online and start trading right away on credit. If you want to trade on margin (that is, with borrowed money) or trade options, you'll need to specify on your forms that you understand exactly what those techniques entail. If you're sending money by check or wire transfer from another brokerage or bank account, the money winds up in a money-market fund at your new brokerage. Then you're off to the races. If there's a problem transferring funds, such as it taking longer than you believe is reasonable, you should consider it a red flag. Countless message-board complaints about online brokerages start with some variation of this line: "I can't believe they lost my paperwork and now no one knows where my money is."

Before you start trading, read the site's online documentation or call an agent to make sure you understand how every button on every form on the trading pages works. It's not brain surgery, but you might find that certain labels for functions have different meanings than you are used to. Also make sure you know your new brokerage's lingo; read its online definitions of terms such as stop limit, stop loss, and buying power. Start out slow, with a single trade, and then branch out and explore every nook of the site. It's your new trading floor—have fun!

Advanced Online Trading—ECNs

When you trade through a conventional online broker, all you're really doing is using the Internet to contact a traditional broker. You still must rely on a human being to execute your trade quickly in the background and at the best possible price. Brokers sometimes experience trading delays, and they sometimes sell orders to market makers who, in turn, might delay placing the trade until they can make a greater profit—at the investor's expense.

Firms such as A.B. Watley (*http://www.abwatley.com*), CyBerCorp (*http://www.cybercorp.com*), and TradeScape.com (*http://www.tradescape.com*) propose to put private, active-trading stock speculators on a par with the pros by allowing them to place trades into the market without intermediaries. Just click the Buy button, and your trade is placed. A.B. Watley claims that orders from its Ultimate Trader service typically reach their destinations in less than a second, and confirmation time averages three to four seconds. This kind of speed might not mean much to the long-term investor, or yeartrader, but it's the sort of thing that daytraders crave.

Perhaps more compelling is the prospect that executions won't just be faster, they'll be better because they're placed through *electronic communications networks,* or ECNs. These are private, alternative stock markets where buyers and sellers are matched up directly. Without an intermediary, there's no spread, which is typically that difference of 15¢ or more between the price you pay for a Nasdaq-traded stock and the price at which you could sell it right away. Thus, direct trades through ECNs can save a daytrader a quarter-point or more per transaction. These amounts add up quickly, particularly for active traders of large blocks of stocks.

Although that sounds cool, there are plenty of caveats. ECNs are new, and most harbor so few traders that they're too illiquid for the real professionals to bother with. It's the Wall Street equivalent of trading stocks directly with people in a single apartment building—sort of an eBay of investments. "Just try to sell 10,000 shares of Yahoo! through an ECN," sneered one private fund manager I know, who won't let anyone but seasoned Wall Street brokerage traders handle his orders. "You can't do it." He said the traditional brokerages might charge a bit more—as much as two cents a share, or $200 for a 10,000-share order—but they know exactly how to play the game of cat and mouse with other traders. The pros, he contended, are picking the pockets of the dilettante daytraders who think they're getting a good deal by going solo on the ECNs.

CyBerCorp and its rivals try to overcome their smaller sizes by placing their customers' trades with several ECNs (and all market makers) at once. Meanwhile, the ECNs are rapidly gaining the scale that they'll need to succeed. They accounted for 18% of all Nasdaq trade executions in the first quarter of 1999, according to an estimate by E-Offering, a new investment bank.

Despite their attractions, the direct-to-ECN brokerages do not benefit most private investors. You don't need an ECN for market orders, for instance, and there's a lot more to understand about person-to-person trading than just real-time pricing. To really mix it up with the active-trading sharks, you need access to (and an understanding of) Nasdaq Level II screens, which list all advertised bids and asks for stocks, as well as the names of the institutions behind them.

Before you scramble to determine whether a Level II screen is exactly what you've been missing, be warned one more time. Even many pros admit it is easy to misinterpret the simplest market data. The more you try to comprehend, the more you end up over-trading your way into costly mistakes. This is especially a problem in the low-volume periods before and after regular Wall Street trading hours. One hedge-fund manager sums up the disconnect between novice stock speculators—who long for cheaper, faster trades—and their real-world results in this manner: "In the end, *when and where* you trade is not as important as *how and what* you trade."

Online Portfolio Managers

After you've made several trades over a few months or a year at one or more brokerages, you'll discover that it can be difficult to determine exactly how you're doing. You may know how much money you started with at each brokerage. But it can be hard to say with authority exactly what your rate of return has been on any particular stock after splits, spin-offs, dividend payments, multiple purchases or sales of the stock, and interest

payments on money-market funds. The task grows exponentially more complex if you try to determine the return on each stock in each of your accounts.

Few, if any, online brokerages provide this data to customers because it's relatively hard for them to track your positions and do the math. Indeed, not many brokerages show much more than your current positions and the most recent day's changes. (Even that data is typically delayed a day.) Oddly, few brokerages keep more than six months of history on your transactions. (Cynics say that the brokerages could do better, but they really don't want you to know how you're doing.)

Moreover, few brokerages help you obtain a good understanding of the technical changes in your stocks' price trends or the fundamental changes in your companies' businesses. After reading Chapters 8 through 11, you might well want to know when your stocks are crossing above or below their moving averages, whether they've been upgraded by analysts, whether their projected earnings growth rate is falling or rising, or whether a company whose shares you own has filed an important SEC document. And you might want to know if there are any lively discussions about your stocks at online bulletin boards.

Only two financial portals on the Web do a great job of helping you analyze your stock and mutual-fund portfolios dynamically and historically: MSN MoneyCentral and ClearStation. All the rest are in third place, though each has its advantages. Yahoo! Finance offers good integration with its Yahoo! Pager alerts and My Yahoo! systems. CBS MarketWatch offers tight integration with BigCharts, insider trades, option chains, and Multex.com research. TheStreet.com offers a nice distinction between long and short positions, options, and mutual funds. Explore them all before you settle on one. I'll shine a spotlight on the top two.

MSN MoneyCentral

The Portfolio Manager section at MSN MoneyCentral, shown in Figure 13-4, wins reviews against its Web rivals every year in the top financial magazines' roundups. This is largely because it is software that tracks *transactions*—not just a Web page that records simple purchases and sales. It can therefore perform all sorts of tricks that Web pages can't, including sorts, dynamic updates, automatic split calculation, currency conversion, multiple views, drag-and-drop column changes, data analysis, and calculation of internal rates of return. In addition, the Portfolio Manager allows you to easily create model portfolios like those I described in Chapters 1 through 4. You can type 10 ticker symbols into a Watch Portfolio dialog box, and specify that you want to allocate $20,000 evenly across their current (or historical) prices. In seconds, you will have an instant portfolio. Finally, Portfolio Manager allows you to download transaction data from most top online brokerages. This feature relieves you of the need to manually type all of your buys and sells. (One caveat: like all MSN MoneyCentral software, the Portfolio Manager does not work on Apple Macintosh or iMac systems.)

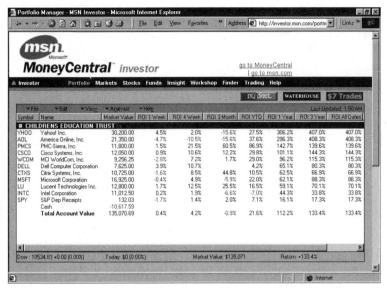

Figure 13-4.   June 25, 1999

The MSN MoneyCentral Portfolio Manager allows you to track numerous types of securities by dozens of criteria, including return on investment, over numerous periods. Here stocks in a portfolio are ranked by year-to-date ROI. Navigation aids to creating accounts or adding stocks are close at hand.

In contrast, most portfolio trackers on the Web present users with a series of empty boxes to fill in with ticker symbols, purchase prices, dates, and commissions. You can then see daily or inception-to-date changes in your portfolio, but you typically cannot sort them, see return calculations, or see more than three or four standard views of the data. None of these trackers handles splits or dividends, and few track options or bonds.

Getting Started

To start tracking a portfolio, visit MSN MoneyCentral (*http://moneycentral.msn.com*) and click the Your Portfolio link. You are required to register with a unique user name and password because you will later be given the option of storing your portfolio on MSN's computers. If you accept this option, you will be able to see your portfolio as you roam throughout the day from your home to your office to an office across the world.

If it's the first time you've visited MSN MoneyCentral, you will also have to download software as instructed; it takes about five minutes over a 28.8-Kbps modem. Once the software is loaded, choose New Account from the File menu. Then follow the directions in the New Account Wizard. You can set up a Regular Account (for stocks you really own), a Watch Account (for stocks you want to observe), or an Imported Account (for

stocks whose data you will pull down from an online broker, Microsoft Money, Quicken, Yahoo! Finance, or Quicken.com).

If you create a Regular Account, you'll need to name the account, press Next, and then type your holdings into the Transactions dialog box that appears next. Explore all the options behind each drop-down box on this page. For instance, in the Symbol box, you can choose from ticker symbols you've entered previously. In the Type box, you can choose among Stock, Bond, Certificate of Deposit, Employee Stock Option, Money Market Fund, Mutual Fund, Option, or Warrant. The Portfolio Manager handles each differently. Next comes the Activity box, in which options include Buy, Sell, Add Shares, Short Sell, Cover Short, and Add Dividends. The Date and Share Price boxes work together; once you enter a transaction date, a button appears that allows you to automatically complete the Share Price box with the closing price of the stock on that date. Complete the Commission box, and then press Record Another to complete your portfolio.

Advisor FYI

If you keep a portfolio at MoneyCentral, you'll notice a little FYI flag occasionally next to some of your stocks. Click that link, and you'll discover one of the most valuable features of the site: a page containing a comprehensive list of interesting technical, fundamental, or news events that have occurred in relation to that company or its stock over the past day, month, and year. For instance, on July 23, 1999, the Advisor FYI for AT&T told me that the company planned to announce earnings on July 29, that the stock's relative strength was decreasing, that its consensus earnings estimate was falling, that a Goldman Sachs analyst had elevated it to his recommended list, that it had filed two SEC documents, that its P/E ratio was well above its industry's average, and that it had been mentioned in five MoneyCentral Investor articles in the past four months.

You can follow up by clicking links to see relevant data (for example, the earnings-estimate page or the SEC document) or clicking a Description link that explains exactly why you should be interested in that bit of information. There's no excuse for being in the dark about your stocks or funds anymore. The feature is also available from the Stock Research area of the site. Click Stocks on the top navigation bar, then click Advisor FYI on the left navigation bar, type a symbol into the text box, and click Go. (To see all stocks that match an Advisor FYI "trigger" at any time, visit the site's Investment Finder, create a screen, and choose from the Advisor FYI criteria listed at the bottom of the Field Name menu. See Appendix A for details on using Investment Finder.)

If you choose to create a Watch Account, you'll need to name the account, and then type the ticker symbols of the stocks you wish to watch into the text box on that page. If you then click the Model Portfolio option, you can choose to either record the purchase of 100 shares, or $10,000 worth, of each stock, or you can create a portfolio that evenly distributes any amount of money across the stocks. Then you can set the date on which those purchases should be made—ranging from the current date to a date in the past. For instance, type the symbols for Microsoft, Cisco Systems, Intel, Dell Computer, and EMC in the first box. Choose Model Portfolio, ask the software to spread $10,000 across those stocks using the last price on January 1, 1991, and press Next. You'll end up on the Portfolio Manager screen, viewing how much that portfolio would have grown by the current date. (Through June 24, 1999, that portfolio value had risen a hundredfold to $1.03 million.)

If you choose Import, follow the instructions for importing your data from the five sources listed above. This is the most convenient way of getting started in the Portfolio Manager because it does not require you to type any data. It makes switching from Yahoo! Finance or Quicken a snap, if you decide that you prefer this portfolio tracker. By the middle of 1999, six brokerages were part of the Open Financial Exchange and therefore capable of exporting transaction data directly to MSN: Charles Schwab, E*Trade, DLJdirect, Waterhouse, Fidelity, and Discover. This feature is so cool that it might well tip the balance if you are otherwise on the fence in choosing between one of these brokers and another.

Advanced Features

Next explore all of the advanced features of the Portfolio Manager by opening the menus across the top of the page (File, Edit, View, and Analysis). If you have questions, explore the Help menu; its How Do I? link leads to a page that describes every feature of the software in step-by-step detail. Here are just a few of the more interesting features:

- From the File menu, choose Export to export data from any or all accounts to a tab-delimited file, which you can then open in Excel and manipulate.

- From the File menu, choose Update Automatically to have the Portfolio Manager grab new prices from the Web at regular intervals. The default interval is five minutes, but you can choose the Preferences option on the Edit menu and change the interval to as short as one minute.

- From the Edit Menu, choose Online Trading when your cursor is on a stock in an account that you've imported from a broker. That broker's home page appears. (You then have to log in to the broker's site to actually trade.)

- From the Edit Menu, choose Investment Details when your cursor is on a stock, and you can see a Summary of returns, all past Transactions for the stock, and a

page of Notes to yourself. On the Notes tab, you can enter a Target Price for the stock that will show up as a column to remind you to buy or sell an investment when the target price is reached.

- From the Analysis Menu, you can jump to any MoneyCentral Investor page of data about a stock, including Historical Charts, News, Advisor FYI, Research Wizard, and Insider Trading. Some of these can also be reached by right-clicking a security in the Portfolio Manager and selecting an option on the pop-up menu. Or you can jump to News and Advisor FYIs instantly by clicking links in their very own Portfolio Manager columns.

- From the Analysis Menu, try the Portfolio Review and Portfolio Charting options. The review shows a highly detailed, X-ray view of your entire portfolio, giving the average market capitalization of your stocks, your risk profile, your asset allocation, and your best and worst trades of the month and year. Figure 13-5 shows an example. If you decide that your asset allocation is out of whack and you'd like to explore it further, click its link. The Portfolio Manager changes its column set to offer you a closer view of your balance between equity, income, and cash. It is remarkable.

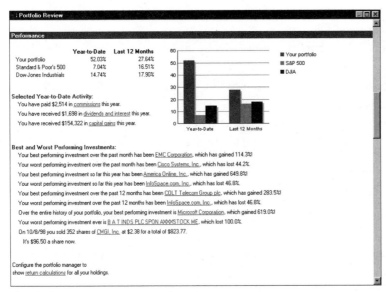

Figure 13-5.   **June 24, 1999**

MSN MoneyCentral's Portfolio Review features clear views of your holdings from many angles, including risk and asset allocation. In the Performance section, you'll learn which investments have done best over various periods. Most clever (or aggravating) is the line listing the security that's done best since you sold it.

- From the Accounts menu, you can select accounts to view, and choose whether to see securities you sold along with your current portfolio. You can also choose to group all of your investments by risk, capitalization, position, or other categories to gain a new perspective on your holdings.

- From the Columns menu, you can choose from nine preset views of your data, including Valuation, Fundamentals, Performance, Return Calculations, and more. You can also mix and match columns from each to create your own custom view. Many investors find the Return Calculations extremely useful. These show how each investment has performed over the past week, month, quarter, year-to-date, one year, or three years. Click a column head to sort all the securities by a particular factor.

- To quickly add a security into any account, type its ticker symbol into the box at the bottom of the page, and then click Enter Symbols.

In summary, this Portfolio Manager—perhaps more than any other software on the Web except Investment Finder—levels the playing field between professional and private investors.

ClearStation

ClearStation sets itself apart from competitors by creating tools that help investors gain perspective on their data. The site's Portfolio Manager, shown in Figure 13-6, is the best on the Web that does not require a software download. What's cool: it does all the hard work for you, particularly for watch portfolios. After clicking the Add A Portfolio link, you can just type the ticker symbols of stocks that interest you in the text box, and then click Create Portfolio. If you accept the default choices, ClearStation automatically builds your portfolio with $10,000 invested in each stock at the market price with a $12 commission.

After you click Finish Portfolio Build, the site creates the portfolio. The initial view is standard, but below your portfolios are lists of messages and news items for each stock. Moreover, every time you return to ClearStation's home page, you'll see a long list of technical alerts on your stocks with topics that range from price breakouts to analyst upgrades to pending split dates.

By now it should be clear that online brokerages and portfolio managers offer terrific advantages to private investors: lower costs, greater visibility, and more convenience. Thus, they have radically changed the rules of the game in the scant six years since the Web exploded into prominence in 1993. Next let's take a look at ways to put all of these concepts together into a trading strategy that achieves your objectives but takes up as little time as possible.

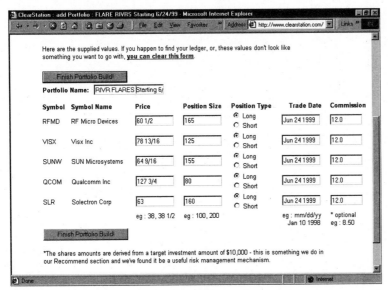

Here are the supplied values. If you happen to find your ledger, or, these values don't look like something you want to go with, **you can clear this form**.

Finish Portfolio Build!

Portfolio Name: RIVR FLARES Starting 6/

Symbol	Symbol Name	Price	Position Size	Position Type	Trade Date	Commission
RFMD	RF Micro Devices	60 1/2	165	● Long ○ Short	Jun 24 1999	12.0
VISX	Visx Inc	78 13/16	125	● Long ○ Short	Jun 24 1999	12.0
SUNW	SUN Microsystems	64 9/16	155	● Long ○ Short	Jun 24 1999	12.0
QCOM	Qualcomm Inc	127 3/4	80	● Long ○ Short	Jun 24 1999	12.0
SLR	Solectron Corp	63	160	● Long ○ Short	Jun 24 1999	12.0
		eg : 38, 38 1/2	eg : 100, 200		eg : mm/dd/yy Jan 10 1998	* optional eg : 8.50

Finish Portfolio Build!

*The shares amounts are derived from a target investment amount of $10,000 - this is something we do in our Recommend section and we've found it be a useful risk management mechanism.

Figure 13-6.   June 25, 1999

ClearStation will create a portfolio if you supply the ticker symbols. If you accept the default values, the software assumes you'll want $10,000 allotments of each stock bought on the current date. You can change those values, but for a watch portfolio, those are all great, time-saving assumptions.

Chapter 14

The 30-Minute Investor

Today we have an unprecedented amount of freedom to set the course of our own financial lives. No longer is investing in public companies a dark art practiced behind closed doors only by specialists for staggering fees. You have learned in this book that anyone with access to the Internet and an inexpensive personal computer can now research stocks from the comfort of home, make trades in a flash, and reap astounding benefits at the intersection of capitalism and communication.

Yet most of us don't want to make careers out of improving and monitoring our investment portfolios. We want to spend enough time to make choices that are good enough, and then we want to go on to other matters such as spending time with our families, friends, and hobbies. The market's gyrations can be entertaining, but they're seldom enthralling.

So here are some suggestions on fitting the online-investing techniques in this book into your lifestyle. Mix and match them to find the right fit for you.

One caveat: you're on your own when it comes to determining how much risk you wish to assume in your portfolio. Just keep in mind that high returns rarely come without high risk, and you may not know how much risk is intolerable until you experience it at exactly the wrong moment.

Creating a Portfolio

There are roughly 8,700 stocks available for purchase on U.S. exchanges at any given time. In the first four chapters of this book, I explained ways to use MSN MoneyCentral's stock-screening engine, called Investment Finder, to apply statistical criteria against all those stocks as a filter—much like a trawler captain uses a net to capture slippery fish in the ocean.

The big idea is to put the odds for success in your favor by using proven statistical stock-picking criteria rather than your instincts about the future of drugs, technology, or industrial policy. If you'll allow me to switch metaphors from sea to sport, you need to become like major-league baseball managers who bring in the southpaw from the bullpen to pitch to the left-handed power hitter because that's the best percentage play. In other words, there's little to be gained from playing hunches.

If you play the percentages, you'll be right more times than you're wrong, and you'll make much more money on your successful stock picks than you'll lose on those that inevitably go sour. Mark Minnervini, chief investment strategist of QuanTech, a quantitative money-management group in Connecticut, said in an interview that "the problem with most investors is that they'd rather be right all the time than make money. Pros don't get personal. They employ strategies. Amateurs let emotions and ego get involved."

Ideal Portfolio: 7 to 15 Names

Most academic studies on managing investment portfolios agree that the typical investor doesn't need to own more than 10 to 20 stocks—even in a portfolio of up to $1 million. The opposing argument contends that owning 50 stocks or more makes it less likely that the collapse of any individual stock will destroy your portfolio. Yet the problem with owning too many stocks is the same as the one you'd have as a teacher with too many children in a classroom: it's hard to keep track of them all. Bill Gates, co-founder of Microsoft, didn't get to be a multi-gazillionaire by owning 30 stocks. He became the world's richest man by essentially owning just one. Warren Buffett, touted as the world's most successful investor, owns meaningful stakes in fewer than 10 public companies at a time.

More specifically, I have tested hundreds of model portfolios against historical data with a varying number of stocks in each. I can affirm without any hesitation that piling on more stocks only detracts from results without diminishing volatility much. If you've got a good concept for a momentum, growth, or value model portfolio, the fewer the number of stocks you own in it (within reason), the better the likely result.

I think it's therefore fair to suggest that 7 to 15 stocks is the right range for most private, independent portfolios managed on the Web. If your portfolio is smaller than

$50,000, you might want to stick to just 7 to 10 names, and if your portfolio is larger than $2 million, you might want as many as 15 to 20 names.

Setting Expectations

How much should you expect to earn in any given year? Here's a quiz: if I were to tell you about a portfolio of five $10 stocks that had a good chance of becoming $12.50 stocks by this time next year, would you be interested? What if I were to tell you about a portfolio of $10 stocks likely to become $20 stocks in *four years*?

My guess is that you'd probably scoff, because turning $10 into $12.50 doesn't sound very exciting. And after nearly a decade of hyped-up expectations, even the idea of waiting four years to double your money sounds kind of lame. But if you were to actually make 25% a year for the next four years—and the next 26 years after that—*Fortune* magazine might put you on its cover in the year 2029 because you would have approximated the record Warren Buffett has established over the past 30 years. Through war, recession, global currency crises, and the baby boom, the Omaha insurance magnate has reportedly scored a 24.7% annual gain in the investments of his holding company.

Model portfolios can help you make that sort of advance over the next 30 years, but first here's the moral of the quiz: capital preservation is *critical* to seasoned investors such as Warren Buffett. One often-overlooked key to Buffett's success is that he has reportedly not lost money in any calendar year since he started investing shareholder's funds. Unlike most of the splendidly dressed money managers you see on financial television shows, the schlumpy septuagenarian from Nebraska does not swing for the fences at every hot new tech stock, foreign stock, or IPO with a neat story to tell. He takes his time and makes choices thoughtfully and carefully. To be sure, Buffett does have a few advantages. He's brilliant, he's experienced in every market environment, and he has no trouble getting a chief executive on the phone to answer a few questions. You, on the other hand, have a computer, the Web, and, hopefully, a spreadsheet program such as Microsoft Excel.

Now let's see what you can do with those tools in a minimal amount of time.

Investing Online in 30 to 60 Minutes a Year

If you want to spend only 30 to 60 minutes a year on your stock investments, bravo! The first four chapters of this book were written just for you. Before you can start to trade, you need to set up an account at an online brokerage, as described in Chapter 13. If you want to make life super easy, choose one that supports Open Financial Exchange, or OFX. After that, follow the steps on the next page.

1. Sometime between the second week of November and the first week of January, choose one to three investment models listed in Chapters 2, 3, and 4 that seem best matched to your appetite for return and tolerance for risk. For instance, consider taking the top three Flare-Out Growth stocks, the top four Redwood or RBI Growth stocks, and the top three Cornerstone Growth or RBI Value stocks. This would give you a mix of momentum, growth, and value styles. (As an alternative, you might consider using these models for just half or a third of your investable funds and putting the rest in a single S&P 500 or Wilshire 5000 index mutual fund.)

2. Visit the Web site MSN MoneyCentral Investor (*http://moneycentral.msn.com/investor*), enter the Investment Finder section, and create each screen as I describe it, step by step, in the relevant chapter.

3. Export the top names netted in each screen to a spreadsheet, as I described in Chapter 1, or print them out. Do not choose more than 20 names.

4. Determine the number of shares of each to buy as described in Chapter 1. (Your goal is to buy approximately an equal dollar amount of each stock you've decided to purchase.)

5. Visit your online broker. Buy the stocks at the current market price.

6. Visit MSN MoneyCentral Investor's Portfolio Manager, and either import data about your stocks via the OFX link (see Chapter 13), or type them in. As an alternative, enter your stocks into the portfolio managers at ClearStation or Yahoo! Finance.

7. Relax and have a nice year. Twelve months later, visit your portfolio manager, check how you've done, and repeat this procedure.

Investing Online in 30 to 60 Minutes a Month

If you want to spend only 30 to 60 minutes a month on your stock investments, you can sneak in a little more sophistication.

1. Complete the first six steps of the preceding section.

2. At least once a month, visit your portfolio tracker at MoneyCentral Investor, ClearStation, or Yahoo! to read news, press releases, and alerts about your stocks. (This is purely for conversational purposes. News should rarely affect the way you think about stocks bought in models.)

3. Also once a month, check whether any of your stocks are approaching their 200-day moving averages, as described in Chapter 11 and Appendix C. If so, set up a MoneyCentral or Yahoo! Pager e-mail alert to warn you if the stock falls to that price. Depending on your tolerance for risk, consider selling if the stocks slips below this important support line.

4. Relax and have a nice month. Repeat in four weeks.

Investing Online in 30 to 60 Minutes a Week

If you want to spend only 30 to 60 minutes a week on your stock investments, you can do a little more prowling on the Web.

1. Complete the first three steps of the preceding section.

2. If it turns out that you actually like reading about stocks, subscribe to Briefing.com, TheStreet.com or Barron's Online, and read a little every day about the market action. See Chapter 5 for sections of those sites to focus on. If you *really* like this stuff, move on to the news and analyst sites I describe in the rest of Chapter 5, in Chapter 6, and in Chapter 10. You might also subscribe to an investment newsletter, as I describe in Chapter 7. If you enjoy lively tech-stock coverage, you might start by subscribing to the free daily Street Life newsletter at Fortune.com and the Weekly Web Report at internetstocks.com.

3. If you're a speed reader and haven't filled up your alloted time, study a few of your stocks' charts at MoneyCentral or BigCharts, as described in Chapter 11. Pay special attention to stocks making new highs. If a stock's money flow or three-year/weekly MACD looks as if it's rolling over at that level, consider taking profits immediately. If you sell, either replace it with a stock ranked among the top three of the screen from which it came—or hold the cash until next year.

4. If you feel very ambitious, run the Great GARP! or Sleepers screens described in Chapter 4, and try researching a couple of those deep-value stocks by employing the resources described in Chapters 8 through 12. Buy one or two with a small amount of your investable funds. Hold at least a year before determining whether you were right or wrong.

5. Relax and have a nice week. Repeat in seven days.

Investing Online in 30 to 60 Minutes a Day

If you want to spend as much as 30 minutes a day on your stock investments, you can research your stocks more thoroughly.

1. Repeat the first four steps of the preceding section.

2. Set up a profile for yourself at FreeEdgar or Edgar Online (see Chapter 9), and review recent 10-Q, 10-K, 13-D, and 13-G forms, as well as proxy filings. Spend 10 minutes a day catching up on these documents. Pace yourself to cover all your stocks over the course of three months, and then start over.

3. Visit bulletin-board discussions that pertain to your stock, as described in Chapter 12. It's rare that you will hear anything critical that will change your mind about your holdings, but it can be fun to enjoy the camaraderie of the boards—especially in obscure stocks.

4. Relax and have a nice day. Repeat in 24 hours.

That wasn't hard, was it? Building and maintaining a terrific portfolio does not have to be hard or time-consuming. It just takes discipline, a computer, the Web, and the barest amount of commitment and interest. Good luck!

Part V

Appendixes

Appendix A

Using MSN MoneyCentral's Investment Finder

The Investment Finder at MSN MoneyCentral is one of the most powerful financial search tools on the Web. You can use it to scan a database of more than 8,500 stocks and 8,500 mutual funds using criteria of your own design—or criteria suggested by the site's editors. It'll help you find new investments or analyze your current holdings. After you master the basic steps, more advanced uses—and creative ideas—will come naturally.

Let's start with the two easiest kinds of search: ones that have been pre-defined by MoneyCentral's editors and ones based on single statistical criteria. Then I'll show you how to create more advanced screens. All procedures in this appendix start in the Investment Finder, which you open by clicking Finder in the top navigation bar of the MSN MoneyCentral Investor home page (*http://moneycentral.msn.com/investor*).

Pre-Defined Screens

The editors at MSN MoneyCentral have created 17 screens that seek stocks conforming to a wide variety of investment interests, such as momentum, value, and low capitalization. The editors have also created 16 screens for mutual funds. The following steps introduce you to these screens:

1. On the left navigation bar of Investment Finder, click Pre-Defined Search to display a list of pre-defined *stock* searches as shown in Figure A-1. If you wish to see pre-defined mutual *fund* searches, click Funds on the submenu that appears.

2. Read the description of each search, and click one that interests you.

3. A list of the top 25 stocks or funds that meet the selected search criteria appears.

4. Use the methods described below to print, export, or learn more about the stocks or funds displayed.

Figure A-1.   May 13, 1999

MSN MoneyCentral's editors have predefined 33 stock and fund screens in Investment Finder. Read the descriptions, and then click titles to view the relevant stocks or funds. To learn how complex screens are created, examine the editors' criteria.

The Ideas Roster

The Ideas Roster is a set of single-criteria queries that can be run against the MSN MoneyCentral stocks and fund database. It allows you to find, for instance, all Nasdaq stocks that are trading at new 52-week highs, all funds that have recently had a change in manager, or all NYSE stocks that have increased their dividends in the past three months. There is no specific investing strategy associated with the Ideas Roster lists; they are intended to inspire further research on your part. Here's how to run an Ideas Roster search:

1. On the left navigation bar of Investment Finder, click Custom Search.

2. On the Finder's File menu, click Open to display the Finder Search dialog box.

3. Click the plus sign (+) next to Ideas Roster to display a list of ideas. Click the plus sign next to an idea to display a list of specific searches. (As shown in Figure A-2, the idea New 52-Week Highs And Lows contains a search for Nasdaq New 52-Week Highs.)

4. Click some of the searches to see definitions for them in the Search Description field.

5. Select a search, and click Open And Run to see the results. As an alternative, click Open And Edit to modify the search criteria to better match your objectives.

6. Once you're viewing the results of a pre-defined search, you can customize the search criteria however you like.

If you have a favorite among the pre-defined searches, you may want to save it as your own search for faster access. The search will then appear under My Saved Searches in the Finder Search dialog box. You may also change any of the criteria in a pre-defined search and save the modified search as your own. (See directions on saving later in this appendix.)

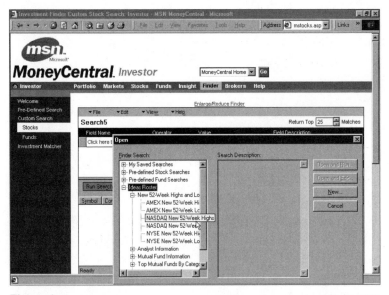

Figure A-2.   May 13, 1999

The Ideas Roster section of Finder allows you to run a variety of simple queries, such as stocks at 52-week highs or companies that have beaten analyst estimates in two straight quarters.

Set Up a Search of Your Own

Now you're ready to discover the coolest way to use Investment Finder: creating your own screens by choosing (and mixing and matching) from more than 500 search criteria. The Finder search criteria range from return-on-equity to price/earnings ratios to five-year dividend-growth rate and more. Once you enter your criteria and run the search, Finder gives you a list of stocks or funds that most closely match your criteria. To see how it all works, give the following sample searches a try.

Simple Stock Search

Let's say you want to create a list of stocks with the greatest price appreciation over the past year. Here's what you do:

1. On the left navigation bar of Investment Finder, click Custom Search.

2. In the Field Name drop-down list, point to Stock Price History, and then click % Price Change Last Year. (Note: To see available options in each criteria group, click the down arrow, and then point to each group in the menu to see the criteria available. If you're not sure what a criterion means, point to it to display a short definition in the upper-right corner of Finder under Field Description. To see the full definition, click More Info at the bottom of the Field Description box.)

3. In the Operator field, click High As Possible.

4. Press the Enter key on your keyboard or click the Run Search button on the screen. The 25 stocks with the greatest price appreciation appear; those with the highest price appreciation appear at the top of the list.

Advanced Stock Searches

Now that you've tried the basics, let's use the Finder to create custom stock searches, such as the ones I mentioned in Part I, that are based on specific investment criteria.

Using Stock Tickers as Criteria

Let's say you like the electronics retailer Best Buy (BBY), but you would like to find companies that are bigger, more profitable, trade in higher volume, and are believed by analysts to have better earnings prospects next year. Start Finder, and then follow this procedure to create the screen shown in Figure A-3:

1. On the left navigation bar of Investment Finder, click Custom Search.

2. In the Field Name drop-down list, point to Company Basics, and then click Market Capitalization. In the Operator field, click >=. In the Value field, click Custom Value, and then type *BBY* (Best Buy's ticker symbol).

3. In the next row under Field Name, point to Analyst Projections, and then click EPS Growth Next Yr. In the Operator field, click >=. In the Value field, click Custom Value, and then type *BBY*.

4. In the next row under Field Name, point to Trading & Volume, and then click Avg. Daily Vol. Last Qtr. In the Operator field, click >=. In the Value field, click Custom Value, and then type *BBY*.

5. In the next row under Field Name, point to Profit Margins, and then click Net Profit Margin. In the Operator field, click >=. In the Value field, click Custom Value, and then type *BBY*.

6. Press Enter on your keyboard, or click Run Search.

A more sophisticated example of this screen can be found under the Investment Matcher link in the left navigation bar of the Finder area. Click Investment Matcher, type a ticker symbol into the text box, and then click Go. You'll see a list of 25 stocks that are similar to your focus stock in market capitalization, valuation, and price appreciation. Click any of the column headings to rank the results by various criteria. The Investment Matcher works for mutual-fund ticker symbols as well.

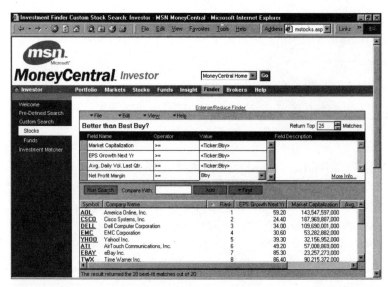

Figure A-3.   May 13, 1999

To find stocks that are similar to ones you are familiar with, but better or worse in specific ways, type their ticker symbols into the Value field.

Here's a simpler example: let's say you just want to find companies that have debt/equity ratios less than 1.0 and price/sales ratios less than 1.5. Here are your search criteria:

1. On the left navigation bar of Investment Finder, click Custom Search.

2. In the Field Name drop-down list, point to Financial Condition, and then click Debt To Equity Ratio. In the Operator field, click <=. In the Value field, click Custom Value, and then type 1.0.

3. In the Field Name drop-down list, point to Price Ratios, and then click Price/Sales Ratio. In the Operator field, click <=. In the Value field, click Custom Value, and then type 1.5.

4. Press Enter on your keyboard or click Run Search.

General Finder Tips

- To display a criterion without it affecting your search, choose the criterion under Field Name, and then select Display Only in the Operator field.

- To rerun a search with changes, simply modify the search criteria as desired, and then click Run Search again.

- To remove a search criterion, right-click the gray box at the far left of the row, and then click Delete Criterion Row or press Delete on your keyboard.

- To get more information on any stock in the list, click its ticker symbol. This displays a Stock Research page with more information.

- To see more or fewer stocks in your result set, change the number in the text box at the top of the Finder labeled "Return Top Matches" to a number ranging from 1 to 100.

- If you search for criteria using the operators High As Possible or Low As Possible, the Finder will use "fuzzy logic" to find the best-fit matches. This can lead to unexpected, and sometimes unsatisfactory, results. It's often best to employ as many "hard" criteria as possible (that is, ones that use greater than, less than, or equal to as the operators) and use High As Possible or Low As Possible to sort the final results on a single criteria. In the Flare-Out Growth screen described in Chapter 2, for example, the operator High As Possible is reserved for the FOG Index formula and employed as a ranking mechanism.

More Advanced Custom Searches

Find Stocks Based on the Dow Dividend Strategy

This search finds the top Dow Dividend Theory stocks, which are used to implement the investing strategy commonly known as "the Dogs of the Dow." Those who follow this technique buy the 5 or 10 stocks with the highest dividend yield among the 30 securities in the Dow Jones Industrial Average. Then they update the portfolio once a year. Follow these steps to let the Finder make the Dow 10 approach easier to execute:

1. On the left navigation bar of Investment Finder, click Custom Search.

2. From the drop-down list under Field Name, point to Company Basics, and then click Dow Jones Membership. Under Operator, leave the default of =. From the drop-down list under Value, click DJ Industrials.

3. Under Field Name, point to Dividends, and then click Current Dividend Yield. Under Operator, click High As Possible. The Value field is grayed out, indicating that it is disabled. The High As Possible operator overrides this field.

4. To evaluate all component members of the Dow Jones Industrial Average, enter 30 in the Return Top field in the upper-right corner of Investment Finder. To limit the results to the 10 stocks with the highest dividend yield, enter 10 in the Return Top field.

5. Click Run Search. The Results Pane lists all component members of the Dow according to their dividend yields. The top 10 companies in the list are the current members of the Dow 10.

A variation of the Dow 10 approach advocated by the Motley Fool requires investors to sort this list by price and then choose the four cheapest. If you do so, limit the screen above to 10 stocks. Under Field Name, point to Stock Price History, and then click Previous Day's Closing Price. Under Operator, click Display. Then click Run Search. Finally, click the column heading for Previous Day's Closing Price to rank the results from low to high. In the Fool 4 method, you would buy the four lowest priced stocks out of the 10 with the highest dividend yields.

Find Stocks Using P/E Ratio, Earnings Growth, and Trading Volume

This search shows you how to find stocks with P/E ratios less than 15, five-year earnings growth of more than 15%, and average daily volumes for the past month at least twice those of a year ago. The purpose of this simple search is to find relatively cheap stocks

with potential for price appreciation based on both technical (trading volume) and fundamental (past earnings growth) indicators.

1. On the left navigation bar of Investment Finder, click Custom Search.

2. From the drop-down list under Field Name, point to Price Ratios, and then click P/E Ratio: Current. Under Operator, click <=. Under Value, click Custom Value, and then type *15*.

3. In the Field Name drop-down list, point to Growth Rates, and then click 5-Year Earnings Growth. Under Operator, click >=. Under Value, click Custom Value, and then type *15*.

4. In the Field Name drop-down list, point to Trading & Volume, and then click Average Daily Volume Last Month. Under Operator, click >=. Under Value, click Custom Value, and type *2 ** (the asterisk symbol, meaning multiplication). From the drop-down list, point to Trading & Volume, and click Average Daily Volume Last Year.

5. Click Run Search. The Results Pane lists the companies that best match the criteria you entered.

Find Stocks Using Criteria Comparisons and Math Formulas

When setting up your searches, you may want to combine search criteria, compare two fields, or introduce equations into the searches. This way, you can extend the standard criteria to fine tune your searches and produce even more powerful results.

Stocks with Low P/E Ratios   Let's say you want to find undervalued stocks with potential for price appreciation, so you decide to seek all stocks with P/E ratios 25% below the S&P 500 average.

1. On the left navigation bar of Investment Finder, click Custom Search.

2. Under Field Name, point to Price Ratios, and then click P/E Ratio: Current. Under Operator, select <=. Under Value, point to Price Ratios, and then click S&P 500 Average P/E Ratio: Current.

3. In the Value field, after S&P 500 Average P/E Ratio: Current, type ** .75*. (This is the decimal equivalent of subtracting 25%.) The Value field should now display: S&P 500 Average P/E Ratio: Current * .75.

4. Enter additional search criteria as desired, and then click Run Search.

Stocks Near Lows Starting to Recover   Now let's say you want to find small stocks that have fallen within 20% of their 52-week lows but that might be in recovery mode because they just crossed above their 200-day moving averages.

1. On the left navigation bar of Investment Finder, click Custom Search.

2. Under Field Name, point to Stock Price History, and then click Previous Day's Closing Price. Under Operator, click <=. Under Value, point to Stock Price History, and then click 52-Week Low. The Value field displays 52-Week Low.

3. In the Value field, after 52-Week Low, type * *1.2.* (This is the decimal equivalent of adding 20%.) The Value field should now display 52-Week Low * 1.2.

4. Under Field Name, point to Company Basics, and then click Market Capitalization. Under Operator, click <=. Under Value, click Custom Value, and then type *$1 billion.*

5. Under Field Name, point to Advisor FYI, point to Trading & Volume, and choose Crossed Above 200-Day Moving Average. Under Operator, keep the default Since. Under Value, choose In the Last Week.

6. Click Run Search.

Stocks with Low PEG Ratios   You may wish to find stocks with low P/E multiples relative to their growth rates, a situation known as having a low PEG (price-earnings ratio/growth rate) ratio. If the market decides the stocks' multiples should expand to be equal to their growth rates, the stocks' price will rise.

1. On the left navigation bar of Investment Finder, click Custom Search.

2. Under Field Name, point to Price Ratios, and then click P/E Ratio: Current. The Field Name displays P/E Ratio: Current. In the Field Name, at the end of P/E Ratio: Current, type a division symbol (*/*).

3. Under Field Name, point to Analyst Projections, and then click EPS Growth Next Yr. The Field Name should now display P/E Ratio: Current/EPS Growth Next Yr.

4. Under Operator, click <=. Under Value, click Custom Value, and then type *1.*

5. Click Run Search.

Creative Query Tips

I find it useful to keep certain criteria—Market Capitalization, Industry Name, and Previous Day's Closing Price—in almost every screen. After those, loosen up and get creative with your queries.

- **Percent off high.** To show the percentage difference between stocks' current price and their 52-week highs, use this query as a single criteria. Under Field Name, point to Stock Price History, and click Previous Day's Closing Price. Then type a division sign, point to Stock Price History again, and click 52-Week High. The Field Name should now display Previous Day's Closing Price/52-Week High. Under Operator,

(continued)

Creative Query Tips, *continued*

choose High As Possible. When you run the screen, the figure that appears in this column in the Results Pane will be the percentage difference between the 52-week high and the current price, expressed as a decimal. That is, the number .82 means the stock is 82% from its 52-week high.

- **Exponential relative strength.** Some market technicians, such as William O'Neil, founder of *Investor's Business Daily*, prefer to overweight the impact of the most recent three months when looking at a stock's 12-month relative strength. To accomplish this in a Finder query, try this: under Field Name, point to Trading & Volume, and click 12-Month Relative Strength. Then type a plus sign (+), a 2, and a multiplication sign (*). Click the down arrow again, point to Trading & Volume, and click 6-Month Relative Strength. Then type a plus sign, a 3, and a multiplication sign. Click the down arrow a third time, point to Trading & Volume, and click 3-Month Relative Strength. The formula should therefore read 12-Month Relative Strength+2*6-Month Relative Strength+3*3-Month Relative Strength as shown in Figure A-4. Under Operator, choose High As Possible. The result will be stocks with the greatest accelerating relative strength.

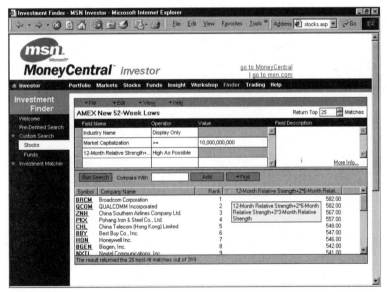

Figure A-4.   May 14, 1999

Create your own measurements in the Finder. In this case, I built an exponential relative-strength measure. To do the same, point, click, type the formula into the Field Name box, and then run the screen. The formula then appears on the heading of the column. (Click the header to sort in ascending or descending order.)

Find Stocks Using Advisor FYI Alerts

The Investment Finder's Advisor FYI feature gives you a way to run quick single-criterion or multiple-criteria searches for data such as P/E ratio well above industry average, relative strength increased, and new 52-week high. The Advisor FYI feature is different from the pre-defined searches in that there is no specific investing strategy involved with the searches. You can use the search results as a starting point for further research. When you use Advisor FYI alerts as search criteria, the result set is a list of securities that currently meet the conditions specified by the alert or alerts selected.

To see a list of all companies whose stock price is up on heavy trading volume in the last week, try this:

1. On the left navigation bar of Investment Finder, click Custom Search.

2. Under Field Name, point to Advisor FYI, then point to Trading & Volume, and then click Price Up On Heavy Volume (as shown in Figure A-5). Under Operator, click Since. In the Value field, click In The Last Week. (The Operator can also be set to "Not Since," and you can type in a specific date in the Value field, if desired.)

3. Enter additional search criteria as desired.

4. Click the Run Search button.

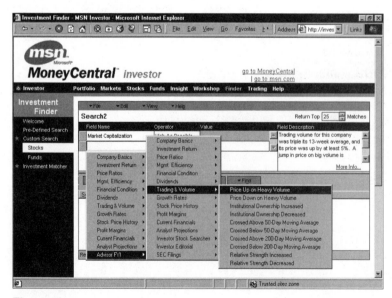

Figures A-5.   May 14, 1999

Advisor FYI criteria in the Finder help you dig deep into the stock market for patterns. To choose an FYI for a screen, you must pass through three dialog boxes. Almost all are based on dates: choose whether you'd like to see events that occurred in the past week, month, quarter, or since a particular date.

Compare Search Results with Specific Stocks

Once you've run a search, you can compare the results to individual stocks and mutual funds of interest to see how they stack up. The criteria you've entered will not affect the stocks or mutual funds you're displaying for comparison.

1. Create or open a search.

2. In the Compare With field, found in the middle of the Finder, enter a stock or mutual-fund symbol, and then click Add.

3. If you don't know the symbol, click the Find button, and click Symbols from the displayed list.

4. The results for your selection are displayed in the Comparison Pane just above the Results Pane. If the stock appears in both panes, it appears in red.

Compare Search Results with Your Portfolio Accounts

If you keep your portfolio in MSN MoneyCentral's portfolio manager, you can compare search results to any of the stocks and mutual funds in your portfolio to see how they stack up. The criteria you've entered will not affect the stocks or mutual funds you're displaying for comparison. Here's how to view this kind of comparison:

1. Create or open a search.

2. Click Find in the middle of Investment Finder to display a list of options. All the accounts you've created in Portfolio Manager are listed under the second separator line.

3. Click the account you want to compare. From the displayed list, you can select individual stocks and mutual funds, or you can choose Add All to add all the stocks and mutual funds from the account to the list.

Comparison Pane Tips

You can easily close the Comparison Pane after you're done comparing data. From the Finder's View menu, click Show Comparison Pane to uncheck it.

You can also quickly remove a security from the Comparison Pane. Right-click the security, and click Delete on the menu that appears.

You can quickly add a security listed in the Results Pane to the Comparison Pane. Right-click the security, and click Compare With on the menu that appears.

---

4. The results of your selection appear in the Comparison Pane, just above the existing Results Pane. (If you try to compare stocks to mutual funds, no results appear in the Comparison Pane.)

5. Compare the data for your selected investments to the data in the Results Pane.

Change the Columns Displayed in Finder

You can customize Investment Finder's column set so that you see the information that interests you most in the exact order you prefer. For example, you might want to remove the Market Capitalization column and add a column for current P/E ratio.

Investment Finder also provides predefined column sets that focus on one aspect of the result set, such as investment return, profit margin, or analyst projection. To customize your column setting:

1. Create or open a search.

2. On the Finder View menu, point to Column Set Displayed, and then click Customize Column Set. The Customize Column Set dialog box appears.

3. Under Available Columns, find and select any column heading you want to display, and then click Add. Repeat this step until you have added all the columns you want to display. (As you select each column heading, the definition appears in the Column Definition box below.)

4. Under Displayed Columns, select any column heading you want to remove, and then click Remove. Repeat this step until you have removed all the columns you don't want to display.

Finder Display Tips

- To adjust a column's width, drag a divider between the column headings. You can also double-click a divider on the right of a column header to automatically resize its width to fit the column's data.

- To sort the result set by any of the displayed columns, click the column heading. To reverse the sort order, click the column heading again. Or from Finder's Edit menu, click Sort Order, and then choose the column by which you want to sort and how you want the results sorted.

- To quickly change the order of the columns in Finder, just drag and drop the column headings to where you want them.

5. Under Displayed Columns, select any column heading you want to move, and then click Move Up or Move Down. (The Symbol, Company Name, and Rank columns always appear. The column heading at the top of the list is the leftmost column displayed after these standard columns.)

6. Click OK to save and display your customized column set.

To select one of Finder's pre-defined column sets:

1. On the Finder View menu, point to Column Set Displayed, and then choose a column set from the submenu. (The Symbol, Company Name, and Rank columns always appear. The column set you choose appears to the right of these standard columns.)

2. To restore the default column settings, open the Finder View menu, point to Column Set Displayed, and then click Default Columns. The default column settings will appear.

Compare Search Results with an Index

Once you've run a search, you can compare the results to a general index, such as the Dow Jones Industrial Average, or an industry-specific index, such as the Personal Computers index, to see how data for individual companies compare to industry averages. The criteria you've entered will not affect the indexes you're displaying for comparison.

1. Create or open a search.

2. Click Find in the middle of the Finder to display a list of options.

3. Select either Industry Indexes or Common Indexes.

4. If you see the index you want, select it from the displayed list. (If you don't see the index you want, point to Industry Indexes, and then click Other Industry Indexes. The Select Industry dialog box appears. Make a selection from the Choose An Industry Category drop-down list. In the Select A Specific Industry list, highlight the specific industry you want to compare.) Click OK.

5. Compare the data for the selected index(es) to the data in the Results Pane. The results appear in the Comparison Pane just above the Results Pane. (Many of the search criteria used to find stocks and mutual funds do not apply to indexes. When you compare search results with an index, the "not applicable" fields will be blank for the index.)

Managing Finder Searches

Save and Rerun a Search

If you've created a search or customized one of Finder's pre-defined searches, you can save the search and run it again later. Each time you run the search, you'll most likely get different output, because the data on individual companies and mutual funds are updated daily.

To save a Finder search:

1. Create a search or open and make changes to an existing one.

2. On the Finder File menu, click Save As. The Save Search dialog box appears.

3. Enter a file name in the Search Name field. The name can include any combination of numbers and letters.

4. In the Search Description field, you can enter a reminder to yourself of what this search does or why you wanted to save it. Click OK.

To open and rerun a Finder search:

1. On the Finder File menu, click Open. The Open dialog box appears.

2. Click the plus sign next to My Saved Searches to display a list.

3. Select the search you want to open. (When you highlight a search, the description you entered when you saved the search appears in the Search Description box.)

4. Click Open And Run to run the search or Open And Edit to modify the search before running it.

Send a Search by E-Mail

Finder makes it easy to share your screens with friends and co-workers by simply sending the search to them by e-mail. You can also transfer a search from one computer to another by sending it through e-mail. (This feature is available only to users who have e-mail installed and are using version 3 or higher of Microsoft Internet Explorer or version 3 or higher of Netscape Navigator on the Windows 95, Windows NT 4, or later operating systems.)

1. Create or open a search.

2. Open the Finder File menu, and click Send To. Finder creates a message with MSN MoneyCentral Investor Finder Search in the subject field and the Web address of the Finder search as the message content.

3. Fill in the address of the recipient, and send the message as you normally would. When the recipients receive the message, they can simply click the Web address and the search will appear exactly as you created it—although the results may change due to data updates.

Export a Result Set to a Spreadsheet Program

Once you have run a Finder search, you can customize the appearance of the results using the specialized features of Microsoft Excel or another spreadsheet program of your choice.

1. Create or open a search.

2. On the Finder File menu, point to Export, and then click Results To Excel. (This option is available only if you have Excel installed on your computer. Click Results To Tab-Delimited File if you want to use a different spreadsheet program.)

3. Finder will start Excel and create a file containing the output from your search.

4. You can use Excel to format or chart the data as you like.

Appendix B

Quarterly Flare-Out Growth Portfolios, 1998–1999

All but one Flare-Out Growth portfolio I created and tracked during 1998 and 1999 in my SuperModels column at MSN MoneyCentral performed well. In Chapter 2, you'll find the the portfolios I created in January 1998 and January 1999. This appendix lists and describes portfolios begun at the start of the second, third, and fourth quarters of 1998, the second quarter of 1999, and on September 4, 1998, for the CNBC Top 100. Each was built in a strictly mechanical fashion from the original Flare-Out Growth screen in Investment Finder, which I describe at the end of this appendix.

1998 Second Quarter

The Flares netted in the second quarter of 1998, shown in Table B-1, were probably the least exciting of the year. Yahoo!, Dell, and Best Buy made great gains over the first three months, but medical-glove maker Safeskin, competitive local exchange carrier Intermedia Communications, and paging-system operator SkyTel meandered. By the time 12 months had gone by, the also-rans had tumbled in a heap. But the 10-stock portfolio still ended the 12-month period ahead by 86%—five times better than the broad market.

Table B-1.   1998 Second Quarter

The Q2 '98 Flare-Out Growth portfolio gained 14.8% from April 1 to June 30, 1998. Through April 1, 1999, the one-year portfolio rose 86%—five times better than the broad market.

	4/1/98 Close	6/30/98 Close	3/31/99 Close	6/30/99 Close	3-Mo. Chg.	12-Mo. Chg.	15-Mo. Chg.
Yahoo!	$24.45	$39.38	$168.38	$172.25	61.0%	588.7%	604.5%
Best Buy	$17.88	$18.06	$52.00	$67.50	1.1%	190.9%	277.6%
Dell Computer	$17.13	$23.20	$40.88	$37.00	35.5%	138.7%	116.1%
Siebel Systems	$28.06	$32.25	$47.50	$66.31	14.9%	69.3%	136.3%
Arterial Vascular*	$39.00	$38.22	$58.38	$58.38	-2.0%	49.7%	49.7%
Citrix Systems	$28.44	$34.19	$38.13	$56.50	20.2%	34.1%	98.7%
SkyTel Comm	$23.38	$23.41	$16.63	$20.94	0.1%	-28.9%	-10.4%
Intermedia	$38.69	$41.94	$26.63	$30.00	8.4%	-31.2%	-22.5%
Tekelec	$22.44	$22.38	$7.31	$12.19	-0.3%	-67.4%	-45.7%
Safeskin	$37.88	$41.13	$7.44	$12.00	8.6%	-80.4%	-68.3%
				Total	14.8%	86.3%	113.6%
				S&P 500	3.0%	17.0%	25.0%

Merged with Medtronic; final price January 28, 1999.

As I'll discuss in Appendix C, more aggressive investors can use a stop-limit order 5% to 10% below any disappointing stock's 200-day moving average. This will prevent the most serious damage from stocks suffering the worst declines. In this portfolio, SkyTel would have been sold in mid-June at around $19, Intermedia would have been sold in August at around $34, Tekelec would have been sold in late July at around $20, and Safeskin would have been sold in mid-September at around $34.

1998 Third Quarter

The third-quarter portfolio, shown in Table B-2, was bought a month before the big summer peak in the market. It answers the question that most people raise with great fear: what if I'm about to buy these momentum stocks near the top? So let's review what did happen.

To be sure, the portfolio had a scary couple of months, with Web media stocks Infoseek, Lycos, CMGI, and Excite all sinking more than 35% from their highs. They hugged their 200-day moving averages for as many as six weeks as the entire market fell apart amid the Asian and Russian financial crises of the summer.

Table B-2. 1998 Third Quarter

The Q3 '98 Flare-Out Growth portfolio sank 10.8% from July 1 to September 30, 1998. Through June 30, 1999, the one-year portfolio rose 167.5%—eight times as much as the broad market.

	7/1/98 Close	9/30/98 Close	6/30/99 Close	3-Mo. Chg.	12-Mo. Chg.
CMGI	$18.94	$13.31	$114.06	-29.7%	502.3%
Yahoo!	$42.47	$64.75	$172.25	52.5%	305.6%
Best Buy	$18.38	$20.81	$67.50	13.3%	267.3%
Excite*	$38.00	$40.88	$133.00	7.6%	250.0%
Amazon.com	$38.04	$37.21	$125.13	-2.2%	228.9%
Lycos	$41.00	$33.81	$91.88	-17.5%	124.1%
Infoseek	$37.81	$24.63	$47.94	-34.9%	26.8%
The Learning Co.**	$29.06	$19.88	$33.38	-31.6%	14.91%
Ballard Power	$33.00	$22.50	$32.00	-31.8%	-3.0%
Lernout & Hauspie	$60.88	$40.19	$35.44	-34.0%	-41.8%
			Total	-10.8%	167.5%
			S&P 500	-11.0%	21.0%

* Merged with AtHome; last price May 28, 1999.

** Merged with Matell; last price May 13, 1999.

But look what incredible fortune befell disciplined investors who hung in with the program and held the stocks for a year. They scored gains of 15% to 502% over the 12-month period following their purchases. Of course, not all the stocks in the portfolio were as lucky. The Learning Company fell decisively below its long-term support in August and could have been sold around $20. Ballard Power plunged below its support in July and could have been sold around $27, and Lernout & Hauspie sank far below its support as well in August and could have been sold around $38. Yet the declines in the latter three would not have badly hurt a yeartrading investor who simply stayed disciplined to the Flare-Out strategy and held all stocks for the full 12 months.

1998 Fourth Quarter

The portfolio created in the fourth quarter of 1998, shown in Table B-3, is a bit less remarkable for its uniform strength—unless you think back to the week that it was created.

The first week of October 1998 was just horrible for investors holding long positions. The broad market had rallied in early and mid-September from terrifying August 31 lows, only to plunge back down in huge steps on September 30 and October 1 to a

low of Dow 7,630. Television programming was rife with pundits predicting total doom for the market, with a fall to Dow 6,000 or even Dow 5,000 not considered out of the question. Phrases like "one more leg down" were used because looming ahead were anniversaries of the late October dates when the market crashed in 1997 and 1987. Tension was palpable. It seemed time to throw in the towel to save whatever equity you had left.

Table B-3. 1998 Fourth Quarter

The Q4 '98 portfolio rose 62% from October 1 to December 31, 1999. Through June 30, 1999, the portfolio gained 99%—2.5 times the broad market.

	10/1/98 Close	12/31/98 Close	6/30/99 Close	3-Mo. Chg.	9-Mo. Chg.
Amazon.com	$34.21	$107.08	$125.13	213.0%	265.8%
Yahoo!	$56.47	$118.47	$172.25	109.8%	205.0%
EMC	$26.50	$42.50	$55.00	60.4%	107.5%
Biogen	$31.00	$41.50	$64.31	33.9%	107.5%
Allegiance*	$26.00	$46.63	$50.25	79.3%	93.3%
Century Comm	$23.19	$31.72	$46.00	36.8%	98.4%
EarthLink Network	$38.25	$57.00	$61.44	49.0%	60.6%
Apple Computer	$37.44	$40.94	$46.31	9.3%	23.7%
Dell Computer	$30.78	$36.59	$37.00	18.9%	20.2%
Schering-Plough	$50.31	$55.25	$52.50	9.8%	4.3%
			Total	62.0%	98.6%
			S&P 500	25.0%	40.0%

Merged with Cardinal Health; last price February 3, 1999.

I was not immune. I'll never forget the helpless feeling I experienced watching the value of my retirement account plunge that week. I gave up on my discipline under pressure from my fears, and I sold off a couple of of my favorite Flare-Out Growth stocks that had already fallen 40% in value. I remember sitting at my desk at home in Seattle, late at night, checking the charts of all my stocks at MSN MoneyCentral, ClearStation, and BigCharts. I determined that no hope remained. My fingers sadly tapped out a couple of sell orders for my online account at Fidelity. Of course, that week of maximum anxiety was the bottom. (Charts always look worst before they turn—a good lesson.) Federal Reserve Chairman Alan Greenspan rode to the rescue and cut interest rates decisively on October 15.

So what happened to our screen-built portfolio? I felt a bit irresponsible publishing the fourth-quarter list because it once again contained such volatile names as Amazon.com, Yahoo!, Dell, and EMC. At the time, all were looking scarier than usual except Yahoo!.

(A truly remarkable stock in 1998, Yahoo! rode through the entire storm with barely a scratch.) But as you can see in Table B-3, Amazon.com closed the quarter with a 213% gain, Yahoo! finished up 110%, and EMC finished up 60%. Even the worst of the bunch, pharmaceutical maker Schering-Plough and computer maker Apple Computer, ended up gaining 9%.

In the end, cool heads who just bought the 10 Flares in the third quarter and went on long vacations ended with a gain of 62%. That was two and a half times better than the S&P 500 Index's gain of 25%. It beat even the remarkable advance of the Nasdaq 100 Index, which exploded by 44% during the quarter. Nine months later, the portfolio was up 99%. The lesson: stick to the Flare discipline for the small part of your portfolio you devote to momentum stocks.

1999 Second Quarter

The Q2 1999 portfolio was perhaps the most mercurial of the past two years: it ran out of the gate on April 1 at top speed and then collapsed in a tangled heap before straightening itself out. The stocks, shown in Table B-4, were collectively up 25% by April 15, but they cratered on April 16 and 19—right after taxes were due and investors needed to pay Uncle Sam. On those two days, the Nasdaq Composite plunged almost 200 points. The portfolio was down 5% by the close of April 19.

Table B-4. 1999 Second Quarter

The Flare-Out Growth portfolio sank 3.6% from April 1, 1999, to June 30, 1999.

	4/1/99 Open	6/30/99 Close	3-Mo. Chg.
Go2Net	$65.44	$91.88	40.4%
Metromedia Fiber Network	$27.38	$35.94	31.3%
CMGI	$93.66	$114.06	21.8%
MindSpring Enterprises	$44.22	$44.31	0.2%
Yahoo!	$179.75	$172.25	-4.2%
Dell Computer	$41.18	$37.00	-10.2%
Network Solutions	$102.44	$79.13	-22.8%
America Online	$150.00	$110.00	-26.7%
Amazon.com	$171.00	$125.13	-26.8%
New Era of Networks	$72.50	$43.94	-39.4%
		Total	-3.6%
		S&P 500	6.0%

But then something interesting and instructive happened: the momentum stocks that were strongest going into the decline were the strongest coming out. All the Flare stocks had phenomenal runs on April 20 and 21. CMGI, Network Solutions, Go2Net, and America Online gained $40.75, $32, $29.38, and $14, respectively, on April 21 alone. They subsequently fell far back to Earth, however, ending the quarter down 3.6% collectively. It will be interesting to see where they end up after a year. If history holds, we'd expect these names to collectively beat the broad market by a factor of three by March 31, 2000.

CNBC Top 100

The Flare-Out Growth stocks netted for the CNBC Top 100 were an eclectic bunch: two cable companies, three financial-services firms, three Internet firms, a data-storage software maker, and a retailer. Over the first month, most of the stocks plunged in value with the rest of the market—but then they were among the first snapped up during the fall recovery. Despite a couple of dogs, the portfolio ended up beating the S&P 500 by a factor of three both by the end of the year and after 10 months.

Table B-5. CNBC Top 100/Flare-Out Growth

By year's end (and 10 months later), the 11 Flare stocks netted for the CNBC Top 100 collectively rose more than three times as much as the broad market.

	9/4/98 Close	12/31/98 Close	6/30/98 Close	4-Mo. Chg.	10-Mo. Chg.
America Online	$21.50	$77.56	$110.00	260.8%	411.6%
Yahoo!	$37.69	$118.47	$172.25	214.3%	357.0%
Amazon.com	$28.75	$107.08	$125.13	272.5%	335.2%
Best Buy	$23.06	$30.69	$67.50	33.1%	192.7%
Capital One Financial	$28.85	$38.33	$55.69	32.9%	93.0%
Cablevision Systems	$34.69	$50.13	$70.00	44.5%	101.8%
Century Comm	$23.63	$31.72	$46.00	34.2%	94.7%
Adelphia Comm	$37.06	$45.75	$63.63	23.4%	71.7%
Legato Systems	$42.00	$65.94	$57.75	57.0%	37.5%
AEGON N.V.	$92.88	$122.25	$73.94	31.6%	-20.4%
First American Financial	$27.44	$32.13	$17.88	17.1%	-34.9%
			Total	92.9%	149.1%
			S&P 500	27.0%	42.0%

Original Flare-Out Growth Screen

Here is the screen recipe I used to create the Flare-Out Growth portfolios in 1998 and 1999. It differs from the screen recipe I described in Chapter 2 by not requiring minimum amounts of volume, sales, or return on equity.

1. **Market capitalization of at least $1 billion.** (In Investment Finder, choose *Company Basics* / Market Capitalization >= $1 billion.) The market of the 1990s prefers larger stocks.

2. **Current price greater than the price three months ago.** (In Investment Finder, choose *Stock Price History* / % Price Change Last Qtr. >= 0.1.) Momentum stocks should be bought above their prices of three months ago.

3. **Current price greater than the 200-day moving average.** (In Investment Finder, choose *Stock Price History* / Previous Day's Closing Price >= *Trading & Volume* / 200-Day Moving Average.) Momentum stocks should be bought above their 200-day moving averages.

4. **Rank these stocks by the Flare-Out Growth Index.** (In Investment Finder, choose *Stock Price History* / % Price Change Last Year - % Price Change Last Qtr. - 3 * % Price Change Last Month. Choose High As Possible as the operator.) The Flare-Out Growth Index, or FOG Index for short, is the momentum formula that mathematically replicates technicians' "bull-flag" chart pattern.

5. **Run the search.** The stocks will be ranked in descending order by the FOG Index.

6. **Buy the top 3 to 10 listed in equal dollar amounts, depending on your risk tolerance.** The fewer the number of stocks you buy, the higher the potential reward (and risk).

Appendix C
Stop Limits for Model Portfolios

"There are no good stocks. They are all bad ... unless they go up."
—William J. O'Neil, *How to Make Money in Stocks*

In Chapters 1 through 4, I suggested that private investors should consider going online to screen for momentum, growth, and value stocks near the beginning of the year and then mechanically buy them in groups of three or four. The big idea is that new software and the Web offer private investors an opportunity to seek and obtain 10 to 15 stocks like the pros do in less time than it takes to watch an episode of "60 Minutes."

It sounds fairly simple, and it is. Especially when all those stocks immediately begin to levitate after you buy them. But what happens if one, two, or more, begin to falter? It's human nature to fret about them—and to want to bail on the strategy. You begin to think you're smarter than the model and that all the historical testing I mentioned bears no relevance to the present situation. And even if you are disciplined, it's just darned hard to watch a stock sink every day for weeks. You just want to step in and stanch the bleeding. You want to *do something*.

My earnest proposal is that you resist the temptation to muck with the model-portfolio strategy you chose and just leave all the stocks alone. Messing with models in midyear is a bumpy road to aggravation and, probably, diminished results. Even seasoned professionals find it difficult to time quick sales and purchases well enough to be consistently successful. But if muck you must, there are smart ways to mechanically go online to protect yourself from the steepest declines.

In this appendix, I'll offer some ideas to potentially enhance model-portfolio results by setting stop limits—brokerage orders to sell a stock at a specified price—on stocks that fail to deliver on their promises.

Placing Stop Limits

Almost everyone new to momentum and growth investing has one legitimate concern: what if the market is plain wrong about these stocks and one day they just plunge to zero?

The glib answer is that none of the stocks historically chosen by the Flare-Out Growth, Redwood Growth, or RBI systems described in Chapters 2 and 3 have actually gone to zero, but a few have fallen quite a lot. And serious losses could have been avoided in almost all cases with a stop-limit order placed at their 200-day moving averages. For many of these stocks, that could be a level substantially below your purchase price. But momentum stocks can be so volatile that placing stops any higher—for example, at their 21-day or 50-day moving averages—will just get in your way. Tighter stops also make you monitor the market closely, negating a strong benefit of yeartrading.

You might recall from Chapter 11 that the 50-day and 200-day moving averages are the average prices paid for a security over the past 50 or 200 trading days. They are also referred to as short-term and long-term "support." These averages tend to provide a floor for stocks trading above them and a ceiling, or "resistance," for stocks trading below them. Stocks that sink below support are in danger of further weakening; stocks that rise above resistance have a shot at new highs.

Typically, you get plenty of warning that a well-loved momentum stock is faltering. Because so many shares are bought every day (probably by institutions), it's rare that one of these stocks plunges through long-term support in a single day. The market's most knowledgeable investors generally start sneaking out of a well-regarded company's shares a little at a time if they suspect that something's wrong with its prospects or believe that it has become wildly overvalued. As these major early investors sell the stock, its money flow and momentum wane, and its price steadily *drifts* lower without actually ever *collapsing*. It may seem to rally occasionally as it slides, but you may note on a chart that it seems to make lower highs and lower lows during those rallies. During this period, you and other long-term investors wait anxiously for buyers to swarm back to the stock first at its 50-day moving average. If no surge of purchasing emerges there, you watch the stock sink toward its next major support level—often the 200-day moving average. That's when you should start to get concerned. If no buying emerges there either, it's a sign that interest in the stock by major investors might be over. Very often, it's a few points below that level that truly catastrophic selling begins.

Very aggressive traders don't wait nearly this long to sell faltering stocks and limit their risks. In his excellent and popular book *How to Make Money in Stocks*, William J. O'Neil contended, using all capital letters, that investors consider a 7% to 8% decline

from their purchase price the "THE ABSOLUTE LIMIT" for patience. He added, "Once you get to that point, you can no longer hesitate. You can't think about it or wait a few more days to see what might happen. It now becomes automatic."

If you are actively trading stocks, his advice is right on. But for yeartrading portfolios, I've determined that it's OK to have a much slower trigger finger. Although the 200-day average is, by no means, a perfect stop-limit level, it offers the best balance between proactivity and laissez-faire that I can suggest. For instance, consider the Flare-Out Growth portfolio created in the first quarter of 1998, as shown in Table 2-1. If you had maintained that portfolio from January 2, 1998, to December 31, 1998, the gain was 138.6%. But if you had sold oil driller Varco International when it crossed decisively below its 200-day moving average on June 1, 1998, you would have recorded a 5% gain for that stock and a 146% gain for the one-year portfolio.

Let's look at how setting stop limits around 200-day moving averages would have affected the Flare-Out Growth portfolios from other quarters. In the portfolio begun in the second quarter of 1998, shown in Table B-1, Safeskin, Tekelec, and SkyTel would have been sold for losses that amounted to 10%, 11%, and 19% rather than losses of 80%, 67%, and 29%. For your trouble, you would have boosted the return of that one-year portfolio from 86% to 100%. In the portfolio begun in the third quarter of 1998, shown in Table B-2, The Learning Co., Ballard Power and Lernout & Hauspie would have been sold for losses that amounted to 31.6%, 31.8%, and 34% rather than a 15% gain for The Learning Co. and losses of 3% and 42% for Ballard Power and Lernout. The portfolio's return would have been diminished, ending the 12-month period with a 161% gain rather than a 167.5% gain. In the portfolio begun on January 2, 1999, New Era of Networks would have sold on April 29 at $35; it ultimately sank to $13.50 three months later.

Among all the stocks that were bought in 1998 quarterly portfolios, only one rebounded powerfully after sinking below its 200-day moving average. CMGI sank by more than 50% from its early August high of $43 to its early October low of $18.75, hugging its long-term moving average for about a month. Ultimately, it never sank *much* below its support, and it climbed a stunning 870% by April 1999.

How can you avoid selling too soon? Set the stop limit about 5% or 10% below the 200-day moving average. Or, alternatively, experiment with the Parabolic SAR indicator described in Chapter 11 to set a closer, more sophisticated stop limit; for instance, try the one-year weekly version of the indicator. More importantly, consider whether the stock's wobbliness is due to a real change in the *company's* story or it is just caught up in a general market malaise. If the latter, it makes more sense to use the long-term average as a "mental stop" rather than a "hard stop." That means that you watch it carefully and sell only if the company is alone in its decline and it falls *decisively* below support.

How to Determine a Stock's 200-Day Moving Average

To determine a stock's 200-day moving average, visit the Company Report page of MSN MoneyCentral Investor (*http://moneycentral.msn.com/investor*), and type in a ticker symbol. The 200-day moving average is listed in the second column under Statistics.

Another, more visual method:

1. Visit the Stocks Research section of MSN MoneyCentral Investor at *http://moneycentral.msn.com/investor/research/welcome.asp* and then click Charts in the left navigation bar.

2. Type in the ticker symbol for your stock in the box, and then click Go.

3. Click Period at the top of the chart control, and then click Year on the menu that appears.

4. Click Analysis at the top of the chart control, point to Moving Averages, and then click 200-Day Moving Average.

5. A line, usually red, appears on the chart. That's the 200-day moving average. Point to the line, and a pop-up box displays, for a couple of seconds, the exact value of the 200-day moving average on the day to which you pointed.

6. To receive an alert if your stock falls to that level, visit the News Alerts section of MSN MoneyCentral Investor's Markets area. Follow instructions there to download and customize the MSNBC News Alert program to monitor your stocks during the day.

7. If a stock in your Flare-Out Growth portfolio slides, keep an eye on where it closes each day relative to that 200-day moving average. If it falls decisively below that level and the rest of the market is fine, consider selling it immediately. If it falls a little bit below the line and runs along it for the next few days or weeks, the stock has found support and might return to its upward path some time over the next few weeks or months. If that fails to happen, consider selling.

Index

Page numbers in italics indicate illustrations.

Keep your
small business
growing!

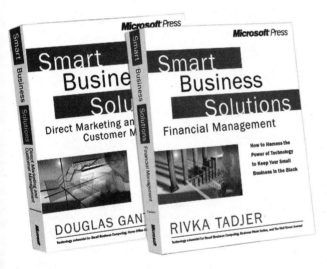

SMART BUSINESS SOLUTIONS books give you practical knowledge about essential software tools you need to efficiently manage a small business. Case studies of successful small businesses, advice from small-business experts, and complete details on how to use the latest technology to your advantage combine to show you how to make your small business prosper.

Smart Business Solutions for Direct Marketing and Customer Management

U.S.A. $29.99, U.K. £27.49, Canada $44.99 [Recommended].
ISBN 0-7356-0683-8.

Smart Business Solutions for Financial Management

U.S.A. $29.99, U.K. £27.49, Canada $44.99 [Recommended].
ISBN: 0-7356-0682-X.

Microsoft®

mspress.microsoft.com

Stay in the *running* for maximum productivity.

These are *the* answer books for business users of Microsoft Office 2000. They are packed with everything from quick, clear instructions for new users to comprehensive answers for power users—the authoritative reference to keep by your computer and use every day. The RUNNING series—learning solutions made by Microsoft.

- RUNNING MICROSOFT® EXCEL 2000
- RUNNING MICROSOFT OFFICE 2000 PREMIUM
- RUNNING MICROSOFT OFFICE 2000 PROFESSIONAL
- RUNNING MICROSOFT OFFICE 2000 SMALL BUSINESS
- RUNNING MICROSOFT WORD 2000
- RUNNING MICROSOFT POWERPOINT® 2000
- RUNNING MICROSOFT ACCESS 2000
- RUNNING MICROSOFT FRONTPAGE® 2000
- RUNNING MICROSOFT OUTLOOK® 2000

mspress.microsoft.com

Register Today!

Return this
Online Investing
registration card today

Microsoft®Press
mspress.microsoft.com

OWNER REGISTRATION CARD   0-7356-0650-1

Online Investing

_____ _____ _____
FIRST NAME   MIDDLE INITIAL   LAST NAME

_____
INSTITUTION OR COMPANY NAME

_____
ADDRESS

_____

_____ _____ _____
CITY   STATE   ZIP

                                                    (   )
_____ _____
E-MAIL ADDRESS   PHONE NUMBER

U.S. and Canada addresses only. Fill in information above and mail postage-free.
Please mail only the bottom half of this page.

For information about Microsoft Press® products, visit our Web site at **mspress.microsoft.com**

Microsoft®*Press*

Books from The Countryman Press
and Backcountry Publications

The Countryman Press and Backcountry Publications, long known
for fine books on travel and outdoor recreation, offer a range of
practical and readable manuals.

Hiking Series
Fifty Hikes in the Adirondacks, Second Edition
Fifty Hikes in Central New York, Second Edition
Fifty Hikes in Central Pennsylvania, Third Edition
Fifty Hikes in Eastern Pennsylvania, Second Edition
Fifty Hikes in the Hudson Valley, Second Edition
Fifty Hikes in Lower Michigan
Fifty Hikes in Massachusetts, Second Edition
Fifty Hikes in New Jersey
Fifty Hikes in the Mountains of North Carolina
Fifty Hikes in Northern Maine
Fifty Hikes in Northern Virginia
Fifty Hikes in Ohio
Fifty Hikes in Southern Maine
Fifty Hikes in Vermont, Fourth Edition
Fifty Hikes in Western New York
Fifty Hikes in Western Pennsylvania, Second Edition
Fifty Hikes in the White Mountains, Fourth Edition
Fifty More Hikes in New Hampshire, Third Edition

Walks & Rambles Series
Walks & Rambles in Dutchess and Putnam Counties
Walks & Rambles in Rhode Island, Second Edition
More Walks & Rambles in Rhode Island
Walks & Rambles in Southwestern Ohio
Walks & Rambles in Westchester & Fairfield Counties, Second Edition
Walks & Rambles on Cape Cod and the Islands
Walks & Rambles on the Delmarva Peninsula
Walks & Rambles in and around St. Louis

We offer many more books on hiking, walking, fishing, and canoeing, plus books on
travel, nature, and many other subjects.

Our books are available at bookstores, or they may be ordered directly from the publisher. For ordering information or for a complete catalog, please contact: The Countryman Press, c/o W.W. Norton & Company, Inc., 800 Keystone Industrial Park, Scranton, PA 18512.

Trail Notes

Trail Notes

Trail Notes

Part III

Researching Investment Ideas Online

Chapter 6
Newspapers and Magazines Online   103

Chapter 7
Newsletters   117

Contents

Part I

Building Model Portfolios

Chapter 1

Introduction to Model Portfolios   **3**

Chapter 2

Momentum Models   **17**

Chapter 3

Growth Investing Models   **33**

PUBLISHED BY
Microsoft Press
A Division of Microsoft Corporation
One Microsoft Way
Redmond, Washington 98052-6399

Library of Congress Cataloging-in-Publication Data
Markman, Jon D., 1958-
       Online Investing : Finding the Right Stock at the Right Time / Jon
    D. Markman.
            p. cm.
       Includes index.
       ISBN 0-7356-0650-1
       1. Investments--Computer network resources.   I. Title.
    HG4515.95.M37   1999
    025.06'3326--dc21   99-37221
                                                              CIP

Printed and bound in the United States of America.

 2 3 4 5 6 7 8 9   QMQM   4 3 2 1 0 9

Distributed in Canada by Penguin Books Canada Limited.

A CIP catalogue record for this book is available from the British Library.

Microsoft Press books are available through booksellers and distributors worldwide. For further information about international editions, contact your local Microsoft Corporation office or contact Microsoft Press International directly at fax (425) 936-7329. Visit our Web site at mspress.microsoft.com.

Acquisitions Editor: Susanne Forderer
Project Editor: Anne Taussig
Technical Editors: Dail Magee Jr., Julie Xiao

ONLINE INVESTING

Jon D. Markman

Introduction

1.

In recent years there has been an effort on the part of the students and critics of Emerson to prove that he was something other than we had thought—that he was, after all, a very human and very modern writer, rather than the cool and somewhat remote spiritual leader that he had seemed to his contemporaries. The real Emerson, it has been argued, can be discovered only in the *Journals,* where we find "Man Thinking"—where we can struggle with him through his own hopes and fears from one personal crisis to another and finally achieve with him a somewhat precarious equilibrium between tensions rather than a static calm. This is an Emerson who can say something to modern man, caught as he is in a world he never made and to which he must constantly readjust in order to survive. This is also the romantic Emerson who, like Carlyle and Wordsworth, Poe and Melville, suffered through storm and stress to emotional resolution in art.

There is so much truth and health in this point of view that it cannot be dismissed lightly. The earlier image of Emerson was caught up, together with those of Bryant and Longfellow, Tennyson and Browning, in the smug certainties of Victorian idealism. Like Pippa, these prophets had only to pass in order to set the world to rights. What insights they had into the deeper strata of human experience were obscured by the glitter of a surface optimism. What artistic mastery they achieved was blurred by an insistence on their "message." All of them had to be "debunked" and reappraised by modern skepticism, and some did not survive the ordeal too well.

Emerson came late to his trial by Van Wyck Brooks, John Jay Chapman, Norman Foerster, Ralph L. Rusk, F. O. Matthiessen, Stephen E. Whicher, and others; and he has gained rather than lost in every re-evaluation; but the new image is still fluent in outline. A satisfactory "modern" Emerson has not yet been discovered; it will never be found in t'

Journals alone or in any collection of paragraphs from his writings. For Emerson was both an intensely reserved man and a careful and deliberate artist; he kept his public and his private lives apart. If he was one of the major artists of his time, those writings to which he devoted his best effort and which he himself gave to the public in spoken or written form must stand on their merits, and they must be studied in the forms in which he presented them.

The work of art should, in the end, be able to stand up to criticism for what it is and what it says without recourse to the author's intentions for excuse. Modern biographers and students of the sage of Concord have done him an immense service in destroying the earlier image and thereby setting his work in a new and more accurate perspective, but there is another ordeal ahead for the poetry, the lectures, and the essays upon which Emerson rested his own bid for immortality. Criticism has not yet done for Emerson's literary work what it has done for *Moby Dick*, the lyrics and tales of Poe, or *The Adventures of Huckleberry Finn*.

This volume is therefore a selection from those writings of Emerson that have best stood the test of time and that represent the various forms of oral and written expression to which he devoted his most careful thought and workmanship. It does not present him primarily as a philosopher, a social critic, or a religious leader, although he was in some sense all of these. It keeps separate his public and his private writings; they should, however, be supplemented by a judicious reading from the *Journals* and *Letters,* no passages from which are here included. The text is that prepared by Emerson himself, as edited in *The Complete Works of Ralph Waldo Emerson* by his son Edward Waldo Emerson, with the assistance of his friend James Eliot Cabot.[1] Except for the lecture, "Human Culture: Introductory," which is here printed from *The Early Lectures of Ralph Waldo Emerson*, Vol. II,[2] with the permission of Harvard University Press, there is little novelty in the selections. Here the reader should find not all the best that Emerson wrote but at least some of the best in each kind of writing that he attempted.

[1] Edward Waldo Emerson (ed.), *The Complete Works of Ralph Waldo Emerson,* Centenary Edition (Boston: Houghton Mifflin Co., 1903–04).

[2] Stephen E. Whicher, Robert E. Spiller, and Wallace E. Williams (eds.), *The Early Lectures of Ralph Waldo Emerson,* Vol. II (Cambridge, Mass.: Harvard University Press, 1963).

2.

From earliest youth, Emerson thought of himself as a poet, and it is to his poetry that we must first turn if we are to discover the roots of his art. "I am a born poet," he confessed in 1835, "of a low class no doubt, but a poet." When the library of his literary father was sold at auction in 1811, it was found to contain the works of Ovid, Pope, Johnson, and Goldsmith. Ralph, then eight years old, was already studying these classical models and practicing the art. It was he who celebrated, often humorously, minor family events in formal verse, and he early wrote verse epistles to his Aunt Mary. His college journals are sprinkled with rhymed couplets, and there is extant at least one formal essay on the beauties of poetry and a long original poem first read before the undergraduate Pythologian Club in April, 1820. An imperfect sympathy with the English romantics, especially Wordsworth, is offset in these journals by a lament for the decline of classical culture and a charge that "the Monks in their cloisters in the dark ages invented Rhyme by which they endeavoured to shackle poetry or the soarings of the mind." [3] The young poet felt this bondage acutely; he had confessedly no ear for music yet he was to struggle throughout his life to confine his soaring thoughts to measured lines despite his early realization that the images of poetry "are nothing but the striking occurrences selected from Nature and Art and [that] it depends a great deal upon the assistance of words to give definiteness and very much resembles algebra in the principle whereon it is founded." [4] The result is that the reader who is accustomed to think of poetry in terms of melody has often turned from his Byron or his Swinburne to find in Emerson's verses an awkwardness and a twisting of phrase or image to make it fit the uncongenial rigidity of English meter and rhyme. But he who starts where Emerson started in his theory of poetry—with the idea that the poet senses the moral law in Nature and gives it expression in exalted word and image—will find in that very awkwardness a vigor and surprise that open fresh vistas of understanding. For Emerson was the first modern American poet to take his

---

[3] William H. Gilman et al. (gen. eds.), *The Journals and Miscellaneous Notebooks of Ralph Waldo Emerson*, Vol. I (Cambridge, Mass.: The Belknap Press of Harvard University Press, 1960), p. 242.

[4] *Ibid.*, p. 64.

primary inspiration from the seventeenth-century English metaphysical poets, and through them to view poetry as a kind of thinking, having as its chief instrument of expression the symbol rather than the metrical foot. For, like algebra, poetry conveyed its abstractions to him through the use of visible symbols and depended upon the eye even more than upon the ear for its reconciliation of nature and mind. When we learn, therefore, that Emerson was an admirer of George Herbert and Sir Thomas Browne, and that Emily Dickinson knew his poetry well and went to the same sources for her own, we do not find it difficult to trace an American heritage for the metaphysical poetry of such modernists as T. S. Eliot and Wallace Stevens.

Students of Emerson's poetry have been somewhat misled by the emphasis he seems to place on sound in his essay on *The Poet.* "For poetry was all written before time was, and whenever we are so finely organized that we can penetrate into that region where the air is music, we hear those primal warblings and attempt to write them down." But it is in this same essay that he calls the poet "the sayer, the namer" and declares that "it is not metres but a metre-making argument that makes a poem." "The poet is the Namer or Language-maker, naming things sometimes after their appearance, sometimes after their essence." "Nature offers all her creatures to to him as a picture language. . . . Things admit of being used as symbols because nature is a symbol, in the whole, and in every part." Thus, in his poem "Each and All," Emerson starts with "the heifer that lows in the upland farm" and concludes, "I yielded myself to the perfect whole"; similarly, in "The Snow-Storm," into what seems at first to be mere description of a winter landscape he unleashes the North Wind, a "fierce artificer" who can mock ages of architecture with his mad "night-work." Emerson's poet,

> The kingly bard
> Must smite the chords rudely and hard
> As with hammer or with mace.
>
> . . . .
>
> Great is the art,
> Great be the manners of the bard.
> He shall not his brain encumber
> With the coil of rhythm and number;   .
>
> . . . .

But mount to paradise
By the stairway of surprise.

This is the Emerson who gave to modern poetry a debt of
freedom even greater than that it owes to Whitman, a freedom to use sound as discord to startle the ear, and an understanding of the visual qualities of language which give to
poetry the mathematician's mastery of the symbol. His poetry
must be seen as well as heard before its meanings can be
grasped.

Thus, even though his output was small—he published
only two volumes of verse during his lifetime—it is to Emerson's poetry that we must first turn if we would read him
aright. Some of his verses are mere epigraphs for his essays
and these tend to rely too heavily on the simple restatement
in meter of ideas better expressed in prose; but the independent poems that are built around images, such as "Days,"
with its single image of time, or "Uriel," with the challenge
of the rebel angel, move directly from the poet's vision to its
meaning as realized in symbolic form.

3.

If Emerson's poetry must be seen as well as heard, his
prose should be heard before it is seen, for it was written first
with an audience in mind and much of it was never committed to print during his lifetime. His sermons, addresses,
lectures, and essays are all variants of the same basic form,
the oral discourse—a form that had a much higher status
as literature a century ago than it would seem to have today.
Those were the days of such preachers as William Ellery
Channing and Lyman Beecher, of orators such as Edward
Everett and Daniel Webster. They were also the great days
of the Lyceum Movement, when each city and town in the
United States had its own public hall where everything from
the lay sermon to the magician's bag of tricks occupied the
long winter months with a continuous variety show.

As the second surviving son of a clergyman, Ralph Waldo
Emerson felt the call to the ministry when his older brother
William decided to go into law. His first prose form, therefore, was the sermon, and he learned the art of public speaking in church and at the Harvard Divinity School. It was an

art of persuasion rather than of logic, an art of direct communication with an audience, in which the structure of meaning was built up from a simple text through expansion,
emphasis, repetition, and illustration to a fuller revelation.
This was the pattern Emerson followed through all the variations that he developed from the basic homiletic form. The
sentence is the first unit; the paragraph (which is normally
an expansion of the sentence) is the second; and the sermon,
lecture, or essay is built up from its slow start, in increasing
tempo, as with building blocks, to a structure that takes form
and balance as it rises from the level ground of common experience into the higher air of moral truth. For this reason,
some students of Emerson's prose have made the mistake
of thinking that his art consists merely in skillful use of the
aphoristic sentence or paragraph, and that they as editors or
anthologists are as free as he seemed to be to lift, shuffle, and
re-form sentence and paragraph in any way that they please.
In such fashion the rhetorical rhythm of his structure is totally
lost, and all that is left is a jumble of parts. Emerson's apparent carelessness of method is wholly deceptive. His art is that
of the composition of meaning by use of the *spoken word,* an
art in which the audience and the occasion are as much a
part of the act of composition as is the speaker.

First, then, the sermon. Emerson won his approbation or
license to preach by delivering a sermon to the Middlesex Association on October 10, 1826, at the age of twenty-three,
and he began assisting the Rev. Henry Ware at the Second
(Unitarian) Church in Boston where, three years later, he
became junior pastor. Through the happy few years of his
marriage to Ellen Tucker, he preached regularly, but he had
always questioned the doctrinal and sacramental phases of
Christianity and, with the demands of regular church responsibility, his doubts increased. Of the many sermons that
survive in manuscript only a few were published in his lifetime, the most memorable of which is the "Farewell Sermon"
of October, 1832, which, like the others, is rather a declaration of independence of view than a call to religious belief
and conformity. Throughout these sermons, the young minister
seems to be debating with his audience and, with their help,
finding his way through the jungle of formalism to a few essential truths. But he was already developing some of the
chief characteristics of his later style: the abrupt statement of

a whole idea or opinion in a single aphoristic sentence, the mounding of illustration upon illustration drawn from both a wide and eclectic reading and a homely experience, the crisp choice of word and image, the rhythm of restrained but ascending emotion.

With his voluntary resignation from his church and the death of his wife, Emersons whole life seemed to fall apart and, in 1832–33, he traveled in Europe. Upon his return he was greeted by friends with an invitation to deliver a lecture in Boston on natural history, or science, on November 5, 1833. With this lecture he began a new life. He married again and settled in Concord, Massachusetts, where he had spent so many of the summers of his youth; he bought the old Coolidge mansion on the Lexington Road; and he became a dominant figure in the life of the town, as his children grew up around him and the local farmers joined the intellectuals in seeking his friendship and guidance.

Like his sermons, his lectures were written for public presentation, and most of them have survived only in manuscript; but they were drawn upon heavily for the published essays, and much of what they contained is thus available in a revised and more polished form. Nevertheless, one must go back to the lectures themselves to hear the voice of Emerson and to appreciate his art. The earlier lectures are somewhat restricted in choice of subject by the fact that they were prepared on short notice on invitation of a lyceum group, but in 1836 he launched out on his own account with a succession of winter series in Boston on "Human Culture," "Human Life," "The Times," and other more congenial subjects.

Each series consisted of from five to twelve lectures on varying aspects of a central theme. They were usually delivered first in a place such as the Masonic Hall in Boston and were then repeated, in whole or in part, in other New England towns. Later Emerson extended his tours to New York and Philadelphia, and finally journeyed as far west as Ohio. On one occasion he accepted an invitation to make a lecture tour of England, where he read the series on "Representative Men." His subjects varied from pure moral abstraction, such as the introductory lecture to the series on "Human Culture," to topics more nearly of the times, such as "The Transcendentalist." Occasionally a specific invitation would elicit an address like "The American Scholar," which was given as the annual oration before the Phi Beta Kappa Society at Harvard, or the controversial address to the Harvard Divinity School in 1838. In every case, however, the form of the lecture was determined by the audience and the occasion. One must know, for example, that "The American Scholar" was the assigned topic for an annual academic oration in order to appreciate the irony and the challenge in Emerson's attack on provincialism and pedantry. Sometimes we hear the thrust and parry of the fencing match in his imperfect sentences and logical *non sequiturs,* or feel the mounting force of persuasion as each idea is sharply or quietly presented and then built up by repetition, emphasis, and rising and falling rhythm to a completion that is not a conclusion. There is a circular or spiral structure in all of Emerson's prose, and to read it well is to hear it spoken.

4.

The final form of Emerson's prose is the reworked essay or book, and Emerson was not by nature a writer of books. Later volumes like *Representative Men* (1850), *English Traits* (1856), and *The Conduct of Life* (1860) were apparently little more than the texts of his lecture series, perhaps considerably edited but otherwise printed much as they had been presented on the platform. Other collections, starting with *Society and Solitude* (1870), were compilations of miscellanies from various periods assembled by either Emerson or his friend James E. Cabot for an importunate publisher. Only the two volumes of collected *Essays* (First Series, 1841; Second Series, 1844) were thought over and thoroughly rewritten with publication in mind, and only *Nature* (1836) was written as a book in the first instance. In these last three works the whole of Emerson's literary method can be traced, starting usually with the passage from the *Journals,* which was reworked for the lecture and then reworked a second time for the essay, each sentence and paragraph polished to clarify its meaning and to strengthen its rhetorical effect, and then the parts woven and rewoven into the texture of the finished lecture or essay. The portrait that has come down to us of the lecturer in his decline shuffling his manuscripts on the lectern with little apparent plan or purpose grossly misrepresents the controlled artistry of his strong and mature years.

This artistry is most apparent in Emerson's first, which was also his last, book. As early as 1833, when he was still in Europe waiting to sail for home, he was planning a statement of what was to be for him the "first philosophy" of a new life. "I like my book about Nature," he wrote in his *Journal*, "and I wish I knew where and how I ought to live. God will show me." Notes on natural history in the same *Journal* list some of the "uses" of Nature that were to provide him with a springboard for both his book and his new way of life.

The book itself did not appear until 1836, after his career as a professional lecturer was well established. It was a slim volume, but in it he had distilled all his experience to date and all his plans for the future. A testament of beauty in poetic prose, it reflects the best of his thinking in the form he had developed in the pulpit and on the platform for its expression. Starting with a definition as text, it establishes at once the dualism of the inner and outer experience that he was here-after to espouse. "Philosophically considered, the Universe is composed of Nature and the Soul." Man is to be the measure of all things, but he must learn to look two ways, and the first is outward into Nature. There follows a series of chapters which, starting on the lowest level of "Commodity," gradually ascend through "Beauty," "Language," and "Discipline" to the upper level of "Spirit," from which the future can be calmly met as a quest for truth. Here the inner vision is fully realized. The ascending thought is closely paralleled by the ascending structure in an almost perfect arc. Uriel's heresy has become the key to the new philosophy and to the form of a new art:

> Line in nature is not found;
> Unit and universe are round.

The cyclic rhythm of life provides the structure and rhythm of the *Essays* as well, although only a few of these adhere strictly to the pattern of the ascending arc. Quarrying the manuscripts of the forty or more lectures that by now had accumulated in his file, Emerson laid out a series of studies of the components of his philosophy of humanism, his view of culture as an organic, continuing, and ever self-renewing experience. In the First Series "History" came first, because the past must first be conquered and made contributory to a living present. Then "Self-Reliance" places man in the center, and "Compensation" and "The Over-Soul" consider his relationship with the worlds of the relative and of the absolute. There is thus a loose plan to the book as a whole, which carries over into the more diverse topics of the Second Series in a descending scale from "The Poet" to "New England Reformers"; but its basic pattern is that of the inventory. Each essay focuses on an aspect of the central truth; taken together they constitute an elaboration and more judicious consideration of that First Philosophy he so passionately stated in *Nature*. No one essay is a doctrinal statement, although Emerson was by now in command of a growing doctrinal system of his own, composed of individualism, intuition, correspondence, compensation, and symbolism. To study the *Essays* as philosophy, one should of course sort out and consider each of these doctrines as well as their interrelationships, but to read and enjoy them as essays, no such effort is called for. Each is a flowing discourse, rising as the sun from a low horizon and shedding its light over a single day, setting a topic and then allowing the topic to develop and expand until it is completed. There are no consecutive arguments and no conclusions. Like experience itself, each essay is a unit only as a single vision of life that comes and goes in its cycle.

If the *Essays*, by their very care of composition, lack some of the fluidity of the spoken word, they compensate for it by their more gemlike perfection. They should first be read fast, and lived in the reading, rather than analyzed piece by piece. Analysis can come later and can be carried down to each single paragraph and sentence with rewarding discoveries. But for Emerson, in his writing as in his life, the way to truth is through living, and not, as Thoreau agreed, "through the having lived."

—ROBERT E. SPILLER

Bibliographical Note

The standard text of Emerson's writings is still the Centenary Edition of *The Complete Works of Ralph Waldo Emerson,* edited by Edward Waldo Emerson, in 12 volumes (Boston: Houghton Mifflin Co., 1903–04). This contains everything that Emerson published in his lifetime plus a selection from manuscripts unpublished at his death. A selection and arrangement of *The Journals of Ralph Waldo Emerson* was edited by Edward Waldo Emerson and Waldo Emerson Forbes, uniform with the Centenary Edition of the *Works,* in 10 volumes (Boston: Houghton Mifflin Co., 1909–14). This text will be superseded for scholarly purposes by the more nearly complete edition, *The Journals and Miscellaneous Notebooks of Ralph Waldo Emerson,* William H. Gilman et al., general editors, in 4 volumes with future volumes in preparation (Cambridge, Mass.: The Belknap Press of Harvard University Press, 1960–64). A definitive 6-volume edition of *The Letters of Ralph Waldo Emerson* was edited by Ralph L. Rusk (New York: Columbia University Press, 1939); and an edition of the early unpublished lectures, *The Early Lectures of Ralph Waldo Emerson,* was edited by Stephen E. Whicher and Robert E. Spiller: Vol. I, 1959; Vol. II, with Wallace E. Williams, 1963 (Cambridge, Mass.: Harvard University Press). Most of the sermons are still unpublished, although a selection of them was offered by Arthur C. McGiffert, Jr., in *Young Emerson Speaks* (Boston: Houghton Mifflin Co., 1938). The collected *Poems* are included as Volume IX of the Centenary Edition of the *Works.*

Selections from Emerson's writings are many, but three deserve mention for their special emphases. *Basic Selections from Emerson,* edited by Eduard C. Lindeman (New York: New American Library of World Literature, 1954; a Mentor paperback) stresses his pragmatic side; *Emerson: A Modern Anthology,* edited by Alfred Kazin and Daniel Aaron (New York: Dell Publishing Co., 1958; a Laurel edition paperback) attempts to order his philosophy by a systematic rearrangement of short passages from his works, letters, and journals; and *Selections from Ralph Waldo Emerson: An Organic Anthology* edited by Stephen E. Whicher (Boston: Houghton Mifflin Co., 1957, Riverside edition) shows his evolving personality by means of chronological presentation of journal passages, closely paralleled by selections from the essays and poems.

The standard biography is *The Life of Ralph Waldo Emerson,* by Ralph L. Rusk (New York: Charles Scribner's Sons, 1949); but James E. Cabot's *A Memoir of Ralph Waldo Emerson,* in 2 volumes (Boston: Houghton Mifflin Co., 1887), is still useful. Among the many critiques are *Emerson: A Statement of New England Transcendentalism as Expressed in the Philosophy of Its Chief Exponent,* by Henry D. Gray (Stanford, Calif.: Stanford University Press, 1917); *Emerson Handbook,* by Frederic Ives Carpenter (New York: Hendricks House, 1953); *Emerson's Angle of Vision,* by Sherman Paul (Cambridge, Mass.: Harvard University Press, 1952); *Freedom and Fate: An Inner Life of Ralph Waldo Emerson,* by Stephen E. Whicher (Philadelphia: University of Pennsylvania Press, 1953); and *Spires of Form: A Study of Emerson's Aesthetic Theory,* by Vivian C. Hopkins (Cambridge, Mass.: Harvard University Press, 1951). Kenneth Walter Cameron has supplied much incidental detail in *Emerson the Essayist,* in 2 volumes (Raleigh, N.C.: Thistle Press, 1945), and in other compilations. See also the periodical *Emerson Society Quarterly,* which first appeared in 1955. For further titles, see *Literary History of the United States,* edited by Robert E. Spiller, et al., in 2 volumes (New York: Macmillan Co., 1963, Third edition, revised.

Part One

POETRY

Poetry

The primary use of a fact is low; the secondary use, as it is a figure or illustration of my thought, is the real worth. First the fact; second its impression, or what I think of it. Hence Nature was called "a kind of adulterated reason." Seas, forests, metals, diamonds and fossils interest the eye, but 't is only with some preparatory or predicting charm. Their value to the intellect appears only when I hear their meaning made plain in the spiritual truth they cover. The mind, penetrated with its sentiment or its thought, projects it outward on whatever it beholds. The lover sees reminders of his mistress in every beautiful object; the saint, an argument for devotion in every natural process; and the facility with which Nature lends itself to the thoughts of man, the aptness with which a river, a flower, a bird, fire, day or night, can express his fortunes, is as if the world were only a disguised man, and, with a change of form, rendered to him all his experience. We cannot utter a sentence in sprightly conversation without a similitude. Note our incessant use of the word *like*—like fire, like a rock, like thunder, like a bee, "like a year without a spring." Conversation is not permitted without tropes; nothing but great weight in things can afford a quite literal speech. It is ever enlivened by inversion and trope. God himself does not speak prose, but communicates with us by hints, omens, inference and dark resemblances in objects lying all around us.

Nothing so marks a man as imaginative expressions. A figurative statement arrests attention, and is remembered and repeated. How often has a phrase of this kind made a reputation. Pythagoras's Golden Sayings were such, and Socrates's, and Mirabeau's, and Burke's, and Bonaparte's. Genius thus makes the transfer from one part of Nature to a remote part, and betrays the rhymes and echoes that pole makes with pole. Imaginative minds cling to their images, and do not wish

3

them rashly rendered into prose reality, as children resent your showing them that their doll Cinderella is nothing but pine wood and rags; and my young scholar does not wish to know what the leopard, the wolf, or Lucia, signify in Dante's Inferno, but prefers to keep their veils on. Mark the delight of an audience in an image. When some familiar truth or fact appears in a new dress, mounted as on a fine horse, equipped with a grand pair of ballooning wings, we cannot enough testify our surprise and pleasure. It is like the new virtue shown in some unprized old property, as when a boy finds that his pocket-knife will attract steel filings and take up a needle; or when the old horse-block in the yard is found to be a Torso Hercules of the Phidian age. Vivacity of expression may indicate this high gift, even when the thought is of no great scope, as when Michel Angelo, praising the *terra cottas,* said, "If this earth were to become marble, woe to the antiques!" A happy symbol is a sort of evidence that your thought is just. I had rather have a good symbol of my thought, or a good analogy, than the suffrage of Kant or Plato. If you agree with me, or if Locke or Montesquieu agree, I may yet be wrong; but if the elm-tree thinks the same thing, if running water, if burning coal, if crystals, if alkalies, in their several fashions say what I say, it must be true. Thus a good symbol is the best argument, and is a missionary to persuade thousands. The Vedas, the Edda, the Koran, are each remembered by their happiest figure. There is no more welcome gift to men than a new symbol. That satiates, transports, converts them. They assimilate themselves to it, deal with it in all ways, and it will last a hundred years. Then comes a new genius, and brings another. Thus the Greek mythology called the sea "the tear of Saturn." The return of the soul to God was described as "a flask of water broken in the sea." Saint John gave us the Christian figure of "souls washed in the blood of Christ." The aged Michel Angelo indicates his perpetual study as in boyhood—"I carry my satchel still." Machiavel described the papacy as "a stone inserted in the body of Italy to keep the wound open." To the Parliament debating how to tax America, Burke exclaimed, "Shear the wolf." Our Kentuckian orator said of his dissent from his companion, "I showed him the back of my hand." And our proverb of the courteous soldier reads: "An iron hand in a velvet glove."

This belief that the higher use of the material world is to furnish us types or pictures to express the thoughts of the mind, is carried to its logical extreme by the Hindoos, who, following Buddha, have made it the central doctrine of their religion that what we call Nature, the external world, has no real existence—is only phenomenal. Youth, age, property, condition, events, persons—self, even—are successive *maias* (deceptions) through which Vishnu mocks and instructs the soul. I think Hindoo books the best gymnastics for the mind, as showing treatment. All European libraries might almost be read without the swing of this gigantic arm being suspected. But these Orientals deal with worlds and pebbles freely.

For the value of a trope is that the hearer is one: and indeed Nature itself is a vast trope, and all particular natures are tropes. As the bird alights on the bough, then plunges into the air again, so the thoughts of God pause but for a moment in any form. All thinking is analogizing, and it is the use of life to learn metonymy. The endless passing of one element into new forms, the incessant metamorphosis, explains the rank which the imagination holds in our catalogue of mental powers. The imagination is the reader of these forms. The poet accounts all productions and changes of Nature as the nouns of language, uses them representatively, too well pleased with their ulterior to value much their primary meaning. Every new object so seen gives a shock of agreeable surprise. The impressions on the imagination make the great days of life: the book, the landscape or the personality which did not stay on the surface of the eye or ear but penetrated to the inward sense, agitates us, and is not forgotten. Walking, working or talking, the sole question is how mamy strokes vibrate on this mystic string—how many diameters are drawn quite through from matter to spirit; for whenever you enunciate a natural law you discover that you have enunciated a law of the mind. Chemistry, geology, hydraulics, are secondary science. The atomic theory is only an interior process *produced,* as geometers say, or the effect of a foregone metaphysical theory. Swedenborg saw gravity to be only an external of the irresistible attractions of affection and faith. Mountains and oceans we think we understand—yes, so long as they are contented to be such, and are safe with the geologist—but when they are melted in Promethean alembics and come out men, and then, melted again, come out words, without any abatement, but with an exaltation of power!

In poetry we say we require the miracle. The bee flies among the flowers, and gets mint and marjoram, and generates a new product, which is not mint and marjoram, but honey; the chemist mixes hydrogen and oxygen to yield a new product, which is not these, but water; and the poet listens to conversation and beholds all objects in Nature, to give back, not them, but a new and transcendent whole.

Poetry is the perpetual endeavor to express the spirit of the thing, to pass the brute body and search the life and reason which causes it to exist; to see that the object is always flowing away, whilst the spirit or necessity which causes it subsists. Its essential mark is that it betrays in every word instant activity of mind, shown in new uses of every fact and image, in preternatural quickness or perception of relations. All its words are poems. It is a presence of mind that gives a miraculous command of all means of uttering the thought and feeling of the moment. The poet squanders on the hour an amount of life that would more than furnish the seventy years of the man that stands next him.

The term "genius," when used with emphasis, implies imagination; use of symbols, figurative speech. A deep insight will always, like Nature, ultimate its thought in a thing. As soon as a man masters a principle and sees his facts in relation to it, fields, waters, skies, offer to clothe his thoughts in images. Then all men understand him; Parthian, Mede, Chinese, Spaniard and Indian hear their own tongue. For he can now find symbols of universal significance, which are readily rendered into any dialect; as a painter, a sculptor, a musician, can in their several ways express the same sentiment of anger, or love, or religion.

The thoughts are few, the forms many; the large vocabulary or many-colored coat of the indigent unity. The *savants* are chatty and vain, but hold them hard to principle and definition, and they become mute and near-sighted. What is motion? what is beauty? what is matter? what is life? what is force? Push them hard and they will not be loquacious. They will come to Plato, Proclus and Swedenborg. The invisible and imponderable is the sole fact. "Why changes not the violet earth into musk?" What is the term of the ever-flowing metamorphosis? I do not know what are the stoppages, but I see that a devouring unity changes all into that which changes not.

The act of imagination is ever attended by pure delight. It infuses a certain volatility and intoxication into all Nature. It has a flute which sets the atoms of our frame in a dance. Our indeterminate size is a delicious secret which it reveals to us. The mountains begin to dislimn, and float in the air. In the presence and conversation of a true poet, teeming with images to express his enlarging thought, his person, his form, grows larger to our fascinated eyes. And thus begins that deification which all nations have made of their heroes in every kind— saints, poets, lawgivers and warriors.

From "Poetry and Imagination" in *Letters and Social Aims*

The Poet

Those who are esteemed umpires of taste are often persons who have acquired some knowledge of admired pictures or sculptures, and have an inclination for whatever is elegant; but if you inquire whether they are beautiful souls, and whether their own acts are like fair pictures, you learn that they are selfish and sensual. Their cultivation is local, as if you should rub a log of dry wood in one spot to produce fire, all the rest remaining cold. Their knowledge of the fine arts is some study of rules and particulars, or some limited judgment of color or form, which is exercised for amusement or for show. It is a proof of the shallowness of the doctrine of beauty as it lies in the minds of our amateurs, that men seem to have lost the perception of the instant dependence of form upon soul. There is no doctrine of forms in our philosophy. We were put into our bodies, as fire is put into a pan to be carried about; but there is no accurate adjustment between the spirit and the organ, much less is the latter the germination of the former. So in regard to other forms, the intellectual men do not believe in any essential dependence of the material world on thought and volition. Theologians think it a pretty air-castle to talk of the spiritual meaning of a ship or a cloud, of a city or a contract, but they prefer to come again to the solid ground of historical evidence; and even the poets are contented with a civil and conformed manner of living, and to write poems from the fancy, at a safe distance from their own experience. But the highest minds of the world have never ceased to explore the double meaning, or shall I say the quadruple or the centuple or much more manifold meaning, of every sensuous fact; Orpheus, Empedocles, Heraclitus, Plato, Plutarch, Dante, Swedenborg, and the masters of sculpture, picture and poetry. For we are not pans and barrows, nor even porters of the fire and torch-bearers, but children of the fire, made of it, and only the same divinity transmuted and at two or three removes, when we know least about it. And this hidden truth, that the fountains whence all this river of Time and its creatures floweth are intrinsically ideal and beautiful, draws us to the consideration of the nature and functions of the Poet, or the man of Beauty; to the means and materials he uses, and to the general aspect of the art in the present time.

The breadth of the problem is great, for the poet is representative. He stands among partial men for the complete man, and apprises us not of his wealth, but of the common wealth. The young man reveres men of genius, because, to speak truly, they are more himself than he is. They receive of the soul as he also receives, but they more. Nature enhances her beauty, to the eye of loving men, from their belief that the poet is beholding her shows at the same time. He is isolated among his contemporaries by truth and by his art, but with this consolation in his pursuits, that they will draw all men sooner or later. For all men live by truth and stand in need of expression. In love, in art, in avarice, in politics, in labor, in games, we study to utter our painful secret. The man is only half himself, the other half is his expression.

Notwithstanding this necessity to be published, adequate expression is rare. I know not how it is that we need an interpreter, but the great majority of men seem to be minors, who have not yet come into possession of their own, or mutes, who cannot report the conversation they have had with nature. There is no man who does not anticipate a supersensual utility in the sun and stars, earth and water. These stand and wait to render him a peculiar service. But there is some obstruction or some excess of phlegm in our constitution, which does not suffer them to yield the due effect. Too feeble fall the impressions of nature on us to make us artists. Every touch should thrill. Every man should be so much an artist that he could report in conversation what had befallen him. Yet, in our experience, the rays or appulses have sufficient force to arrive at the senses, but not enough to reach the quick and compel the reproduction of themselves in speech. The poet is the person in whom these powers are in balance, the man without impediment, who sees and handles that which others dream of, traverses the whole scale of experience, and is representative of man, in virtue of being the largest power to receive and to impart.

For the Universe has three children, born at one time, which reappear under different names in every system of thought, whether they be called cause, operation and effect; or, more poetically, Jove, Pluto, Neptune; or, theologically, the Father, the Spirit and the Son; but which we will call here the Knower, the Doer and the Sayer. These stand respectively for the love of truth, for the love of good, and for the love of beauty. These three are equal. Each is that which he is, essentially, so that he cannot be surmounted or analyzed, and each of these three has the power of the others latent in him and his own, patent.

The poet is the sayer, the namer, and represents beauty. He is a sovereign, and stands on the centre. For the world is not painted or adorned, but is from the beginning beautiful; and God has not made some beautiful things, but Beauty is the creator of the universe. Therefore the poet is not any permissive potentate, but is emperor in his own right. Criticism is infested with a cant of materialism, which assumes that manual skill and activity is the first merit of all men, and disparages such as say and do not, overlooking the fact that some men, namely poets, are natural sayers, sent into the world to the end of expression, and confounds them with those whose province is action but who quit it to imitate the sayers. But Homer's words are as costly and admirable to Homer as Agamemnon's victories are to Agamemnon. The poet does not wait for the hero or the sage, but, as they act and think primarily, so he writes primarily what will and must be spoken, reckoning the others, though primaries also, yet, in respect to him, secondaries and servants; as sitters or models in the studio of a painter, or as assistants who bring building-materials to an architect.

For poetry was all written before time was, and whenever we are so finely organized that we can penetrate into that region where the air is music, we hear those primal warblings and attempt to write them down, but we lose ever and anon a word or a verse and substitute something of our own, and thus miswrite the poem. The men of more delicate ear write down these cadences more faithfully, and these transcripts, though imperfect, become the songs of the nations. For nature is as truly beautiful as it is good, or as it is reasonable, and must as much appear as it must be done, or be known. Words and deeds are quite indifferent modes of the divine energy. Words are also actions, and actions are a kind of words.

The sign and credentials of the poet are that he announces that which no man foretold. He is the true and only doctor; he knows and tells; he is the only teller of news, for he was present and privy to the appearance which he describes. He is a beholder of ideas and an utterer of the necessary and causal. For we do not speak now of men of poetical talents, or of industry and skill in metre, but of the true poet. I took part in a conversation the other day concerning a recent writer of lyrics, a man of subtle mind, whose head appeared to be a music-box of delicate tunes and rhythms, and whose skill and command of language we could not sufficiently praise. But when the question arose whether he was not only a lyrist but a poet, we were obliged to confess that he is plainly a contemporary, not an eternal man. He does not stand out of our low limitations, like a Chimborazo under the line, running up from a torrid base through all the climates of the globe, with belts of the herbage of every latitude on its high and mottled sides; but this genius is the landscape-garden of a modern house, adorned with fountains and statues, with well-bred men and women standing and sitting in the walks and terraces. We hear, through all the varied music, the ground-tone of conventional life. Our poets are men of talents who sing, and not the children of music. The argument is secondary, the finish of the verses is primary.

For it is not metres, but a metre-making argument that makes a poem—a thought so passionate and alive that like the spirit of a plant or an animal it has an architecture of its own, and adorns nature with a new thing. The thought and the form are equal in the order of time, but in the order of genesis the thought is prior to the form. The poet has a new thought; he has a whole new experience to unfold; he will tell us how it was with him, and all men will be richer in his fortune. For the experience of each new age requires a new confession, and the world seems always waiting for its poet. I remember when I was young how much I was moved one morning by tidings that genius had appeared in a youth who sat near me at table. He had left his work and gone rambling none knew whither, and had written hundreds of lines, but could not tell whether that which was in him was therein told; he could tell nothing but that all was changed—man, beast, heaven, earth and sea. How gladly we listened! how credulous! Society seemed to be compromised. We sat in the aurora of a sunrise which was to put out all the stars. Boston seemed to be at twice the distance it had the night before, or was much farther than that. Rome—what was Rome? Plutarch and Shakspeare were in the yellow leaf, and Homer no more should be heard of. It is much to know that poetry has been written this very day, under this very roof, by your side. What! that wonderful spirit has not expired! These stony moments are still sparkling and animated! I had fancied that the oracles were all silent, and nature had spent her fires; and behold! all night, from every pore, these fine auroras have been streaming. Every one has some interest in the advent of the poet, and no one knows how much it may concern him. We know that the secret of the world is profound, but who or what shall be our interpreter, we know not. A mountain ramble, a new style of face, a new person, may put the key into our hands. Of course the value of genius to us is in the veracity of its report. Talent may frolic and juggle; genius realizes and adds. Mankind in good earnest have availed so far in understanding themselves and their work, that the foremost watchman on the peak announces his news. It is the truest word ever spoken, and the phrase will be the fittest, most musical, and the unerring voice of the world for that time.

All that we call sacred history attests that the birth of a poet is the principal event in chronology. Man, never so often deceived, still watches for the arrival of a brother who can hold him steady to a truth until he has made it his own. With what joy I begin to read a poem which I confide in as an inspiration! And now my chains are to be broken; I shall mount above these clouds and opaque airs in which I live—opaque, though they seem transparent—and from the heaven of truth I shall see and comprehend my relations. That will reconcile me to life and renovate nature, to see trifles animated by a tendency, and to know what I am doing. Life will no more be a noise; now I shall see men and woman, and know the signs by which they may be discerned from fools and satans. This day shall be better than my birthday: then I became an animal; now I am invited into the science of the real. Such is the hope, but the fruition is postponed. Oftener it falls that this winged man, who will carry me into the heaven, whirls me into mists, then leaps and frisks about with me as it were from cloud to cloud, still affirming that he is bound heavenward; and I, being myself a novice, am slow in perceiving that he does not know the way into the heavens, and is merely bent that I should admire his skill to rise like a fowl or a flying fish, a little way from the ground or the water; but the all-piercing, all-feeding and ocular air of heaven that man shall never inhabit. I tumble down again soon into my old nooks, and lead the life of exaggerations as before, and have lost my faith in the possibility of any guide who can lead me thither where I would be.

But, leaving these victims of vanity, let us, with new hope, observe how nature, by worthier impulses, has insured the poet's fidelity to his office of announcement and affirming, namely by the beauty of things, which becomes a new and higher beauty when expressed. Nature offers all her creatures to him as a picture-language. Being used as a type, a second wonderful value appears in the object, far better than its old value; as the carpenter's stretched cord, if you hold your ear close enough, is musical in the breeze. "Things more excellent than every image," says Jamblichus, "are expressed through images." Things admit of being used as symbols because nature is a symbol, in the whole, and in every part. Every line we can draw in the sand has expression; and there is no body without its spirit or genius. All form is an effect of character; all condition, of the quality of the life; all harmony, of health; and for this reason a perception of beauty should be sympathetic, or proper only to the good. The beautiful rests on the foundations of the necessary. The soul makes the body, as the wise Spenser teaches:

> So every spirit, as it is more pure,
> And hath in it the more of heavenly light,
> So it the fairer body doth procure
> To habit in, and it more fairly dight,
> With cheerful grace and amiable sight.
> For, of the soul, the body form doth take,
> For soul is form, and doth the body make.[1]

Here we find ourselves suddenly not in a critical speculation but in a holy place, and should go very warily and reverently. We stand before the secret of the world, there where Being passes into Appearance and Unity into Variety.

The Universe is the externization of the soul. Wherever the life is, that bursts into appearance around it. Our science is sensual, and therefore superficial. The earth and the heavenly bodies, physics and chemistry, we sensually treat, as if they were self-existent; but these are the retinue of that Being we have. "The mighty heaven," said Proclus, "exhibits, in its transfigurations, clear images of the splendor of intellectual perceptions; being moved in conjunction with the unapparent periods of intellectual natures." Therefore science always goes abreast with the just elevation of the man, keeping step with religion and metaphysics; or the state of science is an index of our self-knowledge. Since every thing in nature answers to a moral power, if any phenomenon remains brute and dark it is because the corresponding faculty in the observer is not yet active.

No wonder then, if these waters be so deep, that we hover over them with a religious regard. The beauty of the fable proves the importance of the sense; to the poet, and to all others; or, if you please, every man is so far a poet as to be susceptible of these enchantments of nature; for all men have the thoughts whereof the universe is the celebration. I find that the fascination resides in the symbol. Who loves nature? Who does not? Is it only poets, and men of leisure and cultivation, who live with her? No; but also hunters, farmers, grooms and butchers, though they express their affection in

---

[1] Spenser, *An Hymne in Honour of Beautie*, Stanza xix.

their choice of life and not in their choice of words. The writer wonders what the coachman or the hunter values in riding, in horses and dogs. It is not superficial qualities. When you talk with him he holds these at as slight a rate as you. His worship is sympathetic; he has no definitions, but he is commanded in nature by the living power which he feels to be there present. No imitation or playing of these things would content him; he loves the earnest of the north wind, of rain, of stone and wood and iron. A beauty not explicable is dearer than a beauty which we can see to the end of. It is nature the symbol, nature certifying the supernatural, body overflowed by life which he worships with coarse but sincere rites.

The inwardness and mystery of this attachment drive men of every class to the use of emblems. The schools of poets and philosophers are not more intoxicated with their symbols than the populace with theirs. In our political parties, compute the power of badges and emblems. See the great ball which they roll from Baltimore to Bunker Hill! In the political processions, Lowell goes in a loom, and Lynn in a shoe, and Salem in a ship. Witness the cider-barrel, the log-cabin, the hickory-stick, the palmetto, and all the cognizances of party. See the power of national emblems. Some stars, lilies, leopards, a crescent, a lion, an eagle, or other figure which came into credit God knows how, on an old rag of bunting, blowing in the wind on a fort at the ends of the earth, shall make the blood tingle under the rudest or the most conventional exterior. The people fancy they hate poetry, and they are all poets and mystics!

Beyond this universality of the symbolic language, we are apprised of the divineness of this superior use of things, whereby the world is a temple whose walls are covered with emblems, pictures and commandments of the Deity—in this, that there is no fact in nature which does not carry the whole sense of nature; and the distinctions which we make in events and in affairs, of low and high, honest and base, disappear when nature is used as a symbol. Thought makes everything fit for use. The vocabulary of an omniscient man would embrace words and images excluded from polite conversation. What would be base, or even obscene, to the obscene, becomes illustrious, spoken in a new connection of thought. The piety of the Hebrew prophets purges their grossness. The circumcision is an example of the power of poetry to raise the low and offensive. Small and mean things serve as well as great symbols. The meaner the type by which a law is expressed, the more pungent it is, and the more lasting in the memories of men; just as we choose the smallest box or case in which any needful utensil can be carried. Bare lists of words are found suggestive to an imaginative and excited mind; as it is related of Lord Chatham that he was accustomed to read in Bailey's Dictionary when he was preparing to speak in Parliament. The poorest experience is rich enough for all the purposes of expressing thought. Why covet a knowledge of new facts? Day and night, house and garden, a few books, a few actions, serve us as well as would all trades and all spectacles. We are far from having exhausted the significance of the few symbols we use. We can come to use them yet with a terrible simplicity. It does not need that a poem should be long. Every word was once a poem. Every new relation is a new word. Also we use defects and deformities to a sacred purpose, so expressing our sense that the evils of the world are such only to the evil eye. In the old mythology, mythologists observe, defects are ascribed to divine natures, as lameness to Vulcan, blindness to Cupid, and the like—to signify exuberances.

For as it is dislocation and detachment from the life of God that makes things ugly, the poet, who re-attaches things to nature and the Whole—re-attaching even artificial things and violation of nature, to nature, by a deeper insight—disposes very easily of the most disagreeable facts. Readers of poetry see the factory-village and the railway, and fancy that the poetry of the landscape is broken up by these; for these works of art are not yet consecrated in their reading; but the poet sees them fall within the great Order not less than the beehive or the spider's geometrical web. Nature adopts them very fast into her vital circles, and the gliding train of cars she loves like her own. Besides, in a centred mind, it signifies nothing how many mechanical inventions you exhibit. Though you add millions, and never so surprising, the fact of mechanics has not gained a grain's weight. The spiritual fact remains unalterable, by many or by few particulars; as no mountain is of any appreciable height to break the curve of the sphere. A shrewd country-boy goes to the city for the first time, and the complacent citizen is not satisfied with his little wonder. It is not that he does not see all the fine houses and know that he

never saw such before, but he disposes of them as easily as
the poet finds a place for the railway. The chief value of the
new fact is to enhance the great and constant fact of Life,
which can dwarf any and every circumstance, and to which
the belt of wampum and the commerce of America are alike.

The world being thus put under the mind for verb and
noun, the poet is he who can articulate it. For though life is
great, and fascinates and absorbs; and though all men are intelligent of the symbols through which it is named; yet they
cannot originally use them. We are symbols and inhabit symbols; workmen, work, and tools, words and things, birth and
death, all are emblems; but we sympathize with the symbols,
and being infatuated with the economical uses of things, we
do not know that they are thoughts. The poet, by an ulterior
intellectual perception, gives them a power which makes their
old use forgotten, and puts eyes and a tongue into every
dumb and inanimate object. He perceives the independence
of the thought on the symbol, the stability of the thought, the
accidency and fugacity of the symbol. As the eyes of Lyn-
cæus were said to see through the earth, so the poet turns
the world to glass, and shows us all things in their right
series and procession. For through that better perception he
stands one step nearer to things, and sees the flowing or metamorphosis; perceives that thought is multiform; that within
the form of every creature is a force impelling it to ascend
into a higher form; and following with his eyes the life, uses
the forms which express that life, and so his speech flows
with the flowing of nature. All the facts of the animal economy, sex, nutriment, gestation, birth, growth, are symbols of
the passage of the world into the soul of man, to suffer there
a change and reappear a new and higher fact. He uses forms
according to the life, and not according to the form. This is
true science. The poet alone knows astronomy, chemistry,
vegetation and animation, for he does not stop at these facts,
but employs them as signs. He knows why the plain or
meadow of space was strown with these flowers we call suns
and moons and stars; why the great deep is adorned with animals, with men, and gods; for in every word he speaks he
rides on them as the horses of thought.

By virtue of this science the poet is the Namer or Language-
maker, naming things sometimes after their appearance, sometimes after their essence, and giving to every one its own

name and not another's, thereby rejoicing the intellect, which delights in detachment or boundary. The poets made all the words, and therefore language is the archives of history, and, if we must say it, a sort of tomb of the muses. For though the origin of most of our words is forgotten, each word was at first a stroke of genius, and obtained currency because for the moment it symbolized the world to the first speaker and to the hearer. The etymologist finds the deadest word to have been once a brilliant picture. Language is fossil poetry. As the limestone of the continent consists of infinite masses of the shells of animalcules, so language is made up of images or tropes, which now, in their secondary use, have long ceased to remind us of their poetic origin. But the poet names the thing because he sees it, or comes one step nearer to it than any other. This expression or naming is not art, but a second nature, grown out of the first, as a leaf out of a tree. What we call nature is a certain self-regulated motion or change; and nature does all things by her own hands, and does not leave another to baptize her but baptizes herself; and this through the metamorphosis again. I remember that a certain poet described it to me thus:

Genius is the activity which repairs the decays of things, whether wholly or partly of a material and finite kind. Nature, through all her kingdoms, insures herself. Nobody cares for planting the poor fungus; so she shakes down from the gills of one agaric countless spores, any one of which, being preserved, transmits new billions of spores to-morrow or next day. The new agaric of this hour has a chance which the old one had not. This atom of seed is thrown into a new place, not subject to the accidents which destroyed its parent two rods off. She makes a man; and having brought him to ripe age, she will no longer run the risk of losing this wonder at a blow, but she detaches from him a new self, that the kind may be safe from accidents to which the individual is exposed. So when the soul of the poet has come to ripeness of thought, she detaches and sends away from it its poems or songs—a fearless, sleepless, deathless progeny, which is not exposed to the accidents of the weary kingdom of time; a fearless, vivacious offspring, clad with wings (such was the virtue of the soul out of which they came) which carry them fast and far, and infix them irrecoverably into the hearts of men.

These wings are the beauty of the poet's soul. The songs, thus flying immortal from their mortal parent, are pursued by clamorous flights of censures, which swarm in far greater numbers and threaten to devour them; but these last are not winged. At the end of a very short leap they fall plump down and rot, having received from the souls out of which they came no beautiful wings. But the melodies of the poet ascend and leap and pierce into the deeps of infinite time.

So far the bard taught me, using his freer speech. But nature has a higher end, in the production of new individuals, than security, namely *ascension*, or the passage of the soul into higher forms. I knew in my younger days the sculptor who made the statue of the youth which stands in the public garden. He was, as I remember, unable to tell directly what made him happy or unhappy, but by wonderful indirections he could tell. He rose one day, according to his habit, before the dawn, and saw the morning break, grand as the eternity out of which it came, and for many days after, he strove to express this tranquillity, and lo! his chisel had fashioned out of marble the form of a beautiful youth, Phosphorus, whose aspect is such that it is said all persons who look on it become silent. The poet also resigns himself to his mood, and that thought which agitated him is expressed, but *alter idem*, in a manner totally new. The expression is organic, or the new type which things themselves take when liberated. As, in the sun, objects paint their images on the retina of the eye, so they, sharing the aspiration of the whole universe, tend to paint a far more delicate copy of their essence in his mind. Like the metamorphosis of things into higher organic forms is their change into melodies. Over everything stands its dæmon or soul, and, as the form of the thing is reflected by the eye, so the soul of the thing is reflected by a melody. The sea, the mountain-ridge, Niagara, and every flower-bed, pre-exist, or super-exist, in pre-cantations, which sail like odors in the air, and when any man goes by with an ear sufficiently fine, he overhears them and endeavors to write down the notes without diluting or depraving them. And herein is the legitimation of criticism, in the mind's faith that the poems are a corrupt version of some text in nature with which they ought to be made totally. A rhyme in one of our sonnets should not be less pleasing than the iterated nodes of a seashell, or the resembling difference of a group of flowers. The pairing of the birds is an idyl, not tedious as our idyls are; a tempest is a rough ode, without falsehood or rant; a summer, with its harvest sown, reaped and stored, is an epic song, subordinating how many admirably executed parts. Why should not the symmetry and truth that modulate these, glide into our spirits, and we participate the invention of nature?

This insight, which expresses itself by what is called Imagination, is a very high sort of seeing, which does not come by study, but by the intellect being where and what it sees; by sharing the path or circuit of things through forms, and so making them translucid to others. The path of things is silent. Will they suffer a speaker to go with them? A spy they will not suffer; a lover, a poet, is the transcendency of their own nature—him they will suffer. The condition of true naming, on the poet's part, is his resigning himself to the divine *aura* which breathes through forms, and accompanying that.

It is a secret which every intellectual man quickly learns, that beyond the energy of his possessed and conscious intellect he is capable of a new energy (as of an intellect doubled on itself), by abandonment to the nature of things; that beside his privacy of power as an individual man, there is a great public power on which he can draw, by unlocking, at all risks, his human doors, and suffering the ethereal tides to roll and circulate through him; then he is caught up into the life of the Universe, his speech is thunder, his thought is law, and his words are universally intelligible as the plants and animals. The poet knows that he speaks adequately then only when he speaks somewhat wildly, or "with the flower of the mind;" not with the intellect used as an organ, but with the intellect released from all service and suffered to take its direction from its celestial life; or as the ancients were wont to express themselves, not with intellect alone but with the intellect inebriated by nectar. As the traveller who has lost his way throws his reins on his horse's neck and trusts to the instinct of the animal to find his road, so must we do with the divine animal who carries us through this world. For if in any manner we can stimulate this instinct, new passages are opened for us into nature; the mind flows into and through things hardest and highest, and the metamorphosis is possible.

This is the reason why bards love wine, mead, narcotics, coffee, tea, opium, the fumes of sandalwood and tobacco, or whatever other procurers of animal exhilaration. All men avail themselves of such means as they can, to add this extraordinary power to their normal powers; and to this end they prize conversation, music, pictures, sculpture, dancing, theatres, travelling, war, mobs, fires, gaming, politics, or love, or science, or animal intoxication—which are several coarser or finer *quasi*-mechanical substitutes for the true nectar, which is the ravishment of the intellect by coming nearer to the fact. These are auxiliaries to the centrifugal tendency of a man, to his passage out into free space, and they help him to escape the custody of that body in which he is pent up, and of that jail-yard of individual relations in which he is enclosed. Hence a great number of such as were professionally expressers of Beauty, as painters, poets, musicians and actors, have been more than others wont to lead a life of pleasure and indulgence; all but the few who received the true nectar; and, as it was a spurious mode of attaining freedom, as it was an emancipation not into the heavens but into the freedom of baser places, they were punished for that advantage they won, by a dissipation and deterioration. But never can any advantage be taken of nature by a trick. The spirit of the world, the great calm presence of the Creator, comes not forth to the sorceries of opium or of wine. The sublime vision comes to the pure and simple soul in a clean and chaste body. That is not an inspiration, which we owe to narcotics, but some counterfeit excitement and fury. Milton says that the lyric poet may drink wine and live generously, but the epic poet, he who shall sing of the gods and their descent unto men, must drink water out of a wooden bowl. For poetry is not "Devil's wine," but God's wine. It is with this as it is with toys. We fill the hands and nurseries of our children with all manner of dolls, drums and horses; withdrawing their eyes from the plain face and sufficing objects of nature, the sun and moon, the animals, the water and stones, which should be their toys. So the poet's habit of living should be set on a key so low that the common influences should delight him. His cheerfulness should be the gift of the sunlight; the air should suffice for his inspiration, and he should be tipsy with water. That spirit which suffices quiet hearts, which seems to come forth to such from every dry knoll of sere grass, from every pine stump and half-imbedded stone on which the dull March sun shines, comes forth to the poor and hungry, and such as are of simple taste. If thou fill thy brain with Boston and New York, with fashion and covetousness, and wilt stimulate thy jaded senses with wine and French coffee, thou shalt find no radiance of wisdom in the lonely waste of the pine woods.

If the imagination intoxicates the poet, it is not inactive in other men. The metamorphosis excites in the beholder an emotion of joy. The use of symbols has a certain power of emancipation and exhilaration for all men. We seem to be touched by a wand which makes us dance and run about happily, like children. We are like persons who come out of a cave or cellar into the open air. This is the effect on us of tropes, fables, oracles and all poetic forms. Poets are thus liberating gods. Men have really got a new sense, and found within their world another world, or nest of worlds; for, the metamorphosis once seen, we divine that it does not stop. I will not now consider how much this makes the charm of algebra and the mathematics, which also have their tropes, but it is felt in every definition; as when Aristotle defines *space* to be an immovable vessel in which things are contained; or when Plato defines a *line* to be a flowing point, or *figure* to be a bound of solid; and many the like. What a joyful sense of freedom we have when Vitruvius announces the old opinion of artists that no architect can build any house well who does not know something of anatomy. When Socrates, in Charmides, tells us that the soul is cured of its maladies by certain incantations, and that these incantations are beautiful reasons, from which temperance is generated in souls; when Plato calls the world an animal, and Timæus affirms that the plants also are animals; or affirms a man to be a heavenly tree, growing with his root, which is his head, upward; and, as George Chapman, following him, writes,

> So in our tree of man, whose nervie root
> Springs in his top;[2]

when Orpheus speaks of hoariness as "that white flower which marks extreme old age;" when Proclus calls the universe the statue of the intellect; when Chaucer, in his praise of "Gentilesse," compares good blood in mean condition to fire, which,

---

[2] From the Dedication of Chapman's *Homer*.

though carried to the darkest house betwixt this and the mount of Caucasus, will yet hold its natural office and burn as bright as if twenty thousand men did it behold; when John saw, in the Apocalypse, the ruin of the world through evil, and the stars fall from heaven as the fig tree casteth her untimely fruit; when Æsop reports the whole catalogue of common daily relations through the masquerade of birds and beasts—we take the cheerful hint of the immortality of our essence and its versatile habit and escapes, as when the gypsies say of themselves "it is in vain to hang them, they cannot die."

The poets are thus liberating gods. The ancient British bards had for the title of their order, "Those who are free throughout the world." They are free, and they make free. An imaginative book renders us much more service at first, by stimulating us through its tropes, than afterward when we arrive at the precise sense of the author. I think nothing is of any value in books excepting the transcendental and extraordinary. If a man is inflamed and carried away by his thought, to that degree that he forgets the authors and the public and heeds only this one dream which holds him like an insanity, let me read his paper, and you may have all the arguments and histories and criticism. All the value which attaches to Pythagoras, Paracelsus, Cornelius Agrippa, Cardan, Kepler, Swedenborg, Schelling, Oken, or any other who introduces questionable facts into his cosmogony, as angels, devils, magic, astrology, palmistry, mesmerism, and so on, is the certificate we have of departure from routine, and that here is a new witness. That also is the best success in conversation, the magic of liberty, which puts the world like a ball in our hands. How cheap even the liberty then seems; how mean to study, when an emotion communicates to the intellect the power to sap and upheave nature; how great the perspective! Nations, times, systems, enter and disappear like threads in tapestry of large figure and many colors; dream delivers us to dream, and while the drunkenness lasts we will sell our bed, our philosophy, our religion, in our opulence.

There is good reason why we should prize this liberation. The fate of the poor shepherd, who, blinded and lost in the snow-storm, perishes in a drift within a few feet of his cottage door, is an emblem of the state of man. On the brink of the waters of life and truth, we are miserably dying. The inaccessibleness of every thought but that we are in, is wonderful. What if you come near to it; you are as remote when you are nearest as when you are farthest. Every thought is also a prison; every heaven is also a prison. Therefore we love the poet, the inventor, who in any form, whether in an ode or in an action or in looks and behavior, has yielded us a new thought. He unlocks our chains and admits us to a new scene.

This emancipation is dear to all men, and the power to impart it, as it must come from greater depth and scope of thought, is a measure of intellect. Therefore all books of the imagination endure, all which ascend to that truth that the writer sees nature beneath him, and uses it as his exponent. Every verse or sentence possessing this virtue will take care of its own immortality. The religions of the world are the ejaculations of a few imaginative men.

But the quality of the imagination is to flow, and not to freeze. The poet did not stop at the color or the form, but read their meaning; neither may he rest in this meaning, but he makes the same objects exponents of his new thought. Here is the difference betwixt the poet and the mystic, that the last nails a symbol to one sense, which was a true sense for a moment, but soon becomes old and false. For all symbols are fluxional; all language is vehicular and transitive, and is good, as ferries and horses are, for conveyance, not as farms and houses are, for homestead. Mysticism consists in the mistake of an accidental and individual symbol for an universal one. The morning-redness happens to be the favorite meteor to the eyes of Jacob Behmen, and comes to stand to him for truth and faith; and, he believes, should stand for the same realities to every reader. But the first reader prefers as naturally the symbol of a mother and child, or a gardener and his bulb, or a jeweller polishing a gem. Either of these, or of a myriad more, are equally good to the person to whom they are significant. Only they must be held lightly, and be very willingly translated into the equivalent terms which others use. And the mystic must be steadily told, All that you say is just as true without the tedious use of that symbol as with it. Let us have a little algebra, instead of this trite rhetoric—universal signs, instead of these village symbols—and we shall both be gainers. The history of hierarchies seems to show that all religious error consisted in making the symbol too stark and solid, and was at last nothing but an excess of the organ of language.

Swedenborg, of all men in the recent ages, stands eminently for the translator of nature into thought. I do not know the man in history to whom things stood so uniformly for words. Before him the metamorphosis continually plays. Everything on which his eye rests, obeys the impulses of moral nature. The figs become grapes whilst he eats them. When some of his angels affirmed a truth, the laurel twig which they held blossomed in their hands. The noise which at a distance appeared like gnashing and thumping, on coming nearer was found to be the voice of disputants. The men in one of his visions, seen in heavenly light, appeared like dragons, and seemed in darkness; but to each other they appeared as men, and when the light from heaven shone into their cabin, they complained of the darkness, and were compelled to shut the window that they might see.

There was this perception in him which makes the poet or seer an object of awe and terror, namely that the same man or society of men may wear one aspect to themselves and their companions, and a different aspect to higher intelligences. Certain priests, whom he describes as conversing very learnedly together, appeared to the children who were at some distance, like dead horses; and many the like misappearances. And instantly the mind inquires whether these fishes under the bridge, yonder oxen in the pasture, those dogs in the yard, are immutably fishes, oxen and dogs, or only so appear to me, and perchance to themselves appear upright men; and whether I appear as a man to all eyes. The Brahmins and Pythagoras propounded the same question, and if any poet has witnessed the transformation he doubtless found it in harmony with various experiences. We have all seen changes as considerable in wheat and caterpillars. He is the poet and shall draw us with love and terror, who sees through the flowing vest the firm nature, and can declare it.

I look in vain for the poet whom I describe. We do not with sufficient plainness or sufficient profoundness address ourselves to life, nor dare we chaunt our own times and social circumstance. If we filled the day with bravery, we should not shrink from celebrating it. Time and nature yield us many gifts, but not yet the timely man, the new religion, the reconciler, whom all things await. Dante's praise is that he dared to write his autobiography in colossal cipher, or into universality. We have yet had no genius in America, with tyrannous eye, which knew the value of our incomparable materials, and saw, in the barbarism and materialism of the times, another carnival of the same gods whose picture he so much admires in Homer; then in the Middle Age; then in Calvinism. Banks and tariffs, the newspaper and caucus, Methodism and Unitarianism, are flat and dull to dull people, but rest on the same foundations of wonder as the town of Troy and the temple of Delphi, and are as swiftly passing away. Our log-rolling, our stumps and their politics, our fisheries, our Negroes and Indians, our boats and our repudiations, the wrath of rogues and the pusillanimity of honest men, the northern trade, the southern planting, the western clearing, Oregon and Texas, are yet unsung. Yet America is a poem in our eyes; its ample geography dazzles the imagination, and it will not wait long for metres. If I have not found that excellent combination of gifts in my countrymen which I seek, neither could I aid myself to fix the idea of the poet by reading now and then in Chalmers's collection of five centuries of English poets. These are wits more than poets, though there have been poets among them. But when we adhere to the ideal of the poet, we have our difficulties even with Milton and Homer. Milton is too literary, and Homer too literal and historical.

But I am not wise enough for a national criticism, and must use the old largeness a little longer, to discharge my errand from the muse to the poet concerning his art.

Art is the path of the creator to his work. The paths or methods are ideal and eternal, though few men ever see them; not the artist himself for years, or for a lifetime, unless he come into the conditions. The painter, the sculptor, the composer, the epic rhapsodist, the orator, all partake one desire, namely to express themselves symmetrically and abundantly, not dwarfishly and fragmentarily. They found or put themselves in certain conditions, as, the painter and sculptor before some impressive human figures; the orator into the assembly of the people; and the others in such scenes as each has found exciting to his intellect; and each presently feels the new desire. He hears a voice, he sees a beckoning. Then he is apprised, with wonder, what herds of dæmons hem him in. He can no more rest; he says, with the old painter, "By

God it is in me and must go forth of me." He pursues a beauty, half seen, which flies before him. The poet pours out verses in every solitude. Most of the things he says are conventional, no doubt; but by and by he says something which is original and beautiful. That charms him. He would say nothing else but such things. In our way of talking we say "That is yours, this is mine;" but the poet knows well that it is not his; that it is as strange and beautiful to him as to you; he would fain hear the like eloquence at length. Once having tasted this immortal ichor, he cannot have enough of it, and as an admirable creative power exists in these intellections, it is of the last importance that these things get spoken. What a little of all we know is said! What drops of all the sea of our science are baled up! and by what accident it is that these are exposed, when so many secrets sleep in nature! Hence the necessity of speech and song; hence these throbs and heart-beatings in the orator, at the door of the assembly, to the end namely that thought may be ejaculated as Logos, or Word.

Doubt not, O poet, but persist. Say "It is in me, and shall out." Stand there, balked and dumb, stuttering and stammering, hissed and hooted, stand and strive, until at last rage draw out of thee that *dream*-power which every night shows thee is thine own; a power transcending all limit and privacy, and by virtue of which a man is the conductor of the whole river of electricity. Nothing walks, or creeps, or grows, or exists, which must not in turn arise and walk before him as exponent of his meaning. Comes he to that power, his genius is no longer exhaustible. All the creatures by pairs and by tribes pour into his mind as into a Noah's ark, to come forth again to people a new world. This is like the stock of air for our respiration or for the combustion of our fireplace; not a measure of gallons, but the entire atmosphere if wanted. And therefore the rich poets, as Homer, Chaucer, Shakspeare, and Raphael, have obviously no limits to their works except the limits of their lifetime, and resemble a mirror carried through the street, ready to render an image of every created thing.

O poet! a new nobility is conferred in groves and pastures, and not in castles or by the sword-blade any longer. The conditions are hard, but equal. Thou shalt leave the world, and know the muse only. Thou shalt not know any longer the times, customs, graces, politics, or opinions of men, but shalt take all from the muse. For the time of towns is tolled from the world by funereal chimes, but in nature the universal hours are counted by succeeding tribes of animals and plants, and by growth of joy on joy. God wills also that thou abdicate a manifold and duplex life, and that thou be content that others speak for thee. Others shall be thy gentlemen and shall represent all courtesy and worldly life for thee; others shall do the great and resounding actions also. Thou shalt lie close hid with nature, and canst not be afforded to the Capitol or the Exchange. The world is full of renunciations and apprenticeships, and this is thine; thou must pass for a fool and a churl for a long season. This is the screen and sheath in which Pan has protected his well-beloved flower, and thou shalt be known only to thine own, and they shall console thee with tenderest love. And thou shalt not be able to rehearse the names of thy friends in thy verse, for an old shame before the holy ideal. And this is the reward; that the ideal shall be real to thee, and the impressions of the actual world shall fall like summer rain, copious, but not troublesome to thy invulnerable essence. Thou shalt have the whole land for thy park and manor, the sea for thy bath and navigation, without tax and without envy; the woods and the rivers thou shalt own, and thou shalt possess that wherein others are only tenants and boarders. Thou true land-lord! sea-lord! air-lord! Wherever snow falls or water flows or birds fly, wherever day and night meet in twilight, wherever the blue heaven is hung by clouds or sown with stars, wherever are forms with transparent boundaries, wherever are outlets into celestial space, wherever is danger, and awe, and love—there is Beauty, plenteous as rain, shed for thee, and though thou shouldst walk the world over, thou shalt not be able to find a condition inopportune or ignoble.

From *Essays, Second Series*

EACH AND ALL[1]

LITTLE thinks, in the field, you red-cloaked clown
Of thee from the hill-top looking down;
The heifer that lows in the upland farm,
Far-heard, lows not thine ear to charm;
The sexton, tolling his bell at noon,
Deems not that great Napoleon
Stops his horse, and lists with delight,
Whilst his files sweep round yon Alpine height;
Nor knowest thou what argument
Thy life to thy neighbor's creed has lent.
All are needed by each one;
Nothing is fair or good alone.
I thought the sparrow's note from heaven,
Singing at dawn on the alder bough;
I brought him home, in his nest, at even;
He sings the song, but it cheers not now,
For I did not bring home the river and sky;
He sang to my ear—they sang to my eye.
The delicate shells lay on the shore;
The bubbles of the latest wave
Fresh pearls to their enamel gave,
And the bellowing of the savage sea
Greeted their safe escape to me.
I wiped away the weeds and foam,
I fetched my sea-born treasures home;
But the poor, unsightly, noisome things
Had left their beauty on the shore
With the sun and the sand and the wild uproar.
The lover watched his graceful maid,
As 'mid the virgin train she strayed,
Nor knew her beauty's best attire
Was woven still by the snow-white choir.
At last she came to his hermitage,
Like the bird from the woodlands to the cage;

---

[1] This poem, and those that follow, are from *Poems*.

The gay enchantment was undone,
A gentle wife, but fairy none.
Then I said, "I covet truth;
Beauty is unripe childhood's cheat;
I leave it behind with the games of youth:"
As I spoke, beneath my feet
The ground-pine curled its pretty wreath,
Running over the club-moss burrs;
I inhaled the violet's breath;
Around me stood the oaks and firs;
Pine-cones and acorns lay on the ground;
Over me soared the eternal sky,
Full of light and of deity;
Again I saw, again I heard,
The rolling river, the morning bird—
Beauty through my senses stole;
I yielded myself to the perfect whole.

URIEL

IT fell in the ancient periods
  Which the brooding soul surveys,
Or ever the wild Time coined itself
  Into calendar months and days.

This was the lapse of Uriel,
Which in Paradise befell.
Once, among the Pleiads walking,
Seyd overheard the young gods talking;
And the treason, too long pent,
To his ears was evident.
The young deities discussed
Laws of form, and metre just,
Orb, quintessence, and sunbeams,
What subsisteth, and what seems.
One, with low tones that decide,
And doubt and reverend use defied,
With a look that solved the sphere,
And stirred the devils everywhere,

Gave his sentiment divine
Against the being of a line.
"Line in nature is not found;
Unit and universe are round;
In vain produced, all rays return;
Evil will bless, and ice will burn."
As Uriel spoke with piercing eye,
A shudder ran around the sky;
The stern old war-gods shook their heads,
The seraphs frowned from myrtle-beds;
Seemed to the holy festival
The rash word boded ill to all;
The balance-beam of Fate was bent;
The bounds of good and ill were rent;
Strong Hades could not keep his own,
But all slid to confusion.

A sad self-knowledge, withering, fell
On the beauty of Uriel;
In heaven once eminent, the god
Withdrew, that hour, into his cloud;
Whether doomed to long gyration
In the sea of generation,
Or by knowledge grown too bright
To hit the nerve of feebler sight.
Straightway, a forgetting wind
Stole over the celestial kind,
And their lips the secret kept,
If in ashes the fire-seed slept.
But now and then, truth-speaking things
Shamed the angels' veiling wings;
And, shrilling from the solar course,
Or from fruit of chemic force,
Procession of a soul in matter,
Or the speeding change of water,
Or out of the good of evil born,
Came Uriel's voice of cherub scorn,
And a blush tinged the upper sky,
And the gods shook, they knew not why.

THE SPHINX

THE Sphinx is drowsy,
    Her wings are furled:
Her ear is heavy,
    She broods on the world.
"Who'll tell me my secret,
    The ages have kept?
I awaited the seer
    While they slumbered and slept:

"The fate of the man-child,
    The meaning of man;
Known fruit of the unknown;
    Dædalian plan;
Out of sleeping a waking,
    Out of waking a sleep;
Life death overtaking;
    Deep underneath deep?

"Erect as a sunbeam,
    Upspringeth the palm;
The elephant browses,
    Undaunted and calm;
In beautiful motion
    The thrush plies his wings;
Kind leaves of his covert,
    Your silence he sings.

"The waves, unashamèd,
    In difference sweet,
Play glad with the breezes,
    Old playfellows meet;
The journeying atoms,
    Primordial wholes,
Firmly draw, firmly drive,
    By their animate poles.

"Sea, earth, air, sound, silence,
    Plant, quadruped, bird,
By one music enchanted,
    One deity stirred,
Each the other adorning,
    Accompany still;
Night veileth the morning,
    The vapor the hill.

"The babe by its mother
    Lies bathèd in joy;
Glide its hours uncounted,
    The sun is its toy;
Shines the peace of all being,
    Without cloud, in its eyes;
And the sum of the world
    In soft miniature lies.

"But man crouches and blushes,
    Absconds and conceals;
He creepeth and peepeth,
    He palters and steals;
Infirm, melancholy,
    Jealous glancing around,
An oaf, an accomplice,
    He poisons the ground.

"Out spoke the great mother,
    Beholding his fear;
At the sound of her accents
    Cold shuddered the sphere:
'Who has drugged my boy's cup?
    Who has mixed my boy's bread?
Who, with sadness and madness,
    Has turned my child's head?' "

I heard a poet answer
    Aloud and cheerfully,
"Say on, sweet Sphinx! thy dirges
    Are pleasant songs to me.
Deep love lieth under
    These pictures of time;

They fade in the light of
　　Their meaning sublime.

"The fiend that man harries
　　Is love of the Best;
Yawns the pit of the Dragon,
　　Lit by rays from the Blest.
The Lethe of Nature
　　Can't trance him again,
Whose soul sees the perfect,
　　Which his eyes seek in vain.

"To vision profounder,
　　Man's spirit must dive;
His aye-rolling orb
　　At no goal will arrive;
The heavens that now draw him
　　With sweetness untold,
Once found—for new heavens
　　He spurneth the old.

"Pride ruined the angels,
　　Their shame them restores;
Lurks the joy that is sweetest
　　In stings of remorse.
Have I a lover
　　Who is noble and free?
I would he were nobler
　　Than to love me.

"Eterne alternation
　　Now follows, now flies;
And under pain, pleasure,
　　Under pleasure, pain lies.
Love works at the centre,
　　Heart-heaving alway;
Forth speed the strong pulses
　　To the borders of day.

"Dull Sphinx, Jove keep thy five wits;
　　Thy sight is growing blear;

Rue, myrrh and cummin for the Sphinx,
    Her muddy eyes to clear!"
The old Sphinx bit her thick lip,
    Said, "Who taught thee me to name?
I am thy spirit, yoke-fellow;
    Of thine eye I am eyebeam.

"Thou art the unanswered question;
    Couldst see thy proper eye,
Alway it asketh, asketh;
    And each answer is a lie.
So take thy quest through nature,
    It through thousand natures ply;
Ask on, thou clothed eternity;
    Time is the false reply."

Uprose the merry Sphinx,
    And crouched no more in stone;
She melted into purple cloud,
    She silvered in the moon;
She spired into a yellow flame;
    She flowered in blossoms red;
She flowed into a foaming wave:
    She stood Monadnoc's head.

Thorough a thousand voices
    Spoke the universal dame;
"Who telleth one of my meanings
    Is master of all I am."

HAMATREYA

Bulkeley, Hunt, Willard, Hosmer, Meriam, Flint,
Possessed the land which rendered to their toil
Hay, corn, roots, hemp, flax, apples, wool and wood.
Each of these landlords walked amidst his farm,
Saying, " 'T is mine, my children's and my name's.
How sweet the west wind sounds in my own trees!
How graceful climb those shadows on my hill!

I fancy these pure waters and the flags
Know me, as does my dog: we sympathize;
And, I affirm, my actions smack of the soil."

Where are these men? Asleep beneath their grounds:
And strangers, fond as they, their furrows plough.
Earth laughs in flowers, to see her boastful boys
Earth-proud, proud of the earth which is not theirs;
Who steer the plough, but cannot steer their feet
Clear of the grave.
They added ridge to valley, brook to pond,
And sighed for all that bounded their domain;
"This suits me for a pasture; that's my park;
We must have clay, lime, gravel, granite-ledge,
And misty lowland, where to go for peat.
The land is well—lies fairly to the south.
'T is good, when you have crossed the sea and back,
To find the sitfast acres where you left them."
Ah! the hot owner sees not Death, who adds
Him to his land, a lump of mould the more.
Hear what the Earth says:

EARTH-SONG

"Mine and yours;
   Mine, not yours.
Earth endures;
Stars abide—
Shine down in the old sea;
Old are the shores;
But where are old men?
I who have seen much,
Such have I never seen.

"The lawyer's deed
   Ran sure,
   In tail,
To them, and to their heirs
Who shall succeed,
   Without fail,
Forevermore.

"Here is the land,
Shaggy with wood,
With its old valley,
Mound and flood.
But the heritors?
Fled like the flood's foam.
The lawyer, and the laws,
And the kingdom,
Clean swept herefrom.

"They called me theirs,
Who so controlled me;
Yet every one
Wished to stay, and is gone,
How am I theirs,
If they cannot hold me,
But I hold them?"

When I heard the Earth-song
I was no longer brave;
My avarice cooled
Like lust in the chill of the grave.

THE RHODORA:

ON BEING ASKED, WHENCE IS THE FLOWER?

In May, when sea-winds pierced our solitudes,
I found the fresh Rhodora in the woods,
Spreading its leafless blooms in a damp nook,
To please the desert and the sluggish brook.
The purple petals, fallen in the pool,
Made the black water with their beauty gay;
Here might the red-bird come his plumes to cool,
And court the flower that cheapens his array.
Rhodora! if the sages ask thee why
This charm is wasted on the earth and sky,
Tell them, dear, that if eyes were made for seeing,
Then Beauty is its own excuse for being:

Why thou wert there, O rival of the rose!
I never thought to ask, I never knew:
But, in my simple ignorance, suppose
The self-same Power that brought me there brought you.

THE SNOW-STORM

ANNOUNCED by all the trumpets of the sky,
Arrives the snow, and, driving o'er the fields,
Seems nowhere to alight: the whited air
Hides hills and woods, the river, and the heaven,
And veils the farm-house at the garden's end.
The sled and traveller stopped, the courier's feet
Delayed, all friends shut out, the housemates sit
Around the radiant fireplace, enclosed
In a tumultuous privacy of storm.

Come see the north wind's masonry.
Out of an unseen quarry evermore
Furnished with tile, the fierce artificer
Curves his white bastions with projected roof
Round every windward stake, or tree, or door.
Speeding, the myriad-handed, his wild work
So fanciful, so savage, nought cares he
For number or proportion. Mockingly,
On coop or kennel he hangs Parian wreaths;
A swan-like form invests the hidden thorn;
Fills up the farmer's lane from wall to wall,
Maugre the farmer's sighs; and at the gate
A tapering turret overtops the work.
And when his hours are numbered, and the world
Is all his own, retiring, as he were not,
Leaves, when the sun appears, astonished Art
To mimic in slow structures, stone by stone,
Built in an age, the mad wind's night-work,
The frolic architecture of the snow.

WOODNOTES I

1

WHEN the pine tosses its cones
To the song of its waterfall tones,
Who speeds to the woodland walks?
To birds and trees who talks?
Cæsar of his leafy Rome,
There the poet is at home.
He goes to the river-side,
Not hook nor line hath he;
He stands in the meadows wide,
Nor gun nor scythe to see.
Sure some god his eye enchants:
What he knows nobody wants.
In the wood he travels glad,
Without better fortune had,
Melancholy without bad.
Knowledge this man prizes best
Seems fantastic to the rest:
Pondering shadows, colors, clouds;
Grass-buds and caterpillar-shrouds,
Boughs on which the wild bees settle,
Tints that spot the violet's petal,
Why Nature loves the number five,
And why the star-form she repeats:
Lover of all things alive,
Wonderer at all he meets,
Wonderer chiefly at himself,
Who can tell him what he is?
Or how meet in human elf
Coming and past eternities?

2

And such I knew, a forest seer,
A minstrel of the natural year,

Foreteller of the vernal ides,
Wise harbinger of spheres and tides,
A lover true, who knew by heart
Each joy the mountain dales impart;
It seemed that Nature could not raise
A plant in any secret place,
In quaking bog, on snowy hill,
Beneath the grass that shades the rill,
Under the snow, between the rocks,
In damp fields known to bird and fox.
But he would come in the very hour
It opened in its virgin bower,
As if a sunbeam showed the place,
And tell its long-descended race.
It seemed as if the breezes brought him,
It seemed as if the sparrows taught him;
As if by secret sight he knew
Where, in far fields, the orchis grew.
Many haps fall in the field
Seldom seen by wishful eyes,
But all her shows did Nature yield,
To please and win this pilgrim wise.
He saw the partridge drum in the woods;
He heard the woodcock's evening hymn;
He found the tawny thrushes' broods;
And the shy hawk did wait for him;
What others did at distance hear,
And guessed within the thicket's gloom,
Was shown to this philosopher,
And at his bidding seemed to come.

3

In unploughed Maine he sought the lumberers' gang
Where from a hundred lakes young rivers sprang;
He trode the unplanted forest floor, whereon
The all-seeing sun for ages hath not shone;
Where feeds the moose, and walks the surly bear,
And up the tall mast runs the woodpecker.
He saw beneath dim aisles, in odorous beds,
The slight Linnæa hang its twin-born heads,
And blessed the monument of the man of flowers,

Which breathes his sweet fame through the northern bowers.
He heard, when in the grove, at intervals,
With sudden roar the aged pine-tree falls—
One crash, the death-hymn of the perfect tree,
Declares the close of its green century.

ODE

INSCRIBED TO W. H. CHANNING

THOUGH loath to grieve
The evil time's sole patriot,
I cannot leave
My honied thought
For the priest's cant,
Or statesman's rant.

If I refuse
My study for their politique,
Which at the best is trick,
The angry Muse
Puts confusion in my brain.

But who is he that prates
Of the culture of mankind,
Of better arts and life?
Go, blindworm, go,
Behold the famous States
Harrying Mexico
With rifle and with knife!

Or who, with accent bolder,
Dare praise the freedom-loving mountaineer?
I found by thee, O rushing Contoocook!
And in thy valleys, Agiochook!
The jackals of the negro-holder.

The God who made New Hampshire
Taunted the lofty land

With little men;
Small bat and wren
House in the oak:
If earth-fire cleave
The upheaved land, and bury the folk,
The southern crocodile would grieve.
Virtue palters; Right is hence;
Freedom praised, but hid;
Funeral eloquence
Rattles the coffin-lid.

What boots thy zeal,
O glowing friend,
That would indignant rend
The northland from the south?
Wherefore? to what good end?
Boston Bay and Bunker Hill
Would serve things still;
Things are of the snake.

The horseman serves the horse,
The neatherd serves the neat,
The merchant serves the purse,
The eater serves his meat;
'T is the day of the chattel,
Web to weave, and corn to grind;
Things are in the saddle,
And ride mankind.

There are two laws discrete,
Not reconciled—
Law for man, and law for thing;
The last builds town and fleet,
But it runs wild,
And doth the man unking.

'T is fit the forest fall,
The steep be graded,
The mountain tunnelled,
The sand shaded,
The orchard planted,
The glebe tilled,

The prairie granted,
The steamer built.

Let man serve law for man;
Live for friendship, live for love,
For truth's and harmony's behoof;
The state may follow how it can,
As Olympus follows Jove.

Yet do not I implore
The wrinkled shopman to my sounding woods,
Nor bid the unwilling senator
Ask votes of thrushes in the solitudes.
Every one to his chosen work;
Foolish hands may mix and mar;
Wise and sure the issues are.
Round they roll till dark is light,
Sex to sex, and even to odd;
The over-god
Who marries Right to Might,
Who peoples, unpeoples,
He who exterminates
Races by stronger races,
Black by white faces—
Knows to bring honey
Out of the lion;
Grafts gentlest scion
On pirate and Turk.

The Cossack eats Poland,
Like stolen fruit;
Her last noble is ruined,
Her last poet mute:
Straight, into double band
The victors divide;
Half for freedom strike and stand—
The astonished Muse finds thousands at her side.

EROS

THE sense of the world is short,
Long and various the report,
   To love and be beloved;
Men and gods have not outlearned it;
And, how oft soe'er they've turned it,
   Not to be improved.

GIVE ALL TO LOVE

GIVE all to love;
Obey thy heart;
Friends, kindred, days,
Estate, good-fame,
Plans, credit and the Muse—
Nothing refuse.

'T is a brave master;
Let it have scope:
Follow it utterly,
Hope beyond hope:
High and more high
It dives into noon,
With wing unspent,
Untold intent;
But it is a god,
Knows its own path
And the outlets of the sky.

It was never for the mean;
It requireth courage stout.
Souls above doubt,
Valor unbending,
It will reward—

They shall return
More than they were,
And ever ascending.

Leave all for love;
Yet, hear me, yet,
One word more thy heart behoved,
One pulse more of firm endeavor—
Keep thee to-day,
To-morrow, forever,
Free as an Arab
Of thy beloved.

Cling with life to the maid;
But when the surprise,
First vague shadow of surmise
Flits across her bosom young,
Of a joy apart from thee,
Free be she, fancy-free;
Nor thou detain her vesture's hem,
Nor the palest rose she flung
From her summer diadem.

Though thou loved her as thyself,
As a self of purer clay,
Though her parting dims the day,
Stealing grace from all alive;
Heartily know,
When half-gods go,
The gods arrive.

MERLIN

I

Thy trivial harp will never please
Or fill my craving ear;
Its chords should ring as blows the breeze,
Free, peremptory, clear.

No jingling serenader's art,
Nor tinkle of piano strings,
Can make the wild blood start
In its mystic springs.
The kingly bard
Must smite the chords rudely and hard,
As with hammer or with mace;
That they may render back
Artful thunder, which conveys
Secrets of the solar track,
Sparks of the supersolar blaze.
Merlin's blows are strokes of fate,
Chiming with the forest tone,
When boughs buffet boughs in the wood;
Chiming with the gasp and moan
Of the ice-imprisoned flood;
With the pulse of manly hearts;
With the voice of orators;
With the din of city arts;
With the cannonade of wars;
With the marches of the brave;
And prayers of might from martyrs' cave.

Great is the art,
Great be the manners, of the bard.
He shall not his brain encumber
With the coil of rhythm and number;
But, leaving rule and pale forethought,
He shall aye climb
For his rhyme.
"Pass in, pass in," the angels say,
"In to the upper doors,
Nor count compartments of the floors,
But mount to paradise
By the stairway of surprise."

Blameless master of the games,
King of sport that never shames,
He shall daily joy dispense
Hid in song's sweet influence.
Forms more cheerly live and go,
What time the subtle mind

Sings aloud the tune whereto
Their pulses beat,
And march their feet,
And their members are combined.

By Sybarites beguiled,
He shall no task decline;
Merlin's mighty line
Extremes of nature reconciled—
Bereaved a tyrant of his will,
And made the lion mild.
Songs can the tempest still,
Scattered on the stormy air,
Mould the year to fair increase,
And bring in poetic peace.

He shall not seek to weave,
In weak, unhappy times,
Efficacious rhymes;
Wait his returning strength.
Bird that from the nadir's floor
To the zenith's top can soar—
The soaring orbit of the muse exceeds that
          journey's length.
Nor profane affect to hit
Or compass that, by meddling wit,
Which only the propitious mind
Publishes when 't is inclined.
There are open hours
When the God's will sallies free,
And the dull idiot might see
The flowing fortunes of a thousand years;
Sudden, at unawares,
Self-moved, fly-to the doors,
Nor sword of angels could reveal
What they conceal.

II

THE rhyme of the poet
Modulates the king's affairs;
Balance-loving Nature

Made all things in pairs.
To every foot its antipode;
Each color with its counter glowed;
To every tone beat answering tones,
Higher or graver;
Flavor gladly blends with flavor;
Leaf answers leaf upon the bough;
And match the paired cotyledons.
Hands to hands, and feet to feet,
In one body grooms and brides;
Eldest rite, two married sides
In every mortal meet.
Light's far furnace shines,
Smelting balls and bars,
Forging double stars,
Glittering twins and trines.
The animals are sick with love,
Lovesick with rhyme;
Each with all propitious Time
Into chorus wove.

Like the dancers' ordered band,
Thoughts come also hand in hand;
In equal couples mated,
Or else alternated;
Adding by their mutual gage,
One to other, health and age.
Solitary fancies go
Short-lived wandering to and fro,
Most like to bachelors,
Or an ungiven maid,
Not ancestors,
With no posterity to make the lie afraid,
Or keep truth undecayed.
Perfect-paired as eagle's wings,
Justice is the rhyme of things;
Trade and counting use
The self-same tuneful muse;
And Nemesis,
Who with even matches odd,
Who athwart space redresses
The partial wrong,

Fills the just period,
And finishes the song.

Subtle rhymes, with ruin rife,
Murmur in the house of life,
Sung by the Sisters as they spin;
In perfect time and measure they
Build and unbuild our echoing clay.
As the two twilights of the day
Fold us music-drunken in.

BACCHUS

BRING me wine, but wine which never grew
In the belly of the grape,
Or grew on vine whose tap-roots, reaching through
Under the Andes to the Cape,
Suffer no savor of the earth to scape.

Let its grape the morn salute
From a nocturnal root,
Which feels the acrid juice
Of Styx and Erebus;
And turns the woe of Night,
By its own craft, to a more rich delight.

We buy ashes for bread;
We buy diluted wine;
Give me of the true,
Whose ample leaves and tendrils curled
Among the silver hills of heaven
Draw everlasting dew;
Wine of wine,
Blood of the world,
Form of forms, and mould of statures,
That I intoxicated,
And by the draught assimilated,
May float at pleasure through all natures;
The bird-language rightly spell,
And that which roses say so well.

Wine that is shed
Like the torrents of the sun
Up the horizon walls,
Or like the Atlantic streams, which run
When the South Sea calls.

Water and bread,
Food which needs no transmuting,
Rainbow-flowering, wisdom-fruiting,
Wine which is already man,
Food which teach and reason can.

Wine which Music is,
Music and wine are one,
That I, drinking this,
Shall hear far Chaos talk with me;
Kings unborn shall walk with me;
And the poor grass shall plot and plan
What it will do when it is man.
Quickened so, will I unlock
Every crypt of every rock.

I thank the joyful juice
For all I know;
Winds of remembering
Of the ancient being blow,
And seeming-solid walls of use
Open and flow.

Pour, Bacchus! the remembering wine;
Retrieve the loss of me and mine!
Vine for vine be antidote,
And the grape requite the lote!
Haste to cure the old despair—
Reason in Nature's lotus drenched,
The memory of ages quenched;
Give them again to shine;
Let wine repair what this undid;
And where the infection slid,
A dazzling memory revive;
Refresh the faded tints,
Recut the aged prints,

And write my old adventures with the pen
Which on the first day drew,
Upon the tablets blue,
The dancing Pleiads and eternal men.

THRENODY

The South-wind brings
Life, sunshine and desire,
And on every mount and meadow
Breathes aromatic fire;
But over the dead he has no power,
The lost, the lost, he cannot restore;
And, looking over the hills, I mourn
The darling who shall not return.

I see my empty house,
I see my trees repair their boughs;
And he, the wondrous child,
Whose silver warble wild
Outvalued every pulsing sound
Within the air's cerulean round—
The hyacinthine boy, for whom
Morn well might break and April bloom,
The gracious boy, who did adorn
The world whereinto he was born,
And by his countenance repay
The favor of the loving Day—
Has disappeared from the Day's eye;
Far and wide she cannot find him;
My hopes pursue, they cannot bind him.
Returned this day, the South-wind searches,
And finds young pines and budding birches;
But finds not the budding man;
Nature, who lost, cannot remake him;
Fate let him fall, Fate can't retake him;
Nature, Fate, men, him seek in vain.

And whither now, my truant wise and sweet,
O, whither tend thy feet?

I had the right, few days ago,
Thy steps to watch, thy place to know:
How have I forfeited the right?
Hast thou forgot me in a new delight?
I hearken for thy household cheer,
O eloquent child!
Whose voice, an equal messenger,
Conveyed thy meaning mild.
What though the pains and joys
Whereof it spoke were toys
Fitting his age and ken,
Yet fairest dames and bearded men,
Who heard the sweet request,
So gentle, wise and grave,
Bended with joy to his behest
And let the world's affairs go by,
A while to share his cordial game,
Or mend his wicker wagon-frame,
Still plotting how their hungry ear
That winsome voice again might hear;
For his lips could well pronounce
Words that were persuasions.

Gentlest guardians marked serene
His early hope, his liberal mien;
Took counsel from his guiding eyes
To make this wisdom earthly wise.
Ah, vainly do these eyes recall
The school-march, each day's festival,
When every morn my bosom glowed
To watch the convoy on the road;
The babe in willow wagon closed,
With rolling eyes and face composed;
With children forward and behind,
Like Cupids studiously inclined;
And he the chieftain paced beside,
The centre of the troop allied,
With sunny face of sweet repose,
To guard the babe from fancied foes.
The little captain innocent
Took the eye with him as he went;
Each village senior paused to scan

And speak the lovely caravan.
From the window I look out
To mark thy beautiful parade,
Stately marching in cap and coat
To some tune by fairies played—
A music heard by thee alone
To works as noble led thee on.
Now Love and Pride, alas! in vain,
Up and down their glances strain.
The painted sled stands where it stood;
The kennel by the corded wood;
His gathered sticks to stanch the wall
Of the snow-tower, when snow should fall;
The ominous hole he dug in the sand,
And childhood's castles built or planned;
His daily haunts I well discern—
The poultry-yard, the shed, the barn—
And every inch of garden ground
Paced by the blessed feet around,
From the roadside to the brook
Whereinto he loved to look.
Step the meek fowls where erst they ranged;
The wintry garden lies unchanged;
The brook into the stream runs on;
But the deep-eyed boy is gone.

On that shaded day,
Dark with more clouds than tempests are,
When thou didst yield thy innocent breath
In birdlike heavings unto death,
Night came, and Nature had not thee;
I said, "We are mates in misery."
The morrow dawned with needless glow;
Each snowbird chirped, each fowl must crow;
Each tramper started; but the feet
Of the most beautiful and sweet
Of human youth had left the hill
And garden—they were bound and still.
There's not a sparrow or a wren,
There's not a blade of autumn grain,
Which the four seasons do not tend
And tides of life and increase lend;

And every chick of every bird,
And weed and rock-moss is preferred.
O ostrich-like forgetfulness!
O loss of larger in the less!
Was there no star that could be sent,
No watcher in the firmament,
No angel from the countless host
That loiters round the crystal coast,
Could stoop to heal that only child,
Nature's sweet marvel undefiled,
And keep the blossom of the earth,
Which all her harvests were not worth?
Not mine—I never called thee mine,
But Nature's heir—if I repine,
And seeing rashly torn and moved
Not what I made, but what I loved,
Grow early old with grief that thou
Must to the wastes of Nature go—
'T is because a general hope
Was quenched, and all must doubt and grope.
For flattering planets seemed to say
This child should ills of ages stay,
By wondrous tongue, and guided pen,
Bring the flown Muses back to men.
Perchance not he but Nature ailed,
The world and not the infant failed.
It was not ripe yet to sustain
A genius of so fine a strain,
Who gazed upon the sun and moon
As if he came unto his own,
And, pregnant with his grander thought,
Brought the old order into doubt.
His beauty once their beauty tried;
They could not feed him, and he died,
And wandered backward as in scorn,
To wait an æon to be born.
Ill day which made this beauty waste,
Plight broken, this high face defaced!
Some went and came about the dead;
And some in books of solace read;
Some to their friends the tidings say;
Some went to write, some went to pray;

One tarried here, there hurried one;
But their heart abode with none.
Covetous death bereaved us all,
To aggrandize one funeral.
The eager fate which carried thee
Took the largest part of me:
For this losing is true dying;
This is lordly man's down-lying,
This his slow but sure reclining,
Star by star his world resigning.
O child of paradise,
Boy who made dear his father's home,
In whose deep eyes
Men read the welfare of the times to come,
I am too much bereft.
The world dishonored thou hast left.
O truth's and nature's costly lie!
O trusted broken prophecy!
O richest fortune sourly crossed!
Born for the future, to the future lost!

The deep Heart answered, "Weepest thou?
Worthier cause for passion wild
If I had not taken the child.
And deemest thou as those who pore,
With aged eyes, short way before—
Think'st Beauty vanished from the coast
Of matter, and thy darling lost?
Taught he not thee—the man of eld,
Whose eyes within his eyes beheld
Heaven's numerous hierarchy span
The mystic gulf from God to man?
To be alone wilt thou begin
When worlds of lovers hem thee in?
To-morrow, when the masks shall fall
That dizen Nature's carnival,
The pure shall see by their own will,
Which overflowing Love shall fill,
'T is not within the force of fate
The fate-conjoined to separate.
But thou, my votary, weepest thou?
I gave thee sight—where is it now?

I taught thy heart beyond the reach
Of ritual, bible, or of speech;
Wrote in thy mind's transparent table,
As far as the incommunicable;
Taught thee each private sign to raise
Lit by the supersolar blaze.
Past utterance, and past belief,
And past the blasphemy of grief,
The mysteries of Nature's heart;
And though no Muse can these impart,
Throb thine with Nature's throbbing breast,
And all is clear from east to west.

"I came to thee as to a friend;
Dearest, to thee I did not send
Tutors, but a joyful eye,
Innocence that matched the sky,
Lovely locks, a form of wonder,
Laughter rich as woodland thunder,
That thou might'st entertain apart
The richest flowering of all art:
And, as the great all-loving Day
Through smallest chambers takes its way,
That thou might'st break thy daily bread
With prophet, savior and head;
That thou might'st cherish for thine own
The riches of sweet Mary's Son,
Boy-Rabbi, Israel's paragon.
And thoughtest thou such guest
Would in thy hall take up his rest?
Would rushing life forget her laws,
Fate's glowing revolution pause?
High omens ask diviner guess;
Not to be conned to tediousness
And know my higher gifts unbind
The zone that girds the incarnate mind.
When the scanty shores are full
With Thought's perilous, whirling pool;
When frail Nature can no more,
Then the Spirit strikes the hour:
My servant Death, with solving rite,
Pours finite into infinite.

Wilt thou freeze love's tidal flow,
Whose streams through Nature circling go?
Nail the wild star to its track
On the half-climbed zodiac?
Light is light which radiates,
Blood is blood which circulates,
Life is life which generates,
And many-seeming life is one—
Wilt thou transfix and make it none?
Its onward force too starkly pent
In figure, bone and lineament?
Wilt thou, uncalled, interrogate,
Talker! the unreplying Fate?
Nor see the genius of the whole
Ascendant in the private soul,
Beckon it when to go and come,
Self-announced its hour of doom?
Fair the soul's recess and shrine,
Magic-built to last a season;
Masterpiece of love benign,
Fairer that expansive reason
Whose omen 't is, and sign.
Wilt thou not ope thy heart to know
What rainbows teach, and sunsets show?
Verdict which accumulates
From lengthening scroll of human fates,
Voice of earth to earth returned,
Prayers of saints that inly burned,
Saying, *What is excellent,*
As God lives, is permanent;
Hearts are dust, hearts' loves remain;
Heart's love will meet thee again.
Revere the Maker; fetch thine eye
Up to his style, and manners of the sky.
Not of adamant and gold
Built he heaven stark and cold;
No, but a nest of bending reeds,
Flowering grass and scented weeds;
Or like a traveller's fleeing tent,
Or bow above the tempest bent;
Built of tears and sacred flames,
And virtue reaching to its aims;

Built of furtherance and pursuing,
Not of spent deeds, but of doing.
Silent rushes the swift Lord
Through ruined systems still restored,
Broadsowing, bleak and void to bless,
Plants with worlds the wilderness;
Waters with tears of ancient sorrow
Apples of Eden ripe to-morrow.
House and tenant go to ground,
Lost in God, in Godhead found."

CONCORD HYMN
SUNG AT THE COMPLETION OF THE BATTLE
MONUMENT, JULY 4, 1837

By the rude bridge that arched the flood,
  Their flag to April's breeze unfurled,
Here once the embattled farmers stood
  And fired the shot heard round the world.

The foe long since in silence slept;
  Alike the conqueror silent sleeps;
And Time the ruined bridge has swept
  Down the dark stream which seaward creeps.

On this green bank, by this soft stream,
  We set to-day a votive stone;
That memory may their deed redeem,
  When, like our sires, our sons are gone.

Spirit, that made those heroes dare
  To die, and leave their children free,
Bid Time and Nature gently spare
  The shaft we raise to them and thee.

BRAHMA

IF the red slayer think he slays,
  Or if the slain think he is slain,
They know not well the subtle ways
  I keep, and pass, and turn again.

Far or forgot to me is near;
  Shadow and sunlight are the same;
The vanished gods to me appear;
  And one to me are shame and fame.

They reckon ill who leave me out;
  When me they fly, I am the wings;
I am the doubter and the doubt,
  And I the hymn the Brahmin sings.

The strong gods pine for my abode,
  And pine in vain the sacred Seven;
But thou, meek lover of the good!
  Find me, and turn thy back on heaven.

NATURE
MAIA

ILLUSION works impenetrable,
Weaving webs innumerable,
Her gay pictures never fail,
Crowds each on other, veil on veil,
Charmer who will be believed
By man who thirsts to be deceived.

Illusions like the tints of pearl,
Or changing colors of the sky,

Or ribbons of a dancing girl
That mend her beauty to the eye.

The cold gray down upon the quinces lieth
And the poor spinners weave their webs thereon
To share the sunshine that so spicy is.

Samson stark, at Dagon's knee,
Gropes for columns strong as he;
When his ringlets grew and curled,
Groped for axle of the world.

But Nature whistled with all her winds,
Did as she pleased and went her way.

DAYS

DAUGHTERS of Time, the hypocritic Days,
Muffled and dumb like barefoot dervishes,
And marching single in an endless file,
Bring diadems and fagots in their hands.
To each they offer gifts after his will,
Bread, kingdoms, stars, and sky that holds them all.
I, in my pleached garden, watched the pomp,
Forgot my morning wishes, hastily
Took a few herbs and apples, and the Day
Turned and departed silent. I, too late,
Under her solemn fillet saw the scorn.

TERMINUS

IT is time to be old,
To take in sail:
The god of bounds,
Who sets to seas a shore,
Came to me in his fatal rounds,

And said: "No more!
No farther shoot
Thy broad ambitious branches, and thy root.
Fancy departs: no more invent;
Contract thy firmament
To compass of a tent.
There's not enough for this and that,
Make thy option which of two;
Economize the failing river,
Not the less revere the Giver,
Leave the many and hold the few.
Timely wise accept the terms,
Soften the fall with wary foot;
A little while
Still plan and smile,
And—fault of novel germs—
Mature the unfallen fruit.
Curse, if thou wilt, thy sires,
Bad husbands of their fires,
Who, when they gave thee breath,
Failed to bequeath
The needful sinew stark as once,
The Baresark marrow to thy bones,
But left a legacy of ebbing veins,
Inconstant heat and nerveless reins—
Amid the Muses, left thee deaf and dumb,
Amid the gladiators, halt and numb."

As the bird trims her to the gale,
I trim myself to the storm of time,
I man the rudder, reef the sail,
Obey the voice at eve obeyed at prime:
"Lowly faithful, banish fear,
Right onward drive unharmed;
The port, well worth the cruise, is near,
And every wave is charmed."

Part Two

LECTURES AND ADDRESSES

---

scholar = writer? [handwritten annotation]

1. Nature [handwritten annotation]
2. books [handwritten annotation]
3. action [handwritten annotation]

The American Scholar

AN ORATION DELIVERED BEFORE THE PHI BETA
KAPPA SOCIETY, AT CAMBRIDGE,
AUGUST 31, 1837

MR. PRESIDENT AND GENTLEMEN:

I greet you on the recommencement of our literary year. Our
anniversary is one of hope, and, perhaps, not enough of labor.
We do not meet for games of strength or skill, for the recitation of histories, tragedies, and odes, like the ancient Greeks;
for parliaments of love and poesy, like the Troubadours; nor
for the advancement of science, like our contemporaries in
the British and European capitals. Thus far, our holiday has
been simply a friendly sign of the survival of the love of letters
amongst a people too busy to give to letters any more. As
such it is precious as the sign of an indestructible instinct.
Perhaps the time is already come when it ought to be, and
will be, something else; when the sluggard intellect of this
continent will look from under its iron lids and fill the postponed expectation of the word with something better than the
exertions of mechanical skill. Our day of dependence, our
long apprenticeship to the learning of other lands, draws to
a close. The millions that around us are rushing into life, cannot always be fed on the sere remains of foreign harvests.
Events, actions arise, that must be sung, that will sing themselves. Who can doubt that poetry will revive and lead in a
new age, as the star in the constellation Harp, which now
flames in our zenith, astronomers announce, shall one day be
the pole-star for a thousand years?

In this hope I accept the topic which not only usage but
the nature of our association seem to prescribe to this day—
the AMERICAN SCHOLAR. Year by year we come up hither to
read one more chapter of his biography. Let us inquire what

63

light new days and events have thrown on his character and his hopes.

It is one of those fables which out of an unknown antiquity convey an unlooked-for wisdom, that the gods, in the beginning, divided Man into men, that he might be more helpful to himself; just as the hand was divided into fingers, the better to answer its end.

The old fable covers a doctrine ever new and sublime; that there is One Man—present to all particular men only partially, or through one faculty; and that you must take the whole society to find the whole man. Man is not a farmer, or a professor, or an engineer, but he is all. Man is priest, and scholar, and statesman, and producer, and soldier. In the *divided* or social state these functions are parcelled out to individuals, each of whom aims to do his stint of the joint work, whilst each other performs his. The fable implies that the individual, to possess himself, must sometimes return from his own labor to embrace all the other laborers. But, unfortunately, this original unit, this fountain of power, has been so distributed to multitudes, has been so minutely subdivided and peddled out, that it is spilled into drops, and cannot be gathered. The state of society is one in which the members have suffered amputation from the trunk, and strut about so many walking monsters—a good finger, a neck, a stomach, an elbow, but never a man.

Man is thus metamorphosed into a thing, into many things. The planter, who is Man sent out into the field to gather food, is seldom cheered by any idea of the true dignity of his ministry. He sees his bushel and his cart, and nothing beyond, and sinks into the farmer, instead of Man on the farm. The tradesman scarcely ever gives an ideal worth to his work, but is ridden by the routine of his craft, and the soul is subject to dollars. The priest becomes a form; the attorney a statutebook; the mechanic a machine; the sailor a rope of the ship.

In this distribution of functions the scholar is the delegated intellect. In the right state he is *Man Thinking*. In the degenerate state, when the victim of society, he tends to become a mere thinker, or still worse, the parrot of other men's thinking.

In this view of him, as Man Thinking, the theory of his office is contained. Him Nature solicits with all her placid, all her monitory pictures; him the past instructs; him the future invites. Is not indeed every man a student, and do not all things exist for the student's behoof? And, finally, is not the true scholar the only true master? But the old oracle said, "All things have two handles: beware of the wrong one." In life, too often, the scholar errs with mankind and forfeits his privilege. Let us see him in his school, and consider him in reference to the main influences he receives.

1. The first in time and the first in importance of the influences upon the mind is that of nature. Every day, the sun; and, after sunset, Night and her stars. Ever the winds blow; ever the grass grows. Every day, men and women, conversing —beholding and beholden. The scholar is he of all men whom this spectacle most engages. He must settle its value in his mind. What is nature to him? There is never a beginning, there is never an end, to the inexplicable continuity of this web of God, but always circular power returning into itself. Therein it resembles his own spirit, whose beginning, whose ending, he never can find—so entire, so boundless. Far too as her splendors shine, system on system shooting like rays, upward, downward, without centre, without circumference— in the mass and in the particle, Nature hastens to render account of herself to the mind. Classification begins. To the young mind every thing is individual, stands by itself. By and by, it finds how to join two things and see in them one nature; then three, then three thousand; and so, tyrannized over by its own unifying instinct, it goes on tying things together, diminishing anomalies, discovering roots running under ground whereby contrary and remote things cohere and flower out from one stem. It presently learns that since the dawn of history there has been a constant accumulation and classifying of facts. But what is classification but the perceiving that these objects are not chaotic, and are not foreign, but have a law which is also a law of the human mind? The astronomer discovers that geometry, a pure abstraction of the human mind, is the measure of planetary motion. The chemist finds proportions and intelligible method throughout matter: and science is nothing but the finding of analogy, identity, in the most remote parts. The ambitious soul sits down before each refractory fact; one after another reduces all strange constitutions, all new powers, to their class and their law, and

goes on forever to animate the last fibre of organization, the outskirts of nature, by insight.

Thus to him, to this schoolboy under the bending dome of day, is suggested that he and it proceed from one root; one is leaf and one is flower; relation, sympathy, stirring in every vein. And what is that root? Is not that the soul of his soul? A thought too bold; a dream too wild. Yet when this spiritual light shall have revealed the law of more earthly natures— when he has learned to worship the soul, and to see that the natural philosophy that now is, is only the first gropings of its gigantic hand, he shall look forward to an ever expanding knowledge as to a becoming creator. He shall see that nature is the opposite of the soul, answering to it part for part. One is seal and one is print. Its beauty is the beauty of his own mind. Its laws are the laws of his own mind. Nature then becomes to him the measure of his attainments. So much of nature as he is ignorant of, so much of his own mind does he not yet possess. And, in fine, the ancient precept, "Know thyself," and the modern precept, "Study nature," become at last one maxim.

2. The next great influence into the spirit of the scholar is the mind of the Past—in whatever form, whether of literature, of art, of institutions, that mind is inscribed. Books are the best type of the influence of the past, and perhaps we shall get at the truth—learn the amount of this influence more conveniently—by considering their value alone.

The theory of books is noble. The scholar of the first age received into him the world around; brooded thereon; gave it the new arrangement of his own mind, and uttered it again. It came into him life; it went out from him truth. It came to him short-lived actions; it went out from him immortal thoughts. It came to him business; it went from him poetry. It was dead fact; now, it is quick thought. It can stand, and it can go. It now endures, it now flies, it now inspires. Precisely in proportion to the depth of mind from which it issued, so high does it soar, so long does it sing.

Or, I might say, it depends on how far the process had gone, of transmuting life into truth. In proportion to the completeness of the distillation, so will the purity and imperishableness of the product be. But none is quite perfect. As no air-pump can by any means make a perfect vacuum, so neither can any artist entirely exclude the conventional, the local, the perishable from his book, or write a book of pure thought, that shall be as efficient, in all respects, to a remote posterity, as to contemporaries, or rather to the second age. Each age, it is found, must write its own books; or rather, each generation for the next succeeding. The books of an older period will not fit this.

Yet hence arises a grave mischief. The sacredness which attaches to the act of creation, the act of thought, is transferred to the record. The poet chanting was felt to be a divine man: henceforth the chant is divine also. The writer was a just and wise spirit: henceforward it is settled the book is perfect; as love of the hero corrupts into worship of his statue. Instantly the book becomes noxious: the guide is a tyrant. The sluggish and perverted mind of the multitude, slow to open to the incursions of Reason, having once so opened, having once received this book, stands upon it, and makes an outcry if it is disparaged. Colleges are built on it. Books are written on it by thinkers, not by Man Thinking; by men of talent, that is, who start wrong, who set out from accepted dogmas, not from their own sight of principles. Meek young men grow up in libraries, believing it their duty to accept the views which Cicero, which Locke, which Bacon, have given; forgetful that Cicero, Locke, and Bacon were only young men in libraries when they wrote these books.

Hence, instead of Man Thinking, we have the bookworm. Hence the book-learned class, who value books, as such; not as related to nature and the human constitution, but as making a sort of Third Estate with the world and the soul. Hence the restorers of readings, the emendators, the bibliomaniacs of all degrees.

Books are the best of things, well used; abused, among the worst. What is the right use? What is the one end which all means go to effect? They are for nothing but to inspire. I had better never see a book than to be warped by its attraction clean out of my own orbit, and made a satellite instead of a system. The one thing in the world, of value, is the active soul. This every man is entitled to; this every man contains within him, although in almost all men obstructed and as yet unborn. The soul active sees absolute truth and utters truth, or creates. In this action it is genius; not the privilege of here and there a favorite, but the sound estate of every man. In its essence it is progressive. The book, the college, the school of art, the institution of any kind, stop with some past utterance of genius. This is good, say they—let us hold by this. They pin me down. They look backward and not forward. But genius looks forward: the eyes of man are set in his forehead, not in his hindhead: <u>man hopes: genius creates.</u> Whatever talents may be, if the man create not, the pure efflux of the Deity is not his; cinders and smoke there may be, but not yet flame. There are creative manners, there are creative actions, and creative words; manners, actions, words, that is, indicative of no custom or authority, but <u>springing spontaneous from the mind's own sense of good and fair.</u>

On the other part, instead of being its own seer, let it receive from another mind its truth, though it were in torrents of light, without periods of solitude, inquest, and self-recovery, and a fatal disservice is done. <u>Genius is always sufficiently the enemy of genius by over-influence.</u> The literature of every nation bears me witness. <u>The English dramatic poets have Shakspearized now for two hundred years.</u>

Undoubtedly there is a right way of reading, so it be sternly subordinated. Man Thinking must not be subdued by his instruments. <u>Books are for the scholar's idle times.</u> When he can read God directly, the hour is too precious to be wasted in other men's transcripts of their readings. <u>But when the intervals of darkness come, as come they must—when the sun is hid and the stars withdraw their shining—we repair to the lamps which were kindled by their ray, to guide our steps to the East again, where the dawn is. We hear, that we may speak.</u> The Arabian proverb says, "A fig tree, looking on a fig tree, becometh fruitful."

It is remarkable, the character of the pleasure we derive from the best books. They impress us with the conviction that <u>one nature wrote and the same reads.</u> We read the verses of one of the great English poets, of Chaucer, of Marvell, of Dryden, with the most modern joy—with a pleasure, I mean, which is in great part caused by the abstraction of all *time* from their verses. There is some awe mixed with the joy of our surprise, when this poet, who lived in some past world, two or three hundred years ago, says that which lies close to my own soul, that which I also had well-nigh thought and said. But for the evidence thence afforded to the philosophical doctrine of the identity of all minds, <u>we should suppose some preestablished harmony</u>, some foresight of souls that were to be, and some preparation of stores for their future wants, like the fact observed in insects, who lay up food before death for the young grub they shall never see.

I would not be hurried by any love of system, by any exaggeration of instincts, to underrate the Book. We all know, that as the human body can be nourished on any food, though it were boiled grass and the broth of shoes, so the human mind can be fed by any knowledge. And great and heroic men have existed who had almost no other information than by the printed page. I only would say that it needs a strong head to bear that diet. One must be an inventor to read well. As the proverb says, "He that would bring home the wealth of the Indies, must carry out the wealth of the Indies." There is then creative reading as well as creative writing. When the mind is braced by labor and invention, the page of whatever book we read becomes luminous with manifold allusion. Every sentence is doubly significant, and the sense of our author is as broad as the world. We then see, what is always true, that as the seer's hour of vision is short and rare among heavy days and months, so is its record, perchance, the least part of his volume. The discerning will read, in his Plato or Shakspeare, only that least part—only the authentic utterances of the oracle—all the rest he rejects, were it never so many times Plato's and Shakspeare's.

Of course there is a portion of reading quite indispensable to a wise man. History and exact science he must learn by laborious reading. Colleges, in like manner, have their indispensable office—to teach elements. But they can only highly serve us when they aim not to drill, but to create; when they gather from far every ray of various genius to their hospitable halls, and by the concentrated fires, set the hearts of their youth on flame. Thought and knowledge are natures in which apparatus and pretension avail nothing. Gowns and pecuniary foundations, though of towns of gold, can never countervail the least sentence or syllable of wit. Forget this, and our American colleges will recede in their public importance, whilst they grow richer every year.

3. There goes in the world a notion that the scholar should be a recluse, a valetudinarian—as unfit for any handiwork or public labor as a penknife for an axe. The so-called "practical men" sneer at speculative men, as if, because they speculate or *see*, they could do nothing. I have heard it said that the

clergy—who are always, more universally than any other class, the scholars of their day—are addressed as women; that the rough, spontaneous conversation of men they do not hear, but only a mincing and diluted speech. They are often virtually disfranchised; and indeed there are advocates for their celibacy. As far as this is true of the studious classes, it is not just and wise. Action is with the scholar subordinate, but it is essential. Without it he is not yet man. Without it thought can never ripen into truth. Whilst the world hangs before the eye as a cloud of beauty, we cannot even see its beauty. Inaction is cowardice, but there can be no scholar without the heroic mind. The preamble of thought, the transition through which it passes from the unconscious to the conscious, is action. Only so much do I know, as I have lived. Instantly we know whose words are loaded with life, and whose not.

The world—this shadow of the soul, or *other me*—lies wide around. Its attractions are the keys which unlock my thoughts and make me acquainted with myself. I run eagerly into this resounding tumult. I grasp the hands of those next me, and take my place in the ring to suffer and to work, taught by an instinct that so shall the dumb abyss be vocal with speech. I pierce its order; I dissipate its fear: I dispose of it within the circuit of my expanding life. So much only of life as I know by experience, so much of the wilderness have I vanquished and planted, or so far have I extended my being, my dominion. I do not see how any man can afford, for the sake of his nerves and his nap, to spare any action in which he can partake. It is pearls and rubies to his discourse. Drudgery, calamity, exasperation, want, are instructors in eloquence and wisdom. The true scholar grudges every opportunity of action past by, as a loss of power. It is the raw material out of which the intellect moulds her splendid products. A strange process too, this by which experience is converted into thought, as a mulberry leaf is converted into satin. The manufacture goes forward at all hours.

The actions and events of our childhood and youth are now matters of calmest observation. They lie like fair pictures in the air. Not so with our recent actions—with the business which we now have in hand. On this we are quite unable to speculate. Our affections as yet circulate through it. We no more feel or know it than we feel the feet, or the hand, or the brain of our body. The new deed is yet a part of life—remains for a time immersed in our unconscious life. In some contemplative hour it detaches itself from the life like a ripe fruit, to become a thought of the mind. Instantly it is raised, transfigured; the corruptible has put on incorruption. Henceforth it is an object of beauty, however base its origin and neighborhood. Observe too the impossibility of antedating this act. In its grub state, it cannot fly, it cannot shine, it is a dull grub. But suddenly, without observation, the selfsame thing unfurls beautiful wings, and is an angel of wisdom. So is there no fact, no event, in our private history, which shall not, sooner or later, lose its adhesive, inert form, and astonish us by soaring from our body into the empyrean. Cradle and infancy, school and playground, the fear of boys, and dogs, and ferrules, the love of little maids and berries, and many another fact that once filled the whole sky, are gone already; friend and relative, profession and party, town and country, nation and world, must also soar and sing.

Of course, he who has put forth his total strength in fit actions has the richest return of wisdom. I will not shut myself out of this globe of action, and transplant an oak into a flowerpot, there to hunger and pine; nor trust the revenue of some single faculty, and exhaust one vein of thought, much like those Savoyards, who, getting their livelihood by carving shepherds, shepherdesses, and smoking Dutchmen, for all Europe, went out one day to the mountain to find stock, and discovered that they had whittled up the last of their pine trees. Authors we have, in numbers, who have written out their vein, and who, moved by a commendable prudence, sail for Greece or Palestine, follow the trapper into the prairie, or ramble round Algiers, to replenish their merchantable stock.

If it were only for a vocabulary, the scholar would be covetous of action. Life is our dictionary. Years are well spent in country labors; in town; in the insight into trades and manufactures; in frank intercourse with many men and women; in science; in art; to the one end of mastering in all their facts a language by which to illustrate and embody our perceptions. I learn immediately from any speaker how much he has already lived, through the poverty or the splendor of his speech. Life lies behind us as the quarry from whence we get tiles and copestones for the masonry of to-day. This is the way to learn grammar. Colleges and books only copy the language which the field and the work-yard made.

But the final value of action, like that of books, and better than books, is that it is a resource. That great principle of Undulation in nature, that shows itself in the inspiring and expiring of the breath; in desire and satiety; in the ebb and flow of the sea; in day and night; in heat and cold; and, as yet more deeply ingrained in every atom and every fluid, is known to us under the name of Polarity—these "fits of easy transmission and reflection," as Newton called them, are the law of nature because they are the law of spirit.

The mind now thinks, now acts, and each fit reproduces the other. When the artist has exhausted his materials, when the fancy no longer paints, when thoughts are no longer apprehended and books are a weariness—he has always the resource *to live*. Character is higher than intellect. Thinking is the function. Living is the functionary. The stream retreats to its source. A great soul will be strong to live, as well as strong to think. Does he lack organ or medium to impart his truths? He can still fall back on this elemental force of living them. This is a total act, Thinking is a partial act. Let the grandeur of justice shine in his affairs. Let the beauty of affection cheer his lowly roof. Those "far from fame," who dwell and act with him, will feel the force of his constitution in the doings and passages of the day better than it can be measured by any public and designed display. Time shall teach him that the scholar loses no hour which the man lives. Herein he unfolds the sacred germ of his instinct, screened from influence. What is lost in seemliness is gained in strength. Not out of those on whom systems of education have exhausted their culture, comes the helpful giant to destroy the old or to build the new, but out of unhandselled savage nature; out of terrible Druids and Berserkers come at last Alfred and Shakspeare.

I hear therefore with joy whatever is beginning to be said of the dignity and necessity of labor to every citizen. There is virtue yet in the hoe and the spade, for learned as well as for unlearned hands. And labor is everywhere welcome; always we are invited to work; only be this limitation observed, that a man shall not for the sake of wider activity sacrifice any opinion to the popular judgments and modes of action.

I have now spoken of the education of the scholar by nature, by books, and by action. It remains to say somewhat of his duties.

They are such as become Man Thinking. They may all be comprised in self-trust. The office of the scholar is to cheer, to raise, and to guide men by showing them facts amidst appearances. He plies the slow, unhonored, and unpaid task of observation. Flamsteed and Herschel, in their glazed observatories, may catalogue the stars with the praise of all men, and the results being splendid and useful, honor is sure. But he, in his private observatory, cataloguing obscure and nebulous stars of the human mind, which as yet no man has thought of as such—watching days and months sometimes for a few facts; correcting still his old records—must relinquish display and immediate fame. In the long period of his preparation he must betray often an ignorance and shiftlessness in popular arts, incurring the disdain of the able who shoulder him aside. Long he must stammer in his speech; often forego the living for the dead. Worse yet, he must accept—how often!—poverty and solitude. For the ease and pleasure of treading the old road, accepting the fashions, the education, the religion of society, he takes the cross of making his own, and, of course, the self-accusation, the faint heart, the frequent uncertainty and loss of time, which are the nettles and tangling vines in the way of the self-relying and self-directed; and the state of virtual hostility in which he seems to stand to society, and especially to educated society. For all this loss and scorn, what offset? He is to find consolation in exercising the highest functions of human nature. He is one who raises himself from private considerations and breathes and lives on public and illustrious thoughts. He is the world's eye. He is the world's heart. He is to resist the vulgar prosperity that retrogrades ever to barbarism, by preserving and communicating heroic sentiments, noble biographies, melodious verse, and the conclusions of history. Whatsoever oracles the human heart, in all emergencies, in all solemn hours, has uttered as its commentary on the world of actions—these he shall receive and impart. And whatsoever new verdict Reason from her inviolable seat pronounces on the passing men and events of to-day—this he shall hear and promulgate.

These being his functions, it becomes him to feel all confidence in himself, and to defer never to the popular cry. He and he only knows the world. The world of any moment is the merest appearance. Some great decorum, some fetish of a government, some ephemeral trade, or war, or man, is cried up by half mankind and cried down by the other half, as if all depended on this particular up or down. The odds are that the whole question is not worth the poorest thought which the scholar has lost in listening to the controversy. Let him not quit his belief that a popgun is a popgun, though the ancient and honorable of the earth affirm it to be the crack of doom. In silence, in steadiness, in severe abstraction, let him hold by himself; add observation to observation, patient of neglect, patient of reproach, and bide his own time— happy enough if he can satisfy himself alone that this day he has seen something truly. Success treads on every right step. For the instinct is sure, that prompts him to tell his brother what he thinks. He then learns that in going down into the secrets of his own mind he has descended into the secrets of all minds. He learns that he who has mastered any law in his private thoughts, is master to that extent of all men whose language he speaks, and of all into whose language his own can be translated. The poet, in utter solitude remembering his spontaneous thoughts and recording them, is found to have recorded that which men in crowded cities find true for them also. The orator distrusts at first the fitness of his frank confessions, his want of knowledge of the persons he addresses, until he finds that he is the complement of his hearers— that they drink his words because he fulfils for them their own nature; the deeper he dives into his privatest, secretest presentiment, to his wonder he finds this is the most acceptable, most public, and universally true. The people delight in it; the better part of every man feels, This is my music; this is myself.

In self-trust all the virtues are comprehended. Free should the scholar be—free and brave. Free even to the definition of freedom, "without any hindrance that does not arise out of his own constitution." Brave; for fear is a thing which a scholar by his very function puts behind him. Fear always springs from ignorance. It is a shame to him if his tranquillity, amid dangerous times, arise from the presumption that like children and women his is a protected class; or if he seek a temporary peace by the diversion of his thoughts from politics or vexed questions, hiding his head like an ostrich in the flowering bushes, peeping into microscopes, and turning rhymes, as a boy whistles to keep his courage up. So is the danger a danger still; so is the fear worse. Manlike let him turn and face it. Let him look into its eye and search its nature, inspect its origin—see the whelping of this lion—which lies no great way back; he will then find himself a perfect comprehension of its nature and extent; he will have made his hands meet on the other side, and can henceforth defy it and pass on superior. The world is his who can see through its pretension. What deafness, what stone-blind custom, what overgrown error you behold, is there only by sufferance—by your sufferance. See it to be a lie, and you have already dealt it its mortal blow.

Yes, we are the cowed—we the trustless. It is a mischievous notion that we are come late into nature; that the world was finished a long time ago. As the world was plastic and fluid in the hands of God, so it is ever to so much of his attributes as we bring to it. To ignorance and sin, it is flint. They adapt themselves to it as they may; but in proportion as a man has any thing in him divine, the firmament flows before him and takes his signet and form. Not he is great who can alter matter, but he who can alter my state of mind. They are the kings of the world who give the color of their present thought to all nature and all art, and persuade men by the cheerful serenity of their carrying the matter, that this thing which they do is the apple which the ages have desired to pluck, now at last ripe, and inviting nations to the harvest. The great man makes the great thing. Wherever Macdonald sits, there is the head of the table. Linnæus makes botany the most alluring of studies, and wins it from the farmer and the herb-woman; Davy, chemistry; and Cuvier, fossils. The day is always his who works in it with serenity and great aims. The unstable estimates of men crowd to him whose mind is filled with a truth, as the heaped waves of the Atlantic follow the moon.

For this self-trust, the reason is deeper than can be fathomed—darker than can be enlightened. I might not carry with me the feeling of my audience in stating my own belief. But I have already shown the ground of my hope, in adverting to the doctrine that man is one. I believe man has been wronged; he has wronged himself. He has almost lost the light that can lead him back to his prerogatives. Men are become of no account. Men in history, men in the world of to-day, are bugs, are spawn, and are called "the mass" and "the herd." In a century, in a millennium, one or two men; that is to say, one or two approximations to the right state of every man. All the rest behold in the hero or the poet their own green and crude being—ripened; yes, and are content to be less, so *that* may attain to its full stature. What a testimony, full of grandeur, full of pity, is borne to the demands of his own nature, by the poor clansman, the poor partisan, who rejoices in the glory of his chief. The poor and the low find some amends to their immense moral capacity, for their acquiescence in a political and social inferiority. They are content to be brushed like flies from the path of a great person, so that justice shall be done by him to that common nature which it is the dearest desire of all to see enlarged and glorified. They sun themselves in the great man's light, and feel it to be their own element. They cast the dignity of man from their downtrod selves upon the shoulders of a hero, and will perish to add one drop of blood to make that great heart beat, those giant sinews combat and conquer. He lives for us, and we live in him.

Men, such as they are, very naturally seek money or power; and power because it is as good as money—the "spoils," so called, "of office." And why not? for they aspire to the highest, and this, in their sleep-walking, they dream is highest. Wake them and they shall quit the false good and leap to the true, and leave governments to clerks and desks. This revolution is to be wrought by the gradual domestication of the idea of Culture. The main enterprise of the world for splendor, for extent, is the upbuilding of a man. Here are the materials strewn along the ground. The private life of one man shall be a more illustrious monarchy, more formidable to its enemy, more sweet and serene in its influence to its friend, than any kingdom in history. For a man, rightly viewed, comprehendeth the particular natures of all men. Each philosopher, each bard, each actor has only done for me, as by a delegate, what one day I can do for myself. The books which once we valued more than the apple of the eye, we have quite exhausted. What is that but saying that we have come up with the point of view which the universal mind took through the eyes of one scribe; we have been that man, and have passed on. First, one, then another, we drain all cisterns, and waxing greater by all these supplies, we crave a better and more abundant food. The man has never lived that can feed us ever. The human mind cannot be enshrined in a person who shall set a barrier on any one side to this unbounded, unboundable empire. It is one central fire, which, flaming now out of the lips of Etna, lightens the capes of Sicily, and now out of the throat of Vesuvius, illuminates the towers and vineyards of Naples. It is one light which beams out of a thousand stars. It is one soul which animates all men.

But I have dwelt perhaps tediously upon this abstraction of the Scholar. I ought not to delay longer to add what I have to say of nearer reference to the time and to this country.

Historically, there is thought to be a difference in the ideas which predominate over successive epochs, and there are data for marking the genius of the Classic, of the Romantic, and now of the Reflective or Philosophical age. With the views I have intimated of the oneness or the identity of the mind through all individuals, I do not much dwell on these differences. In fact, I believe each individual passes through all three. The boy is a Greek; the youth, romantic; the adult, reflective. I deny not, however, that a revolution in the leading idea may be distinctly enough traced.

Our age is bewailed as the age of Introversion. Must that needs be evil? We, it seems, are critical; we are embarrassed with second thoughts; we cannot enjoy any thing for hankering to know whereof the pleasure consists; we are lined with eyes; we see with our feet; the time is infected with Hamlet's unhappiness—

Sicklied o'er with the pale cast of thought.

It is so bad then? Sight is the last thing to be pitied. Would we be blind? Do we fear lest we should outsee nature and God, and drink truth dry? I look upon the discontent of the literary class as a mere announcement of the fact that they find themselves not in the state of mind of their fathers, and regret the coming state as untried; as a boy dreads the water before he has learned that he can swim. If there is any period one would desire to be born in, is it not the age of Revolution; when the old and the new stand side by side and admit of being compared; when the energies of all men are searched by fear and by hope; when the historic glories of the old can be compensated by the rich possibilities of the new era? This time, like all times, is a very good one, if we but know what to do with it.

I read with some joy of the auspicious signs of the coming days, as they glimmer already through poetry and art, through philosophy and science, through church and state.

One of these signs is the fact that the same movement which effected the elevation of what was called the lowest class in the state, assumed in literature a very marked and as benign an aspect. Instead of the sublime and beautiful, the near, the low, the common, was explored and poetized. That which had been negligently trodden under foot by those who were harnessing and provisioning themselves for long journeys into far countries, is suddenly found to be richer than all foreign parts. The literature of the poor, the feelings of the child, the philosophy of the street, the meaning of household life, are the topics of the time. It is a great stride. It is a sign— is it not?—of new vigor when the extremities are made active, when currents of warm life run into the hands and the feet. I ask not for the great, the remote, the romantic; what is doing in Italy or Arabia; what is Greek art, or Provençal minstrelsy; I embrace the common, I explore and sit at the feet of the familiar, the low. Give me insight into to-day, and you may have the antique and future worlds. What would we really know the meaning of? The meal in the firkin; the milk in the pan; the ballad in the street; the news of the boat; the glance of the eye; the form and the gait of the body—show me the ultimate reason of these matters; show me the sublime presence of the highest spiritual cause lurking, as always it does lurk, in these suburbs and extremities of nature; let me see every trifle bristling with the polarity that ranges it instantly on an eternal law; and the shop, the plough, and the ledger referred to the like cause by which light undulates and poets sing—and the world lies no longer a dull miscellany and lumber-room, but has form and order; there is no trifle, there is no puzzle, but one design unites and animates the farthest pinnacle and the lowest trench.

This idea has inspired the genius of Goldsmith, Burns, Cowper, and, in a newer time, of Goethe, Wordsworth, and

Carlyle. This idea they have differently followed and with various success. In contrast with their writing, the style of Pope, of Johnson, of Gibbon, looks cold and pedantic. This writing is blood-warm. Man is surprised to find that things near are not less beautiful and wondrous than things remote. The near explains the far. The drop is a small ocean. A man is related to all nature. This perception of the worth of the vulgar is fruitful in discoveries. Goethe, in this very thing the most modern of the moderns, has shown us, as none ever did, the genius of the ancients.

There is one man of genius who has done much for this philosophy of life, whose literary value has never yet been rightly estimated—I mean Emanuel Swedenborg. The most imaginative of men, yet writing with the precision of a mathematician, he endeavored to engraft a purely philosophical Ethics on the popular Christianity of his time. Such an attempt of course must have difficulty which no genius could surmount. But he saw and showed the connection between nature and the affections of the soul. He pierced the emblematic or spiritual character of the visible, audible, tangible world. Especially did his shade-loving muse hover over and interpret the lower parts of nature; he showed the mysterious bond that allies moral evil to the foul material forms, and has given in epical parables a theory of insanity, of beasts, of unclean and fearful things.

Another sign of our times, also marked by an analogous political movement, is the new importance given to the single person. Every thing that tends to insulate the individual—to surround him with barriers of natural respect, so that each man shall feel the world is his, and man shall treat with man as a sovereign state with a sovereign state—tends to true union as well as greatness. "I learned," said the melancholy Pestalozzi, "that no man in God's wide earth is either willing or able to help any other man." Help must come from the bosom alone. The scholar is that man who must take up into himself all the ability of the time, all the contributions of the past, all the hopes of the future. He must be an university of knowledges. If there be one lesson more than another which should pierce his ear, it is, The world is nothing, the man is all; in yourself is the law of all nature, and you know not yet how a globule of sap ascends; in yourself slumbers the whole of Reason; it is for you to know all;

it is for you to dare all. Mr. President and Gentlemen, this confidence in the unsearched might of man belongs, by all motives, by all prophecy, by all preparation, to the American Scholar. We have listened too long to the courtly muses of Europe. The spirit of the American freeman is already suspected to be timid, imitative, tame. Public and private avarice make the air we breathe thick and fat. The scholar is decent, indolent, complaisant. See already the tragic consequence. The mind of this country, taught to aim at low objects, eats upon itself. There is no work for any but the decorous and the complaisant. Young men of the fairest promise, who begin life upon our shores, inflated by the mountain winds, shined upon by all the stars of God, find the earth below not in unison with these, but are hindered from action by the disgust which the principles on which business is managed inspire, and turn drudges, or die of disgust, some of them suicides. What is the remedy? They did not yet see, and thousands of young men as hopeful now crowding to the barriers for the career do not yet see, that if the single man plant himself indomitably on his instincts, and there abide, the huge world will come round to him. Patience—patience; with the shades of all the good and great for company; and for solace the perspective of your own infinite life; and for work the study and the communication of principles, the making those instincts prevalent, the conversion of the world. Is it not the chief disgrace in the world, not to be an unit—not to be reckoned one character—not to yield that peculiar fruit which each man was created to bear, but to be reckoned in the gross, in the hundred, or the thousand, of the party, the section, to which we belong; and our opinion predicted geographically, as the north, or the south? Not so, brothers and friends—please God, ours shall not be so. We will walk on our own feet; we will work with our own hands; we will speak our own minds. The study of letters shall be no longer a name for pity, for doubt, and for sensual indulgence. The dread of man and the love of man shall be a wall of defence and a wreath of joy around all. A nation of men will for the first time exist, because each believes himself inspired by the Divine Soul which also inspires all men.

From Nature, Addresses and Lectures

Divinity School Address

DELIVERED BEFORE THE SENIOR CLASS IN DIVINITY
COLLEGE, CAMBRIDGE, SUNDAY EVENING,
JULY 15, 1838

In this refulgent summer, it has been a luxury to draw the
breath of life. The grass grows, the buds burst, the meadow
is spotted with fire and gold in the tint of flowers. The air is
full of birds, and sweet with the breath of the pine, the balm-
of-Gilead, and the new hay. Night brings no gloom to the
heart with its welcome shade. Through the transparent darkness the stars pour their almost spiritual rays. Man under
them seems a young child, and his huge globe a toy. The
cool night bathes the world as with a river, and prepares his
eyes again for the crimson dawn. The mystery of nature was
never displayed more happily. The corn and the wine have
been freely dealt to all creatures, and the never-broken silence
with which the old bounty goes forward has not yielded yet
one word of explanation. One is constrained to respect the
perfection of this world in which our senses converse. How
wide; how rich; what invitation from every property it gives
to every faculty of man! In its fruitful soils; in its navigable
sea; in its mountains of metal and stone; in its forests of all
woods; in its animals; in its chemical ingredients; in the
powers and path of light, heat, attraction and life, it is well
worth the pith and heart of great men to subdue and enjoy
it. The planters, the mechanics, the inventors, the astronomers,
the builders of cities, and the captains, history delights to
honor.

But when the mind opens and reveals the laws which
traverse the universe and make things what they are, then
shrinks the great world at once into a mere illustration and
fable of this mind. What am I? and What is? asks the human

81

spirit with a curiosity new-kindled, but never to be quenched. Behold these out-running laws, which our imperfect apprehension can see tend this way and that, but not come full circle. Behold these infinite relations, so like, so unlike; many, yet one. I would study, I would know, I would admire forever. These works of thought have been the entertainments of the human spirit in all ages.

A more secret, sweet, and overpowering beauty appears to man when his heart and mind open to the sentiment of virtue. Then he is instructed in what is above him. He learns that his being is without bound; that to the good, to the perfect, he is born, low as he now lies in evil and weakness. That which he venerates is still his own, though he has not realized it yet. *He ought.* He knows the sense of that grand word, though his analysis fails to render account of it. When in innocency or when by intellectual perception he attains to say, "I love the Right; Truth is beautiful within and without for evermore. Virtue, I am thine; save me; use me; thee will I serve, day and night, in great, in small, that I may be not virtuous, but virtue;" then is the end of the creation answered, and God is well pleased.

The sentiment of virtue is a reverence and delight in the presence of certain divine laws. It perceives that this homely game of life we play, covers, under what seem foolish details, principles that astonish. The child amidst his baubles is learning the action of light, motion, gravity, muscular force; and in the game of human life, love, fear, justice, appetite, man, and God, interact. These laws refuse to be adequately stated. They will not be written out on paper, or spoken by the tongue. They elude our persevering thought; yet we read them hourly in each other's faces, in each other's actions, in our own remorse. The moral traits which are all globed into every virtuous act and thought—in speech we must sever, and describe or suggest by painful enumeration of many particulars. Yet, as this sentiment is the essence of all religion, let me guide your eye to the precise objects of the sentiment, by an enumeration of some of those classes of facts in which this element is conspicuous.

The intuition of the moral sentiment is an insight of the perfection of the laws of the soul. These laws execute themselves. They are out of time, out of space, and not subject to circumstance. Thus in the soul of man there is a justice

whose retributions are instant and entire. He who does a good
deed is instantly ennobled. He who does a mean deed is by
the action itself contracted. He who puts off impurity, thereby puts on purity. If a man is at heart just, then in so far is
he God; the safety of God, the immortality of God, the
majesty of God do enter into that man with justice. If a man
dissemble, deceive, he deceives himself, and goes out of
acquaintance with his own being. A man in the view of
absolute goodness, adores, with total humility. Every step so
downward, is a step upward. The man who renounces himself, comes to himself.

See how this rapid intrinsic energy worketh everywhere,
righting wrongs, correcting appearances, and bringing up
facts to a harmony with thoughts. Its operation in life,
though slow to the senses, is at last as sure as in the soul.
By it a man is made the Providence to himself, dispensing
good to his goodness, and evil to his sin. Character is always
known. Thefts never enrich; alms never impoverish; murder
will speak out of stone walls. The least admixture of a lie—
for example, the taint of vanity, any attempt to make a good
impression, a favorable appearance—will instantly vitiate
the effect. But speak the truth, and all nature and all spirits
help you with unexpected furtherance. Speak the truth, and
all things alive or brute are vouchers, and the very roots of
the grass underground there do seem to stir and move to
bear you witness. See again the perfection of the Law as it
applies itself to the affections, and becomes the law of
society. As we are, so we associate. The good, by affinity, seek
the good; the vile, by affinity, the vile. Thus of their own
volition, souls proceed into heaven, into hell.

These facts have always suggested to man the sublime
creed that the world is not the product of manifold power,
but of one will, of one mind; and that one mind is everywhere active, in each ray of the star, in each wavelet of the
pool; and whatever opposes that will is everywhere balked
and baffled, because things are made so, and not otherwise.
Good is positive. Evil is merely privative, not absolute: it
is like cold, which is the privation of heat. All evil is so much
death or nonentity. Benevolence is absolute and real. So
much benevolence as a man hath, so much life hath he. For
all things proceed out of this same spirit, which is differently
named love, justice, temperance, in its different applications,

just as the ocean receives different names on the several shores which it washes. All things proceed out of the same spirit, and all things conspire with it. Whilst a man seeks good ends, he is strong by the whole strength of nature. In so far as he roves from these ends, he bereaves himself of power, or auxiliaries; his being shrinks out of all remote channels, he becomes less and less, a mote, a point, until absolute badness is absolute death.

The perception of this law of laws awakens in the mind a sentiment which we call the religious sentiment, and which makes our highest happiness. Wonderful is its power to charm and to command. It is a mountain air. It is the embalmer of the world. It is myrrh and storax, and chlorine and rosemary. It makes the sky and the hills sublime, and the silent song of the stars is it. By it is the universe made safe and habitable, not by science or power. Thought may work cold and intransitive in things, and find no end or unity; but the dawn of the sentiment of virtue on the heart, gives and is the assurance that Law is sovereign over all natures; and the worlds, time, space, eternity, do seem to break out into joy.

This sentiment is divine and deifying. It is the beatitude of man. It makes him illimitable. Through it, the soul first knows itself. It corrects the capital mistake of the infant man, who seeks to be great by following the great, and hopes to derive advantages *from another*, by showing the fountain of all good to be in himself, and that he, equally with every man, is an inlet into the deeps of Reason. When he says, "I ought;" when love warms him; when he chooses, warned from on high, the good and great deed; then, deep melodies wander through his soul from Supreme Wisdom. Then he can worship, and be enlarged by his worship; for he can never go behind this sentiment. In the sublimest flights of the soul, rectitude is never surmounted, love is never outgrown.

This sentiment lies at the foundation of society, and successively creates all forms of worship. The principle of veneration never dies out. Man fallen into superstition, into sensuality, is never quite without the visions of the moral sentiment. In like manner, all the expressions of this sentiment are sacred and permanent in proportion to their purity. The expressions of this sentiment affect us more than all other compositions. The sentences of the oldest time, which ejaculate this piety, are still fresh and fragrant. This thought dwelled always deepest in the minds of men in the devout and contemplative East; not alone in Palestine, where it reached its purest expression, but in Egypt, in Persia, in India, in China. Europe has always owed to oriental genius its divine impulses. What these holy bards said, all sane men found agreeable and true. And the unique impression of Jesus upon mankind, whose name is not so much written as ploughed into the history of this world, is proof of the subtle virtue of this infusion.

Meantime, whilst the doors of the temple stand open, night and day, before every man, and the oracles of this truth cease never, it is guarded by one stern condition; this, namely; it is an intuition. It cannot be received at second hand. Truly speaking, it is not instruction, but provocation, that I can receive from another soul. What he announces, I must find true in me, or reject; and on his word, or as his second, be he who he may, I can accept nothing. On the contrary, the absence of this primary faith is the presence of degradation. As is the flood, so is the ebb. Let this faith depart, and the very words it spake and the things it made become false and hurtful. Then falls the church, the state, art, letters, life. The doctrine of the divine nature being forgotten, a sickness infects and dwarfs the constitution. Once man was all; now he is an appendage, a nuisance. And because the indwelling Supreme Spirit cannot wholly be got rid of, the doctrine of it suffers this perversion, that the divine nature is attributed to one or two persons, and denied to all the rest, and denied with fury. The doctrine of inspiration is lost; the base doctrine of the majority of voices usurps the place of the doctrine of the soul. Miracles, prophecy, poetry, the ideal life, the holy life, exist as ancient history merely; they are not in the belief, nor in the aspiration of society; but, when suggested, seem ridiculous. Life is comic or pitiful as soon as the high ends of being fade out of sight, and man becomes near-sighted, and can only attend to what addresses the senses.

These general views, which, whilst they are general, none will contest, find abundant illustration in the history of religion, and especially in the history of the Christian church. In that, all of us have had our birth and nurture. The truth contained in that, you, my young friends, are now setting forth to teach. As the Cultus, or established worship of the civilized world, it has great historical interest for us. Of its blessed words, which have been the consolation of humanity, you need not that I should speak. I shall endeavor to discharge my duty to you on this occasion, by pointing out two errors in its administration, which daily appear more gross from the point of view we have just now taken.

Jesus Christ belonged to the true race of prophets. He saw with open eye the mystery of the soul. Drawn by its severe harmony, ravished with its beauty, he lived in it, and had his being there. Alone in all history he estimated the greatness of man. One man was true to what is in you and me. He saw that God incarnates himself in man, and evermore goes forth anew to take possession of his World. He said, in this jubilee of sublime emotion, "I am divine. Through me, God acts; through me, speaks. Would you see God, see me; or see thee, when thou also thinkest as I now think." But what a distortion did his doctrine and memory suffer in the same, in the next, and the following ages! There is no doctrine of the Reason which will bear to be taught by the Understanding. The understanding caught this high chant from the poet's lips, and said, in the next age, "This was Jehovah come down out of heaven. I will kill you, if you say he was a man." The idioms of his language and the figures of his rhetoric have usurped the place of his truth; and churches are not built on his principles, but on his tropes. Christianity became a Mythus, as the poetic teaching of Greece and of Egypt, before. He spoke of miracles; for he felt that man's life was a miracle, and all that man doth, and he knew that this daily miracle shines as the character ascends. But the word Miracle, as pronounced by Christian churches, gives a false impression; it is Monster. It is not one with the blowing clover and the falling rain.

He felt respect for Moses and the prophets, but no unfit tenderness at postponing their initial revelations to the hour and the man that now is; to the eternal revelation in the heart. Thus was he a true man. Having seen that the law in us is commanding, he would not suffer it to be commanded. Boldly, with hand, and heart, and life, he declared it was God. Thus is he, as I think, the only soul in history who has appreciated the worth of man.

1. In this point of view we become sensible of the first defect of historical Christianity. Historical Christianity has fallen into the error that corrupts all attempts to communicate

religion. As it appears to us, and as it has appeared for ages, it is not the doctrine of the soul, but an exaggeration of the personal, the positive, the ritual. It has dwelt, it dwells, with noxious exaggeration about the *person* of Jesus. The soul knows no persons. It invites every man to expand to the full circle of the universe, and will have no preferences but those of spontaneous love. But by this eastern monarchy of a Christianity, which indolence and fear have built, the friend of man is made the injurer of man. The manner in which his name is surrounded with expressions which were once sallies of admiration and love, but are now petrified into official titles, kills all generous sympathy and liking. All who hear me, feel that the language that describes Christ to Europe and America is not the style of friendship and enthusiasm to a good and noble heart, but is appropriated and formal— paints a demigod, as the Orientals or the Greeks would describe Osiris or Apollo. Accept the injurious impositions of our early catechetical instruction, and even honesty and self-denial were but splendid sins, if they did not wear the Christian name. One would rather be

A pagan, suckled in a creed outworn,[1]

than to be defrauded of his manly right in coming into nature and finding not names and places, not land and professions, but even virtue and truth foreclosed and monopolized. You shall not be a man even. You shall not own the world; you shall not dare and live after the infinite Law that is in you, and in company with the infinite Beauty which heaven and earth reflect to you in all lovely forms; but you must subordinate your nature to Christ's nature; you must accept our interpretations, and take his portrait as the vulgar draw it.

That is always best which gives me to myself. The sublime is excited in me by the great stoical doctrine, Obey thyself. That which shows God in me, fortifies me. That which shows God out of me, makes me a wart and a wen. There is no longer a necessary reason for my being. Already the long shadows of untimely oblivion creep over me, and I shall decease forever.

The divine bards are the friends of my virtue, of my in-

---

[1] Wordsworth, "The World is Too Much with Us," in *Miscellaneous Sonnets.*

tellect, of my strength. They admonish me that the gleams which flash across my mind are not mine, but God's; that they had the like, and were not disobedient to the heavenly vision. So I love them. Noble provocations go out from them, inviting me to resist evil; to subdue the world; and to Be. And thus, by his holy thoughts, Jesus serves us, and thus only. To aim to convert a man by miracles is a profanation of the soul. A true conversion, a true Christ, is now, as always, to be made by the reception of beautiful sentiments. It is true that a great and rich soul, like his, falling among the simple, does so preponderate, that, as his did, it names the world. The world seems to them to exist for him, and they have not yet drunk so deeply of his sense as to see that only by coming again to themselves, or to God in themselves, can they grow forevermore. It is a low benefit to give me something; it is a high benefit to enable me to do somewhat of myself. The time is coming when all men will see that the gift of God to the soul is not a vaunting, overpowering, excluding sanctity, but a sweet, natural goodness, a goodness like thine and mine, and that so invites thine and mine to be and to grow.

The injustice of the vulgar tone of preaching is not less flagrant to Jesus than to the souls which it profanes. The preachers do not see that they make his gospel not glad, and shear him of the locks of beauty and the attributes of heaven. When I see a majestic Epaminondas, or Washington; when I see among my contemporaries a true orator, an upright judge, a dear friend; when I vibrate to the melody and fancy of a poem; I see beauty that is to be desired. And so lovely, and with yet more entire consent of my human being, sounds in my ear the severe music of the bards that have sung of the true God in all ages. Now do not degrade the life and dialogues of Christ out of the circle of this charm, by insulation and peculiarity. Let them lie as they befell, alive and warm, part of human life and of the landscape and of the cheerful day.

2. The second defect of the traditionary and limited way of using the mind of Christ is a consequence of the first; this, namely; that the Moral Nature, that Law of laws whose revelations introduce greatness—yea, God himself—into the open soul, is not explored as the fountain of the established teaching in society. Men have come to speak of the revelation as somewhat long ago given and done, as if God were dead.

The injury to faith throttles the preacher; and the goodliest of institutions becomes an uncertain and inarticulate voice.

It is very certain that it is the effect of conversation with the beauty of the soul, to beget a desire and need to impart to others the same knowledge and love. If utterance is denied, the thought lies like a burden on the man. Always the seer is a sayer. Somehow his dream is told; somehow he publishes it with solemn joy: sometimes with pencil on canvas, sometimes with chisel on stone, sometimes in towers and aisles of granite, his soul's worship is builded; sometimes in anthems of indefinite music; but clearest and most permanent, in words.

The man enamored of this excellency becomes its priest or poet. The office is coeval with the world. But observe the condition, the spiritual limitation of the office. The spirit only can teach. Not any profane man, not any sensual, not any liar, not any slave can teach, but only he can give, who has; he only can create, who is. The man on whom the soul descends, through whom the soul speaks, alone can teach. Courage, piety, love, wisdom, can teach; and every man can open his door to these angels, and they shall bring him the gift of tongues. But the man who aims to speak as books enable, as synods use, as the fashion guides, and as interest commands, babbles. Let him hush.

To this holy office you propose to devote yourselves. I wish you may feel your call in throbs of desire and hope. The office is the first in the world. It is of that reality that it cannot suffer the deduction of any falsehood. And it is my duty to say to you that the need was never greater of new revelation than now. From the views I have already expressed, you will infer the sad conviction, which I share, I believe, with numbers, of the universal decay and now almost death of faith in society. The soul is not preached. The Church seems to totter to its fall, almost all life extinct. On this occasion, any complaisance would be criminal which told you, whose hope and commission it is to preach the faith of Christ, that the faith of Christ is preached.

It is time that this ill-suppressed murmur of all thoughtful men against the famine of our churches—this moaning of the heart because it is bereaved of the consolation, the hope, the grandeur that come alone out of the culture of the moral nature—should be heard through the sleep of indolence, and over the din of routine. This great and perpetual office of the preacher is not discharged. Preaching is the expression of the moral sentiment in application to the duties of life. In how many churches, by how many prophets, tell me, is man made sensible that he is an infinite Soul; that the earth and heavens are passing into his mind; that he is drinking forever the soul of God? Where now sounds the persuasion, that by its very melody imparadises my heart, and so affirms its own origin in heaven? Where shall I hear words such as in elder ages drew men to leave all and follow—father and mother, house and land, wife and child? Where shall I hear these august laws of moral being so pronounced as to fill my ear, and I feel ennobled by the offer of my uttermost action and passion? The test of the true faith, certainly, should be its power to charm and command the soul, as the laws of nature control the activity of the hands—so commanding that we find pleasure and honor in obeying. The faith should blend with the light of rising and of setting suns, with the flying cloud, the singing bird, and the breath of flowers. But now the priest's Sabbath has lost the splendor of nature; it is unlovely; we are glad when it is done; we can make, we do make, even sitting in our pews, a far better, holier, sweeter, for ourselves.

Whenever the pulpit is usurped by a formalist, then is the worshipper defrauded and disconsolate. We shrink as soon as the prayers begin, which do not uplift, but smite and offend us. We are fain to wrap our cloaks about us, and secure, as best we can, a solitude that hears not. I once heard a preacher who sorely tempted me to say I would go to church no more. Men go, thought I, where they are wont to go, else had no soul entered the temple in the afternoon. A snow-storm was falling around us. The snow-storm was real, the preacher merely spectral, and the eye felt the sad contrast in looking at him, and then out of the window behind him into the beautiful meteor of the snow. He had lived in vain. He had no one word intimating that he had laughed or wept, was married or in love, had been commended, or cheated, or chagrined. If he had ever lived and acted, we were none the wiser for it. The capital secret of his profession, namely, to convert life into truth, he had not learned. Not one fact in all his experience had he yet imported into his doctrine. This man had ploughed and planted and talked and bought and sold; he had read books; he had eaten and drunken; his head aches, his heart throbs; he smiles and suffers; yet was there not a surmise, a hint, in all the discourse, that he had ever lived at all. Not a line did he draw out of real history. The true preacher can be known by this, that he deals out to the people his life— life passed through the fire of thought. But of the bad preacher, it could not be told from his sermon what age of the world he fell in; whether he had a father or a child; whether he was a freeholder or a pauper; whether he was a citizen or a countryman; or any other fact of his biography. It seemed strange that the people should come to church. It seemed as if their houses were very unentertaining, that they should prefer this thoughtless clamor. It shows that there is a commanding attraction in the moral sentiment, that can lend a faint tint of light to dulness and ignorance coming in its name and place. The good hearer is sure he has been touched sometimes; is sure there is somewhat to be reached, and some word that can reach it. When he listens to these vain words, he comforts himself by their relation to his remembrance of better hours, and so they clatter and echo unchallenged.

I am not ignorant that when we preach unworthily, it is not always quite in vain. There is a good ear, in some men, that draws supplies to virtue out of very indifferent nutriment. There is poetic truth concealed in all the commonplaces of prayer and of sermons, and though foolishly spoken, they may be wisely heard; for each is some select expression that broke out in a moment of piety from some stricken or jubilant soul, and its excellency made it remembered. The prayers and even the dogmas of our church are like the zodiac of Denderah and the astronomical monuments of the Hindoos, wholly insulated from anything now extant in the life and business of the people. They mark the height to which the waters once rose. But this docility is a check upon the mischief from the good and devout. In a large portion of the community, the religious service gives rise to quite other thoughts and emotions. We need not chide the negligent servant. We are struck with pity, rather, at the swift retribution of his sloth. Alas for the unhappy man that is called to stand in the pulpit, and *not* give bread of life. Everything that befalls, accuses him. Would he ask contributions for the missions, foreign or domestic? Instantly his face is suffused with shame, to propose to his parish that they should send money a hundred or a thousand miles, to furnish such poor fare as they have at home and would do well to go the hundred or the thousand miles to escape. Would he urge people to a godly way of living—and can he ask a fellow-creature to come to Sabbath meetings, when he and they all know what is the poor uttermost they can hope for therein? Will he invite them privately to the Lord's Supper? He dares not. If no heart warm this rite, the hollow, dry, creaking formality is too plain, than that he can face a man of wit and energy and put the invitation without terror. In the street, what has he to say to the bold village blasphemer? The village blasphemer sees fear in the face, form, and gait of the minister.

Let me not taint the sincerity of this plea by any oversight of the claims of good men. I know and honor the purity and strict conscience of numbers of the clergy. What life the public worship retains, it owes to the scattered company of pious men, who minister here and there in churches, and who sometimes accepting with too great tenderness the tenet of the elders, have not accepted from others, but from their own heart, the genuine impulses of virtue, and so still command our love and awe, to the sanctity of character. Moreover, the exceptions are not so much to be found in a few eminent preachers, as in the better hours, the truer inspirations of all—nay, in the sincere moments of every man. But, with whatever exception, it is still true that tradition characterizes the preaching of this country; that it comes out of the memory, and not out of the soul; that it aims at what is usual, and not at what is necessary and eternal; that thus historical Christianity destroys the power of preaching, by withdrawing it from the exploration of the moral nature of man; where the sublime is, where are the resources of astonishment and power. What a cruel injustice it is to that Law, the joy of the whole earth, which alone can make thought dear and rich; that Law whose fatal sureness the astronomical orbits poorly emulate—that it is travestied and depreciated, that it is behooted and behowled, and not a trait, not a word of it articulated. The pulpit in losing sight of this Law, loses its reason, and gropes after it knows not what. And for want of this culture the soul of the community is sick and faithless. It wants nothing so much as a stern, high, stoical, Christian discipline, to make it know itself and the divinity that speaks through it. Now man is ashamed of himself; he skulks and sneaks through the world, to be tolerated, to be pitied, and scarcely in a thousand years does any man dare to be wise and good, and so draw after him the tears and blessings of his kind.

Certainly there have been periods when, from the inactivity of the intellect on certain truths, a greater faith was possible in names and persons. The Puritans in England and America found in the Christ of the Catholic Church and in the dogmas inherited from Rome, scope for their austere piety and their longings for civil freedom. But their creed is passing away, and none arises in its room. I think no man can go with his thoughts about him into one of our churches, without feeling that what hold the public worship had on men is gone, or going. It has lost its grasp on the affection of the good and the fear of the bad. In the country, neighborhoods, half parishes are *signing off*, to use the local term. It is already beginning to indicate character and religion to withdraw from the religious meetings. I have heard a devout person, who prized the Sabbath, say in bitterness of heart, "On Sundays, it seems wicked to go to church." And the motive that holds the best there is now only a hope and a waiting. What was once a mere circumstance, that the best and the worst men in the parish, the poor and the rich, the learned and the ignorant, young and old, should meet one day as fellows in one house, in sign of an equal right in the soul, has come to be a paramount motive for going thither.

My friends, in these two errors, I think, I find the causes of a decaying church and a wasting unbelief. And what greater calamity can fall upon a nation than the loss of worship? Then all things go to decay. Genius leaves the temple to haunt the senate or the market. Literature becomes frivolous. Science is cold. The eye of youth is not lighted by the hope of other worlds, and age is without honor. Society lives to trifles, and when men die we do not mention them.

And now, my brothers, you will ask, What in these desponding days can be done by us? The remedy is already declared in the ground of our complaint of the Church. We have contrasted the Church with the Soul. In the soul then let the redemption be sought. Wherever a man comes, there comes revolution. The old is for slaves. When a man comes, all books are legible, all things transparent, all religions are forms. He is religious. Man is the wonderworker. He is seen amid miracles. All men bless and curse. He saith yea and nay, only. The stationariness of religion; the assumption that the age of inspiration is past, that the Bible is closed; the fear of degrading the character of Jesus by representing him as a man—indicate with sufficient clearness the falsehood of our theology. It is the office of a true teacher to show us that God is, not was; that He speaketh, not spake. The true Christianity—a faith like Christ's in the infinitude of man—is lost. None believeth in the soul of man, but only in some man or person old and departed. Ah me! no man goeth alone. All men go in flocks to this saint or that poet, avoiding the God who seeth in secret. They cannot see in secret; they love to be blind in public. They think society wiser than their soul, and know not that one soul, and their soul, is wiser than the whole world. See how nations and races flit by on the sea of time and leave no ripple to tell where they floated or sunk, and one good soul shall make the name of Moses, or of Zeno, or of Zoroaster, reverend forever. None assayeth the stern ambition to be the Self of the nation and of nature, but each would be an easy secondary to some Christian scheme, or sectarian connection, or some eminent man. Once leave your own knowledge of God, your own sentiment, and take secondary knowledge, as St. Paul's, or George Fox's, or Swedenborg's, and you get wide from God with every year this secondary form lasts, and if, as now, for centuries—the chasm yawns to that breadth, that men can scarcely be convinced there is in them anything divine.

Let me admonish you, first of all, to go alone; to refuse the good models, even those which are sacred in the imagination of men, and dare to love God without mediator or veil. Friends enough you shall find who will hold up to your emulation Wesleys and Oberlins, Saints and Prophets. Thank God for these good men, but say, "I also am a man." Imitation cannot go above its model. The imitator dooms himself to hopeless mediocrity. The inventor did it because it was natural to him, and so in him it has a charm. In the imitator something else is natural, and he bereaves himself of his own beauty, to come short of another man's.

Yourself a newborn bard of the Holy Ghost, cast behind you all conformity, and acquaint men at first hand with Deity. Look to it first and only, that fashion, custom, authority, pleasure, and money, are nothing to you—are not bandages over your eyes, that you cannot see—but live with the privilege of the immeasurable mind. Not too anxious to visit periodically all families and each family in your parish connection—when you meet one of these men or women, be to them a divine man; be to them thought and virtue; let their timid aspirations find in you a friend; let their trampled instincts be genially tempted out in your atmosphere; let their doubts know that you have doubted, and their wonder feel that you have wondered. By trusting your own heart, you shall gain more confidence in other men. For all our penny-wisdom, for all our soul-destroying slavery to habit, it is not to be doubted that all men have sublime thoughts; that all men value the few real hours of life; they love to be heard; they love to be caught up into the vision of principles. We mark with light in the memory the few interviews we have had, in the dreary years of routine and of sin, with souls that made our souls wiser; that spoke what we thought; that told us what we knew; that gave us leave to be what we inly were. Discharge to men the priestly office, and, present or absent, you shall be followed with their love as by an angel.

And, to this end, let us not aim at common degrees of merit. Can we not leave, to such as love it, the virtue that glitters for the commendation of society, and ourselves pierce the deep solitudes of absolute ability and worth? We easily come up to the standard of goodness in society. Society's praise can be cheaply secured, and almost all men are content with those easy merits; but the instant effect of conversing with God will be to put them away. There are persons who are not actors, not speakers, but influences; persons too great for fame, for display; who disdain eloquence; to whom all we call art and artist, seems too nearly allied to show and by-ends, to the exaggeration of the finite and selfish, and loss of the universal. The orators, the poets, the commanders encroach on us only as fair women do, by our allowance and homage. Slight them by preoccupation of mind, slight them, as you can well afford to do, by high and universal aims, and they instantly feel that you have right, and that it is in lower places that they must shine. They also feel your right; for they with you are open to the influx of the all-knowing Spirit, which annihilates before its broad noon the little shades and gradations of intelligence in the compositions we call wiser and wisest.

In such high communion let us study the grand strokes of rectitude: a bold benevolence, an independence of friends, so that not the unjust wishes of those who love us shall impair our freedom, but we shall resist for truth's sake the freest flow of kindness, and appeal to sympathies far in advance; and—what is the highest form in which we know this beautiful element—a certain solidity of merit, that has nothing to do with opinion, and which is so essentially and manifestly virtue, that it is taken for granted that the right, the brave, the generous step will be taken by it, and nobody thinks of commending it. You would compliment a coxcomb doing a good act, but you would not praise an angel. The silence that accepts merit as the most natural thing in the world, is the highest applause. Such souls, when they appear, are the Imperial Guard of Virtue, the perpetual reserve, the dictators of fortune. One needs not praise their courage—they are the heart and soul of nature. O my friends, there are resources in us on which we have not drawn. There are men who rise refreshed on hearing a threat; men to whom a crisis which intimidates and paralyzes the majority—demanding not the faculties of prudence and thrift, but comprehension, immovableness, the readiness of sacrifice—comes graceful and beloved as a bride. Napoleon said of Massena, that he was not himself until the battle began to go against him; then, when the dead began to fall in ranks around him, awoke his powers of combination, and he put on terror and victory as a robe. So it is in rugged crises, in unweariable endurance, and in aims which put sympathy out of question, that the angel is shown. But these are heights that we can scarce remember and look up to without contrition and shame. Let us thank God that such things exist.

And now let us do what we can to rekindle the smouldering, nigh quenched fire on the altar. The evils of the church that now is are manifest. The question returns, What shall we do? I confess, all attempts to project and establish a Cultus with new rites and forms, seem to me vain. Faith makes us, and not we it, and faith makes its own forms. All attempts to contrive a system are as cold as the new worship introduced by the French to the goddess of Reason—to-day, pasteboard and filigree, and ending to-morrow in madness and murder. Rather let the breath of new life be breathed by you through the forms already existing. For if once you are alive, you shall find they shall become plastic and new. The remedy to their deformity is first, soul, and second, soul, and evermore, soul.

A whole popedom of forms one pulsation of virtue can uplift and vivify. Two inestimable advantages Christianity has given us; first the Sabbath, the jubilee of the whole world, whose light dawns welcome alike into the closet of the philosopher, into the garret of toil, and into prison-cells, and everywhere suggests, even to the vile, the dignity of spiritual being. Let it stand forevermore, a temple, which new love, new faith, new sight shall restore to more than its first splendor to mankind. And secondly, the institution of preaching— the speech of man to men—essentially the most flexible of all organs, of all forms. What hinders that now, everywhere, in pulpits, in lecture-rooms, in houses, in fields, wherever the invitation of men or your own occasions lead you, you speak the very truth, as your life and conscience teach it, and cheer the waiting, fainting hearts of men with new hope and new revelation?

I look for the hour when that supreme Beauty which ravished the souls of those Eastern men, and chiefly of those Hebrews, and through their lips spoke oracles to all time, shall speak in the West also. The Hebrew and Greek Scriptures contain immortal sentences, that have been bread of life to millions. But they have no epical integrity; are fragmentary; are not shown in their order to the intellect. I look for the new Teacher that shall follow so far those shining laws that he shall see them come full circle; shall see their rounding complete grace; shall see the world to be the mirror of the soul; shall see the identity of the law of gravitation with purity of heart; and shall show that the Ought, that Duty, is one thing with Science, with Beauty, and with Joy.

From *Nature, Addresses and Lectures*

The Transcendentalist

A LECTURE READ AT THE MASONIC TEMPLE,
BOSTON, JANUARY, 1842

The first thing we have to say respecting what are called *new views* here in New England, at the present time, is, that they are not new, but the very oldest of thoughts cast into the mould of these new times. The light is always identical in its composition, but it falls on a great variety of objects, and by so falling is first revealed to us, not in its own form, for it is formless, but in theirs; in like manner, thought only appears in the objects it classifies. What is popularly called Transcendentalism among us, is Idealism; Idealism as it appears in 1842. As thinkers, mankind have ever divided into two sects, Materialists and Idealists; the first class founding on experience, the second on consciousness; the first class beginning to think from the data of the senses, the second class perceive that the senses are not final, and say, The senses give us representations of things, but what are the things themselves, they cannot tell. The materialist insists on facts, on history, on the force of circumstances and the animal wants of man; the idealist on the power of Thought and of Will, on inspiration, on miracle, on individual culture. These two modes of thinking are both natural, but the idealist contends that his way of thinking is in higher nature. He concedes all that the other affirms, admits the impressions of sense, admits their coherency, their use and beauty, and then asks the materialist for his grounds of assurance that things are as his senses represent them. But I, he says, affirm facts not affected by the illusions of sense, facts which are of the same nature as the faculty which reports them, and not liable to doubt; facts which in their first appearance to us assume a native superiority to material facts, degrading these into a

98

language by which the first are to be spoken; facts which it only needs a retirement from the senses to discern. Every materialist will be an idealist; but an idealist can never go backward to be a materialist.

The idealist, in speaking of events, sees them as spirits. He does not deny the sensuous fact: by no means; but he will not see that alone. He does not deny the presence of this table, this chair, and the walls of this room, but he looks at these things as the reverse side of the tapestry, as the *other end*, each being a sequel or completion of a spiritual fact which nearly concerns him. This manner of looking at things transfers every object in nature from an independent and anomalous position without there, into the consciousness. Even the materialist Condillac, perhaps the most logical expounder of materialism, was constrained to say, "Though we should soar into the heavens, though we should sink into the abyss, we never go out of ourselves; it is always our own thought that we perceive." What more could an idealist say?

The materialist, secure in the certainty of sensation, mocks at fine-spun theories, at star-gazers and dreamers, and believes that his life is solid, that he at least takes nothing for granted, but knows where he stands, and what he does. Yet how easy it is to show him that he also is a phantom walking and working amid phantoms, and that he need only ask a question or two beyond his daily questions to find his solid universe growing dim and impalpable before his sense. The sturdy capitalist, no matter how deep and square on blocks of Quincy granite he lays the foundations of his banking-house or Exchange, must set it, at last, not on a cube corresponding to the angles of his structure, but on a mass of unknown materials and solidity, red-hot or white-hot perhaps at the core, which rounds off to an almost perfect sphericity, and lies floating in soft air, and goes spinning away, dragging bank and banker with it at a rate of thousands of miles the hour, he knows not whither—a bit of bullet, now glimmering, now darkling through a small cubic space on the edge of an unimaginable pit of emptiness. And this wild balloon, in which his whole venture is embarked, is a just symbol of his whole state and faculty. One thing at least, he says, is certain, and does not give me the headache, that figures do not lie; the multiplication table has been hitherto found unimpeachable truth; and, moreover, if I put a gold eagle in my safe, I find it again to-morrow—but for these thoughts, I know not whence they are. They change and pass away. But ask him why he believes that an uniform experience will continue uniform, or on what grounds he founds his faith in his figures, and he will perceive that his mental fabric is built up on just as strange and quaking foundations as his proud edifice of stone.

In the order of thought, the materialist takes his departure from the external world, and esteems a man as one product of that. The idealist takes his departure from his consciousness, and reckons the world an appearance. The materialist respects sensible masses, Society, Government, social art and luxury, every establishment, every mass, whether majority of numbers, or extent of space, or amount of objects, every social action. The idealist has another measure, which is metaphysical, namely the *rank* which things themselves take in his consciousness; not at all the size or appearance. Mind is the only reality, of which men and all other natures are better or worse reflectors. Nature, literature, history, are only subjective phenomena. Although in his action overpowered by the laws of action, and so, warmly cooperating with men, even preferring them to himself, yet when he speaks scientifically, or after the order of thought, he is constrained to degrade persons into representatives of truths. He does not respect labor, or the products of labor, namely property, otherwise than as a manifold symbol, illustrating with wonderful fidelity of details the laws of being; he does not respect government, except as far as it reiterates the law of his mind; nor the church, nor charities, nor arts, for themselves; but hears, as at a vast distance, what they say, as if his consciousness would speak to him through a pantomimic scene. His thought—that is the Universe. His experience inclines him to behold the procession of facts you call the world, as flowing perpetually outward from an invisible, unsounded centre in himself, centre alike of him and of them, and necessitating him to regard all things as having a subjective or relative existence, relative to that aforesaid Unknown Centre of him.

From this transfer of the world into the consciousness, this beholding of all things in the mind, follow easily his whole ethics. It is simpler to be self-dependent. The height, the deity of man is to be self-sustained, to need no gift, no foreign force. Society is good when it does not violate me, but best when it is likest to solitude. Everything real is self-existent. Everything divine shares the self-existence of Deity. All that you call the world is the shadow of that substance which you are, the perpetual creation of the powers of thought, of those that are dependent and of those that are independent of your will. Do not cumber yourself with fruitless pains to mend and remedy remote effects; let the soul be erect, and all things will go well. You think me the child of my circumstances: I make my circumstance. Let any thought or motive of mine be different from that they are, the difference will transform my condition and economy. I—this thought which is called I— is the mould into which the world is poured like melted wax. The mould is invisible, but the world betrays the shape of the mould. You call it the power of circumstance, but it is the power of me. Am I in harmony with myself? my position will seem to you just and commanding. Am I vicious and insane? my fortunes will seem to you obscure and descending. As I am, so shall I associate, and so shall I act; Cæsar's history will paint out Cæsar. Jesus acted so, because he thought so. I do not wish to overlook or to gainsay any reality; I say I make my circumstance; but if you ask me, Whence am I? I feel like other men my relation to that Fact which cannot be spoken, or defined, nor even thought, but which exists, and will exist.

The Transcendentalist adopts the whole connection of spiritual doctrine. He believes in miracle, in the perpetual openness of the human mind to new influx of light and power; he believes in inspiration, and in ecstasy. He wishes that the spiritual principle should be suffered to demonstrate itself to the end, in all possible applications to the state of man, without the admission of anything unspiritual; that is, anything positive, dogmatic, personal. Thus the spiritual measure of inspiration is the depth of the thought, and never, who said it? And so he resists all attempts to palm other rules and measures on the spirit than its own.

In action he easily incurs the charge of antinomianism by his avowal that he, who has the Law-giver, may with safety not only neglect, but even contravene every written commandment. In the play of Othello, the expiring Desdemona absolves her husband of the murder, to her attendant Emilia. Afterwards, when Emilia charges him with the crime, Othello exclaims,

You heard her say herself it was not I.

Emilia replies,

The more angel she, and thou the blacker devil.

Of this fine incident, Jacobi, the Transcendental moralist, makes use, with other parallel instances, in his reply to Fichte. Jacobi, refusing all measure of right and wrong except the determinations of the private spirit, remarks that there is no crime but has sometimes been a virtue. "I," he says, "am that atheist, that godless person who, in opposition to an imaginary doctrine of calculation, would lie as the dying Desdemona lied; would lie and deceive, as Pylades when he personated Orestes; would assassinate like Timoleon; would perjure myself like Epaminondas and John de Witt; I would resolve on suicide like Cato; I would commit sacrilege with David; yea, and pluck ears of corn on the Sabbath, for no other reason than that I was fainting for lack of food. For I have assurance in myself that in pardoning these faults according to the letter, man exerts the sovereign right which the majesty of his being confers on him; he sets the seal of his divine nature to the grace he accords."

In like manner, if there is anything grand and daring in human thought or virtue, any reliance on the vast, the unknown; any presentiment, any extravagance of faith, the spiritualist adopts it as most in nature. The oriental mind has always tended to this largeness. Buddhism is an expression of it. The Buddhist, who thanks no man, who says, "Do not flatter your benefactors," but who, in his conviction that every good deed can by no possibility escape its reward, will not deceive the benefactor by pretending that he had done more than he should, is a Transcendentalist.

You will see by this sketch that there is no such thing as a Transcendental *party;* that there is no pure Transcendentalist; that we know of none but prophets and heralds of such a philosophy; that all who by strong bias of nature have leaned to the spiritual side in doctrine, have stopped short of their goal. We have had many harbingers and forerunners; but of a purely spiritual life, history has afforded no example. I mean we have yet no man who has leaned entirely on his

character, and eaten angels' food; who, trusting to his sentiments, found life made of miracles; who, working for universal aims, found himself fed, he knew not how; clothed,
sheltered, and weaponed, he knew not how, and yet it was
done by his own hands. Only in the instinct of the lower animal we find the suggestion of the methods of it, and something higher than our understanding. The squirrel hoards nuts
and the bee gathers honey, without knowing what they do,
and they are thus provided for without selfishness or disgrace.

Shall we say then that Transcendentalism is the Saturnalia
or excess of Faith; the presentiment of a faith proper to man
in his integrity, excessive only when his imperfect obedience
hinders the satisfaction of his wish? Nature is transcendental,
exists primarily, necessarily, ever works and advances, yet
takes no thought for the morrow. Man owns the dignity of
the life which throbs around him, in chemistry, and tree, and
animal, and in the involuntary functions of his own body; yet
he is balked when he tries to fling himself into this enchanted
circle, where all is done without degradation. Yet genius and
virtue predict in man the same absence of private ends and
of condescension to circumstances, united with every trait
and talent of beauty and power.

This way of thinking, falling on Roman times, made Stoic
philosophers; falling on despotic times, made patriot Catos
and Brutuses; falling on superstitious times, made prophets
and apostles; on popish times, made protestants and ascetic
monks, preachers of Faith against the preachers of Works;
on prelatical times, made Puritans and Quakers; and falling
on Unitarian and commercial times, makes the peculiar shades
of Idealism which we know.

It is well known to most of my audience that the Idealism
of the present day acquired the name of Transcendental from
the use of that term by Immanuel Kant, of Königsberg, who
replied to the skeptical philosophy of Locke, which insisted
that there was nothing in the intellect which was not previously in the experience of the senses, by showing that there
was a very important class of ideas or imperative forms, which
did not come by experience, but through which experience
was acquired; that these were intuitions of the mind itself;
and he denominated them *Transcendental* forms. The extraordinary profoundness and precision of that man's thinking
have given vogue to his nomenclature, in Europe and Amer-

ica, to that extent that whatever belongs to the class of intuitive thought is popularly called at the present day *Transcendental*.

Although, as we have said, there is no pure Transcendentalist, yet the tendency to respect the intuitions and to give them, at least in our creed, all authority over our experience, has deeply colored the conversation and poetry of the present day; and the history of genius and of religion in these times, though impure, and as yet not incarnated in any powerful individual, will be the history of this tendency.

It is a sign of our times, conspicuous to the coarsest observer, that many intelligent and religious persons withdraw themselves from the common labors and competitions of the market and the caucus, and betake themselves to a certain solitary and critical way of living, from which no solid fruit has yet appeared to justify their separation. They hold themselves aloof: they feel the disproportion between their faculties and the work offered them, and they prefer to ramble in the country and perish of ennui, to the degradation of such charities and such ambitions as the city can propose to them. They are striking work, and crying out for somewhat worthy to do! What they do is done only because they are overpowered by the humanities that speak on all sides; and they consent to such labor as is open to them, though to their lofty dream the writing of Iliads or Hamlets, or the building of cities or empires seems drudgery.

Now every one must do after his kind, be he asp or angel, and these must. The question which a wise man and a student of modern history will ask, is, what that kind is? And truly, as in ecclesiastical history we take so much pains to know what the Gnostics, what the Essenes, what the Manichees, and what the Reformers believed, it would not misbecome us to inquire nearer home, what these companions and contemporaries of ours think and do, at least so far as these thoughts and actions appear to be not accidental and personal, but common to many, and the inevitable flower of the Tree of Time. Our American literature and spiritual history are, we confess, in the optative mood; but whoso knows these seething brains, these admirable radicals, these unsocial worshippers, these talkers who talk the sun and moon away, will believe that this heresy cannot pass away without leaving its mark.

They are lonely; the spirit of their writing and conversation is lonely; they repel influences; they shun general society; they incline to shut themselves in their chamber in the house, to live in the country rather than in the town, and to find their tasks and amusements in solitude. Society, to be sure, does not like this very well; it saith, Whoso goes to walk alone, accuses the whole world; he declares all to be unfit to be his companions; it is very uncivil, nay, insulting; Society will retaliate. Meantime, this retirement does not proceed from any whim on the part of these separators; but if any one will take pains to talk with them, he will find that this part is chosen both from temperament and from principle; with some unwillingness too, and as a choice of the less of two evils; for these persons are not by nature melancholy, sour, and unsocial—they are not stockish or brute—but joyous, susceptible, affectionate; they have even more than others a great wish to be loved. Like the young Mozart, they are rather ready to cry ten times a day, "But are you sure you love me?" Nay, if they tell you their whole thought, they will own that love seems to them the last and highest gift of nature; that there are persons whom in their hearts they daily thank for existing —persons whose faces are perhaps unknown to them, but whose fame and spirit have penetrated their solitude—and for whose sake they wish to exist. To behold the beauty of another character, which inspires a new interest in our own; to behold the beauty lodged in a human being, with such vivacity of apprehension that I am instantly forced home to inquire if I am not deformity itself; to behold in another the expression of a love so high that it assures itself—assures itself also to me against every possible casualty except my unworthiness—these are degrees on the scale of human happiness to which they have ascended; and it is a fidelity to this sentiment which has made common association distasteful to them. They wish a just and even fellowship, or none. They cannot gossip with you, and they do not wish, as they are sincere and religious, to gratify any mere curiosity which you may entertain. Like fairies, they do not wish to be spoken of. Love me, they say, but do not ask who is my cousin and my uncle. If you do not need to hear my thought, because you can read it in my face and behavior, then I will tell it you from sunrise to sunset. If you cannot divine it, you would not understand what I say. I will not molest myself for you. I do not wish to be profaned.

And yet, it seems as if this loneliness, and not this love, would prevail in their circumstances, because of the extravagant demand they make on human nature. That, indeed, constitutes a new feature in their portrait, that they are the most exacting and extortionate critics. Their quarrel with every man they meet is not with his kind, but with his degree. There is not enough of him—that is the only fault. They prolong their privilege of childhood in this wise; of doing nothing, but making immense demands on all the gladiators in the lists of action and fame. They make us feel the strange disappointment which overcasts every human youth. So many promising youths, and never a finished man! The profound nature will have a savage rudeness; the delicate one will be shallow, or the victim of sensibility; the richly accomplished will have some capital absurdity; and so every piece has a crack. 'T is strange, but this masterpiece is the result of such an extreme delicacy that the most unobserved flaw in the boy will neutralize the most aspiring genius, and spoil the work. Talk with a seaman of the hazards to life in his profession and he will ask you, "Where are the old sailors? Do you not see that all are young men?" And we, on this sea of human thought, in like manner inquire, Where are the old idealists? where are they who represented to the last generation that extravagant hope which a few happy aspirants suggest to ours? In looking at the class of counsel, and power, and wealth, and at the matronage of the land, amidst all the prudence and all the triviality, one asks, Where are they who represented genius, virtue, the invisible and heavenly world, to these? Are they dead—taken in early ripeness to the gods— as ancient wisdom foretold their fate? Or did the high idea die out of them, and leave their unperfumed body as its tomb and tablet, announcing to all that the celestial inhabitant, who once gave them beauty, had departed? Will it be better with the new generation? We easily predict a fair future to each new candidate who enters the lists, but we are frivolous and volatile, and by low aims and ill example do what we can to defeat this hope. Then these youths bring us a rough but effectual aid. By their unconcealed dissatisfaction they expose our poverty and the insignificance of man to man. A man is a poor limitary benefactor. He ought to be a shower of benefits

—a great influence, which should never let his brother go, but should refresh old merits continually with new ones; so that though absent he should never be out of my mind, his name never far from my lips; but if the earth should open at my side, or my last hour were come, his name should be the prayer I should utter to the Universe. But in our experience, man is cheap and friendship wants its deep sense. We affect to dwell with our friends in their absence, but we do not; when deed, word, or letter comes not, they let us go. These exacting children advertise us of our wants. There is no compliment, no smooth speech with them; they pay you only this one compliment, of insatiable expectation; they aspire, they severely exact, and if they only stand fast in this watchtower, and persist in demanding unto the end, and without end, then are they terrible friends, whereof poet and priest cannot choose but stand in awe; and what if they eat clouds, and drink wind, they have not been without service to the race of man.

With this passion for what is great and extraordinary, it cannot be wondered at that they are repelled by vulgarity and frivolity in people. They say to themselves, It is better to be alone than in bad company. And it is really a wish to be met—the wish to find society for their hope and religion—which prompts them to shun what is called society. They feel that they are never so fit for friendship as when they have quitted mankind and taken themselves to friend. A picture, a book, a favorite spot in the hills or the woods which they can people with the fair and worthy creation of the fancy, can give them often forms so vivid that these for the time shall seem real, and society the illusion.

But their solitary and fastidious manners not only withdraw them from the conversation, but from the labors of the world; they are not good citizens, not good members of society, unwillingly they bear their part of the public and private burdens; they do not willingly share in the public charities, in the public religious rites, in the enterprises of education, of missions foreign and domestic, in the abolition of the slave-trade, or in the temperance society. They do not even like to vote. The philanthropists inquire whether Transcendentalism does not mean sloth: they had as lief hear that their friend is dead, as that he is a Transcendentalist; for then is he paralyzed, and can never do anything for humanity. What right, cries the good world, has the man of genius to retreat from work, and indulge himself? The popular literary creed seems to be, "I am a sublime genius; I ought not therefore to labor." But genius is the power to labor better and more availably. Deserve thy genius: exalt it. The good, the illuminated, sit apart from the rest, censuring their dulness and vices, as if they thought that by sitting very grand in their chairs, the very brokers, attorneys, and congressmen would see the error of their ways, and flock to them. But the good and wise must learn to act, and carry salvation to the combatants and demagogues in the dusty arena below.

On the part of these children it is replied that life and their faculty seem to them gifts too rich to be squandered on such trifles as you propose to them. What you call your fundamental institutions, your great and holy causes, seem to them great abuses, and, when nearly seen, paltry matters. Each "cause" as it is called—say Abolition, Temperance, say Calvinism, or Unitarianism—becomes speedily a little shop, where the article, let it have been at first never so subtle and ethereal, is now made up into portable and convenient cakes, and retailed in small quantities to suit purchasers. You make very free use of these words "great" and "holy," but few things appear to them such. Few persons have any magnificence of nature to inspire enthusiasm, and the philanthropies and charities have a certain air of quackery. As to the general course of living, and the daily employments of men, they cannot see much virtue in these, since they are parts of this vicious circle; and as no great ends are answered by the men, there is nothing noble in the arts by which they are maintained. Nay, they have made the experiment and found that from the liberal professions to the coarsest manual labor, and from the courtesies of the academy and the college to the conventions of the cotillon-room and the morning call, there is a spirit of cowardly compromise and seeming which intimates a frightful skepticism, a life without love, and an activity without an aim.

Unless the action is necessary, unless it is adequate, I do not wish to perform it. I do not wish to do one thing but once. I do not love routine. Once possessed of the principle, it is equally easy to make four or forty thousand applications of it. A great man will be content to have indicated in any the slightest manner his perception of the reigning Idea of his time, and will leave to those who like it the multiplication of examples. When he has hit the white, the rest may shatter the target. Every thing admonishes us how needlessly long life is. Every moment of a hero so raises and cheers us that a twelvemonth is an age. All that the brave Xanthus brings home from his wars is the recollection that at the storming of Samos, "in the heat of the battle, Pericles smiled on me, and passed on to another detachment." It is the quality of the moment, not the number of days, of events, or of actors, that imports.

New, we confess, and by no means happy, is our condition: if you want the aid of our labor, we ourselves stand in greater want of the labor. We are miserable with inaction. We perish of rest and rust: but we do not like your work.

"Then," says the world, "show me your own."

"We have none."

"What will you do, then?" cries the world.

"We will wait."

"How long?"

"Until the Universe beckons and calls us to work."

"But whilst you wait, you grow old and useless."

"Be it so: I can sit in a corner and *perish* (as you call it), but I will not move until I have the highest command. If no call should come for years, for centuries, then I know that the want of the Universe is the attestation of faith by my abstinence. Your virtuous projects, so called, do not cheer me. I know that which shall come will cheer me. If I cannot work, at least I need not lie. All that is clearly due today is not to lie. In other places other men have encountered sharp trials, and have behaved themselves well. The martyrs were sawn asunder, or hung alive on meat-hooks. Cannot we screw our courage to patience and truth, and without complaint, or even with good-humor, await our turn of action in the Infinite Counsels?"

But to come a little closer to the secret of these persons, we must say that to them it seems a very easy matter to answer the objections of the man of the world, but not so easy to dispose of the doubts and objections that occur to themselves. They are exercised in their own spirit with queries which acquaint them with all adversity, and with the trials of the bravest heroes. When I asked them concerning their private experience, they answered somewhat in this wise: It is not to be denied that there must be some wide difference between my faith and other faith; and mine is a certain brief experience, which surprised me in the highway or in the market, in some place, at some time—whether in the body or out of the body, God knoweth—and made me aware that I had played the fool with fools all this time, but that law existed for me and for all; that to me belonged trust, a child's trust and obedience, and the worship of ideas, and I should never be fool more. Well, in the space of an hour probably, I was let down from this height; I was at my old tricks, the selfish member of a selfish society. My life is superficial, takes no root in the deep world; I ask, When shall I die and be relieved of the responsibility of seeing an Universe which I do not use? I wish to exchange this flash-of-lightning faith for continuous daylight, this fever-glow for a benign climate.

These two states of thought diverge every moment, and stand in wild contrast. To him who looks at his life from these moments of illumination, it will seem that he skulks and plays a mean, shiftless and subaltern part in the world. That is to be done which he has not skill to do, or to be said which others can say better, and he lies by, or occupies his hands with some plaything, until his hour comes again. Much of our reading, much of our labor, seems mere waiting: it was not that we were born for. Any other could do it as well or better. So little skill enters into these works, so little do they mix with the divine life, that it really signifies little what we do, whether we turn a grindstone, or ride, or run, or make fortunes, or govern the state. The worst feature of this double consciousness is, that the two lives, of the understanding and of the soul, which we lead, really show very little relation to each other; never meet and measure each other: one prevails now, all buzz and din; and the other prevails then, all infinitude and paradise; and, with the progress of life, the two discover no greater disposition to reconcile themselves. Yet, what is my faith? What am I? What but a thought of serenity and independence, an abode in the deep blue sky? Presently the clouds shut down again; yet we retain the belief that this petty web we weave will at last be overshot and reticulated with veins of the blue, and that the moments will characterize the days. Patience, then, is for us, is it not? Patience, and still patience. When we pass, as presently we shall, into some new infinitude, out of this Iceland of negations, it will please us to reflect that though we had few virtues or consolations, we bore with our indigence, nor once strove to repair it with hypocrisy or false heat of any kind.

But this class are not sufficiently characterized if we omit to add that they are lovers and worshippers of Beauty. In the eternal trinity of Truth, Goodness, and Beauty, each in its perfection including the three, they prefer to make Beauty the sign and head. Something of the same taste is observable in all the moral movements of the time, in the religious and benevolent enterprises. They have a liberal, even an æsthetic spirit. A reference to Beauty in action sounds, to be sure, a little hollow and ridiculous in the ears of the old church. In politics, it has often sufficed, when they treated of justice, if they kept the bounds of selfish calculation. If they granted restitution, it was prudence which granted it. But the justice which is now claimed for the black, and the pauper, and the drunkard, is for Beauty—is for a necessity to the soul of the agent, not of the beneficiary. I say this is the tendency, not yet the realization. Our virtue totters and trips, does not yet walk firmly. Its representatives are austere; they preach and denounce; their rectitude is not yet a grace. They are still liable to that slight taint of burlesque which in our strange world attaches to the zealot. A saint should be as dear as the apple of the eye. Yet we are tempted to smile, and we flee from the working to the speculative reformer, to escape that same slight ridicule. Alas for these days of derision and criticism! We call the Beautiful the highest, because it appears to us the golden mean, escaping the dowdiness of the good and the heartlessness of the true. They are lovers of nature also, and find an indemnity in the inviolable order of the world for the violated order and grace of man.

There is, no doubt, a great deal of well-founded objection to be spoken or felt against the sayings and doings of this class, some of whose traits we have selected; no doubt they will lay themselves open to criticism and to lampoons, and as ridiculous stories will be to be told of them as of any. There will be cant and pretension; there will be subtilty and moonshine. These persons are of unequal strength, and do not all prosper. They complain that everything around them must be denied; and if feeble, it takes all their strength to deny, before they can begin to lead their own life. Grave seniors insist on their respect to this institution and that usage; to an obsolete history; to some vocation, or college, or etiquette, or beneficiary, or charity, or morning or evening call, which they resist as what does not concern them. But it costs such sleepless nights, alienations and misgivings—they have so many moods about it; these old guardians never change *their* minds; they have but one mood on the subject, namely, that Antony is very perverse—that it is quite as much as Antony can do to assert his rights, abstain from what he thinks foolish, and keep his temper. He cannot help the reaction of this injustice in his own mind. He is braced-up and stilted; all freedom and flowing genius, all sallies of wit and frolic nature are quite out of the question; it is well if he can keep from lying, injustice, and suicide. This is no time for gaiety and grace. His strength and spirits are wasted in rejection. But the strong spirits overpower those around them without effort. Their thought and emotion comes in like a flood, quite withdraws them from all notice of these carping critics; they surrender themselves with glad heart to the heavenly guide, and only by implication reject the clamorous nonsense of the hour. Grave seniors talk to the deaf— church and old book mumble and ritualize to an unheeding, preoccupied and advancing mind, and thus they by happiness of greater momentum lose no time, but take the right road at first.

But all these of whom I speak are not proficients; they are novices; they only show the road in which man should travel, when the soul has greater health and prowess. Yet let them feel the dignity of their charge, and deserve a larger power. Their heart is the ark in which the fire is concealed which shall burn in a broader and universal flame. Let them obey the Genius then most when his impulse is wildest; then most when he seems to lead to uninhabitable deserts of thought and life; for the path which the hero travels alone is the highway of health and benefit to mankind. What is the privilege and nobility of our nature but its persistency, through its power to attach itself to what is permanent?

Society also has its duties in reference to this class, and must behold them with what charity it can. Possibly some benefit may yet accrue from them to the state. In our Mechanics' Fair, there must be not only bridges, ploughs, carpenters' planes, and baking troughs, but also some few finer instruments—rain gauges, thermometers, and telescopes; and in society, besides farmers, sailors, and weavers, there must be a few persons of purer fire kept specially as gauges and meters of character; persons of a fine, detecting instinct, who note the smallest accumulations of wit and feeling in the bystander. Perhaps too there might be room for the exciters and monitors; collectors of the heavenly spark, with power to convey the electricity to others. Or, as the storm-tossed vessel at sea speaks the frigate or "line packet" to learn its longitude, so it may not be without its advantage that we should now and then encounter rare and gifted men, to compare the points of our spiritual compass, and verify our bearings from superior chronometers.

Amidst the downward tendency and proneness of things, when every voice is raised for a new road or another statute or a subscription of stock; for an improvement in dress, or in dentistry; for a new house or a larger business; for a political party, or the division of an estate—will you not tolerate one or two solitary voices in the land, speaking for thoughts and principles not marketable or perishable? Soon these improvements and mechanical inventions will be superseded; these modes of living lost out of memory; these cities rotted, ruined by war, by new inventions, by new seats of trade, or the geologic changes: all gone, like the shells which sprinkle the sea-beach with a white colony to-day, forever renewed to be forever destroyed. But the thoughts which these few hermits strove to proclaim by silence as well as by speech, not only by what they did, but by what they forbore to do, shall abide in beauty and strength, to reorganize themselves in nature, to invest themselves anew in other, perhaps higher endowed and happier mixed clay than ours, in fuller union with the surrounding system.

From *Nature, Addresses and Lectures*

Human Culture: Introductory

A LECTURE READ AT THE MASONIC TEMPLE, BOSTON,
WEDNESDAY EVENING, DECEMBER 6, 1837

There is a historical progress of man. The ideas which predominate at one period are accepted without effort by the next age, which is absorbed in the endeavor to express its own. An attentive observer will easily see by comparing the character of the institutions and books of the present day, with those of any former period—say of ancient Judaea, or the Greek, or the Italian era, or the Reformation, or the Elizabethan age of England—that the tone and aims are entirely changed. The former men acted and spoke under the thought that a shining social prosperity was the aim of men, and compromised ever the individuals to the nation. The modern mind teaches (in extremes) that the nation exists for the individual; for the guardianship and education of every man. The Reformation contained the new thought. The English Revolution is its expansion. The American Declaration of Independence is a formal announcement of it by a nation to nations though a very limited expression. The Church of Calvin and of the Friends have preached it ever. The Missions announce it, which have girdled the globe with their stations "to preach the gospel to every creature." The charity which is thought to distinguish Christendom over ancient paganism, is another expression of the same thought. The Vote—universal suffrage—is another; the downfall of war, the attack upon slavery, are others. The furious democracy which in this country from the beginning of its history, has shown a wish, as the royal governors complained, to leave out men of mark and send illiterate and low persons as deputies—a practice not unknown at this day—is only a perverse or as yet obstructed operation of the same instinct—

a stammering and stuttering out of impatience to articulate the awful words *I am*. The servile statesman who once cried, "Prerogative!" now on every stump and in every caucus has learned to snuffle, "The Poor! the Poor!" Then science has been adopted at last by nations. War is turned out of the throne, and wit is coming in. Instead of piratical voyages sent out by the English crown to hunt the Spanish Manilla galleon, the same crown visits Australasia with gifts, and sends its best blood—keen draughtsmen, post captains, and naturalists, beyond the terminal snowbanks—the farthest step to which mortal Esquimaux or wolverine dared approach the deadly solitude of the Pole. War subsides into engineering. The desperadoes go a whaling or vent their superabundant activity on the bear and catamount-hunt of the frontier. Men say, if there is any interest that is oppressed in large assemblies, it is that of the rich: and lastly, the word is forming, is formed, and is already articulated by legislatures—*Education*.

Thus, in gross, the growth of the new Idea may be observed as it inscribes itself on modern history. Of course, in the mind of the philosopher it has far more precision, and is already attaining a depth and splendor which eclipse all other claims. In the eye of the philosopher, the Individual has ceased to be regarded as a part, and has come to be regarded as a whole. He is the world. Man who has been—in how many tedious ages—esteemed an appendage to a fortune, to a trade, to an army, to a law, to a state, now discovers that property, trade, war, government, geography, nay, the great globe itself and all that it inherits, are but counterparts of mighty faculties which dwell peacefully in his mind, and that it is a state of disease which makes him seem the servant of his auxiliaries and effects. He exists and the world exists to him in a new relation of subject and object, neither of which is valid alone, but only in their marriage have a creative life.

The new view which now tends to remould metaphysics, theology, science, law, trades and professions, and which, in its earnest creation, must modify or destroy the old, has as yet attained no clearer name than *Culture*.

His own Culture, the unfolding of his nature, is the chief end of man. A divine impulse at the core of his being, impels him to this. The only motive at all commensurate with his force, is the ambition to discover *by exercising* his latent power, and to this, the trades and occupations men follow, the connexions they form, their fortunes in the world, and their particular actions are quite subordinate and auxiliary. The true Culture is a discipline so universal as to demonstrate that no part of a man was made in vain. We see men who can do nothing but cipher—dot and carry one; others, who can only fetch and carry; others who can only write or speak; how many who hardly seem to have a right of possession to their legs, their shoulders, and who get the least service out of their eyes. So concentrated to some focal point is their vitality, that the limbs and constitution appear supernumerary. Scholars are noted to be unskilful and awkward. Montaigne says that, "men of supercelestial opinions have subterranean manners." Much oftener, we see men whose emotive, whose intellectual, whose moral faculties, lie dormant.

The philosopher laments the inaction of the higher faculties.

He laments to see men poor who are able to labor.

He laments to see men blind to a beauty that is beaming on every side of them.

He laments to see men offending against laws and paying the penalty, and calling it a visitation of Providence.

He regrets the disproportion so manifest in the minds of men. Cannot a man know the mathematics, and love Shakspeare also? Cannot he unite an eye for beauty, with the ardours of devotion? Can he not join the elegant accomplishments of the gentleman, to the adoration of justice?

He laments the foreign holdings of every man, his dependence for his faith, for his political and religious estimates and opinions, on other men, and on former times.

And from all these oppressions is a wise culture to redeem the soul.

Is it not possible to clear and disencumber a man of a thousand causes of unhappiness; to show him that he has but one interest in the world, that in his own character. Why should he sit groaning there at mischiefs he cannot help? Why should he be a dependent? Why should he be a pretender? Why should he seem and shuffle and apologize any longer, when there is nothing good, nothing lovely, nothing noble and sweet, that is not his own; when he himself is a commander; when with him he has reality; he only is rich; and when the universe is one choral invitation to him to put forth his thousand hands? Culture in the high sense does not consist in polishing and varnishing, but in so presenting the attractions of nature that the slumbering attributes of man may burst their sleep and rush into day. The effect of Culture on the man will not be like the trimming and turfing of gardens, but the educating the eye to the true harmony of the unshorn landscape, with horrid thickets, wide morasses, bald mountains, and the balance of the land and sea.

And what is the foundation on which so vast an ambition rests? How dare we in the face of the miserable world; in the face of all history which records nothing but savage and semisavage life; in the face of the sensual nations, among whom no man puts entire confidence in the virtue of another, scarcely in the virtue of the pure and select souls; and where the heights of self-denial and benevolence are reached always by mixed motives and a winding stair—how can any observer hope so highly of man and reconcile his views with the faces and speech of the mob of men that you shall see pass, if you stand at the corner of a street; with the market and the jail?

I answer the basis of Culture is that part of human nature which in philosophy is called the Ideal. A human being always compares any action or object with somewhat he calls the Perfect: that is to say, not with any action or object now existing in nature, but with a certain Better existing in the mind. That Better we call the Ideal. Ideal is not opposed to Real, but to Actual. The Ideal is the Real. The Actual is but the Apparent and the Temporary. Ideal justice is justice, and not that imperfect, halting compensation which we can attain by courts and juries. The mathematicians say there is no perfect circle in nature and their reasonings are not true of any actual circle but only of the Ideal circle.

The universal presence of this vision of the Better in all parts of life is the characteristic of human nature. The lover enraptured with the new consent of a maiden's affection with his own is instantly sobered by observing that her living form detaches itself from the beautiful image in his mind. They never, never will unite and always in seeing her he must remark deficiency.

The patriot worshipping in his thoughts the pure Republic wherein every citizen should be free, just, and contented, strives evermore to realize his idea upon the green earth, up-heaves the foundations of the state to build his own com-monwealth. Instantly younger men see faults as gross in the new as he in the old and Reform is only a step to Reform.

The pious heart bewails the deadness of religion. Luther, Huss, Cobham, Knox moved by this painful contrast of the actual with the ideal worship, shake down the churches of a thousand years; and already the youthful saint following the same eternal instinct sees the shortcomings of their reforma-tion.

The great works of art are unable to check our criticism. They create a want they do not gratify. They instantly point us to somewhat better than themselves.

In Nature it is no otherwise. No particular form of man or horse or oak entirely satisfies the mind. The physiologist sees ever floating over the individuals the idea which nature never quite successfully executes in any one form.

In human actions the man compares incessantly his deed with what he calls his duty; with the perfect action; and to the best action there is still in the mind a Better.

In human condition the Ideal suggests ever the pictures of Heaven.

In character the mind is constrained ever to refer to a moral Ideal which we call God.

The fruit of this constitutional aspiration is labor. This aspiration is the centrifugal force in moral nature, the principle of expansion resisting the tendency to consolida-tion and rest. The first consequence of a new possession is a new want. The first fruit of a new knowledge is a new curiosity. Much will have more. We cannot go fast enough on our own legs, and so we tame the horse. The horse can no more equal the ideal speed, and so we forge and build the locomotive. The ideal still craves a speed like a cannon ball, a speed like a wish, and the inventive and practical faculties will never cease to toil for this end.

Now what is the disclosure of the mind in regard to the state of society? There is no part of society which conforms to its laws but rather, yawning chasms between. Man, upright, reasoning, royal man the master of the lower world, cannot be found, but instead—a deformed society which confessedly does not aim at an ideal integrity, no longer believes it pos-sible, and only aims by the aid of falsehoods at keeping down universal uproar, at keeping men from each other's throats. The great endeavors of men are paralysed. Men do not imagine that they are anything more than fringes and tassels to the institutions into which they are born. They take the law from things; they serve their property; their trade or profession; books; other men; some religious dogma; some political party or school of opinion that has been palmed upon them; and bow the neck and the knee and the soul to their own creation. I need not specify with accusing finger the unsound parts of our social life. A universal principle of compromise has crept into use. A Routine which no man made and for whose abuses no man holds himself accountable tyrannizes over the spontaneous will and character of all the individuals. A very nice sense of honor would be a very great inconvenience in a career of political, of professional, of commercial activity. A devotion to absolute truth would be unacceptable in the Academy also. An asceticism built on the study and worship of Nature would be rude and harsh to the men of refinement.

The loss of faith is the greatest mischief. We are overpowered by this great Actual which by the numbers, by the extent, by the antiquity lost in darkness of its arrangements daunts our resolution and though condemned by the mind yet we look elsewhere in vain for a realized reform and we say, This is the way of the world, this is necessary, and we accept the yoke and accommodate our feet to the treadmill.

And what temerity is it that refuses this yoke, cries Society always to the aspirant? Art thou better than our father Jacob who gave us this well? Alleviation is all we can expect, not health. "The best of life is just tolerable, it is the most we can make of it." What folly, "says Richard to Robin" and "says Every one" that one man should make himself wiser than the public, than the whole world.

We reply that all the worth that resides in the existing men and institutions was the fruit of successive efforts of this absolute truth to embody itself, and moreover that this is the instinct of the Ideal, its antagonism to numbers, to custom, and the precise mode of its activity.

There is a celebrated property of fluids which is called by natural philosophers the hydrostatic paradox, by reason of which a column of water of the diameter of a needle, is able

to balance the ocean. This fact is a symbol of the relation between one man and all men.

A man may see that his conviction is the natural counter-
balance of the opposite persuasion of any number of men or
of all men. An appeal to his own Reason is good against the
practice of all mankind. Numbers weigh nothing. The ideal
of Right in our mind we know is not less peremptory authority
though not an individual on the face of the earth obeyed its
injunctions. Before the steady gaze of the soul, the whole
life of man, the societies, laws, and property, and pursuits of
men, and the long procession of history do blench and quail.
Before this indomitable soul ever fresh and immortal the
aged world owns its master. There is not among the most
frivolous or sordid a man who is not capable of having his
attention so fastened upon the image of higher life in his
mind that the whole past and the present state of society
shall seem to him a mere circumstance—somewhat defective
and ephemeral in comparison with the Law which they violate. And the clear perception of a single soul that somewhat
universally allowed in society is wrong and rotten, is a prophecy as certain that sooner or later that thing will fall as if
all creatures arose and cried out, It shall end.

This Ideal is the shining side of man. This is the bosom
of discovery. This is the seed of revolutions. This is the Foresight that never slumbers or sleeps. This is the Morrow, ever
dawning, forgetting all the yesterdays that ever shone.

We say that the allegiance of all the faculties is the birth-
right of this; that the denial of its oracles is the death of hope,
is the treason of human nature; that it has been made shame-
fully subservient to the Actual, which is as if the head should
serve the feet. We say the great Reform is to do it justice, to
restore it to the sovereignty. We say that all which is great
and venerable in character is measured by the degree in
which this instinct predominates; that there is always sub-
limity about every the least leaning to its suggestions. It
breathes a fragrancy and grace over the whole manners and
form. Finally we say that it is the property of the Ideal in
man to make him at home everywhere and forever. It belongs
to the inactive mind to honor only the Old or the Remote.
He who can open his mind to the disclosures of the Reason
will see that glory without cloud belongs to the *present*

hour; for the Ideal is the presence of the universal mind to the particular.

And what are the Means of Culture? The means of Culture is the related nature of man. He is so strangely related to every thing that he can go nowhere without meeting objects which solicit his senses, and yield him new meanings. The world treats him ever with a series of symbolical paintings whose moral he gradually finds out. He cannot do the most trivial act but a secret sense is smiling through it which philosophers and poets repeat. The light that shines on his shoes came from the sun, and the entire laws of nature and the soul unite their energies in every moment and every place. There is no trifle in nature. No partiality in her laws. A grain of unregarded dust nature loves with her heart and soul. Out of it goes an attraction which leaps to the planets and from star to star. On it play light, heat, electricity, Gravity, Chemistry, Cohesion, Motion, Rest, so that the history of physical nature might be read from that grain.

So is it with the life of man. It is made up of little parts, but small details are dignified by this pervading relation which connects every point to the brain and the heart. Our culture comes not alone from the grand and beautiful but also from the trivial and sordid. We wash and purify every day for sixty years this temple of the human body. We buy wood and tend our fires and deal with the baker and fisherman and grocer and take a world of pains which nothing but concealed moral and intellectual ends of great worth can exalt to an ideal level.

Natural objects address him. If he look at a flower it awakes in him a pleasing emotion. He cannot see a stone, but his fancy and his understanding are attracted to the varieties of its texture and law of its crystallization, until he finds even this rude body is no stranger to him, and though it cannot speak, yet it is the history of the earth down to the period of written history. He cannot see a star, but instantly this marriage begins of object and subject, of Nature and man, whose offspring is power. In short, it is because of this universally cognate essence of man, that science is possible. The obscure attractions which natural objects have for him are only indications of the truth which appears at last, that the laws of nature preexisted in his mind.

But his relation is not only intellectual to surrounding

things. He is active also. He can hew the tree and hammer the stone and sow the barren ground. That is to say, he is so related to the elements that they are his stock, flexible in his hands; he takes the obedient mountain and puts his own will into it and it becomes a city, temples, and towers. His power is straitly hooped in by a necessity which by constant experiment he touches on every side until at length he learns its arc, which is learning his own nature. An hourly instruction proceeds out of his employment, his disasters, his friends, his antagonists. His life is a series of experiments upon the external world, by every one of which a new power is awaked in his mind. A countryman bred in the woods, cannot go into a crowded city, see its spectacles, and the manners of its inhabitants, and trade in its market and go back to his cabin the same man he left it. A man cannot enter the army and see service and bring home the mind and manners of a boy. He cannot follow the seas without a sea change. He cannot see a mob or hear music or be vexed or frightened; he cannot behold a cataract, a volcano, a meteor, without a new feeling, a new thought. He is as changeable as the face of a looking glass carried through the street, a new creature as he stands in the presence of new objects. Go into a botanical garden; is not that a place of some delight? Go to a muster-field where four or five regiments are marching with flags, music, and artillery; is not that a moving spectacle? Go to a dance, and watch the forms and movement of the youths and maidens; have they nothing of you in keeping? Go to a church where gray old men and matrons stand or sit with the young in serious silence. A new frame of mind. Climb the White Hills; enter the Vatican; descend to the unburied Pompeii; go hearken to the enraged eloquence of Faneuil Hall—each of these shall make a new impression, shall enlarge the scope of the beholder's knowledge and power.

It will be seen at once that in the philosophic view of Human Culture, we look at all things in a new point of view from the popular one, viz., we consider mainly not the things but their effect on the beholder. And this habit of respecting things for their relation to the soul, for their intrinsic and universal effects, it is a part of Culture to form.

It is the office of Culture to domesticate man in his regal place in nature.

A great step is made before the soul can feel itself not a

charity boy, not a bastard or an orphan, not an interloper in the world which exists for it. To most men, a palace, a statue, or a costly book, have an alien and forbidding air, much like a gay equipage, and seem to say like that, who are you, sir? A man is to know that they all are his; suing his notice, petitioners to his faculties that they will come out and take possession; born thralls to his sovereignty; conundrums he alone can guess; chaos until he come like a creator and give them light and order. My position in the world is wholly changed as soon as I see that a picture waits for my verdict and is not to command me but I am to settle its claims to praise. The arts are appeals to my taste. The laws to my understanding. Religion to my Reason. Indeed it is a changed position. Now I come meek but well assured as a youth who comes to the College to be taught, not like an interloper who skulks whilst he gazes at the magnificent ornaments he has broken in to see. That popular fable of the sot who was picked up dead drunk in the street, carried to the duke's house, washed and dressed and put in the duke's bed, and then on his waking treated with all obsequious ceremony like the duke and assured that he had been insane, owes its popularity to the fact that it symbolizes so well the state of man, who is in the actual world a sort of sot and vagabond, but now and then wakes up, exercises his reason, and finds himself a true Prince.

This is the discipline of man in the degrees of Property. He learns that above the merely external rights to the picture, to the park, to the equipage, rights which the law protects, is a spiritual property which is Insight. The kingdom of the Soul transcendeth all the walls and muniments of possession and taketh higher rights not only in the possession but in the possessor, and with this royal reservation, can very well afford to leave the so-called proprietor undisturbed as its keeper or trustee.

Therefore the wise soul cares little to whom belongs the legal ownership of the grand Monadnoc, of the cataract of Niagara, or of the Belvedere Apollo, or whatever else it prizes. It soon finds that no cabinet, though extended along miles of marble colonnade, would suffice to hold the beautiful wonders it has made its own. It has found beauty and wonder progressive, incessant, universal. At last it discovers that the whole world is a museum and that things are more glorious in their order and home than when a few are carried away to glitter alone.

In viewing the relations of objects to the mind we are entitled to disregard entirely those considerations which are of great importance in viewing the relation of things to each other. For example, magnitude, number, nearness of place and time are things of no importance; the spiritual effect is all that concerns us. What moves the mind we are entitled to say was designed to move it, however far off in the apparent chain of cause and effect. Our being floats on the whole culture of the past, on the whole hope of the future. Men dead and buried now for some thousands of years affect my mode of being much more than some of my contemporaries. As things lie in my thought, as they recur to speech and to action—such is their value, and not according to time or to place. How can any thing die to the mind? To this end they all are alive.

To what end existed those gods of Olympus or the tradition so irresistibly embodied in sculpture, architecture, and a perdurable literature that the old names, Jupiter, Apollo, Venus, still haunt us in this cold, Christian, Saxon America and will not be shaken off? To what end the ethical revelation which we call Christianity, with all its history, its corruption, its Reformation; the Revivals of Letters; the press; the planting of America; the conversion of the powers of nature to the domestic service of man, so that the ocean is but a waterwheel and the solar system but a clock? To what end are we distributed into electoral nations; half subject still to England through the dominion of British intellect, and in common with England having not yet mastered or comprehended the astonishing infusions of the Hebrew soul in the morning of the world?

Why is never a local political arrangement made by a Saxon lawgiver for the getting justice in a market or keeping the peace in a village but it drafts a jury today in my county or levies a tax on my house? Why is never a pencil moved in the hand of Rembrandt or Raphael and never a pen in that of Moses or Shakspeare but it communicates emotion and thought to one of us at the end of an age and across the breadth of half a globe. Thus is the prolific power of nature to yield spiritual aliment over a period of 3 or 4000 years epitomized and brought to a focus in the stripling now at school. These things and all things are there for me, and in relation to me. It may not be strictly philosophical—it may be a little beyond strictness of speech to say these all were designed to teach us as they have, but we may affirm that this effect and this action meet as accurately as the splendid lights of morning and evening meet the configuration of the human eye and within that, the more subtle eye of taste.

Once begin to count the problems which invite our research, which answer each to somewhat in the unknown soul, and you find that they are coextensive with the limits of being. Boldly, gladly, the soul plunges into this broad element, not fearing but cheered by the measureless main. Nothing is so old, nothing so mean, nothing so far but it has something for me. The progress of science is to bring the remote near. The kelp which grew neglected on the roaring seabeach of the Orkneys now comes to the shops; the seal, the otter, the ermine, that no man saw but the Indian in the Rocky Mountains, they must come to Long Wharf. The seashells, strombus, turbo, and pearl, that hid a hundred fathoms down in the warm waters of the Gulf, they must take the bait and leave their silent houses and come to Long Wharf also: even the ducks of Labrador that laid their eggs for ages on the rocks, must send their green eggs now to Long Wharf.

So I think it will be the effect of insight to show nearer relations than are yet known between remote periods of history and the present hour. The Assyrian, the Persian, the Egyptian era now fading fast into twilight must reappear and, as a varnish brings out the original colors of an antique picture, so a better understanding of our own time and our own life, will be a sunbeam to search the faintest traces of human character in the first plantation of man. When we consider how much nearer in our own time Egypt, Greece, Homer, and Rome have come to us through Wolf, Niebuhr, Müller, Winkelman, and Champollion, we may believe that Olympus and Memphis, Zoroaster and Tubal Cain have not yet spoken to us their last word.

Having spoken of the aim; the basis; the apparatus; and the scope; I proceed to speak of the scale of Culture. What is the rule that is to introduce a just harmony in the universal school in which it seems we study? Where every being in nature addresses me shall I not be bewildered and without compass or chart?

Proportion certainly is a great end of Culture. A man should ask God morning and evening with the philosopher that he might be instructed to give to every being in the universe its just measure of importance. And it may be thought an obvious objection to views which set so high the hopes and powers of the individual that they foster the prejudices of a private soul which Bacon pointed out as one of the sources of error under the name of the idols of the cave.

But let it not be said that the only way to break up the idols of the cave is conversation with many men and a knowledge of the world. This is also distorting. State Street or the Boulevards of Paris are no truer pictures of the world than is a cloister or a laboratory. The brokers and attorneys are quite as wide of the mark on one side as monks and academicians on the other.

There are two ways of cultivating proportion of character.

1. The habit of attending to all sensations and putting ourselves in a way to receive a variety, as by attending spectacles, visiting theatres, prisons, senates, churches, factories, museums, barracks, ships, hells, a thing impossible to many and except in merest superficiality impossible to any, for a man is not in the place to which he goes unless his mind is there.

But suppose a man goes to all such places as I have named and many more, will he have seen all? What does he know about the miners of Cornwall, or the lumberers of Maine? Is he sure to allow all that is due to the thugs of the desert? Does he appreciate insanity? or know the military life of Russia? or that of the Italian lazzaroni? or the aspirations and tendencies of the Sacs and Foxes? The shortness of life and the limited walks in which most men pass it forbid any hope of multiplying particular observations.

2. The other mode of cultivating gradation and forming a just scale is to compare the depth of thought to which different objects appeal. Nature and the course of life furnish every man the most recluse with a sufficient variety of objects to supply him with the elements and divisions of a scale. Looking back upon any portion of his life he will see that things have entirely lost the relative proportions which they wore to the eye at the moment when they transpired. The once dearest aims of his ambition have sunk out of sight and

some transient shade of thought looms up out of forgotten years.

Proportion is not the effect of circumstances but a habit of mind. The truth is, the mind is a perfect measure of all things and the only measure. I acknowledge that the mind is also a distorting medium so long as its aims are not pure. But the moment the individual declares his independence, takes his life into his own hand, and sets forth in quest of Culture, the love of truth is a sufficient gauge. It is very clear that he can have no other. What external standard, what authority, can teach the paramount rank of truth and justice but the mind's own unvarying instinct. Who shall tell it the claim of other things but Affection and Need and the incessant oracles of the overhanging Ideal? I confess my toleration does not increase to those who do not reverence their own mind. He is not a skeptic who denies a miracle, who denies both angel and resurrection, who does not believe in the existence of such a city as Thebes or Rome; but he is a skeptic who does not think it always an absolute duty to speak the truth, who pretends not to know how to discriminate between a duty and an inclination, and who thinks the mind itself is not a measure of things.

With such views of the aim, of the reason, of the apparatus, of Human Culture I have thought its transcendent claims should be laid before you. I think it the enterprise which out of the urn of God has fallen the lot of the present age. I think the time has come to ask the question, Why are there no heroes? Why is not every man venerable? Why should any be vulgar and vile? I wish that Education should not be trusted to the feeble hand of Societies but we should speak to the individual that which he ought to hear, the voice of faith and of truth. I wish him to perceive that his imitation, his fear, his dependency are child's clothes it is now time to cast off and assume his own vows. I wish him, instead of following with a mendicant admiration the great names that are inscribed on the walls of memory, to know that they are only marks and memoranda for his guidance with which his own experience should come up. Let him know that the stars shone as benignantly on the hour of his advent as on any Milton or Washington or Howard. There is no combination of powers that comes into the world in a child that is not new and that is not needed. No sign indicates beforehand that a great man

—that is, that a true man, has been born. No faculty is marked with a broad arrow beforehand but every gift of noble origin is breathed upon by Hope's perpetual breath. Whoever is alive, may be good and wise. I wish him to adopt this end with a great heart and lay himself generously open to the influences of Heaven and earth. Let him survey in succession his instincts and faculties. Let him examine his senses and his use of them. Is a man's body to be regarded as a philosophic apparatus, a school of science, a generator of power, or is it designed only for the taste of sugar, salt, and wine and for agreeable sensations? Then let him contemplate the Intellect and ask if justice has been done it, if its great instincts have been observed. Let him explore the active powers, and see if he is the able, self-helping, man-helping laborer or an afternoon man and a nuisance. Let him enter the enchanted ground of the Affections and know if he have appropriated their sweetness and health; let him explore the laws of Prudence. Let him learn the higher discipline of the heroic; and ascend to the study and practice of the Holy.

Into these depths I wish to drop my sounding line. Into the several districts of human nature I wish to cast the inquiring glances of one observer. I do not underestimate the difficulties of the task. I see the utter incompetency of a single mind to draw the chart of human nature. I have as much doubt as any one of the value of general rules. There are heights of character to which a man must ascend alone—not to be foreshown—that can only exist by the arrival of the man and the crisis. It is very far from being my belief that teaching can make a hero or that Virtue can be analysed in the lecture room and her deepest secret shown. I rely too much on the inexhaustible Ideal, whose resources always astonish. But I think and I feel that confidence may be inspired in the powers of the will and in the aspirations of the Better by the voice and the faith of a believing man. I wish to inspire hope and shall esteem it the highest success if any ingenuous mind shall own that his scope has been extended; his conscience fortified and that more has been suggested than said.

From *The Early Lectures of Ralph Waldo Emerson, II*

Swedenborg: or, the Mystic

Among eminent persons, those who are most dear to men are not of the class which the economist calls producers: they have nothing in their hands; they have not cultivated corn, nor made bread; they have not led out a colony, nor invented a loom. A higher class, in the estimation and love of this city-building market-going race of mankind, are the poets, who, from the intellectual kingdom, feed the thought and imagination with ideas and pictures which raise men out of the world of corn and money, and console them for the shortcomings of the day and the meanness of labor and traffic. Then, also, the philosopher has his value, who flatters the intellect of this laborer by engaging him with subtleties which instruct him in new faculties. Others may build cities; he is to understand them and keep them in awe. But there is a class who lead us into another region—the world of morals or of will. What is singular about this region of thought is its claim. Wherever the sentiment of right comes in, it takes precedence of every thing else. For other things, I make poetry of them; but the moral sentiment makes poetry of me.

I have sometimes thought that he would render the greatest service to modern criticism, who should draw the line of relation that subsists between Shakspeare and Swedenborg. The human mind stands ever in perplexity, demanding intellect, demanding sanctity, impatient equally of each without the other. The reconciler has not yet appeared. If we tire of the saints, Shakspeare is our city of refuge. Yet the instincts presently teach that the problem of essence must take precedence of all others—the questions of Whence? What? and Whither? and the solution of these must be in a life, and not in a book. A drama or poem is a proximate or oblique

129

reply; but Moses, Menu, Jesus, work directly on this problem. The atmosphere of moral sentiment is a region of grandeur which reduces all material magnificence to toys, yet opens to every wretch that has reason the doors of the universe. Almost with a fierce haste it lays its empire on the man. In the language of the Koran, "God said, The heaven and the earth and all that is between them, think ye that we created them in jest, and that ye shall not return to us?" It is the kingdom of the will, and by inspiring the will, which is the seat of personality, seems to convert the universe into a person—

> The realms of being to no other bow,
> Not only all are thine, but all are Thou.

All men are commanded by the saint. The Koran makes a distinct class of those who are by nature good, and whose goodness has an influence on others, and pronounces this class to be the aim of creation: the other classes are admitted to the feast of being, only as following in the train of this. And the Persian poet exclaims to a soul of this kind—

> Go boldly forth, and feast on being's banquet;
> Thou art the called—the rest admitted with thee.

The privilege of this caste is an access to the secrets and structure of nature by some higher method than by experience. In common parlance, what one man is said to learn by experience, a man of extraordinary sagacity is said, without experience, to divine. The Arabians say, that Abul Khain, the mystic, and Abu Ali Seena, the philosopher, conferred together; and, on parting, the philosopher said, "All that he sees, I know;" and the mystic said, "All that he knows, I see." If one should ask the reason of this intuition, the solution would lead us into that property which Plato denoted as Reminiscence, and which is implied by the Brahmins in the tenet of Transmigration. The soul having been often born, or, as the Hindoos say, "travelling the path of existence through thousands of births," having beheld the things which are here, those which are in heaven and those which are beneath, there is nothing of which she has not gained the knowledge: no wonder that she is able to recollect, in regard to any one thing, what formerly she knew. "For, all things in nature being linked and related, and the soul having heretofore known all, nothing hinders but that any man who has recalled to mind, or according to the common phrase has learned, one thing only, should of himself recover all his ancient knowledge, and find out again all the rest, if he have but courage and faint not in the midst of his researches. For inquiry and learning is reminiscence all." How much more, if he that inquires be a holy and godlike soul! For by being assimilated to the original soul, by whom and after whom all things subsist, the soul of man does then easily flow into all things, and all things flow into it: they mix; and he is present and sympathetic with their structure and law.

This path is difficult, secret and beset with terror. The ancients called it *ecstasy* or absence—a getting out of their bodies to think. All religious history contains traces of the trance of saints—a beatitude, but without any sign of joy; earnest, solitary, even sad; "the flight," Plotinus called it, "of the alone to the alone;" Μύησις, the closing of the eyes—whence our word, *Mystic*. The trances of Socrates, Plotinus, Porphyry, Behmen, Bunyan, Fox, Pascal, Guyon, Swedenborg, will readily come to mind. But what as readily comes to mind is the accompaniment of disease. This beatitude comes in terror, and with shocks to the mind of the receiver.

It o'erinforms the tenement of clay,[1]

and drives the man mad; or gives a certain violent bias which taints his judgment. In the chief examples of religious illumination somewhat morbid has mingled, in spite of the unquestionable increase of mental power. Must the highest good drag after it a quality which neutralizes and discredits it?

Indeed, it takes
From our achievements, when performed at height,
The pith and marrow of our attribute.[2]

Shall we say, that the economical mother disburses so much earth and so much fire, by weight and meter, to make a man,

---

[1] Dryden, *Absalom and Achitophel.*

[2] Shakespeare, *Hamlet*, Act I, scene iv.

and will not add a pennyweight, though a nation is perishing for a leader? Therefore the men of God purchased their science by folly or pain. If you will have pure carbon, carbuncle, or diamond, to make the brain transparent, the trunk and organs shall be so much the grosser: instead of porcelain they are potter's earth, clay, or mud.

In modern times no such remarkable example of this introverted mind has occurred as in Emanuel Swedenborg, born in Stockholm, in 1688. This man, who appeared to his contemporaries a visionary and elixir of moonbeams, no doubt led the most real life of any man then in the world: and now, when the royal and ducal Frederics, Christians and Brunswicks of that day have slid into oblivion, he begins to spread himself into the minds of thousands. As happens in great men, he seemed, by the variety and amount of his powers, to be a composition of several persons—like the giant fruits which are matured in gardens by the union of four or five single blossoms. His frame is on a larger scale and possesses the advantages of size. As it is easier to see the reflection of the great sphere in large globes, though defaced by some crack or blemish, than in drops of water, so men of large calibre, though with some eccentricity or madness, like Pascal or Newton, help us more than balanced mediocre minds.

His youth and training could not fail to be extraordinary. Such a boy could not whistle or dance, but goes grubbing into mines and mountains, prying into chemistry and optics, physiology, mathematics and astronomy, to find images fit for the measure of his versatile and capacious brain. He was a scholar from a child, and was educated at Upsala. At the age of twenty-eight he was made Assessor of the Board of Mines by Charles XII. In 1716, he left home for four years and visited the universities of England, Holland, France and Germany. He performed a notable feat of engineering in 1718, at the siege of Frederikshald, by hauling two galleys, five boats and a sloop, some fourteen English miles overland, for the royal service. In 1721 he journeyed over Europe to examine mines and smelting works. He published in 1716 his Dædalus Hyperboreus, and from this time for the next thirty years was employed in the composition and publication of his scientific works. With the like force he threw himself into theology. In 1743, when he was fifty-four years old, what is called his illumination began. All his metallurgy and transportation of ships overland was absorbed into this ecstasy. He ceased to publish any more scientific books, withdrew from his practical labors and devoted himself to the writing and publication of his voluminous theological works, which were printed at his own expense, or at that of the Duke of Brunswick or other prince, at Dresden, Leipsic, London, or Amsterdam. Later, he resigned his office of Assessor: the salary attached to this office continued to be paid to him during his life. His duties had brought him into intimate acquaintance with King Charles XII., by whom he was much consulted and honored. The like favor was continued to him by his successor. At the Diet of 1751, Count Hopken says, the most solid memorials on finance were from his pen. In Sweden he appears to have attracted a marked regard. His rare science and practical skill, and the added fame of second sight and extraordinary religious knowledge and gifts, drew to him queens, nobles, clergy, shipmasters and people about the ports through which he was wont to pass in his many voyages. The clergy interfered a little with the importation and publication of his religious works, but he seems to have kept the friendship of men in power. He was never married. He had great modesty and gentleness of bearing. His habits were simple; he lived on bread, milk and vegetables; he lived in a house situated in a large garden; he went several times to England, where he does not seem to have attracted any attention whatever from the learned or the emiment; and died at London, March 29, 1772, of apoplexy, in his eighty-fifth year. He is described, when in London, as a man of a quiet, clerical habit, not averse to tea and coffee, and kind to children. He wore a sword when in full velvet dress, and, whenever he walked out, carried a gold-headed cane. There is a common portrait of him in antique coat and wig, but the face has a wandering or vacant air.

The genius which was to penetrate the science of the age with a far more subtle science; to pass the bounds of space and time, venture into the dim spirit-realm, and attempt to establish a new religion in the world—began its lessons in quarries and forges, in the smelting-pot and crucible, in ship-yards and dissecting-rooms. No one man is perhaps able to judge of the merits of his works on so many subjects. One is glad to learn that his books on mines and metals are held in the highest esteem by those who understand these matters. It seems that he anticipated much science of the nineteenth century; anticipated, in astronomy, the discovery of the seventh planet—but, unhappily, not also of the eighth; anticipated the views of modern astronomy in regard to the generation of earths by the sun; in magnetism, some important experiments and conclusions of later students; in chemistry, the atomic theory; in anatomy, the discoveries of Schlichting, Monro and Wilson; and first demonstrated the office of the lungs. His excellent English editor magnanimously lays no stress on his discoveries, since he was too great to care to be original; and we are to judge, by what he can spare, of what remains.

A colossal soul, he lies vast abroad on his times, uncomprehended by them, and requires a long focal distance to be seen; suggests, as Aristotle, Bacon, Selden, Humboldt, that a certain vastness of learning, or *quasi* omnipresence of the human soul in nature, is possible. His superb speculation, as from a tower, over nature and arts, without ever losing sight of the texture and sequence of things, almost realizes his own picture, in the "Principia," of the original integrity of man. Over and above the merit of his particular discoveries, is the capital merit of his self-equality. A drop of water has the properties of the sea, but cannot exhibit a storm. There is beauty of a concert, as well as of a flute; strength of a host, as well as of a hero; and, in Swedenborg, those who are best acquainted with modern books will most admire the merit of mass. One of the missouriums and mastodons of literature, he is not to be measured by whole colleges of ordinary scholars. His stalwart presence would flutter the gowns of an university. Our books are false by being fragmentary: their sentences are *bonmots*, and not parts of natural discourse; childish expressions of surprise or pleasure in nature; or, worse, owing a brief notoriety to their petulance, or aversion from the order of nature—being some curiosity or oddity, designedly not in harmony with nature and purposely framed to excite surprise, as jugglers do by concealing their means. But Swedenborg is systematic and respective of the world in every sentence; all the means are orderly given; his faculties work with astronomic punctuality, and this admirable writing is pure from all pertness or egotism.

Swedenborg was born into an atmosphere of great ideas.

It is hard to say what was his own: yet his life was dignified by noblest pictures of the universe. The robust Aristotelian method, with its breadth and adequateness, shaming our sterile and linear logic by its genial radiation, conversant with series and degree, with effects and ends, skilful to discriminate power from form, essence from accident, and opening, by its terminology and definition, high roads into nature, had trained a race of athletic philosophers. Harvey had shown the circulation of the blood; Gilbert had shown that the earth was a magnet; Descartes, taught by Gilbert's magnet, with its vortex, spiral and polarity, had filled Europe with the leading thought of vortical motion, as the secret of nature. Newton, in the year in which Swedenborg was born, published the "Principia," and established the universal gravity. Malpighi, following the high doctrines of Hippocrates, Leucippus and Lucretius, had given emphasis to the dogma that nature works in leasts—"tota in minimis existit natura." Unrivalled dissectors, Swammerdam, Leuwenhoek, Winslow, Eustachius, Heister, Vesalius, Boerhaave, had left nothing for scalpel or microscope to reveal in human or comparative anatomy: Linnæus, his contemporary, was affirming, in his beautiful science, that "Nature is always like herself:" and, lastly, the nobility of method, the largest application of principles, had been exhibited by Leibnitz and Christian Wolff, in cosmology; whilst Locke and Grotius had drawn the moral argument. What was left for a genius of the largest calibre but to go over their ground and verify and unite? It is easy to see, in these minds, the origin of Swedenborg's studies, and the suggestion of his problems. He had a capacity to entertain and vivify these volumes of thought. Yet the proximity of these geniuses, one or other of whom had introduced all his leading ideas, makes Swedenborg another example of the difficulty, even in a highly fertile genius, of proving originality, the first birth and annunciation of one of the laws of nature.

He named his favorite views the doctrine of Forms, the doctrine of Series and Degrees, the doctrine of Influx, the doctrine of Correspondence. His statement of these doctrines deserves to be studied in his books. Not every man can read them, but they will reward him who can. His theologic works are valuable to illustrate these. His writings would be a sufficient library to a lonely and athletic student; and the "Economy of the Animal Kingdom" is one of those books which, by the sustained dignity of thinking, is an honor to the human race. He had studied spars and metals to some purpose. His varied and solid knowledge makes his style lustrous with points and shooting spiculæ of thought, and resembling one of those winter mornings when the air sparkles with crystals. The grandeur of the topics makes the grandeur of the style. He was apt for cosmology, because of that native perception of identity which made mere size of no account to him. In the atom of magnetic iron he saw the quality which would generate the spiral motion of sun and planet.

The thoughts in which he lived were, the universality of each law in nature; the Platonic doctrine of the scale or degrees; the version or conversion of each into other, and so the correspondence of all the parts; the fine secret that little explains large, and large, little; the centrality of man in nature, and the connection that subsists throughout all things: he saw that the human body was strictly universal, or an instrument through which the soul feeds and is fed by the whole of matter; so that he held, in exact antagonism to the skeptics, that "the wiser a man is, the more will he be a worshipper of the Deity." In short, he was a believer in the Identity-philosophy, which he held not idly, as the dreamers of Berlin or Boston, but which he experimented with and established through years of labor, with the heart and strength of the rudest Viking that his rough Sweden ever sent to battle.

This theory dates from the oldest philosophers, and derives perhaps its best illustration from the newest. It is this, that Nature iterates her means perpetually on successive planes. In the old aphorism, *nature is always self-similar*. In the plant, the eye or germinative point opens to a leaf, then to another leaf, with a power of transforming the leaf into radicle, stamen, pistil, petal, bract, sepal, or seed. The whole art of the plant is still to repeat leaf on leaf without end, the more or less of heat, light, moisture and food determining the form it shall assume. In the animal, nature makes a vertebra, or a spine of vertebræ, and helps herself still by a new spine, with a limited power of modifying its form—spine on spine, to the end of the world. A poetic anatomist, in our own day, teaches that a snake, being a horizontal line, and man, being an erect line, constitute a right angle; and between the lines of this mystical quadrant all animated beings find their place: and he assumes the hair-worm, the span-worm, or the snake, as the type or prediction of the spine. Manifestly, at the end of the spine, Nature puts out smaller spines, as arms; at the end of the arms, new spines, as hands; at the other end, she repeats the process, as legs and feet. At the top of the column she puts out another spine, which doubles or loops itself over, as a span-worm, into a ball, and forms the skull, with extremities again: the hands being now the upper jaw, the feet the lower jaw, the fingers and toes being represented this time by upper and lower teeth. This new spine is destined to high uses. It is a new man on the shoulders of the last. It can almost shed its trunk and manage to live alone, according to the Platonic idea in the Timæus. Within it, on a higher plane, all that was done in the trunk repeats itself. Nature recites her lesson once more in a higher mood. The mind is a finer body, and resumes its functions of feeding, digesting, absorbing, excluding and generating, in a new and ethereal element. Here in the brain is all the process of alimentation repeated, in the acquiring, comparing, digesting and assimilating of experience. Here again is the mystery of generation repeated. In the brain are male and female faculties; here is marriage, here is fruit. And there is no limit to this ascending scale, but series on series. Every thing, at the end of one use, is taken up into the next each series punctually repeating every organ and process of the last. We are adapted to infinity. We are hard to please, and love nothing which ends; and in nature is no end, but every thing at the end of one use is lifted into a superior, and the ascent of these things climbs into dæmonic and celestial natures. Creative force, like a musical composer, goes on unweariedly repeating a simple air or theme, now high, now low, in solo, in chorus, ten thousand times reverberated, till it fills earth and heaven with the chant.

Gravitation, as explained by Newton, is good, but grander when we find chemistry only an extension of the law of masses into particles, and that the atomic theory shows the action of chemistry to be mechanical also. Metaphysics shows us a sort of gravitation operative also in the mental phenomena; and the terrible tabulation of the French statists brings every piece of whim and humor to be reducible also to exact numerical ratios. If one man in twenty thousand, or in thirty thousand, eats shoes or marries his grandmother, then in every twenty thousand or thirty thousand is found

one man who eats shoes or marries his grandmother. What
we call gravitation, and fancy ultimate, is one fork of a
mightier stream for which we have yet no name. Astronomy
is excellent; but it must come up into life to have its full
value, and not remain there in globes and spaces. The globule
of blood gyrates around its own axis in the human veins, as
the planet in the sky; and the circles of intellect relate to
those of the heavens. Each law of nature has the like universality; eating, sleep or hibernation, rotation, generation,
metamorphosis, vortical motion, which is seen in eggs as in
planets. These grand rhymes or returns in nature—the dear,
best-known face startling us at every turn, under a mask so
unexpected that we think it the face of a stranger, and carrying up the semblance into divine forms—delighted the
prophetic eye of Swedenborg; and he must be reckoned a
leader in that revolution, which, by giving to science an idea,
has given to an aimless accumulation of experiments, guidance and form and a beating heart.

I own with some regret that his printed works amount to
about fifty stout octavos, his scientific works being about half
of the whole number; and it appears that a mass of manuscript still unedited remains in the royal library at Stockholm.
The scientific works have just now been translated into English, in an excellent edition.

Swedenborg printed these scientific books in the ten years
from 1734 to 1744, and they remained from that time neglected; and now, after their century is complete, he has at
last found a pupil in Mr. Wilkinson, in London, a philosophic
critic, with a coequal vigor of understanding and imagination
comparable only to Lord Bacon's, who has restored his master's buried books to the day, and transferred them, with
every advantage, from their forgotten Latin into English, to
go round the world in our commercial and conquering tongue.
This startling reappearance of Swedenborg, after a hundred
years, in his pupil, is not the least remarkable fact in his history. Aided it is said by the munificence of Mr. Clissold, and
also by his literary skill, this piece of poetic justice is done.
The admirable preliminary discourses with which Mr. Wilkinson has enriched these volumes, throw all the contemporary philosophy of England into shade, and leave me nothing
to say on their proper grounds.

The "Animal Kingdom" is a book of wonderful merits. It

was written with the highest end—to put science and the soul, long estranged from each other, at one again. It was an anatomist's account of the human body, in the highest style of poetry. Nothing can exceed the bold and brilliant treatment of a subject usually so dry and repulsive. He saw nature "wreathing through an everlasting spiral, with wheels that never dry, on axles that never creak," and sometimes sought "to uncover those secret recesses where Nature is sitting at the fires in the depths of her laboratory;" whilst the picture comes recommended by the hard fidelity with which it is based on practical anatomy. It is remarkable that this sublime genius decides peremptorily for the analytic, against the synthetic method; and, in a book whose genius is a daring poetic synthesis, claims to confine himself to a rigid experience.

He knows, if he only, the flowing of nature, and how wise was that old answer of Amasis to him who bade him drink up the sea—"Yes, willingly, if you will stop the rivers that flow in." Few knew as much about nature and her subtle manners, or expressed more subtly her goings. He thought as large a demand is made on our faith by nature, as by miracles. "He noted that in her proceeding from first principles through her several subordinations, there was no state through which she did not pass, as if her path lay through all things." "For as often as she betakes herself upward from visible phenomena, or, in other words, withdraws herself inward, she instantly as it were disappears, while no one knows what has become of her, or whither she is gone: so that it is necessary to take science as a guide in pursuing her steps."

The pursuing the inquiry under the light of an end or final cause gives wonderful animation, a sort of personality to the whole writing. This book announces his favorite dogmas. The ancient doctrine of Hippocrates, that the brain is a gland; and of Leucippus, that the atom may be known by the mass; or, in Plato, the macrocosm by the microcosm; and, in the verses of Lucretius,

> Ossa videlicet e pauxillis atque minutis
> Ossibus sic et de pauxillis atque minutis
> Visceribus viscus gigni, sanguenque creari
> Sanguinis inter se multis coeuntibus guttis;
> Ex aurique putat micis consistere posse

Aurum, et de terris terram concrescere parvis;
Ignibus ex igneis, humorem humoribus esse.[3]

The principle of all things, entrails made
Of smallest entrails; bone, of smallest bone;
Blood, of small sanguine drops reduced to one;
Gold, of small grains; earth, of small sands compacted;
Small drops to water, sparks to fire contracted:

and which Malpighi had summed in his maxim that "nature exists entire in leasts"—is a favorite thought of Swedenborg. "It is a constant law of the organic body that large, compound, or visible forms exist and subsist from smaller, simpler and ultimately from invisible forms, which act similarly to the larger ones, but more perfectly and more universally; and the least forms so perfectly and universally as to involve an idea representative of their entire universe." The unities of each organ are so many little organs, homogeneous with their compound: the unities of the tongue are little tongues; those of the stomach, little stomachs; those of the heart are little hearts. This fruitful idea furnishes a key to every secret. What was too small for the eye to detect was read by the aggregates; what was too large, by the units. There is no end to his application of the thought. "Hunger is an aggregate of very many little hungers, or losses of blood by the little veins all over the body." It is a key to his theology also. "Man is a kind of very minute heaven, corresponding to the world of spirits and to heaven. Every particular idea of man, and every affection, yea, every smallest part of his affection, is an image and effigy of him. A spirit may be known from only a single thought. God is the grand man."

The hardihood and thoroughness of his study of nature required a theory of forms also. "Forms ascend in order from the lowest to the highest. The lowest form is angular, or the terrestrial and corporeal. The second and next higher form is the circular, which is also called the perpetual-angular, because the circumference of a circle is a perpetual angle. The form above this is the spiral, parent and measure of circular forms: its diameters are not rectilinear, but variously circular, and have a spherical surface for centre; therefore it is called the perpetual-circular. The form above this is the vortical, or

---

[3] Lucretius, *De Rerum Natura* ("On the Nature of Things").

perpetual-spiral: next, the perpetual-vortical, or celestial: last, the perpetual-celestial, or spiritual."

Was it strange that a genius so bold should take the last step also, should conceive that he might attain the science of all sciences, to unlock the meaning of the world? In the first volume of the "Animal Kingdom," he broaches the subject in a remarkable note: "In our doctrine of Representations and Correspondences we shall treat of both these symbolical and typical resemblances, and of the astonishing things which occur, I will not say in the living body only, but throughout nature, and which correspond so entirely to supreme and spiritual things that one would swear that the physical world was purely symbolical of the spiritual world; insomuch that if we choose to express any natural truth in physical and definite vocal terms, and to convert these terms only into the corresponding and spiritual terms, we shall by this means elicit a spiritual truth or theological dogma, in place of the physical truth or precept: although no mortal would have predicted that any thing of the kind could possibly arise by bare literal transposition; inasmuch as the one precept, considered separately from the other, appears to have absolutely no relation to it. I intend hereafter to communicate a number of examples of such correspondences, together with a vocabulary containing the terms of spiritual things, as well as of the physical things for which they are to be substituted. This symbolism pervades the living body."

The fact thus explicitly stated is implied in all poetry, in allegory, in fable, in the use of emblems and in the structure of language. Plato knew it, as is evident from his twice bisected line in the sixth book of the Republic. Lord Bacon had found that truth and nature differed only as seal and print; and he instanced some physical propositions, with their translation into a moral or political sense. Behmen, and all mystics, imply this law in their dark riddle-writing. The poets, in as far as they are poets, use it; but it is known to them only as the magnet was known for ages, as a toy. Swedenborg first put the fact into a detached and scientific statement, because it was habitually present to him, and never not seen. It was involved, as we explained already, in the doctrine of identity and iteration, because the mental series exactly tallies with the material series. It required an insight that could rank things in order and series; or rather it required such rightness of position that the poles of the eye should coincide with the axis of the world. The earth had fed its mankind through five or six millenniums, and they had sciences, religions, philosophies, and yet had failed to see the correspondence of meaning between every part and every other part. And, down to this hour, literature has no book in which the symbolism of things is scientifically opened. One would say that as soon as men had the first hint that every sensible object—animal, rock, river, air—nay, space and time, subsists not for itself, nor finally to a material end, but as a picture-language to tell another story of beings and duties, other science would be put by, and a science of such grand presage would absorb all faculties: that each man would ask of all objects what they mean: Why does the horizon hold me fast, with my joy and grief, in this centre? Why hear I the same sense from countless differing voices, and read one never quite expressed fact in endless picture-language? Yet whether it be that these things will not be intellectually learned, or that many centuries must elaborate and compose so rare and opulent a soul—there is no comet, rock-stratum, fossil, fish, quadruped, spider, or fungus, that, for itself, does not interest more scholars and classifiers than the meaning and upshot of the frame of things.

But Swedenborg was not content with the culinary use of the world. In his fifty-fourth year these thoughts held him fast, and his profound mind admitted the perilous opinion, too frequent in religious history, that he was an abnormal person, to whom was granted the privilege of conversing with angels and spirits; and this ecstasy connected itself with just this office of explaining the moral import of the sensible world. To a right perception, at once broad and minute, of the order of nature, he added the comprehension of the moral laws in their widest social aspects; but whatever he saw, through some excessive determination to form in his constitution, he saw not abstractly, but in pictures, heard it in dialogues, constructed it in events. When he attempted to announce the law most sanely, he was forced to couch it in parable.

Modern psychology offers no similar example of a deranged balance. The principal powers continued to maintain a healthy action, and to a reader who can make due allowance in the report for the reporter's peculiarities, the results are still instructive, and a more striking testimony to the sublime laws he announced than any that balanced dulness could afford. He attempts to give some account of the *modus* of the new state, affirming that "his presence in the spiritual world is attended with a certain separation, but only as to the intellectual part of his mind, not as to the will part;" and he affirms that "he sees, with the internal sight, the things that are in another life, more clearly than he sees the things which are here in the world."

Having adopted the belief that certain books of the Old and New Testaments were exact allegories, or written in the angelic and ecstatic mode, he employed his remaining years in extricating from the literal, the universal sense. He had borrowed from Plato the fine fable of "a most ancient people, men better than we and dwelling nigher to the gods;" and Swedenborg added that they used the earth symbolically; that these, when they saw terrestrial objects, did not think at all about them, but only about those which they signified. The correspondence between thoughts and things henceforward occupied him. "The very organic form resembles the end inscribed on it." A man is in general and in particular an organized justice or injustice, selfishness or gratitude. And the cause of this harmony he assigned in the Arcana: "The reason why all and single things, in the heavens and on earth, are representative, is because they exist from an influx of the Lord, through heaven." This design of exhibiting such correspondences, which, if adequately executed, would be the poem of the world, in which all history and science would play an essential part, was narrowed and defeated by the exclusively theologic direction which his inquiries took. His perception of nature is not human and universal, but is mystical and Hebraic. He fastens each natural object to a theologic notion—a horse signifies carnal understanding; a tree, perception; the moon, faith; a cat means this; an ostrich that; an artichoke this other—and poorly tethers every symbol to a several ecclesiastic sense. The slippery Proteus is not so easily caught. In nature, each individual symbol plays innumerable parts, as each particle of matter circulates in turn through every system. The central identity enables any one symbol to express successively all the qualities and shades of real being. In the transmission of the heavenly waters, every hose fits every hydrant. Nature avenges herself speedily on the hard pedantry that would chain her waves. She is no literalist. Every thing must be taken genially, and we must be at the top of our condition to understand any thing rightly.

His theological bias thus fatally narrowed his interpretation of nature, and the dictionary of symbols is yet to be written. But the interpreter whom mankind must still expect, will find no predecessor who has approached so near to the true problem.

Swedenborg styles himself in the title-page of his books, "Servant of the Lord Jesus Christ;" and by force of intellect, and in effect, he is the last Father in the Church, and is not likely to have a successor. No wonder that his depth of ethical wisdom should give him influence as a teacher. To the withered traditional church, yielding dry catechisms, he let in nature again, and the worshipper, escaping from the vestry of verbs and texts, is surprised to find himself a party to the whole of his religion. His religion thinks for him and is of universal application. He turns it on every side; it fits every part of life, interprets and dignifies every circumstance. Instead of a religion which visited him diplomatically three or four times—when he was born, when he married, when he fell sick and when he died, and, for the rest, never interfered with him—here was a teaching which accompanied him all day, accompanied him even into sleep and dreams; into his thinking, and showed him through what a long ancestry his thoughts descend; into society, and showed by what affinities he was girt to his equals and his counterparts; into natural objects, and showed their origin and meaning, what are friendly, and what are hurtful; and opened the future world by indicating the continuity of the same laws. His disciples allege that their intellect is invigorated by the study of his books.

There is no such problem for criticism as his theological writings, their merits are so commanding, yet such grave deductions must be made. Their immense and sandy diffuseness is like the prairie or the desert, and their incongruities are like the last deliration. He is superfluously explanatory, and his feeling of the ignorance of men, strangely exaggerated. Men take truths of this nature very fast. Yet he abounds in assertions, he is a rich discoverer, and of things which most import us to know. His thought dwells in essential resemblances, like the resemblance of a house to the man who built it. He saw things in their law, in likeness of function, not of structure. There is an invariable method and order in his delivery of his truth, the habitual proceeding of the mind from inmost to outmost. What earnestness and weightiness—his eye never roving, without one swell of vanity, or one look to self in any common form of literary pride! a theoretic or speculative man, but whom no practical man in the universe could affect to scorn. Plato is a gownsman; his garment, though of purple, and almost sky-woven, is an academic robe and hinders action with its voluminous folds. But this mystic is awful to Cæsar. Lycurgus himself would bow.

The moral insight of Swedenborg, the correction of popular errors, the announcement of ethical laws, take him out of comparison with any other modern writer and entitle him to a place, vacant for some ages, among the lawgivers of mankind. That slow but commanding influence which he has acquired, like that of other religious geniuses, must be excessive also, and have its tides, before it subsides into a permanent amount. Of course what is real and universal cannot be confined to the circle of those who sympathize strictly with his genius, but will pass forth into the common stock of wise and just thinking. The world has a sure chemistry, by which it extracts what is excellent in its children and lets fall the infirmities and limitations of the grandest mind.

That metempsychosis which is familiar in the old mythology of the Greeks, collected in Ovid and in the Indian Transmigration, and is there *objective*, or really takes place in bodies by alien will—in Swedenborg's mind has a more philosophic character. It is subjective, or depends entirely upon the thought of the person. All things in the universe arrange themselves to each person anew, according to his ruling love. Man is such as his affection and thought are. Man is man by virtue of willing, not by virtue of knowing and understanding. As he is, so he sees. The marriages of the world are broken up. Interiors associate all in the spiritual world. Whatever the angels looked upon was to them celestial. Each Satan appears to himself a man; to those as bad as he, a comely man; to the purified, a heap of carrion. Nothing can resist states: every thing gravitates: like will to like: what we call poetic justice takes effect on the spot. We have come into a world which is a living poem. Every thing is as I am. Bird and beast is not bird and beast, but emanation and effluvia of the minds and wills of men there present. Every one makes his own house and state. The ghosts are tormented with the fear of death and cannot remember that they have died. They who are in evil and falsehood are afraid of all others. Such as have deprived themselves of charity, wander and flee: the societies which they approach discover their quality and drive them away. The covetous seem to themselves to be abiding in cells where their money is deposited, and these to be infested with mice. They who place merit in good works seem to themselves to cut wood. "I asked such, if they were not wearied? They replied, that they have not yet done work enough to merit heaven."

He delivers golden sayings which express with singular beauty the ethical laws; as when he uttered that famed sentence, that "In heaven the angels are advancing continually to the springtime of their youth, so that the oldest angel appears the youngest:" "The more angels, the more room:" "The perfection of man is the love of use:" "Man, in his perfect form, is heaven:" "What is from Him, is Him:" "Ends always ascend as nature descends." And the truly poetic account of the writing in the inmost heaven, which, as it consists of inflexions according to the form of heaven, can be read without instruction. He almost justifies his claim to preternatural vision, by strange insights of the structure of the human body and mind. "It is never permitted to any one, in heaven, to stand behind another and look at the back of his head; for then the influx which is from the Lord is disturbed." The angels, from the sound of the voice, know a man's love; from the articulation of the sound, his wisdom; and from the sense of the words, his science.

In the "Conjugal Love," he has unfolded the science of marriage. Of this book one would say that with the highest elements it has failed of success. It came near to be the Hymn of Love, which Plato attempted in the "Banquet;" the love, which, Dante says, Casella sang among the angels in Paradise; and which, as rightly celebrated, in its genesis, fruition and effect, might well entrance the souls, as it would lay open the genesis of all institutions, customs and manners. The book had been grand if the Hebraism had been omitted and the law stated without Gothicism, as ethics, and with that scope for ascension of state which the nature of things requires. It is a fine Platonic development of the science of marriage;

teaching that sex is universal, and not local; virility in the male qualifying every organ, act, and thought; and the feminine in woman. Therefore in the real or spiritual world the nuptial union is not momentary, but incessant and total; and chastity not a local, but a universal virtue; unchastity being discovered as much in the trading, or planting, or speaking, or philosophizing, as in generation; and that, though the virgins he saw in heaven were beautiful, the wives were incomparably more beautiful, and went on increasing in beauty evermore.

Yet Swedenborg, after his mode, pinned his theory to a temporary form. He exaggerates the circumstance of marriage; and though he finds false marriages on earth, fancies a wiser choice in heaven. But of progressive souls, all loves and friendships are momentary. *Do you love me?* means, Do you see the same truth? If you do, we are happy with the same happiness: but presently one of us passes into the perception of new truth; we are divorced, and no tension in nature can hold us to each other. I know how delicious is this cup of love—I existing for you, you existing for me; but it is a child's clinging to his toy; an attempt to eternize the fireside and nuptial chamber; to keep the picture-alphabet through which our first lessons are prettily conveyed. The Eden of God is bare and grand: like the out-door landscape remembered from the evening fireside, it seems cold and desolate whilst you cower over the coals, but once abroad again, we pity those who can forego the magnificence of nature for candle-light and cards. Perhaps the true subject of the "Conjugal Love" is *Conversation*, whose laws are profoundly set forth. It is false, if literally applied to marriage. For God is the bride or bridegroom of the soul. Heaven is not the pairing of two, but the communion of all souls. We meet, and dwell an instant under the temple of one thought, and part, as though we parted not, to join another thought in other fellowships of joy. So far from there being anything divine in the low and proprietary sense of *Do you love me?* it is only when you leave and lose me by casting yourself on a sentiment which is higher than both of us, that I draw near and find myself at your side; and I am repelled if you fix your eye on me and demand love. In fact, in the spiritual world we change sexes every moment. You love the worth in me; then I am your husband: but it is not me, but the worth, that fixes the love; and that worth is a drop of the ocean of worth that is beyond me. Meantime I adore the greater worth in another, and so become his wife. He aspires to a higher worth in another spirit, and is wife or receiver of that influence.

Whether from a self-inquisitorial habit that he grew into from jealousy of the sins to which men of thought are liable, he has acquired, in disentangling and demonstrating that particular form of moral disease, an acumen which no conscience can resist. I refer to his feeling of the profanation of thinking to what is good, "from scientifics." "To reason about faith, is to doubt and deny." He was painfully alive to the difference between knowing and doing, and this sensibility is incessantly expressed. Philosophers are, therefore, vipers, cockatrices, asps, hemorrhoids, presters, and flying serpents; literary men are conjurors and charlatans.

But this topic suggests a sad afterthought, that here we find the seat of his own pain. Possibly Swedenborg paid the penalty of introverted faculties. Success, or a fortunate genius, seems to depend on a happy adjustment of heart and brain; on a due proportion, hard to hit, of moral and mental power, which perhaps obeys the law of those chemical ratios which make a proportion in volumes necessary to combination, as when gases will combine in certain fixed rates, but not at any rate. It is hard to carry a full cup; and this man, profusely endowed in heart and mind, early fell into dangerous discord with himself. In his Animal Kingdom he surprised us by declaring that he loved analysis, and not synthesis; and now, after his fiftieth year, he falls into jealousy of his intellect; and though aware that truth is not solitary nor is goodness solitary, but both must ever mix and marry, he makes war on his mind, takes the part of the conscience against it, and, on all occasions, traduces and blasphemes it. The violence is instantly avenged. Beauty is disgraced, love is unlovely, when truth, the half part of heaven, is denied, as much as when a bitterness in men of talent leads to satire and destroys the judgment. He is wise, but wise in his own despite. There is an air of infinite grief and the sound of wailing all over and through this lurid universe. A vampyre sits in the seat of the prophet and turns with gloomy appetite to the images of pain. Indeed, a bird does not more readily weave its nest, or a mole bore into the ground, than this seer of the souls substructs a new hell and pit, each more abominable than the last, round every new crew of offenders. He was let down through a column that seemed of brass, but it was formed of angelic spirits, that he might descend safely amongst the unhappy, and witness the vastation of souls and hear there, for a long continuance, their lamentations: he saw their tormentors who increase and strain pangs to infinity; he saw the hell of the jugglers, the hell of the assassins, the hell of the lascivious; the hell of robbers, who kill and boil men; the infernal tun of the deceitful; the excrementitious hells; the hell of the revengeful, whose faces resembled a round, broad cake, and their arms rotate like a wheel. Except Rabelais and Dean Swift nobody ever had such science of filth and corruption.

These books should be used with caution. It is dangerous to sculpture these evanescing images of thought. True in transition, they become false if fixed. It requires, for his just apprehension, almost a genius equal to his own. But when his visions become the stereotyped language of multitudes of persons of all degrees of age and capacity, they are perverted. The wise people of the Greek race were accustomed to lead the most intelligent and virtuous young men, as part of their education, through the Eleusinian mysteries, wherein, with much pomp and graduation, the highest truths known to ancient wisdom were taught. An ardent and contemplative young man, at eighteen or twenty years, might read once these books of Swedenborg, these mysteries of love and conscience, and then throw them aside for ever. Genius is ever haunted by similar dreams, when the hells and the heavens are opened to it. But these pictures are to be held as mystical, that is, as a quite arbitrary and accidental picture of the truth —not as the truth. Any other symbol would be as good; then this is safely seen.

Swedenborg's system of the world wants central spontaneity; it is dynamic, not vital, and lacks power to generate life. There is no individual in it. The universe is a gigantic crystal, all whose atoms and laminæ lie in uninterrupted order and with unbroken unity, but cold and still. What seems an individual and a will, is none. There is an immense chain of intermediation, extending from centre to extremes, which bereaves every agency of all freedom and character. The universe, in his poem, suffers under a magnetic sleep, and only reflects the mind of the magnetizer. Every thought comes into each mind by influence from a society of spirits that surround it, and into these from a higher society, and so on. All his types mean the same few things. All his figures speak one speech. All his interlocutors Swedenborgize. Be they who they may, to this complexion must they come at last. This Charon ferries them all over in his boat; kings, counsellors, cavaliers, doctors, Sir Isaac Newton, Sir Hans Sloane, King George II., Mahomet, or whomsoever, and all gather one grimness of hue and style. Only when Cicero comes by, our gentle seer sticks a little at saying he talked with Cicero, and with a touch of human relenting remarks, "one whom it was given me to believe was Cicero;" and when the *soi disant* Roman opens his mouth, Rome and eloquence have ebbed away—it is plain theologic Swedenborg like the rest. His heavens and hells are dull; fault of want of individualism. The thousand-fold relation of men is not there. The interest that attaches in nature to each man, because he is right by his wrong, and wrong by his right; because he defies all dogmatizing and classification, so many allowances and contingences and futurities are to be taken into account; strong by his vices, often paralyzed by his virtues—sinks into entire sympathy with his society. This want reacts to the centre of the system. Though the agency of "the Lord" is in every line referred to by name, it never becomes alive. There is no lustre in that eye which gazes from the centre and which should vivify the immense dependency of beings.

The vice of Swedenborg's mind is its theologic determination. Nothing with him has the liberality of universal wisdom, but we are always in a church. That Hebrew muse, which taught the lore of right and wrong to men, had the same excess of influence for him it has had for the nations. The mode, as well as the essence, was sacred. Palestine is ever the more valuable as a chapter in universal history, and ever the less an available element in education. The genius of Swedenborg, largest of all modern souls in this department of thought, wasted itself in the endeavor to reanimate and conserve what had already arrived at its natural term, and, in the great secular Providence, was retiring from its prominence, before Western modes of thought and expression. Swedenborg and Behmen both failed by attaching themselves to the Christian symbol, instead of to the moral sentiment, which carries innumerable christianities, humanities, divinities, in its bosom.

The excess of influence shows itself in the incongruous importation of a foreign rhetoric. "What have I to do," asks the impatient reader, "with jasper and sardonyx, beryl and chalcedony; what with arks and passovers, ephahs and ephods; what with lepers and emerods; what with heave-offerings and unleavened bread, chariots of fire, dragons crowned and horned, behemoth and unicorn? Good for Orientals, these are nothing to me. The more learning you bring to explain them, the more glaring the impertinence. The more coherent and elaborate the system, the less I like it. I say, with the Spartan, 'Why do you speak so much to the purpose, of that which is nothing to the purpose?' [4] My learning is such as God gave me in my birth and habit, in the delight and study of my eyes and not of another man's. Of all absurdities, this of some foreigner proposing to take away my rhetoric and substitute his own, and amuse me with pelican and stork, instead of thrush and robin; palm-trees and shittim-wood, instead of sassafras and hickory—seems the most needless."

Locke said, "God, when he makes the prophet, does not unmake the man." Swedenborg's history points the remark. The parish disputes in the Swedish church between the friends and foes of Luther and Melancthon, concerning "faith alone" and "works alone," intrude themselves into his speculations upon the economy of the universe, and of the celestial societies. The Lutheran bishop's son, for whom the heavens are opened, so that he sees with eyes and in the richest symbolic forms the awful truth of things, and utters again in his books, as under a heavenly mandate, the indisputable secrets of moral nature—with all these grandeurs resting upon him, remains the Lutheran bishop's son; his judgments are those of a Swedish polemic, and his vast enlargements purchased by adamantine limitations. He carries his controversial memory with him in his visits to the souls. He is like Michel Angelo, who, in his frescoes, put the cardinal who had offended him to roast under a mountain of devils; or like Dante, who avenged, in vindictive melodies, all his private wrongs; or perhaps still more like Montaigne's parish priest, who, if a hail-storm passes over the village, thinks the day of doom is

---

[4] Plutarch, *Life of Lycurgus.*

come, and the cannibals already have got the pip. Swedenborg confounds us not less with the pains of Melancthon and
Luther and Wolfius, and his own books, which he advertises
among the angels.

Under the same theologic cramp, many of his dogmas are
bound. His cardinal position in morals is that evils should be
shunned as sins. But he does not know what evil is, or what
good is, who thinks any ground remains to be occupied, after
saying that evil is to be shunned as evil. I doubt not he was
led by the desire to insert the element of personality of Deity.
But nothing is added. One man, you say, dreads erysipelas—
show him that this dread is evil: or, one dreads hell—show
him that *dread* is evil. He who loves goodness, harbors angels,
reveres reverence and lives with God. The less we have to
do with our sins the better. No man can afford to waste his
moments in compunctions. "That is active duty," say the
Hindoos, "which is not for our bondage; that is knowledge,
which is for our liberation: all other duty is good only unto
weariness."

Another dogma, growing out of this pernicious theologic
limitation, is his Inferno. Swedenborg has devils. Evil, according to old philosophers, is good in the making. That pure
malignity can exist is the extreme proposition of unbelief.
It is not to be entertained by a rational agent; it is atheism;
it is the last profanation. Euripides rightly said,

> Goodness and being in the gods are one;
> He who imputes ill to them makes them none.

To what a painful perversion had Gothic theology arrived,
that Swedenborg admitted no conversion for evil spirits! But
the divine effort is never relaxed; the carrion in the sun will
convert itself to grass and flowers; and man, though in
brothels, or jails, or on gibbets, is on his way to all that is
good and true. Burns, with the wild humor of his apostrophe
to poor "auld Nickie Ben,"

> O wad ye tak a thought, and mend! [5]

has the advantage of the vindictive theologian. Every thing
is superficial and perishes but love and truth only. The

---

[5] Burns' poem, "Address to the Devil."

largest is always the truest sentiment, and we feel the more generous spirit of the Indian Vishnu—"I am the same to all mankind. There is not one who is worthy of my love or hatred. They who serve me with adoration—I am in them, and they in me. If one whose ways are altogether evil serve me alone, he is as respectable as the just man; he is altogether well employed; he soon becometh of a virtuous spirit and obtaineth eternal happiness."

For the anomalous pretension of Revelations of the other world—only his probity and genius can entitle it to any serious regard. His revelations destroy their credit by running into detail. If a man say that the Holy Ghost has informed him that the Last Judgment (or the last of the judgments) took place in 1757; or that the Dutch, in the other world, live in a heaven by themselves, and the English in a heaven by themselves; I reply that the Spirit which is holy is reserved, taciturn, and deals in laws. The rumors of ghosts and hobgoblins gossip and tell fortunes. The teachings of the high Spirit are abstemious, and, in regard to particulars, negative. Socrates's Genius did not advise him to act or to find, but if he purposed to do somewhat not advantageous, it dissuaded him. "What God is," he said, "I know not; what he is not, I know." The Hindoos have denominated the Supreme Being, the "Internal Check." The illuminated Quakers explained their Light, not as somewhat which leads to any action, but it appears as an obstruction to any thing unfit. But the right examples are private experiences, which are absolutely at one on this point. Strictly speaking, Swedenborg's revelation is a confounding of planes—a capital offence in so learned a categorist. This is to carry the law of surface into the plane of substance, to carry individualism and its fopperies into the realm of essences and generals—which is dislocation and chaos.

The secret of heaven is kept from age to age. No imprudent, no sociable angel ever dropt an early syllable to answer the longings of saints, the fears of mortals. We should have listened on our knees to any favorite, who, by stricter obedience, had brought his thoughts into parallelism with the celestial currents and could hint to human ears the scenery and circumstance of the newly parted soul. But it is certain that it must tally with what is best in nature. It must not be inferior in tone to the already known works of the artist who sculptures the globes of the firmament and writes the moral law. It must be fresher than rainbows, stabler than mountains, agreeing with flowers, with tides and the rising and setting of autumnal stars. Melodious poets shall be hoarse as street ballads when once the penetrating key-note of nature and spirit is sounded—the earth-beat, sea-beat, heart-beat, which makes the tune to which the sun rolls, and the globule of blood, and the sap of trees.

In this mood we hear the rumor that the seer has arrived, and his tale is told. But there is no beauty, no heaven: for angels, goblins. The sad muse loves night and death and the pit. His Inferno is mesmeric. His spiritual world bears the same relation to the generosities and joys of truth of which human souls have already made us cognizant, as a man's bad dreams bear to his ideal life. It is indeed very like, in its endless power of lurid pictures, to the phenomena of dreaming, which nightly turns many an honest gentleman, benevolent but dyspeptic, into a wretch, skulking like a dog about the outer yards and kennels of creation. When he mounts into the heaven, I do not hear its language. A man should not tell me that he has walked among the angels; his proof is that his eloquence makes me one. Shall the archangels be less majestic and sweet than the figures that have actually walked the earth? These angels that Swedenborg paints give us no very high idea of their discipline and culture: they are all country parsons: their heaven is a *fête champêtre*, an evangelical picnic, or French distribution of prizes to virtuous peasants. Strange, scholastic, didactic, passionless, bloodless man, who denotes classes of souls as a botanist disposes of a carex, and visits doleful hells as a stratum of chalk or hornblende! He has no sympathy. He goes up and down the world of men, a modern Rhadamanthus in gold-headed cane and peruke, and with nonchalance and the air of a referee, distributes souls. The warm, many-weathered, passionate-peopled world is to him a grammar of hieroglyphs, or an emblematic freemason's procession. How different is Jacob Behmen! *he* is tremulous with emotion and listens awe-struck, with the gentlest humanity, to the Teacher whose lessons he conveys; and when he asserts that, "in some sort, love is greater than God," his heart beats so high that the thumping against his leathern coat is audible across the centuries. 'T is a great difference. Behmen is healthily and beautifully wise, notwithstanding the mystical narrowness and incommunicableness. Swedenborg is disagreeably wise, and with all his accumulated gifts, paralyzes and repels.

It is the best sign of a great nature that it opens a foreground, and, like the breath of morning landscapes, invites us onward. Swedenborg is retrospective, nor can we divest him of his mattock and shroud. Some minds are for ever restrained from descending into nature; others are for ever prevented from ascending out of it. With a force of many men, he could never break the umbilical cord which held him to nature, and he did not rise to the platform of pure genius.

It is remarkable that this man, who, by his perception of symbols, saw the poetic construction of things and the primary relation of mind to matter, remained entirely devoid of the whole apparatus of poetic expression, which that perception creates. He knew the grammar and rudiments of the Mother-Tongue—how could he not read off one strain into music? Was he like Saadi, who, in his vision, designed to fill his lap with the celestial flowers, as presents for his friends; but the fragrance of the roses so intoxicated him that the skirt dropped from his hands? or is reporting a breach of the manners of that heavenly society? or was it that he saw the vision intellectually, and hence that chiding of the intellectual that pervades his books? Be it as it may, his books have no melody, no emotion, no humor, no relief to the dead prosaic level. In his profuse and accurate imagery is no pleasure, for there is no beauty. We wander forlorn in a lack-lustre landscape. No bird ever sang in all these gardens of the dead. The entire want of poetry in so transcendent a mind betokens the disease, and like a hoarse voice in a beautiful person, is a kind of warning. I think, sometimes, he will not be read longer. His great name will turn a sentence. His books have become a monument. His laurel so largely mixed with cypress, a charnel-breath so mingles with the temple incense, that boys and maids will shun the spot.

Yet in this immolation of genius and fame at the shrine of conscience, is a merit sublime beyond praise. He lived to purpose: he gave a verdict. He elected goodness as the clue to which the soul must cling in all this labyrinth of nature. Many opinions conflict as to the true centre. In the shipwreck, some cling to running rigging, some to cask and barrel, some to spars, some to mast; the pilot chooses with science—

I plant myself here; all will sink before this; "he comes to land who sails with me." [6] Do not rely on heavenly favor, or on compassion to folly, or on prudence, on common sense, the old usage and main chance of men: nothing can keep you —not fate, nor health, nor admirable intellect; none can keep you, but rectitude only, rectitude for ever and ever! And with a tenacity that never swerved in all his studies, inventions, dreams, he adheres to this brave choice. I think of him as of some transmigrating votary of Indian legend, who says "Though I be dog, or jackal, or pismire, in the last rudiments of nature, under what integument or ferocity, I cleave to right, as the sure ladder that leads up to man and to God."

Swedenborg has rendered a double service to mankind, which is now only beginning to be known. By the science of experiment and use, he made his first steps: he observed and published the laws of nature; and ascending by just degrees from events to their summits and causes, he was fired with piety at the harmonies he felt, and abandoned himself to his joy and worship. This was his first service. If the glory was too bright for his eyes to bear, if he staggered under the trance of delight, the more excellent is the spectacle he saw, the realities of being which beam and blaze through him, and which no infirmities of the prophet are suffered to obscure; and he renders a second passive service to men, not less than the first, perhaps, in the great circle of being—and, in the retributions of spiritual nature, not less glorious or less beautiful to himself.

---

[6] Nathaniel P. Willis' poem, "Lines on Leaving Europe."

From *Representative Men*

Montaigne; or, the Skeptic

Every fact is related on one side to sensation, and on the other to morals. The game of thought is, on the appearance of one of these two sides, to find the other: given the upper, to find the under side. Nothing so thin but has these two faces, and when the observer has seen the obverse, he turns it over to see the reverse. Life is a pitching of this penny—heads or tails. We never tire of this game, because there is still a slight shudder of astonishment at the exhibition of the other face, at the contrast of the two faces. A man is flushed with success, and bethinks himself what this good luck signifies. He drives his bargain in the street; but it occurs that he also is bought and sold. He sees the beauty of a human face, and searches the cause of that beauty, which must be more beautiful. He builds his fortunes, maintains the laws, cherishes his children; but he asks himself, Why? and whereto? This head and this tail are called, in the language of philosophy, Infinite and Finite; Relative and Absolute; Apparent and Real; and many fine names beside.

Each man is born with a predisposition to one or the other of these sides of nature; and it will easily happen that men will be found devoted to one or the other. One class has the perception of difference, and is conversant with facts and surfaces, cities and persons, and the bringing certain things to pass—the men of talent and action. Another class have the perception of identity, and are men of faith and philosophy, men of genius.

Each of these riders drives too fast. Plotinus believes only in philosophers; Fénelon, in saints; Pindar and Byron, in poets. Read the haughty language in which Plato and the Platonists speak of all men who are not devoted to their own shining abstractions: other men are rats and mice. The literary class is usually proud and exclusive. The correspondence of

157

Pope and Swift describes mankind around them as monsters; and that of Goethe and Schiller, in our own time, is scarcely more kind.

It is easy to see how this arrogance comes. The genius is a genius by the first look he casts on any object. Is his eye creative? Does he not rest in angles and colors, but beholds the design?—he will presently undervalue the actual object. In powerful moments, his thought has dissolved the works of art and nature into their causes, so that the works appear heavy and faulty. He has a conception of beauty which the sculptor cannot embody. Picture, statue, temple, railroad, steam-engine, existed first in an artist's mind, without flaw, mistake, or friction, which impair the executed models. So did the Church, the State, college, court, social circle, and all the institutions. It is not strange that these men, remembering what they have seen and hoped of ideas, should affirm disdainfully the superiority of ideas. Having at some time seen that the happy soul will carry all the arts in power, they say, Why cumber ourselves with superfluous realizations? and like dreaming beggars they assume to speak and act as if these values were already substantiated.

On the other part, the men of toil and trade and luxury—the animal world, including the animal in the philosopher and poet also, and the practical world, including the painful drudgeries which are never excused to philosopher or poet any more than to the rest—weigh heavily on the other side. The trade in our streets believes in no metaphysical causes, thinks nothing of the force which necessitated traders and a trading planet to exist: no, but sticks to cotton, sugar, wool and salt. The ward meetings, on election days, are not softened by any misgiving of the value of these ballotings. Hot life is streaming in a single direction. To the men of this world, to the animal strength and spirits, to the men of practical power, whilst immersed in it, the man of ideas appears out of his reason. They alone have reason.

Things always bring their own philosophy with them, that is, prudence. No man acquires property without acquiring with it a little arithmetic also. In England, the richest country that ever existed, property stands for more, compared with personal ability, than in any other. After dinner, a man believes less, denies more: verities have lost some charm. After dinner, arithmetic is the only science: ideas are disturbing, incendiary, follies of young men, repudiated by the solid portion of society: and a man comes to be valued by his athletic and animal qualities. Spence relates that Mr. Pope was with Sir Godfrey Kneller one day, when his nephew, a Guinea trader, came in. "Nephew," said Sir Godfrey, "you have the honor of seeing the two greatest men in the world." "I don't know how great men you may be," said the Guinea man, "but I don't like your looks. I have often bought a man much better than both of you, all muscles and bones, for ten guineas." Thus the men of the senses revenge themselves on the professors and repay scorn for scorn. The first had leaped to conclusions not yet ripe, and say more than is true; the others make themselves merry with the philosopher, and weigh man by the pound. They believe that mustard bites the tongue, that pepper is hot, friction-matches incendiary, revolvers are to be avoided, and suspenders hold up pantaloons; that there is much sentiment in a chest of tea; and a man will be eloquent, if you give him good wine. Are you tender and scrupulous—you must eat more mince-pie. They hold that Luther had milk in him when he said,

> Wer nicht liebt Wein, Weiber, Gesang,
> Der bleibt ein Narr sein Leben lang;

and when he advised a young scholar, perplexed with foreordination and free-will, to get well drunk. "The nerves," says Cabanis, "they are the man." My neighbor, a jolly farmer, in the tavern bar-room, thinks that the use of money is sure and speedy spending. For his part, he says, he puts his down his neck and gets the good of it.

The inconvenience of this way of thinking is that it runs into indifferentism and then into disgust. Life is eating us up. We shall be fables presently. Keep cool: it will be all one a hundred years hence. Life's well enough, but we shall be glad to get out of it, and they will all be glad to have us. Why should we fret and drudge? Our meat will taste to-morrow as it did yesterday, and we may at last have had enough of it. "Ah," said my languid gentleman at Oxford, "there's nothing new or true—and no matter."

With a little more bitterness, the cynic moans; our life is like an ass led to market by a bundle of hay being carried before him; he sees nothing but the bundle of hay. "There is so much trouble in coming into the world," said Lord Bolingbroke, "and so much more, as well as meanness, in going out of it, that 't is hardly worth while to be here at all." I knew a philosopher of this kidney who was accustomed briefly to sum up his experience of human nature in saying, "Mankind is a damned rascal:" and the natural corollary is pretty sure to follow, "The world lives by humbug, and so will I."

The abstractionist and the materialist thus mutually exasperating each other, and the scoffer expressing the worst of materialism, there arises a third party to occupy the middle ground between these two, the skeptic, namely. He finds both wrong by being in extremes. He labors to plant his feet, to be the beam of the balance. He will not go beyond his card. He sees the one-sidedness of these men of the street; he will not be a Gibeonite; he stands for the intellectual faculties, a cool head and whatever serves to keep it cool; no unadvised industry, no unrewarded self-devotion, no loss of the brains in toil. Am I an ox, or a dray?—You are both in extremes, he says. You that will have all solid, and a world of pig-lead, deceive yourselves grossly. You believe yourselves rooted and grounded on adamant; and yet, if we uncover the last facts of our knowledge, you are spinning like bubbles in a river, you know not whither or whence, and you are bottomed and capped and wrapped in delusions. Neither will he be betrayed to a book and wrapped in a gown. The studious class are their own victims; they are thin and pale, their feet are cold, their heads are hot, the night is without sleep, the day a fear of interruption—pallor, squalor, hunger and egotism. If you come near them and see what conceits they entertain— they are abstractionists, and spend their days and nights in dreaming some dream; in expecting the homage of society to some precious scheme, built on a truth, but destitute of proportion in its presentment, of justness in its application, and of all energy of will in the schemer to embody and vitalize it.

But I see plainly, he says, that I cannot see. I know that human strength is not in extremes, but in avoiding extremes. I, at least, will shun the weakness of philosophizing beyond my depth. What is the use of pretending to powers we have not? What is the use of pretending to assurances we have not, respecting the other life? Why exaggerate the power of virtue? Why be an angel before your time? These strings, wound up too high, will snap. If there is a wish for immortality, and no evidence, why not say just that? If there are conflicting evidences, why not state them? If there is not ground for a candid thinker to make up his mind, yea or nay—why not suspend the judgment? I weary of these dogmatizers. I tire of these hacks of routine, who deny the dogmas. I neither affirm nor deny. I stand here to try the case. I am here to consider, σκοπειν, to consider how it is. I will try to keep the balance true. Of what use to take the chair and glibly rattle off theories of society, religion and nature, when I know that practical objections lie in the way, insurmountable by me and by my mates? Why so talkative in public, when each of my neighbors can pin me to my seat by arguments I cannot refute? Why pretend that life is so simple a game, when we know how subtle and elusive the Proteus is? Why think to shut up all things in your narrow coop, when we know there are not one or two only, but ten, twenty, a thousand things, and unlike? Why fancy that you have all the truth in your keeping? There is much to say on all sides.

Who shall forbid a wise skepticism, seeing that there is no practical question on which any thing more than an approximate solution can be had? Is not marriage an open question, when it is alleged, from the beginning of the world, that such as are in the institution wish to get out, and such as are out wish to get in? And the reply of Socrates, to him who asked whether he should choose a wife, still remains reasonable, that "whether he should choose one or not, he would repent it." Is not the State a question? All society is divided in opinion on the subject of the State. Nobody loves it; great numbers dislike it and suffer conscientious scruples to allegiance; and the only defence set up, is the fear of doing worse in disorganizing. Is it otherwise with the Church? Or, to put any of the questions which touch mankind nearest—shall the young man aim at a leading part in law, in politics, in trade? It will not be pretended that a success in either of these kinds is quite coincident with what is best and inmost in his mind. Shall he then, cutting the stays that hold him fast to the social state, put out to sea with no guidance but his genius? There is much to say on both sides. Remember the open question between the present order of "competition" and the friends of "attractive and associated labor." The generous minds embrace the proposition of labor shared by all; it is the only honesty; nothing else is safe. It is from the poor man's hut alone that strength and virtue come: and yet, on the other side, it is alleged that labor impairs the form and breaks the spirit of man, and the laborers cry unanimously, "We have no thoughts." Culture, how indispensable! I cannot forgive you the want of accomplishments; and yet culture will instantly impair that chiefest beauty of spontaneousness. Excellent is culture for a savage; but once let him read in the book, and he is no longer able not to think of Plutarch's heroes. In short, since true fortitude of understanding consists "in not letting what we know be embarrassed by what we do not know," we ought to secure those advantages which we can command, and not risk them by clutching after the airy and unattainable. Come, no chimeras! Let us go abroad; let us mix in affairs; let us learn and get and have and climb. "Men are a sort of moving plants, and, like trees, receive a great part of their nourishment from the air. If they keep too much at home, they pine." Let us have a robust, manly life; let us know what we know, for certain; what we have, let it be solid and seasonable and our own. A world in the hand is worth two in the bush. Let us have to do with real men and women, and not with skipping ghosts.

This then is the right ground of the skeptic—this of consideration, of self-containing; not at all of unbelief; not at all of universal denying, nor of universal doubting—doubting even that he doubts; least of all of scoffing and profligate jeering at all that is stable and good. These are no more his moods than are those of religion and philosophy. He is the considerer, the prudent, taking in sail, counting stock, husbanding his means, believing that a man has too many enemies than that he can afford to be his own foe; that we cannot give ourselves too many advantages in this unequal conflict, with powers so vast and unweariable ranged on one side, and this little conceited vulnerable popinjay that a man is, bobbing up and down into every danger, on the other. It is a position taken up for better defence, as of more safety, and one that can be maintained; and it is one of more opportunity and range: as, when we build a house, the rule is to set it not too high nor too low, under the wind, but out of the dirt.

The philosophy we want is one of fluxions and mobility. The Spartan and Stoic schemes are too stark and stiff for our occasion. A theory of Saint John, and of non-resistance, seems, on the other hand, too thin and aerial. We want some coat woven of elastic steel, stout as the first and limber as the second. We want a ship in these billows we inhabit. An angular, dogmatic house would be rent to chips and splinters in this storm of many elements. No, it must be tight, and fit to the form of man, to live at all; as a shell must dictate the architecture of a house founded on the sea. The soul of man must be the type of our scheme, just as the body of man is the type after which a dwelling-house is built. Adaptiveness is the peculiarity of human nature. We are golden averages, volitant stabilities, compensated or periodic errors, houses founded on the sea. The wise skeptic wishes to have a near view of the best game and the chief players; what is best in the planet; art and nature, places and events; but mainly men. Every thing that is excellent in mankind—a form of grace, an arm of iron, lips of persuasion, a brain of resources, every one skilful to play and win—he will see and judge.

The terms of admission to this spectacle are, that he have a certain solid and intelligible way of living of his own; some method of answering the inevitable needs of human life; proof that he has played with skill and success; that he has evinced the temper, stoutness and the range of qualities which, among his contemporaries and countrymen, entitle him to fellowship and trust. For the secrets of life are not shown except to sympathy and likeness. Men do not confide themselves to boys, or coxcombs, or pedants, but to their peers. Some wise limitation, as the modern phrase is; some condition between the extremes, and having, itself, a positive quality; some stark and sufficient man, who is not salt or sugar, but sufficiently related to the world to do justice to Paris or London, and, at the same time, a vigorous and original thinker, whom cities can not overawe, but who uses them—is the fit person to occupy this ground of speculation.

These qualities meet in the character of Montaigne. And yet, since the personal regard which I entertain for Montaigne may be unduly great, I will, under the shield of this prince of egotists, offer, as an apology for electing him as the representative of skepticism, a word or two to explain how my love began and grew for this admirable gossip.

A single odd volume of Cotton's translation of the Essays remained to me from my father's library, when a boy. It lay long neglected, until, after many years, when I was newly escaped from college, I read the book, and procured the remaining volumes. I remember the delight and wonder in which I lived with it. It seemed to me as if I had myself written the book, in some former life, so sincerely it spoke to my thought and experience. It happened, when in Paris, in 1833, that, in the cemetery of Père Lachaise, I came to a tomb of Auguste Collignon, who died in 1830, aged sixty-eight years, and who, said the monument, "lived to do right, and had formed himself to virtue on the Essays of Montaigne." Some years later, I became acquainted with an accomplished English poet, John Sterling; and, in prosecuting my correspondence, I found that, from a love of Montaigne, he had made a pilgrimage to his chateau, still standing near Castellan, in Périgord, and, after two hundred and fifty years, had copied from the walls of his library the inscriptions which Montaigne had written there. That Journal of Mr. Sterling's, published in the Westminster Review, Mr. Hazlitt has reprinted in the *Prolegomena* to his edition of the Essays. I heard with pleasure that one of the newly-discovered autographs of William Shakspeare was in a copy of Florio's translation of Montaigne. It is the only book which we certainly know to have been in the poet's library. And, oddly enough, the duplicate copy of Florio, which the British Museum purchased with a view of protecting the Shakspeare autograph (as I was informed in the Museum), turned out to have the autograph of Ben Jonson in the fly-leaf. Leigh Hunt relates of Lord Byron, that Montaigne was the only great writer of past times whom he read with avowed satisfaction. Other coincidences, not needful to be mentioned here, concurred to make this old Gascon still new and immortal for me.

In 1571, on the death of his father, Montaigne, then thirty-eight years old, retired from the practice of law at Bordeaux, and settled himself on his estate. Though he had been a man of pleasure and sometimes a courtier, his studious habits now grew on him, and he loved the compass, staidness and independence of the country gentleman's life. He took up his economy in good earnest, and made his farms yield the most. Downright and plain-dealing, and abhorring to be deceived or to deceive, he was esteemed in the country for his sense and probity. In the civil wars of the League, which converted every house into a fort, Montaigne kept his gates open and his house without defence. All parties freely came and went, his courage and honor being universally esteemed. The neighboring lords and gentry brought jewels and papers to him for safe-keeping. Gibbon reckons, in these bigoted times, but two men of liberality in France—Henry IV. and Montaigne.

Montaigne is the frankest and honestest of all writers. His French freedom runs into grossness; but he has anticipated all censure by the bounty of his own confessions. In his times, books were written to one sex only, and almost all were written in Latin; so that in a humorist a certain nakedness of statement was permitted, which our manners, of a literature addressed equally to both sexes, do not allow. But though a biblical plainness coupled with a most uncanonical levity may shut his pages to many sensitive readers, yet the offence is superficial. He parades it: he makes the most of it: nobody can think or say worse of him than he does. He pretends to most of the vices; and, if there be any virtue in him, he says, it got in by stealth. There is no man, in his opinion, who has not deserved hanging five or six times; and he pretends no exception in his own behalf. "Five or six as ridiculous stories," too, he says, "can be told of me, as of any man living." But, with all this really superfluous frankness, the opinion of an invincible probity grows into every reader's mind. "When I the most strictly and religiously confess myself, I find that the best virtue I have has in it some tincture of vice; and I, who am as sincere and perfect a lover of virtue of that stamp as any other whatever, am afraid that Plato, in his purest virtue, if he had listened and laid his ear close to himself, would have heard some jarring sound of human mixture; but faint and remote and only to be perceived by himself."

Here is an impatience and fastidiousness a color or pretence of any kind. He has been in courts so long as to have conceived a furious disgust at appearances; he will indulge himself with a little cursing and swearing; he will talk with sailors and gipsies, use flash and street ballads; he has stayed in-doors till he is deadly sick; he will to the open air, though it rain bullets. He has seen too much of gentlemen of the long robe, until he wishes for cannibals; and is so nervous, by factitious life, that he thinks the more barbarous man is, the better he is. He likes his saddle. You may read theology, and grammar, and metaphysics elsewhere. Whatever you get here shall smack of the earth and of real life, sweet, or smart, or stinging. He makes no hesitation to entertain you with the records of his disease, and his journey to Italy is quite full of that matter. He took and kept this position of equilibrium. Over his name he drew an emblematic pair of scales, and wrote *Que sçais je?* under it. As I look at his effigy opposite the title-page, I seem to hear him say, "You may play old Poz, if you will; you may rail and exaggerate—I stand here for truth, and will not, for all the states and churches and revenues and personal reputations of Europe, overstate the dry fact, as I see it; I will rather mumble and prose about what I certainly know—my house and barns; my father, my wife and my tenants; my old lean bald pate; my knives and forks; what meats I eat and what drinks I prefer, and a hundred straws just as ridiculous— than I will write, with a fine crow-quill, a fine romance. I like gray days, and autumn and winter weather. I am gray and autumnal myself, and think an undress and old shoes that do not pinch my feet, and old friends who do not constrain me, and plain topics where I do not need to strain myself and pump my brains, the most suitable. Our condition as men is risky and ticklish enough. One cannot be sure of himself and his fortune an hour, but he may be whisked off into some pitiable or ridiculous plight. Why should I vapor and play the philosopher, instead of ballasting, the best I can, this dancing balloon? So, at least, I live within compass, keep myself ready for action, and can shoot the gulf at last with decency. If there be anything farcical in such a life, the blame is not mine: let it lie at fate's and nature's door."

The Essays, therefore, are an entertaining soliloquy on every random topic that comes into his head; treating everything without ceremony, yet with masculine sense. There have been men with deeper insight; but, one would say, never a man with such abundance of thoughts: he is never dull, never insincere, and has the genius to make the reader care for all that he cares for.

The sincerity and marrow of the man reaches to his sentences. I know not anywhere the book that seems less written. It is the language of conversation transferred to a book. Cut these words, and they would bleed; they are vascular and alive. One has the same pleasure in it that he feels in listening to the necessary speech of men about their work, when any unusual circumstance gives momentary importance to the dialogue. For blacksmiths and teamsters do not trip in their speech; it is a shower of bullets. It is Cambridge men who correct themselves and begin again at every half sentence, and, moreover, will pun, and refine too much, and swerve from the matter to the expression. Montaigne talks with shrewdness, knows the world and books and himself, and uses the positive degree; never shrieks, or protests, or prays: no weakness, no convulsion, no superlative: does not wish to jump out of his skin, or play any antics, or annihilate space or time, but is stout and solid; tastes every moment of the day; likes pain because it makes him feel himself and realize things; as we pinch ourselves to know that we are awake. He keeps the plain; he rarely mounts or sinks; likes to feel solid ground and the stones underneath. His writing has no enthusiasms, no aspiration; contented, self-respecting and keeping the middle of the road. There is but one exception—in his love for Socrates. In speaking of him, for once his cheek flushes and his style rises to passion.

Montaigne died of a quinsy, at the age of sixty, in 1592. When he came to die he caused the mass to be celebrated in his chamber. At the age of thirty-three, he had been married. "But," he says, "might I have had my own will, I would not have married Wisdom herself, if she would have had me: but 't is to much purpose to evade it, the common custom and use of life will have it so. Most of my actions are guided by example, not choice." In the hour of death, he gave the same weight to custom. *Que sçais je?* What do I know?

This book of Montaigne the world has endorsed by translating it into all tongues and printing seventy-five editions of it in Europe; and that, too, a circulation somewhat chosen, namely among courtiers, soldiers, princes, men of the world and men of wit and generosity.

Shall we say that Montaigne has spoken wisely, and given the right and permanent expression of the human mind, on the conduct of life?

We are natural believers. Truth, or the connection between cause and effect, alone interests us. We are persuaded that a thread runs through all things: all worlds are strung on it, as beads; and men, and events, and life, come to us only because of that thread: they pass and repass only that we may know the direction and continuity of that line. A book or statement which goes to show that there is no line, but random and chaos, a calamity out of nothing, a prosperity and no account of it, a hero born from a fool, a fool from a hero—dispirits us. Seen or unseen, we believe the tie exists. Talent makes counterfeit ties; genius finds the real ones. We hearken to the man of science, because we anticipate the sequence in natural phenomena which he uncovers. We love whatever affirms, connects, preserves; and dislike what scatters or pulls down. One man appears whose nature is to all men's eyes conserving and constructive; his presence supposes a well-ordered society, agriculture, trade, large institutions and empire. If these did not exist, they would begin to exist through his endeavors. Therefore he cheers and comforts men, who feel all this in him very readily. The nonconformist and the rebel say all manner of unanswerable things against the existing republic, but discover to our sense no plan of house or state of their own. Therefore, though the town and state and way of living, which our counsellor contemplated, might be a very modest or musty prosperity, yet men rightly go for him, and reject the reformer so long as he comes only with axe and crowbar.

But though we are natural conservers and causationists, and reject a sour, dumpish unbelief, the skeptical class, which Montaigne represents, have reason, and every man, at some time, belongs to it. Every superior mind will pass through this domain of equilibration—I should rather say, will know how to avail himself of the checks and balances in nature as a natural weapon against the exaggeration and formalism of bigots and blockheads.

Skepticism is the attitude assumed by the student in relation to the particulars which society adores, but which he sees to be reverend only in their tendency and spirit. The ground occupied by the skeptic is the vestibule of the temple. Society does not like to have any breath of question blown on the existing order. But the interrogation of custom at all points is an inevitable stage in the growth of every superior mind, and is the evidence of its perception of the flowing power which remains itself in all changes.

The superior mind will find itself equally at odds with the evils of society and with the projects that are offered to relieve them. The wise skeptic is a bad citizen; no conservative, he sees the selfishness of property and the drowsiness of institutions. But neither is he fit to work with any democratic party that ever was constituted; for parties wish every one committed and he penetrates the popular patriotism. His politics are those of the "Soul's Errand" of Sir Walter Raleigh; or of Krishna, in the Bhagavat, "There is none who is worthy of my love or hatred;" whilst he sentences law, physic, divinity, commerce and custom. He is a reformer; yet he is no better member of the philanthropic association. It turns out that he is not the champion of the operative, the pauper, the prisoner, the slave. It stands in his mind that our life in this world is not of quite so easy interpretation as churches and schoolbooks say. He does not wish to take ground against these benevolences, to play the part of devil's attorney, and blazon every doubt and sneer that darkens the sun for him. But he says, There are doubts.

I mean to use the occasion, and celebrate the calendar-day of our Saint Michel de Montaigne, by counting and describing these doubts or negations. I wish to ferret them out of their holes and sun them a little. We must do with them as the police do with old rogues, who are shown up to the public at the marshal's office. They will never be so formidable when once they have been identified and registered. But I mean honestly by them—that justice shall be done to their terrors. I shall not take Sunday objections, made up on purpose to be put down. I shall take the worst I can find, whether I can dispose of them or they of me.

I do not press the skepticism of the materialist. I know the quadruped opinion will not prevail. 'T is of no importance what bats and oxen think. The first dangerous symptom I report is, the levity of intellect; as if it were fatal to earnestness to know much. Knowledge is the knowing that we can not know. The dull pray; the geniuses are light mockers. How respectable is earnestness on every platform! but intellect kills it. Nay, San Carlo, my subtle and admirable friend, one of the most penetrating of men, finds that all direct ascension, even of lofty piety, leads to this ghastly insight and sends back the votary orphaned. My astonishing San Carlo thought the lawgivers and saints infected. They found the ark empty; saw, and would not tell; and tried to choke off their approaching followers, by saying, "Action, action, my dear fellows, is for you!" Bad as was to me this detection by San Carlo, this frost in July, this blow from a bride, there was still a worse, namely the cloy or satiety of the saints. In the mount of vision, ere they have yet risen from their knees, they say, "We discover that this our homage and beatitude is partial and deformed: we must fly for relief to the suspected and reviled Intellect, to the Understanding, the Mephistopheles, to the gymnastics of talent."

This is hobgoblin the first; and though it has been the subject of much elegy in our nineteenth century, from Byron, Goethe and other poets of less fame, not to mention many distinguished private observers—I confess it is not very affecting to my imagination; for it seems to concern the shattering of baby-houses and crockery-shops. What flutters the Church of Rome, or of England, or of Geneva, or of Boston, may yet be very far from touching any principle of faith. I think that the intellect and moral sentiment are unanimous; and that though philosophy extirpates bugbears, yet it supplies the natural checks of vice, and polarity to the soul. I think that the wiser a man is, the more stupendous he finds the natural and moral economy, and lifts himself to a more absolute reliance.

There is the power of moods, each setting at nought all but its own tissue of facts and beliefs. There is the power of complexions, obviously modifying the dispositions and sentiments. The beliefs and unbeliefs appear to be structural; and as soon as each man attains the poise and vivacity which allow the whole machinery to play, he will not need extreme examples, but will rapidly alternate all opinions in his own life. Our life is March weather, savage and serene in one hour. We go forth austere, dedicated, believing in the iron links of Destiny, and will not turn on our heel to save our life: but a book, or a bust, or only the sound of a name, shoots a spark through the nerves, and we suddenly believe in will: my finger-ring shall be the seal of Solomon; fate is for imbeciles; all is possible to the resolved mind. Presently a new experience gives a new turn to our thoughts: common sense resumes its tyranny; we say, "Well, the army, after all, is the gate to fame, manners and poetry: and, look you—on the whole, selfishness plants best, prunes best, makes the best commerce and the best citizen." Are the opinions of a man on right and wrong, on fate and causation, at the mercy of a broken sleep or an indigestion? Is his belief in God and Duty no deeper than a stomach evidence? And what guaranty for

the permanence of his opinions? I like not the French celerity
—a new Church and State once a week. This is the second
negation; and I shall let it pass for what it will. As far as it
asserts rotation of states of mind, I suppose it suggests its
own remedy, namely in the record of larger periods. What is
the mean of many states; of all the states? Does the general
voice of ages affirm any principle, or is no community of sentiment discoverable in distant times and places? And when it
shows the power of self-interest, I accept that as part of the
divine law and must reconcile it with aspiration the best I can.

The word Fate, or Destiny, expresses the sense of mankind,
in all ages, that the laws of the world do not always befriend,
but often hurt and crush us. Fate, in the shape of *Kinde* or
nature, grows over us like grass. We paint Time with a
scythe; Love and Fortune, blind; and Destiny, deaf. We have
too little power of resistance against this ferocity which
champs us up. What front can we make against these un-
avoidable, victorious, maleficent forces? What can I do
against the influence of Race, in my history? What can I do
against hereditary and constitutional habits; against scrofula,
lymph, impotence? against climate, against barbarism, in my
country? I can reason down or deny every thing, except this
perpetual Belly: feed he must and will, and I cannot make
him respectable.

But the main resistance which the affirmative impulse finds,
and one including all others, is in the doctrine of the Illu-
sionists. There is a painful rumor in circulation that we have
been practised upon in all the principal performances of life,
and free agency is the emptiest name. We have been sopped
and drugged with the air, with food, with woman, with children, with sciences, with events, which leave us exactly
where they found us. The mathematics, 't is complained,
leave the mind where they find it: so do all sciences; and so
do all events and actions. I find a man who has passed
through all the sciences, the churl he was; and, through all
the offices, learned, civil and social, can detect the child.
We are not the less necessitated to dedicate life to them.
In fact we may come to accept it as the fixed rule and
theory of our state of education, that God is a substance, and
his method is illusion. The Eastern sages owned the goddess

Yoganidra, the great illusory energy of Vishnu, by whom, as utter ignorance, the whole world is beguiled.

Or shall I state it thus? The astonishment of life is the absence of any appearance of reconciliation between the theory and practice of life. Reason, the prized reality, the Law, is apprehended, now and then, for a serene and profound moment amidst the hubbub of cares and works which have no direct bearing on it—is then lost for months or years, and again found for an interval, to be lost again. If we compute it in time, we may, in fifty years, have half a dozen reasonable hours. But what are these cares and works the better? A method in the world we do not see, but this parallelism of great and little, which never react on each other, nor discover the smallest tendency to converge. Experiences, fortunes, governings, readings, writings, are nothing to the purpose; as when a man comes into the room it does not appear whether he has been fed on yams or buffalo—he has contrived to get so much bone and fibre as he wants, out of rice or out of snow. So vast is the disproportion between the sky of law and the pismire of performance under it, that whether he is a man of worth or a sot is not so great a matter as we say. Shall I add, as one juggle of this enchantment, the stunning non-intercourse law which makes cooperation impossible? The young spirit pants to enter society. But all the ways of culture and greatness lead to solitary imprisonment. He has been often baulked. He did not expect a sympathy with his thought from the village, but he went with it to the chosen and intelligent, and found no entertainment for it, but mere misapprehension, distaste and scoffing. Men are strangely mistimed and misapplied; and the excellence of each is an inflamed individualism which separates him more.

There are these, and more than these diseases of thought, which our ordinary teachers do not attempt to remove. Now shall we, because a good nature inclines us to virtue's side, say, There are no doubts—and lie for the right? Is life to be led in a brave or in a cowardly manner? and is not the satisfaction of the doubts essential to all manliness? Is the name of virtue to be a barrier to that which is virtue? Can you not believe that a man of earnest and burly habit may find small good in tea, essays and catechism, and want a rougher instruction, want men, labor, trade, farming, war, hunger, plenty, love, hatred, doubt and terror to make things plain to him; and has he not a right to insist on being convinced in his own way? When he is convinced, he will be worth the pains.

Belief consists in accepting the affirmations of the soul; unbelief, in denying them. Some minds are incapable of skepticism. The doubts they profess to entertain are rather a civility or accommodation to the common discourse of their company. They may well give themselves leave to speculate, for they are secure of a return. Once admitted to the heaven of thought, they see no relapse into night, but infinite invitation on the other side. Heaven is within heaven, and sky over sky, and they are encompassed with divinities. Others there are to whom the heaven is brass, and it shuts down to the surface of the earth. It is a question of temperament, or of more or less immersion in nature. The last class must needs have a reflex or parasite faith; not a sight of realities, but an instinctive reliance on the seers and believers of realities. The manners and thoughts of believers astonish them and convince them that these have seen something which is hid from themselves. But their sensual habit would fix the believer to his last position, whilst he as inevitably advances; and presently the unbeliever, for love of belief, burns the believer.

Great believers are always reckoned infidels, impracticable, fantastic, atheistic, and really men of no account. The spiritualist finds himself driven to express his faith by a series of skepticisms. Charitable souls come with their projects and ask his co-operation. How can he hesitate? It is the rule of mere comity and courtesy to agree where you can, and to turn your sentence with something auspicious, and not freezing and sinister. But he is forced to say, "O, these things will be as they must be: what can you do? These particular griefs and crimes are the foliage and fruit of such trees as we see growing. It is vain to complain of the leaf or the berry; cut it off, it will bear another just as bad. You must begin your cure lower down." The generosities of the day prove an intractable element for him. The people's questions are not his; their methods are not his; and against all the dictates of good nature he is driven to say he has no pleasure in them.

Even the doctrines dear to the hope of man, of the divine

Providence and of the immortality of the soul, his neighbors can not put the statement so that he shall affirm it. But he denies out of more faith, and not less. He denies out of honesty. He had rather stand charged with the imbecility of skepticism, than with untruth. I believe, he says, in the moral design of the universe; it exists hospitably for the weal of souls; but your dogmas seem to me caricatures: why should I make believe them? Will any say, This is cold and infidel? The wise and magnanimous will not say so. They will exult in his far-sighted good-will that can abandon to the adversary all the ground of tradition and common belief, without losing a jot of strength. It sees to the end of all transgression. George Fox saw that there was "an ocean of darkness and death; but withal an infinite ocean of light and love which flowed over that of darkness."

The final solution in which skepticism is lost, is in the moral sentiment, which never forfeits its supremacy. All moods may be safely tried, and their weight allowed to all objections: the moral sentiment as easily outweighs them all, as any one. This is the drop which balances the sea. I play with the miscellany of facts, and take those superficial views which we call skepticism; but I know that they will presently appear to me in that order which makes skepticism impossible. A man of thought must feel the thought that is parent of the universe; that the masses of nature do undulate and flow.

This faith avails to the whole emergency of life and objects. The world is saturated with deity and with law. He is content with just and unjust, with sots and fools, with the triumph of folly and fraud. He can behold with serenity the yawning gulf between the ambition of man and his power of performance, between the demand and supply of power, which makes the tragedy of all souls.

Charles Fourier announced that "the attractions of man are proportioned to his destinies;" in other words, that every desire predicts its own satisfaction. Yet all experience exhibits the reverse of this; the incompetency of power is the universal grief of young and ardent minds. They accuse the divine Providence of a certain parsimony. It has shown the heaven and earth to every child and filled him with a desire for the whole; a desire raging, infinite; a hunger, as of space to be filled with planets; a cry of famine, as of devils for souls.

Then for the satisfaction—to each man is administered a single drop, a bead of dew of vital power, *per day*—a cup as large as space, and one drop of the water of life in it. Each man woke in the morning with an appetite that could eat the solar system like a cake; a spirit for action and passion without bounds; he could lay his hand on the morning star; he could try conclusions with gravitation or chemistry; but, on the first motion to prove his strength—hands, feet, senses, gave way and would not serve him. He was an emperor deserted by his states, and left to whistle by himself, or thrust into a mob of emperors, all whistling: and still the sirens sang, "The attractions are proportioned to the destinies." In every house, in the heart of each maiden and of each boy, in the soul of the soaring saint, this chasm is found—between the largest promise of ideal power, and the shabby experience.

The expansive nature of truth comes to our succor, elastic, not to be surrounded. Man helps himself by larger generalizations. The lesson of life is practically to generalize; to believe what the years and the centuries say, against the hours; to resist the usurpation of particulars; to penetrate to their catholic sense. Things seem to say one thing, and say the reverse. The appearance is immoral; the result is moral. Things seem to tend downward, to justify despondency, to promote rogues, to defeat the just; and by knaves as by martyrs the just cause is carried forward. Although knaves win in every political struggle, although society seems to be delivered over from the hands of one set of criminals into the hands of another set of criminals, as fast as the government is changed, and the march of civilization is a train of felonies—yet, general ends are somehow answered. We see, now, events forced on which seem to retard or retrograde the civility of ages. But the world-spirit is a good swimmer, and storms and waves cannot drown him. He snaps his finger at laws: and so, throughout history, heaven seems to affect low and poor means. Through the years and the centuries, through evil agents, through toys and atoms, a great and beneficent tendency irresistibly streams.

Let a man learn to look for the permanent in the mutable and fleeting; let him learn to bear the disappearance of things he was wont to reverence without losing his reverence; let him learn that he is here, not to work but to be worked upon;

and that, though abyss open under abyss, and opinion displace opinion, all are at last contained in the Eternal Cause:

If my bark sink, 't is to another sea.[1]

_____

[1] Channing's poem, "A Poet's Hope."

From *Representative Men*

Part Three

NATURE

Introduction

Our age is retrospective. It builds the sepulchres of the fathers. It writes biographies, histories, and criticism. The foregoing generations beheld God and nature face to face; we, through their eyes. Why should not we also enjoy an original relation to the universe? Why should not we have a poetry and philosophy of insight and not of tradition, and a religion by revelation to us, and not the history of theirs? Embosomed for a season in nature, whose floods of life stream around and through us, and invite us, by the powers they supply, to action proportioned to nature, why should we grope among the dry bones of the past, or put the living generation into masquerade out of its faded wardrobe? The sun shines to-day also. There is more wool and flax in the fields. There are new lands, new men, new thoughts. Let us demand our own works and laws and worship.

Undoubtedly we have no questions to ask which are unanswerable. We must trust the perfection of the creation so far as to believe that whatever curiosity the order of things has awakened in our minds, the order of things can satisfy. Every man's condition is a solution in hieroglyphic to those inquiries he would put. He acts it as life, before he apprehends it as truth. In like manner, nature is already, in its forms and tendencies, describing its own design. Let us interrogate the great apparition that shines so peacefully around us. Let us inquire, to what end is nature?

All science has one aim, namely, to find a theory of nature. We have theories of races and of functions, but scarcely yet a remote approach to an idea of creation. We are now so far from the road to truth, that religious teachers dispute and hate each other, and speculative men are esteemed unsound and frivolous. But to a sound judgment, the most abstract truth is the most practical. Whenever a true theory appears,

179

it will be its own evidence. Its test is, that it will explain all phenomena. Now many are thought not only unexplained but inexplicable; as language, sleep, madness, dreams, beasts, sex.

Philosophically considered, <u>the universe is composed of Nature and the Soul</u>. Strictly speaking, therefore, all that is separate from us, all which Philosophy distinguishes as the NOT ME, that is, both nature and art, all other men and my own body, must be ranked under this name, NATURE. In enumerating the values of nature and casting up their sum, I shall use the word in both senses—in its common and in its philosophical import. In inquiries so general as our present one, the inaccuracy is not material; no confusion of thought will occur. <u>*Nature,* in the common sense, refers to essences unchanged by man; space, the air, the river, the leaf.</u> *Art* is applied to the mixture of his will with the same things, as in a house, a canal, a statue, a picture. But his operations taken together are so insignificant, a little chipping, baking, patching, and washing, that in an impression so grand as that of the world on the human mind, they do not vary the result.

Nature

I

To go into solitude, a man needs to retire as much from his chamber as from society. I am not solitary whilst I read and write, though nobody is with me. <u>But if a man would be alone, let him look at the stars.</u> The rays that come from those heavenly worlds will separate between him and what he touches. One might think the atmosphere was made transparent with this design, to give man, in the heavenly bodies, the perpetual presence of the sublime. Seen in the streets of cities, how great they are! <u>If the stars should appear one night in a thousand years, how would men believe and adore;</u> and preserve for many generations the remembrance of the city of God which had been shown! But every night come out these envoys of beauty, and light the universe with their admonishing smile.

The stars awaken a certain reverence, because though always present, they are inaccessible; but all natural objects make a kindred impression, when the mind is open to their influence. Nature never wears a mean appearance. Neither does the wisest man extort her secret, and lose his curiosity by finding out all her perfection. Nature never became a toy to a wise spirit. The flowers, the animals, the mountains, reflected the wisdom of his best hour, as much as they had delighted the simplicity of his childhood.

When we speak of nature in this manner, we have a distinct but most poetical sense in the mind. We mean the integrity of impression made by manifold natural objects. It is this which distinguishes the stick of timber of the wood-cutter from the tree of the poet. The charming landscape which I saw this morning is indubitably made up of some twenty or thirty farms. Miller owns this field, Locke that, and Manning the woodland beyond. But none of them owns the landscape. There is a property in the horizon which no man has but he whose eye can integrate all the parts, that is, the poet. This is the best part of these men's farms, yet to this their warranty-deeds give no title.

To speak truly, few adult persons can see nature. Most persons do not see the sun. At least they have a very superficial seeing. The sun illuminates only the eye of the man, but shines into the eye and the heart of the child. The lover of nature is he whose inward and outward senses are still truly adjusted to each other; who has retained the spirit of infancy even into the era of manhood. His intercourse with heaven and earth becomes part of his daily food. In the presence of nature a wild delight runs through the man, in spite of real sorrows. Nature says—he is my creature, and maugre all his impertinent griefs, he shall be glad with me. Not the sun or the summer alone, but every hour and season yields its tribute of delight; for every hour and change corresponds to and authorizes a different state of the mind, from breathless noon to grimmest midnight. Nature is a setting that fits equally well a comic or a mourning piece. In good health, the air is a cordial of incredible virtue. Crossing a bare common, in snow puddles, at twilight, under a clouded sky, without having in my thoughts any occurrence of special good fortune, I have enjoyed a perfect exhilaration. I am glad to the brink of fear. In the woods, too, a man casts off his years, as the snake his slough, and at what period soever of life is always a child. In the woods is perpetual youth. Within these plantations of God, a decorum and sanctity reign, a perennial festival is dressed, and the guest sees not how he should tire of them in a thousand years. In the woods, we return to reason and faith. There I feel that nothing can befall me in life—no disgrace, no calamity (leaving me my eyes), which nature cannot repair. Standing on the bare ground—my head bathed by the blithe air and uplifted into infinite space—all mean egotism vanishes. I become a transparent eyeball; I am nothing; I see all; the currents of the Universal Being circulate through me; I am part or parcel of God. The name of the nearest friend sounds then foreign and accidental: to be brothers, to be acquaintances, master or servant, is then a trifle and a disturbance. I am the lover of uncontained and immortal beauty. In the wilderness, I find something more dear and connate than in streets or villages. In the tranquil landscape, and especially in the distant line of the horizon, man beholds somewhat as beautiful as his own nature.

The greatest delight which the fields and woods minister is the suggestion of an occult relation between man and the vegetable. I am not alone and unacknowledged. They nod to me, and I to them. The waving of the boughs in the storm is new to me and old. It takes me by surprise, and yet is not unknown. Its effect is like that of a higher thought or a better emotion coming over me, when I deemed I was thinking justly or doing right.

Yet it is certain that the power to produce this delight does not reside in nature, but in man, or in a harmony of both. It is necessary to use these pleasures with great temperance. For nature is not always tricked in holiday attire, but the same scene which yesterday breathed perfume and glittered as for the frolic of the nymphs is overspread with melancholy to-day. Nature always wears the colors of the spirit. To a man laboring under calamity, the heat of his own fire hath sadness in it. Then there is a kind of contempt of the landscape felt by him who has just lost by death a dear friend. The sky is less grand as it shuts down over less worth in the population.

Commodity

II

Whoever considers the final cause of the world will discern a multitude of uses that enter as parts into that result. They all admit of being thrown into one of the following classes: Commodity; Beauty; Language; and Discipline.

Under the general name of commodity, I rank all those advantages which our senses owe to nature. This, of course, is a benefit which is temporary and mediate, not ultimate, like its service to the soul. Yet although low, it is perfect in its kind, and is the only use of nature which all men apprehend. The misery of man appears like childish petulance, when we explore the steady and prodigal provision that has been made for his support and delight on this green ball which floats him through the heavens. What angels invented these splendid ornaments, these rich conveniences, this ocean of air above, this ocean of water beneath, this firmament of earth between? this zodiac of lights, this tent of dropping clouds, this striped coat of climates, this fourfold year? Beasts, fire, water, stones, and corn serve him. The field is at once his floor, his work-yard, his play-ground, his garden, and his bed.

> More servants wait on man
> Than he'll take notice of.[1]

Nature, in its ministry to man, is not only the material, but is also the process and the result. All the parts incessantly

---

[1] George Herbert's poem "Man."

work into each other's hands for the profit of man. The wind sows the seed; the sun evaporates the sea; the wind blows the vapor to the field; the ice, on the other side of the planet, condenses rain on this; the rain feeds the plant; the plant feeds the animal; and thus the endless circulations of the divine charity nourish man.

The useful arts are reproductions or new combinations by the wit of man, of the same natural benefactors. He no longer waits for favoring gales, but by means of steam, he realizes the fable of Æolus's bag, and carries the two and thirty winds in the boiler of his boat. To diminish friction, he paves the road with iron bars, and, mounting a coach with a ship-load of men, animals, and merchandise behind him, he darts through the country, from town to town, like an eagle or a swallow through the air. By the aggregate of these aids, how is the face of the world changed, from the era of Noah to that of Napoleon! The private poor man hath cities, ships, canals, bridges, built for him. He goes to the post-office, and the human race run on his errands; to the book-shop, and the human race read and write of all that happens for him; to the court-house, and nations repair his wrongs. He sets his house upon the road, and the human race go forth every morning, and shovel out the snow, and cut a path for him.

But there is no need of specifying particulars in this class of uses. The catalogue is endless, and the examples so obvious, that I shall leave them to the reader's reflection, with the general remark, that this mercenary benefit is one which has respect to a farther good. A man is fed, not that he may be fed, but that he may work,

Beauty

III

A nobler want of man is served by nature, namely, the love of Beauty.

The ancient Greeks called the world κόσμος, beauty. Such is the constitution of all things, or such the plastic power of the human eye, that the primary forms, as the sky, the mountain, the tree, the animal, give us a delight *in and for themselves;* a pleasure arising from outline, color, motion, and grouping. This seems partly owing to the eye itself. The eye is the best of artists. By the mutual action of its structure and of the laws of light, perspective is produced, which integrates every mass of objects, of what character soever, into a well colored and shaded globe, so that where the particular objects are mean and unaffecting, the landscape which they compose is round and symmetrical. And as the eye is the best composer, so light is the first of painters. There is no object so foul that intense light will not make beautiful. And the stimulus it affords to the sense, and a sort of infinitude which it hath, like space and time, make all matter gay. Even the corpse has its own beauty. But besides this general grace diffused over nature, almost all the individual forms are agreeable to the eye, as is proved by our endless imitations of some of them, as the acorn, the grape, the pine-cone, the wheat-ear, the egg, the wings and forms of most birds, the lion's claw, the serpent, the butterfly, sea-shells, flames, clouds, buds, leaves, and the forms of many trees, as the palm.

For better consideration, we may distribute the aspects of Beauty in a threefold manner.

1. First, the simple perception of natural forms is a delight. The influence of the forms and actions in nature is so needful to man, that, in its lowest functions, it seems to lie on the confines of commodity and beauty. To the body and mind which have been cramped by noxious work or company,

nature is medicinal and restores their tone. The tradesman, the attorney, comes out of the din and craft of the street and sees the sky and the woods, and is a man again. In their eternal calm, he finds himself. The health of the eye seems to demand a horizon. We are never tired, so long as we can see far enough.

But in other hours, Nature satisfies by its loveliness, and without any mixture of corporeal benefit. I see the spectacle of morning from the hilltop over against my house, from daybreak to sunrise with emotions which an angel might share. The long slender bars of cloud float like fishes in the sea of crimson light. From the earth, as a shore, I look out into that silent sea. I seem to partake its rapid transformations; the active enchantment reaches my dust, and I dilate and conspire with the morning wind. How does Nature deify us with a few and cheap elements! Give me health and a day, and I will make the pomp of emperors ridiculous. The dawn is my Assyria; the sunset and moonrise my Paphos, and unimaginable realms of faerie; broad noon shall be my England of the senses and the understanding; the night shall be my Germany of mystic philosophy and dreams.

Not less excellent, except for our less susceptibility in the afternoon, was the charm, last evening, of a January sunset. The western clouds divided and subdivided themselves into pink flakes modulated with tints of unspeakable softness, and the air had so much life and sweetness that it was a pain to come within doors. What was it that nature would say? Was there no meaning in the live repose of the valley behind the mill, and which Homer or Shakspeare could not re-form for me in words? The leafless trees become spires of flame in the sunset, with the blue east for their background, and the stars of the dead calices of flowers, and every withered stem and stubble rimed with frost, contribute something to the mute music.

The inhabitants of cities suppose that the country landscape is pleasant only half the year. I please myself with the graces of the winter scenery, and believe that we are as much touched by it as by the genial influences of summer. To the attentive eye, each moment of the year has its own beauty, and in the same field, it beholds, every hour, a picture which was never seen before, and which shall never be seen again. The heavens change every moment, and reflect their glory or gloom on the plains beneath. The state of the crop in the surrounding farms alters the expression of the earth from week to week. The succession of native plants in the pastures and roadsides, which makes the silent clock by which time tells the summer hours, will make even the divisions of the day sensible to a keen observer. The tribes of birds and insects, like the plants punctual to their time, follow each other, and the year has room for all. By water-courses, the variety is greater. In July, the blue pontederia or pickerel-weed blooms in large beds in the shallow parts of our pleasant river, and swarms with yellow butterflies in continual motion. Art cannot rival this pomp of purple and gold. Indeed the river is a perpetual gala, and boasts each month a new ornament.

But this beauty of Nature which is seen and felt as beauty, is the least part. The shows of day, the dewy morning, the rainbow, mountains, orchards in blossom, stars, moonlight, shadows in still water, and the like, if too eagerly hunted, become shows merely, and mock us with their unreality. Go out of the house to see the moon, and 't is mere tinsel; it will not please as when its light shines upon your necessary journey. The beauty that shimmers in the yellow afternoons of October, who ever could clutch it? Go forth to find it, and it is gone; 't is only a mirage as you look from the windows of diligence.

2. The presence of a higher, namely, of the spiritual element is essential to its perfection. The high and divine beauty which can be loved without effeminacy, is that which is found in combination with the human will. Beauty is the mark God sets upon virtue. Every natural action is graceful. Every heroic act is also decent, and causes the place and the bystanders to shine. We are taught by great actions that the universe is the property of every individual in it. Every rational creature has all nature for his dowry and estate. It is his, if he will. He may divest himself of it; he may creep into a corner, and abdicate his kingdom, as most men do, but he is entitled to the world by his constitution. In proportion to the energy of his thought and will, he takes up the world into himself. "All those things for which men plough, build, or sail, obey virtue;" said Sallust. "The winds and waves," said Gibbon, "are always on the side of the ablest navigators." So are the sun and moon and all the stars of heaven. When

a noble act is done—perchance in a scene of great natural beauty; when Leonidas and his three hundred martyrs consume one day in dying, and the sun and moon come each and look at them once in the steep defile of Thermopylæ; when Arnold Winkelried, in the high Alps, under the shadow of the avalanche, gathers in his side a sheaf of Austrian spears to break the line for his comrades; are not these heroes entitled to add the beauty of the scene to the beauty of the deed? When the bark of Columbus nears the shore of America —before it the beach lined with savages, fleeing out of all their huts of cane; the sea behind; and the purple mountains of the Indian Archipelago around, can we separate the man from the living picture? Does not the New World clothe his form with her palmgroves and savannahs as fit drapery? Ever does natural beauty steal in like air, and envelope great actions. When Sir Harry Vane was dragged up the Tower-hill, sitting on a sled, to suffer death as the champion of the English laws, one of the multitude cried out to him, "You never satè on so glorious a seat!" Charles II, to intimidate the citizens of London, caused the patriot Lord Russell to be drawn in an open coach through the principal streets of the city on his way to the scaffold. "But," his biographer says, "the multitude imagined they saw liberty and virtue sitting by his side." In private places, among sordid objects, an act of truth or heroism seems at once to draw to itself the sky as its temple, the sun as its candle. Nature stretches out her arms to embrace man, only let his thoughts be of equal greatness. Willingly does she follow his steps with the rose and the violet, and bend her lines of grandeur and grace to the decoration of her darling child. Only let his thoughts be of equal scope, and the frame will suit the picture. A virtuous man is in unison with her works, and makes the central figure of the visible sphere. Homer, Pindar, Socrates, Phocion, associate themselves fitly in our memory with the geography and climate of Greece. The visible heavens and earth sympathize with Jesus. And in common life whosoever has seen a person of powerful character and happy genius, will have remarked how easily he took all things along with him—the persons, the opinions, and the day, and nature became ancillary to a man.

3. There is still another aspect under which the beauty of the world may be viewed, namely, as it becomes an object

of the intellect. Beside the relation of things to virtue, they have a relation to thought. The intellect searches out the absolute order of things as they stand in the mind of God, and without the colors of affection. The intellectual and the active powers seem to succeed each other; and the exclusive activity of the one generates the exclusive activity of the other. There is something unfriendly in each to the other, but they are like the alternate periods of feeding and working in animals; each prepares and will be followed by the other. Therefore does beauty, which, in relation to actions, as we have seen, comes unsought, and comes because it is unsought, remain for the apprehension and pursuit of the intellect; and then again, in its turn, of the active power. Nothing divine dies. All good is eternally reproductive. The beauty of nature re-forms itself in the mind, and not for barren contemplation, but for new creation.

All men are in some degree impressed by the face of the world; some men even to delight. This love of beauty is Taste. Others have the same love in such excess, that, not content with admiring, they seek to embody it in new forms. The creation of beauty is Art.

The production of a work of art throws a light upon the mystery of humanity. A work of art is an abstract or epitome of the world. It is the result or expression of nature, in miniature. For although the works of nature are innumerable and all different, the result or the expression of them all is similar and single. Nature is a sea of forms radically alike and even unique. A leaf, a sunbeam, a landscape, the ocean, make an analogous impression on the mind. What is common to them all—that perfectness and harmony, is beauty. The standard of beauty is the entire circuit of natural forms—the totality of nature; which the Italians expressed by defining beauty "il più nell' uno." Nothing is quite beautiful alone; nothing but is beautiful in the whole. A single object is only so far beautiful as it suggests this universal grace. The poet, the painter, the sculptor, the musician, the architect, seek each to concentrate this radiance of the world on one point, and each in his several work to satisfy the love of beauty which stimulates him to produce. Thus is Art a nature passed through the alembic of man. Thus in art does Nature work through the will of a man filled with the beauty of her first works.

The world thus exists to the soul to satisfy the desire of

beauty. This element I call an ultimate end. No reason can be asked or given why the soul seeks beauty. Beauty, in its largest and profoundest sense, is one expression for the universe. God is the all-fair. Truth, and goodness, and beauty, are but different faces of the same All. But beauty in nature is not ultimate. It is the herald of inward and eternal beauty, and is not alone a solid and satisfactory good. It must stand as a part, and not as yet the last or highest expression of the final cause of Nature.

Language

IV

Language is a third use which Nature subserves to man. Nature is the vehicle of thought, and in a simple, double, and three-fold degree.

1. Words are signs of natural facts.
2. Particular natural facts are symbols of particular spiritual facts.
3. Nature is the symbol of spirit.

1. Words are signs of natural facts. The use of natural history is to give us aid in supernatural history; the use of the outer creation, to give us language for the beings and changes of the inward creation. Every word which is used to express a moral or intellectual fact, if traced to its root, is found to be borrowed from some material appearance. *Right* means *straight; wrong* means *twisted. Spirit* primarily means *wind; transgression*, the crossing of a *line; supercilious*, the *raising of the eyebrow*. We say the *heart* to express emotion, the *head* to denote thought; and *thought* and *emotion* are words borrowed from sensible things, and now appropriated to spiritual nature. Most of the process by which this transformation is made, is hidden from us in the remote time when language was framed; but the same tendency may be daily

observed in children. Children and savages use only nouns or names of things, which they convert into verbs, and apply to analogous mental acts.

2. But this origin of all words that convey a spiritual import—so conspicuous a fact in the history of language—is our least debt to nature. It is not words only that are emblematic; it is things which are emblematic. Every natural fact is a symbol of some spiritual fact. Every appearance in nature corresponds to some state of the mind, and that state of the mind can only be described by presenting that natural appearance as its picture. An enraged man is a lion, a cunning man is a fox, a firm man is a rock, a learned man is a torch. A lamb is innocence; a snake is subtle spite; flowers express to us the delicate affections. Light and darkness are our familiar expression for knowledge and ignorance; and heat for love. Visible distance behind and before us, is respectively our image of memory and hope.

Who looks upon a river in a meditative hour and is not reminded of the flux of all things? Throw a stone into the stream, and the circles that propagate themselves are the beautiful type of all influence. Man is conscious of a universal soul within or behind his individual life, wherein, as in a firmament, the natures of Justice, Truth, Love, Freedom, arise and shine. This universal soul he calls Reason: it is not mine, or thine, or his, but we are its; we are its property and men. And the blue sky in which the private earth is buried, the sky with its eternal calm, and full of everlasting orbs, is the type of Reason. That which intellectually considered we call Reason, considered in relation to nature, we call Spirit. Spirit is the Creator. Spirit hath life in itself. And man in all ages and countries embodies it in his language as the FATHER.

It is easily seen that there is nothing lucky or capricious in these analogies, but that they are constant, and pervade nature. These are not the dreams of a few poets, here and there, but man is an analogist, and studies relations in all objects. He is placed in the centre of beings, and a ray of relation passes from every other being to him. And neither can man be understood without these objects, nor these objects without man. All the facts in natural history taken by themselves, have no value, but are barren, like a single sex. But marry it to human history, and it is full of life. Whole floras, all Linnæus' and Buffon's volumes, are dry catalogues of facts; but the most trivial of these facts, the habit of a plant, the organs, or work, or noise of an insect, applied to the illustration of a fact in intellectual philosophy, or in any way associated to human nature, affects us in the most lively and agreeable manner. The seed of a plant—to what affecting analogies in the nature of man is that little fruit made use of, in all discourse, up to the voice of Paul, who calls the human corpse a seed—"It is sown a natural body; it is raised a spiritual body." The motion of the earth round its axis and round the sun, makes the day and the year. These are certain amounts of brute light and heat. But is there no intent of an analogy between man's life and the seasons? And do the seasons gain no grandeur or pathos from that analogy? The instincts of the ant are very unimportant considered as the ant's; but the moment a ray of relation is seen to extend from it to man, and the little drudge is seen to be a monitor, a little body with a mighty heart, then all its habits, even that said to be recently observed, that it never sleeps, become sublime.

Because of this radical correspondence between visible things and human thoughts, savages, who have only what is necessary, converse in figures. As we go back in history, language becomes more picturesque, until its infancy, when it is all poetry; or all spiritual facts are represented by natural symbols. The same symbols are found to make the original elements of all languages. It has moreover been observed, that the idioms of all languages approach each other in passages of the greatest eloquence and power. And as this is the first language, so is it the last. This immediate dependence of language upon nature, this conversion of an outward phenomenon into a type of somewhat in human life, never loses its power to affect us. It is this which gives that piquancy to the conversation of a strong-natured farmer or backwoodsman, which all men relish.

A man's power to connect his thought with its proper symbol, and so to utter it, depends on the simplicity of his character, that is, upon his love of truth and his desire to communicate it without loss. The corruption of man is followed by the corruption of language. When simplicity of character and the sovereignty of ideas is broken up by the prevalence of secondary desires—the desire of riches, of pleasure, of power, and of praise—and duplicity and falsehood take place of simplicity and truth, the power over nature as an interpreter of the will is in a degree lost; new imagery ceases to be created, and old words are perverted to stand for things which are not; a paper currency is employed, when there is no bullion in the vaults. In due time the fraud is manifest, and words lose all power to stimulate the understanding or the affections. Hundreds of writers may be found in every long-civilized nation who for a short time believe and make others believe that they see and utter truths, who do not of themselves clothe one thought in its natural garment, but who feed unconsciously on the language created by the primary writers of the country, those, namely, who hold primarily on nature.

But wise men pierce this rotten diction and fasten words again to visible things; so that picturesque language is at once a commanding certificate that he who employs it is a man in alliance with truth and God. The moment our discourse rises above the ground line of familiar facts and is inflamed with passion or exalted by thought, it clothes itself in images. A man conversing in earnest, if he watch his intellectual processes, will find that a material image more or less luminous arises in his mind, contemporaneous with every thought, which furnishes the vestment of the thought. Hence, good writing and brilliant discourse are perpetual allegories. This imagery is spontaneous. It is the blending of experience with the present action of the mind. It is proper creation. It is the working of the Original Cause through the instruments he has already made.

These facts may suggest the advantage which the country life possesses, for a powerful mind, over the artificial and curtailed life of cities. We know more from nature than we can at will communicate. Its light flows into the mind evermore, and we forget its presence. The poet, the orator, bred in the woods, whose senses have been nourished by their fair and appeasing changes, year after year, without design and without heed—shall not lose their lesson altogether, in the roar of cities or the broil of politics. Long hereafter amidst agitation and terror in national councils—in the hour of revolution—these solemn images shall reappear in their morning lustre, as fit symbols and words of the thoughts which the passing events shall awaken. At the call of a noble sentiment, again the woods wave, the pines murmur, the river rolls and shines, and the cattle low upon the mountains, as he saw and heard them in his infancy. And with these forms, the spells of persuasion, the keys of power are put into his hands.

3. We are thus assisted by natural objects in the expression of particular meanings. But how great a language to convey such pepper-corn informations! Did it need such noble races of creatures, this profusion of forms, this host of orbs in heaven, to furnish man with the dictionary and grammar of his municipal speech? Whilst we use this grand cipher to expedite the affairs of our pot and kettle, we feel that we have not yet put it to its use, neither are able. We are like travellers using the cinders of a volcano to roast their eggs. Whilst we see that it always stands ready to clothe what we would say, we cannot avoid the question whether the characters are not significant of themselves. Have mountains, and waves, and skies, no significance but what we consciously give them when we employ them as emblems of our thoughts? The world is emblematic. Parts of speech are metaphors, because the whole of nature is a metaphor of the human mind. The laws of moral nature answer to those of matter as face to face in a glass. "The visible world and the relation of its parts, is the dial plate of the invisible." The axioms of physics translate the laws of ethics. Thus, "the whole is greater than its parts;" "reaction is equal to action;" "the smallest weight may be made to lift the greatest, the difference of weight being compensated by time;" and many the like propositions, which have an ethical as well as physical sense. These propositions have a much more extensive and universal sense when applied to human life, than when confined to technical use.

In like manner, the memorable words of history and the proverbs of nations consist usually of a natural fact, selected as a picture or parable of a moral truth. Thus; A rolling stone gathers no moss; A bird in the hand is worth two in the bush; A cripple in the right way will beat a racer in the wrong; Make hay while the sun shines; 'T is hard to carry a full cup even; Vinegar is the son of wine; The last ounce broke the camel's back; Long-lived trees make roots first; and the like. In their primary sense these are trivial facts, but we repeat them for the value of their analogical import. What is true of proverbs, is true of all fables, parables, and allegories.

This relation between the mind and matter is not fancied

by some poet, but stands in the will of God, and so is free to be known by all men. It appears to men, or it does not appear. When in fortunate hours we ponder this miracle, the wise man doubts if at all other times he is not blind and deaf;

> Can such things be,
> And overcome us like a summer's cloud,
> Without our special wonder? [2]

for the universe becomes transparent, and the light of higher laws than its own shines through it. It is the standing problem which has exercised the wonder and the study of every fine genius since the world began; from the era of the Egyptians and the Brahmins to that of Pythagoras, of Plato, of Bacon, of Leibnitz, of Swedenborg. There sits the Sphinx at the road-side, and from age to age, as each prophet comes by, he tries his fortune at reading her riddle. There seems to be a necessity in spirit to manifest itself in material forms; and day and night, river and storm, beast and bird, acid and alkali, preëxist in necessary Ideas in the mind of God, and are what they are by virtue of preceding affections in the world of spirit. A Fact is the end or last issue of spirit. The visible creation is the terminus or the circumference of the invisible world. "Material objects," said a French philosopher, "are necessarily kinds of *scoriæ* of the substantial thoughts of the Creator, which must always preserve an exact relation to their first origin; in other words, visible nature must have a spiritual and moral side."

This doctrine is abstruse, and though the images of "garment," "scoriæ," "mirror," etc., may stimulate the fancy, we must summon the aid of subtler and more vital expositors to make it plain. "Every scripture is to be interpreted by the same spirit which gave it forth"—is the fundamental law of criticism. A life in harmony with Nature, the love of truth and of virtue, will purge the eyes to understand her text. By degrees we may come to know the primitive sense of the permanent objects of nature, so that the world shall be to us an open book, and every form significant of its hidden life and final cause.

A new interest surprises us, whilst, under the view now suggested, we contemplate the fearful extent and multitude

---

[2] Shakespeare, *Macbeth*, Act III, scene iv.

of objects; since "every object rightly seen, unlocks a new faculty of the soul." That which was unconscious truth, becomes, when interpreted and defined in an object, a part of the domain of knowledge—a new weapon in the magazine of power.

Discipline

V

In view of the significance of nature, we arrive at once at a new fact, that nature is a discipline. This use of the world includes the preceding uses, as parts of itself.

Space, time, society, labor, climate, food, locomotion, the animals, the mechanical forces, give us sincerest lessons, day by day, whose meaning is unlimited. They educate both the Understanding and the Reason. Every property of matter is a school for the understanding—its solidity or resistance, its inertia, its extension, its figure, its divisibility. The understanding adds, divides, combines, measures, and finds nutriment and room for its activity in this worthy scene. Meantime, Reason transfers all these lessons into its own world of thought, by perceiving the analogy that marries Matter and Mind.

1. Nature is a discipline of the understanding in intellectual truths. Our dealing with sensible objects is a constant exercise in the necessary lessons of difference, of likeness, of order, of being and seeming, of progressive arrangement; of ascent from particular to general; of combination to one end of manifold forces. Proportioned to the importance of the organ to be formed, is the extreme care with which its tuition is provided—a care pretermitted in no single case. What tedious training, day after day, year after year, never ending, to form the common sense; what continual reproduction of annoyances, inconveniences, dilemmas; what rejoicing over us of

little men; what disputing of prices, what reckonings of interest—and all to form the Hand of the mind—to instruct us that "good thoughts are no better than good dreams, unless they be executed!"

The same good office is performed by Property and its filial systems of debt and credit. Debt, grinding debt, whose iron face the widow, the orphan, and the sons of genius fear and hate—debt, which consumes so much time, which so cripples and disheartens a great spirit with cares that seem so base, is a preceptor whose lessons cannot be foregone, and is needed most by those who suffer from it most. Moreover, property, which has been well compared to snow—"if it fall level to-day, it will be blown into drifts to-morrow"—is the surface action of internal machinery, like the index on the face of a clock. Whilst now it is the gymnastics of the understanding, it is hiving, in the foresight of the spirit, experience in profounder laws.

The whole character and fortune of the individual are affected by the least inequalities in the culture of the understanding; for example, in the perception of differences. Therefore is Space, and therefore Time, that man may know that things are not huddled and lumped, but sundered and individual. A bell and a plough have each their use, and neither can do the office of the other. Water is good to drink, coal to burn, wool to wear; but wool cannot be drunk, nor water spun, nor coal eaten. The wise man shows his wisdom in separation, in gradation, and his scale of creatures and of merits is as wide as nature. The foolish have no range in their scale, but suppose every man is as every other man. What is not good they call the worst, and what is not hateful, they call the best.

In like manner, what good heed Nature forms in us! She pardons no mistakes. Her yea is yea, and her nay, nay.

The first steps in Agriculture, Astronomy, Zoölogy (those first steps which the farmer, the hunter, and the sailor take), teach that Nature's dice are always loaded; that in her heaps and rubbish are concealed sure and useful results.

How calmly and genially the mind apprehends one after another the laws of physics! What noble emotions dilate the mortal as he enters into the councils of the creation, and feels by knowledge the privilege to Be! His insight refines him. The beauty of nature shines in his own breast. Man is greater that he can see this, and the universe less, because Time and Space relations vanish as laws are known.

Here again we are impressed and even daunted by the immense Universe to be explored. "What we know is a point to what we do not know." Open any recent journal of science, and weigh the problems suggested concerning Light, Heat, Electricity, Magnetism, Physiology, Geology, and judge whether the interest of natural science is likely to be soon exhausted.

Passing by many particulars of the discipline of nature, we must not omit to specify two.

The exercise of the Will, or the lesson of power, is taught in every event. From the child's successive possession of his several senses up to the hour when he saith, "Thy will be done!" he is learning the secret that he can reduce under his will not only particular events but great classes, nay, the whole series of events, and so conform all facts to his character. Nature is thoroughly mediate. It is made to serve. It receives the dominion of man as meekly as the ass on which the Saviour rode. It offers all its kingdoms to man as the raw material which he may mould into what is useful. Man is never weary of working it up. He forges the subtile and delicate air into wise and melodious words, and gives them wing as angels of persuasion and command. One after another his victorious thought comes up with and reduces all things, until the world becomes at last only a realized will—the double of the man.

2. Sensible objects conform to the premonitions of Reason and reflect the conscience. All things are moral; and in their boundless changes have an unceasing reference to spiritual nature. Therefore is nature glorious with form, color, and motion; that every globe in the remotest heaven, every chemical change from the rudest crystal up to the laws of life, every change of vegetation from the first principle of growth in the eye of a leaf, to the tropical forest and ante-diluvian coal-mine, every animal function from the sponge up to Hercules, shall hint or thunder to man the laws of right and wrong, and echo the Ten Commandments. Therefore is Nature ever the ally of Religion: lends all her pomp and riches to the religious sentiment. Prophet and priest, David, Isaiah, Jesus, have drawn deeply from this source. This ethical character so penetrates the bone and marrow of

nature, as to seem the end for which it was made. Whatever private purpose is answered by any member or part, this is its public and universal function, and is never omitted. Nothing in nature is exhausted in its first use. When a thing has served an end to the uttermost, it is wholly new for an ulterior service. In God, every end is converted into a new means. Thus the use of commodity, regarded by itself, is mean and squalid. But it is to the mind an education in the doctrine of Use, namely, that a thing is good only so far as it serves; that a conspiring of parts and efforts to the production of an end is essential to any being. The first and gross manifestation of this truth is our inevitable and hated training in values and wants, in corn and meat.

It has already been illustrated, that every natural process is a version of a moral sentence. The moral law lies at the centre of nature and radiates to the circumference. It is the pith and marrow of every substance, every relation, and every process. All things with which we deal, preach to us. What is a farm but a mute gospel? The chaff and the wheat, weeds and plants, blight, rain, insects, sun—it is a sacred emblem from the first furrow of spring to the last stack which the snow of winter overtakes in the fields. But the sailor, the shepherd, the miner, the merchant, in their several resorts, have each an experience precisely parallel, and leading to the same conclusion: because all organizations are radically alike. Nor can it be doubted that this moral sentiment which thus scents the air, grows in the grain, and impregnates the waters of the world, is caught by man and sinks into his soul. The moral influence of nature upon every individual is that amount of truth which it illustrates to him. Who can estimate this? Who can guess how much firmness the sea-beaten rock has taught the fisherman? how much tranquillity has been reflected to man from the azure sky, over whose unspotted deeps the winds forevermore drive flocks of stormy clouds, and leave no wrinkle or stain? how much industry and providence and affection we have caught from the pantomime of brutes? What a searching preacher of self-command is the varying phenomenon of Health!

Herein is especially apprehended the unity of Nature— the unity in variety—which meets us everywhere. All the endless variety of things make an identical impression. Xenophanes complained in his old age, that, look where he would, all things hastened back to Unity. He was weary of seeing the same entity in the tedious variety of forms. The fable of Proteus has a cordial truth. A leaf, a drop, a crystal, a moment of time, is related to the whole, and partakes of the perfection of the whole. Each particle is a microcosm, and faithfully renders the likeness of the world.

Not only resemblances exist in things whose analogy is obvious, as when we detect the type of the human hand in the flipper of the fossil saurus, but also in objects wherein there is great superficial unlikeness. Thus architecture is called "frozen music," by De Staël and Goethe. Vitruvius thought an architect should be a musician. "A Gothic church," said Coleridge, "is a petrified religion." Michael Angelo maintained, that, to an architect, a knowledge of anatomy is essential. In Haydn's oratorios, the notes present to the imagination not only motions, as of the snake, the stag, and the elephant, but colors also; as the green grass. The law of harmonic sounds reappears in the harmonic colors. The granite is differenced in its laws only by the more or less of heat from the river that wears it away. The river, as it flows, resembles the air that flows over it; the air resembles the light which traverses it with more subtile currents; the light resembles the heat which rides with it through Space. Each creature is only a modification of the other; the likeness in them is more than the difference, and their radical law is one and the same. A rule of one art, or a law of one organization, holds true throughout nature. So intimate is this Unity, that, it is easily seen, it lies under the undermost garment of Nature, and betrays its source in Universal Spirit. For it pervades Thought also. Every universal truth which we express in words, implies or supposes every other truth. *Omne verum vero consonat*. It is like a great circle on a sphere, comprising all possible circles; which, however, may be drawn and comprise it in like manner. Every such truth is the absolute Ens seen from one side. But it has innumerable sides.

The central Unity is still more conspicuous in actions. Words are finite organs of the infinite mind. They cannot cover the dimensions of what is in truth. They break, chop, and impoverish it. An action is the perfection and publication of thought. A right action seems to fill the eye, and to be related to all nature. "The wise man, in doing one thing, does all; or, in the one thing he does rightly, he sees the likeness of all which is done rightly."

Words and actions are not the attributes of brute nature. They introduce us to the human form, of which all other organizations appear to be degradations. When this appears among so many that surround it, the spirit prefers it to all others. It says, "From such as this have I drawn joy and knowledge; in such as this have I found and beheld myself; I will speak to it; it can speak again; it can yield me thought already formed and alive." In fact, the eye—the mind—is always accompanied by these forms, male and female; and these are incomparably the richest informations of the power and order that lie at the heart of things. Unfortunately every one of them bears the marks as of some injury; is marred and superficially defective. Nevertheless, far different from the deaf and dumb nature around them, these all rest like fountain-pipes on the unfathomed sea of thought and virtue whereto they alone, of all organizations, are the entrances.

It were a pleasant inquiry to follow into detail their ministry to our education, but where would it stop? We are associated in adolescent and adult life with some friends, who, like skies and waters, are coextensive with our idea; who, answering each to a certain affection of the soul, satisfy our desire on that side; whom we lack power to put at such focal distance from us, that we can mend or even analyze them. We cannot choose but love them. When much intercourse with a friend has supplied us with a standard of excellence, and has increased our respect for the resources of God who thus sends a real person to outgo our ideal; when he has, moreover, become an object of thought, and, whilst his character retains all its unconscious effect, is converted in the mind into solid and sweet wisdom—it is a sign to us that his office is closing, and he is commonly withdrawn from our sight in a short time.

Idealism

VI

Thus is the unspeakable but intelligible and practicable meaning of the world conveyed to man, the immortal pupil, in every object of sense. To this one end of Discipline, all parts of nature conspire.

A noble doubt perpetually suggests itself—whether this end be not the Final Cause of the Universe; and whether nature outwardly exists. It is a sufficient account of that Appearance we call the World, that God will teach a human mind, and so makes it the receiver of a certain number of congruent sensations, which we call sun and moon, man and woman, house and trade. In my utter impotence to test the authenticity of the report of my senses, to know whether the impressions they make on me correspond with outlying objects, what difference does it make, whether Orion is up there in heaven, or some god paints the image in the firmament of the soul? The relations of parts and the end of the whole remaining the same, what is the difference, whether land and sea interact, and worlds revolve and intermingle without number or end—deep yawning under deep, and galaxy balancing galaxy, throughout absolute space—or whether, without relations of time and space, the same appearances are inscribed in the constant faith of man? Whether nature enjoy a substantial existence without, or is only in the apocalypse of the mind, it is alike useful and alike venerable to me. Be it what it may, it is ideal to me so long as I cannot try the accuracy of my senses.

The frivolous make themselves merry with the Ideal theory, as if its consequences were burlesque; as if it affected the stability of nature. It surely does not. God never jests with us, and will not compromise the end of nature by permitting any inconsequence in its procession. Any distrust of the permanence of laws would paralyze the faculties of man. Their permanence is sacredly respected, and his faith therein is perfect. The wheels and springs of man are all set to the hypothesis of the permanence of nature. We are not built like a ship to be tossed, but like a house to stand. It is a natural consequence of this structure, that so long as the active powers predominate over the reflective, we resist with indignation any hint that nature is more short-lived or mutable than spirit. The broker, the wheelwright, the carpenter, the tollman, are much displeased at the intimation.

But whilst we acquiesce entirely in the permanence of natural laws, the question of the absolute existence of nature still remains open. It is the uniform effect of culture on the human mind, not to shake our faith in the stability of particular phenomena, as of heat, water, azote; but to lead us to regard nature as phenomenon, not a substance; to attribute necessary existence to spirit; to esteem nature as an accident and an effect.

To the senses and the unrenewed understanding, belongs a sort of instinctive belief in the absolute existence of nature. In their view man and nature are indissolubly joined. Things are ultimates, and they never look beyond their sphere. The presence of Reason mars this faith. The first effort of thought tends to relax this despotism of the senses which binds us to nature as if we were a part of it, and shows us nature aloof, and, as it were, afloat. Until this higher agency intervened, the animal eye sees, with wonderful accuracy, sharp outlines and colored surfaces. When the eye of Reason opens, to outline and surface are at once added grace and expression. These proceed from imagination and affection, and abate somewhat of the angular distinctness of objects. If the Reason be stimulated to more earnest vision, outlines and surfaces become transparent, and are no longer seen; causes and spirits are seen through them. The best moments of life are these delicious awakenings of the higher powers, and the reverential withdrawing of nature before its God. *transcendental moments*

Let us proceed to indicate the effects of culture.

1. Our first institution in the Ideal philosophy is a hint from Nature herself.

Nature is made to conspire with spirit to emancipate us. Certain mechanical changes, a small alteration in our local position, apprizes us of a dualism. We are strangely affected by seeing the shore from a moving ship, from a balloon, or through the tints of an unusual sky. <u>The least change in our point of view gives the whole world a pictorial air.</u> A man who seldom rides, needs only to get into a coach and traverse his own town, to turn the street into a puppet-show. The men, the women—talking, running, bartering, fighting—the earnest mechanic, the lounger, the beggar, the boys, the dogs, are unrealized at once, or, at least, wholly detached from all relation to the observer, and seen as apparent, not substantial beings. What new thoughts are suggested by seeing a face of country quite familiar, in the rapid movement of the railroad car! Nay, <u>the most wonted objects,</u> (make a very slight change in the point of vision,) <u>please us most.</u> In a camera obscura, the butcher's cart, and the figure of one of our own family amuse us. So a portrait of a well-known face gratifies us. <u>Turn the eyes</u> upside down, by looking at the landscape <u>through your legs, and how agreeable is the picture,</u> though you have seen it any time these twenty years!

In these cases, by mechanical means, is suggested the difference between the observer and the spectacle—between man and nature. Hence arises a pleasure mixed with awe; I may say, a low degree of the sublime is felt, from the fact, probably, that man is hereby apprized that whilst the world is a spectacle, something in himself is stable.

2. In a higher manner the poet communicates the same pleasure. By a few strokes he delineates, as on air, the sun, the mountain, the camp, the city, the hero, the maiden, not different from what we know them, but only lifted from the ground and afloat before the eye. <u>He unfixes the land and the sea,</u> makes them revolve around the axis of his primary thought, and disposes them anew. <u>Possessed himself</u> by a heroic passion, he uses matter as symbols of it. The sensual <u>man conforms thoughts to things; the poet conforms things to his thoughts.</u> The one esteems nature as rooted and fast; the other, as fluid, and impresses his being thereon. To him, the refractory world is ductile and flexible; he invests dust and stones with humanity, and makes them the words of the Reason. The Imagination may be defined to be the use which the Reason makes of the material world. Shakspeare possesses the power of subordinating nature for the purposes of expression, beyond all poets. His imperial muse tosses the crea-

tion like a bauble from hand to hand, and uses it to embody
any caprice of thought that is uppermost in his mind. The
remotest spaces of nature are visited, and the farthest sundered
things are brought together, by a subtile spiritual connection.
We are made aware that magnitude of material things is
relative, and all objects shrink and expand to serve the passion
of the poet. Thus in his sonnets, the lays of birds, the scents
and dyes of flowers he finds to be the *shadow* of his beloved;
time, which keeps her from him, is his *chest*; the suspicion
she has awakened, is her *ornament*;

> The ornament of beauty is Suspect,
> A crow which flies in heaven's sweetest air.[3]

His passion is not the fruit of chance; it swells, as he speaks,
to a city, or a state.

> No, it was builded far from accident;
> It suffers not in smiling pomp, nor falls
> Under the brow of thralling discontent;
> It fears not policy, that heretic,
> That works on leases of short numbered hours,
> But all alone stands hugely politic.[4]

In the strength of his constancy, the Pyramids seem to him
recent and transitory. The freshness of youth and love dazzles
him with its resemblance to morning;

> Take those lips away
> Which so sweetly were forsworn;
> And those eyes—the break of day,
> Lights that do mislead the morn.[5]

The wild beauty of this hyperbole, I may say in passing, it
would not be easy to match in literature.

This transfiguration which all material objects undergo
through the passion of the poet—this power which he exerts
to dwarf the great, to magnify the small—might be illustrated
by a thousand examples from his Plays. I have before me
the Tempest, and will cite only these few lines.

[3] Shakespeare, Sonnet lxx.

[4] Shakespeare, Sonnet cxxiv.

[5] Shakespeare, *Measure for Measure*, Act IV, scene i.

ARIEL. The strong based promontory
Have I made shake, and by the spurs plucked up
The pine and cedar.

Prospero calls for music to soothe the frantic Alonzo, and his companions;

A solemn air, and the best comforter
To an unsettled fancy, cure thy brains
Now useless, boiled within thy skull.

Again;

The charm dissolves apace,
And, as the morning steals upon the night,
Melting the darkness, so their rising senses
Begin to chase the ignorant fumes that mantle
Their clearer reason.
Their understanding
Begins to swell: and the approaching tide
Will shortly fill the reasonable shores
That now lie foul and muddy.

The perception of real affinities between events (that is to say, of *ideal* affinities, for those only are real), enables the poet thus to make free with the most imposing forms and phenomena of the world, and to assert the predominance of the soul.

3. Whilst thus the poet animates nature with his own thoughts, he differs from the philosopher only herein, that the one proposes Beauty as his main end; the other Truth. But the philosopher, not less than the poet, postpones the apparent order and relations of things to the empire of thought. "The problem of philosophy," according to Plato, "is, for all that exists conditionally, to find a ground unconditioned and absolute." It proceeds on the faith that a law determines all phenomena, which being known, the phenomena can be predicted. That law, when in the mind, is an idea. Its beauty is infinite. The true philosopher and the true poet are one, and a beauty, which is truth, and a truth, which is beauty, is the aim of both. Is not the charm of one of Plato's or Aristotle's definitions strictly like that of the Antigone of Sophocles? It

is, in both cases, that a spiritual life has been imparted to nature; that the solid seeming block of matter has been pervaded and dissolved by a thought; that this feeble human being has penetrated the vast masses of nature with an informing soul, and recognized itself in their harmony, that is, seized their law. In physics, when this is attained, the memory disburthens itself of its cumbrous catalogues of particulars, and carries centuries of observation in a single formula.

Thus even in physics, the material is degraded before the spiritual. The astronomer, the geometer, rely on their irrefragable analysis, and disdain the results of observation. The sublime remark of Euler on his law of arches, "This will be found contrary to all experience, yet is true;" had already transferred nature into the mind, and left matter like an outcast corpse.

4. Intellectual science has been observed to beget invariably a doubt of the existence of matter. Turgot said, "He that has never doubted the existence of matter, may be assured he has no aptitude for metaphysical inquiries." It fastens the attention upon immortal necessary uncreated natures, that is, upon Ideas; and in their presence we feel that the outward circumstance is a dream and a shade. Whilst we wait in this Olympus of gods, we think of nature as an appendix to the soul. We ascend into their region, and know that these are the thoughts of the Supreme Being. "These are they who were set up from everlasting, from the beginning, or ever the earth was. When he prepared the heavens, they were there; when he established the clouds above, when he strengthened the fountains of the deep. Then they were by him, as one brought up with him. Of them took he counsel."

Their influence is proportionate. As objects of science they are accessible to few men. Yet all men are capable of being raised by piety or by passion, into their region. And no man touches these divine natures, without becoming, in some degree, himself divine. Like a new soul, they renew the body. We become physically nimble and lightsome; we tread on air; life is no longer irksome, and we think it will never be so. No man fears age or misfortune or death in their serene company, for he is transported out of the district of change. Whilst we behold unveiled the nature of Justice and Truth, we learn the difference between the absolute and the conditional or relative. We apprehend the absolute. As it were, for the first time, *we exist*. We become immortal, for we learn that time and space are relations of matter; that with a perception of truth or a virtuous will they have no affinity.

5. Finally, religion and ethics, which may be fitly called the practice of ideas, or the introduction of ideas into life, have an analogous effect with all lower culture, in degrading nature and suggesting its dependence on spirit. Ethics and religion differ herein; that the one is the system of human duties commencing from man; the other, from God. Religion includes the personality of God; Ethics does not. They are one to our present design. They both put nature under foot. The first and last lesson of religion is, "The things that are seen, are temporal; the things that are unseen, are eternal." It puts an affront upon nature. It does that for the unschooled, which philosophy does for Berkeley and Viasa. The uniform language that may be heard in the churches of the most ignorant sects is, "Contemn the unsubstantial shows of the world; they are vanities, dreams, shadows, unrealities; seek the realities of religion." The devotee flouts nature. Some theosophists have arrived at a certain hostility and indignation towards matter, as the Manichean and Plotinus. They distrusted in themselves any looking back to these flesh-pots of Egypt. Plotinus was ashamed of his body. In short, they might all say of matter, what Michel Angelo said of external beauty, "It is the frail and weary weed, in which God dresses the soul which he has called into time."

It appears that motion, poetry, physical and intellectual science, and religion, all tend to affect our convictions of the reality of the external world. But I own there is something ungrateful in expanding too curiously the particulars of the general proposition, that all culture tends to imbue us with idealism. I have no hostility to nature, but a child's love to it. I expand and live in the warm day like corn and melons. Let us speak her fair. I do not wish to fling stones at my beautiful mother, nor soil my gentle nest. I only wish to indicate the true position of nature in regard to man, wherein to establish man all right education tends; as the ground which to attain is the object of human life, that is, of man's connection with nature. Culture inverts the vulgar views of nature, and brings the mind to call that apparent which it uses to call real, and that real which it uses to call visionary. Children, it is true, believe in the external world. The belief that it appears only, is an afterthought, but with culture this faith will as surely arise on the mind as did the first.

The advantage of the ideal theory over the popular faith is this, that it presents the world in precisely that view which is most desirable to the mind. It is, in fact, the view which Reason, both speculative and practical, that is, philosophy and virtue, take. For seen in the light of thought, the world always is phenomenal; and virtue subordinates it to the mind. Idealism sees the world in God. It beholds the whole circle of persons and things, of actions and events, of country and religion, not as painfully accumulated, atom after atom, act after act, in an aged creeping Past, but as one vast picture which God paints on the instant eternity for the contemplation of the soul. Therefore the soul holds itself off from a too trivial and microscopic study of the universal tablet. It respects the end too much to immerse itself in the means. It sees something more important in Christianity than the scandals of ecclesiastical history or the niceties of criticism; and, very incurious concerning persons or miracles, and not at all disturbed by chasms of historical evidence, it accepts from God the phenomenon, as it finds it, as the pure and awful form of religion in the world. It is not hot and passionate at the appearance of what it calls its own good or bad fortune, at the union or opposition of other persons. No man is its enemy. It accepts whatsoever befalls, as part of its lesson. It is a watcher more than a doer, and it is a doer, only that it may the better watch.

Spirit

VII

It is essential to a true theory of nature and of man, that it should <u>contain somewhat progressive.</u> Uses that are exhausted or that may be, and facts that end in the statement, cannot be all that is true of this brave lodging wherein man is harbored, and wherein all his faculties find appropriate and endless exercise. And all the uses of nature admit of being summed in one, which yields the activity of man an infinite scope. Through all its kingdoms, to the suburbs and outskirts of things, it is faithful to the cause whence it had its origin. It always speaks of Spirit. It suggests the absolute. It is a perpetual effect. It is a great shadow pointing always to the sun behind us.

The aspect of Nature is devout. Like the figure of Jesus, she stands with bended head, and hands folded upon the breast. The happiest man is he who learns from nature the lesson of worship.

Of that ineffable essence which we call Spirit, he that thinks most, will say least. We can foresee God in the coarse, and, as it were, distant phenomena of matter; but when we try to define and describe himself, both language and thought desert us, and we are as helpless as fools and savages. That essence refuses to be recorded in propositions, but when man has worshipped him intellectually, the noblest ministry of nature is to stand as the apparition of God. It is the organ through which the universal spirit speaks to the individual, and strives to lead back the individual to it.

When we consider Spirit, we see that the views already presented do not include the whole circumference of man. We must add some related thoughts.

Three problems are put by nature to the mind: What is matter? Whence is it? and Whereto? The first of these questions only, the ideal theory answers. Idealism saith: matter is a phenomenon, not a substance. Idealism acquaints us with the total disparity between the evidence of our own being and the evidence of the world's being. The one is perfect; the other, incapable of any assurance; the mind is a part of the nature of things; the world is a divine dream, from which we may presently awake to the glories and certainties of day. Idealism is a hypothesis to account for nature by other principles than those of carpentry and chemistry. Yet, if it only deny the existence of matter, it does not satisfy the demands of the spirit. It leaves God out of me. It leaves me in the splendid labyrinth of my perceptions, to wander without end. Then the heart resists it, because it balks the affections in denying substantive being to men and women. Nature is so pervaded with human life that there is something of humanity in all and in every particular. But this theory makes nature foreign to me, and does not account for that consanguinity which we acknowledge to it.

Let it stand then, in the present state of our knowledge, merely as a useful introductory hypothesis, serving to apprize us of the eternal distinction between the soul and the world.

But when, following the invisible steps of thought, we come to inquire, Whence is matter? and Whereto? many truths arise to us out of the recesses of consciousness. We learn that the highest is present to the soul of man; that the dread universal essence, which is not wisdom, or love, or beauty, or power, but all in one, and each entirely, is that for which all things exist, and that by which they are; that spirit creates; that behind nature, throughout nature, spirit is present; one and not compound it does not act upon us from without, that is, in space and time, but spiritually, or through ourselves: therefore, that spirit, that is, the Supreme Being, does not build up nature around us, but puts it forth through us, as the life of the tree puts forth new branches and leaves through the pores of the old. As a plant upon the earth, so a man rests upon the bosom of God; he is nourished by unfailing fountains, and draws at his need inexhaustible power. Who can set bounds to the possibilities of man? Once inhale the upper air, being admitted to behold the absolute natures of justice and truth, and we learn that man has access to the entire mind of the Creator, is himself the creator in the finite. This view, which admonishes me where the sources of wisdom and power lie, and points to virtue as to

> The golden key
> Which opes the palace of eternity,[6]

carries upon its face the highest certificate of truth, because it animates me to create my own world through the purification of my soul.

The world proceeds from the same spirit as the body of man. It is a remoter and inferior incarnation of God, a projection of God in the unconscious. But it differs from the body in one important respect. It is not, like that, now subjected to the human will. Its serene order is inviolable by us. It is,

---

[6] Milton, *Comus*, A Mask Presented at Ludlow Castle, 1634, lines 13, 14.

therefore, to us, the present expositor of the divine mind. It
is a fixed point whereby we may measure our departure. As
we degenerate, the contrast between us and our house is
more evident. We are as much strangers in nature as we are
aliens from God. We do not understand the notes of birds.
The fox and the deer run away from us; the bear and tiger
rend us. We do not know the uses of more than a few plants,
as corn and the apple, the potato and the vine. Is not the
landscape, every glimpse of which hath a grandeur, a face of
him? Yet this may show us what discord is between man
and nature, for you cannot freely admire a noble landscape
if laborers are digging in the field hard by. The poet finds
something ridiculous in his delight until he is out of the sight
of men.

Prospects

VIII

In inquiries respecting the laws of the world and the frame
of things, the highest reason is always the truest. That which
seems faintly possible, it is so refined, is often faint and dim
because it is deepest seated in the mind among the eternal
verities. Empirical science is apt to cloud the sight, and by
the very knowledge of functions and processes to bereave the
student of the manly contemplation of the whole. The savant
becomes unpoetic. But the best read naturalist who lends an
entire and devout attention to truth, will see that there remains much to learn of his relation to the world, and that
it is not to be learned by any addition or subtraction or other
comparison of known quantities, but is arrived at by untaught
sallies of the spirit, by a continual self-recovery, and by entire
humility. He will perceive that there are far more excellent
qualities in the student than preciseness and infallibility; that
a guess is often more fruitful than an indisputable affirmation,

and that a dream may let us deeper into the secret of nature
than a hundred concerted experiments.

For the problems to be solved are precisely those which
the physiologist and the naturalist omit to state. It is not so
pertinent to man to know all the individuals of the animal
kingdom, as it is to know whence and whereto is this tyrannizing unity in his constitution, which evermore separates
and classifies things, endeavoring to reduce the most diverse
to one form. When I behold a rich landscape, it is less to my
purpose to recite correctly the order and superposition of the
strata, than to know why all thought of multitude is lost in a
tranquil sense of unity. I cannot greatly honor minuteness in
details, so long as there is no hint to explain the relation between things and thoughts; no ray upon the *metaphysics* of
conchology, of botany, of the arts, to show the relation of the
forms of flowers, shells, animals, architecture, to the mind,
and build science upon ideas. In a cabinet of natural history,
we become sensible of a certain occult recognition and sympathy in regard to the most unwieldy and eccentric forms of
beast, fish, and insect. The American who has been confined,
in his own country, to the sight of buildings designed after
foreign models, is surprised on entering York Minster or St.
Peter's at Rome, by the feeling that these structures are
imitations also—faint copies of an invisible archetype. Nor
has science sufficient humanity, so long as the naturalist overlooks that wonderful congruity which subsists between man
and the world; of which he is lord, not because he is the
most subtile inhabitant, but because he is its head and heart,
and finds something of himself in every great and small thing,
in every mountain stratum, in every new law of color, fact
of astronomy, or atmospheric influence which observation or
analysis lays open. A perception of this mystery inspires the
muse of George Herbert, the beautiful psalmist of the seven-
teenth century. The following lines are part of his little poem
on Man.

> Man is all symmetry,
> Full of proportions, one limb to another,
> And all to all the world besides.
> Each part may call the farthest, brother;
> For head with foot hath private amity,
> And both with moons and tides.

Nothing hath got so far
But man hath caught and kept it as his prey;
His eyes dismount the highest star:
He is in little all the sphere.
Herbs gladly cure our flesh, because that they
Find their acquaintance there.

For us, the winds do blow,
The earth doth rest, heaven move, and fountains flow;
Nothing we see, but means our good,
As our delight, or as our treasure;
The whole is either our cupboard of food,
Or cabinet of pleasure.

The stars have us to bed:
Night draws the curtain; which the sun withdraws,
Music and light attend our head.
All things unto our flesh are kind,
In their descent and being; to our mind,
In their ascent and cause.

More servants wait on man
Than he'll take notice of. In every path,
He treads down that which doth befriend him
When sickness makes him pale and wan.
Oh mighty love! Man is one world, and hath
Another to attend him.

The perception of this class of truths makes the attraction which draws men to science, but the end is lost sight of in attention to the means. In view of this half-sight of science, we accept the sentence of Plato, that "poetry comes nearer to vital truth than history." Every surmise and vaticination of the mind is entitled to a certain respect, and we learn to prefer imperfect theories, and sentences which contain glimpses of truth, to digested systems which have no one valuable suggestion. A wise writer will feel that the ends of study and composition are best answered by announcing undiscovered regions of thought, and so communicating, through hope, new activity to the torpid spirit.

I shall therefore conclude this essay with some traditions of man and nature, which a certain poet sang to me; and which, as they have always been in the world, and perhaps reappear to every bard, may be both history and prophecy.

"The foundations of man are not in matter, but in spirit. But the element of spirit is eternity. To it, therefore, the longest series of events, the oldest chronologies are young and recent. In the cycle of the universal man, from whom the known individuals proceed, centuries are points, and all history is but the epoch of one degradation.

"We distrust and deny inwardly our sympathy with nature. We own and disown our relation to it, by turns. We are like Nebuchadnezzar, dethroned, bereft of reason, and eating grass like an ox. But who can set limits to the remedial force of spirit?

"A man is a god in ruins. When men are innocent, life shall be longer, and shall pass into the immortal as gently as we awake from dreams. Now, the world would be insane and rabid, if these disorganizations should last for hundreds of years. It is kept in check by death and infancy. Infancy is the perpetual Messiah, which comes into the arms of fallen men, and pleads with them to return to paradise.

"Man is the dwarf of himself. Once he was permeated and dissolved by spirit. He filled nature with his overflowing currents. Out from him sprang the sun and moon; from man the sun, from woman the moon. The laws of his mind, the periods of his actions externized themselves into day and night, into the year and the seasons. But, having made for himself this huge shell, his waters retired; he no longer fills the veins and veinlets; he is shrunk to a drop. He sees that the structure still fits him, but fits him colossally. Say, rather, once it fitted him, now it corresponds to him from far and on high. He adores timidly his own work. Now is man the follower of the sun, and woman the follower of the moon. Yet sometimes he starts in his slumber, and wonders at himself and his house, and muses strangely at the resemblance betwixt him and it. He perceives that if his law is still paramount, if still he have elemental power, if his word is sterling yet in nature, it is not conscious power, it is not inferior but superior to his will. It is instinct." Thus my Orphic poet sang.

At present, man applies to nature but half his force. He works on the world with his understanding alone. He lives in it and masters it by a penny-wisdom; and he that works most in it is but a half-man, and whilst his arms are strong and his digestion good, his mind is imbruted, and he is a selfish savage. His relation to nature, his power over it, is through the understanding, as by manure; the economic use of fire, wind, water, and the mariner's needle; steam, coal, chemical agriculture; the repairs of the human body by the dentist and the surgeon. This is such a resumption of power as if a banished king should buy his territories inch by inch, instead of vaulting at once into his throne. Meantime, in the thick darkness, there are not wanting gleams of a better light —occasional examples of the action of man upon nature with his entire force—with reason as well as understanding. Such examples are, the traditions of miracles in the earliest antiquity of all nations; the history of Jesus Christ; the achievements of a principle, as in religious and political revolutions, and in the abolition of the slave-trade; the miracles of enthusiasm, as those reported of Swedenborg, Hohenlohe, and the Shakers; many obscure and yet contested facts, now arranged under the name of Animal Magnetism; prayer; eloquence; self-healing; and the wisdom of children. These are examples of Reason's momentary grasp of the sceptre; the exertions of a power which exists not in time or space, but an instantaneous in-streaming causing power. The difference between the actual and the ideal force of man is happily figured by the schoolmen, in saying, that the knowledge of man is an evening knowledge, *vespertina cognitio*, but that of God is a morning knowledge, *matutina cognitio*.

The problem of restoring to the world original and eternal beauty is solved by the redemption of the soul. The ruin or the blank that we see when we look at nature, is in our own eye. The axis of vision is not coincident with the axis of things, and so they appear not transparent but opaque. The reason why the world lacks unity, and lies broken and in heaps, is because man is disunited with himself. He cannot be a naturalist until he satisfies all the demands of the spirit. Love is as much its demand as perception. Indeed, neither can be perfect without the other. In the uttermost meaning of the words, thought is devout, and devotion is thought. Deep calls unto deep. But in actual life, the marriage is not celebrated. There are innocent men who worship God after the tradition of their fathers, but their sense of duty has not yet extended to the use of all their faculties. And there are patient naturalists, but they freeze their subject under the wintry light of the understanding. Is not prayer also a study of truth—a sally of the soul into the unfound infinite? No man ever prayed heartily without learning something. But when a faithful thinker, resolute to detach every object from personal relations and see it in the light of thought, shall, at the same time, kindle science with the fire of the holiest affections, then will God go forth anew into the creation.

It will not need, when the mind is prepared for study, to search for objects. The invariable mark of wisdom is to see the miraculous in the common. What is a day? What is a year? What is summer? What is woman? What is a child? What is sleep? To our blindness, these things seem unaffecting. We make fables to hide the baldness of the fact and conform it, as we say, to the higher law of the mind. But when the fact is seen under the light of an idea, the gaudy fable fades and shrivels. We behold the real higher law. To the wise, therefore, a fact is true poetry, and the most beautiful of fables. These wonders are brought to our own door. You also are a man. Man and woman and their social life, poverty, labor, sleep, fear, fortune, are known to you. Learn that none of these things is superficial, but that each phenomenon has its roots in the faculties and affections of the mind. Whilst the abstract question occupies your intellect, nature brings it in the concrete to be solved by your hands. It were a wise inquiry for the closet, to compare, point by point, especially at remarkable crises in life, our daily history with the rise and progress of ideas in the mind.

So shall we come to look at the world with new eyes. It shall answer the endless inquiry of the intellect—What is truth? and of the affections—What is good? by yielding itself passive to the educated Will. Then shall come to pass what my poet said: "Nature is not fixed but fluid. Spirit alters, moulds, makes it. The immobility or bruteness of nature is the absence of spirit; to pure spirit it is fluid, it is volatile, it is obedient. Every spirit builds itself a house, and beyond its house a world, and beyond its world a heaven. Know then that the world exists for you. For you is the phenomenon perfect. What we are, that only can we see. All that Adam had, all that Cæsar could, you have and can do. Adam called his house, heaven and earth; Cæsar called his house, Rome; you perhaps call yours, a cobbler's trade; a hundred acres of ploughed land; or a scholar's garret. Yet line for line and point for point your dominion is as great as theirs, though without fine names. Build therefore your own world. As fast as you conform your life to the pure idea in your mind, that will unfold its great proportions. A correspondent revolution in things will attend the influx of the spirit. So fast will disagreeable appearances, swine, spiders, snakes, pests, madhouses, prisons, enemies, vanish; they are temporary and shall be no more seen. The sordor and filths of nature, the sun shall dry up and the wind exhale. As when the summer comes from the south the snow-banks melt and the face of the earth becomes green before it, so shall the advancing spirit create its ornaments along its path, and carry with it the beauty it visits and the song which enchants it; it shall draw beautiful faces, warm hearts, wise discourse, and heroic acts, around its way, until evil is no more seen. The kingdom of man over nature, which cometh not with observation— a dominion such as now is beyond his dream of God—he shall enter without more wonder than the blind man feels who is gradually restored to perfect sight."

From *Addresses, Essays, and Lectures*

Part Four

ESSAYS

History

There is one mind common to all individual men. Every man
is an inlet to the same and to all of the same. He that is once
admitted to the right of reason is made a freeman of the
whole estate. What Plato has thought, he may think; what a
saint has felt, he may feel; what at any time has befallen any
man, he can understand. Who hath access to this universal
mind is a party to all that is or can be done, for this is the
only and sovereign agent.

Of the works of this mind history is the record. Its genius
is illustrated by the entire series of days. Man is explicable
by nothing less than all his history. Without hurry, without
rest, the human spirit goes forth from the beginning to
embody every faculty, every thought, every emotion which
belongs to it, in appropriate events. But the thought is always
prior to the fact; all the facts of history preëxist in the mind
as laws. Each law in turn is made by circumstances predominant, and the limits of nature give power to but one
at a time. A man is the whole encyclopædia of facts. The
creation of a thousand forests is in one acorn, and Egypt,
Greece, Rome, Gaul, Britain, America, lie folded already in
the first man. Epoch after epoch, camp, kingdom, empire,
republic, democracy, are merely the application of his manifold spirit to the manifold world.

This human mind wrote history, and this must read it.
The Sphinx must solve her own riddle. If the whole of history is in one man, it is all to be explained from individual
experience. There is a relation between the hours of our life
and the centuries of time. As the air I breathe is drawn from
the great repositories of nature, as the light on my book is
yielded by a star a hundred millions of miles distant, as the
poise of my body depends on the equilibrium of centrifugal
and centripetal forces, so the hours should be instructed by

the ages and the ages explained by the hours. Of the universal mind each individual man is one more incarnation. All its properties consist in him. Each new fact in his private experience flashes a light on what great bodies of men have done, and the crises of his life refer to national crises. Every revolution was first a thought in one man's mind, and when the same thought occurs to another man, it is the key to that era. Every reform was once a private opinion, and when it shall be a private opinion again it will solve the problem of the age. The fact narrated must correspond to something in me to be credible or intelligible. We, as we read, must become Greeks, Romans, Turks, priest and king, martyr and executioner; must fasten these images to some reality in our secret experience, or we shall learn nothing rightly. What befell Asdrubal or Cæsar Borgia is as much an illustration of the mind's powers and depravations as what has befallen us. Each new law and political movement has a meaning for you. Stand before each of its tablets and say, "Under this mask did my Proteus nature hide itself." This remedies the defect of our too great nearness to ourselves. This throws our actions into perspective—and as crabs, goats, scorpions, the balance and the waterpot lose their meanness when hung as signs in the zodiac, so I can see my own vices without heat in the distant persons of Solomon, Alcibiades, and Catiline.

It is the universal nature which gives worth to particular men and things. Human life, as containing this, is mysterious and inviolable, and we hedge it round with penalties and laws. All laws derive hence their ultimate reason; all express more or less distinctly some command of this supreme, illimitable essence. Property also holds of the soul, covers great spiritual facts, and instinctively we at first hold to it with swords and laws and wide and complex combinations. The obscure consciousness of this fact is the light of all our day, the claim of claims; the plea for education, for justice, for charity; the foundation of friendship and love and of the heroism and grandeur which belong to acts of self-reliance. It is remarkable that involuntarily we always read as superior beings. Universal history, the poets, the romancers, do not in their stateliest pictures—in the sacerdotal, the imperial palaces, in the triumphs of will or of genius—anywhere lose our ear, anywhere make us feel that we intrude, that this is for better men; but rather is it true that in their grandest strokes we feel most at home. All that Shakspeare says of the king, yonder slip of a boy that reads in the corner feels to be true of himself. We sympathize in the great moments of history, in the great discoveries, the great resistances, the great prosperities of men—because there law was enacted, the sea was searched, the land was found, or the blow was struck, *for us*, as we ourselves in that place would have done or applauded.

We have the same interest in condition and character. We honor the rich because they have externally the freedom, power, and grace which we feel to be proper to man, proper to us. So all that is said of the wise man by Stoic or Oriental or modern essayist, describes to each reader his own idea, describes his unattained but attainable self. All literature writes the character of the wise man. Books, monuments, pictures, conversation, are portraits in which he finds the lineaments he is forming. The silent and the eloquent praise him and accost him, and he is stimulated wherever he moves as by personal allusions. A true aspirant therefore never needs look for allusions personal and laudatory in discourse. He hears the commendation, not of himself, but, more sweet, of that character he seeks, in every word that is said concerning character, yet further in every fact and circumstance—in the running river and the rustling corn. Praise is looked, homage tendered, love flows, from mute nature, from the mountains and the lights of the firmament.

These hints, dropped as it were from sleep and night, let us use in broad day. The student is to read history actively and not passively; to esteem his own life the text, and books the commentary. Thus compelled, the Muse of history will utter oracles as never to those who do not respect themselves. I have no expectation that any man will read history aright who thinks that what was done in a remote age, by men whose names have resounded far, has any deeper sense than what he is doing to-day.

The world exists for the education of each man. There is no age or state of society or mode of action in history to which there is not somewhat corresponding in his life. Every thing tends in a wonderful manner to abbreviate itself and yield its own virtue to him. He should see that he can live all history in his own person. He must sit solidly at home, and not suffer himself to be bullied by kings or empires, but know that he is greater than all the geography and all the government of the world; he must transfer the point of view from which history is commonly read, from Rome and Athens and London, to himself, and not deny his conviction that he is the court, and if England or Egypt have anything to say to him he will try the case; if not, let them forever be silent. He must attain and maintain that lofty sight where facts yield their secret sense, and poetry and annals are alike. The instinct of the mind, the purpose of nature, betrays itself in the use we make of the signal narrations of history. Time dissipates to shining ether the solid angularity of facts. No anchor, no cable, no fences avail to keep a fact a fact. Babylon, Troy, Tyre, Palestine, and even early Rome are passing already into fiction. The Garden of Eden, the sun standing still in Gibeon, is poetry thenceforward to all nations. Who cares what the fact was, when we have made a constellation of it to hang in heaven an immortal sign? London and Paris and New York must go the same way. "What is history," said Napoleon, "but a fable agreed upon?" This life of ours is stuck round with Egypt, Greece, Gaul, England, War, Colonization, Church, Court and Commerce, as with so many flowers and wild ornaments grave and gay. I will not make more account of them. I believe in Eternity. I can find Greece, Asia, Italy, Spain and the Islands—the genius and creative principle of each and of all eras, in my own mind.

We are always coming up with the emphatic facts of history in our private experience and verifying them here. All history becomes subjective; in other words there is properly no history, only biography. Every mind must know the whole lesson for itself—must go over the whole ground. What it does not see, what it does not live, it will not know. What the former age has epitomized into a formula or rule for manipular convenience, it will lose all the good of verifying for itself, by means of the wall of that rule. Somewhere, sometime, it will demand and find compensation for that loss, by doing the work itself. Ferguson discovered many things in astronomy which had long been known. The better for him.

History must be this or it is nothing. Every law which the state enacts indicates a fact in human nature; that is all. We must in ourselves see the necessary reason of every fact—see how it could and must be. So stand before every public and private work; before an oration of Burke, before a victory of Napoleon, before a martyrdom of Sir Thomas More, of

Sidney, of Marmaduke Robinson; before a French Reign of Terror, and a Salem hanging of witches; before a fanatic Revival and the Animal Magnetism in Paris, or in Providence. We assume that we under like influence should be alike affected, and should achieve the like; and we aim to master intellectually the steps and reach the same height or the same degradation that our fellow, our proxy, has done.

All inquiry into antiquity, all curiosity respecting the Pyramids, the excavated cities, Stonehenge, the Ohio Circles, Mexico, Memphis—is the desire to do away this wild, savage, and preposterous There or Then, and introduce in its place the Here and the Now. Belzoni digs and measures in the mummy-pits and pyramids of Thebes until he can see the end of the difference between the monstrous work and himself. When he has satisfied himself, in general and in detail, that it was made by such a person as he, so armed and so motived, and to ends to which he himself should also have worked, the problem is solved; his thought lives along the whole line of temples and sphinxes and catacombs, passes through them all with satisfaction, and they live again to the mind, or are *now*.

A Gothic cathedral affirms that it was done by us and not done by us. Surely it was by man, but we find it not in our man. But we apply ourselves to the history of its production. We put ourselves into the place and state of the builder. We remember the forest-dwellers, the first temples, the adherence to the first type, and the decoration of it as the wealth of the nation increased; the value which is given to wood by carving led to the carving over the whole mountain of stone of a cathedral. When we have gone through this process, and added thereto the Catholic Church, its cross, its music, its processions, its Saints' days and image-worship, we have as it were been the man that made the minster; we have seen how it could and must be. We have the sufficient reason.

The difference between men is in their principle of association. Some men classify objects by color and size and other accidents of appearance; others by intrinsic likeness, or by the relation of cause and effect. The progress of the intellect is to the clearer vision of causes, which neglects surface differences. To the poet, to the philosopher, to the saint, all things are friendly and sacred, all events profitable, all days holy, all men divine. For the eye is fastened on the life, and slights the circumstance. Every chemical substance, every plant, every animal in its growth, teaches the unity of cause, the variety of appearance.

Upborne and surrounded as we are by this all-creating nature, soft and fluid as a cloud or the air, why should we be such hard pedants, and magnify a few forms? Why should we make account of time, or of magnitude, or of figure? The soul knows them not, and genius, obeying its law, knows how to play with them as a young child plays with graybeards and in churches. Genius studies the causal thought, and far back in the womb of things sees the rays parting from one orb, that diverge, ere they fall, by infinite diameters. Genius watches the monad through all his masks as he performs the metempsychosis of nature. Genius detects through the fly, through the caterpillar, through the grub, through the egg, the constant individual; through countless individuals the fixed species, through many species the genus; through all genera the steadfast type; through all the kingdoms of organized life the eternal unity. Nature is a mutable cloud which is always and never the same. She casts the same thought into troops of forms, as a poet makes twenty fables with one moral. Through the bruteness and toughness of matter, a subtle spirit bends all things to its own will. The adamant streams into soft but precise form before it, and whilst I look at it its outline and texture are changed again. Nothing is so fleeting as form; yet never does it quite deny itself. In man we still trace the remains or hints of all that we esteem badges of servitude in the lower races; yet in him they enhance his nobleness and grace; as Io, in Æschylus, transformed to a cow, offends the imagination; but how changed when as Isis in Egypt she meets Osiris-Jove, a beautiful woman with nothing of the metamorphosis left but the lunar horns as the splendid ornament of her brows!

The identity of history is equally intrinsic, the diversity equally obvious. There is, at the surface, infinite variety of things; at the centre there is simplicity of cause. How many are the acts of one man in which we recognize the same character! Observe the sources of our information in respect to the Greek genius. We have the *civil history* of that people, as Herodotus, Thucydides, Xenophon, and Plutarch have given it; a very sufficient account of what manner of persons they were and what they did. We have the same national mind expressed for us again in their *literature*, in epic and lyric poems, drama, and philosophy; a very complete form. Then we have it once more in their *architecture*, a beauty as of temperance itself, limited to the straight line and the square—a builded geometry. Then we have it once again in *sculpture*, the "tongue on the balance of expression," a multitude of forms in the utmost freedom of action and never transgressing the ideal serenity; like votaries performing some religious dance before the gods, and, though in convulsive pain or mortal combat, never daring to break the figure and decorum of their dance. Thus of the genius of one remarkable people we have a fourfold representation: and to the senses what more unlike than an ode of Pindar, a marble centaur, the peristyle of the Parthenon, and the last actions of Phocion?

Every one must have observed faces and forms which, without any resembling feature, make a like impression on the beholder. A particular picture or copy of verses, if it do not awaken the same train of images, will yet superinduce the same sentiment as some wild mountain walk, although the resemblance is nowise obvious to the senses, but is occult and out of the reach of the understanding. Nature is an endless combination and repetition of a very few laws. She hums the old well-known air through innumerable variations.

Nature is full of a sublime family likeness throughout her works, and delights in startling us with resemblances in the most unexpected quarters. I have seen the head of an old sachem of the forest which at once reminded the eye of a bald mountain summit, and the furrows of the brow suggested the strata of the rock. There are men whose manners have the same essential splendor as the simple and awful sculpture on the friezes of the Parthenon and the remains of the earliest Greek art. And there are compositions of the same strain to be found in the books of all ages. What is Guido's Rospigliosi Aurora but a morning thought, as the horses in it are only a morning cloud? If any one will but take pains to observe the variety of actions to which he is equally inclined in certain moods of mind, and those to which he is averse, he will see how deep is the chain of affinity.

A painter told me that nobody could draw a tree without in some sort becoming a tree; or draw a child by studying the outlines of its form merely—but by watching for a time his motions and plays, the painter enters into his nature and can then draw him at will in every attitude. So Roos "entered into the inmost nature of a sheep." I knew a draughtsman employed in a public survey who found that he could not sketch the rocks until their geological structure was first explained to him. In a certain state of thought is the common origin of very diverse works. It is the spirit and not the fact that is identical. By a deeper apprehension, and not primarily by a painful acquisition of many manual skills, the artist attains the power of awakening other souls to a given activity.

It has been said that "common souls pay with what they do, nobler souls with that which they are." And why? Because a profound nature awakens in us by its actions and words, by its very looks and manners, the same power and beauty that a gallery of sculpture or of pictures addresses.

Civil and natural history, the history of art and of literature, must be explained from individual history, or must remain words. There is nothing but is related to us, nothing that does not interest us—kingdom, college, tree, horse, or iron shoe—the roots of all things are in man. Santa Croce and the Dome of St. Peter's are lame copies after a divine model. Strasburg Cathedral is a material counterpart of the soul of Erwin of Steinbach. The true poem is the poet's mind; the true ship is the ship-builder. In the man, could we lay him open, we should see the reason for the last flourish and tendril of his work; as every spine and tint in the sea-shell preëxists in the secreting organs of the fish. The whole of heraldry and of chivalry is in courtesy. A man of fine manners shall pronounce your name with all the ornament that titles of nobility could ever add.

The trivial experience of every day is always verifying some old prediction to us and converting into things the words and signs which we had heard and seen without heed. A lady with whom I was riding in the forest said to me that the woods always seemed to her *to wait,* as if the genii who inhabit them suspended their deeds until the wayfarer had passed onward; a thought which poetry has celebrated in the dance of the fairies, which breaks off on the approach of human feet. The man who has seen the rising moon break out of the clouds at midnight, has been present like an archangel at the creation of light and of the world. I remember one summer day in the fields my companion pointed out to me

a broad cloud, which might extend a quarter of a mile
parallel to the horizon, quite accurately in the form of a
cherub as painted over churches—a round block in the centre,
which it was easy to animate with eyes and mouth, supported
on either side by wide-stretched symmetrical wings. What
appears once in the atmosphere may appear often, and it
was undoubtedly the archetype of that familiar ornament.
I have seen in the sky a chain of summer lightning which at
once showed to me that the Greeks drew from nature when
they painted the thunderbolt in the hand of Jove. I have seen
a snow-drift along the sides of the stone wall which obviously
gave the idea of the common architectural scroll to abut a
tower.

By surrounding ourselves with the original circumstances
we invent anew the orders and the ornaments of architecture,
as we see how each people merely decorated its primitive
abodes. The Doric temple preserves the semblance of the
wooden cabin in which the Dorian dwelt. The Chinese
pagoda is plainly a Tartar tent. The Indian and Egyptian
temples still betray the mounds and subterranean houses of
their forefathers. "The custom of making houses and tombs
in the living rock," says Heeren in his Researches on the
Ethiopians, "determined very naturally the principal character
of the Nubian Egyptian architecture to the colossal form
which it assumed. In these caverns, already prepared by
nature, the eye was accustomed to dwell on huge shapes and
masses, so that when art came to the assistance of nature
it could not move on a small scale without degrading itself.
What would statues of the usual size, or neat porches and
wings have been, associated with those gigantic halls before
which only Colossi could sit as watchmen or lean on the
pillars of the interior?"

The Gothic church plainly originated in a rude adaptation
of the forest trees, with all their boughs, to a festal or solemn
arcade; as the bands about the cleft pillars still indicate the
green withes that tied them. No one can walk in a road cut
through pine woods, without being struck with the architectural appearance of the grove, especially in winter, when
the barrenness of all other trees shows the low arch of the
Saxons. In the woods in a winter afternoon one will see as
readily the origin of the stained glass window, with which
the Gothic cathedrals are adorned, in the colors of the

western sky seen through the bare and crossing branches of the forest. Nor can any lover of nature enter the old piles of Oxford and the English cathedrals, without feeling that the forest overpowered the mind of the builder, and that his chisel, his saw and plane still reproduced its ferns, its spikes of flowers, its locust, elm, oak, pine, fir and spruce.

The Gothic cathedral is a blossoming in stone subdued by the insatiable demand of harmony in man. The mountain of granite blooms into an eternal flower, with the lightness and delicate finish as well as the aerial proportions and perspective of vegetable beauty.

In like manner all public facts are to be individualized, all private facts are to be generalized. Then at once History becomes fluid and true, and Biography deep and sublime. As the Persian imitated in the slender shafts and capitals of his architecture the stem and flower of the lotus and palm, so the Persian court in its magnificent era never gave over the nomadism of its barbarous tribes, but travelled from Ecbatana, where the spring was spent, to Susa in summer and to Babylon for the winter.

In the early history of Asia and Africa, Nomadism and Agriculture are the two antagonist facts. The geography of Asia and of Africa necessitated a nomadic life. But the nomads were the terror of all those whom the soil or the advantages of a market had induced to build towns. Agriculture therefore was a religious injunction, because of the perils of the state from nomadism. And in these late and civil countries of England and America these propensities still fight out the old battle, in the nation and in the individual. The nomads of Africa were constrained to wander, by the attacks of the gad-fly, which drives the cattle mad, and so compels the tribe to emigrate in the rainy season and to drive off the cattle to the higher sandy regions. The nomads of Asia follow the pasturage from month to month. In America and Europe the nomadism is of trade and curiosity; a progress, certainly, from the gad-fly of Astaboras to the Anglo and Italomania of Boston Bay. Sacred cities, to which a periodical religious pilgrimage was enjoined, or stringent laws and customs tending to invigorate the national bond, were the check on the old rovers; and the cumulative values of long residence are the restraints on the itinerancy of the present day. The antagonism of the two tendencies is not less active in individuals, as the love of adventure or the love of repose happens to predominate. A man of rude health and flowing spirits has the faculty of rapid domestication, lives in his wagon and roams through all latitudes as easily as a Calmuc. At sea, or in the forest, or in the snow, he sleeps as warm, dines with as good appetite, and associates as happily as beside his own chimneys. Or perhaps his facility is deeper seated, in the increased range of his faculties of observation, which yield him points of interest wherever fresh objects meet his eyes. The pastoral nations were needy and hungry to desperation; and this intellectual nomadism, in its excess, bankrupts the mind through the dissipation of power on a miscellany of objects. The home-keeping wit, on the other hand, is that continence or content which finds all the elements of life in its own soil; and which has its own perils of monotony and deterioration, if not stimulated by foreign infusions.

Every thing the individual sees without him corresponds to his states of mind, and every thing is in turn intelligible to him, as his onward thinking leads him into the truth to which that fact or series belongs.

The primeval world—the Fore-World, as the Germans say —I can dive to it in myself as well as grope for it with researching fingers in catacombs, libraries, and the broken reliefs and torsos of ruined villas.

What is the foundation of that interest all men feel in Greek history, letters, art and poetry, in all its periods from the Heroic or Homeric age down to the domestic life of the Athenians and Spartans, four or five centuries later? What but this, that every man passes personally through a Grecian period. The Grecian state is the era of the bodily nature, the perfection of the senses—of the spiritual nature unfolded in strict unity with the body. In it existed those human forms which supplied the sculptor with his models of Hercules, Phœbus, and Jove; not like the forms abounding in the streets of modern cities, wherein the face is a confused blur of features, but composed of incorrupt, sharply defined and symmetrical features, whose eye-sockets are so formed that it would be impossible for such eyes to squint and take furtive glances on this side and on that, but they must turn the whole head. The manners of that period are plain and fierce. The reverence exhibited is for personal qualities; courage, address, self-command, justice, strength, swiftness, a loud voice, a broad chest. Luxury and elegance are not known. A sparse population and want make every man his own valet, cook, butcher and soldier, and the habit of supplying his own needs educates the body to wonderful performances. Such are the Agamemnon and Diomed of Homer, and not far different is the picture Xenophon gives of himself and his compatriots in the Retreat of the Ten Thousand. "After the army had crossed the river Teleboas in Armenia, there fell much snow, and the troops lay miserably on the ground covered with it. But Xenophon arose naked, and taking an axe, began to split wood; whereupon others rose and did the like." Throughout his army exists a boundless liberty of speech. They quarrel for plunder, they wrangle with the generals on each new order, and Xenophon is as sharp-tongued as any and sharper-tongued than most, and so gives as good as he gets. Who does not see that this is a gang of great boys, with such a code of honor and such lax discipline as great boys have?

The costly charm of the ancient tragedy, and indeed of all the old literature, is that the persons speak simply—speak as persons who have great good sense without knowing it, before yet the reflective habit has become the predominant habit of the mind. Our admiration of the antique is not admiration of the old, but of the natural. The Greeks are not reflective, but perfect in their senses and in their health, with the finest physical organization in the world. Adults acted with the simplicity and grace of children. They made vases, tragedies and statues, such as healthy senses should—that is, in good taste. Such things have continued to be made in all ages, and are now, wherever a healthy physique exists; but, as a class, from their superior organization, they have surpassed all. They combine the energy of manhood with the engaging unconsciousness of childhood. The attraction of these manners is that they belong to man, and are known to every man in virtue of his being once a child; besides that there are always individuals who retain these characteristics. A person of child-like genius and inborn energy is still a Greek, and revives our love of the Muse of Hellas. I admire the love of nature in the Philoctetes. In reading those fine apostrophes to sleep, to the stars, rocks, mountains and waves, I feel time passing away as an ebbing sea. I feel the eternity of man, the identity of his thought. The Greek had, it seems, the same fellow-beings as I. The sun and moon, water and fire, met his heart precisely as they meet mine. Then the vaunted distinction between Greek and English, between Classic and Romantic schools, seems superficial and pedantic. When a thought of Plato becomes a thought to me—when a truth that fired the soul of Pindar fires mine, time is no more. When I feel that we two meet in a perception, that our two souls are tinged with the same hue, and do as it were run into one, why should I measure degrees of latitude, why should I count Egyptian years?

The student interprets the age of chivalry by his own age of chivalry, and the days of maritime adventure and circumnavigation by quite parallel miniature experiences of his own. To the sacred history of the world he has the same key. When the voice of a prophet out of the deeps of antiquity merely echoes to him a sentiment of his infancy, a prayer of his youth, he then pierces to the truth through all the confusion of tradition and the caricature of institutions.

Rare, extravagant spirits come by us at intervals, who disclose to us new facts in nature. I see that men of God have from time to time walked among men and made their commissions felt in the heart and soul of the commonest hearer. Hence evidently the tripod, the priest, the priestess inspired by the divine afflatus.

Jesus astonishes and overpowers sensual people. They cannot unite him to history, or reconcile him with themselves. As they come to revere their intuitions and aspire to live holily, their own piety explains every fact, every word.

How easily these old worships of Moses, of Zoroaster, of Menu, of Socrates, domesticate themselves in the mind. I cannot find any antiquity in them. They are mine as much as theirs.

I have seen the first monks and anchorets, without crossing seas or centuries. More than once some individual has appeared to me with such negligence of labor and such commanding contemplation, a haughty beneficiary begging in the name of God, as made good to the nineteenth century Simeon the Stylite, the Thebais, and the first Capuchins.

The priestcraft of the East and West, of the Magian, Brahmin, Druid, and Inca, is expounded in the individual's private life. The cramping influence of a hard formalist on a young child, in repressing his spirits and courage, paralyzing the understanding, and that without producing indignation, but only fear and obedience, and even much sympathy with the tyranny—is a familiar fact, explained to the child when he becomes a man, only by seeing that the oppressor of his youth is himself a child tyrannized over by those names and words and forms of whose influence he was merely the organ to the youth. The fact teaches him how Belus was worshipped and how the Pyramids were built, better than the discovery by Champollion of the names of all the workmen and the cost of every tile. He finds Assyria and the Mounds of Cholula at his door, and himself has laid the courses.

Again, in that protest which each considerate person makes against the superstition of his times, he repeats step for step the part of old reformers, and in the search after truth finds, like them, new perils to virtue. He learns again what moral vigor is needed to supply the girdle of a superstition. A great licentiousness treads on the heels of a reformation. How many times in the history of the world has the Luther of the day had to lament the decay of piety in his own household! "Doctor," said his wife to Martin Luther, one day, "how is it that whilst subject to papacy we prayed so often and with such fervor, whilst now we pray with the utmost coldness and very seldom?"

The advancing man discovers how deep a property he has in literature—in all fable as well as in all history. He finds that the poet was no odd fellow who described strange and impossible situations, but that universal man wrote by his pen a confession true for one and true for all. His own secret biography he finds in lines wonderfully intelligible to him dotted down before he was born. One after another he comes up in his private adventures with every fable of Æsop, of Homer, of Hafiz, of Ariosto, of Chaucer, of Scott, and verifies them with his own head and hands.

The beautiful fables of the Greeks, being proper creations of the imagination and not of the fancy, are universal verities. What a range of meanings and what perpetual pertinence has the story of Prometheus! Besides its primary value as the first chaper of the history of Europe (the mythology thinly veiling authentic facts, the invention of the mechanic arts and the migration of colonies), it gives the history of religion, with some closeness to the faith of later ages. Prometheus is the

Jesus of the old mythology. He is the friend of man; stands between the unjust "justice" of the Eternal Father and the race of mortals, and readily suffers all things on their account. But where it departs from the Calvinistic Christianity and exhibits him as the defier of Jove, it represents a state of mind which readily appears wherever the doctrine of Theism is taught in a crude, objective form, and which seems the self-defence of man against this untruth, namely a discontent with the believed fact that a God exists, and a feeling that the obligation of reverence is onerous. It would steal if it could the fire of the Creator, and live apart from him and independent of him. The Prometheus Vinctus is the romance of skepticism. Not less true to all time are the details of that stately apologue. Apollo kept the flocks of Admetus, said the poets. When the gods come among men, they are not known. Jesus was not; Socrates and Shakspeare were not. Antæus was suffocated by the gripe of Hercules, but every time he touched his mother-earth his strength was renewed. Man is the broken giant, and in all his weakness both his body and his mind are invigorated by habits of conversation with nature. The power of music, the power of poetry, to unfix and as it were clap wings to solid nature, interprets the riddle of Orpheus. The philosophical perception of identity through endless mutations of form makes him know the Proteus. What else am I who laughed or wept yesterday, who slept last night like a corpse, and this morning stood and ran? And what see I on any side but the transmigrations of Proteus? I can symbolize my thought by using the name of any creature, of any fact, because every creature is man agent or patient. Tantalus is but a name for you and me. Tantalus means the impossibility of drinking the waters of thought which are always gleaming and waving within sight of the soul. The transmigration of souls is no fable. I would it were; but men and women are only half human. Every animal of the barnyard, the field and the forest, of the earth and of the waters that are under the earth, has contrived to get a footing and to leave the print of its features and form in some one or other of these upright, heaven-facing speakers. Ah! brother, stop the ebb of thy soul—ebbing downward into the forms into whose habits thou hast now for many years slid. As near and proper to us is also that old fable of the Sphinx, who was said to sit in the road-side and put riddles to every passenger.

If the man could not answer, she swallowed him alive. If he could solve the riddle, the Sphinx was slain. What is our life but an endless flight of winged facts or events? In splendid variety these changes come, all putting questions to the human spirit. Those men who cannot answer by a superior wisdom these facts or questions of time, serve them. Facts encumber them, tyrannize over them, and make the men of routine, the men of *sense*, in whom a literal obedience to facts has extinguished every spark of that light by which man is truly man. But if the man is true to his better instincts or sentiments, and refuses the dominion of facts, as one that comes of a higher race; remains fast by the soul and sees the principle, then the facts fall aptly and supple into their places; they know their master, and the meanest of them glorifies him.

See in Goethe's Helena the same desire that every word should be a thing. These figures, he would say, these Chirons, Griffins, Phorkyas, Helen and Leda, are somewhat, and do exert a specific influence on the mind. So far then are they eternal entities, as real to-day as in the first Olympiad. Much revolving them he writes out freely his humor, and gives them body to his own imagination. And although that poem be as vague and fantastic as a dream, yet is it much more attractive than the more regular dramatic pieces of the same author, for the reason that it operates a wonderful relief to the mind from the routine of customary images—awakens the reader's invention and fancy by the wild freedom of the design, and by the unceasing succession of brisk shocks of surprise.

The universal nature, too strong for the petty nature of the bard, sits on his neck and writes through his hand; so that when he seems to vent a mere caprice and wild romance, the issue is an exact allegory. Hence Plato said that "poets utter great and wise things which they do not themselves understand." All the fictions of the Middle Age explain themselves as a masked or frolic expression of that which in grave earnest the mind of that period toiled to achieve. Magic and all that is ascribed to it is a deep presentiment of the powers of science. The shoes of swiftness, the sword of sharpness, the power of subduing the elements, of using the secret virtues of minerals, of understanding the voices of birds, are the obscure efforts of the mind in a right direction. The preternatural prowess of the hero, the gift of perpetual youth, and the like, are alike the endeavor of the human spirit "to bend the shows of things to the desires of the mind."

In Perceforest and Amadis de Gaul a garland and a rose bloom on the head of her who is faithful, and fade on the brow of the inconstant. In the story of the Boy and the Mantle even a mature reader may be surprised with a glow of virtuous pleasure at the triumph of the gentle Venelas; and indeed all the postulates of elfin annals—that the fairies do not like to be named; that their gifts are capricious and not to be trusted; that who seeks a treasure must not speak; and the like—I find true in Concord, however they might be in Cornwall or Bretagne.

Is it otherwise in the newest romance? I read the Bride of Lammermoor. Sir William Ashton is a mask for a vulgar temptation, Ravenswood Castle a fine name for proud poverty, and the foreign mission of state only a Bunyan disguise for honest industry. We may all shoot a wild bull that would toss the good and beautiful, by fighting down the unjust and sensual. Lucy Ashton is another name for fidelity, which is always beautiful and always liable to calamity in this world.

But along with the civil and metaphysical history of man, another history goes daily forward—that of the external world —in which he is not less strictly implicated. He is the compend of time; he is also the correlative of nature. His power consists in the multitude of his affinities, in the fact that his life is intertwined with the whole chain of organic and inorganic being. In old Rome the public roads beginning at the Forum proceeded north, south, east, west, to the centre of every province of the empire, making each market-town of Persia, Spain and Britain pervious to the soldiers of the capital: so out of the human heart go as it were highways to the heart of every object in nature, to reduce it under the dominion of man. A man is a bundle of relations, a knot of roots, whose flower and fruitage is the world. His faculties refer to natures out of him and predict the world he is to inhabit, as the fins of the fish foreshow that water exists, or the wings of an eagle in the egg presuppose air. He cannot live without a world. Put Napoleon in an island prison, let his faculties find no men to act on, no Alps to climb, no stake to play for, and he would beat the air, and appear stupid. Transport him to large countries, dense population, complex

interests and antagonist power, and you shall see that the
man Napoleon, bounded that is by such a profile and outline,
is not the virtual Napoleon. This is but Talbot's shadow—

> His substance is not here.
> For what you see is but the smallest part
> And least proportion of humanity;
> But were the whole frame here,
> It is of such a spacious, lofty pitch,
> Your roof were not sufficient to contain it.[1]

Columbus needs a planet to shape his course upon. Newton
and Laplace need myriads of age and thick-strewn celestial
areas. One may say a gravitating solar system is already proph-
esied in the nature of Newton's mind. Not less does the
brain of Davy or of Gay-Lussac, from childhood exploring
the affinities and repulsions of particles, anticipate the laws of
organization. Does not the eye of the human embryo predict
the light? the ear of Handel predict the witchcraft of
harmonic sound? Do not the constructive fingers of Watt,
Fulton, Whittemore, Arkwright, predict the fusible, hard, and
temperable texture of metals, the properties of stone, water,
and wood? Do not the lovely attributes of the maiden child
predict the refinements and decorations of civil society? Here
also we are reminded of the action of man on man. A mind
might ponder its thoughts for ages and not gain so much
self-knowledge as the passion of love shall teach it in a day.
Who knows himself before he has been thrilled with indignation at an outrage, or has heard an eloquent tongue, or has
shared the throb of thousands in a national exultation or
alarm? No man can antedate his experience, or guess what
faculty or feeling a new object shall unlock, any more than he
can draw to-day the face of a person whom he shall see
to-morrow for the first time.

I will not now go behind the general statement to explore
the reason of this correspondency. Let it suffice that in the
light of these two facts, namely, that the mind is One, and
that nature is its correlative, history is to be read and written.

Thus in all ways does the soul concentrate and reproduce
its treasures for each pupil. He too shall pass through the

---

[1] Shakespeare, *Henry VI, First Part*, Act II, scene iii.

whole cycle of experience. He shall collect into a focus the rays of nature. History no longer shall be a dull book. It shall walk incarnate in every just and wise man. You shall not tell me by languages and titles a cataloque of the volumes you have read. You shall make me feel what periods you have lived. A man shall be the Temple of Fame. He shall walk, as the poets have described that goddess, in a robe painted all over with wonderful events and experiences; his own form and features by their exalted intelligence shall be that variegated vest. I shall find in him the Foreworld; in his childhood the Age of Gold, the Apples of Knowledge, the Argonautic Expedition, the calling of Abraham, the building of the Temple, the Advent of Christ, Dark Ages, the Revival of Letters, the Reformation, the discovery of new lands, the opening of new sciences and new regions in man. He shall be the priest of Pan, and bring with him into humble cottages the blessing of the morning stars, and all the recorded benefits of heaven and earth.

Is there somewhat overweening in this claim? Then I reject all I have written, for what is the use of pretending to know what we know not? But it is the fault of our rhetoric that we cannot strongly state one fact without seeming to belie some other. I hold our actual knowledge very cheap. Hear the rats in the wall, see the lizard on the fence, the fungus under foot, the lichen on the log. What do I know sympathetically, morally, of either of these worlds of life? As old as the Caucasian man—perhaps older—these creatures have kept their counsel beside him, and there is no record of any word or sign that has passed from one to the other. What connection do the books show between the fifty or sixty chemical elements and the historical eras? Nay, what does history yet record of the metaphysical annals of man? What light does it shed on those mysteries which we hide under the names Death and Immortality? Yet every history should be written in a wisdom which divined the range of our affinities and looked at facts as symbols. I am ashamed to see what a shallow village tale our so-called History is. How many times we must say Rome, and Paris, and Constantinople! What does Rome know of rat and lizard? What are Olympiads and Consulates to these neighboring systems of being? Nay, what food or experience or succor have they for the Esqui-

maux seal-hunter, for the Kanàka in his canoe, for the fisherman, the stevedore, the porter?

Broader and deeper we must write our annals—from an
ethical reformation, from an influx of the ever new, ever
sanative conscience—if we would trulier express our central
and wide-related nature, instead of this old chronology of
selfishness and pride to which we have too long lent our eyes.
Already that day exists for us, shines in on us at unawares,
but the path of science and of letters is not the way into
nature. The idiot, the Indian, the child and unschooled
farmer's boy stand nearer to the light by which nature is to
be read, than the dissector or the antiquary.

From *Essays, First Series*

Self-Reliance

I read the other day some verses written by an eminent
painter which were original and not conventional. The soul
always hears an admonition in such lines, let the subject
be what it may. The sentiment they instil is of more value
than any thought they may contain. To believe your own
thought, to believe that what is true for you in your private
heart is true for all men—that is genius. Speak your latent
conviction, and it shall be the universal sense: for the inmost in due time becomes the outmost, and our first thought
is rendered back to us by the trumpets of the Last Judgment.
Familiar as the voice of the mind is to each, the highest merit
we ascribe to Moses, Plato and Milton is that they set at
naught books and traditions, and spoke not what men, but
what *they* thought. A man should learn to detect and watch
that gleam of light which flashes across his mind from within,
more than the lustre of the firmament of bards and sages. Yet
he dismisses without notice his thought, because it is his. In
every work of genius we recognize our own rejected thoughts;
they come back to us with a certain alienated majesty. Great

works of art have no more affecting lesson for us than this. They teach us to abide by our spontaneous impression with good-humored inflexibility then most when the whole cry of voices is on the other side. Else to-morrow a stranger will say with masterly good sense precisely what we have thought and felt all the time, and we shall be forced to take with shame our own opinion from another.

There is a time in every man's education when he arrives at the conviction that envy is ignorance; that imitation is suicide; that he must take himself for better for worse as his portion; that though the wide universe is full of good, no kernel of nourishing corn can come to him but through his toil bestowed on that plot of ground which is given to him to till. The power which resides in him is new in nature, and none but he knows what that is which he can do, nor does he know until he has tried. Not for nothing one face, one character, one fact, makes much impression on him, and another none. This sculpture in the memory is not without preëstablished harmony. The eye was placed where one ray should fall, that it might testify of that particular ray. We but half express ourselves, and are ashamed of that divine idea which each of us represents. It may be safely trusted as proportionate and of good issues, so it be faithfully imparted, but God will not have his work made manifest by cowards. A man is relieved and gay when he has put his heart into his work and done his best; but what he has said or done otherwise shall give him no peace. It is a deliverance which does not deliver. In the attempt his genius deserts him; no muse befriends; no invention, no hope.

Trust thyself: every heart vibrates to that iron string. Accept the place the divine providence has found for you, the society of your contemporaries, the connection of events. Great men have always done so, and confided themselves childlike to the genius of their age, betraying their perception that the absolutely trustworthy was seated at their heart, working through their hands, predominating in all their being. And we are now men, and must accept in the highest mind the same transcendent destiny; and not minors and invalids in a protected corner, not cowards fleeing before a revolution, but guides, redeemers and benefactors, obeying the Almighty effort and advancing on Chaos and the Dark.

What pretty oracles nature yields us on this text in the

face and behavior of children, babes, and even brutes! That divided and rebel mind, that distrust of a sentiment because our arithmetic has computed the strength and means opposed to our purpose, these have not. Their mind being whole, their eye is as yet unconquered, and when we look in their faces we are disconcerted. Infancy conforms to nobody; all conform to it; so that one babe commonly makes four or five out of the adults who prattle and play to it. So God has armed youth and puberty and manhood no less with its own piquancy and charm, and made it enviable and gracious and its claims not to be put by, if it will stand by itself. Do not think the youth has no force, because he cannot speak to you and me. Hark! in the next room his voice is sufficiently clear and emphatic. It seems he knows how to speak to his contemporaries. Bashful or bold then, he will know how to make us seniors very unnecessary.

The nonchalance of boys who are sure of a dinner, and would disdain as much as a lord to do or say aught to conciliate one, is the healthy attitude of human nature. A boy is in the parlor what the pit is in the playhouse; independent, irresponsible, looking out from his corner on such people and facts as pass by, he tries and sentences them on their merits, in the swift, summary way of boys, as good, bad, interesting, silly, eloquent, troublesome. He cumbers himself never about consequences, about interests; he gives an independent, genuine verdict. You must court him; he does not court you. But the man is as it were clapped into jail by his consciousness. As soon as he has once acted or spoken with *éclat* he is a committed person, watched by the sympathy or the hatred of hundreds, whose affections must now enter into his account. There is no Lethe for this. Ah, that he could pass again into his neutrality! Who can thus avoid all pledges and, having observed, observe again from the same unaffected, unbiased, unbribable, unaffrighted innocence—must always be formidable. He would utter opinions on all passing affairs, which being seen to be not private but necessary, would sink like darts into the ear of men and put them in fear.

These are the voices which we hear in solitude, but they grow faint and inaudible as we enter into the world. Society everywhere is in conspiracy against the manhood of every one of its members. Society is a joint-stock company, in which the members agree, for the better securing of his bread to each shareholder, to surrender the liberty and culture of the eater. The virtue in most request is conformity. Self-reliance is its aversion. It loves not realities and creators, but names and customs.

Whoso would be a man, must be a nonconformist. He who would gather immortal palms must not be hindered by the name of goodness, but must explore if it be goodness. Nothing is at last sacred but the integrity of your own mind. Absolve you to yourself, and you shall have the suffrage of the world. I remember an answer which when quite young I was prompted to make to a valued adviser who was wont to importune me with the dear old doctrines of the church. On my saying, "What have I to do with the sacredness of traditions, if I live wholly from within?" my friend suggested, "But these impulses may be from below, not from above." I replied, "They do not seem to me to be such; but if I am the Devil's child, I will live then from the Devil." No law can be sacred to me but that of my nature. Good and bad are but names very readily transferable to that or this; the only right is what is after my constitution; the only wrong what is against it. A man is to carry himself in the presence of all opposition as if every thing were titular and ephemeral but he. I am ashamed to think how easily we capitulate to badges and names, to large societies and dead institutions. Every decent and well-spoken individual affects and sways me more than is right. I ought to go upright and vital, and speak the rude truth in all ways. If malice and vanity wear the coat of philanthropy, shall that pass? If an angry bigot assumes this bountiful cause of Abolition, and comes to me with his last news from Barbadoes, why should I not say to him, "Go love thy infant; love thy wood-chopper; be good-natured and modest; have that grace; and never varnish your hard, uncharitable ambition with this incredible tenderness for black folk a thousand miles off. Thy love afar is spite at home." Rough and graceless would be such greeting, but truth is handsomer than the affectation of love. Your goodness must have some edge to it—else it is none. The doctrine of hatred must be preached, as the counteraction of the doctrine of love, when that pules and whines. I shun father and mother and wife and brother when my genius calls me. I would write on the lintels of the door-post, *Whim*. I hope it is somewhat better than whim at last, but we cannot spend the day in explanation. Expect me not to show cause why I seek or why I exclude company. Then again, do not tell me, as a good man did to-day, of my obligation to put all poor men in good situations. Are they *my* poor? I tell thee, thou foolish philanthropist, that I grudge the dollar, the dime, the cent I give to such men as do not belong to me and to whom I do not belong. There is a class of persons to whom by all spiritual affinity I am bought and sold; for them I will go to prison if need be; but your miscellaneous popular charities; the education at college of fools; the building of meeting-houses to the vain end to which many now stand; alms to sots, and the thousand-fold Relief Societies—though I confess with shame I sometimes succumb and give the dollar, it is a wicked dollar, which by and by I shall have the manhood to withhold.

Virtues are, in the popular estimate, rather the exception than the rule. There is the man *and* his virtues. Men do what is called a good action, as some piece of courage or charity, much as they would pay a fine in expiation of daily non-appearance on parade. Their works are done as an apology or extenuation of their living in the world—as invalids and the insane pay a high board. Their virtues are penances. I do not wish to expiate, but to live. My life is for itself and not for a spectacle. I much prefer that it should be of a lower strain, so it be genuine and equal, than that it should be glittering and unsteady. I wish it to be sound and sweet, and not to need diet and bleeding. I ask primary evidence that you are a man, and refuse this appeal from the man to his actions. I know that for myself it makes no difference whether I do or forbear those actions which are reckoned excellent. I cannot consent to pay for a privilege where I have intrinsic right. Few and mean as my gifts may be, I actually am, and do not need for my own assurance or the assurance of my fellows any secondary testimony.

What I must do is all that concerns me, not what the people think. This rule, equally arduous in actual and in intellectual life, may serve for the whole distinction between greatness and meanness. It is the harder because you will always find those who think they know what is your duty better than you know it. It is easy in the world to live after the world's opinion; it is easy in solitude to live after our own; but the great man is he who in the midst of the crowd keeps with perfect sweetness the independence of solitude.

The objection to conforming to usages that have become dead to you is that it scatters your force. It loses your time and blurs the impression of your character. If you maintain a dead church, contribute to a dead Bible-society, vote with a great party either for the government or against it, spread your table like base housekeepers—under all these screens I have difficulty to detect the precise man you are: and of course so much force is withdrawn from your proper life. But do your work, and I shall know you. Do your work, and you shall reinforce yourself. A man must consider what a blindman's-buff is this game of conformity. If I know your sect I anticipate your argument. I hear a preacher announce for his text and topic the expediency of one of the institutions of his church. Do I not know beforehand that not possibly can he say a new and spontaneous word? Do I not know that with all this ostentation of examining the grounds of the institution he will do no such thing? Do I not know that he is pledged to himself not to look but at one side, the permitted side, not as a man, but as a parish minister? He is a retained attorney, and these airs of the bench are the emptiest affectation. Well, most men have bound their eyes with one or another hand-kerchief, and attached themselves to some one of these communities of opinion. This conformity makes them not false in a few particulars, authors of a few lies, but false in all particulars. Their every truth is not quite true. Their two is not the real two, their four not the real four; so that every word they say chagrins us and we know not where to begin to set them right. Meantime nature is not slow to equip us in the prison-uniform of the party to which we adhere. We come to wear one cut of face and figure, and acquire by degrees the gentlest asinine expression. There is a mortifying experience in particular, which does not fail to wreak itself also in the general history; I mean "the foolish face of praise," the forced smile which we put on in company where we do not feel at ease, in answer to conversation which does not interest us. The muscles, not spontaneously moved but moved by a low usurping wilfulness, grow tight about the outline of the face, with the most disagreeable sensation.

For nonconformity the world whips you with its displeasure. And therefore a man must know how to estimate a sour face. The by-standers look askance on him in the public street or in the friend's parlor. If this aversion had its origin in contempt and resistance like his own he might well go home with a sad countenance; but the sour faces of the multitude, like their sweet faces, have no deep cause, but are put on and off as the wind blows and a newspaper directs. Yet is the discontent of the multitude more formidable than that of the senate and the college. It is easy enough for a firm man who knows the world to brook the rage of the cultivated classes. Their rage is decorous and prudent, for they are timid, as being very vulnerable themselves. But when to their feminine rage the indignation of the people is added, when the ignorant and the poor are aroused, when the unintelligent brute force that lies at the bottom of society is made to growl and mow, it needs the habit of magnanimity and religion to treat it godlike as a trifle of no concernment.

The other terror that scares us from self-trust is our consistency; a reverence for our past act or word because the eyes of others have no other data for computing our orbit than our past acts, and we are loth to disappoint them.

But why should you keep your head over your shoulder? Why drag about this corpse of your memory, lest you contradict somewhat you have stated in this or that public place? Suppose you should contradict yourself; what then? It seems to be a rule of wisdom never to rely on your memory alone, scarcely even in acts of pure memory, but to bring the past for judgment into the thousand-eyed present, and live ever in a new day. In your metaphysics you have denied personality to the Deity, yet when the devout motions of the soul come, yield to them heart and life, though they should clothe God with shape and color. Leave your theory, as Joseph his coat in the hand of the harlot, and flee.

A foolish consistency is the hobgoblin of little minds, adored by little statesmen and philosophers and divines. With consistency a great soul has simply nothing to do. He may as well concern himself with his shadow on the wall. Speak what you think now in hard words and to-morrow speak what to-morrow thinks in hard words again, though it contradict every thing you said to-day. "Ah, so you shall be sure to be misunderstood." Is it so bad then to be misunderstood? Pythagoras was misunderstood, and Socrates, and Jesus, and Luther, and Copernicus, and Galileo, and Newton, and every pure and wise spirit that ever took flesh. To be great is to be misunderstood.

I suppose no man can violate his nature. All the sallies of his will are rounded in by the law of his being, as the inequalities of Andes and Himmaleh are insignificant in the curve of the sphere. Nor does it matter how you gauge and try him. A character is like an acrostic or Alexandrian stanza— read it forward, backward, or across, it still spells the same thing. In this pleasing contrite wood-life which God allows me, let me record day by day my honest thought without prospect or retrospect, and, I cannot doubt, it will be found symmetrical, though I mean it not and see it not. My book should smell of pines and resound with the hum of insects. The swallow over my window should interweave that thread or straw he carries in his bill into my web also. We pass for what we are. Character teaches above our wills. Men imagine that they communicate their virtue or vice only by overt actions, and do not see that virtue or vice emit a breath every moment.

There will be an agreement in whatever variety of actions, so they be each honest and natural in their hour. For of one will, the actions will be harmonious, however unlike they seem. These varieties are lost sight of at a little distance, at a little height of thought. One tendency unites them all. The voyage of the best ship is a zigzag line of a hundred tacks. See the line from a sufficient distance, and it straightens itself to the average tendency. Your genuine action will explain itself and will explain your other genuine actions. Your conformity explains nothing. Act singly, and what you have already done singly will justify you now. Greatness appeals to the future. If I can be firm enough to-day to do right and scorn eyes, I must have done so much right before as to defend me now. Be it how it will, do right now. Always scorn appearances and you always may. The force of character is cumulative. All the foregone days of virtue work their health into this. What makes the majesty of the heroes of the senate and the field, which so fills the imagination? The consciousness of a train of great days and victories behind. They shed a united light on the advancing actor. He is attended as by a visible escort of angels. That is it which throws thunder into Chatham's voice, and dignity into Washington's port, and America into Adams's eye. Honor is venerable to us because it is no ephemera. It is always ancient virtue. We worship it to-day because it is not of to-day. We love it and pay it homage because it is not a trap for our love and homage, but is self-dependent, self-derived, and therefore of an old immaculate pedigree, even if shown in a young person.

I hope in these days we have heard the last of conformity and consistency. Let the words be gazetted and ridiculous henceforward. Instead of the gong for dinner, let us hear a whistle from the Spartan fife. Let us never bow and apologize more. A great man is coming to eat at my house. I do not wish to please him; I wish that he should wish to please me. I will stand here for humanity, and though I would make it kind, I would make it true. Let us affront and reprimand the smooth mediocrity and squalid contentment of the times, and hurl in the face of custom and trade and office, the fact which is the upshot of all history, that there is a great responsible Thinker and Actor working wherever a man works; that a true man belongs to no other time or place, but is the centre of things. Where he is, there is nature. He measures you and all men and all events. Ordinarily, every body in society reminds us of somewhat else, or of some other person. Character, reality, reminds you of nothing else; it takes place of the whole creation. The man must be so much that he must make all circumstances indifferent. Every true man is a cause, a country, and an age; requires infinite spaces and numbers and time fully to accomplish his design; and posterity seem to follow his steps as a train of clients. A man Cæsar is born, and for ages after we have a Roman Empire. Christ is born, and millions of minds so grow and cleave to his genius that he is confounded with virtue and the possible of man. An institution is the lengthened shadow of one man; as, Monachism, of the Hermit Antony; the Reformation, of Luther; Quakerism, of Fox; Methodism, of Wesley; Abolition, of Clarkson. Scipio, Milton called "the height of Rome;" and all history resolves itself very easily into the biography of a few stout and earnest persons.

Let a man then know his worth, and keep things under his feet. Let him not peep or steal, or skulk up and down with the air of a charity-boy, a bastard, or an interloper in the world which exists for him. But the man in the street, finding no worth in himself which corresponds to the force which built a tower or sculptured a marble god, feels poor when he looks on these. To him a palace, a statue, or a costly book have an alien and forbidding air, much like a gay equipage,

and seem to say like that, "Who are you, Sir?" Yet they all
are his, suitors for his notice, petitioners to his faculties that
they will come out and take possession. The picture waits for
my verdict; it is not to command me, but I am to settle its
claims to praise. That popular fable of the sot who was
picked up dead-drunk in the street, carried to the duke's
house, washed and dressed and laid in the duke's bed, and,
on his waking, treated with all obsequious ceremony like the
duke, and assured that he had been insane, owes its popularity
to the fact that it symbolizes so well the state of man, who
is in the world a sort of sot, but now and then wakes up,
exercises his reason and finds himself a true prince.

Our reading is mendicant and sycophantic. In history our
imagination plays us false. Kingdom and lordship, power and
estate, are a gaudier vocabulary than private John and Edward in a small house and common day's work; but the things
of life are the same to both; the sum total of both is the
same. Why all this deference to Alfred and Scanderbeg and
Gustavus? Suppose they were virtuous; did they wear out
virtue? As great a stake depends on your private act to-day
as followed their public and renowned steps. When private
men shall act with original views, the lustre will be transferred from the actions of kings to those of gentlemen.

The world has been instructed by its kings, who have so
magnetized the eyes of nations. It has been taught by this
colossal symbol the mutual reverence that is due from man
to man. The joyful loyalty with which men have everywhere
suffered the king, the noble, or the great proprietor to walk
among them by a law of his own, make his own scale of men
and things and reverse theirs, pay for benefits not with money
but with honor, and represent the law in his person, was the
hieroglyphic by which they obscurely signified their consciousness of their own right and comeliness, the right of
every man.

The magnetism which all original action exerts is explained
when we inquire the reason of self-trust. Who is the Trustee?
What is the aboriginal Self, on which a universal reliance may
be grounded? What is the nature and power of that science-
baffling star, without parallax, without calculable elements,
which shoots a ray of beauty even into trivial and impure
actions, if the least mark of independence appear? The inquiry leads us to that source, at once the essence of genius,

of virtue, and of life, which we call Spontaneity or Instinct. We denote this primary wisdom as Intuition, whilst all later teachings are tuitions. In that deep force, the last fact behind which analysis cannot go, all things find their common origin. For the sense of being which in calm hours rises, we know not how, in the soul, is not diverse from things, from space, from light, from time, from man, but one with them and proceeds obviously from the same source whence their life and being also proceed. We first share the life by which things exist and afterwards see them as appearances in nature and forget that we have shared their cause. Here is the fountain of action and of thought. Here are the lungs of that inspiration which giveth man wisdom and which cannot be denied without impiety and atheism. We lie in the lap of immense intelligence, which makes us receivers of its truth and organs of its activity. When we discern justice, when we discern truth, we do nothing of ourselves, but allow a passage to its beams. If we ask whence this comes, if we seek to pray into the soul that causes, all philosophy is at fault. Its presence or its absence is all we can affirm. Every man discriminates between the voluntary acts of his mind and his involuntary perceptions, and knows that to his involuntary perceptions a perfect faith is due. He may err in the expression of them, but he knows that these things are so, like day and night, not to be disputed. My wilful actions and acquisitions are but roving; the idlest reverie, the faintest native emotion, command my curiosity and respect. Thoughtless people contradict as readily the statement of perceptions as of opinions, or rather much more readily; for they do not distinguish between perception and notion. They fancy that I choose to see this or that thing. But perception is not whimsical, but fatal. If I see a trait, my children will see it after me, and in course of time all mankind—although it may chance that no one has seen it before me. For my perception of it is as much a fact as the sun.

The relations of the soul to the divine spirit are so pure that it is profane to seek to interpose helps. It must be that when God speaketh he should communicate, not one thing, but all things; should fill the world with his voice; should scatter forth light, nature, time, souls, from the centre of the present thought; and new date and new create the whole. Whenever a mind is simple and receives a divine wisdom, old things pass away—means, teachers, texts, temples fall;

it lives now, and absorbs past and future into the present hour. All things are made sacred by relation to it—one as much as another. All things are dissolved to their centre by their cause, and in the universal miracle petty and particular miracles disappear. If therefore a man claims to know and speak of God and carries you backward to the phraseology of some old mouldered nation in another country, in another world, believe him not. Is the acorn better than the oak which is its fulness and completion? Is the parent better than the child into whom he has cast his ripened being? Whence then this worship of the past? The centuries are conspirators against the sanity and authority of the soul. Time and space are but physiological colors which the eye makes, but the soul is light: where it is, is day; where it was, is night; and history is an impertinence and an injury if it be any thing more than a cheerful apologue or parable of my being and becoming.

Man is timid and apologetic; he is no longer upright; he dares not say "I think," "I am," but quotes some saint or sage. He is ashamed before the blade of grass or the blowing rose. These roses under my window make no reference to former roses or to better ones; they are for what they are; they exist with God to-day. There is no time to them. There is simply the rose; it is perfect in every moment of its existence. Before a leaf-bud has burst, its whole life acts; in the full-blown flower there is no more; in the leafless root there is no less. Its nature is satisfied and it satisfies nature in all moments alike. But man postpones or remembers; he does not live in the present, but with reverted eye laments the past, or, heedless of the riches that surround him, stands on tiptoe to foresee the future. He cannot be happy and strong until he too lives with nature in the present, above time.

This should be plain enough. Yet see what strong intellects dare not yet hear God himself unless he speak the phraseology of I know not what David, or Jeremiah, or Paul. We shall not always set so great a price on a few texts, on a few lives. We are like children who repeat by rote the sentences of grandames and tutors, and as they grow older, of the men of talents and character they chance to see—painfully recollecting the exact words they spoke; afterwards, when they come into the point of view which those had who uttered these sayings, they understand them and are willing to let the words go; for at any time they can use words as good when occasion comes. If we live truly, we shall see truly. It is as easy for the strong man to be strong, as it is for the weak to be weak. When we have new perception, we shall gladly disburden the memory of its hoarded treasures as old rubbish. When a man lives with God, his voice shall be as sweet as the murmur of the brook and the rustle of the corn.

And now at last the highest truth on this subject remains unsaid; probably cannot be said; for all that we say is the far-off remembering of the intuition. That thought by what I can now nearest approach to say it, is this. When good is near you, when you have life in yourself, it is not by any known or accustomed way; you shall not discern the footprints of any other; you shall not see the face of man; you shall not hear any name—the way, the thought, the good, shall be wholly strange and new. It shall exclude example and experience. You take the way from man, not to man. All persons that ever existed are its forgotten ministers. Fear and hope are alike beneath it. There is somewhat low even in hope. In the hour of vision there is nothing that can be called gratitude, nor properly joy. The soul raised over passion beholds identity and eternal causation, perceives the self-existence of Truth and Right, and calms itself with knowing that all things go well. Vast spaces of nature, the Atlantic Ocean, the South Sea; long intervals of time, years, centuries, are of no account. This which I think and feel underlay every former state of life and circumstances, as it does underlie my present, and what is called life and what is called death.

Life only avails, not the having lived. Power ceases in the instant of repose; it resides in the moment of transition from a past to a new state, in the shooting of the gulf, in the darting to an aim. This one fact the world hates; that the soul *becomes;* for that forever degrades the past, turns all riches to poverty, all reputation to a shame, confounds the saint with the rogue, shoves Jesus and Judas equally aside. Why then do we prate of self-reliance? Inasmuch as the soul is present there will be power not confident but agent. To talk of reliance is a poor external way of speaking. Speak rather of that which relies because it works and is. Who has more obedience than I masters me, though he should not raise his finger. Round him I must revolve by the gravitation of spirits. We fancy it rhetoric when we speak of eminent virtue. We do not yet see that virtue is Height, and that a man or a company of men, plastic and permeable to principles, by the law of nature must overpower and ride all cities, nations, kings, rich men, poets, who are not.

This is the ultimate fact which we so quickly reach on this, as on every topic, the resolution of all into the ever-blessed ONE. Self-existence is the attribute of the Supreme Cause, and it constitutes the measure of good by the degree in which it enters into all lower forms. All things real are so by so much virtue as they contain. Commerce, husbandry, hunting, whaling, war, eloquence, personal weight, are somewhat, and engage my respect as examples of its presence and impure action. I see the same law working in nature for conservation and growth. Power is, in nature, the essential measure of right. Nature suffers nothing to remain in her kingdoms which cannot help itself. The genesis and maturation of a planet, its poise and orbit, the bended tree recovering itself from the strong wind, the vital resources of every animal and vegetable, are demonstrations of the self-sufficing and therefore self-relying soul.

Thus all concentrates: let us not rove; let us sit at home with the cause. Let us stun and astonish the intruding rabble of men and books and institutions by a simple declaration of the divine fact. Bid the invaders take the shoes from off their feet, for God is here within. Let our simplicity judge them, and our docility to our own law demonstrate the poverty of nature and fortune beside our native riches.

But now we are a mob. Man does not stand in awe of man, nor is his genius admonished to stay at home, to put itself in communication with the internal ocean, but it goes abroad to beg a cup of water of the urns of other men. We must go alone. I like the silent church before the service begins, better than any preaching. How far off, how cool, how chaste the persons look, begirt each one with a precinct or sanctuary! So let us always sit. Why should we assume the faults of our friend, or wife, or father, or child, because they sit around our hearth, or are said to have the same blood? All men have my blood and I all men's. Not for that will I adopt their petulance or folly, even to the extent of being ashamed of it. But your isolation must not be mechanical, but spiritual, that is, must be elevation. At times the whole world seems to be in conspiracy to importune you with emphatic trifles.

Friend, client, child, sickness, fear, want, charity, all knock at once at thy closet door and say, "Come out unto us." But keep thy state; come not into their confusion. The power men possess to annoy me I give them by a weak curiosity. No man can come near me but through my act. "What we love that we have, but by desire we bereave ourselves of the love."

If we cannot at once rise to the sanctities of obedience and faith, let us at least resist our temptations; let us enter into the state of war and wake Thor and Woden, courage and constancy, in our Saxon breasts. This is to be done in our smooth times by speaking the truth. Check this lying hospitality and lying affection. Live no longer to the expectation of these deceived and deceiving people with whom we converse. Say to them, "O father, O mother, O wife, O brother, O friend, I have lived with you after appearances hitherto. Henceforward I am the truth's. Be it known unto you that henceforward I obey no law less than the eternal law. I will have no covenants but proximities. I shall endeavor to nourish my parents, to support my family, to be the chaste husband of one wife—but these relations I must fill after a new and unprecedented way. I appeal from your customs. I must be myself. I cannot break myself any longer for you, or you. If you can love me for what I am, we shall be the happier. If you cannot, I will still seek to deserve that you should. I will not hide my tastes or aversions. I will so trust that what is deep is holy, that I will do strongly before the sun and moon whatever inly rejoices me and the heart appoints. If you are noble, I will love you; if you are not, I will not hurt you and myself by hypocritical attentions. If you are true, but not in the same truth with me, cleave to your companions; I will seek my own. I do this not selfishly but humbly and truly. It is alike your interest, and mine, and all men's, however long we have dwelt in lies, to live in truth. Does this sound harsh to-day? You will soon love what is dictated by your nature as well as mine, and if we follow the truth it will bring us out safe at last." But so may you give these friends pain. Yes, but I cannot sell my liberty and my power, to save their sensibility. Besides, all persons have their moments of reason, when they look out into the region of absolute truth; then will they justify me and do the same thing.

The populace think that your rejection of popular standards

is a rejection of all standards, and mere antinomianism; and the bold sensualist will use the name of philosophy to gild his crimes. But the law of consciousness abides. There are two confessionals, in one or the other of which we must be shriven. You may fulfil your round of duties by clearing yourself in the *direct*, or in the *reflex* way. Consider whether you have satisfied your relations to father, mother, cousin, neighbor, town, cat and dog—whether any of these can upbraid you. But I may also neglect this reflex standard and absolve me to myself. I have my own stern claims and perfect circle. It denies the name of duty to many offices that are called duties. But if I can discharge its debts it enables me to dispense with the popular code. If any one imagines that this law is lax, let him keep its commandment one day.

And truly it demands something godlike in him who has cast off the common motives of humanity and has ventured to trust himself for a taskmaster. High be his heart, faithful his will, clear his sight, that he may in good earnest be doctrine, society, law, to himself, that a simple purpose may be to him as strong as iron necessity is to others!

If any man consider the present aspects of what is called by distinction *society*, he will see the need of these ethics. The sinew and heart of man seem to be drawn out, and we are become timorous, desponding whimperers. We are afraid of truth, afraid of fortune, afraid of death, and afraid of each other. Our age yields no great and perfect persons. We want men and women who shall renovate life and our social state, but we see that most natures are insolvent, cannot satisfy their own wants, have an ambition out of all proportion to their practical force and do lean and beg day and night continually. Our housekeeping is mendicant, our arts, our occupations, our marriages, our religion we have not chosen, but society has chosen for us. We are parlor soldiers. We shun the rugged battle of fate, where strength is born.

If our young men miscarry in their first enterprises they lose all heart. If the young merchant fails, men say he is *ruined*. If the finest genius studies at one of our colleges and is not installed in an office within one year afterwards in the cities or suburbs of Boston or New York, it seems to his friends and to himself that he is right in being disheartened and in complaining the rest of his life. A sturdy lad from New Hampshire or Vermont, who in turn tries all the professions, who *teams it, farms it, peddles*, keeps a school, preaches, edits a newspaper, goes to Congress, buys a township, and so forth, in successive years, and always like a cat falls on his feet, is worth a hundred of these city dolls. He walks abreast with his days and feels no shame in not "studying a profession," for he does not postpone his life, but lives already. He has not one chance, but a hundred chances. Let a Stoic open the resources of man and tell men they are not leaning willows, but can and must detach themselves; that with the exercise of self-trust, new powers shall appear; that a man is the word made flesh, born to shed healing to the nations; that he should be ashamed of our compassion, and that the moment he acts from himself, tossing the laws, the books, idolatries and customs out of the window, we pity him no more but thank and revere him—and that teacher shall restore the life of man to splendor and make his name dear to all history.

It is easy to see that a greater self-reliance must work a revolution in all the offices and relations of men; in their religion; in their education; in their pursuits; their modes of living; their association; in their property; in their speculative views.

1. In what prayers do men allow themselves! That which they call a holy office is not so much as brave and manly. Prayer looks abroad and asks for some foreign addition to come through some foreign virtue, and loses itself in endless mazes of natural and supernatural, and mediatorial and miraculous. Prayer that craves a particular commodity, anything less than all good, is vicious. Prayer is the contemplation of the facts of life from the highest point of view. It is the soliloquy of a beholding and jubilant soul. It is the spirit of God pronouncing his works good. But prayer as a means to effect a private end is meanness and theft. It supposes dualism and not unity in nature and consciousness. As soon as the man is at one with God, he will not beg. He will then see prayer in all action. The prayer of the farmer kneeling in his field to weed it, the prayer of the rower kneeling with the stroke of his oar, are true prayers heard throughout nature, though for cheap ends. Caratach, in Fletcher's "Bonduca," when admonished to inquire the mind of the god Audate, replies,

> His hidden meaning lies in our endeavors;
> Our valors are our best gods.

Another sort of false prayers are our regrets. Discontent is the want of self-reliance: it is infirmity of will. Regret calamities if you can thereby help the sufferer; if not, attend your own work and already the evil begins to be repaired. Our sympathy is just as base. We come to them who weep foolishly and sit down and cry for company, instead of imparting to them truth and health in rough electric shocks, putting them once more in communication with their own reason. The secret of fortune is joy in our hands. Welcome evermore to gods and men is the self-helping man. For him all doors are flung wide; him all tongues greet, all honors crown, all eyes follow with desire. Our love goes out to him and embraces him because he did not need it. We solicitously and apologetically caress and celebrate him because he held on his way and scorned our disapprobation. The gods love him because men hated him. "To the persevering mortal," said Zoroaster, "the blessed Immortals are swift."

As men's prayers are a disease of the will, so are their creeds a disease of the intellect. They say with those foolish Israelites, "Let not God speak to us, lest we die. Speak thou, speak any man with us, and we will obey." Everywhere I am hindered of meeting God in my brother, because he has shut his own temple doors and recites fables merely of his brother's, or his brother's brother's God. Every new mind is a new classification. If it prove a mind of uncommon activity and power, a Locke, a Lavoisier, a Hutton, a Bentham, a Fourier, it imposes its classification on other men, and lo! a new system. In proportion to the depth of the thought, and so to the number of the objects it touches and brings within reach of the pupil, is his complacency. But chiefly is this apparent in creeds and churches, which are also classifications of some powerful mind acting on the elemental thought of duty and man's relation to the Highest. Such is Calvinism, Quakerism, Swedenborgism. The pupil takes the same delight in subordinating every thing to the new terminology as a girl who has just learned botany in seeing a new earth and new seasons thereby. It will happen for a time that the pupil will find his intellectual power has grown by the study of his master's mind. But in all unbalanced minds the classification is idolized, passes for the end and not for a speedily exhaustible means, so that the walls of the system blend to their eye in the remote horizon with the walls of the universe; the luminaries of heaven seem to them hung on the arch their master built. They cannot imagine how you aliens have any right to see— how you can see; "It must be somehow that you stole the light from us." They do not yet perceive that light, unsystematic, indomitable, will break into any cabin, even into theirs. Let them chirp awhile and call it their own. If they are honest and do well, presently their neat new pinfold will be too strait and low, will crack, will lean, will rot and vanish, and the immortal light, all young and joyful, million-orbed, million-colored, will beam over the universe as on the first morning.

2. It is for want of self-culture that the superstition of Travelling, whose idols are Italy, England, Egypt, retains its fascination for all educated Americans. They who made England, Italy, or Greece venerable in the imagination, did so by sticking fast where they were, like an axis of the earth. In manly hours we feel that duty is our place. The soul is no traveller; the wise man stays at home, and when his necessities, his duties, on any occasion call him from his house, or into foreign lands, he is at home still and shall make men sensible by the expression of his countenance that he goes, the missionary of wisdom and virtue, and visits cities and men like a sovereign and not like an interloper or a valet.

I have no churlish objection to the circumnavigation of the globe for the purposes of art, of study, and benevolence, so that the man is first domesticated, or does not go abroad with the hope of finding somewhat greater than he knows. He who travels to be amused, or to get somewhat which he does not carry, travels away from himself, and grows old even in youth among old things. In Thebes, in Palmyra, his will and mind have become old and dilapidated as they. He carries ruins to ruins.

Travelling is a fool's paradise. Our first journeys discover to us the indifference of places. At home I dream that at Naples, at Rome, I can be intoxicated with beauty and lose my sadness. I pack my trunk, embrace my friends, embark on the sea and at last wake up in Naples, and there beside me is the stern fact, the sad self, unrelenting, identical, that I fled from. I seek the Vatican and the palaces. I affect to be intoxicated with sights and suggestions, but I am not intoxicated. My giant goes with me wherever I go.

3. But the rage of travelling is a symptom of a deeper un-

soundness affecting the whole intellectual action. The intellect is vagabond, and our system of education fosters restlessness. Our minds travel when our bodies are forced to stay at home. We imitate; and what is imitation but the travelling of the mind? Our houses are built with foreign taste; our shelves are garnished with foreign ornaments; our opinions, our tastes, our faculties, lean, and follow the Past and the Distant. The soul created the arts wherever they have flourished. It was in his own mind that the artist sought his model. It was an application of his own thought to the thing to be done and the conditions to be observed. And why need we copy the Doric or the Gothic model? Beauty, convenience, grandeur of thought and quaint expression are as near to us as to any, and if the American artist will study with hope and love the precise thing to be done by him, considering the climate, the soil, the length of the day, the wants of the people, the habit and form of the government, he will create a house in which all these will find themselves fitted, and taste and sentiment will be satisfied also.

Insist on yourself; never imitate. Your own gift you can present every moment with the cumulative force of a whole life's cultivation; but of the adopted talent of another you have only an extemporaneous half possession. That which each can do best, none but his Maker can teach him. No man yet knows what it is, nor can, till that person has exhibited it. Where is the master who could have taught Shakspeare? Where is the master who could have instructed Franklin, or Washington, or Bacon, or Newton? Every great man is a unique. The Scipionism of Scipio is precisely that part he could not borrow. Shakspeare will never be made by the study of Shakspeare. Do that which is assigned you, and you cannot hope too much or dare too much. There is at this moment for you an utterance brave and grand as that of the colossal chisel of Phidias, or trowel of the Egyptians, or the pen of Moses or Dante, but different from all these. Not possibly will the soul, all rich, all eloquent, with thousand-cloven tongue, deign to repeat itself; but if you can hear what these patriarchs say, surely you can reply to them in the same pitch of voice; for the ear and the tongue are two organs of one nature. Abide in the simple and noble regions of thy life, obey thy heart, and thou shalt reproduce the Fore-world again.

4. As our Religion, our Education, our Art look abroad, so does our spirit of society. All men plume themselves on the improvement of society, and no man improves.

Society never advances. It recedes as fast on one side as it gains on the other. It undergoes continual changes; it is barbarous, it is civilized, it is christianized, it is rich, it is scientific; but this change is not amelioration. For every thing that is given something is taken. Society acquires new arts and loses old instincts. What a contrast between the well-clad, reading, writing, thinking American, with a watch, a pencil and a bill of exchange in his pocket, and the naked New Zealander, whose property is a club, a spear, a mat and an undivided twentieth of a shed to sleep under! But compare the health of the two men and you shall see that the white man has lost his aboriginal strength. If the traveller tell us truly, strike the savage with a broad-axe and in a day or two the flesh shall unite and heal as if you struck the blow into soft pitch, and the same blow shall send the white to his grave.

The civilized man has built a coach, but has lost the use of his feet. He is supported on crutches, but lacks so much support of muscle. He has a fine Geneva watch, but he fails of the skill to tell the hour by the sun. A Greenwich nautical almanac he has, and so being sure of the information when he wants it, the man in the street does not know a star in the sky. The solstice he does not observe; the equinox he knows as little; and the whole bright calendar of the year is without a dial in his mind. His note-books impair his memory; his libraries overload his wit; the insurance-office increases the number of accidents; and it may be a question whether machinery does not encumber; whether we have not lost by refinement some energy, by a Christianity, entrenched in establishments and forms, some vigor of wild virtue. For every Stoic was a Stoic; but in Christendom where is the Christian?

There is no more deviation in the moral standard than in the standard of height or bulk. No greater men are now than ever were. A singular equality may be observed between the great men of the first and of the last ages; nor can all the science, art, religion, and philosophy of the nineteenth century avail to educate greater men than Plutarch's heroes, three or four and twenty centuries ago. Not in time is the race progressive. Phocion, Socrates, Anaxagoras, Diogenes, are great men, but they leave no class. He who is really of their class will not be called by their name, but will be his own man, and in his turn the founder of a sect. The arts and inventions of each period are only its costume and do not invigorate men. The harm of the improved machinery may compensate its good. Hudson and Behring accomplished so much in their fishing-boats as to astonish Parry and Franklin, whose equipment exhausted the resources of science and art. Galileo, with an opera-glass, discovered a more splendid series of celestial phenomena than any one since. Columbus found the New World in an undecked boat. It is curious to see the periodical disuse and perishing of means and machinery which were introduced with loud laudation a few years or centuries before. The great genius returns to essential man. We reckoned the improvements of the art of war among the triumphs of science, and yet Napoleon conquered Europe by the bivouac, which consisted of falling back on naked valor and disencumbering it of all aids. The Emperor held it impossible to make a perfect army, says Las Cases, "without abolishing our arms, magazines, commissaries and carriages, until, in imitation of the Roman custom, the soldier should receive his supply of corn, grind it in his hand-mill and bake his bread himself."

Society is a wave. The wave moves onward, but the water of which it is composed does not. The same particle does not rise from the valley to the ridge. Its unity is only phenomenal. The persons who make up a nation to-day, next year die, and their experience dies with them.

And so the reliance on Property, including the reliance on governments which protect it, is the want of self-reliance. Men have looked away from themselves and at things so long that they have come to esteem the religious, learned and civil institutions as guards of property, and they deprecate assaults on these, because they feel them to be assaults on property. They measure their esteem of each other by what each has, and not by what each is. But a cultivated man becomes ashamed of his property, out of new respect for his nature. Especially he hates what he has if he see that it is accidental —came to him by inheritance, or gift, or crime; then he feels that it is not having; it does not belong to him, has no root in him and merely lies there because no revolution or no robber takes it away. But that which a man is, does always by necessity acquire; and what the man acquires, is living property, which does not wait the beck of rulers, or mobs, or revolutions, or fire, or storm, or bankruptcies, but perpetually renews itself wherever the man breathes. "Thy lot or portion of life," said the Caliph Ali, "is seeking after thee; therefore be at rest from seeking after it." Our dependence on these foreign goods leads us to our slavish respect for numbers. The political parties meet in numerous conventions; the greater the concourse and with each new uproar of announcement, The delegation from Essex! The Democrats from New Hampshire! The Whigs of Maine! the young patriot feels himself stronger than before by a new thousand of eyes and arms. In like manner the reformers summon conventions and vote and resolve in multitude. Not so, O friends! will the God deign to enter and inhabit you, but by a method precisely the reverse. It is only as a man puts off all foreign support and stands alone that I see him to be strong and to prevail. He is weaker by every recruit to his banner. Is not a man better than a town? Ask nothing of men, and, in the endless mutation, thou only firm column must presently appear the upholder of all that surrounds thee. He who knows that power is inborn, that he is weak because he has looked for good out of him and elsewhere, and, so perceiving, throws himself unhesitatingly on his thought, instantly rights himself, stands in the erect position, commands his limbs, works miracles; just as a man who stands on his feet is stronger than a man who stands on his head.

So use all that is called Fortune. Most men gamble with her, and gain all, and lose all, as her wheel rolls. But do thou leave as unlawful these winnings, and deal with Cause and Effect, the chancellors of God. In the Will work and acquire, and thou hast chained the wheel of Chance, and shall sit hereafter out of fear from her rotations. A political victory, a rise of rents, the recovery of your sick or the return of your absent friend, or some other favorable event raises your spirits, and you think good days are preparing for you. Do not believe it. Nothing can bring you peace but yourself. Nothing can bring you peace but the triumph of principles.

From *Essays, First Series*

Compensation

Ever since I was a boy I have wished to write a discourse on Compensation; for it seemed to me when very young that on this subject life was ahead of theology and the people knew more than the preachers taught. The documents too from which the doctrine is to be drawn, charmed my fancy by their endless variety, and lay always before me, even in sleep; for they are the tools in our hands, the bread in our basket, the transactions of the street, the farm and the dwelling-house; greetings, relations, debts and credits, the influence of character, the nature and endowment of all men. It seemed to me also that in it might be shown men a ray of divinity, the present action of the soul of this world, clean from all vestige of tradition; and so the heart of man might be bathed by an inundation of eternal love, conversing with that which he knows was always and always must be, because it really is now. It appeared moreover that if this doctrine could be stated in terms with any resemblance to those bright intuitions in which this truth is sometimes revealed to us, it would be a star in many dark hours and crooked passages in our journey, that would not suffer us to lose our way.

I was lately confirmed in these desires by hearing a sermon at church. The preacher, a man esteemed for his orthodoxy, unfolded in the ordinary manner the doctrine of the Last Judgment. He assumed that judgment is not executed in this world; that the wicked are successful; that the good are miserable; and then urged from reason and from Scripture a compensation to be made to both parties in the next life. No offence appeared to be taken by the congregation at this doctrine. As far as I could observe when the meeting broke up they separated without remark on the sermon.

Yet what was the import of this teaching? What did the

preacher mean by saying that the good are miserable in the present life? Was it that houses and lands, offices, wine, horses, dress, luxury, are had by unprincipled men, whilst the saints are poor and despised; and that a compensation is to be made to these last hereafter, by giving them the like gratifications another day—bank-stock and doubloons, venison and champagne? This must be the compensation intended; for what else? Is it that they are to have leave to pray and praise? to love and serve men? Why, that they can do now. The legitimate inference the disciple would draw was, "We are to have *such* a good time as the sinners have now; "or, or, to push it to its extreme import, "You sin now, we shall sin by and by; we would sin now, if we could; not being successful we expect our revenge to-morrow."

The fallacy lay in the immense concession that the bad are successful; that justice is not done now. The blindness of the preacher consisted in deferring to the base estimate of the market of what constitutes a manly success, instead of confronting and convicting the world from the truth; announcing the presence of the soul; the omnipotence of the will; and so establishing the standard of good and ill, of success and falsehood.

I find a similar base tone in the popular religious works of the day and the same doctrines assumed by the literary men when occasionally they treat the related topics. I think that our popular theology has gained in decorum, and not in principle, over the superstitions it has displaced. But men are better than their theology. Their daily life gives it the lie. Every ingenuous and aspiring soul leaves the doctrine behind him in his own experience, and all men feel sometimes the falsehood which they cannot demonstrate. For men are wiser than they know. That which they hear in schools and pulpits without afterthought, if said in conversation would probably be questioned in silence. If a man dogmatize in a mixed company on Providence and the divine laws, he is answered by a silence which conveys well enough to an observer the dissatisfaction of the hearer, but his incapacity to make his own statement.

I shall attempt in this and the following chapter to record some facts that indicate the path of the law of Compensation; happy beyond my expectation if I shall truly draw the smallest arc of this circle.

Polarity, or action and reaction, we meet in every part of nature; in darkness and light; in heat and cold; in the ebb and flow of waters; in male and female; in the inspiration and expiration of plants and animals; in the equation of quantity and quality in the fluids of the animal body; in the systole and diastole of the heart; in the undulations of fluids and of sound; in the centrifugal and centripetal gravity; in electricity, galvanism, and chemical affinity. Superinduce magnetism at one end of a needle, the opposite magnetism takes place at the other end. If the south attracts, the north repels. To empty here, you must condense there. An inevitable dualism bisects nature, so that each thing is a half, and suggests another thing to make it whole; as, spirit, matter; man, woman; odd, even; subjective, objective; in, out; upper, under; motion, rest; yea, nay.

Whilst the world is thus dual, so is every one of its parts. The entire system of things gets represented in every particle. There is somewhat that resembles the ebb and flow of the sea, day and night, man and woman, in a single needle of the pine, in a kernel of corn, in each individual of every animal tribe. The reaction, so grand in the elements, is repeated within these small boundaries. For example, in the animal kingdom the physiologist has observed that no creatures are favorites, but a certain compensation balances every gift and every defect. A surplusage given to one part is paid out of a reduction from another part of the same creature. If the head and neck are enlarged, the trunk and extremities are cut short.

The theory of the mechanic forces is another example. What we gain in power is lost in time, and the converse. The periodic or compensating errors of the planets is another instance. The influences of climate and soil in political history is another. The cold climate invigorates. The barren soil does not breed fevers, crocodiles, tigers or scorpions.

The same dualism underlies the nature and condition of man. Every excess causes a defect; every defect an excess. Every sweet hath its sour; every evil its good. Every faculty which is a receiver of pleasure has an equal penalty put on its abuse. It is to answer for its moderation with its life. For every grain of wit there is a grain of folly. For every thing you have missed, you have gained something else; and for every thing you gain, you lose something. If riches increase, they are increased that use them. If the gatherer gathers too much, Nature takes out of the man what she puts into his chest; swells the estate, but kills the owner. Nature hates monopolies and exceptions. The waves of the sea do not more speedily seek a level from their loftiest tossing than the varieties of condition tend to equalize themselves. There is always some levelling circumstance that puts down the overbearing, the strong, the rich, the fortunate, substantially on the same ground with all others. Is a man too strong and fierce for society and by temper and position a bad citizen—a morose ruffian, with a dash of the pirate in him? Nature sends him a troop of pretty sons and daughters who are getting along in the dame's classes at the village school, and love and fear for them smooths his grim scowl to courtesy. Thus she contrives to intenerate the granite and felspar, takes the boar out and puts the lamb in and keeps her balance true.

The farmer imagines power and place are fine things. But the President has paid dear for his White House. It has commonly cost him all his peace, and the best of his manly attributes. To preserve for a short time so conspicuous an appearance before the world, he is content to eat dust before the real masters who stand erect behind the throne. Or do men desire the more substantial and permanent grandeur of genius? Neither has this an immunity. He who by force of will or of thought is great and overlooks thousands, has the charges of that eminence. With every influx of light comes new danger. Has he light? he must bear witness to the light, and always outrun that sympathy which gives him such keen satisfaction, by his fidelity to new revelations of the incessant soul. He must hate father and mother, wife and child. Has he all that the world loves and admires and covets? he must cast behind him their admiration and afflict them by faithfulness to his truth and become a byword and a hissing.

This law writes the laws of cities and nations. It is in vain to build or plot or combine against it. Things refuse to be mismanaged long. *Res nolunt diu male administrari.* Though no checks to a new evil appear, the checks exist, and will appear. If the government is cruel, the governor's life is not safe. If you tax too high, the revenue will yield nothing. If you make the criminal code sanguinary, juries will not convict. If the law is too mild, private vengeance comes in. If the government is a terrific democracy, the pressure is resisted by an over-charge of energy in the citizen, and life glows with a fiercer flame. The true life and satisfactions of man seem to elude the utmost rigors or felicities of condition and to establish themselves with great indifference under all varieties of circumstances. Under all governments the influence of character remains the same—in Turkey and in New England about alike. Under the primeval despots of Egypt, history honestly confesses that man must have been as free as culture could make him.

These appearances indicate the fact that the universe is represented in every one of its particles. Every thing in nature contains all the powers of nature. Every thing is made of one hidden stuff; as the naturalist sees one type under every metamorphosis, and regards a horse as a running man, a fish as a swimming man, a bird as a flying man, a tree as a rooted man. Each new form repeats not only the main character of the type, but part for part all the details, all the aims, furtherances, hindrances, energies and whole system of every other. Every occupation, trade, art, transaction, is a compend of the world and a correlative of every other. Each one is an entire emblem of human life; of its good and ill, its trials, its enemies, its course and its end. And each one must somehow accommodate the whole man and recite all his destiny.

The world globes itself in a drop of dew. The microscope cannot find the animalcule which is less perfect for being little. Eyes, ears, taste, smell, motion, resistance, appetite, and organs of reproduction that take hold on eternity—all find room to consist in the small creature. So do we put our life into every act. The true doctrine of omnipresence is that God reappears with all his parts in every moss and cobweb. The value of the universe contrives to throw itself into every point. If the good is there, so is the evil; if the affinity, so the repulsion; if the force, so the limitation.

Thus is the universe alive. All things are moral. That soul which within us is a sentiment, outside of us is a law. We feel its inspiration; but there in history we can see its fatal strength. "It is in the world, and the world was made by it." Justice is not postponed. A perfect equity adjusts its balance in all parts of life. Ἀεὶ γὰρ εὖ πίπτουσιν οἱ Διὸς κύβοι, The dice of God are always loaded. The world looks like a multi-plication-table, or a mathematical equation, which, turn it how you will, balances itself. Take what figure you will, its exact value, nor more nor less, still returns to you. Every secret is told, every crime is punished, every virtue rewarded, every wrong redressed, in silence and certainty. What we call retribution is the universal necessity by which the whole appears wherever a part appears. If you see smoke, there must be fire. If you see a hand or a limb, you know that the trunk to which it belongs is there behind.

Every act rewards itself, or in other words integrates itself, in a twofold manner; first in the thing, or in real nature; and secondly in the circumstance, or in apparent nature. Men call the circumstance the retribution. The causal retribution is in the thing and is seen by the soul. The retribution in the circumstance is seen by the understanding; it is inseparable from the thing, but is often spread over a long time and so does not become distinct until after many years. The specific stripes may follow late after the offence, but they follow because they accompany it. Crime and punishment grow out of one stem. Punishment is a fruit that unsuspected ripens within the flower of the pleasure which concealed it. Cause and effect, means and ends, seed and fruit, cannot be severed; for the effect already blooms in the cause, the end preëxists in the means, the fruit in the seed.

Whilst thus the world will be whole and refuses to be disparted, we seek to act partially, to sunder, to appropriate; for example—to gratify the senses we sever the pleasure of the senses from the needs of the character. The ingenuity of man has always been dedicated to the solution of one problem—how to detach the sensual sweet, the sensual strong, the sensual bright, etc., from the moral sweet, the moral deep, the moral fair; that is, again, to contrive to cut clean off this upper surface so thin as to leave it bottomless; to get a *one end*, without an *other end*. The soul says, "Eat;" the body would feast. The soul says, "The man and woman shall be one flesh and one soul;" the body would join the flesh only. The soul says, "Have dominion over all things to the ends of virtue;" the body would have the power over things to its own ends.

The soul strives amain to live and work through all things. It would be the only fact. All things shall be added unto it— power, pleasure, knowledge, beauty. The particular man aims to be somebody; to set up for himself; to truck and higgle for a private good; and, in particulars, to ride that he may ride; to dress that he may be dressed; to eat that he may eat;

and to govern, that he may be seen. Men seek to be great; they would have offices, wealth, power, and fame. They think that to be great is to possess one side of nature—the sweet, without the other side, the bitter.

This dividing and detaching is steadily counteracted. Up to this day it must be owned no projector has had the smallest success. The parted water reunites behind our hand. Pleasure is taken out of pleasant things, profit out of profitable things, power out of strong things, as soon as we seek to separate them from the whole. We can no more halve things and get the sensual good, by itself, than we can get an inside that shall have no outside, or a light without a shadow. "Drive out Nature with a fork, she comes running back."

Life invests itself with inevitable conditions, which the unwise seek to dodge, which one and another brags that he does not know, that they do not touch him; but the brag is on his lips, the conditions are in his soul. If he escapes them in one part they attack him in another more vital part. If he has escaped them in form and in the appearance, it is because he has resisted his life and fled from himself, and the retribution is so much death. So signal is the failure of all attempts to make this separation of the good from the tax, that the experiment would not be tried—since to try it is to be mad—but for the circumstance that when the disease began in the will, of rebellion and separation, the intellect is at once infected, so that the man ceases to see God whole in each object, but is able to see the sensual allurement of an object and not see the sensual hurt; he sees the mermaid's head but not the dragon's tail, and thinks he can cut off that which he would have from that which he would not have. "How secret art thou who dwellest in the highest heavens in silence, O thou only great God, sprinkling with an unwearied providence certain penal blindnesses upon such as have unbridled desires!" [1]

The human soul is true to these facts in the painting of fable, of history, of law, of proverbs, of conversation. It finds a tongue in literature unawares. Thus the Greeks called Jupiter, Supreme Mind; but having traditionally ascribed to him many base actions, they involuntarily made amends to reason by tying up the hands of so bad a god. He is made as helpless as a king of England. Prometheus knows one secret which

---

[1] *Confessions* of St. Augustine, Book I.

Jove must bargain for; Minerva, another. He cannot get his own thunders; Minerva keeps the key of them:—

> Of all the gods, I only know the keys
> That ope the solid doors within whose vaults
> His thunders sleep.[2]

A plain confession of the in-working of the All and of its moral aim. The Indian mythology ends in the same ethics; and it would seem impossible for any fable to be invented and get any currency which was not moral. Aurora forgot to ask youth for her lover, and though Tithonus is immortal, he is old. Achilles is not quite invulnerable; the sacred waters did not wash the heel by which Thetis held him. Siegfried, in the Nibelungen, is not quite immortal, for a leaf fell on his back whilst he was bathing in the dragon's blood, and that spot which it covered is mortal. And so it must be. There is a crack in every thing God has made. It would seem there is always this vindictive circumstance stealing in at unawares even into the wild poesy in which the human fancy attempted to make bold holiday and to shake itself free of the old laws—this back-stroke, this kick of the gun, certifying that the law is fatal; that in nature nothing can be given, all things are sold.

This is that ancient doctrine of Nemesis, who keeps watch in the universe and lets no offence go unchastised. The Furies, they said, are attendants on justice, and if the sun in heaven should transgress his path they would punish him. The poets related that stone walls and iron swords and leathern thongs had an occult sympathy with the wrongs of their owners; that the belt which Ajax gave Hector dragged the Trojan hero over the field at the wheels of the car of Achilles, and the sword which Hector gave Ajax was that on whose point Ajax fell. They recorded that when the Thasians erected a statue to Theagenes, a victor in the games, one of his rivals went to it by night and endeavored to throw it down by repeated blows, until at last he moved it from its pedestal and was crushed to death beneath its fall.

This voice of fable has in it somewhat divine. It came from thought above the will of the writer. That is the best part of each writer which has nothing private in it; that

---

[2] Aeschylus, *Prometheus*.

which he does not know; that which flowed out of his constitution and not from his too active invention; that which in
the study of a single artist you might not easily find, but in
the study of many you would abstract as the spirit of them
all. Phidias it is not, but the work of man in that early
Hellenic world that I would know. The name and circumstance of Phidias, however convenient for history, embarrass
when we come to the highest criticism. We are to see that
which man was tending to do in a given period, and was
hindered, or, if you will, modified in doing, by the interfering
volitions of Phidias, of Dante, of Shakspeare, the organ whereby man at the moment wrought.

Still more striking is the expression of this fact in the
proverbs of all nations, which are always the literature of
reason, or the statements of an absolute truth without qualifi-
cation. Proverbs, like the sacred books of each nation, are
the sanctuary of the intuitions. That which the droning world,
chained to appearances, will not allow the realist to say in
his own words, it will suffer him to say in proverbs without
contradiction. And this law of laws, which the pulpit, the
senate and the college deny, is hourly preached in all markets
and workshops by flights of proverbs, whose teaching is as
true and as omnipresent as that of birds and flies.

All things are double, one against another. Tit for tat; an
eye for an eye; tooth for a tooth; blood for blood; measure
for measure; love for love. Give, and it shall be given you.
He that watereth shall be watered himself. What will you
have? quoth God; pay for it and take it. Nothing venture,
nothing have. Thou shalt be paid exactly for what thou hast
done, no more, no less. Who doth not work shall not eat.
Harm watch, harm catch. Curses always recoil on the head
of him who imprecates them. If you put a chain around the
neck of a slave, the other end fastens itself around your own.
Bad counsel confounds the adviser. The Devil is an ass.

It is thus written, because it is thus in life. Our action is
overmastered and characterized above our will by the law of
nature. We aim at a petty end quite aside from the public
good but our act arranges itself by irresistible magnetism in
a line with the poles of the world.

A man cannot speak but he judges himself. With his will
or against his will he draws his portrait to the eye of his
companions by every word. Every opinion reacts on him who

utters it. It is a thread-ball thrown at a mark, but the other end remains in the thrower's bag. Or rather it is a harpoon hurled at the whale, unwinding, as it flies, a coil of cord in the boat, and, if the harpoon is not good, or not well thrown, it will go nigh to cut the steersman in twain or to sink the boat.

You cannot do wrong without suffering wrong. "No man had ever a point of pride that was not injurious to him," said Burke. The exclusive in fashionable life does not see that he excludes himself from enjoyment, in the attempt to appropriate it. The exclusionist in religion does not see that he shuts the door of heaven on himself, in striving to shut out others. Treat men as pawns and ninepins and you shall suffer as well as they. If you leave out their heart, you shall lose your own. The senses would make things of all persons; of women, of children, of the poor. The vulgar proverb, "I will get it from his purse or get it from his skin," is sound philosophy.

All infractions of love and equity in our social relations are speedily punished. They are punished by fear. Whilst I stand in simple relations to my fellow-man, I have no displeasure in meeting him. We meet as water meets water, or as two currents of air mix, with perfect diffusion and interpenetration of nature. But as soon as there is any departure from simplicity and attempt at halfness, or good for me that is not good for him, my neighbor feels the wrong; he shrinks from me as far as I have shrunk from him; his eyes no longer seek mine; there is war between us; there is hate in him and fear in me.

All the old abuses in society, universal and particular, all unjust accumulations of property and power, are avenged in the same manner. Fear is an instructor of great sagacity and the herald of all revolutions. One thing he teaches, that there is rottenness where he appears. He is a carrion crow, and though you see not well what he hovers for, there is death somewhere. Our property is timid, our laws are timid, our cultivated classes are timid. Fear for ages has boded and mowed and gibbered over government and property. That obscene bird is not there for nothing. He indicates great wrongs which must be revised.

Of the like nature is that expectation of change which instantly follows the suspension of our voluntary activity. The terror of cloudless noon, the emerald of Polycrates, the awe of prosperity, the instinct which leads every generous soul to impose on itself tasks of a noble asceticism and vicarious virtue, are the tremblings of the balance of justice through the heart and mind of man.

Experienced men of the world know very well that it is best to pay scot and lot as they go along, and that a man often pays dear for a small frugality. The borrower runs in his own debt. Has a man gained any thing who has received a hundred favors and rendered none? Has he gained by borrowing, through indolence or cunning, his neighbor's wares, or horses, or money? There arises on the deed the instant acknowledgment of benefit on the one part and of debt on the other; that is, of superiority and inferiority. The transaction remains in the memory of himself and his neighbor; and every new transaction alters according to its nature their relation to each other. He may soon come to see that he had better have broken his own bones than to have ridden in his neighbor's coach, and that "the highest price he can pay for a thing is to ask for it."

A wise man will extend this lesson to all parts of life, and know that it is the part of prudence to face every claimant and pay every just demand on your time, your talents, or your heart. Always pay; for first or last you must pay your entire debt. Persons and events may stand for a time between you and justice, but it is only a postponement. You must pay at last your own debt. If you are wise you will dread a prosperity which only loads you with more. Benefit is the end of nature. But for every benefit which you receive, a tax is levied. He is great who confers the most benefits. He is base— and that is the one base thing in the universe—to receive favors and render none. In the order of nature we cannot render benefits to those from whom we receive them, or only seldom. But the benefit we receive must be rendered again, line for line, deed for deed, cent for cent, to somebody. Beware of too much good staying in your hand. It will fast corrupt and worm worms. Pay it away quickly in some sort.

Labor is watched over by the same pitiless laws. Cheapest, say the prudent, is the dearest labor. What we buy in a broom, a mat, a wagon, a knife, is some application of good sense to a common want. It is best to pay in your land a skilful gardener, or to buy good sense applied to gardening; in your sailor, good sense applied to navigation; in the house, good sense applied to cooking, sewing, serving; in your agent, good sense applied to accounts and affairs. So do you multiply your presence, or spread yourself throughout your estate. But because of the dual constitution of things, in labor as in life there can be no cheating. The thief steals from himself. The swindler swindles himself. For the real price of labor is knowledge and virtue, whereof wealth and credit are signs. These signs, like paper money, may be counterfeited or stolen, but that which they represent, namely, knowledge and virtue, cannot be counterfeited or stolen. These ends of labor cannot be answered but by real exertions of the mind, and in obedience to pure motives. The cheat, the defaulter, the gambler, cannot extort the knowledge of material and moral nature which his honest care and pains yield to the operative. The law of nature is, Do the thing, and you shall have the power; but they who do not the thing have not the power.

Human labor, through all its forms, from the sharpening of a stake to the construction of a city or an epic, is one immense illustration of the perfect compensation of the universe. The absolute balance of Give and Take, the doctrine that every thing has its price—and if that price is not paid, not that thing but something else is obtained, and that it is impossible to get anything without its price—is not less sublime in the columns of a leger than in the budgets of states, in the laws of light and darkness, in all the action and reaction of nature. I cannot doubt that the high laws which each man sees implicated in those processes with which he is conversant, the stern ethics which sparkle on his chisel-edge, which are measured out by his plumb and foot-rule, which stand as manifest in the footing of the shop-bill as in the history of a state—do recommend to him his trade, and though seldom named, exalt his business to his imagination.

The league between virtue and nature engages all things to assume a hostile front to vice. The beautiful laws and substances of the world persecute and whip the traitor. He finds that things are arranged for truth and benefit, but there is no den in the wide world to hide a rogue. Commit a crime, and the earth is made of glass. Commit a crime, and it seems as if a coat of snow fell on the ground, such as reveals in the woods the track of every partridge and fox and squirrel and mole. You cannot recall the spoken word, you cannot wipe out the foot-track, you cannot draw up the ladder, so as to leave no inlet or clew. Some damning circumstance always transpires. The laws and substances of nature—water, snow, wind, gravitation—become penalties to the thief.

On the other hand the law holds with equal sureness for all right action. Love, and you shall be loved. All love is mathematically just, as much as the two sides of an algebraic equation. The good man has absolute good, which like fire turns every thing to its own nature, so that you cannot do him any harm; but as the royal armies sent against Napoleon, when he approached cast down their colors and from enemies became friends, so disasters of all kinds, as sickness, offence, poverty, prove benefactors:

> Winds blow and waters roll
> Strength to the brave and power and deity,
> Yet in themselves are nothing.[3]

The good are befriended even by weakness and defect. As no man had ever a point of pride that was not injurious to him, so no man had ever a defect that was not somewhere made useful to him. The stag in the fable admired his horns and blamed his feet, but when the hunter came, his feet saved him, and afterwards, caught in the thicket, his horns destroyed him. Every man in his lifetime needs to thank his faults. As no man thoroughly understands a truth until he has contended against it, so no man has a thorough acquaintance with the hindrances or talents of men until he has suffered from the one and seen the triumph of the other over his own want of the same. Has he a defect of temper that unfits him to live in society? Thereby he is driven to entertain himself alone and acquire habits of self-help; and thus, like the wounded oyster, he mends his shell with pearl.

Our strength grows out of our weakness. The indignation which arms itself with secret forces does not awaken until we are pricked and stung and sorely assailed. A great man is always willing to be little. Whilst he sits on the cushion of advantages, he goes to sleep. When he is pushed, tormented, defeated, he has a chance to learn something; he has been put on his wits, on his manhood; he has gained facts; learns his ignorance; is cured of the insanity of conceit; has got moderation and real skill. The wise man throws himself on

---

[3] Wordsworth, "September, 1802," in *Sonnets to Liberty.*

the side of his assailants. It is more his interest than it is theirs to find his weak point. The wound cicatrizes and falls off from him like a dead skin, and when they would triumph, lo! he has passed on invulnerable. Blame is safer than praise. I hate to be defended in a newspaper. As long as all that is said is said against me, I feel a certain assurance of success. But as soon as honeyed words of praise are spoken for me I feel as one that lies unprotected before his enemies. In general, every evil to which we do not succumb is a benefactor. As the Sandwich Islander believes that the strength and valor of the enemy he kills passes into himself, so we gain the strength of the temptation we resist.

The same guards which protect us from disaster, defect and enmity, defend us, if we will, from selfishness and fraud. Bolts and bars are not the best of our institutions, nor is shrewdness in trade a mark of wisdom. Men suffer all their life long under the foolish superstition that they can be cheated. But it is as impossible for a man to be cheated by any one but himself, as for a thing to be and not to be at the same time. There is a third silent party to all our bargains. The nature and soul of things takes on itself the guaranty of the fulfilment of every contract, so that honest service cannot come to loss. If you serve an ungrateful master, serve him the more. Put God in your debt. Every stroke shall be repaid. The longer the payment is withholden, the better for you; for compound interest on compound interest is the rate and usage of this exchequer.

The history of persecution is a history of endeavors to cheat nature, to make water run up hill, to twist a rope of sand. It makes no difference whether the actors be many or one, a tyrant or a mob. A mob is a society of bodies voluntarily bereaving themselves of reason and traversing its work. The mob is man voluntarily descending to the nature of the beast. Its fit hour of activity is night. Its actions are insane, like its whole constitution. It persecutes a principle; it would whip a right; it would tar and feather justice, by inflicting fire and outrage upon the houses and persons of those who have these. It resembles the prank of boys, who run with fire-engines to put out the ruddy aurora streaming to the stars. The inviolate spirit turns their spite against the wrongdoers. The martyr cannot be dishonored. Every lash inflicted is a tongue of fame; every prison a more illustrious abode; every burned book or house enlightens the world; every suppressed or expunged word reverberates through the earth from side to side. Hours of sanity and consideration are always arriving to communities, as to individuals, when the truth is seen and the martyrs are justified.

Thus do all things preach the indifference of circumstances. The man is all. Every thing has two sides, a good and an evil. Every advantage has its tax. I learn to be content. But the doctrine of compensation is not the doctrine of indifference. The thoughtless say, on hearing these representations, What boots it to do well? there is one event to good and evil; if I gain any good I must pay for it; if I lose any good I gain some other; all actions are indifferent.

There is a deeper fact in the soul than compensation, to wit, its own nature. The soul is not a compensation, but a life. The soul *is.* Under all this running sea of circumstance, whose waters ebb and flow with perfect balance, lies the aboriginal abyss of real Being. Essence, or God, is not a relation or a part, but the whole. Being is the vast affirmative, excluding negation, self-balanced, and swallowing up all relations, parts and times within itself. Nature, truth, virtue, are the influx from thence. Vice is the absence or departure of the same. Nothing, Falsehood, may indeed stand as the great Night or shade on which as a background the living universe paints itself forth, but no fact is begotten by it; it cannot work, for it is not. It cannot work any good; it cannot work any harm. It is harm inasmuch as it is worse not to be than to be.

We feel defrauded of the retribution due to evil acts, because the criminal adheres to his vice and contumacy and does not come to a crisis or judgment anywhere in visible nature. There is no stunning confutation of his nonsense before men and angels. Has he therefore outwitted the law? Inasmuch as he carries the malignity and the lie with him he so far deceases from nature. In some manner there will be a demonstration of the wrong to the understanding also; but, should we not see it, this deadly deduction makes square the eternal account.

Neither can it be said, on the other hand, that the gain of rectitude must be bought by any loss. There is no penalty to virtue; no penalty to wisdom; they are proper additions of being. In a virtuous action I properly *am;* in a virtuous act I add to the world; I plant into deserts conquered from Chaos and Nothing and see the darkness receding on the limits of the horizon. There can be no excess to love, none to knowledge, none to beauty, when these attributes are considered in the purest sense. The soul refuses limits, and always affirms an Optimism, never a Pessimism.

Man's life is a progress, and not a station. His instinct is trust. Our instinct uses "more" and "less" in application to man, of the *presence of the soul*, and not of its absence; the brave man is greater than the coward; the true, the benevolent, the wise, is more a man and not less, than the fool and knave. There is no tax on the good of virtue, for that is the incoming of God himself, or absolute existence, without any comparative. Material good has its tax, and if it came without desert or sweat, has no root in me, and the next wind will blow it away. But all the good of nature is the soul's, and may be had if paid for in nature's lawful coin, that is, by labor which the heart and the head allow. I no longer wish to meet a good I do not earn, for example to find a pot of buried gold, knowing that it brings with it new burdens. I do not wish more external goods—neither possessions, nor honors, nor powers, nor persons. The gain is apparent; the tax is certain. But there is no tax on the knowledge that the compensation exists and that it is not desirable to dig up treasure. Herein I rejoice with a serene eternal peace. I contract the boundaries of possible mischief. I learn the wisdom of St. Bernard, "Nothing can work me damage except myself; the harm that I sustain I carry about with me, and never am a real sufferer but by my own fault."

In the nature of the soul is the compensation for the inequalities of condition. The radical tragedy of nature seems to be the distinction of More and Less. How can Less not feel the pain; how not feel indignation or malevolence towards More? Look at those who have less faculty, and one feels sad and knows not well what to make of it. He almost shuns their eye; he fears they will upbraid God. What should they do? It seems a great injustice. But see the facts nearly and these mountainous inequalities vanish. Love reduces them as the sun melts the iceberg in the sea. The heart and soul of all men being one, this bitterness of *His* and *Mine* ceases. His is mine. I am my brother and my brother is me. If I feel overshadowed and outdone by great neighbors, I can yet love; I can still receive; and he that loveth maketh his own the grandeur he loves. Thereby I make the discovery that my brother is my guardian, acting for me with the friendliest designs, and the estate I so admired and envied is my own. It is the nature of the soul to appropriate all things. Jesus and Shakspeare are fragments of the soul, and by love I conquer and incorporate them in my own conscious domain. His virtue—is not that mine? His wit—if it cannot be made mine, it is not wit.

Such also is the natural history of calamity. The changes which break up at short intervals the prosperity of men are advertisements of a nature whose law is growth. Every soul is by this intrinsic necessity quitting its whole system of things, its friends and home and laws and faith, as the shellfish crawls out of its beautiful but stony case, because it no longer admits of its growth, and slowly forms a new house. In proportion to the vigor of the individual these revolutions are frequent, until in some happier mind they are incessant and all worldly relations hang very loosely about him, becoming as it were a transparent fluid membrane through which the living form is seen, and not, as in most men, an indurated heterogeneous fabric of many dates and of no settled character, in which the man is imprisoned. Then there can be enlargement, and the man of to-day scarcely recognizes the man of yesterday. And such should be the outward biography of man in time, a putting off of dead circumstances day by day, as he renews his raiment day by day. But to us, in our lapsed estate, resting, not advancing, resisting, not coöperating with the divine expansion, this growth comes by shocks.

We cannot part with our friends. We cannot let our angels go. We do not see that they only go out that archangels may come in. We are idolaters of the old. We do not believe in the riches of the soul, in its proper eternity and omnipresence. We do not believe there is any force in to-day to rival or recreate that beautiful yesterday. We linger in the ruins of the old tent where once we had bread and shelter and organs, nor believe that the spirit can feed, cover, and nerve us again. We cannot again find aught so dear, so sweet, so graceful. But we sit and weep in vain. The voice of the Almighty saith, "Up and onward for evermore!" We cannot stay amid the ruins. Neither will we rely on the new; and so we walk ever with reverted eyes, like those monsters who look backwards.

And yet the compensations of calamity are made apparent to the understanding also, after long intervals of time. A fever, a mutilation, a cruel disappointment, a loss of wealth, a loss of friends, seems at the moment unpaid loss, and unpayable. But the sure years reveal the deep remedial force that underlies all facts. The death of a dear friend, wife, brother, lover, which seemed nothing but privation, somewhat later assumes the aspect of a guide or genius; for it commonly operates revolutions in our way of life, terminates an epoch of infancy or of youth which was waiting to be closed, breaks up a wonted occupation, or a household, or style of living, and allows the formation of new ones more friendly to the growth of character. It permits or constrains the formation of new acquaintances and the reception of new influences that prove of the first importance to the next years; and the man or woman who would have remained a sunny garden-flower, with no room for its roots and too much sunshine for its head, by the falling of the walls and the neglect of the gardener is made the banian of the forest, yielding shade and fruit to wide neighborhoods of men.

From *Essays, First Series*

The Over-Soul

There is a difference between one and another hour of life in their authority and subsequent effect. Our faith comes in moments; our vice is habitual. Yet there is a depth in those brief moments which constrains us to ascribe more reality to them than to all other experiences. For this reason the argument which is always forthcoming to silence those who conceive extraordinary hopes of man, namely the appeal to experience, is for ever invalid and vain. We give up the past to the objector, and yet we hope. He must explain this hope. We grant that human life is mean, but how did we find out that it was mean? What is the ground of this uneasiness of ours; of this old discontent? What is the universal sense of want and ignorance, but the fine innuendo by which the soul makes its enormous claim? Why do men feel that the natural history of man has never been written, but he is always leaving behind what you have said of him, and it becomes old, and books of metaphysics worthless? The philosophy of six thousand years has not searched the chambers and magazines of the soul. In its experiments there has always remained, in the last analysis, a residuum it could not resolve. Man is a stream whose source is hidden. Our being is descending into us from we know not whence. The most exact calculator has no prescience that somewhat incalculable may not balk the very next moment. I am constrained every moment to acknowledge a higher origin for events than the will I call mine.

As with events, so is it with thoughts. When I watch that flowing river, which, out of regions I see not, pours for a season its streams into me, I see that I am a pensioner; not a cause but a surprised spectator of this ethereal water; that I desire and look up and put myself in the attitude of reception, but from some alien energy the visions come.

The Supreme Critic on the errors of the past and the present, and the only prophet of that which must be, is that great nature in which we rest as the earth lies in the soft arms of the atmosphere; that Unity, that Over-Soul, within which every man's particular being is contained and made one with all other; that common heart of which all sincere conversation is the worship, to which all right action is submission; that overpowering reality which confutes our tricks and talents, and constrains every one to pass for what he is, and to speak from his character and not from his tongue, and which evermore tends to pass into our thought and hand and become wisdom and virtue and power and beauty. We live in succession, in division, in parts, in particles. Meantime within man is the soul of the whole; the wise silence; the universal beauty, to which every part and particle is equally related; the eternal ONE. And this deep power in which we exist and whose beatitude is all accessible to us, is not only self-sufficing and perfect in every hour, but the act of seeing and the thing seen, the seer and the spectacle, the subject and the object, are one. We see the world piece by piece, as the sun, the moon, the animal, the tree; but the whole, of which these are the shining parts, is the soul. Only by the vision of that Wisdom can the horoscope of the ages be read, and by falling back on our better thoughts, by yielding to the spirit of prophecy which is innate in every man, we can know what it saith. Every man's words who speaks from that life must sound vain to those who do not dwell in the same thought on their own part. I dare not speak for it. My words do not carry its august sense; they fall short and cold. Only itself can inspire whom it will, and behold! their speech shall be lyrical, and sweet, and universal as the rising of the wind. Yet I desire, even by profane words, if I may not use sacred, to indicate the heaven of this deity and to report what hints I have collected of the transcendent simplicity and energy of the Highest Law.

If we consider what happens in conversation, in reveries, in remorse, in times of passion, in surprises, in the instructions of dreams, wherein often we see ourselves in masquerade—the droll disguises only magnifying and enhancing a real element and forcing it on our distant notice—we shall catch many hints that will broaden and lighten into knowledge of the secret of nature. All goes to show that the soul in man is not an organ, but animates and exercises all the organs; is not a function, like the power of memory, of calculation, of comparison, but uses these as hands and feet; is not a faculty, but a light; is not the intellect or the will, but the master of the intellect and the will; is the background of our being, in which they lie—an immensity not possessed and that cannot be possessed. From within or from behind, a light shines through us upon things and makes us aware that we are nothing, but the light is all. A man is the façade of a temple wherein all wisdom and all good abide. What we commonly call man, the eating, drinking, planting, counting man, does not, as we know him, represent himself, but misrepresents himself. Him we do not respect, but the soul, whose organ he is, would he let it appear through his action, would make our knees bend. When it breathes through his intellect, it is genius; when it breathes through his will, it is virtue; when it flows through his affection, it is love. And the blindness of the intellect begins when it would be something of itself. The weakness of the will begins when the individual would be something of himself. All reform aims in some one particular to let the soul have its way through us; in other words, to engage us to obey.

Of this pure nature every man is at some time sensible. Language cannot paint it with his colors. It is too subtle. It is undefinable, unmeasurable; but we know that it pervades and contains us. We know that all spiritual being is in man. A wise old proverb says, "God comes to see us without bell;" that is, as there is no screen or ceiling between our heads and the infinite heavens, so is there no bar or wall in the soul, where man, the effect, ceases, and God, the cause, begins. The walls are taken away. We lie open on one side to the deeps of spiritual nature, to the attributes of God. Justice we see and know, Love, Freedom, Power. These natures no man ever got above, but they tower over us, and most in the moment when our interests tempt us to wound them.

The sovereignty of this nature whereof we speak is made known by its independency of those limitations which circumscribe us on every hand. The soul circumscribes all things. As I have said, it contradicts all experience. In like manner it abolishes time and space. The influence of the senses has in most men overpowered the mind to that degree that the walls of time and space have come to look real and insurmountable; and to speak with levity of these limits is, in the world, the sign of insanity. Yet time and space are but inverse measures of the force of the soul. The spirit sports with time—

Can crowd eternity into an hour,
Or stretch an hour to eternity.[1]

We are often made to feel that there is another youth and age than that which is measured from the year of our natural birth. Some thoughts always find us young, and keep us so. Such a thought is the love of the universal and eternal beauty. Every man parts from that contemplation with the feeling that it rather belongs to ages than to mortal life. The least activity of the intellectual powers redeems us in a degree from the conditions of time. In sickness, in languor, give us a strain of poetry or a profound sentence, and we are refreshed; or produce a volume of Plato or Shakspeare, or remind us of their names, and instantly we come into a feeling of longevity. See how the deep divine thought reduces centuries and millenniums, and makes itself present through all ages. Is the teaching of Christ less effective now than it was

---

[1] William Blake, "Auguries of Innocence."

when first his mouth was opened? The emphasis of facts and persons in my thought has nothing to do with time. And so always the soul's scale is one, the scale of the senses and the understanding is another. Before the revelations of the soul, Time, Space and Nature shrink away. In common speech we refer all things to time, as we habitually refer the immensely sundered stars to one concave sphere. And so we say that the Judgment is distant or near, that the Millennium approaches, that a day of certain political, moral, social reforms is at hand, and the like, when we mean that in the nature of things one of the facts we contemplate is external and fugitive, and the other is permanent and connate with the soul. The things we now esteem fixed shall, one by one, detach themselves like ripe fruit from our experience, and fall. The wind shall blow them none knows whither. The landscape, the figures, Boston, London, are facts as fugitive as any institution past, or any whiff of mist or smoke, and so is society, and so is the world. The soul looketh steadily forwards, creating a world before her, leaving worlds behind her. She has no dates, nor rites, nor persons, nor specialties, nor men. The soul knows only the soul; the web of events is the flowing robe in which she is clothed.

After its own law and not by arithmetic is the rate of its progress to be computed. The soul's advances are not made by gradation, such as can be represented by motion in a straight line, but rather by ascension of state, such as can be represented by metamorphosis—from the egg to the worm, from the worm to the fly. The growths of genius are of a certain *total* character, that does not advance the elect individual first over John, then Adam, then Richard, and give to each the pain of discovered inferiority—but by every throe of growth the man expands there where he works, passing, at each pulsation, classes, populations, of men. With each divine impulse the mind rends the thin rinds of the visible and finite, and comes out into eternity, and inspires and expires its air. It converses with truths that have always been spoken in the world, and becomes conscious of a closer sympathy with Zeno and Arrian than with persons in the house.

This is the law of moral and of mental gain. The simple rise as by specific levity not into a particular virtue, but into the region of all the virtues. They are in the spirit which contains them all. The soul requires purity, but purity is not

it; requires justice, but justice is not that; requires benefi-
cence, but is somewhat better; so that there is a kind of
descent and accommodation felt when we leave speaking of
moral nature to urge a virtue which enjoins. To the well-born
child all the virtues are natural, and not painfully acquired.
Speak to his heart, and the man becomes suddenly virtuous.

Within the same sentiment is the germ of intellectual
growth, which obeys the same law. Those who are capable
of humility, of justice, of love, of aspiration, stand already on
a platform that commands the sciences and arts, speech and
poetry, action and grace. For whoso dwells in this moral beatitude already anticipates those special powers which men
prize so highly. The lover has no talent, no skill, which passes
for quite nothing with his enamored maiden, however little
she may possess of related faculty; and the heart which
abandons itself to the Supreme Mind finds itself related to all
its works, and will travel a royal road to particular knowledges and powers. In ascending to this primary and aboriginal
sentiment we have come from our remote station on the circumference instantaneously to the centre of the world, where,
as in the closet of God, we see causes, and anticipate the universe, which is but a slow effect.

One mode of the divine teaching is the incarnation of the
spirit in a form—in forms, like my own. I live in society;
with persons who answer to thoughts in my own mind, or
express a certain obedience to the great instincts to which I
live. I see its presence to them. I am certified of a common
nature; and these other souls, these separated selves, draw
me as nothing else can. They stir in me the new emotions we
call passion; of love, hatred, fear, admiration, pity; thence
come conversation, competition, persuasion, cities and war.
Persons are supplementary to the primary teaching of the
soul. In youth we are mad for persons. Childhood and youth
see all the world in them. But the larger experience of man
discovers the identical nature appearing through them all.
Persons themselves acquaint us with the impersonal. In all
conversation between two persons tacit reference is made, as
to a third party, to a common nature. That third party or
common nature is not social; it is impersonal; is God. And
so in groups where debate is earnest, and especially on high
questions, the company become aware that the thought rises
to an equal level in all bosoms, that all have a spiritual prop-

erty in what was said, as well as the sayer. They all become wiser than they were. It arches over them like a temple, this unity of thought in which every heart beats with nobler sense of power and duty, and thinks and acts with unusual solemnity. All are conscious of attaining to a higher self-possession. It shines for all. There is a certain wisdom of humanity which is common to the greatest men with the lowest, and which our ordinary education often labors to silence and obstruct. The mind is one, and the best minds, who love truth for its own sake, think much less of property in truth. They accept it thankfully everywhere, and do not label or stamp it with any man's name, for it is theirs long beforehand, and from eternity. The learned and the studious of thought have no monopoly of wisdom. Their violence of direction in some degree disqualifies them to think truly. We owe many valuable observations to people who are not very acute or profound, and who say the thing without effort which we want and have long been hunting in vain. The action of the soul is oftener in that which is felt and left unsaid than in that which is said in any conversation. It broods over every society, and they unconsciously seek for it in each other. We know better than we do. We do not yet possess ourselves, and we know at the same time that we are much more. I feel the same truth how often in my trivial conversation with my neighbors, that somewhat higher in each of us overlooks this by-play, and Jove nods to Jove from behind each of us.

Men descend to meet. In their habitual and mean service to the world, for which they forsake their native nobleness, they resemble those Arabian sheiks who dwell in mean houses and affect an external poverty, to escape the rapacity of the Pacha, and reserve all their display of wealth for their interior and guarded retirements.

As it is present in all persons, so it is in every period of life. It is adult already in the infant man. In my dealing with my child, my Latin and Greek, my accomplishments and my money stead me nothing; but as much soul as I have avails. If I am wilful, he sets his will against mine, one for one, and leaves me, if I please, the degradation of beating him by my superiority of strength. But if I renounce my will and act for the soul, setting that up as umpire between us two, out of his young eyes looks the same soul; he reveres and loves with me.

The soul is the perceiver and revealer of truth. We know truth when we see it, let sceptic and scoffer say what they choose. Foolish people ask you, when you have spoken what they do not wish to hear, "How do you know it is truth, and not an error of your own?" We know truth when we see it, from opinion, as we know when we are awake that we are awake. It was a grand sentence of Emanuel Swedenborg, which would alone indicate the greatness of that man's perception—"It is no proof of a man's understanding to be able to affirm whatever he pleases; but to be able to discern that what is true is true, and that what is false is false—this is the mark and character of intelligence." In the book I read, the good thought returns to me, as every truth will, the image of the whole soul. To the bad thought which I find in it, the same soul becomes a discerning, separating sword, and lops it away. We are wiser than we know. If we will not interfere with our thought, but will act entirely, or see how the thing stands in God, we know the particular thing, and every thing, and every man. For the Maker of all things and all persons stands behind us and casts his dread omniscience through us over things.

But beyond this recognition of its own in particular passages of the individual's experience, it also reveals truth. And here we should seek to reinforce ourselves by its very presence, and to speak with a worthier, loftier strain of that advent. For the soul's communication of truth is the highest event in nature, since it then does not give somewhat from itself, but it gives itself, or passes into and becomes that man whom it enlightens; or in proportion to that truth he receives, it takes him to itself.

We distinguish the announcements of the soul, its manifestations of its own nature, by the term *Revelation*. These are always attended by the emotion of the sublime. For this communication is an influx of the Divine mind into our mind. It is an ebb of the individual rivulet before the flowing surges of the sea of life. Every distinct apprehension of this central commandment agitates men with awe and delight. A thrill passes through all men at the reception of new truth, or at the performance of a great action, which comes out of the heart of nature. In these communications the power to see is not separated from the will to do, but the insight proceeds from obedience, and the obedience proceeds from a joyful perception. Every moment when the individual feels himself invaded by it is memorable. By the necessity of our constitution a certain enthusiasm attends the individual's consciousness of that divine presence. The character and duration of this enthusiasm vary with the state of the individual, from an ecstasy and trance and prophetic inspiration—which is its rarer appearance—to the faintest glow of virtuous emotion, in which form it warms, like our household fires, all the families and associations of men, and makes society possible. A certain tendency to insanity has always attended the opening of the religious sense in men, as if they had been "blasted with excess of light." [2] The trances of Socrates, the "union" of Plotinus, the vision of Porphyry, the conversion of Paul, the aurora of Behmen, the convulsions of George Fox and his Quakers, the illumination of Swedenborg, are of this kind. What was in the case of these remarkable persons a ravishment, has, in innumerable instances in common life, been exhibited in less striking manner. Everywhere the history of religion betrays a tendency to enthusiasm. The rapture of the Moravian and Quietist; the opening of the eternal sense of the Word, in the language of the New Jerusalem Church; the *revival* of the Calvinistic churches; the *experiences* of the Methodists, are varying forms of that shudder of awe and delight with which the individual soul always mingles with the universal soul.

The nature of these revelations is the same; they are perceptions of the absolute law. They are solutions of the soul's own questions. They do not answer the questions which the understanding asks. The soul answers never by words, but by the thing itself that is inquired after.

Revelation is the disclosure of the soul. The popular notion of a revelation is that it is a telling of fortunes. In past oracles of the soul the understanding seeks to find answers to sensual questions, and undertakes to tell from God how long men shall exist, what their hands shall do and who shall be their company, adding names and dates and places. But we must pick no locks. We must check this low curiosity. An answer in words is delusive; it is really no answer to the questions you ask. Do not require a description of the countries towards which you sail. The description does not describe them to you,

---

[2] Gray, *Progress of Poesy.*

and to-morrow you arrive there and know them by inhabiting them. Men ask concerning the immortality of the soul, the employments of heaven, the state of the sinner, and so forth. They even dream that Jesus has left replies to precisely these interrogatories. Never a moment did that sublime spirit speak in their *patois*. To truth, justice, love, the attributes of the soul, the idea of immutableness is essentially associated. Jesus, living in these moral sentiments, heedless of sensual fortunes, heeding only the manifestations of these, never made the separation of the idea of duration from the essence of these attributes, nor uttered a syllable concerning the duration of the soul. It was left to his disciples to sever duration from the moral elements, and to teach the immortality of the soul as a doctrine, and maintain it by evidences. The moment the doctrine of the immortality is separately taught, man is already fallen. In the flowing of love, in the adoration of humility, there is no question of continuance. No inspired man ever asks this question or condescends to these evidences. For the soul is true to itself, and the man in whom it is shed abroad cannot wander from the present, which is infinite, to a future which would be finite.

These questions which we lust to ask about the future are a confession of sin. God has no answer for them. No answer in words can reply to a question of things. It is not in an arbitrary "decree of God," but in the nature of man, that a veil shuts down on the facts of to-morrow; for the soul will not have us read any other cipher than that of cause and effect. By this veil which curtains events it instructs the children of men to live in to-day. The only mode of obtaining an answer to these questions of the senses is to forego all low curiosity, and, accepting the tide of being which floats us into the secret of nature, work and live, work and live, and all unawares the advancing soul has built and forged for itself a new condition, and the question and the answer are one.

By the same fire, vital, consecrating, celestial, which burns until it shall dissolve all things into the waves and surges of an ocean of light, we see and know each other, and what spirit each is of. Who can tell the grounds of his knowledge of the character of the several individuals in his circle of friends? No man. Yet their acts and words do not disappoint him. In that man, though he knew no ill of him, he put no trust. In that other, though they had seldom met, authentic signs had yet passed, to signify that he might be trusted as one who had an interest in his own character. We know each other very well—which of us has been just to himself and whether that which we teach or behold is only an aspiration or is our honest effort also.

We are all discerners of spirits. That diagnosis lies aloft in our life or unconscious power. The intercourse of society, its trade, its religion, its friendships, its quarrels, is one wide judicial investigation of character. In full court, or in small committee, or confronted face to face, accuser and accused, men offer themselves to be judged. Against their will they exhibit those decisive trifles by which character is read. But who judges? and what? Not our understanding. We do not read them by learning or craft. No; the wisdom of the wise man consists herein, that he does not judge them; he lets them judge themselves and merely reads and records their own verdict.

By virtue of this inevitable nature, private will is overpowered, and, maugre our efforts or our imperfections, your genius will speak from you, and mine from me. That which we are, we shall teach, not voluntarily but involuntarily. Thoughts come into our minds by avenues which we never left open, and thoughts go out of our minds through avenues which we never voluntarily opened. Character teaches over our head. The infallible index of true progress is found in the tone the man takes. Neither his age, nor his breeding, nor company, nor books, nor actions, nor talents, nor all together can hinder him from being deferential to a higher spirit than his own. If he have not found his home in God, his manners, his forms of speech, the turn of his sentences, the build, shall I say, of all his opinions will involuntarily confess it, let him brave it out how he will. If he have found his centre, the Deity will shine through him, through all the disguises of ignorance, of ungenial temperament, of unfavorable circumstance. The tone of seeking is one, and the tone of having is another.

The great distinction between teachers sacred or literary—between poets like Herbert, and poets like Pope—between philosophers like Spinoza, Kant and Coleridge, and philosophers like Locke, Paley, Mackintosh and Stewart—between men of the world who are reckoned accomplished talkers, and here and there a fervent mystic, prophesying half insane under the infinitude of his thought—is that one class speak *from within,* or from experience, as parties and possessors of the fact; and the other class *from without,* as spectators merely, or perhaps as acquainted with the fact on the evidence of third persons. It is of no use to preach to me from without. I can do that too easily myself. Jesus speaks always from within, and in a degree that transcends all others. In that is the miracle. I believe beforehand that it ought so to be. All men stand continually in the expectation of the appearance of such a teacher. But if a man do not speak from within the veil, where the word is one with that it tells of, let him lowly confess it.

The same Omniscience flows into the intellect and makes what we call genius. Much of the wisdom of the world is not wisdom, and the most illuminated class of men are no doubt superior to literary fame, and are not writers. Among the multitude of scholars and authors we feel no hallowing presence; we are sensible of a knack and skill rather than of inspiration; they have a light and know not whence it comes and call it their own; their talent is some exaggerated faculty, some overgrown member, so that their strength is a disease. In these instances the intellectual gifts do not make the impression of virtue, but almost of vice; and we feel that a man's talents stand in the way of his advancement in truth. But genius is religious. It is a larger imbibing of the common heart. It is not anomalous, but more like and not less like other men. There is in all great poets a wisdom of humanity which is superior to any talents they exercise. The author, the wit, the partisan, the fine gentleman, does not take place of the man. Humanity shines in Homer, in Chaucer, in Spenser, in Shakspeare, in Milton. They are content with truth. They use the positive degree. They seem frigid and phlegmatic to those who have been spiced with the frantic passion and violent coloring of inferior but popular writers. For they are poets by the free course which they allow to the informing soul, which through their eyes beholds again and blesses the things which it hath made. The soul is superior to its knowledge, wiser than any of its works. The great poet makes us feel our own wealth, and then we think less of his compositions. His best communication to our mind is to teach us to despise all he has done. Shakspeare carries us to such a lofty strain of intelligent activity as to suggest a wealth which beggars his own; and we then feel that the splendid works which he has created, and which in other hours we extol as a sort of self-existent poetry, take no stronger hold of real nature than the shadow of a passing traveller on the rock. The inspiration which uttered itself in Hamlet and Lear could utter things as good from day to day for ever. Why then should I make account of Hamlet and Lear, as if we had not the soul from which they fell as syllables from the tongue?

This energy does not descend into individual life on any other condition than entire possession. It comes to the lowly and simple; it comes to whomsoever will put off what is foreign and proud; it comes as insight; it comes as serenity and grandeur. When we see those whom it inhabits, we are apprised of new degrees of greatness. From that inspiration the man comes back with a changed tone. He does not talk with men with an eye to their opinion. He tries them. It requires of us to be plain and true. The vain traveller attempts to embellish his life by quoting my lord and the prince and the countess, who thus said or did to *him*. The ambitious vulgar show you their spoons and brooches and rings, and preserve their cards and compliments. The more cultivated, in their account of their own experience, cull out the pleasing, poetic circumstance—the visit to Rome, the man of genius they saw, the brilliant friend they know; still further on perhaps the gorgeous landscape, the mountain lights, the mountain thoughts they enjoyed yesterday—and so seek to throw a romantic color over their life. But the soul that ascends to worship the great God is plain and true; has no rose-color, no fine friends, no chivalry, no adventures; does not want admiration; dwells in the hour that now is, in the earnest experience of the common day—by reason of the present moment and the mere trifle having become porous to thought and bibulous of the sea of light.

Converse with a mind that is grandly simple, and literature looks like word-catching. The simplest utterances are worthiest to be written, yet are they so cheap and so things of course, that in the infinite riches of the soul it is like gathering a few pebbles off the ground, or bottling a little air in a phial, when the whole earth and the whole atmosphere are ours. Nothing can pass there, or make you one of the circle, but the casting aside your trappings and dealing man to man in naked truth, plain confession and omniscient affirmation.

Souls such as these treat you as gods would, walk as gods in the earth, accepting without any admiration your wit, your bounty, your virtue even—say rather your act of duty, for your virtue they own as their proper blood, royal as themselves, and over-royal, and the father of the gods. But what rebuke their plain fraternal bearing casts on the mutual flattery with which authors solace each other and wound themselves! These flatter not. I do not wonder that these men go to see Cromwell and Christina and Charles the Second and James the First and the Grand Turk. For they are, in their own elevation, the fellows of kings, and must feel the servile tone of conversation in the world. They must always be a godsend to princes, for they confront them, a king to a king, without ducking or concession, and give a high nature the refreshment and satisfaction of resistance, of plain humanity, of even companionship and of new ideas. They leave them wiser and superior men. Souls like these make us feel that sincerity is more excellent than flattery. Deal so plainly with man and woman as to constrain the utmost sincerity and destroy all hope of trifling with you. It is the highest compliment you can pay. Their "highest praising," said Milton, "is not flattery, and their plainest advice is a kind of praising."

Ineffable is the union of man and God in every act of the soul. The simplest person who in his integrity worships God, becomes God; yet for ever and ever the influx of this better and universal self is new and unsearchable. It inspires awe and astonishment. How dear, how soothing to man, arises the idea of God, peopling the lonely place, effacing the scars of our mistakes and disappointments! When we have broken our god of tradition and ceased from our god of rhetoric, then may God fire the heart with his presence. It is the doubling of the heart itself, nay, the infinite enlargement of the heart with a power of growth to a new infinity on every side. It inspires in man an infallible trust. He has not the conviction, but the sight, that the best is the true, and may in that thought easily dismiss all particular uncertainties and fears, and adjourn to the sure revelation of time the solution of his private riddles. He is sure that his welfare is dear to the heart of being. In the presence of law to his mind he is overflowed with a reliance so universal that it sweeps away all cherished hopes and the most stable projects of mortal condition in its flood. He believes that he cannot escape from his good. The things that are really for thee gravitate to thee. You are running to seek your friend. Let your feet run, but your mind need not. If you do not find him, will you not acquiesce that it is best you should not find him? for there is a power, which, as it is in you, is in him also, and could therefore very well bring you together, if it were for the best. You are preparing with eagerness to go and render a service to which your talent and your taste invite you, the love of men and the hope of fame. Has it not occurred to you that you have no right to go, unless you are equally willing to be prevented from going? O, believe, as thou livest, that every sound that is spoken over the round world, which thou oughtest to hear, will vibrate on thine ear! Every proverb, every book, every byword that belongs to thee for aid or comfort, shall surely come home through open or winding passages. Every friend whom not thy fantastic will but the great and tender heart in thee craveth, shall lock thee in his embrace. And this because the heart in thee is the heart of all; not a valve, not a wall, not an intersection is there anywhere in nature, but one blood rolls uninterruptedly an endless circulation through all men, as the water of the globe is all one sea, and, truly seen, its tide is one.

Let man then learn the revelation of all nature and all thought to his heart; this, namely; that the Highest dwells with him; that the sources of nature are in his own mind, if the sentiment of duty is there. But if he would know what the great God speaketh, he must "go into his closet and shut the door," as Jesus said. God will not make himself manifest to cowards. He must greatly listen to himself, withdrawing himself from all the accents of other men's devotion. Even their prayers are hurtful to him, until he have made his own. Our religion vulgarly stands on numbers of believers. Whenever the appeal is made—no matter how indirectly—to numbers, proclamation is then and there made that religion is not. He that finds God a sweet enveloping thought to him never counts his company. When I sit in that presence, who shall dare to come in? When I rest in perfect humility, when I burn with pure love, what can Calvin or Swedenborg say?

It makes no difference whether the appeal is to numbers

or to one. The faith that stands on authority is not faith. The reliance on authority measures the decline of religion, the withdrawal of the soul. The position men have given to Jesus, now for many centuries of history, is a position of authority. It characterizes themselves. It cannot alter the eternal facts. Great is the soul, and plain. It is no flatterer, it is no follower; it never appeals from itself. It believes in itself. Before the immense possibilities of man all mere experience, all past biography, however spotless and sainted, shrinks away. Before that heaven which our presentiments foreshow us, we cannot easily praise any form of life we have seen or read of. We not only affirm that we have few great men, but, absolutely speaking, that we have none; that we have no history, no record of any character or mode of living that entirely contents us. The saints and demigods whom history worships we are constrained to accept with a grain of allowance. Though in our lonely hours we draw a new strength out of their memory, yet, pressed on our attention, as they are by the thoughtless and customary, they fatigue and invade. The soul gives itself, alone, original and pure, to the Lonely, Original and Pure, who, on that condition, gladly inhabits, leads and speaks through it. Then is it glad, young and nimble. It is not wise, but it sees through all things. It is not called religious, but it is innocent. It calls the light its own, and feels that the grass grows and the stone falls by a law inferior to, and dependent on, its nature. Behold, it saith, I am born into the great, the universal mind. I, the imperfect, adore my own Perfect. I am somehow receptive of the great soul, and thereby I do overlook the sun and the stars and feel them to be the fair accidents and effects which change and pass. More and more the surges of everlasting nature enter into me, and I become public and human in my regards and actions. So come I to live in thoughts and act with energies which are immortal. Thus revering the soul, and learning, as the ancient said, that "its beauty is immense," man will come to see that the world is the perennial miracle which the soul worketh, and be less astonished at particular wonders; he will learn that there is no profane history; that all history is sacred; that the universe is represented in an atom, in a moment of time. He will weave no longer a spotted life of shreds and patches, but he will live with a divine unity. He will cease from what is base and frivolous in his life and be content with all places and with any service he can render. He will calmly front the morrow in the negligency of that trust which carries God with it and so hath already the whole future in the bottom of the heart.

From *Essays, First Series*

Experience

Where do we find ourselves? In a series of which we do not know the extremes, and believe that it has none. We wake and find ourselves on a stair; there are stairs below us, which we seem to have ascended; there are stairs above us, many a one, which go upward and out of sight. But the Genius which according to the old belief stands at the door by which we enter, and gives us the lethe to drink, that we may tell no tales, mixed the cup too strongly, and we cannot shake off the lethargy now at noonday. Sleep lingers all our lifetime about our eyes, as night hovers all day in the boughs of the fir-tree. All things swim and glitter. Our life is not so much threatened as our perception. Ghostlike we glide through nature, and should not know our place again. Did our birth fall in some fit of indigence and frugality in nature, that she was so sparing of her fire and so liberal of her earth that it appears to us that we lack the affirmative principle, and though we have health and reason, yet we have no superfluity of spirit for new creation? We have enough to live and bring the year about, but not an ounce to impart or to invest. Ah that our Genius were a little more of a genius! We are like millers on the lower levels of a stream, when the factories above them have exhausted the water. We too fancy that the upper people must have raised their dams.

If any of us knew what we were doing, or where we are going, then when we think we best know! We do not know to-day whether we are busy or idle. In times when we thought ourselves indolent, we have afterwards discovered that much was accomplished and much was begun in us. All our days are so unprofitable while they pass, that 't is wonderful where or when we ever got anything of this which we call wisdom, poetry, virtue. We never got it on any dated calendar day. Some heavenly days must have been intercalated somewhere, like those that Hermes won with dice of the Moon, that Osiris might be born. It is said all martyrdoms looked mean when they were suffered. Every ship is a romantic object, except that we sail in. Embark, and the romance quits our vessel and hangs on every other sail in the horizon. Our life looks trivial, and we shun to record it. Men seem to have learned of the horizon the art of perpetual retreating and reference. "Yonder uplands are rich pasturage, and my neighbor has fertile meadow, but my field," says the querulous farmer, "only holds the world together." I quote another man's saying; unluckily that other withdraws himself in the same way, and quotes me. 'T is the trick of nature thus to degrade to-day; a good deal of buzz, and somewhere a result slipped magically in. Every roof is agreeable to the eye until it is lifted; then we find tragedy and moaning women and hard-eyed husbands and deluges of lethe, and the men ask, "What's the news?" as if the old were so bad. How many individuals can we count in society? how many actions? how many opinions? So much of our time is preparation, so much is routine, and so much retrospect, that the pith of each man's genius contracts itself to a very few hours. The history of literature—take the net result of Tiraboschi, Warton, or Schlegel—is a sum of very few ideas and of very few original tales; all the rest being variation of these. So in this great society wide lying around us, a critical analysis would find very few spontaneous actions. It is almost all custom and gross sense. There are even few opinions, and these seem organic in the speakers, and do not disturb the universal necessity.

What opium is instilled into all disaster! It shows formidable as we approach it, but there is at last no rough rasping friction, but the most slippery sliding surfaces; we fall soft on a thought; *Ate Dea* is gentle,

> Over men's heads walking aloft,
> With tender feet treading so soft.[1]

---

[1] Source unknown.

People grieve and bemoan themselves, but it is not half so bad with them as they say. There are moods in which we court suffering, in the hope that here at least we shall find reality, sharp peaks and edges of truth. But it turns out to be scene-painting and counterfeit. The only thing grief has taught me is to know how shallow it is. That, like all the rest, plays about the surface, and never introduces me into the reality, for contact with which we would even pay the costly price of sons and lovers. Was it Boscovich who found out that bodies never come in contact? Well, souls never touch their objects. An innavigable sea washes with silent waves between us and the things we aim at and converse with. Grief too will make us idealists. In the death of my son, now more than two years ago, I seem to have lost a beautiful estate— no more. I cannot get it nearer to me. If to-morrow I should be informed of the bankruptcy of my principal debtors, the loss of my property would be a great inconvenience to me, perhaps, for many years; but it would leave me as it found me—neither better nor worse. So is it with this calamity; it does not touch me; something which I fancied was a part of me, which could not be torn away without tearing me nor enlarged without enriching me, falls off from me and leaves no scar. It was caducous. I grieve that grief can teach me nothing, nor carry me one step into real nature. The Indian who was laid under a curse that the wind should not blow on him, nor water flow to him, nor fire burn him, is a type of us all. The dearest events are summer-rain, and we the Para coats that shed every drop. Nothing is left us now but death. We look to that with a grim satisfaction, saying, There at least is reality that will not dodge us.

I take this evanescence and lubricity of all objects, which lets them slip through our fingers then when we clutch hardest, to be the most unhandsome part of our condition. Nature does not like to be observed, and likes that we should be her fools and playmates. We may have the sphere for our cricket-ball, but not a berry for our philosophy. Direct strokes she never gave us power to make; all our blows glance, all our hits are accidents. Our relations to each other are oblique and casual.

Dream delivers us to dream, and there is no end to illusion. Life is a train of moods like a string of beads, and as we pass through them they prove to be many-colored lenses which paint the world their own hue, and each shows only what lies in its focus. From the mountain you see the mountain. We animate what we can, and we see only what we animate. Nature and books belong to the eyes that see them. It depends on the mood of the man whether he shall see the sunset or the fine poem. There are always sunsets, and there is always genius; but only a few hours so serene that we can relish nature or criticism. The more or less depends on structure or temperament. Temperament is the iron wire on which the beads are strung. Of what use is fortune or talent to a cold and defective nature? Who cares what sensibility or discrimination a man has at some time shown, if he falls asleep in his chair? or if he laugh and giggle? or if he apologize? or is infected with egotism? or thinks of his dollar? or cannot go by food? or has gotten a child in his boyhood? Of what use is genius, if the organ is too convex or too concave and cannot find a focal distance within the actual horizon of human life? Of what use, if the brain is too cold or too hot, and the man does not care enough for results to stimulate him to experiment, and hold him up in it? or if the web is too finely woven, too irritable by pleasure and pain, so that life stagnates from too much reception without due outlet? Of what use to make heroic vows of amendment, if the same old law-breaker is to keep them? What cheer can the religious sentiment yield, when that is suspected to be secretly dependent on the seasons of the year and the state of the blood? I knew a witty physician who found the creed in the biliary duct, and used to affirm that if there was disease in the liver, the man became a Calvinist, and if that organ was sound, he became a Unitarian. Very mortifying is the reluctant experience that some unfriendly excess or imbecility neutralizes the promise of genius. We see young men who owe us a new world, so readily and lavishly they promise, but they never acquit the debt; they die young and dodge the account; or if they live they lose themselves in the crowd.

Temperament also enters fully into the system of illusions and shuts us in a prison of glass which we cannot see. There is an optical illusion about every person we meet. In truth they are all creatures of given temperament, which will appear in a given character, whose boundaries they will never pass; but we look at them, they seem alive, and we presume there is impulse in them. In the moment it seems impulse; in the year, in the lifetime, it turns out to be a certain uniform tune which the revolving barrel of the music-box must play. Men resist the conclusion in the morning, but adopt it as the evening wears on, that temper prevails over everything of time, place and condition, and is inconsumable in the flames of religion. Some modifications the moral sentiment avails to impose, but the individual texture holds its dominion, if not to bias the moral judgments, yet to fix the measure of activity and of enjoyment.

I thus express the law as it is read from the platform of ordinary life, but must not leave it without noticing the capital exception. For temperament is a power which no man willingly hears any one praise but himself. On the platform of physics we cannot resist the contracting influences of so-called science. Temperament puts all divinity to rout. I know the mental proclivity of physicians. I hear the chuckle of the phrenologists. Theoretic kidnappers and slave-drivers, they esteem each man the victim of another, who winds him round his finger by knowing the law of his being; and, by such cheap signboards as the color of his beard or the slope of his occiput, reads the inventory of his fortunes and character. The grossest ignorance does not disgust like this impudent knowingness. The physicians say they are not materialists; but they are: Spirit is matter reduced to an extreme thinness: O so thin! But the definition of *spiritual* should be, *that which is its own evidence.* What notions do they attach to love! what to religion! One would not willingly pronounce these words in their hearing, and give them the occasion to profane them. I saw a gracious gentleman who adapts his conversation to the form of the head of the man he talks with! I had fancied that the value of life lay in its inscrutable possibilities; in the fact that I never know, in addressing myself to a new individual, what may befall me. I carry the keys of my castle in my hand, ready to throw them at the feet of my lord, whenever and in what disguise soever he shall appear. I know he is in the neighborhood, hidden among vagabonds. Shall I preclude my future by taking a high seat and kindly adapting my conversation to the shape of heads? When I come to that, the doctors shall buy me for a cent. "But, sir, medical history; the report to the Institute; the proven facts!" I distrust the facts and the inferences. Temperament is the veto or limitation-power in the constitution, very justly applied to restrain an opposite excess in the constitution, but absurdly offered as a bar to original equity. When virtue is in presence, all subordinate powers sleep. On its own level, or in view of nature, temperament is final. I see not, if one be once caught in this trap of so-called sciences, any escape for the man from the links of the chain of physical necessity. Given such an embryo, such a history must follow. On this platform one lives in a sty of sensualism, and would soon come to suicide. But it is impossible that the creative power should exclude itself. Into every intelligence there is a door which is never closed, through which the creator passes. The intellect, seeker of absolute truth, or the heart, lover of absolute good, intervenes for our succor, and at one whisper of these high powers we awake from ineffectual struggles with this nightmare. We hurl it into its own hell, and cannot again contract ourselves to so base a state.

The secret of the illusoriness is in the necessity of a succession of moods or objects. Gladly we would anchor, but the anchorage is quicksand. This onward trick of nature is too strong for us: *Pero si muove.* When at night I look at the moon and stars, I seem stationary, and they to hurry. Our love of the real draws us to permanence, but health of body consists in circulation, and sanity of mind in variety or facility of association. We need change of objects. Dedication to one thought is quickly odious. We house with the insane, and must humor them; then conversation dies out. Once I took such delight in Montaigne that I thought I should not need any other book; before that, in Shakspeare; then in Plutarch; then in Plotinus; at one time in Bacon; afterwards in Goethe; even in Bettine; but now I turn the pages of either of them languidly, whilst I still cherish their genius. So with pictures; each will bear an emphasis of attention once, which it cannot retain, though we fain would continue to be pleased in that manner. How strongly I have felt of pictures that when you have seen one well, you must take your leave of it; you shall never see it again. I have had good lessons from pictures which I have since seen without emotion or remark. A deduction must be made from the opinion which even the wise express on a new book or occurrence. Their opinion gives me tidings of their mood, and some vague guess at the new fact, but is nowise to be trusted as the lasting relation between that intellect and that thing. The child asks, "Mamma, why don't I like the story as well as when you told it me yesterday?" Alas! child, it is even so with the oldest cherubim of knowledge. But will it answer thy question to say, Because thou wert born to a whole and this story is a particular? The reason of the pain this discovery causes us (and we make it late in respect to works of art and intellect) is the plaint of tragedy which murmurs from it in regard to persons, to friendship and love.

That immobility and absence of elasticity which we find in the arts, we find with more pain in the artist. There is no power of expansion in men. Our friends early appear to us as representatives of certain ideas which they never pass·or exceed. They stand on the brink of the ocean of thought and power, but they never take the single step that would bring them there. A man is like a bit of Labrador spar, which has no lustre as you turn it in your hand until you come to a particular angle; then it shows deep and beautiful colors. There is no adaptation or universal applicability in men, but each has his special talent, and the mastery of successful men consists in adroitly keeping themselves where and when that turn shall be oftenest to be practised. We do what we must, and call it by the best names we can, and would fain have the praise of having intended the result which ensues. I cannot recall any form of man who is not superfluous sometimes. But is not this pitiful? Life is not worth the taking, to do tricks in.

Of course it needs the whole society to give the symmetry we seek. The party-colored wheel must revolve very fast to appear white. Something is earned too by conversing with so much folly and defect. In fine, whoever loses, we are always of the gaining party. Divinity is behind our failures and follies also. The plays of children are nonsense, but very educative nonsense. So it is with the largest and solemnest things, with commerce, government, church, marriage, and so with the history of every man's bread, and the ways by which he is to come by it. Like a bird which alights nowhere, but hops perpetually from bough to bough, is the Power which abides in no man and in no woman, but for a moment speaks from this one, and for another moment from that one.

But what help from these fineries or pedantries? What help from thought? Life is not dialectics. We, I think, in these times, have had lessons enough of the futility of criticism. Our young people have thought and written much on labor and reform, and for all that they have written, neither the world nor themselves have got on a step. Intellectual tasting of life will not supersede muscular activity. If a man should consider the nicety of the passage of a piece of bread down his throat, he would starve. At Education Farm the noblest theory of life sat on the noblest figures of young men and maidens, quite powerless and melancholy. It would not rake or pitch a ton of hay; it would not rub down a horse; and the men and maidens it left pale and hungry. A political orator wittily compared our party promises to western roads, which opened stately enough, with planted trees on either side to tempt the traveller, but soon became narrow and narrower and ended in a squirrel-track and ran up a tree. So does culture with us; it ends in headache. Unspeakably sad and barren does life look to those who a few months ago were dazzled with the splendor of the promise of the times. "There is now no longer any right course of action nor any self-devotion left among the Iranis." Objections and criticism we have had our fill of. There are objections to every course of life and action, and the practical wisdom infers an indifferency, from the omnipresence of objection. The whole frame of things preaches indifferency. Do not craze yourself with thinking, but go about your business anywhere. Life is not intellectual or critical, but sturdy. Its chief good is for well-mixed people who can enjoy what they find, without question. Nature hates peeping, and our mothers speak her very sense when they say, "Children, eat your victuals, and say no more of it." To fill the hour—that is happiness; to fill the hour and leave no crevice for a repentance or an approval. We live amid surfaces, and the true art of life is to skate well on them. Under the oldest mouldiest conventions a man of native force prospers just as well as in the newest world, and that by skill of handling and treatment. He can take hold anywhere. Life itself is a mixture of power and form, and will not bear the least excess of either. To finish the moment, to find the journey's end in every step of the road, to live the greatest number of good hours, is wisdom. It is not the part of men, but of fanatics, or of mathematicians if you will, to say that, the shortness of life considered, it is not worth caring whether for so short a duration we were sprawling in want or sitting high. Since our office is with moments, let us husband them. Five minutes of to-day are worth as much to me as five minutes in the next millennium. Let us be poised, and wise, and our own, to-day. Let us treat the men and women well; treat them as if they were real; perhaps they are. Men live in their fancy, like drunkards whose hands are too soft and tremulous for successful labor. It is a tempest of fancies, and the only ballast I know is a respect to the present hour. Without any shadow of doubt, amidst this vertigo of shows and politics, I settle myself ever the firmer in the creed that we should not postpone and refer and wish, but do broad justice where we are, by whomsoever we deal with, accepting our actual companions and circumstances, however humble or odious, as the mystic officials to whom the universe has delegated its whole pleasure for us. If these are mean and malignant, their contentment, which is the last victory of justice, is a more satisfying echo to the heart than the voice of poets and the casual sympathy of admirable persons. I think that however a thoughtful man may suffer from the defects and absurdities of his company, he cannot without affectation deny to any set of men and women a sensibility to extraordinary merit. The coarse and frivolous have an instinct of superiority, if they have not a sympathy, and honor it in their blind capricious way with sincere homage.

The fine young people despise life, but in me, and in such as with me are free from dyspepsia, and to whom a day is a sound and solid good, it is a great excess of politeness to look scornful and to cry for company. I am grown by sympathy a little eager and sentimental, but leave me alone and I should relish every hour and what it brought me, the potluck of the day, as heartily as the oldest gossip in the bar-room. I am thankful for small mercies. I compared notes with one of my friends who expects everything of the universe and is disappointed when anything is less than the best, and I found that I begin at the other extreme, expecting nothing, and am always full of thanks for moderate goods. I accept the clangor and jangle of contrary tendencies. I find my account in sots and bores also. They give a reality to the circumjacent picture which such a vanishing meteorous appearance can ill spare. In the morning I awake and find the old world, wife, babes and mother, Concord and Boston, the dear old spiritual world and even the dear old devil not far off. If we will take the good we find, asking no questions, we shall have heaping measures. The great gifts are not got by analysis. Everything good is on the highway. The middle region of our being is the temperate zone. We may climb into the thin and cold realm of pure geometry and lifeless science, or sink into that of sensation. Between these extremes is the equator of life, of thought, of spirit, of poetry—a narrow belt. Moreover, in popular experience everything good is on the highway. A collector peeps into all the picture-shops of Europe for a landscape of Poussin, a crayon-sketch of Salvator; but the Transfiguration, the Last Judgment, the Communion of Saint Jerome, and what are as transcendent as these, are on the walls of the Vatican, the Uffizi, or the Louvre, where every footman may see them; to say nothing of Nature's pictures in every street, of sunsets and sunrises every day, and the sculpture of the human body never absent. A collector recently bought at public auction, in London, for one hundred and fifty-seven guineas, an autograph of Shakspeare; but for nothing a school-boy can read Hamlet and can detect secrets of highest concernment yet unpublished therein. I think I will never read any but the commonest books—the Bible, Homer, Dante, Shakspeare and Milton. Then we are impatient of so public a life and planet, and run hither and thither for nooks and secrets. The imagination delights in the woodcraft of Indians, trappers and bee-hunters. We fancy that we are strangers, and not so intimately domesticated in the planet as the wild man and the wild beast and bird. But the exclusion reaches them also; reaches the climbing, flying, gliding, feathered and four-footed man. Fox and woodchuck, hawk and snipe and bittern, when nearly seen, have no more root in the deep world than man, and are just such superficial tenants of the globe. Then the new molecular philosophy shows astronomical interspaces betwixt atom and atom, shows that the world is all outside; it has no inside.

The mid-world is best. Nature, as we know her, is no saint. The lights of the church, the ascetics, Gentoos and corn-eaters, she does not distinguish by any favor. She comes eating and drinking and sinning. Her darlings, the great, the strong, the beautiful, are not children of our law; do not come out of the Sunday School, nor weigh their food, nor punctually keep the commandments. If we will be strong with her strength we must not harbor such disconsolate consciences, borrowed too from the consciences of other nations. We must set up the strong present tense against all the rumors of wrath, past or to come. So many things are unsettled which it is of the first importance to settle; and, pending their settlement, we will do as we do. Whilst the debate goes forward on the equity of commerce, and will not be closed for a century or two, New and Old England may keep shop. Law of copyright and international copyright is to be discussed, and in the interim we will sell our books for the most we can. Expediency of literature, reason of literature, lawfulness of writing down a thought, is questioned; much is to say on both sides, and, while the fight waxes hot, thou, dearest scholar, stick to thy foolish task, add a line every hour, and between whiles add a line. Right to hold land, right of property, is disputed, and the conventions convene, and before the vote is taken, dig away in your garden, and spend your earnings as a waif or godsend to all serene and beautiful purposes. Life itself is a bubble and a scepticism, and a sleep within a sleep. Grant it, and as much more as they will— but thou, God's darling! heed thy private dream; thou wilt not be missed in the scorning and scepticism; there are enough of them; stay there in thy closet and toil until the rest are agreed what to do about it. Thy sickness, they say, and thy puny habit require that thou do this or avoid that, but know that thy life is a flitting state, a tent for a night, and do thou, sick or well, finish that stint. Thou art sick, but shalt not be worse, and the universe, which holds thee dear, shall be the better.

Human life is made up of the two elements, power and form, and the proportion must be invariably kept if we would have it sweet and sound. Each of these elements in excess makes a mischief as hurtful as its defect. Everything runs to excess; every good quality is noxious if unmixed, and, to carry the danger to the edge of ruin, nature causes each man's peculiarity to superabound. Here, among the farms, we adduce the scholars as examples of this treachery. They are nature's victims of expression. You who see the artist, the orator, the poet, too near, and find their life no more excellent than that of mechanics or farmers, and themselves victims of partiality, very hollow and haggard, and pronounce them failures, not heroes, but quacks—conclude very reasonably that these arts are not for man, but are disease. Yet nature will not bear you out. Irresistible nature made men such, and makes legions more of such, every day. You love the boy reading in a book, gazing at a drawing or a cast; yet what are these millions who read and behold, but incipient writers and sculptors? Add a little more of that quality which now reads and sees, and they will seize the pen and chisel. And if one remembers how innocently he began to be an artist, he perceives that nature joined with his enemy. A man is a golden impossibility. The line he must walk is a hair's breadth. The wise through excess of wisdom is made a fool.

How easily, if fate would suffer it, we might keep forever these beautiful limits, and adjust ourselves, once for all, to the perfect calculation of the kingdom of known cause and effect. In the street and in the newspapers, life appears so plain a business that manly resolution and adherence to the multiplication-table through all weathers will insure success. But ah! presently comes a day, or is it only a half-hour, with its angel-whispering—which discomfits the conclusions of nations and of years! To-morrow again every thing looks real and angular, the habitual standards are reinstated, common-sense is as rare as genius—is the basis of genius, and experience is hands and feet to every enterprise—and yet, he who should do his business on this understanding would be quickly bankrupt. Power keeps quite another road than the turnpikes of choice and will; namely the subterranean and invisible tunnels and channels of life. It is ridiculous that we are diplomatists, and doctors, and considerate people; there are no dupes like these. Life is a series of surprises, and would not be worth taking or keeping if it were not. God delights to isolate us every day, and hide from us the past and the future. We would look about us, but with grand politeness he draws down before us an impenetrable screen of purest sky, and another behind us of purest sky. "You will not remember," he seems to say, "and you will not expect." All good conversation, manners and action come from a spontaneity which forgets usages and makes the moment great. Nature hates calculators; her methods are saltatory and impulsive. Man lives by pulses; our organic movements are such; and the chemical and ethereal agents are undulatory and alternate; and the mind goes antagonizing on, and never prospers but by fits. We thrive by casualties. Our chief experiences have been casual. The most attractive class of people are those who are powerful obliquely and not by the direct stroke; men of genius, but not yet accredited; one gets the cheer of their light without paying too great a tax. Theirs is the beauty of the bird or the morning light, and not of art. In the thought of genius there is always a surprise; and the moral sentiment is well called "the newness," for it is never other; as new to the oldest intelligence as to the young child— "the kingdom that cometh without observation." In like manner, for practical success, there must not be too much design. A man will not be observed in doing that which he can do best. There is a certain magic about his properest action which stupefies your powers of observation, so that though it is done before you, you wist not of it. The art of life has a pudency, and will not be exposed. Every man is an impossibility until he is born; every thing impossible until we see a success. The ardors of piety agree at last with the coldest scepticism—that nothing is of us or our works—that all is of God. Nature will not spare us the smallest leaf of laurel. All writing comes by the grace of God, and all doing and having. I would gladly be moral and keep due metes and bounds, which I dearly love, and allow the most to the will of man; but I have set my heart on honesty in this chapter, and I can see nothing at last, in success or failure, than more or less of vital force supplied from the Eternal. The results of life are uncalculated and uncalculable. The years teach much which the days never know. The persons who compose our company converse, and come and go, and design and execute many things, and somewhat comes of it all, but an unlooked-for result. The individual is always mistaken. He designed many things, and drew in other persons as coadjutors, quarrelled with some or all, blundered much, and something is done; all are a little advanced, but the individual is always mistaken. It turns out somewhat new and very unlike what he promised himself.

The ancients, struck with this irreducibleness of the elements of human life to calculation, exalted Chance into a divinity; but that is to stay too long at the spark, which glitters truly at one point, but the universe is warm with the latency of the same fire. The miracle of life which will not be expounded but will remain a miracle, introduces a new element. In the growth of the embryo, Sir Everard Home I think noticed that the evolution was not from one central point, but coactive from three or more points. Life has no memory. That which proceeds in succession might be remembered, but that which is coexistent, or ejaculated from a deeper cause, as yet far from being conscious, knows not its own tendency. So is it with us, now sceptical or without unity, because immersed in forms and effects all seeming to be of equal yet hostile value, and now religious, whilst in the reception of spiritual law. Bear with these distractions, with this coetaneous growth of the parts; they will one day be *members*, and obey one will. On that one will, on that secret cause, they nail our attention and hope. Life is hereby melted into an expectation or a religion. Underneath the inharmonious trivial particulars, is a musical perfection; the Ideal journeying always with us, the heaven without rent or seam. Do but observe the mode of our illumination. When I converse with a profound mind, or if at any time being alone I have good thoughts, I do not at once arrive at satisfactions, as when, being thirsty, I drink water; or go to the fire, being cold; no! but I am at first apprised of my vicinity to a new and excellent region of life. By persisting to read or to think, this region gives further sign of itself, as it were in flashes of light, in sudden discoveries of its profound beauty and repose, as if the clouds that covered it parted at intervals and showed the approaching traveller the inland mountains, with the tranquil eternal meadows spread at their base, whereon flocks graze and shepherds pipe and dance. But every insight from this realm of thought is felt as initial, and promises a sequel. I do not make it; I arrive there, and behold what was there already. I make! O no! I clap my hands in infantine joy and amazement before the first opening to me of this august magnificence, old with the love and homage of innumerable ages, young with the life of life, the sunbright Mecca of the desert. And what a future it opens! I feel a new heart beating with the love of the new beauty. I am ready to die out of nature and be born again into this new yet unapproachable America I have found in the West:

Since neither now nor yesterday began
These thoughts, which have been ever, nor yet can
A man be found who their first entrance knew.[2]

If I have described life as a flux of moods, I must now add that there is that in us which changes not and which ranks all sensations and states of mind. The consciousness in each man is a sliding scale, which identifies him now with the First Cause, and now with the flesh of his body; life above life, in infinite degrees. The sentiment from which it sprung determines the dignity of any deed, and the question ever is, not what you have done or forborne, but at whose command you have done or forborne it.

Fortune, Minerva, Muse, Holy Ghost—these are quaint names, too narrow to cover this unbounded substance. The baffled intellect must still kneel before this cause, which refuses to be named—ineffable cause, which every fine genius has essayed to represent by some emphatic symbol, as, Thales by water, Anaximenes by air, Anaxagoras by (Νοῦς) thought, Zoroaster by fire, Jesus and the moderns by love; and the metaphor of each has become a national religion. The Chinese Mencius has not been the least successful in his generalization. "I fully understand language," he said, "and nourish well my vast-flowing vigor." "I beg to ask what you call vast-flowing vigor?" said his companion. "The explanation," replied Mencius, "is difficult. This vigor is supremely great, and in the highest degree unbending. Nourish it correctly and do it no injury, and it will fill up the vacancy between heaven and earth. This vigor accords with and assists justice and reason, and leaves no hunger." In our more correct writing we give to this generalization the name of Being, and thereby confess that we have arrived as far as we can go. Suffice it for the joy of the universe that we have not arrived at a wall, but at interminable oceans. Our life seems not present so much as prospective; not for the affairs on which it is wasted, but as a hint of this vast-flowing vigor. Most of life seems to be mere advertisement of faculty; information is given us not to sell ourselves cheap; that we are very great. So, in particulars, our greatness is always in a tendency or direction, not in an action. It is for us to believe in the rule, not in the exception.

---

[2] Sophocles, *Antigone*, contains lines similar to these.

The noble are thus known from the ignoble. So in accepting the leading of the sentiments, it is not what we believe concerning the immortality of the soul or the like, but *the universal impulse to believe*, that is the material circumstance and is the principal fact in the history of the globe. Shall we describe this cause as that which works directly? The spirit is not helpless or needful of mediate organs. It has plentiful powers and direct effects. I am explained without explaining, I am felt without acting, and where I am not. Therefore all just persons are satisfied with their own praise. They refuse to explain themselves, and are content that new actions should do them that office. They believe that we communicate without speech and above speech, and that no right action of ours is quite unaffecting to our friends, at whatever distance; for the influence of action is not to be measured by miles. Why should I fret myself because a circumstance has occurred which hinders my presence where I was expected? If I am not at the meeting, my presence where I am should be as useful to the commonwealth of friendship and wisdom, as would be my presence in that place. I exert the same quality of power in all places. Thus journeys the mighty Ideal before us; it never was known to fall into the rear. No man ever came to an experience which was satiating, but his good is tidings of a better. Onward and onward! In liberated moments we know that a new picture of life and duty is already possible; the elements already exist in many minds around you of a doctrine of life which shall transcend any written record we have. The new statement will comprise the scepticisms as well as the faiths of society, and out of unbeliefs a creed shall be formed. For scepticisms are not gratuitous or lawless, but are limitations of the affirmative statement, and the new philosophy must take them in and make affirmations outside of them, just as much as it must include the oldest beliefs.

It is very unhappy, but too late to be helped, the discovery we have made that we exist. That discovery is called the Fall of Man. Ever afterwards we suspect our instruments. We have learned that we do not see directly, but mediately, and that we have no means of correcting these colored and distorting lenses which we are, or of computing the amount of their errors. Perhaps these subject-lenses have a creative power; perhaps there are no objects. Once we lived in what we saw; now, the rapaciousness of this new power, which threatens to absorb all things, engages us. Nature, art, persons, letters, religions, objects, successively tumble in, and God is but one of its ideas. Nature and literature are subjective phenomena; every evil and every good thing is a shadow which we cast. The street is full of humiliations to the proud. As the fop contrived to dress his bailiffs in his livery and make them wait on his guests at table, so the chagrins which the bad heart gives off as bubbles, at once take form as ladies and gentlemen in the street, shopmen or barkeepers in hotels, and threaten or insult whatever is threatenable and insultable in us. 'T is the same with our idolatries. People forget that it is the eye which makes the horizon, and the rounding mind's eye which makes this or that man a type or representative of humanity, with the name of hero or saint. Jesus, the "providential man," is a good man on whom many people are agreed that these optical laws shall take effect. By love on one part and by forbearance to press objection on the other part, it is for a time settled that we will look at him in the centre of the horizon, and ascribe to him the properties that will attach to any man so seen. But the longest love or aversion has a speedy term. The great and crescive self, rooted in absolute nature, supplants all relative existence and ruins the kingdom of mortal friendship and love. Marriage (in what is called the spiritual world) is impossible, because of the inequality between every subject and every object. The subject is the receiver of Godhead, and at every comparison must feel his being enhanced by that cryptic might. Though not in energy, yet by presence, this magazine of substance cannot be otherwise than felt; nor can any force of intellect attribute to the object the proper deity which sleeps or wakes forever in every subject. Never can love make consciousness and ascription equal in force. There will be the same gulf between every me and thee as between the original and the picture. The universe is the bride of the soul. All private sympathy is partial. Two human beings are like globes, which can touch only in a point, and whilst they remain in contact all other points of each of the spheres are inert; their turn must also come, and the longer a particular union lasts the more energy of appetency the parts not in union acquire.

Life will be imaged, but cannot be divided nor doubled.

Any invasion of its unity would be chaos. The soul is not twin-born but the only begotten, and though revealing itself as child in time, child in appearance, is of a fatal and universal power, admitting no co-life. Every day, every act betrays the ill-concealed deity. We believe in ourselves as we do not believe in others. We permit all things to ourselves, and that which we call sin in others is experiment for us. It is an instance of our faith in ourselves that men never speak of crime as lightly as they think; or every man thinks a latitude safe for himself which is nowise to be indulged to another. The act looks very differently on the inside and on the outside; in its quality and in its consequences. Murder in the murderer is no such ruinous thought as poets and romancers will have it; it does not unsettle him or fright him from his ordinary notice of trifles; it is an act quite easy to be contemplated; but in its sequel it turns out to be a horrible jangle and confounding of all relations. Especially the crimes that spring from love seem right and fair from the actor's point of view, but when acted are found destructive of society. No man at last believes that he can be lost, or that the crime in him is as black as in the felon. Because the intellect qualifies in our own case the moral judgments. For there is no crime to the intellect. That is antinomian or hypernomian, and judges law as well as fact. "It is worse than a crime, it is a blunder," said Napoleon, speaking the language of the intellect. To it, the world is a problem in mathematics or the science of quantity, and it leaves out praise and blame and all weak emotions. All stealing is comparative. If you come to absolutes, pray who does not steal? Saints are sad, because they behold sin (even when they speculate) from the point of view of the conscience, and not of the intellect; a confusion of thought. Sin, seen from the thought, is a diminution, or *less;* seen from the conscience or will, it is pravity or *bad.* The intellect names it shade, absence of light, and no essence. The conscience must feel it as essence, essential evil. This it is not; it has an objective existence, but no subjective.

Thus inevitably does the universe wear our color, and every object fall successively into the subject itself. The subject exists, the subject enlarges; all things sooner or later fall into place. As I am, so I see; use what language we will, we can never say anything but what we are; Hermes, Cadmus, Columbus, Newton, Bonaparte, are the mind's ministers. Instead of feeling a poverty when we encounter a great man, let us treat the new-comer like a travelling geologist who passes through our estate and shows us good slate, or limestone, or anthracite, in our brush pasture. The partial action of each strong mind in one direction is a telescope for the objects on which it is pointed. But every other part of knowledge is to be pushed to the same extravagance, ere the soul attains her due sphericity. Do you see that kitten chasing so prettily her own tail? If you could look with her eyes you might see her surrounded with hundreds of figures performing complex dramas, with tragic and comic issues, long conversations, many characters, many ups and downs of fate—and meantime it is only puss and her tail. How long before our masquerade will end its noise of tambourines, laughter and shouting, and we shall find it was a solitary performance? A subject and an object—it takes so much to make the galvanic circuit complete, but magnitude adds nothing. What imports it whether it is Kepler and the sphere, Columbus and America, a reader and his book, or puss with her tail?

It is true that all the muses and love and religion hate these developments, and will find a way to punish the chemist who publishes in the parlor the secrets of the laboratory. And we cannot say too little of our constitutional necessity of seeing things under private aspects, or saturated with our humors. And yet is the God the native of these bleak rocks. That need makes in morals the capital virtue of self-trust. We must hold hard to this poverty, however scandalous, and by more vigorous self-recoveries, after the sallies of action, possess our axis more firmly. The life of truth is cold and so far mournful; but it is not the slave of tears, contritions and perturbations. It does not attempt another's work, nor adopt another's facts. It is a main lesson of wisdom to know your own from another's. I have learned that I cannot dispose of other people's facts; but I possess such a key to my own as persuades me, against all their denials, that they also have a key to theirs. A sympathetic person is placed in the dilemma of a swimmer among drowning men, who all catch at him, and if he give so much as a leg or a finger they will drown him. They wish to be saved from the mischiefs of their vices, but not from their vices. Charity would be wasted on this poor waiting on the symptoms. A wise and hardy physician will say, *Come out of that,* as the first condition of advice.

In this our talking America we are ruined by our good nature and listening on all sides. This compliance takes away the power of being greatly useful. A man should not be able to look other than directly and forthright. A preoccupied attention is the only answer to the importunate frivolity of other people; an attention, and to an aim which makes their wants frivolous. This is a divine answer, and leaves no appeal and no hard thoughts. In Flaxman's drawing of the Eumenides of Æschylus, Orestes supplicates Apollo, whilst the Furies sleep on the threshold. The face of the god expresses a shade of regret and compassion, but is calm with the conviction of the irreconcilableness of the two spheres. He is born into other politics, into the eternal and beautiful. The man at his feet asks for his interest in turmoils of the earth, into which his nature cannot enter. And the Eumenides there lying express pictorially this disparity. The god is surcharged with his divine destiny.

Illusion, Temperament, Succession, Surface, Surprise, Reality, Subjectiveness—these are threads on the loom of time, these are the lords of life. I dare not assume to give their order, but I name them as I find them in my way. I know better than to claim any completeness for my picture. I am a fragment, and this is a fragment of me. I can very confidently announce one or another law, which throws itself into relief and form, but I am too young yet by some ages to compile a code. I gossip for my hour concerning the eternal politics. I have seen many fair pictures not in vain. A wonderful time I have lived in. I am not the novice I was fourteen, nor yet seven years ago. Let who will ask, Where is the fruit? I find a private fruit sufficient. This is a fruit—that I should not ask for a rash effect from meditations, counsels and the hiving of truths. I should feel it pitiful to demand a result on this town and county, an overt effect on the instant month and year. The effect is deep and secular as the cause. It works on periods in which mortal lifetime is lost. All I know is reception; I am and I have: but I do not get, and when I have fancied I had gotten anything, I found I did not. I worship with wonder the great Fortune. My reception has been so large, that I am not annoyed by receiving this or that superabundantly. I say to the Genius, if he will pardon the proverb, *In for a mill, in for a million*. When I receive a new gift,

I do not macerate my body to make the account square, for if I should die I could not make the account square. The benefit overran the merit the first day, and has overrun the merit ever since. The merit itself, so-called, I reckon part of the receiving.

Also that hankering after an overt or practical effect seems to me an apostasy. In good earnest I am willing to spare this most unnecessary deal of doing. Life wears to me a visionary face. Hardest roughest action is visionary also. It is but a choice between soft and turbulent dreams. People disparage knowing and the intellectual life, and urge doing. I am very content with knowing, if only I could know. That is an august entertainment, and would suffice me a great while. To know a little would be worth the expense of this world. I hear always the law of Adrastia, "that every soul which had acquired any truth, should be safe from harm until another period."

I know that the world I converse with in the city and in the farms, is not the world I *think*. I observe that difference, and shall observe it. One day I shall know the value and law of this discrepance. But I have not found that much was gained by manipular attempts to realize the world of thought. Many eager persons successively make an experiment in this way, and make themselves ridiculous. They acquire democratic manners, they foam at the mouth, they hate and deny. Worse, I observe that in the history of mankind there is never a solitary example of success—taking their own tests of success. I say this polemically, or in reply to the inquiry, Why not realize your world? But far be from me the despair which prejudges the law by a paltry empiricism— since there never was a right endeavor but it succeeded. Patience and patience, we shall win at the last. We must be very suspicious of the deceptions of the element of time. It takes a good deal of time to eat or to sleep, or to earn a hundred dollars, and a very little time to entertain a hope and an insight which becomes the light of our life. We dress our garden, eat our dinners, discuss the household with our wives, and these things make no impression, are forgotten next week; but, in the solitude to which every man is always returning, he has a sanity and revelations which in his passage into new worlds he will carry with him. Never mind the ridicule, never mind the defeat; up again, old heart!—it seems to say—there is victory yet for all justice; and the true romance which the world exists to realize will be the transformation of genius into practical power.

From *Essays, Second Series*

Politics

In dealing with the State we ought to remember that its institutions are not aboriginal, though they existed before we were born; that they are not superior to the citizen; that every one of them was once the act of a single man; every law and usage was a man's expedient to meet a particular case; that they all are imitable, all alterable; we may make as good, we may make better. Society is an illusion to the young citizen. It lies before him in rigid repose, with certain names, men and institutions rooted like oak-trees to the centre, round which all arrange themselves the best they can. But the old statesman knows that society is fluid; there are no such roots and centres, but any particle may suddenly become the centre of the movement and compel the system to gyrate round it; as every man of strong will, like Pisistratus or Cromwell, does for a time, and every man of truth, like Plato or Paul, does forever. But politics rest on necessary foundations, and cannot be treated with levity. Republics abound in young civilians who believe that the laws make the city, that grave modifications of the policy and modes of living and employments of the population, that commerce, education and religion may be voted in or out; and that any measure, though it were absurd, may be imposed on a people if only you can get sufficient voices to make it a law. But the wise know that foolish legislation is a rope of sand which perishes in the twisting; that the State must follow and not lead the character and progress of the citizen; the strongest usurper is quickly got rid of; and they only who build on Ideas, build for eternity; and that the form of government which prevails is the expression of what cultivation exists in the population which permits it. The law is only a memorandum. We are superstitious, and esteem the statute somewhat: so much life as it has in the character of living men is its force. The statute stands there to say, Yesterday we agreed so and so, but how feel ye this article to-day? Our statute is a currency which we stamp with our own portrait: it soon becomes unrecognizable, and in process of time will return to the mint. Nature is not democratic, nor limited-monarchical, but despotic, and will not be fooled or abated of any jot of her authority by the pertest of her sons; and as fast as the public mind is opened to more intelligence, the code is seen to be brute and stammering. It speaks not articulately, and must be made to. Meantime the education of the general mind never stops. The reveries of the true and simple are prophetic. What the tender poetic youth dreams, and prays, and paints to-day, but shuns the ridicule of saying aloud, shall presently be the resolutions of public bodies; then shall be carried as grievance and bill of rights through conflict and war, and then shall be triumphant law and establishment for a hundred years, until it gives place in turn to new prayers and pictures. The history of the State sketches in coarse outline the progress of thought, and follows at a distance the delicacy of culture and of aspiration.

The theory of politics which has possessed the mind of men, and which they have expressed the best they could in their laws and in their revolutions, considers persons and property as the two objects for whose protection government exists. Of persons, all have equal rights, in virtue of being identical in nature. This interest of course with its whole power demands a democracy. Whilst the rights of all as persons are equal, in virtue of their access to reason, their rights in property are very unequal. One man owns his clothes, and another owns a county. This accident, depending primarily on the skill and virtue of the parties, of which there is every degree, and secondarily on patrimony, falls unequally, and its rights of course are unequal. Personal rights, universally the same, demand a government framed on the ratio of census; property demands a government framed on the ratio of owners and of owning. Laban, who has flocks and herds, wishes them looked after by an officer on the frontiers, lest the Midianites shall drive them off; and pays a tax to that end. Jacob has no flocks or herds and no fear of the Midianites, and pays no tax to the officer. It seemed fit that Laban and Jacob should have equal rights to elect the officer who is to defend their persons, but that Laban and not Jacob should elect the officer who is to guard the sheep and cattle. And if question arise whether additional officers or watch-towers should be provided, must not Laban and Isaac, and those who must sell part of their herds to buy protection for the rest, judge better of this, and with more right, than Jacob, who, because he is a youth and a traveller, eats their bread and not his own?

In the earliest society the proprietors made their own wealth, and so long as it comes to the owners in the direct way, no other opinion would arise in any equitable community than that property should make the law for property, and persons the law for persons.

But property passes through donation or inheritance to those who do not create it. Gift, in one case, makes it as really the new owner's as labor made it the first owner's: in the other case, of patrimony, the law makes an ownership which will be valid in each man's view according to the estimate which he sets on the public tranquillity.

It was not, however, found easy to embody the readily admitted principle that property should make law for property, and persons for persons; since persons and property mixed themselves in every transaction. At last it seemed settled that the rightful distinction was that the proprietors should have more elective franchise than non-proprietors, on the Spartan principle of "calling that which is just, equal; not that which is equal, just."

That principle no longer looks so self-evident as it appeared in former times, partly because doubts have arisen whether too much weight had not been allowed in the laws to property, and such a structure given to our usages as allowed the rich to encroach on the poor, and to keep them poor; but mainly because there is an instinctive sense, however obscure and yet inarticulate, that the whole constitution of property, on its present tenures, is injurious, and its influence on persons deteriorating and degrading; that truly the only interest for the consideration of the State is persons; that property will always follow persons; that the highest end of government is the culture of men; and that if men can be educated, the institutions will share their improvement and the moral sentiment will write the law of the land.

If it be not easy to settle the equity of this question, the peril is less when we take note of our natural defences. We are kept by better guards than the vigilance of such magistrates as we commonly elect. Society always consists in greatest part of young and foolish persons. The old, who have seen through the hypocrisy of courts and statesmen, die and leave no wisdom to their sons. They believe their own newspaper, as their fathers did at their age. With such an ignorant and deceivable majority, States would soon run to ruin, but that there are limitations beyond which the folly and ambition of governors cannot go. Things have their laws, as well as men; and things refuse to be trifled with. Property will be protected. Corn will not grow unless it is planted and manured; but the farmer will not plant or hoe it unless the chances are a hundred to one that he will cut and harvest it. Under any forms, persons and property must and will have their just sway. They exert their power, as steadily as matter its attraction. Cover up a pound of earth never so cunningly, divide and subdivide it; melt it to liquid, convert it to gas; it will always weigh a pound; it will always attract and resist other matter by the full virtue of one pound weight: and the attributes of a person, his wit and his moral energy, will exercise, under any law or extinguishing tyranny, their proper force— if not overtly, then covertly; if not for the law, then against it; if not wholesomely, then poisonously; with right, or by might.

The boundaries of personal influence it is impossible to fix, as persons are organs of moral or supernatural force. Under the dominion of an idea which possesses the minds of multitudes, as civil freedom, or the religious sentiment, the powers of persons are no longer subjects of calculation. A nation of men unanimously bent on freedom or conquest can easily confound the arithmetic of statists, and achieve extravagant actions, out of all proportion to their means; as the Greeks, the Saracens, the Swiss, the Americans, and the French have done.

In like manner to every particle of property belongs its own attraction. A cent is the representative of a certain quantity of corn or other commodity. Its value is in the necessities of the animal man. It is so much warmth, so much bread, so much water, so much land. The law may do what it will with the owner of property; its just power will still attach to the cent. The law may in a mad freak say that all shall have power except the owners of property; they shall have no vote. Nevertheless, by a higher law, the property will, year after year, write every statute that respects property. The non-proprietor will be the scribe of the proprietor. What the owners wish to do, the whole power of property will do, either through the law or else in defiance of it. Of course I speak of all the property, not merely of great estates. When the rich are outvoted, as frequently happens, it is the joint treasury of the poor which exceeds their accumulations. Every man owns something, if it is only a cow, or a wheelbarrow, or his arms, and so has that property to dispose of.

The same necessity which secures the rights of person and property against the malignity or folly of the magistrate, determines the form and methods of governing, which are proper to each nation and to its habit of thought, and nowise transferable to other states of society. In this country we are very vain of our political institutions, which are singular in this, that they sprung, within the memory of living men, from the character and condition of the people, which they still express with sufficient fidelity—and we ostentatiously prefer them to any other in history. They are not better, but only fitter for us. We may be wise in asserting the advantage in modern times of the democratic form, but to other states of society, in which religion consecrated the monarchical, that and not this was expedient. Democracy is better for us, because the religious sentiment of the present time accords better with it. Born democrats, we are nowise qualified to judge of monarchy, which, to our fathers living in the monarchical idea, was also relatively right. But our institutions, though in coincidence with the spirit of the age, have not any exemption from the practical defects which have discredited other forms. Every actual State is corrupt. Good men must not obey the laws too well. What satire on government can equal the severity of censure conveyed in the word *politic*, which now for ages has signified *cunning*, intimating that the State is a trick?

The same benign necessity and the same practical abuse appear in the parties, into which each State divides itself, of opponents and defenders of the administration of the govern-

ment. Parties are also founded on instincts, and have better
guides to their own humble aims than the sagacity of their
leaders. They have nothing perverse in their origin, but rudely
mark some real and lasting relation. We might as wisely re-
prove the east wind or the frost, as a political party, whose
members, for the most part, could give no account of their
position, but stand for the defence of those interests in which
they find themselves. Our quarrel with them begins when
they quit this deep natural ground at the bidding of some
leader, and obeying personal considerations, throw themselves
into the maintenance and defence of points nowise belonging
to their system. A party is perpetually corrupted by personality. Whilst we absolve the association from dishonesty, we
cannot extend the same charity to their leaders. They reap
the rewards of the docility and zeal of the masses which they
direct. Ordinarily our parties are parties of circumstance, and
not of principle; as the planting interest in conflict with the
commercial; the party of capitalists and that of operatives:
parties which are identical in their moral character, and
which can easily change ground with each other in the support of many of their measures. Parties of principle, as, religious sects, or the party of free-trade, of universal suffrage, of
abolition of slavery, of abolition of capital punishment—degenerate into personalities, or would inspire enthusiasm. The
vice of our leading parties in this country (which may be cited
as a fair specimen of these societies of opinion) is that they
do not plant themselves on the deep and necessary grounds
to which they are respectively entitled, but lash themselves to
fury in the carrying of some local and momentary measure,
nowise useful to the commonwealth. Of the two great parties
which at this hour almost share the nation between them, I
should say that one has the best cause, and the other contains the best men. The philosopher, the poet, or the religious
man, will of course wish to cast his vote with the democrat,
for free-trade, for wide suffrage, for the abolition of legal
cruelties in the penal code, and for facilitating in every manner the access of the young and the poor to the sources of
wealth and power. But he can rarely accept the persons
whom the so-called popular party propose to him as representatives of these liberalities. They have not at heart the
ends which give to the name of democracy what hope and
virtue are in it. The spirit of our American radicalism is de-

structive and aimless: it is not loving; it has no ulterior and divine ends, but is destructive only out of hatred and selfishness. On the other side, the conservative party, composed of the most moderate, able and cultivated part of the population, is timid, and merely defensive of property. It vindicates no right, it aspires to no real good, it brands no crime, it proposes no generous policy; it does not build, nor write, nor cherish the arts, nor foster religion, nor establish schools, nor encourage science, nor emancipate the slave, nor befriend the poor, or the Indian, or the immigrant. From neither party, when in power, has the world any benefit to expect in science, art, or humanity, at all commensurate with the resources of the nation.

I do not for these defects despair of our republic. We are not at the mercy of any waves of chance. In the strife of ferocious parties, human nature always finds itself cherished; as the children of the convicts at Botany Bay are found to have as healthy a moral sentiment as other children. Citizens of feudal states are alarmed at our democratic institutions lapsing into anarchy, and the older and more cautious among ourselves are learning from Europeans to look with some terror at our turbulent freedom. It is said that in our license of construing the Constitution, and in the despotism of public opinion, we have no anchor; and one foreign observer thinks he has found the safeguard in the sanctity of Marriage among us; and another thinks he has found it in our Calvinism. Fisher Ames expressed the popular security more wisely, when he compared a monarchy and a republic, saying that a monarchy is a merchantman, which sails well, but will sometimes strike on a rock and go to the bottom; whilst a republic is a raft, which would never sink, but then your feet are always in water. No forms can have any dangerous importance whilst we are befriended by the laws of things. It makes no difference how many tons' weight of atmosphere presses on our heads, so long as the same pressure resists it within the lungs. Augment the mass a thousand-fold, it cannot begin to crush us, as long as reaction is equal to action. The fact of two poles, of two forces, centripetal and centrifugal, is universal, and each force by its own activity develops the other. Wild liberty develops iron conscience. Want of liberty, by strengthening law and decorum, stupefies conscience. "Lynch-law" prevails only where there is greater hardihood and self-subsistency in the leaders. A mob cannot be a permanency; everybody's interest requires that it should not exist, and only justice satisfies all.

We must trust infinitely to the beneficent necessity which shines through all laws. Human nature expresses itself in them as characteristically as in statues, or songs, or railroads; and an abstract of the codes of nations would be a transcript of the common conscience. Governments have their origin in the moral identity of men. Reason for one is seen to be reason for another, and for every other. There is a middle measure which satisfies all parties, be they never so many or so resolute for their own. Every man finds a sanction for his simplest claims and deeds, in decisions of his own mind, which he calls Truth and Holiness. In these decisions all the citizens find a perfect agreement, and only in these; not in what is good to eat, good to wear, good use of time, or what amount of land or of public aid each is entitled to claim. This truth and justice men presently endeavor to make application of to the measuring of land, the apportionment of service, the protection of life and property. Their first endeavors, no doubt, are very awkward. Yet absolute right is the first governor; or, every government is an impure theocracy. The idea after which each community is aiming to make and mend its law, is the will of the wise man. The wise man it cannot find in nature, and it makes awkward but earnest efforts to secure his government by contrivance; as by causing the entire people to give their voices on every measure; or by a double choice to get the representation of the whole; or by a selection of the best citizens; or to secure the advantages of efficiency and internal peace by confiding the government to one, who may himself select his agents. All forms of government symbolize an immortal government, common to all dynasties and independent of numbers, perfect where two men exist, perfect where there is only one man.

Every man's nature is a sufficient advertisement to him of the character of his fellows. My right and my wrong is their right and their wrong. Whilst I do what is fit for me, and abstain from what is unfit, my neighbor and I shall often agree in our means, and work together for a time to one end. But whenever I find my dominion over myself not sufficient for me, and undertake the direction of him also, I overstep the truth, and come into false relations to him. I may have so much more skill or strength than he that he cannot express adequately his sense of wrong, but it is a lie, and hurts like a lie both him and me. Love and nature cannot maintain the assumption; it must be executed by a practical lie, namely by force. This undertaking for another is the blunder which stands in colossal ugliness in the governments of the world. It is the same thing in numbers, as in a pair, only not quite so intelligible. I can see well enough a great difference between my setting myself down to a self-control, and my going to make somebody else act after my views; but when a quarter of the human race assume to tell me what I must do, I may be too much disturbed by the circumstances to see so clearly the absurdity of their command. Therefore all public ends look vague and quixotic beside private ones. For any laws but those which men make for themselves are laughable. If I put myself in the place of my child, and we stand in one thought and see that things are thus or thus, that perception is law for him and me. We are both there, both act. But if, without carrying him into the thought, I look over into his plot, and, guessing how it is with him, ordain this or that, he will never obey me. This is the history of governments— one man does something which is to bind another. A man who cannot be acquainted with me, taxes me; looking from afar at me ordains that a part of my labor shall go to this or that whimsical end—not as I, but as he happens to fancy. Behold the consequence. Of all debts men are least willing to pay the taxes. What a satire is this on government! Everywhere they think they get their money's worth, except for these.

Hence the less government we have the better—the fewer laws, and the less confided power. The antidote to this abuse of formal government is the influence of private character, the growth of the Individual; the appearance of the principal to supersede the proxy; the appearance of the wise man; of whom the existing government is, it must be owned, but a shabby imitation. That which all things tend to educe; which freedom, cultivation, intercourse, revolutions, go to form and deliver, is character; that is the end of Nature, to reach unto this coronation of her king. To educate the wise man the State exists, and with the appearance of the wise man the State expires. The appearance of character makes the State unnecessary. The wise man is the State. He needs no army, fort, or navy—he loves men too well; no bribe, or feast, or palace, to draw friends to him; no vantage ground, no favorable circumstance. He needs no library, for he has not done thinking; no church, for he is a prophet; no statute-book, for he has the lawgiver; no money, for he is value; no road, for he is at home where he is; no experience, for the life of the creator shoots through him, and looks from his eyes. He has no personal friends, for he who has the spell to draw the prayer and piety of all men unto him needs not husband and educate a few to share with him a select and poetic life. His relation to men is angelic; his memory is myrrh to them; his presence, frankincense and flowers.

We think our civilization near its meridian, but we are yet only at the cock-crowing and the morning star. In our barbarous society the influence of character is in its infancy. As a political power, as the rightful lord who is to tumble all rulers from their chairs, its presence is hardly yet suspected. Malthus and Ricardo quite omit it; the Annual Register is silent; in the Conversations' Lexicon it is not set down; the President's Message, the Queen's Speech, have not mentioned it; and yet it is never nothing. Every thought which genius and piety throw into the world, alters the world. The gladiators in the lists of power feel, through all their frocks of force and simulation, the presence of worth. I think the very strife of trade and ambition is confession of this divinity; and successes in those fields are the poor amends, the fig-leaf with which the shamed soul attempts to hide its nakedness. I find the like unwilling homage in all quarters. It is because we know how much is due from us that we are impatient to show some petty talent as a substitute for worth. We are haunted by a conscience of this right to grandeur of character, and are false to it. But each of us has some talent, can do somewhat useful, or graceful, or formidable, or amusing, or lucrative. That we do, as an apology to others and to ourselves for not reaching the mark of a good and equal life. But it does not satisfy *us*, whilst we thrust it on the notice of our companions. It may throw dust in their eyes, but does not smooth our own brow, or give us the tranquillity of the strong when we walk abroad. We do penance as we go. Our talent is a sort of expiation, and we are constrained to reflect on our splendid moment with a certain humiliation, as somewhat too fine, and not as one act of many acts, a fair expression of our permanent energy. Most persons of ability meet in society with a kind of tacit appeal. Each seems to say, "I am not all here." Senators and presidents have climbed so high with pain enough, not because they think the place specially agreeable, but as an apology for real worth, and to vindicate their manhood in our eyes. This conspicuous chair is their compensation to themselves for being of a poor, cold, hard nature. They must do what they can. Like one class of forest animals, they have nothing but a prehensile tail; climb they must, or crawl. If a man found himself so rich-natured that he could enter into strict relations with the best persons and make life serene around him by the dignity and sweetness of his behavior, could he afford to circumvent the favor of the caucus and the press, and covet relations so hollow and pompous as those of a politician? Surely nobody would be a charlatan who could afford to be sincere.

The tendencies of the times favor the idea of self-government, and leave the individual, for all code, to the rewards and penalties of his own constitution; which work with more energy than we believe whilst we depend on artificial restraints. The movement in this direction has been very marked in modern history. Much has been blind and discreditable, but the nature of the revolution is not affected by the vices of the revolters; for this is a purely moral force. It was never adopted by any party in history, neither can be. It separates the individual from all party, and unites him at the same time to the race. It promises a recognition of higher rights than those of personal freedom, or the security of property. A man has a right to be employed, to be trusted, to be loved, to be revered. The power of love, as the basis of a State, has never been tried. We must not imagine that all things are lapsing into confusion if every tender protestant be not compelled to bear his part in certain social conventions; nor doubt that roads can be built, letters carried, and the fruit of labor secured, when the government of force is at an end. Are our methods now so excellent that all competition is hopeless? could not a nation of friends even devise better ways? On the other hand, let not the most conservative and timid fear anything from a premature surrender of the bayonet and the system of force. For, according to the order of nature, which is quite superior to our will, it stands thus; there will always be a government of force where men are selfish; and when they are pure enough to abjure the code of force they will be wise enough to see how these public ends of the post-office, of the highway, of commerce and the exchange of property, of museums and libraries, of institutions of art and science can be answered.

We live in a very low state of the world, and pay unwilling tribute to governments founded on force. There is not, among the most religious and instructed men of the most religious and civil nations, a reliance on the moral sentiment and a sufficient belief in the unity of things, to persuade them that society can be maintained without artificial restraints, as well as the solar system; or that the private citizen might be reasonable and a good neighbor, without the hint of a jail or a confiscation. What is strange too, there never was in any man sufficient faith in the power of rectitude to inspire him with the broad design of renovating the State on the principle of right and love. All those who have pretended this design have been partial reformers, and have admitted in some manner the supremacy of the bad State. I do not call to mind a single human being who has steadily denied the authority of the laws, on the simple ground of his own moral nature. Such designs, full of genius and full of faith as they are, are not entertained except avowedly as air-pictures. If the individual who exhibits them dare to think them practicable, he disgusts scholars and churchmen; and men of talent and women of superior sentiments cannot hide their contempt. Not the less does nature continue to fill the heart of youth with suggestions of this enthusiasm, and there are now men—if indeed I can speak in the plural number—more exactly, I will say, I have just been conversing with one man, to whom no weight of adverse experience will make it for a moment appear impossible that thousands of human beings might exercise towards each other the grandest and simplest sentiments, as well as a knot of friends, or a pair of lovers.

From *Essays, Second Series* Volume III.

Fate

It chanced during one winter a few years ago, that our cities were bent on discussing the theory of the Age. By an odd coincidence, four or five noted men were each reading a discourse to the citizens of Boston or New York, on the Spirit of the Times. It so happened that the subject had the same prominence in some remarkable pamphlets and journals issued in London in the same season. To me, however, the question of the times resolved itself into a practical question of the conduct of life. How shall I live? We are incompetent to solve the times. Our geometry cannot span the huge orbits of the prevailing ideas, behold their return and reconcile their opposition. We can only obey our own polarity. 'T is fine for us to speculate and elect our course, if we must accept an irresistible dictation.

In our first steps to gain our wishes we come upon immovable limitations. We are fired with the hope to reform men. After many experiments we find that we must begin earlier—at school. But the boys and girls are not docile; we can make nothing of them. We decide that they are not of good stock. We must begin our reform earlier still—at generation: that is to say, there is Fate, or laws of the world.

But if there be irresistible dictation, this dictation understands itself. If we must accept Fate, we are not less compelled to affirm liberty, the significance of the individual, the grandeur of duty, the power of character. This is true, and that other is true. But our geometry cannot span these extreme points and reconcile them. What to do? By obeying each thought frankly, by harping, or, if you will, pounding on each string, we learn at last its power. By the same obedience to other thoughts we learn theirs, and then comes some reasonable hope of harmonizing them. We are sure that, though we know not how, necessity does comport with liberty, the individual with the world, my polarity with the spirit of the times. The riddle of the age has for each a private solution. If one would study his own time, it must be by this method of taking up in turn each of the leading topics which belong to our scheme of human life, and by firmly stating all that is agreeable to experience on one, and doing the same justice to the opposing facts in the others, the true limitations will appear. Any excess of emphasis on one part would be corrected, and a just balance would be made.

But let us honestly state the facts. Our America has a bad name for superficialness. Great men, great nations, have not been boasters and buffoons, but perceivers of the terror of life, and have manned themselves to face it. The Spartan, embodying his religion in his country, dies before its majesty without a question. The Turk, who believes his doom is written on the iron leaf in the moment when he entered the world, rushes on the enemy's sabre with undivided will. The Turk; the Arab, the Persian, accepts the foreordained fate:

> On two days, it steads not to run from thy grave,
>   The appointed, and the unappointed day;
> On the first, neither balm nor physician can save,
>   Nor thee, on the second, the Universe slay.[1]

The Hindoo under the wheel is as firm. Our Calvinists in the last generation had something of the same dignity. They felt that the weight of the Universe held them down to their place. What could *they* do? Wise men feel that there is something which cannot be talked or voted away—a strap or belt which girds the world:

> The Destinee, ministre general,
> That executeth in the world over al,
> The purveiance that God hath seen beforne,
> So strong it is, that though the world had sworne
> The contrary of a thing by yea or nay,
> Yet sometime it shall fallen on a day
> That falleth not oft in a thousand yeer;
> For certainly, our appetités here,
> Be it or warre, or pees, or hate, or love,
> All this is ruled by the sight above.
>   CHAUCER: *The Knighte's Tale.*

---

[1] From a Persian distich by Ali ben Abu Taleb.

The Greek Tragedy expressed the same sense. "Whatever is fated that will take place. The great immense mind of Jove is not to be transgressed."

Savages cling to a local god of one tribe or town. The broad ethics of Jesus were quickly narrowed to village theologies, which preach an election or favoritism. And now and then an amiable parson, like Jung Stilling or Robert Huntington, believes in pistareen-Providence, which, whenever the good man wants a dinner, makes that somebody shall knock at his door and leave a half-dollar. But Nature is no sentimentalist—does not cosset or pamper us. We must see that the world is rough and surly, and will not mind drowning a man or a woman, but swallows your ship like a grain of dust. The cold, inconsiderate of persons, tingles your blood, benumbs your feet, freezes a man like an apple. The diseases, the elements, fortune, gravity, lightning, respect no persons. The way of Providence is a little rude. The habit of snake and spider, the snap of the tiger and other leapers and bloody jumpers, the crackle of the bones of his prey in the coil of the anaconda—these are in the system, and our habits are like theirs. You have just dined, and however scrupulously the slaughter-house is concealed in the graceful distance of miles, there is complicity, expensive races—race living at the expense of race. The planet is liable to shocks from comets, perturbations from planets, rendings from earthquake and volcano, alterations of climate, precessions of equinoxes. Rivers dry up by opening of the forest. The sea changes its bed. Towns and counties fall into it. At Lisbon an earthquake killed men like flies. At Naples three years ago ten thousand persons were crushed in a few minutes. The scurvy at sea, the sword of the climate in the west of Africa, at Cayenne, at Panama, at New Orleans, cut off men like a massacre. Our western prairie shakes with fever and ague. The cholera, the small-pox, have proved as mortal to some tribes as a frost to the crickets, which, having filled the summer with noise, are silenced by a fall of the temperature of one night. Without uncovering what does not concern us, or counting how many species of parasites hang on a bombyx, or groping after intestinal parasites or infusory biters, or the obscurities of alternate generation—the forms of the shark, the *labrus*, the jaw of the sea-wolf paved with crushing teeth, the weapons of the grampus, and other warriors hidden in the sea, are hints of ferocity in the interiors of nature. Let us not deny it up and down. Providence has a wild, rough, incalculable road to its end, and it is of no use to try to whitewash its huge, mixed instrumentalities, or to dress up that terrific benefactor in a clean shirt and white neckcloth of a student in divinity.

Will you say, the disasters which threaten mankind are exceptional, and one need not lay his account for cataclysms every day? Aye, but what happens once may happen again, and so long as these strokes are not to be parried by us they must be feared.

But these shocks and ruins are less destructive to us than the stealthy power of other laws which act on us daily. An expense of ends to means is fate—organization tyrannizing over character. The menagerie, or forms and powers of the spine, is a book of fate; the bill of the bird, the skull of the snake, determines tyrannically its limits. So is the scale of races, of temperaments; so is sex; so is climate; so is the reaction of talents imprisoning the vital power in certain directions. Every spirit makes its house; but afterwards the house confines the spirit.

The gross lines are legible to the dull; the cabman is phrenologist so far, he looks in your face to see if his shilling is sure. A dome of brow denotes one thing, a pot-belly another; a squint, a pug-nose, mats of hair, the pigment of the epidermis, betray character. People seem sheathed in their tough organization. Ask Spurzheim, ask the doctors, ask Quetelet if temperaments decide nothing? or if there be anything they do not decide? Read the description in medical books of the four temperaments and you will think you are reading your own thoughts which you had not yet told. Find the part which black eyes and which blue eyes play severally in the company. How shall a man escape from his ancestors, or draw off from his veins the black drop which he drew from his father's or his mother's life? It often appears in a family as if all the qualities of the progenitors were potted in several jars —some ruling quality in each son or daughter of the house; and sometimes the unmixed temperament, the rank unmitigated elixir, the family vice is drawn off in a separate individual and the others are proportionally relieved. We sometimes see a change of expression in our companion and say his father or his mother comes to the windows of his eyes, and sometimes a remote relative. In different hours a man represents each of several of his ancestors, as if there were seven or eight of us rolled up in each man's skin—seven or eight ancestors at least; and they constitute the variety of notes for that new piece of music which his life is. At the corner of the street you read the possibility of each passenger in the facial angle, in the complexion, in the depth of his eye. His parentage determines it. Men are what their mothers made them. You may as well ask a loom which weaves huckabuck why it does not make cashmere, as expect poetry from this engineer, or a chemical discovery from that jobber. Ask the digger in the ditch to explain Newton's laws; the fine organs of his brain have been pinched by overwork and squalid poverty from father to son for a hundred years. When each comes forth from his mother's womb, the gate of gifts closes behind him. Let him value his hands and feet, he has but one pair. So he has but one future, and that is already predetermined in his lobes and described in that little fatty face, pig-eye, and squat form. All the privilege and all the legislation of the world cannot meddle or help to make a poet or a prince of him.

Jesus said, "When he looketh on her, he hath committed adultery." But he is an adulterer before he has yet looked on the woman, by the superfluity of animal and the defect of thought in his constitution. Who meets him, or who meets her, in the street, sees that they are ripe to be each other's victim.

In certain men digestion and sex absorb the vital force, and the stronger these are, the individual is so much weaker. The more of these drones perish, the better for the hive. If, later, they give birth to some superior individual, with force enough to add to this animal a new aim and a complete apparatus to work it out, all the ancestors are gladly forgotten. Most men and most women are merely one couple more. Now and then one has a new cell or camarilla opened in his brain—an architectural, a musical, or a philological knack; some stray taste or talent for flowers, or chemistry, or pigments, or storytelling; a good hand for drawing, a good foot for dancing, an athletic frame for wide journeying, etc.—which skill nowise alters rank in the scale of nature, but serves to pass the time; the life of sensation going on as before. At last these hints and tendencies are fixed in one or in a succession. Each absorbs so much food and force as to become itself a new centre. The new talent draws off so rapidly the vital force that not enough remains for the animal functions, hardly enough for health; so that in the second generation, if the like genius appear, the health is visibly deteriorated and the generative force impaired.

People are born with the moral or with the material bias— uterine brothers with this diverging destination; and I suppose, with high magnifiers, Mr. Frauenhofer or Dr. Carpenter might come to distinguish in the embryo, at the fourth day— this is a Whig, and that a Freesoiler.

It was a poetic attempt to lift this mountain of Fate, to reconcile this despotism of race with liberty, which led the Hindoos to say, "Fate is nothing but the deeds committed in a prior state of existence." I find the coincidence of the extremes of Eastern and Western speculation in the daring statement of Schelling, "There is in every man a certain feeling that he had been what he is from all eternity, and by no means became such in time." To say it less sublimely—in the history of the individual is always an account of his condition, and he knows himself to be a party to his present estate.

A good deal of our politics is physiological. Now and then a man of wealth in the heyday of youth adopts the tenet of broadest freedom. In England there is always some man of wealth and large connection, planting himself, during all his years of health, on the side of progress, who, as soon as he begins to die, checks his forward play, calls in his troops and becomes conservative. All conservatives are such from personal defects. They have been effeminated by position or nature, born hålt and blind, through luxury of their parents, and can only, like invalids, act on the defensive. But strong natures, backwoodsmen, New Hampshire giants, Napoleons, Burkes, Broughams, Websters, Kossuths, are inevitable patriots, until their life ebbs and their defects and gout, palsy and money, warp them.

The strongest idea incarnates itself in majorities and nations, in the healthiest and strongest. Probably the election goes by avoirdupois weight, and if you could weigh bodily the tonnage of any hundred of the Whig and the Democratic party in a town on the Dearborn balance, as they passed the hay-scales, you could predict with certainty which party would carry it. On the whole it would be rather the speediest way of deciding the vote, to put the selectmen or the mayor and aldermen at the hay-scales.

In science we have to consider two things: power and circumstance. All we know of the egg, from each successive discovery, is, *another vesicle;* and if, after five hundred years you get a better observer or a better glass, he finds, within the last observed, another. In vegetable and animal tissue it is just alike, and all that the primary power or spasm operates is still vesicles, vesicles. Yes—but the tyrannical Circumstance! A vesicle in new circumstances, a vesicle lodged in darkness, Oken thought, became animal; in light, a plant. Lodged in the parent animal, it suffers changes which end in unsheathing miraculous capability in the unaltered vesicle, and it unlocks itself to fish, bird, or quadruped, head and foot, eye and claw. The Circumstance is Nature. Nature is what you may do. There is much you may not. We have two things— the circumstance, and the life. Once we thought positive power was all. Now we learn that negative power, or circumstance, is half. Nature is the tyrannous circumstance, the thick skull, the sheathed snake, the ponderous, rock-like jaw; necessitated activity; violent direction; the conditions of a tool, like the locomotive, strong enough on its track, but which can do nothing but mischief off of it; or skates, which are wings on the ice but fetters on the ground.

The book of Nature is the book of Fate. She turns the gigantic pages—leaf after leaf—never re-turning one. One leaf she lays down, a floor of granite; then a thousand ages, and a bed of slate; a thousand ages, and a measure of coal; a thousand ages, and a layer of marl and mud: vegetable forms appear; her first misshapen animals, zoöphyte, trilobium, fish; then, saurians—rude forms, in which she has only blocked her future statue, concealing under these unwieldy monsters the fine type of her coming king. The face of the planet cools and dries, the races meliorate, and man is born. But when a race has lived its term, it comes no more again.

The population of the world is a conditional population; not the best, but the best that could live now; and the scale of tribes, and the steadiness with which victory adheres to one tribe and defeat to another, is as uniform as the superposition of strata. We know in history what weight belongs to race. We see the English, French, and Germans planting themselves on every shore and market of America and Australia, and monopolizing the commerce of these countries. We like the nervous and victorious habit of our own branch of the family. We follow the step of the Jew, of the Indian, of the Negro. We see how much will has been expended to extinguish the Jew, in vain. Look at the unpalatable conclusions of Knox, in his Fragment of Races—a rash and unsatisfactory writer, but charged with pungent and unforgetable truths. "Nature respects race, and not hybrids." "Every race has its own *habitat*." "Detach a colony from the race, and it deteriorates to the crab." See the shades of the picture. The German and Irish millions, like the Negro, have a great deal of guano in their destiny. They are ferried over the Atlantic and carted over America, to ditch and to drudge, to make corn cheap and then to lie down prematurely to make a spot of green grass on the prairie.

One more fagot of these adamantine bandages is the new science of Statistics. It is a rule that the most casual and extraordinary events, if the basis of population is broad enough, become matter of fixed calculation. It would not be safe to say when a captain like Bonaparte, a singer like Jenny Lind, or a navigator like Bowditch would be born in Boston; but, on a population of twenty or two hundred millions, something like accuracy may be had.

'T is frivolous to fix pedantically the date of particular inventions. They have all been invented over and over fifty times. Man is the arch machine of which all these shifts drawn from himself are toy models. He helps himself on each emergency by copying or duplicating his own structure, just so far as the need is. 'T is hard to find the right Homer, Zoroaster, or Menu; harder still to find the Tubal Cain, or Vulcan, or Cadmus, or Copernicus, or Fust, or Fulton; the indisputable inventor. There are scores and centuries of them. "The air is full of men." This kind of talent so abounds, this constructive tool-making efficiency, as if it adhered to the chemic atoms; as if the air he breathes were made of Vaucansons, Franklins, and Watts.

Doubtless in every million there will be an astronomer, a mathematician, a comic poet, a mystic. No one can read the history of astronomy without perceiving that Copernicus, Newton, Laplace, are not new men, or a new kind of men, but that Thales, Anaximenes, Hipparchus, Empedocles, Aristarchus, Pythagoras, Œnipodes, had anticipated them; each had the same tense geometrical brain, apt for the same vigorous computation and logic; a mind parallel to the movement of the world. The Roman mile probably rested on a measure of a degree of the meridian. Mahometan and Chinese know what we know of leap-year, of the Gregorian calendar, and of the precession of the equinoxes. As in every barrel of cowries brought to New Bedford there shall be one *orangia*, so there will, in a dozen millions of Malays and Mahometans, be one or two astronomical skulls. In a large city, the most casual things, and things whose beauty lies in their casualty, are produced as punctually and to order as the baker's muffin for breakfast. Punch makes exactly one capital joke a week; and the journals contrive to furnish one good piece of news every day.

And not less work the laws of repression, the penalities of violated functions. Famine, typhus, frost, war, suicide and effete races must be reckoned calculable parts of the system of the world.

These are pebbles from the mountain, hints of the terms by which our life is walled up, and which show a kind of mechanical exactness, as of a loom or mill in what we call casual or fortuitous events.

The force with which we resist these torrents of tendency looks so ridiculously inadequate that it amounts to little more than a criticism or protest made by a minority of one, under compulsion of millions. I seemed in the height of a tempest to see men overboard struggling in the waves, and driven about here and there. They glanced intelligently at each other, but 't was little they could do for one another; 't was much if each could keep afloat alone. Well, they had a right to their eye-beams, and all the rest was Fate.

We cannot trifle with this reality, this cropping-out in our planted gardens of the core of the world. No picture of life can have any veracity that does not admit the odious facts. A man's power is hooped in by a necessity which, by many experiments, he touches on every side until he learns its arc. The element running through entire nature, which we popularly call Fate, is known to us as limitation. Whatever limits us we call Fate. If we are brute and barbarous, the fate takes a brute and dreadful shape. As we refine, our checks become finer. If we rise to spiritual culture, the antagonism takes a spiritual form. In the Hindoo fables, Vishnu follows Maya through all her ascending changes, from insect and crawfish up to elephant; whatever form she took, he took the male form of that kind, until she became at last woman and goddess, and he a man and a god. The limitations refine as the soul purifies, but the ring of necessity is always perched at the top.

When the gods in the Norse heaven were unable to bind the Fenris Wolf with steel or with weight of mountains—the one he snapped and the other he spurned with his heel—they put round his foot a limp band softer than silk or cobweb, and this held him; the more he spurned it the stiffer it drew. So soft and so stanch is the ring of Fate. Neither brandy, nor nectar, nor sulphuric ether, nor hell-fire, nor ichor, nor poetry, nor genius, can get rid of this limp band. For if we give it the high sense in which the poets use it, even thought itself is not above Fate; that too must act according to eternal laws, and all that is wilful and fantastic in it is in opposition to its fundamental essence.

And last of all, high over thought, in the world of morals, Fate appears as vindicator, levelling the high, lifting the low, requiring justice in man, and always striking soon or late when justice is not done. What is useful will last, what is hurtful will sink. "The doer must suffer," said the Greeks; "you would soothe a Deity not to be soothed." "God himself cannot procure good for the wicked," said the Welsh triad. "God may consent, but only for a time," said the bard of Spain. The limitation is impassable by any insight of man. In its last and loftiest ascensions, insight itself and the freedom of the will is one of its obedient members. But we must not run into generalizations too large, but show the natural bounds or essential distinctions, and seek to do justice to the other elements as well.

Thus we trace Fate in matter, mind, and morals; in race, in retardations of strata, and in thought and character as well. It is everywhere bound or limitation. But Fate has its lord; limitation its limits—is different seen from above and from below, from within and from without. For though Fate is immense, so is Power, which is the other fact in the dual world, immense. If Fate follows and limits Power, Power attends and antagonizes Fate. We must respect Fate as natural history, but there is more than natural history. For who and what is this criticism that pries into the matter? Man is not order of

nature, sack and sack, belly and members, link in a chain,
nor any ignominious baggage; but a stupendous antagonism, a
dragging together of the poles of the Universe. He betrays
his relation to what is below him—thick-skulled, small-
brained, fishy, quadrumanous, quadruped ill-disguised, hardly
escaped into biped—and has paid for the new powers by
loss of some of the old ones. But the lightning which ex-
plodes and fashions planets, maker of planets and suns, is in
him. On one side elemental order, sandstone and granite,
rock-ledges, peat-bog, forest, sea and shore; and on the other
part thought, the spirit which composes and decomposes nature—here they are, side by side, god and devil, mind and
matter, king and conspirator, belt and spasm, riding peacefully together in the eye and brain of every man.

Nor can he blink the freewill. To hazard the contradiction
—freedom is necessary. If you please to plant yourself on the
side of Fate, and say, Fate is all; then we say, a part of Fate
is the freedom of man. Forever wells up the impulse of choosing and acting in the soul. Intellect annuls Fate. So far as a
man thinks, he is free. And though nothing is more disgusting
than the crowing about liberty by slaves, as most men are,
and the flippant mistaking for freedom of some paper preamble like a Declaration of Independence or the statute right
to vote, by those who have never dared to think or to act—
yet it is wholesome to man to look not at Fate, but the other
way: the practical view is the other. His sound relation to
these facts is to use and command, not to cringe to them.
"Look not on Nature, for her name is fatal," said the oracle.
The too much contemplation of these limits induces meanness.
They who talk much of destiny, their birth-star, etc., are in a
lower dangerous plane, and invite the evils they fear.

I cited the instinctive and heroic races as proud believers
in Destiny. They conspire with it; a loving resignation is with
the event. But the dogma makes a different impression when
it is held by the weak and lazy. 'T is weak and vicious people who cast the blame on Fate. The right use of Fate is to
bring up our conduct to the loftiness of nature. Rude and
invincible except by themselves are the elements. So let man
be. Let him empty his breast of his windy conceits, and show
his lordship by manners and deeds on the scale of nature.
Let him hold his purpose as with the tug of gravitation. No
power, no persuasion, no bribe shall make him give up his

point. A man ought to compare advantageously with a river, an oak, or a mountain. He shall have not less the flow, the expansion, and the resistance of these.

'T is the best use of Fate to teach a fatal courage. Go face the fire at sea, or the cholera in your friend's house, or the burglar in your own, or what danger lies in the way of duty —knowing you are guarded by the cherubim of Destiny. If you believe in Fate to your harm, believe it at least for your good.

For if Fate is so prevailing, man also is part of it, and can confront fate with fate. If the Universe have these savage accidents, our atoms are as savage in resistance. We should be crushed by the atmosphere, but for the reaction of the air within the body. A tube made of a film of glass can resist the shock of the ocean if filled with the same water. If there be omnipotence in the stroke, there is omnipotence of recoil.

1. But Fate against Fate is only parrying and defence: there are also the noble creative forces. The revelation of Thought takes man out of servitude into freedom. We rightly say of ourselves, we were born and afterward we were born again, and many times. We have successive experiences so important that the new forgets the old, and hence the mythology of the seven or the nine heavens. The day of days, the great day of the feast of life, is that in which the inward eye opens to the Unity in things, to the omnipresence of law: sees that what is must be and ought to be, or is the best. This beatitude dips from on high down on us and we see. It is not in us so much as we are in it. If the air come to our lungs, we breathe and live; if not, we die. If the light come to our eyes, we see; else not. And if truth come to our mind we suddenly expand to its dimensions, as if we grew to worlds. We are as lawgivers; we speak for Nature; we prophesy and divine.

This insight throws us on the party and interest of the Universe, against all and sundry; against ourselves as much as others. A man speaking from insight affirms of himself what is true of the mind: seeing its immortality, he says, I am immortal; seeing its invincibility, he says, I am strong. It is not in us, but we are in it. It is of the maker, not of what is made. All things are touched and changed by it. This uses and is not used. It distances those who share it from those who share it not. Those who share it not are flocks and herds. It dates from itself; not from former men or better men, gospel, or constitution, or college, or custom. Where it shines, Nature is no longer intrusive, but all things make a musical or pictorial impression. The world of men show like a comedy without laughter: populations, interests, government, history; 't is all toy figures in a toy house. It does not overvalue particular truths. We hear eagerly every thought and word quoted from an intellectual man. But in his presence our own mind is roused to activity, and we forget very fast what he says, much more interested in the new play of our own thought than in any thought of his. 'T is the majesty into which we have suddenly mounted, the impersonality, the scorn of egotisms, the sphere of laws, that engage us. Once we were stepping a little this way and a little that way; now we are as men in a balloon, and do not think so much of the point we have left, or the point we would make, as of the liberty and glory of the way.

Just as much intellect as you add, so much organic power. He who sees through the design, presides over it, and must will that which must be. We sit and rule, and, though we sleep, our dream will come to pass. Our thought, though it were only an hour old, affirms an oldest necessity, not to be separated from thought, and not to be separated from will. They must always have coexisted. It apprises us of its sovereignty and godhead, which refuse to be severed from it. It is not mine or thine, but the will of all mind. It is poured into the souls of all men, as the soul itself which constitutes them men. I know not whether there be, as is alleged, in the upper region of our atmosphere, a permanent westerly current which carries with it all atoms which rise to that height, but I see that when souls reach a certain clearness of perception they accept a knowledge and motive above selfishness. A breath of will blows eternally through the universe of souls in the direction of the Right and Necessary. It is the air which all intellects inhale and exhale, and it is the wind which blows the worlds into order and orbit.

Thought dissolves the material universe by carrying the mind up into a sphere where all is plastic. Of two men, each obeying his own thought, he whose thought is deepest will be the strongest character. Always one man more than another represents the will of Divine Providence to the period.

2. If thought makes free, so does the moral sentiment. The

mixtures of spiritual chemistry refuse to be analyzed. Yet we can see that with the perception of truth is joined the desire that it shall prevail; that affection is essential to will. Moreover, when a strong will appears, it usually results from a certain unity of organization, as if the whole energy of body and mind flowed in one direction. All great force is real and elemental. There is no manufacturing a strong will. There must be a pound to balance a pound. Where power is shown in will, it must rest on the universal force. Alaric and Bonaparte must believe they rest on a truth, or their will can be bought or bent. There is a bribe possible for any finite will. But the pure sympathy with universal ends is an infinite force, and cannot be bribed or bent. Whoever has had experience of the moral sentiment cannot choose but believe in unlimited power. Each pulse from that heart is an oath from the Most High. I know not what the word *sublime* means, if it be not the intimations, in this infant, of a terrific force. A text of heroism, a name and anecdote of courage, are not arguments but sallies of freedom. One of these is the verse of the Persian Hafiz, "'T is written on the gate of Heaven, 'Woe unto him who suffers himself to be betrayed by Fate!'" Does the reading of history make us fatalists? What courage does not the opposite opinion show! A little whim of will to be free gallantly contending against the universe of chemistry.

But insight is not will, nor is affection will. Perception is cold, and goodness dies in wishes. As Voltaire said, 't is the misfortune of worthy people that they are cowards; "*un des plus grands malheurs des honnêtes gens c'est qu'ils sont des lâches.*" There must be a fusion of these two to generate the energy of will. There can be no driving force except through the conversion of the man into his will, making him the will, and the will him. And one may say boldly that no man has a right perception of any truth who has not been reacted on by it so as to be ready to be its martyr.

The one serious and formidable thing in nature is a will. Society is servile from want of will, and therefore the world wants saviours and religions. One way is right to go; the hero sees it, and moves on that aim, and has the world under him for root and support. He is to others as the world. His approbation is honor; his dissent, infamy. The glance of his eye has the force of sunbeams. A personal influence towers up in memory only worthy, and we gladly forget numbers, money, climate, gravitation, and the rest of Fate.

We can afford to allow the limitation, if we know it is the meter of the growing man. We stand against Fate, as children stand up against the wall in their father's house and notch their height from year to year. But when the boy grows to man, and is master of the house, he pulls down that wall and builds a new and bigger. 'T is only a question of time. Every brave youth is in training to ride and rule this dragon. His science is to make weapons and wings of these passions and retarding forces. Now whether, seeing these two things, fate and power, we are permitted to believe in unity? The bulk of mankind believe in two gods. They are under one dominion here in the house, as friend and parent, in social circles, in letters, in art, in love, in religion; but in mechanics, in dealing with steam and climate, in trade, in politics, they think they come under another; and that it would be a practical blunder to transfer the method and way of working of one sphere into the other. What good, honest, generous men at home, will be wolves and foxes on 'Change! What pious men in the parlor will vote for what reprobates at the polls! To a certain point, they believe themselves the care of a Providence. But in a steamboat, in an epidemic, in war, they believe a malignant energy rules.

But relation and connection are not somewhere and sometimes, but everywhere and always. The divine order does not stop where their sight stops. The friendly power works on the same rules in the next farm and the next planet. But where they have not experience they run against it and hurt themselves. Fate then is a name for facts not yet passed under the fire of thought; for causes which are unpenetrated.

But every jet of chaos which threatens to exterminate us is convertible by intellect into wholesome force. Fate is unpenetrated causes. The water drowns ship and sailor like a grain of dust. But learn to swim, trim your bark, and the wave which drowned it will be cloven by it and carry it like its own foam, a plume and a power. The cold is inconsiderate of persons, tingles your blood, freezes a man like a dewdrop. But learn to skate, and the ice will give you a graceful, sweet, and poetic motion. The cold will brace your limbs and brain to genius, and make you foremost men of time. Cold and sea will train an imperial Saxon race, which nature cannot bear to lose, and after cooping it up for a thousand years in yonder England, gives a hundred Englands, a hundred Mexicos. All the bloods it shall absorb and domineer: and more than Mexicos, the secrets of water and steam, the spasms of electricity, the ductility of metals, the chariot of the air, the ruddered balloon are awaiting you.

The annual slaughter from typhus far exceeds that of war; but right drainage destroys typhus. The plague in the sea-service from scurvy is healed by lemon juice and other diets portable or procurable; the depopulation by cholera and small-pox is ended by drainage and vaccination; and every other pest is not less in the chain of cause and effect, and may be fought off. And whilst art draws out the venom, it commonly extorts some benefit from the vanquished enemy. The mischievous torrent is taught to drudge for man; the wild beasts he makes useful for food, or dress, or labor; the chemic explosions are controlled like his watch. These are now the steeds on which he rides. Man moves in all modes, by legs of horses, by wings of wind, by steam, by gas of balloon, by electricity, and stands on tiptoe threatening to hunt the eagle in his own element. There's nothing he will not make his carrier.

Steam was till the other day the devil which we dreaded. Every pot made by any human potter or brazier had a hole in its cover, to let off the enemy, lest he should lift pot and roof and carry the house away. But the Marquis of Worcester, Watt, and Fulton bethought themselves that where was power was not devil, but was God; that it must be availed of, and not by any means let off and wasted. Could he lift pots and roofs and houses so handily? He was the workman they were in search of. He could be used to lift away, chain and compel other devils far more reluctant and dangerous, namely, cubic miles of earth, mountains, weight or resistance of water, machinery, and the labors of all men in the world; and time he shall lengthen, and shorten space.

It has not fared much otherwise with higher kinds of steam. The opinion of the million was the terror of the world, and it was attempted either to dissipate it, by amusing nations, or to pile it over with strata of society—a layer of soldiers, over that a layer of lords, and a king on the top; with clamps and hoops of castles, garrisons, and police. But sometimes the religious principle would get in and burst the hoops and rive every mountain laid on top of it. The Fultons and Watts of politics, believing in unity, saw that it was a power, and by satisfying it (as justice satisfies everybody), through a different disposition of society—grouping it on a level instead of piling it into a mountain—they have contrived to make of this terror the most harmless and energetic form of a State.

Very odious, I confess, are the lessons of Fate. Who likes to have a dapper phrenologist pronouncing on his fortunes? Who likes to believe that he has, hidden in his skull, spine, and pelvis, all the vices of a Saxon or Celtic race, which will be sure to pull him down—with what grandeur of hope and resolve he is fired—into a selfish, huckstering, servile, dodging animal? A learned physician tells us the fact is invariable with the Neapolitan, that when mature he assumes the forms of the unmistakable scoundrel. That is a little overstated—but may pass.

But these are magazines and arsenals. A man must thank his defects, and stand in some terror of his talents. A transcendent talent draws so largely on his forces as to lame him; a defect pays him revenues on the other side. The sufferance which is the badge of the Jew, has made him, in these days, the ruler of the rulers of the earth. If Fate is ore and quarry, if evil is good in the making, if limitation is power that shall be, if calamities, oppositions, and weights are wings and means—we are reconciled.

Fate involves the melioration. No statement of the Universe can have any soundness which does not admit its ascending effort. The direction of the whole and of the parts is toward benefit, and in proportion to the health. Behind every individual closes organization; before him opens liberty—the Better, the Best. The first and worse races are dead. The second and imperfect races are dying out, or remain for the maturing of higher. In the latest race, in man, every generosity, every new perception, the love and praise he extorts from his fellows, are certificates of advance out of fate into freedom. Liberation of the will from the sheaths and clogs of organization which he has outgrown, is the end and aim of this world. Every calamity is a spur and valuable hint; and where his endeavors do not yet fully avail, they tell as tendency. The whole circle of animal life—tooth against tooth, devouring war, war for food, a yelp of pain and a grunt of triumph, until at last the whole menagerie, the whole chemical mass is mellowed and refined for higher use—pleases at a sufficient perspective.

But to see how fate slides into freedom and freedom into fate, observe how far the roots of every creature run, or find if you can a point where there is no thread of connection. Our life is consentaneous and far-related. This knot of nature is so well tied that nobody was ever cunning enough to find the two ends. Nature is intricate, overlapped, interweaved and endless. Christopher Wren said of the beautiful King's College chapel, that "if anybody would tell him where to lay the first stone, he would build such another." But where shall we find the first atom in this house of man, which is all consent, inosculation and balance of parts?

The web of relation is shown in *habitat*, shown in hibernation. When hibernation was observed, it was found that whilst some animals became torpid in winter, others were torpid in summer: hibernation then was a false name. The *long sleep* is not an effect of cold, but is regulated by the supply of food proper to the animal. It becomes torpid when the fruit or prey it lives on is not in season, and regains its activity when its food is ready.

Eyes are found in light; ears in auricular air; feet on land; fins in water; wings in air; and each creature where it was meant to be, with a mutual fitness. Every zone has its own *Fauna*. There is adjustment between the animal and its food, its parasite, its enemy. Balances are kept. It is not allowed to diminish in numbers, nor to exceed. The like adjustments exist for man. His food is cooked when he arrives; his coal in the pit; the house ventilated; the mud of the deluge dried; his companions arrived at the same hour, and awaiting him with love, concert, laughter and tears. These are coarse adjustments, but the invisible are not less. There are more belongings to every creature than his air and his food. His instincts must be met, and he has predisposing power that bends and fits what is near him to his use. He is not possible until the invisible things are right for him, as well as the visible. Of what changes then in sky and earth, and in finer skies and earths, does the appearance of some Dante or Columbus apprise us!

How is this effected? Nature is no spendthrift, but takes

the shortest way to her ends. As the general says to his soldiers, "If you want a fort, build a fort," so nature makes every creature do its own work and get its living—is it planet, animal or tree. The planet makes itself. The animal cell makes itself—then, what it wants. Every creature, wren or dragon, shall make its own lair. As soon as there is life, there is self-direction and absorbing and using of material. Life is freedom—life in the direct ratio of its amount. You may be sure the new-born man is not inert. Life works both voluntarily and supernaturally in its neighborhood. Do you suppose he can be estimated by his weight in pounds, or that he is contained in his skin—this reaching, radiating, jaculating fellow? The smallest candle fills a mile with its rays, and the papillæ of a man run out to every star.

When there is something to be done, the world knows how to get it done. The vegetable eye makes leaf, pericarp, root, bark, or thorn, as the need is; the first cell converts itself into stomach, mouth, nose, or nail, according to the want; the world throws its life into a hero or a shepherd, and puts him where he is wanted. Dante and Columbus were Italians, in their time; they would be Russians or Americans to-day. Things ripen, new men come. The adaptation is not capricious. The ulterior aim, the purpose beyond itself, the correlation by which planets subside and crystallize, then animate beasts and men—will not stop but will work into finer particulars, and from finer to finest.

The secret of the world is the tie between person and event. Person makes event, and event person. The "times," "the age," what is that but a few profound persons and a few active persons who epitomize the times? Goethe, Hegel, Metternich, Adams, Calhoun, Guizot, Peel, Cobden, Kossuth, Rothschild, Astor, Brunel, and the rest. The same fitness must be presumed between a man and the time and event, as between the sexes, or between a race of animals and the food it eats, or the inferior races it uses. He thinks his fate alien, because the copula is hidden. But the soul contains the event that shall befall it; for the event is only the actualization of its thoughts, and what we pray to ourselves for is always granted. The event is the print of your form. It fits you like your skin. What each does is proper to him. Events are the children of his body and mind. We learn that the soul of Fate is the soul of us, as Hafiz sings,

Alas! till now I had not known,
My guide and fortune's guide are one.

All the toys that infatuate men and which they play for—
houses, land, money, luxury, power, fame, are the selfsame
thing, with a new gauze or two of illusion overlaid. And of all
the drums and rattles by which men are made willing to have
their heads broke, and are led out solemnly every morning
to parade—the most admirable is this by which we are
brought to believe that events are arbitrary and independent
of actions. At the conjuror's, we detect the hair by which
he moves his puppet, but we have not eyes sharp enough to
descry the thread that ties cause and effect.

Nature magically suits the man to his fortunes, by making
these the fruit of his character. Ducks take to the water,
eagles to the sky, waders to the sea margin, hunters to the forest, clerks to counting-rooms, soldiers to the frontier. Thus
events grow on the same stem with persons; are sub-persons.
The pleasure of life is according to the man that lives it, and
not according to the work or the place. Life is an ecstasy.
We know what madness belongs to love—what power to
paint a vile object in hues of heaven. As insane persons are
indifferent to their dress, diet, and other accommodations, and
as we do in dreams, with equanimity, the most absurd acts,
so a drop more of wine in our cup of life will reconcile us to
strange company and work. Each creature puts forth from
itself its own condition and sphere, as the slug sweats out its
slimy house on the pear-leaf, and the woolly aphides on the
apple perspire their own bed, and the fish its shell. In youth
we clothe ourselves with rainbows and go as brave as the
zodiac. In age we put out another sort of perspiration—gout,
fever, rheumatism, caprice, doubt, fretting and avarice.

A man's fortunes are the fruit of his character. A man's
friends are his magnetisms. We go to Herodotus and Plutarch
for examples of Fate; but we are examples. "*Quisque suos
patimur manes.*" [2] The tendency of every man to enact all that
is in his constitution is expressed in the old belief that the
efforts which we make to escape from our destiny only serve
to lead us into it: and I have noticed a man likes better
to be complimented on his position, as the proof of the last
or total excellence, than on his merits.

[2] Virgil, *Aeneid.*

A man will see his character emitted in the events that seem to meet, but which exude from and accompany him. Events expand with the character. As once he found himself among toys, so now he plays a part in colossal systems, and his growth is declared in his ambition, his companions and his performance. He looks like a piece of luck, but is a piece of causation; the mosaic, angulated and ground to fit into the gap he fills. Hence in each town there is some man who is, in his brain and performance, an explanation of the tillage, production, factories, banks, churches, ways of living and society of that town. If you do not chance to meet him, all that you see will leave you a little puzzled; if you see him it will become plain. We know in Massachusetts who built New Bedford, who built Lynn, Lowell, Lawrence, Clinton, Fitchburg, Holyoke, Portland, and many another noisy mart. Each of these men, if they were transparent, would seem to you not so much men as walking cities, and wherever you put them they would build one.

History is the action and reaction of these two—Nature and Thought; two boys pushing each other on the curbstone of the pavement. Everything is pusher or pushed; and matter and mind are in perpetual tilt and balance, so. Whilst the man is weak, the earth takes up him. He plants his brain and affections. By and by he will take up the earth, and have his gardens and vineyards in the beautiful order and productiveness of his thought. Every solid in the universe is ready to become fluid on the approach of the mind, and the power to flux it is the measure of the mind. If the wall remain adamant, it accuses the want of thought. To a subtle force it will stream into new forms, expressive of the character of the mind. What is the city in which we sit here, but an aggregate of incongruous materials which have obeyed the will of some man? The granite was reluctant, but his hands were stronger, and it came. Iron was deep in the ground and well combined with stone, but could not hide from his fires. Wood, lime, stuffs, fruits, gums, were dispersed over the earth and sea, in vain. Here they are, within reach of every man's day-labor, what he wants of them. The whole world is the flux of matter over the wires of thought to the poles or points where it would build. The races of men rise out of the ground, preoccupied with a thought which rules them, and divided into parties ready armed and angry to fight for this metaphysical abstraction. The quality of the thought differences the Egyptian and the Roman, the Austrian and the American. The men who come on the stage at one period are all found to be related to each other. Certain ideas are in the air. We are all impressionable, for we are made of them; all impressionable, but some more than others, and these first express them. This explains the curious contemporaneousness of inventions and discoveries. The truth is in the air, and the most impressionable brain will announce it first, but all will announce it a few minutes later. So women, as most susceptible, are the best index of the coming hour. So the great man, that is, the man most imbued with the spirit of the time, is the impressionable man —of a fibre irritable and delicate, like iodine to light. He feels the infinitesimal attractions. His mind is righter than others because he yields to a current so feeble as can be felt only by a needle delicately poised.

The correlation is shown in defects. Möller, in his Essay on Architecture, taught that the building which was fitted accurately to answer its end would turn out to be beautiful though beauty had not been intended. I find the like unity in human structures rather virulent and pervasive; that a crudity in the blood will appear in the argument; a hump in the shoulder will appear in the speech and handiwork. If his mind could be seen, the hump would be seen. If a man has a see-saw in his voice, it will run into his sentences, into his poem, into the structure of his fable, into his speculation, into his charity. And as every man is hunted by his own dæmon, vexed by his own disease, this checks all his activity.

So each man, like each plant, has his parasites. A strong, astringent, bilious nature has more truculent enemies than the slugs and moths that fret my leaves. Such an one has curculios, borers, knife-worms; a swindler ate him first, then a client, then a quack, then smooth, plausible gentlemen, bitter and selfish as Moloch.

This correlation really existing can be divined. If the threads are there, thought can follow and show them. Especially when a soul is quick and docile, as Chaucer sings:

> Or if the soule of proper kind
> Be so parfite as men find,
> That is wot what is to come,
> And that he warneth all and some

> Of everiche of hir aventures,
> By avisions or figures;
> But that our flesh hath no might
> To understand it aright
> For it is warned too derkely.

Some people are made up of rhyme, coincidence, omen, periodicity, and presage: they meet the person they seek; what their companion prepares to say to them, they first say to him; and a hundred signs apprise them of what is about to befall.

Wonderful intricacy in the web, wonderful constancy in the design this vagabond life admits. We wonder how the fly finds its mate, and yet year after year, we find two men, two women, without legal or carnal tie, spend a great part of their best time within a few feet of each other. And the moral is that what we seek we shall find; what we flee from flees from us; as Goethe said, "what we wish for in youth, comes in heaps on us in old age," too often cursed with the granting of our prayer: and hence the high caution, that since we are sure of having what we wish, we beware to ask only for high things.

One key, one solution to the mysteries of human condition, one solution to the old knots of fate, freedom, and foreknowledge, exists; the propounding, namely, of the double consciousness. A man must ride alternately on the horses of his private and his public nature, as the equestrians in the circus throw themselves nimbly from horse to horse, or plant one foot on the back of one and the other foot on the back of the other. So when a man is the victim of his fate, has sciatica in his loins and cramp in his mind; a club-foot, and a club in his wit; a sour face and a selfish temper; a strut in his gait and a conceit in his affection; or is ground to powder by the vice of his race—he is to rally on his relation to the Universe, which his ruin benefits. Leaving the dæmon who suffers, he is to take sides with the Deity who secures universal benefit by his pain.

To offset the drag of temperament and race, which pulls down, learn this lesson, namely, that by the cunning co-presence of two elements, which is throughout nature, whatever lames or paralyzes you draws in with it the divinity, in some form, to repay. A good intention clothes itself with sudden power. When a god wishes to ride, any chip or pebble will bud and shoot out winged feet and serve him for a horse.

Let us build altars to the Blessed Unity which holds nature and souls in perfect solution, and compels every atom to serve an universal end. I do not wonder at a snow-flake, a shell, a summer landscape, or the glory of the stars; but at the necessity of beauty under which the universe lies; that all is and must be pictorial; that the rainbow and the curve of the horizon and the arch of the blue vault are only results from the organism of the eye. There is no need for foolish amateurs to fetch me to admire a garden of flowers, or a sungilt cloud, or a waterfall, when I cannot look without seeing splendor and grace. How idle to choose a random sparkle here or there, when the indwelling necessity plants the rose of beauty on the brow of chaos, and discloses the central intention of Nature to be harmony and joy.

Let us build altars to the Beautiful Necessity. If we thought men were free in the sense that in a single exception one fantastical will could prevail over the law of things, it were all one as if a child's hand could pull down the sun. If in the least particular one could derange the order of nature—who would accept the gift of life?

Let us build altars to the Beautiful Necessity, which secures that all is made of one piece; that plaintiff and defendant, friend and enemy, animal and planet, food and eater are of one kind. In astronomy is vast space but no foreign system; in geology, vast time but the same laws as to-day. Why should we be afraid of Nature, which is no other than "philosophy and theology embodied"? Why should we fear to be crushed by savage elements, we who are made up of the same elements? Let us build to the Beautiful Necessity, which makes man brave in believing that he cannot shun a danger that is appointed, nor incur one that is not; to the Necessity which rudely or softly educates him to the perception that there are no contingencies; that Law rules throughout existence; a Law which is not intelligent but intelligence; not personal nor impersonal—it disdains words and passes understanding; it dissolves persons; it vivifies nature; yet solicits the pure in heart to draw on all its omnipotence.

From *Conduct of Life*

Illusions

Some years ago, in company with an agreeable party, I spent a long summer day in exploring the Mammoth Cave in Kentucky. We traversed, through spacious galleries affording a solid masonry foundation for the town and county overhead, the six or eight black miles from the mouth of the cavern to the innermost recess which tourists visit—a niche or grotto made of one seamless stalactite, and called, I believe, Serena's Bower. I lost the light of one day. I saw high domes and bottomless pits; heard the voice of unseen waterfalls; paddled three quarters of a mile in the deep Echo River, whose waters are peopled with the blind fish; crossed the streams "Lethe" and "Styx;" plied with music and guns the echoes in these alarming galleries; saw every form of stalagmite and stalactite in the sculptured and fretted chambers—icicle, orange-flower, acanthus, grapes and snowball. We shot Bengal lights into the vaults and groins of the sparry cathedrals and examined all the masterpieces which the four combined engineers, water, limestone, gravitation and time, could make in the dark.

The mysteries and scenery of the cave had the same dignity that belongs to all natural objects, and which shames the fine things to which we foppishly compare them. I remarked especially the mimetic habit with which nature, on new instruments, hums her old tunes, making night to mimic day, and chemistry to ape vegetation. But I then took notice and still chiefly remember that the best thing which the cave had to offer was an illusion. On arriving at what is called the "Star-Chamber," our lamps were taken from us by the guide and extinguished or put aside, and, on looking upwards, I saw or seemed to see the night heaven thick with stars glimmering more or less brightly over our heads, and even what seemed a comet flaming among them. All the party were touched with astonishment and pleasure. Our musical friends sung with much feeling a pretty song, "The stars are in the quiet sky," etc., and I sat down on the rocky floor to enjoy the serene picture. Some crystal specks in the black ceiling high overhead, reflecting the light of a half-hid lamp, yielded this magnificent effect.

I own I did not like the cave so well for eking out its sublimities with this theatrical trick. But I have had many experiences like it, before and since; and we must be content to be pleased without too curiously analyzing the occasions. Our conversation with nature is not just what it seems. The cloud-rack, the sunrise and sunset glories, rainbows and Northern Lights are not quite so spheral as our childhood thought them, and the part our organization plays in them is too large. The senses interfere everywhere and mix their own structure with all they report of. Once we fancied the earth a plane, and stationary. In admiring the sunset we do not yet deduct the rounding, coördinating, pictorial powers of the eye.

The same interference from our organization creates the most of our pleasure and pain. Our first mistake is the belief that the circumstance gives the joy which we give to the circumstance. Life is an ecstasy. Life is sweet as nitrous oxide; and the fisherman dripping all day over a cold pond, the switchman at the railway intersection, the farmer in the field, the negro in the rice-swamp, the fop in the street, the hunter in the woods, the barrister with the jury, the belle at the ball, all ascribe a certain pleasure to their employment, which they themselves give it. Health and appetite impart the sweetness to sugar, bread and meat. We fancy that our civilization has got on far, but we still come back to our primers.

We live by our imaginations, by our admirations, by our sentiments. The child walks amid heaps of illusions, which he does not like to have disturbed. The boy, how sweet to him is his fancy! how dear the story of barons and battles! What a hero he is, whilst he feeds on his heroes! What a debt is his to imaginative books! He has no better friend or influence than Scott, Shakspeare, Plutarch and Homer. The man lives to other objects, but who dare affirm that they are more real? Even the prose of the streets is full of refractions. In the life of the dreariest alderman, fancy enters into all details and colors them with rosy hue. He imitates the air and actions of people whom he admires, and is raised in his own eyes. He pays a debt quicker to a rich man than to a poor man. He wishes the bow and compliment of some leader in the state or in society; weighs what he says; perhaps he never comes nearer to him for that, but dies at last better contented for this amusement of his eyes and his fancy.

The world rolls, the din of life is never hushed. In London, in Paris, in Boston, in San Francisco, the carnival, the masquerade is at its height. Nobody drops his domino. The unities, the fictions of the piece it would be an impertinence to break. The chapter of fascinations is very long. Great is paint; nay, God is the painter; and we rightly accuse the critic who destroys too many illusions. Society does not love its unmaskers. It was wittily if somewhat bitterly said by D'Alembert, "*qu'un état de vapeur était un état très fâcheux, parcequ'il nous faisait voir les choses comme elles sont.*" I find men victims of illusion in all parts of life. Children, youths, adults and old men, all are led by one bauble or another. Yoganidra, the goddess of illusion, Proteus, or Momus, or Gylfi's Mocking—for the Power has many names—is stronger than the Titans, stronger than Apollo. Few have overheard the gods or surprised their secret. Life is a succession of lessons which must be lived to be understood. All is riddle, and the key to a riddle is another riddle. There are as many pillows of illusion as flakes in a snow-storm. We wake from one dream into another dream. The toys to be sure are various, and are graduated in refinement to the quality of the dupe. The intellectual man requires a fine bait; the sots are easily amused. But everybody is drugged with his own frenzy, and the pageant marches at all hours, with music and banner and badge.

Amid the joyous troop who give in to the charivari, comes now and then a sad-eyed boy whose eyes lack the requisite refractions to clothe the show in due glory, and who is afflicted with a tendency to trace home the glittering miscellany of fruits and flowers to one root. Science is a search after identity, and the scientific whim is lurking in all corners. At the State Fair a friend of mine complained that all the varieties of fancy pears in our orchards seem to have been selected by somebody who had a whim for a particular kind of pear, and only cultivated such as had that perfume; they were all alike. And I remember the quarrel of another youth

with the confectioners, that when he racked his wit to choose
the best comfits in the shops, in all the endless varieties of
sweetmeat he could find only three flavors, or two. What
then? Pears and cakes are good for something; and because
you unluckily have an eye or nose too keen, why need you
spoil the comfort which the rest of us find in them? I knew
a humorist who in a good deal of rattle had a grain or two
of sense. He shocked the company by maintaining that the
attributes of God were two—power and risibility, and that it
was the duty of every pious man to keep up the comedy. And
I have known gentlemen of great stake in the community,
but whose sympathies were cold—presidents of colleges and
governors and senators—who held themselves bound to sign
every temperance pledge, and act with Bible societies and
missions and peace-makers, and cry *Hist-a-boy!* to every
good dog. We must not carry comity too far, but we all have
kind impulses in this direction. When the boys come into
my yard for leave to gather horse-chestnuts, I own I enter
into nature's game, and affect to grant the permission reluctantly, fearing that any moment they will find out the im-
posture of that showy chaff. But this tenderness is quite unnecessary; the enchantments are laid on very thick. Their
young life is thatched with them. Bare and grim to tears is
the lot of the children in the hovel I saw yesterday; yet not
the less they hung it round with frippery romance, like the
children of the happiest fortune, and talked of "the dear
cottage where so many joyful hours had flown." Well, this
thatching of hovels is the custom of the country. Women,
more than all, are the element and kingdom of illusion. Being
fascinated, they fascinate. They see through Claude-Lorraines.
And how dare any one, if he could, pluck away the *coulisses*,
stage effects and ceremonies, by which they live? Too pathetic,
too pitiable, is the region of affection, and its atmosphere always liable to *mirage*.

We are not very much to blame for our bad marriages. We
live amid hallucinations; and this especial trap is laid to trip
up our feet with, and all are tripped up first or last. But the
mighty Mother who had been so sly with us, as if she felt
that she owed us some indemnity, insinuates into the Pandora-
box of marriage some deep and serious benefits and some
great joys. We find a delight in the beauty and happiness of
children that makes the heart too big for the body. In the

worst-assorted connections there is ever some mixture of true marriage. Teague and his jade get some just relations of mutual respect, kindly observation, and fostering of each other; learn something, and would carry themselves wiselier if they were now to begin.

'T is fine for us to point at one or another fine madman, as if there were any exempts. The scholar in his library is none. I, who have all my life heard any number of orations and debates, read poems and miscellaneous books, conversed with many geniuses, am still the victim of any new page; and if Marmaduke, or Hugh, or Moosehead, or any other, invent a new style or mythology, I fancy that the world will be all brave and right if dressed in these colors, which I had not thought of. Then at once I will daub with this new paint; but it will not stick. 'T is like the cement which the peddler sells at the door; he makes broken crockery hold with it, but you can never buy of him a bit of the cement which will make it hold when he is gone.

Men who make themselves felt in the world avail themselves of a certain fate in their constitution which they know how to use. But they never deeply interest us unless they lift a corner of the curtain, or betray, never so slightly, their penetration of what is behind it. 'T is the charm of practical men that outside of their practicality are a certain poetry and play, as if they led the good horse Power by the bridle, and preferred to walk, though they can ride so fiercely. Bonaparte is intellectual, as well as Cæsar; and the best soldiers, sea-captains and railway men have a gentleness when off duty, a good-natured admission that there are illusions, and who shall say that he is not their sport? We stigmatize the cast-iron fellows who cannot so detach themselves, as "dragon-ridden," "thunder-stricken," and fools of fate, with whatever powers endowed.

Since our tuition is through emblems and indirections, it is well to know that there is method in it, a fixed scale and rank above rank in the phantasms. We begin low with coarse masks and rise to the most subtle and beautiful. The red men told Columbus "they had an herb which took away fatigue;" but he found the illusion of "arriving from the east at the Indies" more composing to his lofty spirit than any tobacco. Is not our faith in the impenetrability of matter more sedative than narcotics? You play with jackstraws, balls, bowls, horse and gun, estates and politics; but there are finer games before you. Is not time a pretty toy? Life will show you masks that are worth all your carnivals. Yonder mountain must migrate into your mind. The fine star-dust and nebulous blur in Orion, "the portentous year of Mizar and Alcor," must come down and be dealt with in your household thought. What if you shall come to discern that the play and playground of all this pompous history are radiations from yourself, and that the sun borrows his beams? What terrible questions we are learning to ask! The former men believed in magic, by which temples, cities and men were swallowed up, and all trace of them gone. We are coming on the secret of a magic which sweeps out of men's minds all vestige of theism and beliefs which they and their fathers held and were framed upon.

There are deceptions of the senses, deceptions of the passions, and the structural, beneficent illusions of sentiment and of the intellect. There is the illusion of love, which attributes to the beloved person all which that person shares with his or her family, sex, age or condition, nay, with the human mind itself. 'T is these which the lover loves, and Anna Matilda gets the credit of them. As if one shut up always in a tower, with one window through which the face of heaven and earth could be seen, should fancy that all the marvels he beheld belonged to that window. There is the illusion of time, which is very deep; who has disposed of it? or come to the conviction that what seems the *succession* of thought is only the distribution of wholes into causal series? The intellect sees that every atom carries the whole of nature; that the mind opens to omnipotence; that, in the endless striving and ascents, the metamorphosis is entire, so that the soul doth not know itself in its own act when that act is perfected. There is illusion that shall deceive even the elect. There is illusion that shall deceive even the performer of the miracle. Though he make his body, he denies that he makes it. Though the world exist from thought, thought is daunted in presence of the world. One after the other we accept the mental laws, still resisting those which follow, which however must be accepted. But all our concessions only compel us to new profusion. And what avails it that science has come to treat space and time as simply forms of thought, and the material world as hypothetical, and withal our pretension of *property* and even of self-hood are fading with the rest, if, at last, even our thoughts are not finalities, but the incessant flowing and ascension reach these also, and each thought which yesterday was a finality, to-day is yielding to a larger generalization?

With such volatile elements to work in, 't is no wonder if our estimates are loose and floating. We must work and affirm, but we have no guess of the value of what we say or do. The cloud is now as big as your hand, and now it covers a county. That story of Thor, who was set to drain the drink-ing-horn in Asgard and to wrestle with the old woman and to run with the runner Lok, and presently found that he had been drinking up the sea, and wrestling with Time, and rac-ing with Thought—describes us, who are contending, amid these seeming trifles, with the supreme energies of nature. We fancy we have fallen into bad company and squalid con-dition, low debts, shoe-bills, broken glass to pay for, pots to buy, butcher's meat, sugar, milk and coal. "Set me some great task, ye gods! and I will show my spirit." "Not so," says the good Heaven; "plod and plough, vamp your old coats and hats, weave a shoestring; great affairs and the best wine by and by." Well, 't is all phantasm; and if we weave a yard of tape in all humility and as well as we can, long hereafter we shall see it was no cotton tape at all but some galaxy which we braided, and that the threads were Time and Nature.

We cannot write the order of the variable winds. How can we penetrate the law of our shifting moods and susceptibility? Yet they differ as all and nothing. Instead of the firmament of yesterday, which our eyes require, it is to-day an egg-shell which coops us in; we cannot even see what or where our stars of destiny are. From day to day the capital facts of human life are hidden from our eyes. Suddenly the mist rolls up and reveals them, and we think how much good time is gone that might have been saved had any hint of these things been shown. A sudden rise in the road shows us the system of mountains, and all the summits, which have been just as near us all the year, but quite out of mind. But these alterna-tions are not without their order, and we are parties to our various fortune. If life seem a succession of dreams, yet poetic justice is done in dreams also. The visions of good men are good; it is the undisciplined will that is whipped with bad thoughts and bad fortunes. When we break the laws, we lose our hold on the central reality. Like sick men in hospitals, we change only from bed to bed, from one folly to another; and it cannot signify much what becomes of such castaways, wailing, stupid, comatose creatures, lifted from bed to bed, from the nothing of life to the nothing of death.

In this kingdom of illusions we grope eagerly for stays and foundations. There is none but a strict and faithful dealing at home and a severe barring out of all duplicity or illusion there. Whatever games are played with us, we must play no games with ourselves, but deal in our privacy with the last honesty and truth. I look upon the simple and childish virtues of veracity and honesty as the root of all that is sublime in character. Speak as you think, be what you are, pay your debts of all kinds. I prefer to be owned as sound and solvent, and my word as good as my bond, and to be what cannot be skipped, or dissipated, or undermined, to all the *éclat* in the universe. This reality is the foundation of friendship, religion, poetry and art. At the top or at the bottom of all illusions, I set the cheat which still leads us to work and live for appearances; in spite of our conviction, in all sane hours, that it is what we really are that avails with friends, with strangers, and with fate or fortune.

One would think from the talk of men that riches and poverty were a great matter; and our civilization mainly respects it. But the Indians say that they do not think the white man, with his brow of care, always toiling, afraid of heat and cold, and keeping within doors, has any advantage of them. The permanent interest of every man is never to be in a false position, but to have the weight of nature to back him in all that he does. Riches and poverty are a thick or thin costume; and our life—the life of all of us—identical. For we transcend the circumstance continually and taste the real quality of existence; as in our employments, which only differ in the manifestations but express the same laws; or in our thoughts, which wear no silks and taste no ice-creams. We see God face to face every hour, and know the savor of nature.

The early Greek philosophers Heraclitus and Xenophanes measured their force on this problem of identity. Diogenes of Apollonia said that unless the atoms were made of one stuff, they could never blend and act with one another. But the Hindoos, in their sacred writings, express the liveliest feeling, both of the essential identity and of that illusion which they conceive variety to be. "The notions, '*I am*,' and '*This is mine*,' which influence mankind, are but delusions of the mother of the world. Dispel, O Lord of all creatures! the conceit of knowledge which proceeds from ignorance." And the beatitude of man they hold to lie in being freed from fascination.

The intellect is stimulated by the statement of truth in a trope, and the will by clothing the laws of life in illusions. But the unities of Truth and of Right are not broken by the disguise. There need never be any confusion in these. In a crowded life of many parts and performers, on a stage of nations, or in the obscurest hamlet in Maine or California, the same elements offer the same choices to each new comer, and, according to his election, he fixes his fortune in absolute Nature. It would be hard to put more mental and moral philosophy than the Persians have thrown into a sentence—

> Fooled thou must be, though wisest of the wise:
> Then be the fool of virtue, not of vice.

There is no chance and no anarchy in the universe. All is system and gradation. Every god is there sitting in his sphere. The young mortal enters the hall of the firmament; there is he alone with them alone, they pouring on him benedictions and gifts, and beckoning him up to their thrones. On the instant, and incessantly, fall snow-storms of illusions. He fancies himself in a vast crowd which sways this way and that and whose movement and doings he must obey: he fancies himself poor, orphaned, insignificant. The mad crowd drives hither and thither, now furiously commanding this thing to be done, now that. What is he that he should resist their will, and think or act for himself? Every moment new changes and new showers of deceptions to baffle and distract him. And when, by and by, for an instant, the air clears and the cloud lifts a little, there are the gods still sitting around him on their thrones—they alone with him alone.

From *Conduct of Life*

Part Five

PEOPLE

Ability

The Saxon and the Northman are both Scandinavians. History does not allow us to fix the limits of the application of these names with any accuracy, but from the residence of a portion of these people in France, and from some effect of that powerful soil on their blood and manners, the Norman has come popularly to represent in England the aristocratic, and the Saxon the democratic principle. And though, I doubt not, the nobles are of both tribes, and the workers of both, yet we are forced to use the names a little mythically, one to represent the worker and the other the enjoyer.

The island was a prize for the best race. Each of the dominant races tried its fortune in turn. The Phœnician, the Celt and the Goth had already got in. The Roman came, but in the very day when his fortune culminated. He looked in the eyes of a new people that was to supplant his own. He disembarked his legions, erected his camps and towers—presently he heard bad news from Italy, and worse and worse, every year; at last, he made a handsome compliment of roads and walls, and departed. But the Saxon seriously settled in the land, builded, tilled, fished and traded, with German truth and adhesiveness. The Dane came and divided with him. Last of all the Norman or French-Dane arrived, and formally conquered, harried and ruled the kingdom. A century later it came out that the Saxon had the most bottom and longevity, had managed to make the victor speak the language and accept the law and usage of the victim; forced the baron to dictate Saxon terms to Norman kings; and, step by step, got all the essential securities of civil liberty invented and confirmed. The genius of the race and the genius of the place conspired to this effect. The island is lucrative to free labor, but not worth possession on other terms. The race was so intellectual that a feudal or military tenure could not last longer than the war. The power of the Saxon-Danes, so thoroughly beaten in the war that the name of English and villein were synonymous, yet so vivacious as to extort charters from the kings, stood on the strong personality of these people. Sense and economy must rule in a world which is made of sense and economy, and the banker, with his seven per cent., drives the earl out of his castle. A nobility of soldiers cannot keep down a commonalty of shrewd scientific persons. What signifies a pedigree of a hundred links, against a cotton-spinner with steam in his mill; or against a company of broad-shouldered Liverpool merchants, for whom Stephenson and Brunel are contriving locomotives and a tubular bridge?

These Saxons are the hands of mankind. They have the taste for toil, a distaste for pleasure or repose, and the telescopic appreciation of distant gain. They are the wealth-makers—and by dint of mental faculty which has its own conditions. The Saxon works after liking, or only for himself; and to set him at work and to begin to draw his monstrous values out of barren Britain, all dishonor, fret and barrier must be removed, and then his energies begin to play.

The Scandinavian fancied himself surrounded by Trolls— a kind of goblin men with vast power of work and skilful production—divine stevedores, carpenters, reapers, smiths and masons, swift to reward every kindness done them, with gifts of gold and silver. In all English history this dream comes to pass. Certain Trolls or working brains, under the names of Alfred, Bede, Caxton, Bracton, Camden, Drake, Selden, Dugdale, Newton, Gibbon, Brindley, Watt, Wedgwood, dwell in the troll-mounts of Britain and turn the sweat of their face to power and renown.

If the race is good, so is the place. Nobody landed on this spellbound island with impunity. The enchantments of barren shingle and rough weather transformed every adventurer into a laborer. Each vagabond that arrived bent his neck to the yoke of gain, or found the air too tense for him. The strong survived, the weaker went to the ground. Even the pleasure-hunters and sots of England are of a tougher texture. A hard temperament had been formed by Saxon and Saxon-Dane, and such of these French or Normans as could reach it were naturalized in every sense.

All the admirable expedients or means hit upon in England

must be looked at as growths or irresistible offshoots of the expanding mind of the race. A man of that brain thinks and acts thus; and his neighbor, being afflicted with the same kind of brain, though he is rich and called a baron or a duke, thinks the same thing, and is ready to allow the justice of the thought and act in his retainer or tenant, though sorely against his baronial or ducal will.

The island was renowned in antiquity for its breed of mastiffs, so fierce that when their teeth were set you must cut their heads off to part them. The man was like his dog. The people have that nervous bilious temperament which is known by medical men to resist every means employed to make its possessor subservient to the will of others. The English game is main force to main force, the planting of foot to foot, fair play and open field—a rough tug without trick or dodging, till one or both come to pieces. King Ethelwald spoke the language of his race when he planted himself at Wimborne and said he "would do one of two things, or there live, or there lie." They hate craft and subtlety. They neither poison, nor waylay, nor assassinate; and when they have pounded each other to a poultice, they will shake hands and be friends for the remainder of their lives.

You shall trace these Gothic touches at school, at country fairs, at the hustings and in parliament. No artifice, no breach of truth and plain dealing—not so much as secret ballot, is suffered in the island. In parliament, the tactics of the opposition is to resist every step of the government by a pitiless attack: and in a bargain, no prospect of advantage is so dear to the merchant as the thought of being tricked is mortifying.

Sir Kenelm Digby, a courtier of Charles and James, who won the sea-fight of Scanderoon, was a model Englishman in his day. "His person was handsome and gigantic, he had so graceful elocution and noble address, that, had he been dropt out of the clouds in any part of the world, he would have made himself respected: he was skilled in six tongues, and master of arts and arms." Sir Kenelm wrote a book, Of Bodies and of Souls, in which he propounds, that "syllogisms do breed, or rather are all the variety of man's life. They are the steps by which we walk in all our businesses. Man, as he is man, doth nothing else but weave such chains. Whatsoever he doth, swerving from this work, he doth as deficient from the nature of man: and, if he do aught beyond this, by breaking out into divers sorts of exterior actions, he findeth, nevertheless, in this linked sequel of simple discourses, the art, the cause, the rule, the bounds and the model of it."

There spoke the genius of the English people. There is a necessity on them to be logical. They would hardly greet the good that did not logically fall—as if it excluded their own merit, or shook their understandings. They are jealous of minds that have much facility of association, from an instinctive fear that the seeing many relations to their thought might impair this serial continuity and lucrative concentration. They are impatient of genius, or of minds addicted to contemplation, and cannot conceal their contempt for sallies of thought, however lawful, whose steps they cannot count by their wonted rule. Neither do they reckon better a syllogism that ends in syllogism. For they have a supreme eye to facts, and theirs is a logic that brings salt to soup, hammer to nail, oar to boat; the logic of cooks, carpenters and chemists, following the sequence of nature, and one on which words make no impression. Their mind is not dazzled by its own means, but locked and bolted to results. They love men who, like Samuel Johnson, a doctor in the schools, would jump out of his syllogism the instant his major proposition was in danger, to save that at all hazards. Their practical vision is spacious, and they can hold many threads without entangling them. All the steps they orderly take; but with the high logic of never confounding the minor and major proposition; keeping their eye on their aim, in all the complicity and delay incident to the several series of means they employ. There is room in their minds for this and that—a science of degrees. In the courts the independence of the judges and the loyalty of the suitors are equally excellent. In parliament they have hit on that capital invention of freedom, a constitutional opposition. And when courts and parliament are both deaf, the plaintiff is not silenced. Calm, patient, his weapon of defence from year to year is the obstinate reproduction of the grievance, with calculations and estimates. But, meantime, he is drawing numbers and money to his opinion, resolved that if all remedy fails, right of revolution is at the bottom of his charter-box. They are bound to see their measure carried, and stick to it through ages of defeat.

Into this English logic, however, an infusion of justice enters, not so apparent in other races—a belief in the existence of two sides, and the resolution to see fair play. There is on every question an appeal from the assertion of the parties to the proof of what is asserted. They kiss the dust before a fact. Is it a machine, is it a charter, is it a boxer in the ring, is it a candidate on the hustings—the universe of Englishmen will suspend their judgment until the trial can be had. They are not to be led by a phrase, they want a working plan, a working machine, a working constitution, and will sit out the trial and abide by the issue and reject all preconceived theories. In politics they put blunt questions, which must be answered; Who is to pay the taxes? What will you do for trade? What for corn? What for the spinner?

This singular fairness and its results strike the French with surprise. Philip de Commines says, "Now, in my opinion, among all the sovereignties I know in the world, that in which the public good is best attended to, and the least violence exercised on the people, is that of England." Life is safe, and personal rights; and what is freedom without security? whilst, in France, "fraternity," "equality," and "indivisible unity" are names for assassination. Montesquieu said, "England is the freest country in the world. If a man in England had as many enemies as hairs on his head, no harm would happen to him."

Their self-respect, their faith in causation, and their realistic logic or coupling of means to ends, have given them the leadership of the modern world. Montesquieu said, "No people have true common-sense but those who are born in England." This common-sense is a perception of all the conditions of our earthly existence; of laws that can be stated, and of laws that cannot be stated, or that are learned only by practice, in which allowance for friction is made. They are impious in their skepticism of theory, and in high departments they are cramped and sterile. But the unconditional surrender to facts, and the choice of means to reach their ends, are as admirable as with ants and bees.

The bias of the nation is a passion for utility. They love the lever, the screw and pulley, the Flanders draught-horse, the waterfall, wind-mills, tide-mills; the sea and the wind to bear their freight ships. More than the diamond Koh-i-noor, which glitters among their crown jewels, they prize that dull pebble which is wiser than a man, whose poles turn themselves to the poles of the world, and whose axis is parallel to the axis of the world. Now, their toys are steam and galvanism. They are heavy at the fine arts, but adroit at the coarse; not good in jewelry or mosaics, but the best iron-masters, colliers, wool-combers and tanners in Europe. They apply themselves to agriculture, to draining, to resisting encroachments of sea, wind, travelling sands, cold and wet sub-soil; to fishery, to manufacture of indispensable staples—salt, plumbago, leather, wool, glass, pottery and brick—to bees and silkworms; and by their steady combinations they succeed. A manufacturer sits down to dinner in a suit of clothes which was wool on a sheep's back at sunrise. You dine with a gentleman on venison, pheasant, quail, pigeons, poultry, mushrooms and pine-apples, all the growth of his estate. They are neat husbands for ordering all their tools pertaining to house and field. All are well kept. There is no want and no waste. They study use and fitness in their building, in the order of their dwellings and in their dress. The Frenchman invented the ruffle; the Englishman added the shirt. The Englishman wears a sensible coat buttoned to the chin, of rough but solid and lasting texture. If he is a lord, he dresses a little worse than a commoner. They have diffused the taste for plain substantial hats, shoes and coats through Europe. They think him the best dressed man whose dress is so fit for his use that you cannot notice or remember to describe it.

They secure the essentials in their diet, in their arts and manufactures. Every article of cutlery shows, in its shape, thought and long experience of workmen. They put the expense in the right place, as, in their sea-steamers, in the solidity of the machinery and the strength of the boat. The admirable equipment of their arctic ships carries London to the pole. They build roads, aqueducts; warm and ventilate houses. And they have impressed their directness and practical habit on modern civilization.

In trade, the Englishman believes that nobody breaks who ought not to break; and that if he do not make trade everything, it will make him nothing; and acts on this belief. The spirit of system, attention to details, and the subordination of details, or the not driving things too finely (which is charged on the Germans), constitute that dispatch of business which makes the mercantile power of England.

In war, the Englishman looks to his means. He is of the

opinion of Civilis, his German ancestor, whom Tacitus reports as holding that "the gods are on the side of the strongest;" a sentence which Bonaparte unconsciously translated, when he said that "he had noticed that Providence always favored the heaviest battalion." Their military science propounds that if the weight of the advancing column is greater than that of the resisting, the latter is destroyed. Therefore Wellington, when he came to the army in Spain, had every man weighed, first with accoutrements, and then without; believing that the force of an army depended on the weight and power of the individual soldiers, in spite of cannon. Lord Palmerston told the House of Commons that more care is taken of the health and comfort of English troops than of any other troops in the world; and that hence the English can put more men into the rank, on the day of action, on the field of battle, than any other army. Before the bombardment of the Danish forts in the Baltic, Nelson spent day after day, himself, in the boats, on the exhausting service of sounding the channel. Clerk of Eldin's celebrated manœuvre of breaking the line of sea-battle, and Nelson's feat of *doubling*, or stationing his ships one on the outer bow, and another on the outer quarter of each of the enemy's, were only translations into naval tactics of Bonaparte's rule of concentration. Lord Collingwood was accustomed to tell his men that if they could fire three well-directed broadsides in five minutes, no vessel could resist them; and from constant practice they came to do it in three minutes and a half.

But conscious that no race of better men exists, they rely most on the simplest means, and do not like ponderous and difficult tactics, but delight to bring the affair hand to hand; where the victory lies with the strength, courage and endurance of the individual combatants. They adopt every improvement in rig, in motor, in weapons, but they fundamentally believe that the best stratagem in naval war is to lay your ship close alongside of the enemy's ship and bring all your guns to bear on him, until you or he go to the bottom. This is the old fashion, which never goes out of fashion, neither in nor out of England.

It is not usually a point of honor, nor a religious sentiment, and never any whim, that they will shed their blood for; but usually property, and right measured by property, that breeds revolution. They have no Indian taste for a tomahawk-dance, no French taste for a badge or a proclamation. The Englishman is peaceably minding his business and earning his day's wages. But if you offer to lay hand on his day's wages, on his cow, or his right in common, or his shop, he will fight to the Judgment. Magna-charta, jury-trial, *habeas-corpus,* star-chamber, ship-money, Popery, Plymouth colony, American Revolution, are all questions involving a yeoman's right to his dinner, and except as touching that, would not have lashed the British nation to rage and revolt.

Whilst they are thus instinct with a spirit of order and of calculation, it must be owned they are capable of larger views; but the indulgence is expensive to them, costs great crises, or accumulations of mental power. In common, the horse works best with blinders. Nothing is more in the line of English thought than our unvarnished Connecticut question, "Pray, sir, how do you get your living when you are at home?" The questions of freedom, of taxation, of privilege, are money questions. Heavy fellows, steeped in beer and fleshpots, they are hard of hearing and dim of sight. Their drowsy minds need to be flagellated by war and trade and politics and persecution. They cannot well read a principle, except by the light of fagots and of burning towns.

Tacitus says of the Germans, "Powerful only in sudden efforts, they are impatient of toil and labor." This highly destined race, if it had not somewhere added the chamber of patience to its brain, would not have built London. I know not from which of the tribes and temperaments that went to the composition of the people this tenacity was supplied, but they clinch every nail they drive. They have no running for luck, and no immoderate speed. They spend largely on their fabric, and await the slow return. Their leather lies tanning seven years in the vat. At Rogers's mills, in Sheffield, where I was shown the process of making a razor and a penknife, I was told there is no luck in making good steel; that they make no mistakes, every blade in the hundred and in the thousand is good. And that is characteristic of all their work —no more is attempted than is done.

When Thor and his companions arrive at Utgard, he is told that "nobody is permitted to remain here, unless he understand some art, and excel in it all other men." The same question is still put to the posterity of Thor. A nation of laborers, every man is trained to some one art or detail and aims at perfection in that; not content unless he has something in which he thinks he surpasses all other men. He would rather not do anything at all than not do it well. I suppose no people have such thoroughness—from the highest to the lowest, every man meaning to be master of his art.

"To show capacity," a Frenchman described as the end of a speech in debate: "No," said an Englishman, "but to set your shoulder at the wheel—to advance the business." Sir Samuel Romilly refused to speak in popular assemblies, confining himself to the House of Commons, where a measure can be carried by a speech. The business of the House of Commons is conducted by a few persons, but these are hard-worked. Sir Robert Peel "knew the Blue Books by heart." His colleagues and rivals carry Hansard in their heads. The high civil and legal offices are not beds of ease, but posts which exact frightful amounts of mental labor. Many of the great leaders, like Pitt, Canning, Castlereagh, Romilly, are soon worked to death. They are excellent judges in England of a good worker, and when they find one, like Clarendon, Sir Philip Warwick, Sir William Coventry, Ashley, Burke, Thurlow, Mansfield, Pitt, Eldon, Peel, or Russell, there is nothing too good or too high for him.

They have a wonderful heat in the pursuit of a public aim. Private persons exhibit, in scientific and antiquarian researches, the same pertinacity as the nation showed in the coalitions in which it yoked Europe against the empire of Bonaparte, one after the other defeated, and still renewed, until the sixth hurled him from his seat.

Sir John Herschel, in completion of the work of his father, who had made the catalogue of the stars of the northern hemisphere, expatriated himself for years at the Cape of Good Hope, finished his inventory of the southern heaven, came home, and redacted it in eight years more—a work whose value does not begin until thirty years have elapsed, and thenceforward a record to all ages of the highest import. The Admiralty sent out the Arctic expeditions year after year, in search of Sir John Franklin, until at last they have threaded their way through polar pack and Behring's Straits and solved the geographical problem. Lord Elgin, at Athens, saw the imminent ruin of the Greek remains, set up his scaffoldings, in spite of epigrams, and, after five years' labor to collect them, got his marbles on ship-board. The ship struck a rock and went to the bottom. He had them all fished up by divers, at a vast expense, and brought to London; not knowing that Haydon, Fuseli and Canova, and all good heads in all the world, were to be his applauders. In the same spirit, were the excavation and research by Sir Charles Fellowes for the Xanthian monument, and of Layard for his Nineveh sculptures.

The nation sits in the immense city they have builded, a London extended into every man's mind, though he live in Van Dieman's Land or Capetown. Faithful performance of what is undertaken to be performed, they honor in themselves, and exact in others, as certificate of equality with themselves. The modern world is theirs. They have made and make it day by day. The commercial relations of the world are so intimately drawn to London, that every dollar on earth contributes to the strength of the English government. And if all the wealth in the planet should perish by war or deluge, they know themselves competent to replace it.

They have approved their Saxon blood, by their sea-going qualities; their descent from Odin's smiths, by their hereditary skill in working in iron; their British birth, by husbandry and immense wheat harvests; and justified their occupancy of the centre of habitable land, by their supreme ability and cosmopolitan spirit. They have tilled, builded, forged, spun and woven. They have made the island a thoroughfare, and London a shop, a law-court, a record-office and scientific bureau, inviting to strangers; a sanctuary to refugees of every political and religious opinion; and such a city that almost every active man, in any nation, finds himself at one time or other forced to visit it.

In every path of practical activity they have gone even with the best. There is no secret of war in which they have not shown mastery. The steam-chamber of Watt, the locomotive of Stephenson, the cotton-mule of Roberts, perform the labor of the world. There is no department of literature, of science, or of useful art, in which they have not produced a first-rate book. It is England whose opinion is waited for on the merit of a new invention, an improved science. And in the complications of the trade and politics of their vast empire, they have been equal to every exigency, with counsel and with conduct. Is it their luck, or is it in the chambers of their brain—it is their commercial advantage that whatever light appears in better method or happy invention, breaks out *in their race.* They are a family to which a destiny attaches, and the Banshee has sworn that a male heir shall never be wanting. They have a wealth of men to fill important posts, and the vigilance of party criticism insures the selection of a competent person.

A proof of the energy of the British people is the highly artificial construction of the whole fabric. The climate and geography, I said, were factitious, as if the hands of man had arranged the conditions. The same character pervades the whole kingdom. Bacon said, "Rome was a state not subject to paradoxes;" but England subsists by antagonisms and contradictions. The foundations of its greatness are the rolling waves; and from first to last it is a museum of anomalies. This foggy and rainy country furnishes the world with astronomical observations. Its short rivers do not afford water-power, but the land shakes under the thunder of the mills. There is no gold-mine of any importance, but there is more gold in England than in all other countries. It is too far north for the culture of the vine, but the wines of all countries are in its docks. The French Comte de Lauraguais said, "No fruit ripens in England but a baked apple;" but oranges and pine-apples are as cheap in London as in the Mediterranean. The Mark-Lane Express, or the Custom House Returns, bear out to the letter the vaunt of Pope,

> Let India boast her palms, nor envy we
> The weeping amber, nor the spicy tree,
> While, by our oaks, those precious loads are borne,
> And realms commanded which those trees adorn.[1]

The native cattle are extinct, but the island is full of artificial breeds. The agriculturist Bakewell created sheep and cows and horses to order, and breeds in which every thing was omitted but what is economical. The cow is sacrificed to her bag, the ox to his sirloin. Stall-feeding makes sperm-mills of the cattle, and converts the stable to a chemical factory. The rivers, lakes and ponds, too much fished, or obstructed by factories, are artificially filled with the eggs of salmon, turbot and herring.

Chat Moss and the fens of Lincolnshire and Cambridge-

---

[1] From Pope's "Windsor Forest" (quoted by Emerson from memory and differing slightly from the original).

shire are unhealthy and too barren to pay rent. By cylindrical tiles and gutta-percha tubes, five millions of acres of bad land have been drained and put on equality with the best, for rape-culture and grass. The climate too, which was already believed to have become milder and drier by the enormous consumption of coal, is so far reached by this new action, that fogs and storms are said to disappear. In due course, all England will be drained and rise a second time out of the waters. The latest step was to call in the aid of steam to agriculture. Steam is almost an Englishman. I do not know but they will send him to Parliament next, to make laws. He weaves, forges, saws, pounds, fans, and now he must pump, grind, dig and plough for the farmer. The markets created by the manufacturing population have erected agriculture into a great thriving and spending industry. The value of the houses in Britain is equal to the value of the soil. Artificial aids of all kinds are cheaper than the natural resources. No man can afford to walk, when the parliamentary-train carries him for a penny a mile. Gas-burners are cheaper than daylight in numberless floors in the cities. All the houses in London buy their water. The English trade does not exist for the exportation of native products, but on its manufactures, or the making well every thing which is ill-made elsewhere. They make ponchos for the Mexican, bandannas for the Hindoo, ginseng for the Chinese, beads for the Indian, laces for the Flemings, telescopes for astronomers, cannons for kings.

The Board of Trade caused the best models of Greece and Italy to be placed within the reach of every manufacturing population. They caused to be translated from foreign languages and illustrated by elaborate drawings, the most approved works of Munich, Berlin and Paris. They have ransacked Italy to find new forms, to add a grace to the products of their looms, their potteries and their foundries.

The nearer we look, the more artificial is their social system. Their law is a network of fictions. Their property, a scrip or certificate of right to interest on money that no man ever saw. Their social classes are made by statute. Their ratios of power and representation are historical and legal. The last Reform-bill took away political power from a mound, a ruin and a stone wall, whilst Birmingham and Manchester, whose mills paid for the wars of Europe, had no representative. Purity in the elective Parliament is secured by the purchase of seats. Foreign power is kept by armed colonies; power at home, by a standing army of police. The pauper lives better than the free laborer, the thief better than the pauper, and the transported felon better than the one under imprisonment. The crimes are factitious; as smuggling, poaching, nonconformity, heresy and treason. The sovereignty of the seas is maintained by the impressment of seamen. "The impressment of seamen," said Lord Eldon, "is the life of our navy." Solvency is maintained by means of a national debt, on the principle, "If you will not lend me the money, how can I pay you?" For the administration of justice, Sir Samuel Romilly's expedient for clearing the arrears of business in Chancery was, the Chancellor's staying away entirely from his court. Their system of education is factitious. The Universities galvanize dead languages into a semblance of life. Their church is artificial. The manners and customs of society are artificial—made-up men with made-up manners—and thus the whole is Birminghamized, and we have a nation whose existence is a work of art—a cold, barren, almost arctic isle being made the most fruitful, luxurious and imperial land in the whole earth.

Man in England submits to be a product of political economy. On a bleak moor a mill is built, a banking-house is opened, and men come in as water in a sluice-way, and towns and cities rise. Man is made as a Birmingham button. The rapid doubling of the population dates from Watt's steam-engine. A landlord who owns a province says, "The tenantry are unprofitable; let me have sheep." He unroofs the houses and ships the population to America. The nation is accustomed to the instantaneous creation of wealth. It is the maxim of their economists, "that the greater part in value of the wealth now existing in England has been produced by human hands within the last twelve months." Meantime, three or four days' rain will reduce hundreds to starving in London.

One secret of their power is their mutual good understanding. Not only good minds are born among them, but all the people have good minds. Every nation has yielded some good wit, if, as has chanced to many tribes, only one. But the intellectual organization of the English admits a communicableness of knowledge and ideas among them all. An electric touch by any of their national ideas, melts them into one family and brings the hoards of power which their individuality is always hiving, into use and play for all. Is it the smallness of the country, or is it the pride and affection of race—they have solidarity, or responsibleness, and trust in each other.

Their minds, like wool, admit of a dye which is more lasting than the cloth. They embrace their cause with more tenacity than their life. Though not military, yet every common subject by the poll is fit to make a soldier of. These private, reserved, mute family-men can adopt a public end with all their heat, and this strength of affection makes the romance of their heroes. The difference of rank does not divide the national heart. The Danish poet Oehlenschläger complains that who writes in Danish writes to two hundred readers. In Germany there is one speech for the learned, and another for the masses, to that extent that, it is said, no sentiment or phrase from the works of any great German writer is ever heard among the lower classes. But in England, the language of the noble is the language of the poor. In Parliament, in pulpits, in theatres, when the speakers rise to thought and passion, the language becomes idiomatic; the people in the street best understand the best words. And their language seems drawn from the Bible, the Common Law and the works of Shakspeare, Bacon, Milton, Pope, Young, Cowper, Burns and Scott. The island has produced two or three of the greatest men that ever existed, but they were not solitary in their own time. Men quickly embodied what Newton found out, in Greenwich observatories and practical navigation. The boys know all that Hutton knew of strata, or Dalton of atoms, or Harvey of blood-vessels; and these studies, once dangerous, are in fashion. So what is invented or known in agriculture, or in trade, or in war, or in art, or in literature and antiquities. A great ability, not amassed on a few giants, but poured into the general mind, so that each of them could at a pinch stand in the shoes of the other; and they are more bound in character than differenced in ability or in rank. The laborer is a possible lord. The lord is a possible basket-maker. Every man carries the English system in his brain, knows what is confided to him and does therein the best he can. The chancellor carries England on his mace, the midshipman at the point of his dirk, the smith on his hammer, the cook in the bowl of his spoon; the postilion cracks his whip for England, and the sailor times his oars to "God save the King!" The very felons have their pride in each other's English stanchness. In politics and in war they hold together as by hooks of steel. The charm in Nelson's history is the unselfish greatness, the assurance of being supported to the uttermost by those whom he supports to the uttermost. Whilst they are some ages ahead of the rest of the world in the art of living; whilst in some directions they do not represent the modern spirit but constitute it—this vanguard of civility and power they coldly hold, marching in phalanx, lockstep, foot after foot, file after file of heroes, ten thousand deep.

From *English Traits*

Thoreau

Henry David Thoreau was the last male descendant of a French ancestor who came to this country from the Isle of Guernsey. His character exhibited occasional traits drawn from this blood, in singular combination with a very strong Saxon genius.

He was born in Concord, Massachusetts, on the 12th of July, 1817. He was graduated at Harvard College in 1837, but without any literary distinction. An iconoclast in literature, he seldom thanked colleges for their service to him, holding them in small esteem, whilst yet his debt to them was important. After leaving the University, he joined his brother in teaching a private school, which he soon renounced. His father was a manufacturer of lead-pencils, and Henry applied himself for a time to this craft, believing he could make a better pencil than was then in use. After completing his experiments, he exhibited his work to chemists and artists in Boston, and having obtained their certificates to its excellence and to its equality with the best London manufacture, he returned home contented. His friends congratulated him that he had now opened his way to fortune. But he replied that he should never make another pencil. "Why should I? I would not do again what I have done once." He resumed his endless walks and miscellaneous studies, making every day some new acquaintance with Nature, though as yet never speaking of zoölogy or botany, since, though very studious of natural facts, he was incurious of technical and textual science.

At this time, a strong, healthy youth, fresh from college, whilst all his companions were choosing their profession, or eager to begin some lucrative employment, it was inevitable that his thoughts should be exercised on the same question, and it required rare decision to refuse all the accustomed paths and keep his solitary freedom at the cost of disappointing the natural expectations of his family and friends: all the more difficult that he had a perfect probity, was exact in securing his own independence, and in holding every man to the like duty. But Thoreau never faltered. He was a born protestant. He declined to give up his large ambition of knowledge and action for any narrow craft or profession, aiming at a much more comprehensive calling, the art of living well. If he slighted and defied the opinions of others, it was only that he was more intent to reconcile his practice with his own belief. Never idle or self-indulgent, he preferred, when he wanted money, earning it by some piece of manual labor agreeable to him, as building a boat or a fence, planting, grafting, surveying or other short work, to any long engagements. With his hardy habits and few wants, his skill in wood-craft, and his powerful arithmetic, he was very competent to live in any part of the world. It would cost him less time to supply his wants than another. He was therefore secure of his leisure.

A natural skill for mensuration, growing out of his mathematical knowledge and his habit of ascertaining the measures and distances of objects which interested him, the size of trees, the depth and extent of ponds and rivers, the height of mountains and the air-line distance of his favorite summits—this, and his intimate knowledge of the territory about Concord, made him drift into the profession of land-surveyor. It had the advantage for him that it led him continually into new and secluded grounds, and helped his studies of Nature. His accuracy and skill in this work were readily appreciated, and he found all the employment he wanted.

He could easily solve the problems of the surveyor, but he was daily beset with graver questions, which he manfully confronted. He interrogated every custom, and wished to settle all his practice on an ideal foundation. He was a

protestant *à outrance,* and few lives contain so many renunciations. He was bred to no profession; he never married; he
lived alone; he never went to church; he never voted; he
refused to pay a tax to the State; he ate no flesh, he drank no
wine, he never knew the use of tobacco; and, though a naturalist, he used neither trap nor gun. He chose, wisely no doubt
for himself, to be the bachelor of thought and Nature. He had
no talent for wealth, and knew how to be poor without the
least hint of squalor or inelegance. Perhaps he fell into his way
of living without forecasting it much, but approved it with
later wisdom. "I am often reminded," he wrote in his journal,
"that if I had bestowed on me the wealth of Crœsus, my aims
must be still the same, and my means essentially the same."
He had no temptations to fight against—no appetites, no passions, no taste for elegant trifles. A fine house, dress, the
manners and talk of highly cultivated people were all thrown
away on him. He much preferred a good Indian, and considered these refinements as impediments to conversation, wish-
ing to meet his companion on the simplest terms. He declined
invitations to dinner-parties, because there each was in every
one's way, and he could not meet the individuals to any purpose. "They make their pride," he said, "in making their
dinner cost much; I make my pride in making my dinner
cost little." When asked at table what dish he preferred, he
answered, "The nearest." He did not like the taste of wine,
and never had a vice in his life. He said, "I have a faint
recollection of pleasure derived from smoking dried lily-stems,
before I was a man. I had commonly a supply of these. I
have never smoked anything more noxious."

He chose to be rich by making his wants few, and supplying them himself. In his travels, he used the railroad only to
get over so much country as was unimportant to the present
purpose, walking hundreds of miles, avoiding taverns, buying a lodging in farmers' and fishermen's houses, as cheaper,
and more agreeable to him, and because there he could better
find the men and the information he wanted.

There was somewhat military in his nature, not to be subdued, always manly and able, but rarely tender, as if he
did not feel himself except in opposition. He wanted a fallacy
to expose, a blunder to pillory, I may say required a little
sense of victory, a roll of the drum, to call his powers into
full exercise. It cost him nothing to say No; indeed he found

it much easier than to say Yes. It seemed as if his first instinct on hearing a proposition was to controvert it, so impatient was he of the limitations of our daily thought. This
habit, of course, is a little chilling to the social affections;
and though the companion would in the end acquit him of
any malice or untruth, yet it mars conversation. Hence, no
equal companion stood in affectionate relations with one so
pure and guileless. "I love Henry," said one of his friends,
"but I cannot like him; and as for taking his arm, I should as
soon think of taking the arm of an elm-tree."

Yet, hermit and stoic as he was, he was really fond of
sympathy, and threw himself heartily and childlike into the
company of young people whom he loved, and whom he delighted to entertain, as he only could, with the varied and
endless anecdotes of his experiences by field and river: and
he was always ready to lead a huckleberry-party or a search
for chestnuts or grapes. Talking, one day, of a public discourse, Henry remarked that whatever succeeded with the
audience was bad. I said, "Who would not like to write something which all can read, like Robinson Crusoe? and who does
not see with regret that his page is not solid with a right
materialistic treatment, which delights everybody?" Henry
objected, of course, and vaunted the better lectures which
reached only a few persons. But, at supper, a young girl,
understanding that he was to lecture at the Lyceum, sharply
asked him, "Whether his lecture would be a nice, interesting
story, such as she wished to hear, or whether it was one of
those old philosophical things that she did not care about."
Henry turned to her, and bethought himself, and, I saw, was
trying to believe that he had matter that might fit her and
her brother, who were to sit up and go to the lecture, if it
was a good one for them.

He was a speaker and actor of the truth, born such, and
was ever running into dramatic situations from this cause.
In any circumstance it interested all bystanders to know
what part Henry would take, and what he would say; and he
did not disappoint expectation, but used an original judgment on each emergency. In 1845 he built himself a small
framed house on the shores of Walden Pond, and lived there
two years alone, a life of labor and study. This action was
quite native and fit for him. No one who knew him would
tax him with affectation. He was more unlike his neighbors in

his thought than in his action. As soon as he had exhausted the advantages of that solitude, he abandoned it. In 1847, not approving some uses to which the public expenditure was applied, he refused to pay his town tax, and was put in jail. A friend paid the tax for him, and he was released. The like annoyance was threatened the next year. But as his friends paid the tax, notwithstanding his protest, I believe he ceased to resist. No opposition or ridicule had any weight with him. He coldly and fully stated his opinion without affecting to believe that it was the opinion of the company. It was of no consequence if every one present held the opposite opinion. On one occasion he went to the University Library to procure some books. The librarian refused to lend them. Mr. Thoreau repaired to the President, who stated to him the rules and usages, which permitted the loan of books to resident graduates, to clergymen who were alumni, and to some others resident within a circle of ten miles' radius from the College. Mr. Thoreau explained to the President that the railroad had destroyed the old scale of distances— that the library was useless, yes, and President and College useless, on the terms of his rules—that the one benefit he owed to the College was its library—that, at this moment, not only his want of books was imperative, but he wanted a large number of books, and assured him that he, Thoreau and not the librarian, was the proper custodian of these. In short, the President found the petitioner so formidable, and the rules getting to look so ridiculous, that he ended by giving him a privilege which in his hands proved unlimited thereafter.

No truer American existed than Thoreau. His preference of his country and condition was genuine, and his aversation from English and European manners and tastes almost reached contempt. He listened impatiently to news or *bonmots* gleaned from London circles; and though he tried to be civil, these anecdotes fatigued him. The men were all imitating each other, and on a small mould. Why can they not live as far apart as possible, and each be a man by himself? What he sought was the most energetic nature; and he wished to go to Oregon, not to London. "In every part of Great Britain," he wrote in his diary, "are discovered traces of the Romans, their funereal urns, their camps, their roads, their dwellings. But New England, at least, is not based on any Roman ruins.

We have not to lay the foundations of our houses on the ashes of a former civilization."

But idealist as he was, standing for abolition of slavery, abolition of tariffs, almost for abolition of government, it is needless to say he found himself not only unrepresented in actual politics, but almost equally opposed to every class of reformers. Yet he paid the tribute of his uniform respect to the Anti-Slavery party. One man, whose personal acquaintance he had formed, he honored with exceptional regard. Before the first friendly word had been spoken for Captain John Brown, he sent notices to most houses in Concord that he would speak in a public hall on the condition and character of John Brown, on Sunday evening, and invited all people to come. The Republican Committee, the Abolitionist Committee, sent him word that it was premature and not advisable. He replied—"I did not send to you for advice, but to announce that I am to speak." The hall was filled at an early hour by people of all parties, and his earnest eulogy of the hero was heard by all respectfully, by many with a sympathy that surprised themselves.

It was said of Plotinus that he was ashamed of his body, and 't is very likely he had good reason for it—that his body was a bad servant, and he had not skill in dealing with the material world, as happens often to men of abstract intellect. But Mr. Thoreau was equipped with a most adapted and serviceable body. He was of short stature, firmly built, of light complexion, with strong, serious blue eyes, and a grave aspect—his face covered in the late years with a becoming beard. His senses were acute, his frame well-knit and hardy, his hands strong and skilful in the use of tools. And there was a wonderful fitness of body and mind. He could pace sixteen rods more accurately than another man could measure them with rod and chain. He could find his path in the woods at night, he said, better by his feet than his eyes. He could estimate the measure of a tree very well by his eye; he could estimate the weight of a calf or a pig, like a dealer. From a box containing a bushel or more of loose pencils, he could take up with his hands fast enough just a dozen pencils at every grasp. He was a good swimmer, runner, skater, boatman, and would probably outwalk most countrymen in a day's journey. And the relation of body to mind was still finer than we have indicated. He said he wanted every stride his legs made. The length of his walk uniformly made the length of his writing. If shut up in the house he did not write at all.

He had a strong common sense, like that which Rose Flammock, the weaver's daughter in Scott's romance, commends in her father, as resembling a yardstick, which, whilst it measures dowlas and diaper, can equally well measure tapestry and cloth of gold. He had always a new resource. When I was planting forest trees, and had procured half a peck of acorns, he said that only a small portion of them would be sound, and proceeded to examine them and select the sound ones. But finding this took time, he said, "I think if you put them all into water the good ones will sink;" which experiment we tried with success. He could plan a garden or a house or a barn; would have been competent to lead a "Pacific Exploring Expedition;" could give judicious counsel in the gravest private or public affairs.

He lived for the day, not cumbered and mortified by his memory. If he brought you yesterday a new proposition, he would bring you to-day another not less revolutionary. A very industrious man, and setting, like all highly organized men, a high value on his time, he seemed the only man of leisure in town, always ready for any excursion that promised well, or for conversation prolonged into late hours. His trenchant sense was never stopped by his rules of daily prudence, but was always up to the new occasion. He liked and used the simplest food, yet, when some one urged a vegetable diet, Thoreau thought all diets a very small matter, saying that "the man who shoots the buffalo lives better than the man who boards at the Graham House." He said, "You can sleep near the railroad, and never be disturbed: Nature knows very well what sounds are worth attending to, and has made up her mind not to hear the railroad-whistle. But things respect the devout mind, and a mental ecstasy was never interrupted." He noted what repeatedly befell him, that, after receiving from a distance a rare plant, he would presently find the same in his own haunts. And those pieces of luck which happen only to good players happened to him. One day, walking with a stranger, who inquired where Indian arrowheads could be found, he replied, "Everywhere," and, stooping forward, picked one on the instant from the ground. At Mount Washington, in Tuckerman's Ravine, Thoreau had a bad fall, and sprained his foot. As he was in the act of getting up from his fall, he saw for the first time the leaves of the *Arnica mollis*.

His robust common sense, armed with stout hands, keen perceptions and strong will, cannot yet account for the superiority which shone in his simple and hidden life. I must add the cardinal fact, that there was an excellent wisdom in him, proper to a rare class of men, which showed him the material world as a means and symbol. This discovery, which sometimes yields to poets a certain casual and interrupted light, serving for the ornament of their writing, was in him an unsleeping insight; and whatever faults or obstructions of temperament might cloud it, he was not disobedient to the heavenly vision. In his youth, he said, one day, "The other world is all my art; my pencils will draw no other; my jack-knife will cut nothing else; I do not use it as a means." This was the muse and genius that ruled his opinions, conversation, studies, work and course of life. This made him a searching judge of men. At first glance he measured his companion, and, though insensible to some fine traits of culture, could very well report his weight and calibre. And this made the impression of genius which his conversation sometimes gave.

He understood the matter in hand at a glance, and saw the limitations and poverty of those he talked with, so that nothing seemed concealed from such terrible eyes. I have repeatedly known young men of sensibility converted in a moment to the belief that this was the man they were in search of, the man of men, who could tell them all they should do. His own dealing with them was never affectionate, but superior, didactic, scorning their petty ways—very slowly conceding, or not conceding at all, the promise of his society at their houses, or even at his own. "Would he not walk with them?" "He did not know. There was nothing so important to him as his walk; he had no walks to throw away on company." Visits were offered him from respectful parties, but he declined them. Admiring friends offered to carry him at their own cost to the Yellowstone River—to the West Indies—to South America. But though nothing could be more grave or considered than his refusals, they remind one, in quite new relations, of that fop Brummell's reply to the gentleman who offered him his carriage in a shower, "But where will *you* ride, then?" and what accusing silences, and what searching and irresistible speeches, battering down all defences, his companions can remember!

Mr. Thoreau dedicated his genius with such entire love to the fields, hills and waters of his native town, that he made them known and interesting to all reading Americans, and to people over the sea. The river on whose banks he was born and died he knew from its springs to its confluence with the Merrimack. He had made summer and winter observations on it for many years, and at every hour of the day and night. The result of the recent survey of the Water Commissioners appointed by the State of Massachusetts he had reached by his private experiments, several years earlier. Every fact which occurs in the bed, on the banks or in the air over it; the fishes, and their spawning and nests, their manners, their food; the shad-flies which fill the air on a certain evening once a year, and which are snapped at by the fishes so ravenously that many of these die of repletion; the conical heaps of small stones on the river-shallows, the huge nests of small fishes, one of which will sometimes overfill a cart; the birds which frequent the stream, heron, duck, sheldrake, loon, osprey; the snake, muskrat, otter, woodchuck and fox, on the banks; the turtle, frog, hyla and cricket, which make the banks vocal—were all known to him, and, as it were, townsmen and fellow creatures; so that he felt an absurdity or violence in any narrative of one of these by itself apart, and still more of its dimensions on an inch-rule, or in the exhibition of its skeleton, or the specimen of a squirrel or a bird in brandy. He liked to speak of the manners of the river, as itself a lawful creature, yet with exactness, and always to an observed fact. As he knew the river, so the ponds in this region.

One of the weapons he used, more important to him than microscope or alcohol-receiver to other investigators, was a whim which grew on him by indulgence, yet appeared in gravest statement, namely, of extolling his own town and neighborhood as the most favored centre for natural observation. He remarked that the Flora of Massachusetts embraced almost all the important plants of America—most of the oaks, most of the willows, the best pines, the ash, the maple, the beech, the nuts. He returned Kane's Arctic Voyage to a friend of whom he had borrowed it, with the remark, that "Most of the phenomena noted might be observed in Concord." He seemed a little envious of the Pole, for the coincident sunrise and sunset, or five minutes' day after six months: a splendid fact, which Annursnuc had never afforded him. He found red snow in one of his walks, and told me that he expected to find yet the *Victoria regia* in Concord. He was the attorney of the indigenous plants, and owned to a preference of the weeds to the imported plants, as of the Indian to the civilized man, and noticed, with pleasure, that the willow bean-poles of his neighbor had grown more than his beans. "See these weeds," he said, "which have been hoed at by a million farmers all spring and summer, and yet have prevailed, and just now come out triumphant over all lanes, pastures, fields and gardens, such is their vigor. We have insulted them with low names, too—as Pigweed, Wormwood, Chickweed, Shad-blossom." He says, "They have brave names, too—Ambrosia, Stellaria, Amelanchier, Amaranth, etc."

I think his fancy for referring everything to the meridian of Concord did not grow out of any ignorance or depreciation of other longitudes or latitudes, but was rather a playful expression of his conviction of the indifferency of all places, and that the best place for each is where he stands. He expressed it once in this wise: "I think nothing is to be hoped from you, if this bit of mould under your feet is not sweeter to you to eat than any other in this world, or in any world."

The other weapon with which he conquered all obstacles in science was patience. He knew how to sit immovable, a part of the rock he rested on, until the bird, the reptile, the fish, which had retired from him, should come back and resume its habits, nay, moved by curiosity, should come to him and watch him.

It was a pleasure and a privilege to walk with him. He knew the country like a fox or a bird, and passed through it as freely by paths of his own. He knew every track in the snow or on the ground, and what creature had taken this path before him. One must submit abjectly to such a guide, and the reward was great. Under his arm he carried an old music-book to press plants; in his pocket, his diary and pencil, a spy-glass for birds, microscope, jack-knife and twine. He wore a straw hat, stout shoes, strong gray trousers, to brave scrub-oaks and smilax, and to climb a tree for a hawk's or a squirrel's nest. He waded into the pool for the water plants, and his strong legs were no insignificant part of his armor. On the day I speak of he looked for the Menyanthes, detected it across the wide pool, and, on examination of the florets, decided that it had been in flower five days. He drew out of his breast-pocket his diary, and read the names of all the plants that should bloom on this day, whereof he kept account as a banker when his notes fall due. The Cypripedium not due till to-morrow. He thought that, if waked up from a trance, in this swamp, he could tell by the plants what time of the year it was within two days. The redstart was flying about, and presently the fine grosbeaks, whose brilliant scarlet "makes the rash gazer wipe his eye," and whose fine clear note Thoreau compared to that of a tanager which has got rid of its hoarseness. Presently he heard a note which he called that of the night-warbler, a bird he had never identified, had been in search of twelve years, which always, when he saw it, was in the act of diving down into a tree or bush, and which it was vain to seek; the only bird which sings indifferently by night and by day. I told him he must beware of finding and booking it, lest life should have nothing more to show him. He said, "What you seek in vain for, half your life, one day you come full upon, all the family at dinner. You seek it like a dream, and as soon as you find it you become its prey."

His interest in the flower or the bird lay very deep in his mind, was connected with Nature, and the meaning of Nature was never attempted to be defined by him. He would not offer a memoir of his observations to the Natural History Society. "Why should I? To detach the description from its connections in my mind would make it no longer true or valuable to me: and they do not wish what belongs to it." His power of observation seemed to indicate additional senses. He saw as with microscope, heard as with ear-trumpet, and his memory was a photographic register of all he saw and heard. And yet none knew better than he that it is not the fact that imports, but the impression or effect of the fact on your mind. Every fact lay in glory in his mind, a type of the order and beauty of the whole.

His determination on Natural History was organic. He confessed that he sometimes felt like a hound or a panther, and, if born among Indians, would have been a fell hunter. But, restrained by his Massachusetts culture, he played out the game in this mild form of botany and ichthyology. His intimacy with animals suggested what Thomas Fuller records of Butler, the apiologist, that "either he had told the bees things or the bees had told him." Snakes coiled round his legs; the fishes swam into his hand, and he took them out of the water; he pulled the woodchuck out of its hole by the tail, and took the foxes under his protection from the hunters. Our naturalist had perfect magnanimity; he had no secrets: he would carry you to the heron's haunt, or even to his most prized botanical swamp—possibly knowing that you could never find it again, yet willing to take his risks.

No college ever offered him a diploma, or a professor's chair; no academy made him its corresponding secretary, its discoverer or even its member. Perhaps these learned bodies feared the satire of his presence. Yet so much knowledge of Nature's secret and genius few others possessed; none in a more large and religious synthesis. For not a particle of respect had he to the opinions of any man or body of men, but homage solely to the truth itself; and as he discovered everywhere among doctors some leaning of courtesy, it discredited them. He grew to be revered and admired by his townsmen, who had at first known him only as an oddity. The farmers who employed him as a surveyor soon discovered his rare accuracy and skill, his knowledge of their lands, of trees, of birds, of Indian remains and the like, which enabled him to tell every farmer more than he knew before of his own farm; so that he began to feel a little as if Mr. Thoreau had better rights in his land than he. They felt, too, the superiority of character which addressed all men with a native authority.

Indian relics abound in Concord—arrowheads, stone chisels, pestles and fragments of pottery; and on the river-bank, large heaps of clam-shells and ashes mark spots which the savages frequented. These, and every circumstance touching the Indian, were important in his eyes. His visits to Maine were chiefly for love of the Indian. He had the satisfaction of seeing the manufacture of the bark canoe, as well as of trying his hand in its management on the rapids. He was inquisitive about the making of the stone arrow-head, and in his last days charged a youth setting out for the Rocky Mountains to find an Indian who could tell him that: "It was well worth a visit to California to learn it." Occasionally, a small party of Penobscot Indians would visit Concord, and pitch their tents for a few weeks in summer on the riverbank. He failed not to make acquaintance with the best of them; though he well knew that asking questions of Indians is like catechizing beavers and rabbits. In his last visit to Maine he had great satisfaction from Joseph Polis, an intelligent Indian of Old-town, who was his guide for some weeks.

He was equally interested in every natural fact. The depth of his perception found likeness of law throughout Nature, and I know not any genius who so swiftly inferred universal law from the single fact. He was no pedant of a department. His eye was open to beauty, and his ear to music. He found these, not in rare conditions, but wheresoever he went. He thought the best of music was in single strains; and he found poetic suggestion in the humming of the telegraph-wire.

His poetry might be bad or good; he no doubt wanted a lyric facility and technical skill, but he had the source of poetry in his spiritual perception. He was a good reader and critic, and his judgment on poetry was to the ground of it. He could not be deceived as to the presence or absence of the poetic element in any composition, and his thirst for this made him negligent and perhaps scornful of superficial graces. He would pass by many delicate rhythms, but he would have detected every live stanza or line in a volume and knew very well where to find an equal poetic charm in prose. He was so enamoured of the spiritual beauty that he held all actual written poems in very light esteem in the comparison. He admired Æschylus and Pindar; but when some one was commending them, he said that Æschylus and the Greeks, in describing Apollo and Orpheus, had given no song, or no good one. "They ought not to have moved trees, but to have chanted to the gods such a hymn as would have sung all their old ideas out of their heads, and new ones in." His own verses are often rude and defective. The gold does not yet run pure, is drossy and crude. The thyme and marjoram are not yet honey. But if he want lyric fineness and technical merits, if he have not the poetic temperament, he never lacks the causal thought, showing that his genius was better than his talent. He knew the worth of the Imagination for the uplifting and consolation of human life, and liked to throw every thought into a symbol. The fact you tell is of no value, but only the impression. For this reason his presence was poetic, always piqued the curiosity to know more deeply the secrets of his mind. He had many reserves, an unwillingness to exhibit to profane eyes what was still sacred in his own, and knew well how to throw a poetic veil over his experience. All readers of Walden will remember his mythical record of his disappointments:

"I long ago lost a hound, a bay horse and a turtle-dove, and am still on their trail. Many are the travellers I have spoken concerning them, describing their tracks, and what calls they answered to. I have met one or two who have heard the hound, and the tramp of the horse, and even seen the dove disappear behind a cloud; and they seemed as anxious to recover them as if they had lost them themselves."

His riddles were worth the reading, and I confide that if at any time I do not understand the expression, it is yet just. Such was the wealth of his truth that it was not worth his while to use words in vain. His poem entitled "Sympathy" reveals the tenderness under that triple steel of stoicism, and the intellectual subtility it could animate. His classic poem on "Smoke" suggests Simonides, but is better than any poem of Simonides. His biography is in his verses. His habitual thought makes all his poetry a hymn to the Cause of causes, the Spirit which vivifies and controls his own:

> I hearing get, who had but ears,
> And sight, who had but eyes before;
> I moments live, who lived but years,
> And truth discern, who knew but learning's lore.

And still more in these religious lines:

> Now chiefly is my natal hour,
> And only now my prime of life;
> I will not doubt the love untold,
> Which not my worth nor want have bought,
> Which wooed me young, and wooes me old,
> And to this evening hath me brought.[1]

Whilst he used in his writings a certain petulance of remark in reference to churches or churchmen, he was a person of a rare, tender and absolute religion, a person incapable of any profanation, by act or by thought. Of course, the same isolation which belonged to his original thinking and living detached him from the social religious forms. This is neither

[1] These lines and those above are from Thoreau's poem "Inspiration."

to be censured nor regretted. Aristotle long ago explained it, when he said, "One who surpasses his fellow citizens in virtue is no longer a part of the city. Their law is not for him, since he is a law to himself."

Thoreau was sincerity itself, and might fortify the convictions of prophets in the ethical laws by his holy living. It was an affirmative experience which refused to be set aside. A truth-speaker he, capable of the most deep and strict conversation; a physician to the wounds of any soul; a friend, knowing not only the secret of friendship, but almost worshipped by those few persons who resorted to him as their confessor and prophet, and knew the deep value of his mind and great heart. He thought that without religion or devotion of some kind nothing great was ever accomplished: and he thought that the bigoted sectarian had better bear this in mind.

His virtues, of course, sometimes ran into extremes. It was easy to trace to the inexorable demand on all for exact truth that austerity which made this willing hermit more solitary even than he wished. Himself of a perfect probity, he required not less of others. He had a disgust at crime, and no worldly success would cover it. He detected paltering as readily in dignified and prosperous persons as in beggars, and with equal scorn. Such dangerous frankness was in his dealing that his admirers called him "that terrible Thoreau," as if he spoke when silent, and was still present when he had departed. I think the severity of his ideal interfered to deprive him of a healthy sufficiency of human society.

The habit of a realist to find things the reverse of their appearance inclined him to put every statement in a paradox. A certain habit of antagonism defaced his earlier writings— a trick of rhetoric not quite outgrown in his later, of substituting for the obvious word and thought its diametrical opposite. He praised wild mountains and winter forests for their domestic air, in snow and ice he would find sultriness, and commended the wilderness for resembling Rome and Paris. "It was so dry, that you might call it wet."

The tendency to magnify the moment, to read all the laws of Nature in the one object or one combination under your eye, is of course comic to those who do not share the philosopher's perception of identity. To him there was no such thing as size. The pond was a small ocean; the Atlantic, a large Walden Pond. He referred every minute fact to cosmical laws. Though he meant to be just, he seemed haunted by a certain chronic assumption that the science of the day pretended completeness, and he had just found out that the *savants* had neglected to discriminate a particular botanical variety, had failed to describe the seeds or count the sepals. "That is to say," we replied, "the blockheads were not born in Concord; but who said they were? It was their unspeakable misfortune to be born in London, or Paris, or Rome; but, poor fellows, they did what they could, considering that they never saw Bateman's Pond, or Nine-Acre Corner, or Becky Stow's Swamp; besides, what were you sent into the world for, but to add this observation?"

Had his genius been only contemplative, he had been fitted to his life, but with his energy and practical ability he seemed born for great enterprise and for command; and I so much regret the loss of his rare powers of action, that I cannot help counting it a fault in him that he had no ambition. Wanting this, instead of engineering for all America, he was the captain of a huckleberry-party. Pounding beans is good to the end of pounding empires one of these days; but if, at the end of years, it is still only beans!

But these foibles, real or apparent, were fast vanishing in the incessant growth of a spirit so robust and wise, and which effaced its defeats with new triumphs. His study of Nature was a perpetual ornament to him, and inspired his friends with curiosity to see the world through his eyes, and to hear his adventures. They possessed every kind of interest.

He had many elegancies of his own, whilst he scoffed at conventional elegance. Thus, he could not bear to hear the sound of his own steps, the grit of gravel; and therefore never willingly walked in the road, but in the grass, on mountains and in woods. His senses were acute, and he remarked that by night every dwelling-house gives out bad air, like a slaughter-house. He liked the pure fragrance of melilot. He honored certain plants with special regard, and, over all, the pond-lily—then, the gentian, and the *Mikania scandens*, and "life-everlasting," and a basstree which he visited every year when it bloomed, in the middle of July. He thought the scent a more oracular inquisition than the sight—more oracular and trustworthy. The scent, of course, reveals what is concealed from the other senses. By it he detected earthiness. He delighted in echoes, and said they were almost the only kind of kindred voices that he heard. He loved Nature so well, was so happy in her solitude, that he became very jealous of cities and the sad work which their refinements and artifices made with man and his dwelling. The axe was always destroying his forest. "Thank God," he said, "they cannot cut down the clouds!" "All kinds of figures are drawn on the blue ground with this fibrous white paint."

I subjoin a few sentences taken from his unpublished manuscripts, not only as records of his thought and feeling, but for their power of description and literary excellence:

"Some circumstantial evidence is very strong, as when you find a trout in the milk."

"The chub is a soft fish, and tastes like boiled brown paper salted."

"The youth gets together his materials to build a bridge to the moon, or, perchance, a palace or temple on the earth, and, at length the middle-aged man concludes to build a wood-shed with them."

"The locust z-ing."

"Devil's-needles zigzagging along the Nut-Meadow brook."

"Sugar is not so sweet to the palate as sound to the healthy ear."

"I put on some hemlock-boughs, and the rich salt crackling of their leaves was like mustard to the ear, the crackling of uncountable regiments. Dead trees love the fire."

"The bluebird carries the sky on his back."

"The tanager flies through the green foliage as if it would ignite the leaves."

"If I wish for a horse-hair for my compass-sight I must go to the stable; but the hair-bird, with her sharp eyes, goes to the road."

"Immortal water, alive even to the superficies."

"Fire is the most tolerable third party."

"Nature made ferns for pure leaves, to show what she could do in that line."

"No tree has so fair a bole and so handsome an instep as the beech."

"How did these beautiful rainbow-tints get into the shell of the fresh-water clam, buried in the mud at the bottom of our dark river?"

"Hard are the times when the infant's shoes are second-foot."

"We are strictly confined to our men to whom we give liberty."

"Nothing is so much to be feared as fear. Atheism may comparatively be popular with God himself."

"Of what significance the things you can forget? A little thought is sexton to all the world."

"How can we expect a harvest of thought who have not had a seed-time of character?"

"Only he can be trusted with gifts who can present a face of bronze to expectations."

"I ask to be melted. You can only ask of the metals that they be tender to the fire that melts them. To nought else can they be tender."

There is a flower known to botanists, one of the same genus with our summer plant called "Life-Everlasting," a *Gnaphalium* like that, which grows on the most inaccessible cliffs of the Tyrolese mountains, where the chamois dare hardly venture, and which the hunter, tempted by its beauty, and by his love (for it is immensely valued by the Swiss maidens), climbs the cliffs to gather, and is sometimes found dead at the foot, with the flower in his hand. It is called by botanists the *Gnaphalium leontopodium,* but by the Swiss *Edelweisse,* which signifies *Noble Purity.* Thoreau seemed to me living in the hope to gather this plant, which belonged to him of right. The scale on which his studies proceeded was so large as to require longevity, and we were the less prepared for his sudden disappearance. The country knows not yet, or in the least part, how great a son it has lost. It seems an injury that he should leave in the midst his broken task which none else can finish, a kind of indignity to so noble a soul that he should depart out of Nature before yet he has been really shown to his peers for what he is. But he, at least, is content. His soul was made for the noblest society; he had in a short life exhausted the capabilities of this world; wherever there is knowledge, wherever there is virtue, wherever there is beauty, he will find a home.

From *Lectures and Biographical Sketches*